AF352144

PATRICK WHITE

A Bibliography

Brian Hubber

&

Vivian Smith

Quiddlers Press
in association with
Oak Knoll Press

2004

Published in Australia and New Zealand by
Quiddlers Press
P.O. Box 3034
Auburn, Vic. 3123
Australia

Published in the U.S.A. and Canada by
Oak Knoll Press
310 Delaware Street
New Castle, DE 19720
U.S.A.

Jacket image: George Matoulas, *Patrick at Centennial*, mixed media on paper, 2003; by permission of the artist.
Frontispiece: Louis Kahan, *Patrick White*, pen and ink, n.d. (c.1960). Print Collection, Baillieu Library, University of Melbourne; reproduction rights administered by VISCOPY.
Designed and typeset by Quiddlers Press.
Printed by BPA Print Group, Burwood, Vic. 3125, Australia.

ISBN 0-9581949-2-0 (Quiddlers Press)
ISBN 1-58456-143-2 (Oak Knoll Press)

CATALOGUING IN PUBLICATION (NATIONAL LIBRARY OF AUSTRALIA)

Patrick White : a bibliography.

Includes index.

ISBN 0-9581949-2-0

1. White, Patrick, 1912-1990 - Bibliography. 2. Authors, Australian - Bibliography. I. Hubber, Brian. II. Smith, Vivian, 1933- .

016.8233

Library of Congress CIP information is available from Oak Knoll Press

C O N T E N T S

Introduction

When Patrick White heard that this bibliography was in progress, he took it for granted that it was a task that had to be done and that he would not be alive to see its completion. White's relationship to the world of scholarship was as complex as the man himself. He was often scornful of academic attempts to analyse narrative, to categorise his work, to uncover or expose the well-springs of his creative powers. But he cultivated personal friendships with Australian critics whose work he approved of, he read avidly everything that was written about him, at least until his final years, and he understood extremely well the role that consistent critical attention can play in the advancement of a writer's name and reputation. He resented the ill-informed, pretentious and hostile notices that some of his novels received, but he could be extraordinarily helpful and encouraging to young scholars and readers, and he liked hearing what those who genuinely admired his work had to say. David Marr records White reading his biography: 'He confessed he found the book so painful that he often found himself reading through tears. He did not ask me to cut or change a line.' (Marr, *Life* p.646)

White was sympathetic towards the present undertaking, but it could have none of the importance for him of his biography. Nevertheless, he consistently maintained that he should be judged by his published output and not by other factors such as his lifestyle, his politics, or the creative processes which resulted in the novels and plays: 'I can't let you have my 'papers' because I don't keep any. My mss are destroyed as soon as the books are printed. I put very little into notebooks, don't keep my friends' letters as I urge them not to keep mine, and anything unfinished when I die is to be burnt. The final versions of my books are what I want people to see and if there is anything of importance in me, it will be in those.' (To Dr George Chandler, Director-General, National Library of Australia, 9 April 1977). A true understanding then of White's work must begin with an accurate inventory of his published output.

Moreover – and perhaps the following contention is truer of White than of most authors – he was always alert to the look and feel of the published work, from his first commercially published volume (*The Ploughman*, a limited edition in 300 copies) and his first novel ('My apologies for the War-and-Peace build-up on the jacket [of *Happy Valley*]. This has only appeared with the second printing. The first had a nice blue jacket, with white lettering, and not so much blurb ...' To Spud Johnson, 24 July 1939).

White was also alert to what has become known as the paratext. As we have seen he was sensitive to the extravagant blurb on the *Happy Valley* dustjacket. At other times he edited blurbs: 'Thank you for the draft blurb, which I have torn into considerably, as you will see. I think my version may whet the curiosity slightly more than yours; perhaps you will object to the introduction of characters' names, but to me they work up into a kind of incantation'. (To Juliet Page, Jonathan Cape, 4 February 1970) The title itself was an even more crucial part of the book, and so White always resisted attempts to change the title: 'A book grows with its title. If one starts to mess around with the latter afterwards, the whole thing begins to look a bit like a bad Hollywood film'. (To Ben Huebsch, 7 May 1957, on suggestions that the title of *Voss* might be changed.) Dedications were also important – as a thank-you, as a recognition of the part the person played in the creation of the novel, or recognition of a broader contribution. And White was not above removing a dedication. *The Living and the Dead* was dedicated ('for his selflessness and patience') to Joe Rankin, in whose New York apartment White had typed up the third and final draft. When he left New York to sign up for the air force, White's letters were ignored by Rankin. White dropped the dedication to Rankin from the second edition of *The Living and the Dead*, published by Eyre & Spottiswoode in 1962 (see D3a below) and the dedication has been absent ever since.

It is not surprising that an author like White, who had a life-long interest in the visual arts, was involved in the appearance of his books. As early as 1948 he suggested the use of Roy de Maistre's 'The Garden' on the dustjacket of *The Aunt's Story*. Later, disappointed with the jacket on *The Tree of Man* (he described it as a 'filthy jacket'), White approached Sidney Nolan to do the jacket for *Voss*. While White approved an initial sketch, he was disappointed with the end result ('that fat amiable botanist'); nevertheless the 'botanist' continued to appear on the Penguin edition of *Voss* right through into the 1980s. Nolan produced a number of jacket designs for White's books, including the Penguin edition of *The Aunt's Story* (1963), the U.K. first edition of *Riders in the Chariot* (1961), the U.K. second edition of *The Living and the Dead* (1962), the Penguin edition of *The Living and the Dead* (1967), and the U.K. first edition of *The Burnt Ones* (1964); moreover, it was a Nolan painting from the Mrs Fraser series which appeared on the U.K. first edition of *A Fringe of Leaves* (1976).

White also fruitfully collaborated with the painter and designer Desmond Digby and the designer Luciana Arrighi. Digby designed the sets for a number of productions of White's plays, and was also responsible for the jackets of the U.K. first editions of *Four Plays* (1965), *The Solid Mandala* (1966), *The Eye of the Storm* (1973) and *The Cockatoos* (1974). The Arrighis were both cousins and good friends of White, and Luciana Arrighi has been described by Marr as 'a kind of prodigal daughter' to White. However, Luciana was an established designer in her own right and was responsible for the designs on White's film *The Night the Prowler* (1978) and the opera *Voss* (1986) as well as the jacket for *The Twyborn Affair* (1979).

There is no doubt then that White exercised considerable control over the visual and physical qualities of his published works – and not just the first editions but also the paperbacks and at times the translations. If White put so much of himself into the artefact, it is incumbent on the bibliographer to describe – and the literary scholar to analyse – the level and nature of this authorial input.

Why a bibliography?

The present bibliography describes, in varying degrees of detail, the many elements of each of White's books, whether an edition, subedition, issue or translation up to 1994. By this accumulation of detail, scholars are now better able to understand a number of aspects of White's influence: the quantitative impact of each of White's books from the first edition through subsequent editions, subeditions and issues; the geographical and linguistic extent of White's work; the qualitative assessment of the reception of White's books; the visual and tactile qualities of the books themselves; and the sequence of editions and translations and the degree to which White exercised authority over them.

A descriptive bibliography has a variety of uses and potential users. It will assist booksellers to identify accurately the books they are putting up for sale. It will help collectors – both private and institutional – in the same way, as well as assisting them conceive and form their collections. Textual critics will be able to reconstruct accurate stemma of editions. Literary historians and historians of the book will have the aggregate data which define the physical output and influence of Australia's pre-eminent novelist. Literary critics and scholars will have at their fingertips reference to the published output so they can easily consult White's various texts. Readers will find that the bibliography can assist with their systematic reading of White's *œuvre*.

Apart from being a reference work, the present bibliography aggregates the data that are known about White's published output. The evidence of print runs, numbers of editions and issues, prices, reviews etc. is now brought together in a single digest. We hope that this aggregated data will raise new questions regarding the influence of White.

It is an old adage that writers don't write books – they write manuscripts. Books are made by the combined talents and skills of a great variety of people. A descriptive bibliography is a tribute and a recognition of the work of hundreds of people – the agents, publishers, publisher's readers, editors, copy editors, proof readers, artists, graphic designers, photographers, printers, binders, paper makers, distributors, booksellers, reviewers and scholars – who actually brought White's work into the marketplace. And White was keenly aware of this complex process. For all his irascibility, he was loyal to his agents and publishers. He stayed with the literary agent Curtis Brown for fifty years and only changed when the agency dismissed their Sydney representative, Barbara Mobbs, in 1987. White stayed with Mobbs. He was also loyal to his publishers. He stayed with Viking all his life and changed his English publisher only once, in the late 1960s, when he thought Eyre & Spottiswoode's attention to his requirements was inadequate. White did appreciate the efforts of the publishing industry's footsoldiers, and on occasion he expressed his appreciation warmly. In September 1965 he wrote to Marshall Best of Viking: 'I believe the proof corrector of *The Solid Mandala* is the same one I have always had. One day you must tell me about him or her'.

Finally, it should also be remembered that the book – that is, the physical artefact – can be an object of study in its own right. It is now recognised not only that the book is the intermediate object between the reader and the writer but also that the book is more than a text. It is also a physical artefact with visual and tactile qualities. There is a paratextual apparatus (binding design, typography, title and half-title page, dedications, epigraphs, blurbs, design work, running titles, etc.) which mediates and influences the reading of a text. The book is after all (even in this age of the Worldwide Web) the dominant cultural and intellectual artefact of Western society.

Organisation of the bibliography

The body of the bibliography consists of 27 'chapters', each devoted to a single book. Essentially, each 'chapter' treats a discrete work in its first published manifestation. Thus *Collected Plays Volume II* gets a chapter of its own because it contained the first publication of *Shepherd on the Rocks*. *Collected Plays Volume I* however is a re-issue of *Four Plays* and is therefore treated in the chapter devoted to that work. Similarly, *Night on Bald Mountain* (1996) is treated in the chapter on *Four Plays*. *Patrick White: Selected Writings* has its own chapter because, while it is largely a reprint of previously published material, it includes some major uncollected short pieces.

There are also seven appendices. The first lists each of White's poems, giving brief information on its composition, and first and later publication. The second treats the short stories, giving information on composition, first and later publication, reviews and translations. The third treats the performance history of each of the plays and sketches; for convenience sake the motion picture *The Night the Prowler* is included in this section. Again, the sorts of things treated are composition, details of first and later performances, the existence of manuscripts or typescripts, publication and translation. The fourth appendix treats a number of musical adaptations of White's work. The fifth lists White's miscellaneous and occasional pieces, totalling more than 100 separate items. (This is a small number for a modern author, indicative of the fact that White was a wealthy man independently of his literary success: he did not have to rely on a secondary income from the frequent publication of short pieces.) Appendix 6 provides a summary of translations, and Appendix 7 records all known White literary manuscripts.

What data does each 'chapter' contain? Each chapter attempts to detail the 'life' of the designated title. There is an introduction that summarises the story of the composition of the work, its pre-publication, publishing, reception and later publishing history. The body of the chapter comprises bibliographic descriptions of the various editions, subeditions and issues of the title. The following example is taken from the very complex publishing history of *Voss*.

The organising principle is the edition, defined as being from the same setting of type. A subedition is from the same setting, but is published either by a different publisher or at a different time. Thus, the Canadian subedition by Macmillan (G1d) is the Canadian issue of the U.S. first edition. The Viking subedition of 1974 (G1e) has been so defined because, although it is from the same setting as the first edition and by the same publisher, it is published at a significantly later date. In fact, it is published in a pseudo collected works edition designed to exploit the publicity surrounding the Nobel Prize.

The third level in the hierarchy is the issue. An issue is defined as all copies of a book printed by any one run of the press. Second and subsequent issues of an edition receive only brief descriptions.

The section on translations gives a clear view of the publishing history of White in translation. *Voss*, for instance, has been translated into 20 languages to date. Some of these translations have complex publishing histories of their own, being known in multiple editions and issues. The German translation of *Voss* by John Stickforth was first published in 1958 (only a year after the first English publication), a second issue coming out almost immediately. In 1973 and 1974 this same edition was reissued in paperback. A second edition – what might be called the 'book-club' edition – was published in 1962 and reissued in 1974. Finally, a third edition was published in Leipzig in 1987, perhaps a symptom of the opening up of East Germany prior to re-unification.

The printed work may be issued in different formats, and these are described at the end of each chapter in a Miscellaneous sequence. *Voss* for instance was issued in Braille and as a number of sound recordings.

What data are included in each description? A full description can be subdivided into various elements. The heading contains a reference number which in a coded form indicates the title, the edition and the issue; for example, the First U.K. Edition Second Issue is designated by the reference number 'G2b', where 'G' = Voss, '2' = the 'Second' or U.K. edition, and 'b' = second issue. A summary of the edition and issue is also given along with publication details.

Introduction

The title is given in a quasi-facsimile transcription, with line endings and different fonts indicated.

The collation formula gives the external dimensions of the book, a statement of signatures (where applicable) and the total number of leaves, and a statement of pagination.

The next paragraph gives a detailed summary of the contents of the book. Where possible the contents are described in the words of the book. Text deliberately omitted is indicated by an ellipsis in square brackets, thus [...]. Because modern books often give details of publication on the verso of the title page, care has been taken in transcribing this information from the many re-issues of White's books.

The binding is next described, generally in terms of cased, sewn or perfect. Details of colour and fabric are given in subjective terms. This is a shortcoming in that the colour and fabric of the binding is not given in exact terms – for instance, with reference to a standard colour chart. This has been necessary because much of this data was collected early in the project, and it would have been too time-consuming to go back over this ground. The next paragraph describes the dustjacket, often the source of information on prices and the status of the issue. Also, the dustjacket is the most important design feature of the outside of the book.

A summary paragraph is often given regarding the edition's publishing history. Information given includes publication date, price on publication, the size of the print run and the ISBN. This information has been gleaned both from the book and from archival sources where possible. We have been fortunate that a colleague, Judith Scurfield of the State Library of Victoria, was kind enough to inspect the Eyre & Spottiswoode and Jonathan Cape archives at the University of Reading. Although Marr reports that The Viking Press archives and the Curtis Brown papers at Columbia University do have figures for U.S. sales, it has not been possible to inspect these archives.

Reviews are listed in the next paragraph. Not all reviews have been inspected or searched out methodically. They have been taken from secondary sources where these are available – e.g. *Book Review Digest*, *Book Review Index*, the Austlit database, and review indexes at the State Library of New South Wales and the State Library of Victoria.

The Notes paragraph contains miscellaneous notes, such as details of pre-publication versions of the text (manuscripts, proof copies) and the provenance of specific copies.

The final paragraph indicates the location of copies that have been sighted in compiling the bibliographic description. These locations have been listed for editions only and as a rule not for subeditions or issues. The rule-of-thumb was that as many copies should be inspected as necessary in order to establish the discrete nature of the edition or issue. In practice, about half-a-dozen copies of the first editions were inspected, but only one or two copies of many of the subsequent subeditions, issues and translations. Locations are indicated by standard abbreviations, given in full in the list of 'Abbreviations' on p.xvii.

As is the established practice, only editions and the more important subeditions have been supplied with a full bibliographic description. Clearly, it would not be possible to provide this level of detail for every issue of every title. Most subeditions and issues are given only brief descriptions. Minimal information might consist of only the statement of issue. More frequently however there is also information about the binding, the dimensions of the book if it changes from one issue to the next (as it did in the 1980s for Penguins), price and publication date.

That leaves the question of how to treat the translations. In some bibliographies – e.g. B.J. Kirkpatrick's *A Bibliography of Katherine Mansfield* (Oxford, 1989) – translations are given only brief descriptions. For several reasons, it has been decided to give translations full descriptions. Firstly, it can be argued that a translation is a new edition. What is more, it may well have been produced with authorial input. There are several instances of White being consulted by translators, and he was always willing to oblige them by explaining colloquialisms, characterisation, plot, and what he is trying to do in the work. The *Letters* includes correspondence of this kind, and there may be scope for further research in the archives of Gallimard, Bonniers, and Kiepenheuer & Witsch. Secondly, translations have proved important in White's development as a writer. For example, the French translation of *Happy Valley* was undertaken by Marie Viton in the late 1940s. In the ensuing correspondence with White, Viton encouraged and cajoled the depressed writer and may have been the catalyst for his return to writing. The result was *The Tree of Man*. White directly acknowledged Viton's influence in a letter to James Stern (24 September 1958): 'I felt that I was getting nowhere, and that there was not much point in my continuing to write. Nobody read what I had to say. I was up to my ears in the place at Castle Hill. However, [Viton] continued to pester me by correspondence, and I suppose it was her efforts as much as anything else that decided me to embark on *The Tree of Man*.' One might also refer to the Bölls' translation of *The Tree of Man* (1957), which was very important in introducing White to a European audience.

Acknowledgements

In acknowledging the work of others, bibliographical scholars should first notice work in the same discipline. The first systematic analysis was compiled by staff of the Fryer Memorial Library at the University of Queensland, entitled *Patrick White, 1912: a Bibliography* (Brisbane, 1962). Two supplements to this work were published by the National Library of Australia, the first in October 1965 and the second in October 1966. A new bibliography was compiled by Janette Finch of the Public Library of South Australia, entitled *Bibliography of Patrick White* (Adelaide, 1966), but this was soon superseded by Alan Lawson's (at the time) definitive bibliography, entitled *Patrick White* (Melbourne, 1974) and published in the Australian Bibliographies series. Continuing bibliographical work has been published in the supplement to the fourth issue each year of the *Index to Australian Book Reviews* and the bibliography published in the May issue of *Australian Literary Studies*. This accumulated bibliographical knowledge has been invaluable to the present project.

Even more invaluable has been the biographical work of David Marr. While the editors have not been directly in touch with Marr, his *Patrick White: a Life* (1991) and his edition of White's *Letters* (1994) have provided much of the essential context of the composition, publication and reception of White's literary works. These two volumes have been used extensively and are not only indispensable source books, they are two of the classics of modern Australian writing.

It has been said many times that a bibliographic work of this nature is not possible without considerable assistance from colleagues, friends and interested people. Not in any order we would like to thank the following: Jan

McDonald, Judith Scurfield and colleagues at the State Library of Victoria, who so generously gave of their time, their expertise and their books; Paul Brunton and Jerelynn Brown at the State Library of New South Wales; Professor Boyd Rayward of the University of New South Wales for vital logistical support; James Fairfax for financial support; Humphrey McQueen and Dr Geoffrey Cains for access to their collections, and to the latter for permission to quote from White's letter of 18 October 1970 to G.C. Ingleton; Jonathan Wantrup of New Century Antiquarian Books; Marie-Louise Ayres and staff of the Australian Defence Force Academy Library; Margaret Dent, Christopher Harrison and staff of National Library of Australia; the late Manoly Lascaris for his hospitality and for making Patrick White's own library available.

Brian Hubber would like to thank his wife, Julie Duffy, and three children, Duncan, Edward and Angus, for their patience and encouragement since 1994 when he first agreed to take on this project. He has written the introductions to each chapter and his work for this book is dedicated to the memory of his father, Gerry Hubber, born 5 February 1923, died 26 September 1994.

This bibliography started in the Department of Australian Literature at the University of Sydney, and Vivian Smith would like to thank Debra Adelaide, Elizabeth Harrower, Noel Rowe, Sybille Smith, Elizabeth Webby and David Weston for their valuable assistance. He would also like to thank Brian Hubber for coming in as co-editor at a crucial stage in the development of the work.

* * * * *

In writing a preface for F.T. Bason's *A Bibliography of the Writings of Somerset Maugham* (London, 1931), Maugham observed: 'it gives me a shiver to turn the pages, as though somebody were walking over my grave …When I look at it, well printed and smartly bound, I seem to look at my own tombstone'. White, of course, has no tombstone; David Marr relates that his ashes were scattered near one of the small lakes in Centennial Park. The editors would like to think that the present bibliography is in some small way a memorial to Patrick White's life's work as a writer.

Abbreviations

ABC	Australian Broadcasting Corporation
ADFA	Australian Defence Force Academy Library
ANL	National Library of Australia
b&w	black and white
c	circa
cm	centimetre
col.	Colour
comp.	compiled
ed.	edition or edited (depending on the context)
eds.	editions
illust.	Illustration(s)
ISBN	International Standard Book Number
Lawson	Alan Lawson, *Patrick White* (Melbourne: Oxford University Press, 1974)
Letters	*Patrick White: Letters*, edited by David Marr (Milson's Point, NSW: Random House Australia, 1994)
Marr	David Marr, *Patrick White: A Life* (Milson's Point, NSW: Random House, 1991)
min.	minutes
ML	State Library of New South Wales, Mitchell Library
ms	manuscript
n.d.	no date
n.p.	no publisher or no place (depending on the context)
NBD	National Bibliographic Database
no.	number
NSL	State Library of New South Wales
NU	University of Sydney Library
NUCOM	National Union Catalogue of Monographs
p.	page
pp.	pages
PW	Patrick White
trans.	translated
ts	typescript
U.K.	United Kingdom
U.S.	United State of America
v.	volume
VGRL	Geelong Regional Libraries
VMOU	Monash University Library
vol.	volume
vols.	volumes
VSL	State Library of Victoria
VU	University of Melbourne Library

A Thirteen Poems (1929/1930)

In 1922, aged ten, Patrick White had written some letters to the Sydney *Sunday Times* (January 1922; 22 October 1922). His mother, Ruth, took this as proof of her son's genius. At 13 he was taken by his parents to England and placed in the prestigious public school at Cheltenham where he stayed for the next four years. During these four years he wrote regularly to his parents who had returned to Australia. Often he would include a poem, and it was these poems which Ruth gathered together and published as *Thirteen Poems*. Of the dated poems, the first was composed at Christmas 1927 and the last, 7 August 1929. White returned to Australia late in 1929 but years later could not remember whether *Thirteen Poems* had been issued before or after his return. *Thirteen Poems* was probably produced in a small number of copies as it was circulated to family members. Only two copies are known to be extant. The University of Sydney copy was found in 1969 among the books and papers of collector, Colin Berckelman. The second copy came to light in 1992 when it was discovered by the lessees of Dogwoods, White's former home at Castle Hill. It was apparently White's own copy, judging from the bookplate. This copy again came on the market in 1996 and was purchased by the State Library of New South Wales for $25,000. Other copies are rumoured to be in private hands in Canada and England.

* * * * *

A1 Australian First Edition ([Sydney], [privately published], [1929/1930])

[in black letter] <u>Thirteen Poems</u> | <u>By P. V. M. White.</u>

24.1 x 17.4 cm. Unsigned: 24 leaves (numbered and printed on recto only). ll.*2 3-22 23-24.*

1 title page; *2* 'INDEX'; 3-4 'A RUSTIC ECLOGUE.'; 5-6 'LONG AGO: A REMINISCENCE.'; 7 'TREES IN WINTER.'; 8 'SHADOW PLAY.'; 9 'SUSAN.'; 10 'THE WINDOW.'; 11-13 'THE DEATH OF ARABELLA CHEYNE.'; 14 'IN NIHIL IBIMUS.'; 15 'REQUIEM.'; 16-17 'THE BIRDS.'; 18 'ORCHARD ROW.'; 19-20 'SERAPHITA.'; 21-22 'ST. JACQUES, DIEPPE.'; *23* blank; *24* blank.

Bound in thick grey-brown paper wrappers, saddle-stapled and tied with a brown silk cord through two punched holes. Front: [in black letter] 'Thirteen Poems | By P. V. M. White.'. Back: blank. Inside front and back covers: blank.

Notes: The University of Sydney copy has the ex libris of the book collector, Colin B. Berckelman. Leon Cantrell in *Australian Literary Studies* v.6, October 1974, p.434-436 reported the discovery of this first known copy of *Thirteen Poems*. It is said that White himself visited the Library of the University of Sydney and demanded the return of the book. A compromise was reached which restricted access to the item.

The State Library of New South Wales copy has a book label: 'PATRICK WHITE' | [in pencil ms at bottom right] 'Adrian Feint'. Accessioned by the State Library of New South Wales, 4 June 1996. Cost: $25,000. Purchased from Nicholas Pounder, bookseller, who was the agent for a private vendor.

Copies: NU: RB 1630.19; NSL: Mitchell Library (SAFE 1/160).

B   The Ploughman and Other Poems (1935)

While at Cambridge, Patrick White had published two poems – 'The Ploughman' and 'Meeting Again' – in the *London Mercury* (June 1934, pp.104-105): 'The other day I had a very reassuring surprise: in the shape of the proof of two poems I had sent to the *London Mercury*'. Publication of these two poems inspired Ruth and Victor, White's parents, to find a publisher for a collection of their son's poetry. Each invested £50 in P.R. Stephensen & Company, and Stephensen set to work on the collection. He was also approached about publishing one of White's early novels, 'Finding Heaven', but he thought that it needed revision. Stephensen's financial difficulties, however, were chronic, and in July 1934 the Whites invested another £200 to keep him solvent. W.T. Baker & Co. had already been contracted to do the printing, but proofs did not reach White until October. At this point White recast the collection dropping two poems and including five of his more recent poems.

(Surviving in the National Library of Australia, Manuscript Collection, MS 8649, is a small notebook – No.2 from the "Canvas" Series, being 203 x 127 mm and containing 200 pages – which contains some thirty poems. On the front endpaper is the inscription: 'Poems by P.V.M. White Given to EGW [i.e. Elizabeth 'Betty' Withycombe, White's cousin]'. Twenty-eight of the poems were subsequently published in *The Ploughman*; the two remaining poems – 'Soirée' and 'Interpretation' – have never been published. It might be wondered whether this notebook was seen by Stephensen, because *The Ploughman* was eventually covered in a very similar canvas cloth.)

Stephensen, in the meantime, was again in financial trouble and was concentrating on publishing Xavier Herbert's *Capricornia*. (Could this have been the source of White's scorn of Herbert in later years?) The company went into liquidation early in February. Within a few weeks Ruth had arranged for Boylan & Co. to print the book and it came out under the Beacon Press imprint. (Apart from *Life*, see also Craig Munro's *Wild Man of Letters: The Story of P.R. Stephensen* (Melbourne, 1984), p.137 and 143-144.) L. Roy Davies did the woodcuts. The price was five shillings and the edition was limited to three hundred. The critical reception exhibited some goodwill but little enthusiasm.

In 1971 Geoffrey Ingleton, the book collector, asked White about the circumstances behind the publishing of *The Ploughman*. Ingleton had located two copies: one in the Mackaness collection, and Guy Moore's copy, which sold at auction in October 1971 for $120. White replied that he wished the poems in

The Ploughman had never been published as they were 'embarrassingly' bad. He further claimed that before leaving Castle Hill he had burnt a suitcase full of the books and he hoped that he might find and destroy any other existing copies. (To Geoffrey Ingleton, 18 October 1971, State Library of New South Wales MLMSS 6625X)

White's suitcase full of *The Ploughman* had been gathered together by the Sydney bookseller, Berkelouw, under a standing order. In 1978 White wrote to Ms Janice Kenny of the National Library of Australia, refusing permission for the Library to make a copy of *The Ploughman* for an overseas graduate student. White (only half seriously) threatened to go to Canberra and 'contrive to steal and destroy the book you have'. In a gentler manner, White discouraged Elizabeth Falkenberg from undertaking a translation of the early poems (To Elizabeth Falkenberg, 4 October 1976, National Library of Australia, MS 8234).

* * * * *

B1 Australian First Edition (Sydney, Beacon Press, 1935)

THE PLOUGHMAN | and | Other Poems | By | PATRICK WHITE | ILLUSTRATIONS | By | L. ROY DAVIES | [Beacon Press device] | SYDNEY, N.S.W. | 1935

19.4 x 13 cm. Unsigned [A-D^8 E^6]: 38 leaves. Unpaginated (text is printed on the recto only). ll.[38].

Endpaper; [1] 'THE PLOUGHMAN'; [2] blank; [3] title page; [4] blank; [5] 'DEDICATED | TO MY MOTHER'; [6] [illust. of] '"THE PLOUGHMAN"'; [7] 'THE PLOUGHMAN | [text] | *Polperro, Dec.,* 1933.'; [8] blank; [9] [illust.] | 'MEETING AGAIN | [text] | *Winchester, January,* 1934.'; [10] blank; [11] 'LINES WRITTEN ON LEAVING THE SCILLY | ISLANDS | [text] | *S.S. "Scillonian" off St. Mary's,* 3.1.33.'; [12] blank; [13] [illust.] | 'IF I COULD TELL YOU | [text] | 1.1.33, *St. Mary's.*'; [14] blank; [15] [illust.] | 'ISLES OF SCILLY | [text] | 18.12.32, *St. Martin's.*'; [16] blank; [17] [illust. | 'FUTILITY | [text] | 25.12.32, *St. Mary's.*'; [18] blank; [19] 'AFTER RAIN | [text] | *Hanover, August* 1933.'; [20] blank; [21] [illust.] | 'WHEN THOUGHTS ARE STILL AND FORMLESS | [text] | *Hanover, August* 1933.'; [22] blank; [23] 'RAIN IN SUMMER | [text] | *Heidelberg, July,* 1933.'; [24] blank; [25] 'IF YOU WOULD SEE | [text] | *Heidelberg, July,* 1933.'; [26] blank; [27] [illust.] | 'I WALKED IN THE GARDEN | [text] | *Heidelberg, July,* 1933.'; [28] blank; [29] [illust.] | 'LOVELY, LOVELY YOU MAY BE | [text] | *Cambridge, October,* 1933.'; [30] blank; [31] [illust.] | 'HE LOOKED FOR LOVE | [text] | *Cambridge, October* 1933.'; [32] blank; [33] 'LINES WRITTEN AFTER AN ENCOUNTER WITH | DEATH IN A COUNTRY LANE | [text] | *Polperro, Dec.,* 1933.'; [34] blank; [35] [illust.] | 'BITTER WERE THE TEARS SHE WEPT | [text] | *Zennor, Dec.,* 1933.'; [36] blank; [37] [illust.] | 'LAMENT IN WINTER | [text] | *Zennor, Dec.,* 1933.'; [38] blank; [39] 'RESURRECTION'; [40] blank; [41] ['Resurrection' continues] | *Winchester, Dec.,* 1933.' | [illust].; [42] blank; [43] 'THEY HELD OUT THEIR HANDS

TO ME | [text] | *Cambridge, October, 1933.*'; [*44*] blank; [*45*] [illust.] | 'O COLD, COLD RAIN | [text] | *Cambridge, November, 1933.*'; [*46*] blank; [*47*] [illust.] | 'SECOND LIFE | [text] | *Cambridge, November, 1933.*'; [*48*] blank; [*49*] [illust.] | 'ALONE | [text] | *Cambridge, Jan., 1934.*'; [*50*] blank; [*51*] [illust.] | 'GODSTOW ABBEY | [text] | *Oxford, Jan., 1934.*'; [*52*] blank; [*53*] 'THE BELLS | [text] | *Cambridge, February, 1934.*'; [*54*] blank; [*55*] [illust.] | 'THE BRIDGE | [text] | *Cambridge, February, 1934.*'; [*56*] blank; [*57*] [illust.] | 'TRIO | [text] | *Cambridge, February, 1934.*'; [*58*] blank; [*59*] [illust.] | 'WISDOM FOR THE WISE | [text] | *Hanover, March, 1934.*'; [*60*] blank; [*61*] [illust.] | 'OCTOBER | [text] | *London, October, 1934.*'; [*62*] blank; [*63*] 'EARLY AUTUMN | [text] | *Cambridge, October, 1934.*'; [*64*] blank; [*65*] [illust.] | 'DIRGE | [text] | *Wimborne, September, 1934.*'; [*66*] blank; [*67*] 'ORAM'S GRAVE | [text] | *Salisbury, September, 1934.*'; [*68*] blank; [*69*] 'INTERLUDE | [text] | *London, September, 1934.*'; [*70*] blank; [*71*] [illust.] | 'MORNING SOLILOQUY | [text] | *Corfe Castle, August, 1934.*'; [*72*] blank; [*73*] [illust.] | 'TO A GULL BLOWN INLAND BY THE STORM | [text] | *Corfe Castle, August, 1934.*'; [*74*] blank; [*75*] 'The Ploughman and other Poems | produced by The Beacon Press of | Sydney, N.S.W., and limited to 300 | numbered copies, was completed | in the month of February, 1935. | This is Copy No. ....'; [*76*] blank; endpaper.

Cased in light brown canvas with light brown wove endpapers. Front and back: blank. Spine: [running down:] [in brown] 'THE PLOUGHMAN   PATRICK WHITE'.

Light brown textured dustjacket. Front: [woodcut illust. of ploughman] | 'THE PLOUGH-MAN | and Other Poems | By | PATRICK WHITE'. Back, spine and inside front and back flap: blank.

Reviews: *The Opinion: the Australis topical and literary magazine* v.1 no.1, 1935, p.5.

Notes: Copy no.116 has a bookplate: 'EX LIBRIS | BOUNTIANA | DR GEORGE | MACKANESS | AUSTRALIANA'. Copy no.54 has in ms on front free endpaper: 'Lilian A White'. Copy no.41 has in ms on front free endpaper: 'To "Jeanie Deans" Patrick White London April 1935'. Copy no.95 has the bookplate of Patrick White very lightly tipped in; the illustration of "The Ploughman" is signed in blue ink by L. Roy Davies. Copy no.108 has the bookplate of Harry Hastings Pearce; and in ms on the inside front flap of the dustjacket: 'Mackaness no2 1968 $10.50' and 'In 1980 I [i.e. Harry Hastings Pearce] was offered £100 for this book by a 2nd Hand Dealer and refused it'.

In the National Library of Australia (Manuscripts Collection, MS 8649) there is a notebook of Patrick White's that contains 28 of the 33 poems published in *The Ploughman*.

Copies: NU: RB1635.6 (Copy no.298 "For copyright") (lacks dustjacket); NU: RB 1635.6 (Copy no.86) (lacks dustjacket); Personal collection (Copy no.116); NSL: Mitchell Library A821/W (Copy no.295 'For copyright') (lacks dustjacket); NSL: Mitchell Library 821.914/W587/1 (Copy no. 54) (lacks dustjacket); VMOU: *A820.5 W587 A6/P1 (Copy no.41); ANL: SR 821A WHI (Copy no.296 'For copyright') (lacks dustjacket); ANL: HHP 796 (Copy no.108); ADFA (Copy no.95); VU: McL L/A-P White (Copy no.76) (lacks dustjacket).

C Happy Valley (1939)

The origins of *Happy Valley* lie in a stint of jackarooing Patrick White did in the Snowy Mountains in 1930-1931. At the time White wrote a number of 'jackaroo' novels – another, entitled 'Finding Heaven', was offered to P.R. Stephensen in 1934 – and one of these was reworked into *Happy Valley* by White in London in 1936 and 1937. The manuscript was turned down by some eight publishers before the poet Geoffrey Grigson persuaded Harrap to publish it (see *The Bookseller* 26 January 1939, p.84). *Happy Valley* appeared early in 1939 to much acclaim. White went to New York to seek a publisher and was able to interest Ben Huebsch of The Viking Press. The Viking edition came out in June 1940, again to a favourable critical reception. Huebsch, in fact, was most influential in White's early career and The Viking Press published White's books right to the end of his career.

Both the United Kingdom and the United States editions had limited commercial success: the Harrap edition went into a second printing and then came out in the Harrap Fiction Library. Five hundred copies had been shipped to Australia where, it is said, Dymocks had a monopoly over distribution. (Members of the Sydney booktrade report that copies of *Happy Valley* without the dustjacket were appearing on the Sydney market in the early 1960s – as if a box of them had been found in some bookseller's store-room). The critical reception in Australia was only lukewarm.

Happy Valley has never been re-issued in either paperback or hardback. It was omitted from The Viking Press uniform edition of White's works, published after the winning of the Nobel Prize. In 1959, in a letter to Geoffrey Dutton, White claimed he could not read *Happy Valley* or *The Living and the Dead* 'if I were shut up in a cell with them.' He later explained 'it is too full of obvious stylistic enthusiasms.' (To Manfred McKenzie, 5 January 1963) Even later, White wrote to one of his French translators that he had not allowed a reissue of *Happy Valley* for two reasons: the first was because he feared a libel suit from a Chinese-Australian family whose history he had drawn on for the novel, 'the other is because there are too many influences, too many styles as I cast about trying to find a style of my own.' (To Jean Lambert, 30 January 1983)

It is slightly inconsistent then that White allowed a French translation. Perhaps he thought that he was unlikely to be sued over a foreign language version of the novel. The translation was mainly due to the persistent enthusiasm of Marie Viton who had persuaded Gallimard to take out options on White's first three novels. *Eden-Ville* was published in 1951 but, according to White, was such a flop that the publisher did not bother to forward the reviews. (To James Stern, 24 September 1958) It is remarkable then that *Eden-Ville* apparently went through at least five issues. It is said by Marr (*Life* p.546) that an Italian translation and a another French translation were published in the wake of White's Nobel Prize, but no copies of these works or any other references to them have been sighted.

* * * * *

C1a U.K. First Edition First Issue (London: Harrap, 1939)

HAPPY VALLEY | *A Novel* | By | PATRICK WHITE | [at bottom:] [publisher's device] | GEORGE G. HARRAP & CO. LTD. | LONDON TORONTO BOMBAY SYDNEY

13.8 x 20.4 cm. [A]⁸ B-U⁸ X⁴: 164 leaves. pp.*8* 9-112 *113-114* 115-326 *327-328*.

Endpaper; *1* 'HAPPY VALLEY'; *2* blank; *3* title page; *4* '*First published* 1939 | *by* GEORGE G. HARRAP & CO. LTD. | 182 *High Holborn, London, W.C.1* | *Copyright. All rights reserved* | [at bottom:] [rule] | *Made in Great Britain. Printed by Western Printing Services, Ltd.* | *Bristol*'; *5* 'TO | ROY DE MAISTRE'; *6* 'It is impossible to do away with the law of suffering, which | is the one indispensible condition of our being. Progress is | to be measured by the amount of suffering undergone … | the purer the suffering, the greater is the progress. | MAHATMA GANDHI'; *7* 'PART I'; *8* 'NOTE | *All the characters in this book are fictitious.*'; 9-112 text of Part I; *113* 'PART II'; *114* blank; 115-326 *327* text of Part II; *328* blank; endpaper.

Cased in tan cloth with off-white endpapers. Front and back: blank. Spine: [in blue] 'HAPPY | VALLEY | PATRICK | WHITE | HARRAP'. Inside front and back covers: blank.

Blue paper dustjacket. Front: [in light blue] '*Happy* | *Valley* | *A NOVEL* | S[in black]now in Australia is | not what one thinks of, | but it is in a snowbound | public-house in the | mountains of New | South Wales that this | very remarkable novel | begins. | [*Turn to front flap* [in light blue] [pointing hand] | *PATRICK WHITE*'. Back: [in black] '*Two Outstanding New Harrap Novels* | [swelled rule] | HUMPHREY CHESTERMAN | [in light blue] Penny World | [in black] [blurb and quotations, 8 lines] | HANS HABE | [in light blue] Three over the Frontier | [in black] *Translated by Eric Sutton* | [blurb and quotations, 9 lines] | *Recommended by the Book Society*' | [swelled rule]. Spine: [in light blue] *Happy* | *Valley* | *A NOVEL* | *by* | *PATRICK* | *WHITE* | *HARRAP*'. Inside front flap: [in light blue] 'HAPPY VALLEY | [blurb, 38 lines] | [biography, 8 lines] | [at bottom right:] 8/6 | NET'. Inside back flap: [in box:] 'INVITATION | Thousands of readers all | over the world regularly | receive, free, the *Harrap* | *Book News*. Are you among | them? If not − and assuming | that you will be interested in | this lively and well-illus- | trated newspaper which | gives extracts from new | books, reviews by distin- | guished writers, information | about authors, etc. − send a | postcard to | HARRAP | 182, High Holborn, | London, W.C.I'.

Published 2 February 1939. Price: 8s 6d. Print run: the first issue of 2,000 was sold out within the month thus requiring a second issue (see C1b below). Some 500 copies were sent to Australia, and it is said (by John Holroyd of Melbourne, quoted by David Marr in *Life*) that Dymocks had a monopoly over distribution in Australia. Price: 8s 6d.

Reviews: J.D. Beresford *Manchester Guardian* 3 February 1939, p.7 (370w); V.S. Pritchett *Bystander* 8 February 1939, p.206; *Times Literary Supplement* 11 February 1939, p.91 (260w); Desmond Shawe-Taylor *New Statesman and Nation* v.17, 11 February 1939, p.212 (260w); Pamela Hansford Johnson *Liverpool Post* 13 February 1939; Kate O'Brien *The Spectator* v.162, 17 February 1939, p.276 (450w); *Herald* (Melbourne) 18 February 1939, p.36; *Adelaide Mail* 18 March 1939, p.9; Richard Church *John O'London's Weekly* 1939; *Bonniers Litterära Magasin* May 1939, p.352-353; 'Furnley Maurice' [Frank Wilmot] *Bohemia* June 1939, p.18; *Desiderata* no.39, 1939, p.15; S. Mackenzie *Desiderata* no.40, 1939, p.19-20 (reprinted in *Weekend Australian* 6-7 July 1985, p.12); Harold J. Oliver *Australian National Review* v.5 no.29, May 1939, p.90.

Notes: Winner of the Australian Literature Society Gold Medal, 1939. One of the copies in a personal collection has an inscription in White's hand: 'To Hilda Richardson with my best wishes, and thanks for many services admirably rendered, Patrick White 4th February 1939'. Hilda Richardson was White's housekeeper in London. The ADFA copy has the following inscription in White's hand on the front endpaper: 'To Roy [de Maistre], a second dedication | Patrick White 2nd February 1939'.

Copies: VSL: *LT 819.93 W582H (lacks dustjacket); Personal collections (2 copies); NU: 1639.1 (lacks dustjacket); NSL: Mitchell Library 823.914/W587/55 (lacks dustjacket); NSL: Mitchell Library A823/W587/1A1 (lacks dustjacket); VU: McL L/A-F White.

C1b U.K. First Edition Second Issue (London: Harrap, 1939)

Notes: p.*4* '*First published February* 1939 | *by* GEORGE G. HARRAP & CO. LTD. | 182 *High Holborn, London, W.C.*1 | *Reprinted February* 1939 | *Copyright. All rights reserved* | [at bottom:] [rule] | *Made in Great Britain. Printed by Western Printing Services, Ltd.,* | *Bristol*'. Dappled brown paper dustjacket. Published in February 1939. Price: 8/6.

One copy in a personal collection has in manuscript on the front endpaper: 'For Mrs Untermeyer | with best wishes | Patrick White | Dec 1939'.

Copies: VSL: La Trobe Library Moir Collection (lacks dustjacket); Personal collections (2 copies); NU: RB 1639.1 (copy 2); NSL: Mitchell Library [PW].

C1c U.K. First Edition Third Issue (London: Harrap, 1940)

Notes: (Harrap's Fiction Library). Published July 1940. Price: 4s. (*The English Catalogue of Books 1935-1941* London, 1945).

C2 U.S. First Edition (New York: Viking, 1940)

HAPPY VALLEY | A NOVEL BY | Patrick White | [publisher's device] | THE VIKING PRESS | NEW YORK · 1940

21 x 14 cm. Unsigned: 160 leaves. pp.*10* 11-110 *111-112* 113-317 *318-320*.

Endpaper; *1* 'HAPPY VALLEY'; *2* blank; *3* title page; *4* [at bottom:] 'ALL RIGHTS RESERVED | PRINTED IN THE UNITED STATES OF AMERICA | PUBLISHED IN MAY 1940'; *5* 'TO | ROY DE MAISTRE'; *6* 'NOTE | *All the characters in this book are fictitious.*'; *7* '*It is impossible to do away with the law of* | *suffering, which is the one indispensible condition* | *of our being. Progress is to be measured by the* | *amount of suffering undergone ... the purer the* | *suffering, the greater is the progress.* | MAHATMA GANDHI'; *8* blank; *9* 'Part One'; *10* blank; 11-110 text of Part One; *111* 'Part Two'; *112* blank; 113-317 text of Part Two; *318-320* blank; endpaper.

Cased in black calico grain cloth with top edge in red and with white endpapers. Front: [on inlaid panel:] [in white on red] '*HAPPY* | *VALLEY* | A NOVEL BY | *Patrick White*'. Back: blank. Spine: [on panel:] [in white on red] '*Patrick* | *White* | [rule] | [running down:] HAPPY VALLEY | [upright:] [rule] | *The* | *Viking* | *Press*'.

White paper dustjacket with green illust. of man walking and woman on horse across front and spine; signed 'Hallock'. Front: [in white on red panel:] '*Happy* | *Valley* | [in black] A NOVEL BY | [in white] *Patrick White*'. Back: [in green on white] '"*I have read it with the very greatest interest, excitement, and admi-* | *ration. The characterization, atmosphere, and gen-* | *eral swing of the* | *plot seem to me first rate.*" —ELIZABETH BOWEN. | [in red] [ornamental rule] | [in green] *Happy Valley* | [in red] BY PATRICK WHITE | [in green] [blurb, 18 lines] | "*Interests me both because of its technique and its shrewd yet sensitive* | *penetration into the secrecies of human nature.*" | —RICHARD CHURCH, *John o'London's Weekly.* | (SEE ALSO FRONT FLAP OF THIS JACKET) | [in red] THE VIKING PRESS · PUBLISHERS'. Spine: [running down:] [in white] 'WHITE *Happy Valley* VIKING'. Inside front flap: [in green] 'HAPPY VALLEY $2.50 | [in red] *Patrick White* | [in green] [biography, 20 lines] | [in red] *Happy Valley* | [in green] CRITICAL ESTIMATES | [quotation of four lines from] — *Evening Standard* (London). | [quotation of four lines from] —*The Spectator* (London). | [quotation of four lines from] —HERBERT READ. | [quotation of two lines from] —GRAHAM GREENE. | [in red] THE VIKING PRESS | 18 East 48th Street | New York City'. Inside back flap: [in red] '*Masters of Fiction* | [in green] *A brief list of the current books of in-* | *terna- tionally popular novelists whose* | *works appear under the Viking imprint* | [list of six titles] | *De- scriptive list of other current books* | *sent free on request* | [in red] THE VIKING PRESS | 18 East 48th Street | New York City'.

Published in May 1940. Price: $2.50.

Reviews: J.S. Southron *New York Times Book Review* 26 May 1940, p.7 (850w); J.S. Mabon *New York Herald Tribune Books* 2 June 1940, p.2 (650w); Marian Wiggin *Boston Transcript* 22 June 1940, p.2 (380w); *New Republic* v.103, 1 July 1940, p.103 (30w); L.B. Salomon *Nation* v.151, 7 September 1940, p.198 (230w).

Copies: NSL: Mitchell Library A823/W587/61 (lacks dustjacket); Personal collections (2 copies); VU: AX A823.3 White.

C.t1a French First Edition First Issue (Paris: Gallimard, 1951)

DU MONDE ENTIER | PATRICK WHITE | EDEN-VILLE | (HAPPY VALLEY) | *traduit de l'anglais par* | *MARIE VITON* | roman | [publisher's device] | *nrf* | GALLIMARD

20.9 x 14.1 cm. [1]⁸ 2-22⁸ 23⁴: 180 leaves. pp.7 8 *9-15* 16-354 *355-360* (the first page of each chapter is unnumbered).

1-2 blank; *3* 'EDEN-VILLE'; *4* blank; *5* title page; *6* '*Il a été tiré de cet ouvrage cent sept exemplaires sur vélin | pur fil Lafuma-Navarre, dont cent numérotés de 1 à 100, et | sept, hors commerce, marqués de A à G.* | EXEMPLAIRE | *Tous droits de traduction, de reproduction et d'adaptation | réservés pour tous les pays y compris la Russie.* | *Copyright by Librairie Gallimard, 1951.*'; *7 8* 'NOTE BIOGRAPHIQUE'; *9* '*à ROY DE MAISTRE*'; *10* blank; *11* [epigraph of five lines from] 'Mᴀʜᴀᴛᴍᴀ Gᴀɴᴅʜɪ'; *12* blank; *13* 'PREMIERE PARTIE'; *14* blank; *15* 16-354 text; *355* 'TABLE'; *356* blank; *357* 'ACHEVÉ D'IMPRIMER | EN OCTOBRE 1951 PAR | EMMANUEL GREVIN et FILS | A LAGNY-SUR-MARNE | *Dépôt légal : 4ᵉ trimestre 1951.* | Nᵒ *d'Éd.* 2668. – Nᵒ *d'Imp.* 2377. | *Imprimé en France.*'; *358-360* blank.

Sewn in off-white paper covers. Front: 'DU MONDE ENTIER | [in red] CXI | PATRICK WHITE | [in black] [publisher's device] | [in red] EDEN-VILLE | [in black] *traduit de l'anglais par* | MARIE VITON | [in red] *nrf* | [in black] GALLIMARD'. Back: [in red] '"DU MONDE ENTIER" | [in black] *Dernières Publications* | [list of 72 titles in two columns] | PUR FIL'. Spine: 'DU MONDE | ENTIER | CXI | [in red] EDEN | VILLE | [in black] par | PATRICK | WHITE | *nrf* | Gallimard'.

Glassine wrapper. Blank.

Published in October 1951.

Notes: Copies in the trade edition have a different binding. It is sewn in off-white paper covers. Front: 'DU MONDE ENTIER | PATRICK WHITE | [in red] EDEN-VILLE [in black] | *traduit de l'anglais par* | *Marie Viton* | roman | [publisher's device] | [in red] *nrf* | [in black] GALLIMARD'. Back: 'S.P. | PATRICK WHITE | [in red] EDEN-VILLE | [in black] [blurb, 16 lines] | [in red] • *COLLECTION DU "MONDE ENTIER"* | (Dernières Publications)' | [list of 9 titles]. Spine: 'DU MONDE | ENTIER | PATRICK WHITE | [in red] EDEN | VILLE | [in black] *nrf* | Gallimard'.

The practice of bringing out an edition on several grades of paper was well-known in France, perhaps the most famous example being Sylvia Beach's first edition of James Joyce's *Ulysses* (1922) in one thousand copies – 100 on Dutch handmade paper, 150 on vergé d'Arches paper, and 750 on handmade paper. Gallimard continued the practice; for example, in 1950 they published an edition of Joyce's *Les Exiles* in an edition of 1,255 copies, 205 on Lafuma Navarre and 1,050 on alfa Marais. (John J. Slocum and Herbert Cahoon, *A Bibliography of James Joyce [1882-1941]* (New Haven: Yales University Press, 1953)).

Copies: Personal collection (Copy no.60); NSL: Mitchell Library A823/W587/1C1 (Copy no.70) (lacks original spine); NSL: Mitchell Library [PW]; NSL: Mitchell Library [PW] (Copy no.A); ADFA (2 copies, Copy no.E and Copy no.99); VU: AX A823.3 White (Copy no.6).

C.t1b French First Edition Second Issue (Paris: Gallimard, 1951)

Notes: p.5 '*Deuxième édition*'.

Copies: ANL: N A823.3 W587ed-2 (acquired 1988).

C.t1c French First Edition Third Issue (Paris: Gallimard, 1951)

Not seen, but a copy is in the Biblioteca Nacional (Portugal) at call no. 820 WHI HV

C.t1d French First Edition Fourth Issue (Paris: Gallimard, 1951)

Not seen, but assumed on the basis of C.t1c and C.t1e

C.t1e French First Edition Fifth Issue (Paris: Gallimard, 1951)

DU MONDE ENTIER | PATRICK WHITE | EDEN-VILLE | (HAPPY VALLEY) | *traduit de l'anglais par* | *MARIE VITON* | roman | [publisher's device] | *nrf* | GALLIMARD | *cinquième édition*

Copies: Personal collection.

D The Living and the Dead (1941)

Patrick White commenced writing *The Living and the Dead* while staying at Sandwich on Cape Cod, Massachusetts, in July 1939: 'It all came suddenly pouring out – a novel that has been fermenting for the last three years.' (*Life* p.188, quoting a letter to Spud Johnson, 24 July 1939). He worked in 'fits and starts … at what promises to be a *very* long novel.' (To Spud Johnson, 17 August 1939) White returned to London in October 1939, working on the novel on the *TSS Vandyck*. The first draft of 150,000 words was finished on the 15 February 1940. At this time White confided to Pepe Mamblas that he was 'thinking of calling the novel *The Living and the Dead*. I'm more and more conscious anyway in this country, of people being divided into two categories – the people who are aware and the people who are – well, just dead.' (To Pepe Mamblas, 15 February 1940)

White set to work on the revision immediately but began to have mixed feelings about the novel: 'It should have been the Novel of London, but haste made it only a sketch.' (*Life* p.194, quoting a letter to Marcel Aurrousseau, 23 May 1962) When White returned to New York early in 1940 he brought with him the second draft. He typed the third draft in Dr Joe Rankin's apartment (*The Living and the Dead* was dedicated to Rankin 'for his selflessness and patience') while awaiting the publication of *Happy Valley* by The Viking Press. By July the typescript had been submitted and accepted by Viking: 'I have just got the Viking Press to say they will publish my new book, *The Living and the Dead*, though I have not yet signed a contract. Still, I know that Huebsch personally is enthusiastic.' (To Spud Johnson, 26 July 1940)

A copy of the typescript had also been submitted to Harrap in London but they rejected it, as did Faber, Chatto, Jonathan Cape and Heinemann. Eventually, it was read by Herbert Read, a powerful cultural critic and an editorial director of George Routledge & Sons. Routledge accepted Read's recommendation to publish *The Living and the Dead*; it appeared in July 1941. Only 1,428 copies were printed for the British and overseas market. It sold out within the year – 354 to the colonial markets – but a second printing was cancelled because of war paper shortages.

While Curtis Brown was trying to place *The Living and the Dead* in London, White had been called up and posted to Africa. He noted in his diary (24 March 1941) that *The Living and the Dead* was to be published by Routledge early in the summer. He was in Alexandria when he wrote to Huebsch acknowledging receipt of the New York edition: 'I am delighted with the way you have done the book, binding, type, and the jacket all very good.' (To Ben Huebsch, 17 April 1942)

The Living and the Dead was reissued in 1962 by Eyre & Spottiswoode, apparently as part of a uniform edition of the novels. The dedication to Joe Rankin was omitted from this and subsequent editions, issues and translations.

A paperback edition was published by Penguin in 1967. It was reissued by Penguin in 1974 in both the United Kingdom and Australia, presumably to meet the demand generated by the 1973 Nobel Prize.

A small number of translations of *The Living and the Dead* have appeared, over which White appears to have exercised some control. Marie Viton's enthusiasm for White's work resulted in Gallimard publishing *Happy Valley*, but Viton's translation of *The Living and the Dead* never saw the light of day. A Polish translation was forwarded to White: 'I must send [it to] Tania when I find the energy to do it up. Or perhaps she can no longer read Polish.' (To James Stern, 27 May 1966) Late in life White developed a strong rapport with Jean Lambert who translated a number of White's works into French. And so in 1989 White was re-reading chunks of the novel to assist Lambert. This translation was published by Gallimard in 1990.

* * * * *

D1a U.S. First Edition First Issue (New York: Viking, 1941)

THE | *LIVING AND* | *THE DEAD* | [at bottom:] *PATRICK WHITE* | 1941 | *NEW YORK • THE VIKING PRESS*

20.8 x 13.8 cm. Unsigned: 196 leaves. p.[*8*] *1* 2-383 *384*.

Endpaper; [*1*] '*THE LIVING AND THE DEAD*'; [*2*] '*By the same author* | HAPPY VALLEY'; [*3*] title page; [*4*] 'Copyright 1941 by Patrick White | Printed in the U.S.A. by the Vail-Ballou Press | First published in February 1941 | Published on the same day in the Dominion of Canada | by the Macmillan Company of Canada Limited'; [*5*] '*To* | JOE RANKIN | *for his selflessness* | *and patience*'; [*6*] blank; [*7*] 'Je te mets sous la garde du plaisir et de la douleur; l'un et | autre veilleront à tes pensées, à tes actions; engendreront tes | passions, exciteront tes aversions, tes amitiés, tes tendresses, | tes fureurs; allumeront tes désirs, tes craintes, tes espérances; | te dévoileront des vérités, te plongeront dans des erreurs; et | aprés t'avoir fait enfanter mille systèmes absurdes et différ- | ents de morale at de législation, te découvriront un jour les | principes simples, au développement desquels sont attachés | l'ordre et le bonheur du monde moral. —HELVÉTIUS'; [*8*] blank; *1* 2-181 text for Part I; *182* blank; 183-383 text for Part II; *384* blank; endpaper.

Cased in pale, dust red cloth with top edge in graphite and with off-white endpapers. Front: [stamped in blind] [publisher's device]. Back: blank. Spine: [in black on gold paper inlaid panel:] '*PATRICK* | *WHITE* | The | LIVING | and the | DEAD | *THE* | *VIKING PRESS*'.

White paper dustjacket printed with purple background and blue and white illust. of stars and clouds. Front: [in purple] 'THE | [in white] LIVING | AND THE DEAD | [in grey] BY PATRICK WHITE | AUTHOR OF "HAPPY VALLEY"'. Back: [in purple] [hollow type] 'THE LIVING | AND THE DEAD | [in grey] BY PATRICK WHITE | [in purple] [solid type] [blurb, 28 lines] | [in grey] [hollow type] THE VIKING PRESS | NEW YORK CITY'. Spine: [in grey] 'THE | [in orange] LIVING | [in grey] AND | THE | [in orange] DEAD | PATRICK WHITE | [in grey] THE | [in orange] VIKING | [in grey] PRESS'. Inside front flap: [in blue] 'The Living and the Dead $2.50 | [in purple] *Also by Patrick White* | [in blue] [hollow type] HAPPY VALLEY | [at right] $2.50 | [in purple] [quotation of three lines from] —RALPH THOMPSON, *New York Times.* | [quotation of four lines from] —GRAHAM GREENE. | [quotation of two lines from] —ELIZABETH BOWEN. | [quotation of four lines from] —LOUIS B. SALOMON, *Nation.* | [quotation of two lines from] —JOHN SCOTT MABON, *New | York Herald Tribune Books.* | [quotation of three lines from] —HERBERT READ. | [in grey] [swelled rule] | [in blue] *Jacket design by E. McKnight Kauffer* | [in grey] [hollow type] THE VIKING PRESS'. Inside back flap: [in purple] [hollow type] 'FINE VINTAGE | [in blue] The Cat's Cradle Book | [in purple] SYLVIA TOWNSEND WARNER | [in blue] *Illustrated by Bertram Hartman $2.50* | [quotation of four lines from] —JANE SPENCE | SOUTHRON, *New York Times Book Review.* | [quotation of three lines from] —JAMES BRANCH CABELL. | [quotation of two lines from] —CARL VAN VECHTEN. | [in blue] [swelled rule] | Presenting Moonshine | [in purple] JOHN COLLIER [in blue] $2.50 | [in purple] [blurb, 7 lines] | [in blue] *Descriptive list of other | current books upon request* | THE VIKING PRESS | 18 East 48th Street | New York City'.

Reviews: Iris Barry *New York Herald Tribune Books* 4 February 1941, p.8 (320w); J.S. Southron *New York Times Book Review* 9 February 1941, p.6 (750w); *Time* v.37, 10 February 1941, p.74 (300w); *New Yorker* v.17, 15 February 1941, p.6 (60w); R.L. Nathan *Saturday Review of Literature* v.23, 15 February 1941, p.11 (500w); L.B. Salomon *Nation* v. 152, 8 March 1941, p.276 (500w).

Published in February 1941. Price: $2.50.

Copies: NSL: Mitchell Library [PW] (lacks dustjacket); Personal collections (2 copies); VU: AX A823.2 White.

D1b Canadian Subedition (Toronto, Macmillan Canada, 1941)

Not seen, but referred to in D1a and in the *Cumulative Book Index*. Price: CAN$3.

D1c AMS Subedition (New York: AMS, 1979)

Notes: p.[4] 'First AMS edition published in 1979. | [...] | Reprinted by arrangement with the Viking Press, Inc. | Reprinted from the edition of 1941, New York.'. Cased in tan linen cloth boards. Dustjacket not seen.

D2a U.K. First Edition First Issue (London: Routledge, 1941)

THE | *LIVING AND* | *THE DEAD* | [at bottom:] *PATRICK WHITE* | *GEORGE ROUTLEDGE & SONS, LTD.* | *LONDON* – 68-74 *CARTER LANE, E.C.*4.

19.4 x 12.8 cm. [A]⁴ B-M¹⁶ ²H¹⁶: 196 leaves. p.[8] *1* 2-181 *182-183* 184-383 *384.*

Endpaper; [*1*] *'THE LIVING AND THE DEAD'*; [*2*] *'By the same author* | HAPPY VALLEY'; [*3*] title page; [*4*] *'First published in England*, 1941. | [at bottom:] PRINTED IN GREAT BRITAIN BY | LOWE AND BRYDONE PRINTERS LIMITED, LONDON, N.W.10'; [*5*] *'To* | JOE RANKIN | *for his selflessness* | *and patience'*; [*6*] blank; [*7*] [ten-line quotation in French from] 'HELVÉTIUS'; [*8*] blank; 1-181 text for Part I; *182* blank; *183* 184-383 text for Part II; *384* blank; endpaper.

Cased in black cloth with white endpapers. Front and back: blank. Spine: [in green] *'THE* | *LIVING* | *AND THE* | *DEAD* | *Patrick* | *White* | [at bottom:] *ROUTLEDGE'.*

Pale green dustjacket with thin white horizontal lines. Front: [in black] *'THE LIVING* | *AND* | *THE DEAD* | [illust. of two soldiers in a trench] | [at bottom:] *Patrick* | *White'.* Back: [publisher's device] | [advertisements for four books in Routledge's International Fiction Library] | [publisher's device]. Spine: *'THE* | *LIVING* | *AND THE* | *DEAD* | *Patrick* | *White* | [publisher's device] | *ROUTLEDGE'.* Inside front flap: [blurb, 23 lines]. Inside back flap: blank.

Published in July 1941. Price: 10s 6d. After the typescript had been rejected by Harrap (the publisher in 1939 of *Happy Valley*), Faber, Chatto, Jonathan Cape and Heinemann, it was read by Herbert Read who accepted it on behalf of Routledge. The first print run of 1,428 was sold out within a year. The second printing was cancelled due to war shortages. Fewer than 350 copies were sent to Australia. White's total royalties amounted to £55 11s 2d.

Reviews: William Gibson *Manchester Guardian* 4 July 1941, p.8 (320w); *Times Literary Supplement* 5 July 1941, p.321 (750w); Kate O'Brien *The Spectator* v.167, 11 July 1941, p.44 (140w); Edwin Muir *Listener* 31 July 1941, p.175; Anthony West *New Statesman and Nation* v.22, 2 August 1941, p.114 (300w); Douglas Stewart *Bulletin* 22 October 1941, p.2.

Notes: The University of Sydney copy has a card with: 'Best Wishes from Patrick White', the ex libris of Colin B. Berckelman, and a booklabel of Angus & Robertson Ltd. The copy in the personal collection is a well-travelled copy, with the following provenances: Bookstamp: 'Ashwoods Pitt St. Sydney'; Bookstamp: 'Waterloo Book Stall Wodehouse Road. Fort, Bombay'; and in manuscript on title page: 'Patrick White 1984'. ADFA has an 'Advance Copy' sewn in blue paper. Front: 'THE LIVING | AND THE DEAD | [oxford rule] | Patrick White | [oxford rule] | ADVANCE COPY | Eyre & Spottiswoode • Publishers • Ltd | Large Crown 8vo pp 336 About 22s 6d net | Probable publication November 1962'.

Copies: NSL: Mitchell Library [PW]; NU: RB 1641.4; VSL: SLT A823.3 W585L (lacks dustjacket); VSL: La Trobe Library Moir Collection (lacks dustjacket); Personal collection (lacks dustjacket); VU: AX A 823.3 White (lacks dustjacket).

D2b U.K. First Edition Second Issue (London: Routledge, 1941)

Not seen, but referred to in the *Cumulative Book Index 1938-1942*. Published in December 1941. Price: 9s.

D3a U.K. Second Edition First Issue (London: Eyre & Spottiswoode, 1962)

PATRICK WHITE | * * * | The Living and the Dead | [at bottom:] 1962 | EYRE & SPOTTISWOODE | *London*

20.5 x 13.7 cm. [A]^8 B-V^8: 168 leaves. pp.*10* 11-163 *164-166* 167-334 *335-336*.

Endpaper; *1-2* blank; *3* 'The Living and the Dead' | [blurb, repeating some of that on inside front flap, 18 lines]; *4* '*Also by Patrick White* | HAPPY VALLEY | THE AUNT'S STORY | THE TREE OF MAN | VOSS | RIDERS IN THE CHARIOT'; *5* title page; *6* '*First published in 1941 by* | *The Viking Press, New York* | *First published in Great Britain in 1962 by* | *Eyre & Spottiswoode (Publishers) Ltd* | *22 Henrietta Street, Covent Garden, WC2* | *Printed in Great Britain by* | *Northumberland Press Ltd, Gateshead-on-Tyne* | *Catalogue No. 6/4278/2*'; *7* [epigraph from] 'HELVÉTIUS'; *8* blank; *9* 'PART I'; *10* blank; 11-163 text for Part I; *164* blank; *165* 'PART II'; *166* blank; 167-334 *335* text for Part II; *336* blank; endpaper.
Cased in dark blue imitation cloth with off-white endpapers. Front and back: blank. Spine: [in gold] [cursive] '*The* | *Living* | *and the* | *Dead* | [ornament] | *Patrick* | *White* | [at bottom:] *E & S*.

White laminated paper dustjacket with red illust. of two heads. Front: [in green] 'THE LIVING | AND THE | DEAD | [illust.] | [at bottom:] PATRICK | WHITE'. Back: [in red] '*The novels of Patrick White* | [in green] *RIDERS IN THE CHARIOT* | [quotation of five lines from] | A. ALVAREZ *New Statesman* | *VOSS* | [quotation of four lines from] | WALTER ALLEN *New Statesman* | *THE TREE OF MAN* | [quotation of three lines from] | JOHN DAVENPORT *Observer* | *THE AUNT'S STORY* | [quotation of two lines from] | K. W. GRANSDEN *Encounter* | [in red] EYRE & SPOTTISWOODE LTD · 22 HENRIETTA STREET · LONDON W.C.2'. Spine: [in green] 'PATRICK | WHITE | [running down:] [in red] THE LIVING AND THE DEAD | [at bottom:] [upright:] [in green] E & S'. Inside front flap: [blurb, 28 lines] | [in red] 'JACKET ILLUSTRATION BY | SIDNEY NOLAN | [in green] [at left:] 6/4278/2 | [at right:] PRICE IN U.K. | 22s 6d net'. Inside back flap: [at bottom:] 'PRINTED IN GREAT BRITAIN'.

Published 8 November 1962. Price: 22s 6d.
Reviews: H.G. Kippax *Sydney Morning Herald* 19 January 1963.
Notes: Four of the seven copies examined have a pasteover on p.*6* which is as follows: '*First published in Great Britain 1941* | *This edition published by* | *Eyre & Spottiswoode (Publishers) Ltd 1962* | *Printed in Great Britain by* | *Northumberland Press Ltd, Gateshead-on-Tyne* | *Catalogue No. 6/4278/2*'. A State Library of New South Wales copy (NSL: JFR/066951) has the text of the pasteover actually printed on p.*6* indicating that it is either a separate issue or has had an in-press correction.
Copies: NU: RB IMP 7307; NSL: Mitchell Library A823/W587/2B1 (lacks dustjacket); NSL: JFR/066951; VSL: SLT A823.3 W585L (1962); Personal collections (3 copies).

D3b U.K. Second Edition Second Issue (London: Eyre & Spottiswoode, 1962)

Notes: p.*6* '*First printed in Great Britain in 1941* | *This edition published by* | *Eyre & Spottis-woode (Publishers) Ltd 1962* | *Reprinted 1962* | *Printed in Great Britain by* | *Northumberland Press Ltd, Gateshead-on-Tyne* | *Catalogue No. 6/4278/2*'.

D4a Penguin Edition First Issue (Harmondsworth: Penguin, 1967)

Patrick White | The Living and the Dead | Penguin Books | in association | with Eyre & Spottiswoode

18.2 x 11.1 cm. [A]^{16} B-E^{16} F-H^8 I-N^{16}: 184 leaves. pp.[2] *1-6* 7-357 *358-366*.

[*1-2*] blank; *1* 'Penguin Book 2623 | The Living and the Dead' | [biography, 22 lines]; *2* blank; *3* title page; *4* 'Penguin Books Ltd, Harmondsworth, | Middlesex, England | Penguin Books Pty Ltd, Ringwood, | Victoria, Australia | First published in 1941 | This edition published by Eyre & Spottiswoode 1962 | Published in Penguin Books 1967 | Copyright © Patrick White, 1941 | Made and printed in Great Britain by | Cox & Wyman Ltd, London, Reading & Fakenham | Set in Monotype Bembo | [publisher's conditions, 8 lines]'; *5* [epigraph from] 'HELVÉTIUS'; *6* blank; 7-172 text of Part One; 173-357, *358* text of Part Two; *359* 'More about Penguins'; *360* blank; *361* 'Voss'; *362* 'The Aunt's Story'; *363* 'The Tree of Man'; *364* 'Riders in the Chariot'; *365* 'Short Stories by Patrick White | The Burnt Ones'; *366* 'The Fetish and other Stories | *Alberto Moravia*'.

Perfectbound in white paper and printed in colour. Front: [at top left:] [publisher's device] | [in orange] 'A PENGUIN BOOK | [in black] PATRICK WHITE | [in orange] THE LIVING | AND THE DEAD' | [col. illust. of a man and a dove]. Back: [in white on orange] [blurb, 13 lines] | 'Cover design by Jack Larkin | [in black on orange] For copyright reasons this edition is not for sale in | the U.S.A. or Canada | United Kingdom 7/6 | Australia $1.30 | New Zealand $1.00 | South Africa R1.00'. Spine: [running down:] [in white on orange] 'Patrick White [in black on orange] The Living and the Dead | [upright:] [publisher's device] | 2623'. Inside front and back covers: blank.

Price: 7/6, AU$1.30, NZ$1.00, R1.00.

Copies: VSL: Kilvington Collection; NSL: Mitchell Library A823/W587/2C1.

D4b Penguin Edition Second Issue (Harmondsworth: Penguin, 1974)

Notes: p.*4* 'Published in Penguin Books in 1967 | Reprinted 1974 | [...] | Made and printed in Great Britain by | Cox & Wyman Ltd, London, Reading & Fakenham | Set in Monotype Bembo'. Cover design by Jack Larkin. Price: 40p, AU$1.35, NZ$1.35. ISBN 0 1400 2623 1.

D4c Penguin Edition Australian Issue (Harmondsworth: Penguin, 1974)

Notes: p.*4* 'Published in Penguin Books in 1967 | Reprinted 1974 | Copyright © Patrick White, 1941 | Made and printed in Australia at | The Dominion Press, North Blackburn,

Victoria | Set in Monotype Bembo'. Cover design by Jack Larkin. Price: AU$1.80, NZ$1.80. ISBN 0 1400.2623 1.

D4d Penguin Edition Third Issue (Harmondsworth: Penguin, 1975)

Notes: p.*4* 'Published in Penguin Books 1967 | Reprinted in 1974, 1975 | Copyright © Patrick White, 1941 | Made and printed in Great Britain by | Cox & Wyman Ltd, London, Reading and Fakenham | Set in Monotype Bembo'. Cover design by Jack Larkin. Price: 90p, NZ$3.05. ISBN 0 1400.2623 1.

D4e Penguin Edition Fourth Issue (Harmondsworth: Penguin, 1977)

Notes: p.*4* 'Published in Penguin Books in 1967 | Reprinted 1974, 1975, 1977 | [...] | Made and printed in Great Britain by | Cox & Wyman Ltd, London, Reading and Fakenham | Set in Monotype Bembo'. Cover design by Jack Larkin.

D4f Penguin Edition Fifth Issue (Harmondsworth: Penguin, 1983)

Notes: 19.8 cm x 12.9 cm. Page *4* 'Published in Penguin Books in 1967 | Reprinted 1974, 1975, 1977, 1983 | [...] | Printed and bound in Great Britain by | Cox & Wyman Ltd, Reading | Set in Monotype Bembo'. Cover design by Neil Stuart. Cover illustration by Mel Odom. Price: £2.95, AU$6.95, CAN$6.95, US$5.95. ISBN 0 1400.2623 1.

D4g Penguin Edition Sixth Issue (Harmondsworth: Penguin, n.d.)

Notes: not seen, but assumed given statement on p.*4* of D4h below.

D4h Penguin Edition Seventh Issue (Harmondsworth: Penguin, [1992])

Notes: p.*4* 'Published in Penguin Books 1967 | 10 9 8 7 | [...] | Printed in England by Clays Ltd, St Ives plc | Set in Monotype Bembo'. The cover shows *Backs of Houses, Chelsea* by Malcolm Drummond in the Southampton City Art Gallery. Published in the United Kingdom in January and in Australia in March 1992. Price: £6.99, AU$16.95, CAN$13.99, US$10.95. ISBN 0-14-018526-7.

D.t1 Polish First Edition (Warsaw: PIW, 1966)

Patrick White | ŻYWI I UMARLI | Przełożyla | MARIA SKIBNIEWSKA | Państwowy Instytut Wydawniczy

$[1]^8$ 2-28^8 29^2 ($2 signed): 226 leaves. pp.*8* 9-216 *217-220* 221-450 *451-452*.

1 [publisher's device] | 'WHITE | ŻYWI I UMARLI'; *2* blank; *3* title page; *4* 'Tytuł oryginału | «THE LIVING AND THE DEAD» | Okładke projektowała | EWA FRYSZTAK'; *5* [epigraph from] *'Helvetius'*; *6* blank; *7* 'CZĘŚĆ PIERWSZA'; *8* blank; 9-216 *217* text of Part I; *218* blank; *219* 'CZĘŚĆ DRUGA'; *220* blank; 221-450 *451* text of Part II; *452* 'Printed in Poland | Państwowy Instytut Wydawniczy, Warszawa 1966 r. | Wydanie pierwsze. Nakład 20 000 + 290 egz. Ark. | wyd. 21,3. Ark. druk. 28,25. Papier sat. kl. V, 60 g, | 82X104 cm. z Fabryki Papieru we Włocławku. Od- | dano do składania 12. VIII. 1965 r. Podpisano do | druku 23. XII. 1965 r. Druk ukończono w stycz- | niu 1966 r. Łódzka Drukarnia Dziełowa, Łódz, | ul. Rewolucji 1905 Roku 45. Zam. nr 394/A/65. E-81. | Cena zł 25.- | w prenumeracie zł 20.-'.

Sewn in off-white paper printed in crimson, black and olive. Front: [at top left:] [series device] | [in white] 'Patrick White [in black] ŻYWI I UMARLI' | [illust. of two women on a crimson background]. Back: 'Cena zł 25.- | w prenumeracie zł 20.-'. Spine: [running down:] 'PATRICK WHITE · ŻYWI I UMARLI ·' | [at bottom:] [upright:] [publisher's device]. Front flap: [Oxford rule] | 'KIK | KLUB | INTERESUJACAJ | KSIAŹKI' | [biography, 5 lines] | [blurb, 34 lines]. Back flap: 'Tytuły serii dziewiątej | *Patrick White* | ŻYWI I UMARLI | * | *Halldór Laxness* | CZYSTY TON | * | *Magda Szabo* | PIŁAT | * | *Martin Walser* | MAŁŻEŃSTWA | W PHILLIPPSBURGU | * | *Mika Waltari* | KARIN CÓRKA MAGNUSA | * | *John Oliver Killens* | A POTEM USŁYSZELIŚMY | GRZMOT | Cena kompletu w prenumeracie | na rok 1966 wynosi 90 zł + 10 zł | na opłatę połowy kosztów porta, | czyli zł 100.- | Sumę tę należy wpłacić na konto: | PKO Warszawa I-6-100022 Księgar- | nia „Oświata" KIK, podając czy- | telnie nazwisko i adres. | Książki wysylane są pocztą.' | [Oxford rule].

Copies: VSL: La Trobe Library SLT 819.93 W582LS; NSL: Mitchell Library A823/ W587/ 2D1 (lacks original spine); NSL: Mitchell Library [PW].

D.t2 Turkish First Edition (Istanbul: Sander Yayinlari, 1973)

PATRICK WHITE | YAŞAYANLAR VE ÖLÜLER | (THE LIVING AND THE DEAD) | ROMAN | Türkçesi : | BELKIS BAYSAL | SANDER YAYINLARI — ISTANBUL

18.5 x 13.5 cm. Unsigned: 188 leaves. pp.*9* 10-181 *182-183* 184-373 *374-376*.

1-2 blank; *3* 'SANDER YAYINLARI | ÇAĞDAS DÜNYA | YAZARLARI DIZISI : 13 | YAŞAYANLAR VE ÖLÜLER | (THE LIVING AND THE DEAD) | ROMAN | (1973 NOBEL | EDEBIYAT ÖDÜLÜ)'; *4* blank; *5* title page; *6* 'SANDER YAYINLARI | ISTANBUL | Halâskârgazi Caddesi 275-277, Osmanbey | Tel.: 48 32 09 | Yayin ve Dağitim : Kiraği Sokak 62-2, Osmanbey | Tel : 40 84 75 | Lâtin Matbaasi - Tel. : 26 47 81 Istanbul, Kasim 1973'; *7* [nine-line quotation from] 'HELVETIUS'; *8* blank; *9* 10-181 text of 'BIRINCI BÖLÜM'; *182* blank; *183* 184-373 text of 'IKINCI BÖLÜM'; 374 [*2*] blank.

Perfectbound in glossy white paper. Front: 'patrick white | [in red] NOBEL 1973 | yaşayanlar ve ölüler | [in grey] roman | [col. illust.] | [in black] sander yayinlari – istanbul' [publisher's device]. Back: [at top left:] [b&w photograph of the author] | 'Çağdaş Dünya Yazarlari Dizisi: 13 | Patrick White | YAŞAYANLAR VE ÖLÜLER | (The Living and the

Dead) | Roman | [biography, 7 lines] | [blurb, 11 lines] | [at centre:] ÇETIN [publisher's device] OFSET | 27 32 87 ISTANBUL | [at right:] Kapak düzeni: Mehmet Aksel'. Spine: 'Çağdaş | dünya | yazarlari | dizisi | [in circle:] 13 | [running down:] [in black] PATRICK WHITE YAŞAYANLAR VE ÖLÜLER' | [upright:] [publisher's device]. Inside front and back covers: blank.

Copies: VSL: La Trobe Library SLT A823.3 W582LB

D.t3 Spanish First Edition (Barcelona: Barral Editores, 1974)

PATRICK WHITE | LOS VIVOS | Y LOS MUERTOS | [publisher's device] | BREVE | BIBLIOTECA DE LITERATURAS | BARRAL EDITORES | 1974

19.3 x 12.5 cm. [1]^8 2-26^8 ($1 signed): 208 leaves. pp.*8* 9-195 *196-198* 199-413 *414-416*.

1-2 blank; *3* 'LOS VIVOS Y LOS MUERTOS'; *4* blank; *5* title page; *6* 'Titulo de la edición original: | *The Living and the Dead* | Traducción de: | *Idalia Cordero* | Primera edición: junio, 1974 | © Patrick White | © de los derechos en lengua castellana y de la traducción española: | BARRAL EDITORES, S.A. - Barcelona, 1973 | ISBN 84-211-0308-3 | Depósito Legal: B. 25549 - 1974   Printed in Spain | Gráficas Diamante, Zamora, 83. Barcelona - 5'; *7* 'PRIMERA PARTE'; *8* blank; 9-195 text of Part I; *196* blank; *197* 'SEGUNDA PARTE'; *198* blank; 199-413 text of Part II; *414* blank; *415* 'Impreso en el mes | de mayo de 1974 | en los talleres de | Gráficas Diamante | Zamora, 83, Barcelona'; *416* blank.

Sewn in grey paper printed in full colour. Front: [in box:] 'PATRICK WHITE | LOS VIVOS | Y LOS MUERTOS | [col. illust. of man in a room] [printed over the col. illust.] [publisher's device] BARRAL'. Back: [col. illust. of man coming out of the illust. of the room] | [blurb, 11 lines] | [in box:] 'SERIES DE RESPUESTA 108 | BREVE BIBLIOTECA DE LITERATURAS 19 | [publisher's device] BARRAL EDITORES'. Spine: [running down:] 'PATRICK WHITE LOS VIVOS Y LOS MUERTOS | [at bottom:] [upright:] 108' | [publisher's device]. Inside front flap: [photograph of the author] | [biography, 18 lines] | 'Bibliografia' | [9 lines]. Inside back flap: '*TITULOS PUBLICADOS*'.

Black paper wrap-around: [in silver] 'OTRA GRAN NOVELA | DE PATRICK WHITE | PREMIO NOBEL 1973'.

Copies: NSL: Mitchell Library A823/W587/34; NSL: Mitchell Library [PW]; Personal collection.

D.t4 French First Edition (Paris: Gallimard, 1990)

PATRICK WHITE | DES MORTS | ET DES VIVANTS | roman | *Traduit de l'anglais* | *par Jean Lambert* | [publisher's device] | GALLIMARD

20.4 x 14 cm. Unsigned: 204 leaves. pp.*12* 13-406 *407-408* (the last page of each chapter is unnumbered).

1-3 blank; *4* 'DU MÊME AUTEUR | *Aux Éditions Gallimard* | EDEN-VILLE | LE CHAR DES ÉLUS | VOSS | LES ÉCHAUDÉS | LE MYSTÉRIEUX MANDALA |

LŒIL DU CYCLONE | LE VIVISECTEUR | UNE CEINTURE DE FEUILLES | LES INCARNATIONS D'EDDIE TWYBORN | DÉFAUTS DANS LE MIROIR : Un autoportrait. | MÉMOIRES ÉCLATÉS D'ALEX XENOPHON DEMIRJIAN GRAY'; *5* '*Du monde entier*'; *6* blank; *7* title page; *8* '*Titre original :* | THE LIVING AND THE DEAD | © *Patrick White, 1941.* | © *Éditions Gallimard, 1990, pour la traduction française.*'; *9* [epigraph]; *10* blank; *11* '*Première partie*'; *12* blank; 13-406 *407* text; *408* 'Composé et achevé d'imprimer | par la Société Nouvelle Firmin-Didot | à Mesnil-Sur-l'Estrée, le 28 septembre 1990. | Dépôt légal : septembre 1990. | Numéro d'imprimeur : 13081. | ISBN 2-07-071791-7 | Imprimé en France | 50054'.

Sewn in buff coloured card. Front: 'DU MONDE ENTIER | PATRICK WHITE | [in red] ROMAN | TRADUIT DE L'ANGLAIS | PAR JEAN LAMBERT | [series device] | [in red] [publisher's device] | [in black] GALLIMARD'. Back: 'PATRICK WHITE | [in red] Des morts et des vivants | [in black] [description, 34 lines] | [barcode] [device] 90-X A71791   ISBN 2-07-071791-7   180FF   tc'. Spine: [in red] '*du monde* | *entier*' | [in black] PATRICK | WHITE | [in red] DES MORTS | ET DES VIVANTS | [in black] [publisher's device] | GALLIMARD'.

Published in October 1990. Price: 180 FF.

Copies: VSL: SLT A823.3/W585LL.

D.m1 Sound Recording (Hobart: Hear-a-Book, 1983)

The Living and the Dead (11 audiocassettes).

Read by Harry Dodson from the Eyre & Spottiswoode edition of 1962.

E The Aunt's Story (1948)

Patrick White appears to have conceived the idea of *The Aunt's Story* sometime in 1939, and the exercise book which contained his war diary for several months of 1941 also contained sketches for *The Aunt's Story*. In 1946 White bought Roy de Maistre's painting entitled 'The Figure in the Garden (The Aunt)'. White later claimed that 'Long before it [*The Aunt's Story*] was written I was seeing it in terms of Klee'. (For more on Klee and the writing of *The Aunt's Story*, see Helen Hewitt, *Patrick White, Painter Manqué*, Melbourne University Press, 2002.)

White was demobbed in London in January 1946; he immediately set to work on *The Aunt's Story*. 'My creative self, frozen silent by the war years began to thaw … I can't say it poured on to the paper after the years of drought; it was more like a foreign substance torn out by ugly handfuls' (*Flaws* p.127). The first part of *The Aunt's Story* was written in London, the second part in Alexandria and the third on board the *Strathmore* as it sailed for Australia. By January 1947 the final draft was complete and the typescript was sent to Ben Huebsch (The Viking Press) in New York and to Routledge in London. Both publishers accepted the novel for publication. Routledge was said to be 'extremely enthusiastic' but could not give a publication date because there was a continuing paper shortage in Britain. Huebsch wrote: 'The book will surely add to your reputation among the discerning' (19 May 1947).

A number of problems arose with The Viking Press edition. Firstly, a new title, *Theo's Story*, was suggested by Huebsch. This was rejected by White. Secondly, Viking wanted to change the name of the character John Holstius because they thought the real John Holstius of San Francisco might object. White wrote to Holstius and he raised no objection. The third problem was that Viking did not intend to send proofs to White. White insisted and then proceeded to make 31 corrections. Fourteen of these were accepted and an errata slip was added to the first printing. In the second printing the errors were corrected.

The United States edition was published by The Viking Press early in 1948. The reviews were favourable although White believed they showed that the book would have a limited market. In fact, the first printing of 6,000 sold out in a week, and a second, corrected printing was issued.

The United Kingdom edition was published by Routledge in August 1948. The English reviews were respectful but not enthusiastic. Sales were slow. Of 4,000 copies in the first printing, half were remaindered in 1951. In Australia, reviews were off-hand. Supplies took nearly four months to arrive. 'White flicked through library copies and saw by their pages where his readers' interest had run dry in the gravel of the *jardin exotique*' (*Life* p.258).

The Aunt's Story was later republished in 1958 by Eyre & Spottiswoode, apparently as part of Eyre & Spottiswoode's series of White's novels. It was a modest commercial, though strong critical success, vindicating White's own sense that the novel was an artistic achievement.

As early as August 1948 White had heard that Gallimard was doing French translations of both *Happy Valley* and *The Aunt's Story*, though at this time he did not know who would be the translator. (To Ben Huebsch, 6 August 1948) Almost four years later White received a presentation copy of *Eden-Ville* and was being pestered by the translator, Marie Viton [Marie d'Estournelles de Constant] about *The Aunt's Story*. After the perceived failure of *Eden-Ville* (although it apparently went through five printings) Gallimard lost interest in White, renouncing options on his early novels. Viton was by this stage critically ill and died in May 1954. As Viton worked on her French translation, Casini published an Italian translation in 1951. White had not received a single query about this translation and was concerned about how it had been done. A number of other translations appeared after the Nobel Prize, including Turkish (1973), Spanish (1974), Japanese (1976), Serbo-Croatian (1979), Greek (1988) and Swedish (1991).

White always considered *The Aunt's Story* as a favourite and was delighted to hear that Allen Lane had decided to do the novel as a Penguin, just as he was delighted in 1975 when Glenda Jackson proposed a film version, and in 1989 when it was produced as a radio play.

Concerning the physical appearance of his books, White was always prepared to give an opinion. He thought The Viking Press edition *looked* very striking, though he abhorred the errors. The Routledge edition, while more modestly presented due to wartime shortages, reproduced on the jacket de Maistre's painting which had so influenced White. The jacket on the Eyre & Spottiswoode edition of 1958 had a Nolan painting which White liked 'in itself (I have the original hanging in my living room), but it is not my character'. White's criticisms must have been heeded by Nolan who was again commissioned for the Penguin edition. 'I had seen an early painting of his which seemed to convey much more of Theodora Goodman than the jacket he did for the E&S hardcover edition, and now he is going to do something along the lines of that early painting of a woman caught in her net veil.' (To the Moores, 27 April 1963)

* * * * *

E1a U.S. First Edition First Issue (New York: Viking Press, 1948)

Patrick White | The | Aunt's | Story | New York 1948 | The Viking Press

20.8 x 13.7 cm. [A]^8 B-I^{16} K^8 (χ_1 [= errata] is inserted after A$_3$): 145 leaves. pp.[8] *1-2* 3-125 *126-128* 129-246 *247-248* 249-281 *282*.

Endpaper; [1] 'The Aunt's Story'; [2] 'By the same author | THE LIVING | AND THE DEAD | HAPPY VALLEY'; [3] title page; [4] 'For | Betty Withycombe | COPYRIGHT 1948 | BY PATRICK WHITE | FIRST PUBLISHED | BY THE VIKING PRESS | IN JANUARY 1948 | PUBLISHED ON THE SAME DAY | IN THE DOMINION OF CANADA | BY THE MACMILLAN COMPANY | OF CANADA LIMITED | SET IN | CASLON AND JANSON TYPES | AND PRINTED IN U.S.A. | BY THE VAIL-BALLOU PRESS, INC.'; [5] 'Contents | PART ONE 1 | Meroë | PART TWO 127 | Jardin Exotique | PART THREE 247 | Holstius'; [6] 'All the characters of this story are | wholly imaginary and have no ref- | erence whatever to actual people.'; [7] 'ERRATA'; [8] blank; *1* 'Part One | Meroë | *She thought of the narrow-* | *ness of the limits within which a* | *hu-* *man soul may speak and be* | *understood by its nearest of* | *mental kin, of how soon it* | *reaches that* *solitary land of the* | *individual experience, in which* | *no fellow footfall is ever heard.* | OLIVE SCHREINER'; *2* blank; 3-125 text for Part One; *126* blank; *127* 'Part Two | Jardin | Ex-otique | *Henceforward we walk split* | *into myriad fragments, like an* | *insect with a hundred feet, a* | *centipede with soft-stirring feet* | *that drinks in the atmosphere;* | *we walk with sensitive filaments* | *that drink avidly of past and fu-* | *ture, and all things melt into* | *music and sorrow; we walk* | *against a united world, asserting* | *our dividedness. All things, as* | *we walk, splitting with us into* | *a myriad iridescent fragments.* | *The great fragmentation of ma-* | *turity.* | HENRY MILLER'; *128* blank; 129-246 text for Part Two; *247* 'Part Three | Holstius | *When your life is most real,* | *to me you are mad.* | OLIVE SCHREINER'; *248* blank; 249-281 text for Part Three; *282* blank; endpaper.

Cased in beige calico boards with off-white endpapers. Front: [in beige on olive green panel:] 'The | AUNT's | Story'. Back: blank. Spine: [in olive green] 'PATRICK | WHITE | [in beige on olive green] The | AUNT's | Story | [in olive green] Viking'. Inside front and back covers: blank.

White paper dustjacket printed in olive green and black and signed 'Bill English'. Front: [in white on black square] 'The | [in olive green] AUNT[in white]'s | Story | [in black] a | novel by | PATRICK WHITE'. Back: [in olive green box:] [quotation of six lines from] '— ALFRED KAZAN | [in black] [blurb, 27 lines] | [at left:] [in olive green box:] THE | AUNT'S | STORY | BY | PATRICK WHITE | [at bottom:] [in olive green box:] [quotation of five lines from] —JOHN WOODBURN'. Inside front flap: '*The Aunt's Story* $3.00 | *FROM THE BOOK, PAGES 230-31*' | [quotation of 38 lines]. Inside back flap: [b&w photograph of the author] | 'PHOTO BY BASIL GREEN | [in green] *Patrick White* | [in black] [biography, 7 lines] | [in green] THE VIKING PRESS | 18 East 48 Street | New York, New York | [in black] PRINTED IN THE U.S.A. | PATRICK WHITE | *The Aunt's Story* | VIKING'.

Published in October 1948. Price: $3. Run: 6,000.

Reviews: *Kirkus* v.15, 1 November 1947, p.607 (210w); E.H. Kennedy *Library Journal* v.72, 1 December 1947, p.1686 (80w); Walter Havighurst *Saturday Review of Literature* v.31, 3 January 1948, p.11 (650w); Iris Barry *New York Herald Tribune Weekly Book Review* 4 January 1948, p.2 (550w); Feike Feikema *Chicago Sun* 6 January 1948, (410w); Hamilton Basso *New Yorker* v.23, 10 January 1948, p.80 (280w); James Stern *New York Times Book Review* 11 January 1948, p.5 (750w); *Booklist* v.44, 15 February 1948, p.217 (410w); John Woodburn *New Republic* v.118, 16 February 1948, p.27 (1200w); Diana Trilling *Nation* v.166, 21 February 1948, p.219 (1300w).

Copies: NSL: Mitchell Library 823.914/W587/34 (lacks dustjacket); NSL: Mitchell Library [PW]; VU: A823.3 White; Personal collection (3 copies).

E1b U.S. First Edition Second Issue (New York: Viking, 1948)

Not seen, but referred to in the Compass Paperback Edition (1962) for which see E1d below.

E1c Canadian Subedition (Toronto: Macmillan, 1948)

Published simultaneously with E1a. Price: CAN$3.25. (*Cumulative Book Index*).

E1d Compass Subedition (New York: Viking Press, 1962)

Patrick White | The | Aunt's | Story | New York | The Viking Press

19.5 x 13 cm. Unsigned: 144 leaves. pp.[*6*] *1-2* 3-125 *126-128* 129-246 *247-248* 249-281 *282*.

Notes: p.*4* 'FIRST PUBLISHED IN 1948 | BY THE VIKING PRESS, INC. | SECOND PRINTING 1948 | COMPASS BOOKS EDITION | ISSUED IN 1962 | BY THE VIKING PRESS, INC. | 625 MADISON AVENUE | NEW YORK 22, NEW YORK | PUBLISHED ON THE SAME DAY | IN THE DOMINION OF CANADA | BY THE MACMILLAN COMPANY | OF CANADA LIMITED | PRINTED IN THE U.S.A. BY | THE MURRAY PRINTING COMPANY'. Perfectbound in white card. Cover design [illust. of woman seated by a fern] by James and Ruth McCrea. Price: US$1.45, CAN$1.69.

Copies: NSL: Mitchell Library [PW].

E1e U.S. First Edition Viking Subedition (New York: Viking Press, 1974)

Notes: p.[*4*] [floral ornament] [dedication] 'FOR BETTY WITHYCOMBE | Copyright 1948 by Patrick White | All rights reserved | First published in 1948 by The Viking Press, Inc. | 625 Madison Avenue, New York, N.Y. 10022 | Published simultaneously in Canada by | The Macmillan Company of Canada Limited | SBN 670-14168-2 | Library of Congress catalog card number: 48-5103 | Printed in U.S.A.'. Cased in black calico cloth stamped on spine in metallic red. Yellow paper dustjacket printed in black. Published in 1974. Price: US$7.95. Reprint of the 1948 edition. Uniform with White's other titles, published in 1974 after the awarding of the Nobel Prize.

Copies: NSL: Mitchell Library [PW].

E2 U.K. First Edition First Issue (London: Routledge & Kegan Paul, 1948)

Patrick White | [swelled rule] | THE AUNT'S STORY | *A NOVEL* | [at bottom:] ROUTLEDGE & KEGAN PAUL LIMITED

18.9 x 12.7 cm. [1]^{16} 2-11^{16} ($1 signed): 176 leaves. pp.[*8*] 3-154 *155-156* 157-302 *303-304* 305-346.

Endpaper; [*1*] 'THE AUNT'S STORY | By PATRICK WHITE. Author of "The Living and the Dead."'; [*2*] '*By the same Author* | HAPPY VALLEY | THE LIVING AND THE DEAD'; [*3*] title page; [*4*] '*First published in England by* | ROUTLEDGE & KEGAN PAUL LTD. | Broadway House, 68-74 Carter Lane, | London, E.C.4 | 1948 | for | BETTY WITHYCOMBE | THIS BOOK IS PRODUCED IN COMPLETE | CONFORMITY WITH THE AUTHORISED | ECONOMY STANDARDS | Printed and bound in England by William Clowes and Sons Limited | London and Beccles'; [*5*] 'CONTENTS | PART I. MEROE . . . . . 3 | PART II. JARDIN EXOTIQUE . . . . 157 | PART III. HOLSTIUS . . . . . 305'; [*6*] blank; [*7*] 'PART I | MEROË | [epigraph of five lines from] OLIVE SCHREINER'; [*8*] blank; 3-154 text of Part I; *155* 'PART II | JARDIN EXOTIQUE | [epigraph of eight lines from] HENRY MILLER'; *156* blank; 157-302 text of Part II; *303* 'PART III | HOLSTIUS | [epigraph of one line from] OLIVE SCHREINER'; *304* blank; 305-346 text of Part III; endpaper.

Cased in dark blue cloth with white endpapers. Front and back: blank. Spine: [in gold] '*THE | AUNT'S | STORY | Patrick | White | ROUTLEDGE & | KEGAN PAUL*'.

White glossy paper dustjacket with black and white illust. by Roy de Maistre on front. Front: [in white] 'THE | AUNT'S | STORY | *by* | PATRICK | WHITE'. Back: 'THE AUNT'S STORY | [blurb, 24 lines] | *See flaps of jacket for biographical sketch and photo of the author* | PATRICK WHITE'. Spine: 'THE | AUNT'S | STORY | *by* | PATRICK | WHITE | [at bottom:] Routledge | & | Kegan | Paul'. Inside front flap: [b&w photograph of the author] | 'PATRICK WHITE | [biography, 18 lines] | [*continued on back flap* | 10s. 6d. net'. Inside back flap: '*continued from front flap*] | [biography continues, 25 lines] | WORKS | NOVELS. *Happy Valley* (Harrap 1938). Won gold | medal for best Australian novel of its year. | *The Living and the Dead* (Routledge 1941). | *The Aunt's Story* (Routledge 1948). All three novels have been published in the | United States by the Viking Press. | SHORT STORIES have been published in the | *London Mercury* and *Horizon* as well as in Australian | publications. | SKETCHES & LYRICS have appeared in West | End Theatrical Revues. | VERSE has been published by the *London Mercury*, | *New Verse* and Australian publications. | [rule] | JACKET. The jacket is a reproduction in black and | white of a picture by Roy de Maistre, "The Garden".'.

Published in September 1948. Price: 10s 6d. Run: 4,000.

Reviews: *Times Literary Supplement* 2 October 1948, p.553 (180w); *Age Literary Supplement* 12 February 1949, p.6; John Betjeman *Daily Herald* 21 September 1948; *Sydney Morning Herald* 7 August 1948, p.6; *Southerly* 1950, p.209-210.

Notes: An uncorrected proof copy has been sighted in private collection. It is sewn in a plain brown paper wrapper with white paper paste-on on front: 'WILLIAM CLOWES AND SONS | LIMITED | [at left:] [in red] | [printer's device] | [at right:] [in black] CAXTON

PRESS | BECCLES | SUFFOLK | *Telephone Beccles 2103* | [swelled rule] | TITLE [in typescript] THE AUNT'S STORY | SIZE [in typescript] Crown 8vo EXTENT [in typescript] i-vi & 1-346 | TYPE [in typescript] 12 pt. Bembo | DATE [in typescript] 12.3.48 STAGE [in typescript] Revise'.

Copies: NSL: Mitchell Library [PW]; NSL: Mitchell Library A823/W587/3A1 (lacks dustjacket); NSL: GRL N828.99943/W587/9 (lacks dustjacket); VSL: SLT 819.93/W582A (lacks dustjacket); Personal collection (2 copies).

E3a U.K. Second Edition First Issue (London: Eyre & Spottiswoode, 1958)

[hollow type] THE | AUNT'S | STORY | [solid type] Patrick White | 1958 | EYRE & SPOTTISWOODE | LONDON

20.6 x 13.3 cm. [1]⁸ 2-19⁸ ($1 signed): 152 leaves. pp.*8* 9-137 *138-140* 141-265 *266-268* 269-302 *303-304*.

Endpaper; *1* 'THE AUNT'S STORY' | [blurb, 14 lines, repeated in part from the inside front flap]; *2* 'By the same author | THE LIVING AND THE DEAD | HAPPY VALLEY | THE TREE OF MAN | VOSS'; *3* title page; *4* 'For Betty Withycombe | All the characters in this story are | wholly imaginary and have no | reference whatever to actual people | FIRST PUBLISHED 1948 | THIS EDITION PUBLISHED 1958 | BY EYRE & SPOTTISWOODE | CATALOGUE NO 6/4174 | PRINTED IN GREAT BRITAIN BY | HAZELL WATSON AND VINEY LTD | AYLESBURY AND SLOUGH'; *5* 'Contents'; *6* blank; *7* 'Part One MEROË | [ornamented rule] | [epigraph from] OLIVE SCHREINER'; *8* blank; 9-137 text of Part One; *138* blank; *139* 'Part Two | JARDIN EXOTIQUE | [ornamented rule] | [epigraph from] HENRY MILLER'; *140* blank; 141-265 text of Part Two; *266* blank; *267* 'Part Three HOLSTIUS | [ornamented rule] | [epigraph from] OLIVE SCHREINER'; *268* blank; 269-302 *303* text of Part Three; *304* blank; endpaper.

Cased in dark blue linen with white endpapers. Front and back: blank. Spine: [in gold] '*The | Aunt's | Story* | [ornament] | *Patrick | White* | [at bottom:] *E & S*.

White paper wrappers with a brown illust. of a woman's head on front and spine. Front: [in white] '*The | Aunt's | Story* | [illust.] | *Patrick White*'. Back: 'PATRICK WHITE | is also the author of *The Tree of Man* and *Voss* | [quotation of 12 lines from] EILEEN FRASER | *Twentieth Century.* | [quotation of six lines from] WALTER ALLEN *New Statesman.* | [quotation of three lines from] GERALD BULLETT *The Bookman.* | [quotation of four lines from] JOHN DAVENPORT *Observer.* | [quotation of five lines from] JAMES STERN *New York Times Book Review.* | [quotation of three lines from] KENNETH YOUNG *Daily Telegraph.* | Eyre & Spottiswoode · Publishers · Ltd'. Spine: [in brown] '*The | Aunt's | Story* | [in white] *Patrick | White* | [in brown] *E & S*. Inside front flap: 'The Aunt's Story | PATRICK WHITE | [blurb, 32 lines] | JACKET DESIGN BY SIDNEY NOLAN | [at bottom left:] 6/4174' | [price clipped]. Inside back flap: blank.

Published 4 December 1958. Price: 16s. Print run: 7,500. By 31 December 1959, 5,678 copies had been sold – 3,129 in the U.K. and 2,549 in the colonies, mainly Australia. Remained in print until 1974.

Reviews: *Advertiser* (Adelaide) 27 December 1958, p. 8; C. Kelly *Advertiser* (Adelaide) 17 January 1959, p. 24; *Age Literary Supplement* 19 April 1959; *Times Literary Supplement* 2 January 1959, p.5; *Southerly* v.20 no.1, 1959, p.51-55; *Quadrant* no.3, Spring 1959, p.91-92; *Bulletin* 4 November 1959, p.59; Peter Coleman *Observer* vol.2 no.3, 7 February 1959.

Notes: The original painting which was the basis for the dustjacket design is held in the Mitchell Library, State Library of New South Wales (ML 745). Oil? on paper, 24.3 x 19.6 cm. Signed and dated 'Nolan '58' at bottom right. Presented by White, August 1974.

Copies: NU: RB; NSL: Mitchell Library [PW]; VSL: 819.93/W582A; Personal collection (2 copies); NSL: Mitchell Library A823/W587/3B1.

E3b U.K. Second Edition Second Issue (London: Eyre & Spottiswoode, 1958)

Notes: not seen but referred to in Eyre & Spottiswoode archive, University of Reading. Published in February 1959. Print run: 2,775.

E3c U.K. Second Edition Third Issue (London: Eyre & Spottiswoode, 1969)

[hollow type] THE | AUNT'S | STORY | [solid type] Patrick White | EYRE & SPOTTISWOODE | LONDON

20.6 x 13.3 cm. [1]^8 2-14^8 [15]^8 [16]-[17]^{16} ([1]^8 2-14^8 gathered in sixteens): 152 leaves. pp.*8* 9-137 *138-140* 141-265 *266-268* 269-302 *303-304*.

Notes: p.*4* 'FIRST PUBLISHED 1949 [sic] | THIS EDITION PUBLISHED 1958 | BY EYRE & SPOTTISWOODE | REPRINTED 1969 | REPRODUCED AND PRINTED IN GREAT BRITAIN BY | REDWOOD PRESS LIMITED | TROWBRIDGE & LONDON | S.B.N. 423 41740 9'. Cased in blue cloth. White paper dustjacket with a brown illust. of a woman's head on front and spine. Price: £2.

Copies: NSL: JFR/066946.

E4a Penguin Edition First Australian Issue (Harmondsworth: Penguin, 1963)

PATRICK WHITE | THE AUNT'S STORY | PENGUIN BOOKS

18 x 11 cm. Unsigned: 152 leaves. pp.*10* 11-137 *138-140* 141-262 *263-264* 265-299 *300-304*.

1 'PENGUIN BOOKS | AU5 | THE AUNT'S STORY | PATRICK WHITE' | [publisher's device flanked by two boomerangs]; *2* blank; *3* title page; *4* 'Penguin Books Ltd, Harmondsworth, Middlesex, England | Penguin Books Pty Ltd, Mitcham, Victoria, Australia | [rule] | First Published by Eyre & Spottiswoode [sic] 1948 | Published in Penguin Books 1963 | [rule] | Printed in Australia for Penguin Books Pty Ltd | at The Griffin Press, Adelaide | Set in Intertype Garamond | [publisher's conditions, 7 lines]; *5* '*For* | BETTY

WITHYCOMBE'; *6* 'All the characters in this story are wholly | imaginary and have no reference whatever | to actual people'; *7* 'CONTENTS'; *8* blank; *9* '*Part One* MEROË | [quotation from] | OLIVE SCHREINER'; *10* blank; 11-137 text of Part One; *138* blank; *139* '*Part Two* JARDIN EXOTIQUE | [quotation of 9 lines from] | HENRY MILLER'; *140* blank; 141-262 text of Part Two; *263* '*Part Three* HOLSTIUS | [quotation of one line from] | OLIVE SCHREINER'; *264* blank; 265-299 text of Part Three; *300* blank; *301* [publisher's device] | '*The other novels by* | PATRICK WHITE | *which are available in Penguins | are described on the | next page*'; *302* blank; *303* 'PATRICK WHITE IN PENGUINS | VOSS | [blurb, 10 lines] | [quotation of two lines from] –Walter Allen in the *New Statesman* | [quotation of two lines from] –John Davenport in *The Observer* | THE TREE OF MAN | [blurb, 7 lines] | [quotation of two lines from] –Peter Green in *The Daily* | *Telegraph* | [quotation of three lines from] –John Davenport in *The Observer*'; *304* blank.

Perfectbound in white paper printed in orange, brown and black. Front: [at top left:] [publisher's device] 'a Penguin Book [at top right] 4/6 | [rule] | The Aunt's Story | [rule] | [in white] Patrick White' | [brown illust. of a woman's head wearing a hat]. Back: [at top right:] [publisher's device] 'a Penguin Book | [rule] | [in white] The Aunt's Story | [in black] [blurb, 17 lines] | [quotation of two lines from] –John Davenport in The *Observer* | [quotation of two lines from] – | Peter Green in The *Daily Telegraph* | [quotation of three lines from] –Phyllis Young in | The *Yorkshire Post* | *For copyright reasons this edition is not for sale in U.S.A. or Canada*'. Spine: [running down:] [in white] 'Patrick White [in black] The Aunt's Story | [upright:] [publisher's device] | AU5'. Inside front cover: [b&w photograph of author] | [biography, 25 lines] | 'Cover illustration by Sidney Nolan | *For a complete list of books available | please write to Penguin Books | whose address can be found on the | back of the title page*'. Inside back cover: 'SOME OTHER | AUSTRALIAN PENGUIN BOOKS | TO THE ISLANDS | *Randolph Stow* | [blurb, 6 lines] | * | KANGAROO TALES | *edited by Rosemary Wighton* | [blurb, 3 lines] | * | THREE AUSTRALIAN PLAYS | This volume in the famous Penguin Plays Series contains— | THE ONE DAY OF THE YEAR *by Alan Seymour* | NED KELLY *by Douglas Stewart* | THE TOWER *by Hal Porter* | The volume has an authoritative introduction to Australian drama | by H. Kippax ('Brek' of *Nation*). | * | THE AUSTRALIAN UGLINESS | *Robin Boyd*' | [blurb, 6 lines].

Price: 4/6 and 7s.

Reviews: Z. Ghose *Spectator* v.212, 17 April 1964, p.523.

Notes: The original artwork which was the basis for the cover design is held in the Mitchell Library, State Library of New South Wales. Sepia ripolin?, 29.8 x 24.7 cm. Initialled 'N' at bottom left. Untitled. Presented by White, August 1974. A number of copies of this issue have a different state of the binding, i.e. the price is given as 7s. The different treatment and pricing may indicate that the publishers had specific markets in mind. In which case it might be supposed that the 7s copies were aimed at the Australian market.

Copies: Personal collection; NSL: Mitchell Library A823/W587/3D1; VSL: Kilvington Collection; VSL: SLT 819.93/W582A (1963) Copy 1; NSL: Mitchell Library A823/W587/3C1; Personal collection.

E4b Penguin Edition Second Australian Issue (Harmondsworth: Penguin, 1969)
Notes: 18 x 11 cm. Page *4* 'Published in Penguin Books 1963 | Reprinted 1969 | [rule] |
Printed in Australia for Penguin Books Australia Ltd | at The Griffin Press, Adelaide | Set in
Intertype Garamond'. Cover design by Jack Larkin. Price: AU$1.25.

E4c Penguin Edition Third Australian Issue (Harmondsworth: Penguin, 1971)
Notes: p.*4* 'Published in Penguin Books 1963 | Reprinted 1969, 1971 | [rule] | Copyright ©
Patrick White, 1948 | [rule] | Printed in Australia for Penguin Books Australia Ltd | at Hal-
stead Press, Sydney | Set in Intertype Garamond'. Price: AU$1.25. SBN 1 4 007005 6.

E4d Penguin Edition Fourth Australian Issue (Harmondsworth: Penguin, 1974)
Notes: p.*4* 'Published in Penguin Books 1963 | Reprinted 1969, 1971, 1974 | [rule] | Copy-
right © Patrick White, 1948 | [rule] | Printed in Australia for Penguin Books Australia Ltd |
by Alexander Brothers, Mentone, Victoria | Set in Intertype Garamond'. Cover design by
Jack Larkin. There are two states of the binding of this issue. The first makes no mention of
White's Nobel Prize of 1973, while the second mentions it in the biography and on the back
cover. Price: AU$1.35 (sold for AU$2.50 in the late 1970s), NZ$1.35. ISBN 0 1407 00.05 6.

E4e Penguin Edition Fifth Australian Issue (Harmondsworth: Penguin, 1981)
Notes: p.*4* 'Published in Penguin Books, 1963 | Reprinted 1969, 1971, 1974, 1981 | Copy-
right © Patrick White, 1948 | Made and printed in Australia at | The Dominion Press,
Blackburn, Victoria | Set in Intertype Garamond'. The cover shows a detail from *Eileen* by
Tom Roberts, reproduced by permission of the Art Gallery | of New South Wales. Price:
AU$5.95.

E5a Penguin Edition First English Issue (Harmondsworth: Penguin Books, 1963)
Not seen, but referred to in E5e below. However, it may be that the reference in E5e is to
E4a; that is, the first issue printed in the United Kingdom was in fact E5e

E5b Penguin Edition Second English Issue (Harmondsworth: Penguin, 1969)
Not seen.

E5c Penguin Edition Third English Issue (Harmondsworth: Penguin Books, 1971)
Not seen.

E5d Penguin Edition Fourth English Issue (Harmondsworth: Penguin Books, 1974)
Not seen.

E5e Penguin Edition Fifth English Issue (Harmondsworth: Penguin Books, 1976)
PATRICK WHITE | THE AUNT'S STORY | [publisher's device] | PENGUIN BOOKS
18.1 x 11.1 cm. [1]^{12}2-12^{12} ($1 signed): 144 leaves. pp.*10* 11-131 *132-134* 135-251 *252-254*
255-286 287-288.

Notes: p.*4* 'Published in Penguin Books 1963 | Reprinted 1969, 1971, 1974, 1976 | [short
rule] | Copyright © Patrick White, 1948 | [short rule] | Made and printed in Great Britain

by | Hazell Watson & Viney Ltd, Aylesbury, Bucks | Set in Lintotype Granjon'. Cover design by Jack Larkin. Price: 75p, NZ$2.55. ISBN 0 1400 4145 1.

E5f Penguin Edition Sixth English Issue (Harmondsworth: Penguin, 1977)
Notes: p.*4* 'Published in Penguin Books 1963 | Reprinted 1969, 1971, 1974, 1976, 1977 | [short rule] | Copyright 1948 by Patrick White | All rights reserved | [short rule] | Made and printed in Great Britain | by Hazell Watson & Viney Ltd, | Aylesbury, Bucks | Set in Lintotype Granjon'. Price: AU$2.50.

E5g Penguin Edition Seventh English Issue (Harmondsworth: Penguin, 1982)
Not seen.

E5h Penguin Edition Eighth English Issue (Harmondsworth: Penguin, 1985)
Notes: 19.6 x 12.7 cm. Page *4* 'Published in Penguin Books 1963 | Reprinted 1969, 1971, 1974, 1976, 1977, 1982, 1985 | [rule] | Copyright © 1948 by Patrick White | Copyright © renewed Patrick White, 1976 | All rights reserved | [rule] | Made and printed in Great Britain by | Hazell Watson & Viney Limited, | member of the BPCC Group, | Aylesbury, Bucks | Set in Linotype Granjon'.

E5i Penguin Edition Ninth English Issue (Harmondsworth: Penguin, 1987)
Notes: 19.6 x 12.7 cm. Page *4* 'Published in Penguin Books 1963 | Reprinted 1969, 1971, 1974, 1976, 1977, 1978, 1985, 1987 | Copyright 1948 by Patrick White | Copyright © renewed by Patrick White, 1976 | All rights reserved | Made and printed in Great Britain by | Hazell Watson & Viney Limited, | Member of BPCC Group | Aylesbury, Bucks | Set in Lintotype Granjon'. The cover shows a detail from *Eileen* by Tom Roberts, reproduced by kind permission of the Art Gallery of New South Wales. Price: £3.95, AU$9.95, NZ$14.99, CAN$8.95, US$6.95. ISBN 0-14-004145-1.

E5j Penguin Edition Tenth English Issue (Harmondsworth: Penguin, [1988])
Notes: 19.6 x 12.7 cm. Page *4* 'Published in Penguin Books 1963 | 10 | Copyright 1948 by Patrick White | Copyright © renewed by Patrick White, 1976 | All rights reserved | Made and printed in Great Britain by | Hazell Watson & Viney Limited | Member of BPCC Limited | Aylesbury, Bucks, England | Set in Lintotype Granjon'. The cover shows a detail from *Eileen* by Tom Roberts, reproduced by kind permission of the Art Gallery of New South Wales. Price: £4.99, AU$11.99, NZ$18.95, CAN$12.95. ISBN 0-14-004145-1.

E5k Penguin Edition Eleventh English Issue (Harmondsworth: Penguin, [1993])
Notes: p.*4* 'Published in Penguin Books 1963 | 11 13 15 17 19 20 18 16 14 12 | Printed in England by Clays Ltd, St Ives plc | Set In Linotype Granjon'. The cover shows a detail from *Eileen* by Tom Roberts, reproduced by kind permission of the Art Gallery of New South Wales. Published in May 1993. Price: £6.99, CAN$12.99, AU$14.95, US$10.95. ISBN 0 1401 8653 0.

E5l Vintage Subedition First Issue (London: Vintage, 1994)
Notes: p.*4* 'Published by Vintage 1994 | 2 4 6 8 10 9 7 5 3 1 | [...] | Printed and bound in Great Britain by | Cox & Wyman, Reading, Berkshire'. Price: £5.99, AU$12.95. ISBN 0-09-932401-6.

E5m Vintage Subedition Second Issue (London: Vintage, n.d)
Notes: p.*4* 'Published by Vintage 1994 | 2 4 6 8 10 9 7 5 3'.

E.t1 Italian First Edition (Rome: Casini, 1951)

PATRICK WHITE | [in red] MAI UN PASSO AMICO | GHERARDO CASINI EDITORE ROMA

19.1 x 12.5 cm. [1]⁴ 2⁸ 3/5/7/9/11/13¹⁶ 15⁸ 16/18/20¹⁶ ($1 signed): 164 leaves. pp.[*4*] *1-2* 3-140 *141-142* 143-277 *278-280* 281-319 *320-324*.

[*1*] 'I ROMANZI DELL'AMBRA / 9'; [*2*] blank; [*3*] title page; [*4*] 'PROPRIETÀ LETTERARIA RISERVATA GHERARDO CASINI EDITORE | ROMA 1951 | [rule] | Traduzione dall'Inglese di Emma Cremonese | *Titolo originale dell'opera:* | THE AUNT'S STORY | STAMPATO IN ITALIA'; *1* 'Parte Prima | MEROË' | [epigraph]; *2* blank; 3-140 text of Part I; *141* 'Parte Seconda | JARDIN EXOTIQUE' | [epigraph]; *142* blank; 143-277 text of Part II; *278* blank; *279* 'Parte Terza | HOLSTIUS' | [epigraph]; *280* blank; 281-319 text of Part III; *320* blank; *321* 'INDICE'; *322* blank; *323* '*Stampato nelle Officine Grafiche Fratelli Stianti | Sancasciano Val di Pesa (Firenze) | —Dicembre 1951—*'; *324* blank.

Sewn in white paper. Front: [in red] '*Mai | un passo amico | di* | PATRICK WHITE | [publisher's device] | CASINI'. Back: [in red] [at bottom right:] 'Prezzo Lire 1200'. Spine: [in red] '*P. WHITE* MAI UN PASSO AMICO | [at bottom:] [upright:] 9'.

White paper dustjacket printed in light green, red and black. Front: [in red] 'PATRICK WHITE | MAI UN PASSO | AMICO | CASINI'. Back: [at top left:] [b&w photograph of author] | [biography, 36 lines] | [blurb, 14 lines] | [double rule] | 'Prezzo Lire 1200'. Spine: [in red] '*P. WHITE* MAI UN PASSO AMICO | [at bottom:] [upright:] 9'. Inside front flap: [blurb, 16 lines] | 'In sopracoperta: | G. BOLDINI, *La cravatta a puntini.*'. Inside back flap: 'I ROMANZI DELL'AMBRIA' | [13 titles follow] | GHERARDO CASINI EDITORE | *Lungotevere A. Da Brescia 15 - Roma*'. On inside of dustjacket: [advertisements].

Published in December 1951. Price: Lire 1200.

Copies: NSL: Mitchell Library [PW].

E.t2 Italian Second Edition (Rome: Club degli Editori, 1974)

Patrick White | MAI UN PASSO AMICO | [publisher's device] | CLUB DEGLI EDITORI – MILANO

20.9 x 13.2 cm. Unsigned: 180 leaves. pp.*6* 7-159 *160-162* 163-312 *313-314* 315-357 *358-360*.

Endpaper; *1 'Narrativa* | UN LIBRO AL MESE | P 3 | Spedizione in a. p. a tariffa ridotta editoriale | Autorizz. Dirpostel Brescia - n. 17325/RD dell'8-6-1971 | N. 20 - Marzo 1974'; *2* blank; *3* title page; *4 'Titulo originale:* | THE AUNT'S STORY | © 1974, by Club degli Editori | TRADUZIONE DI | EMMA CREMONESE | EDIZIONE RISERVATA AGLI ADERENTI AL CLUB DEGLI EDITORI'; *5* 'Parte Prima | MEROË'; *6* blank; *7-159* text of Part I; *160* blank; *161* 'Parte Seconda | JARDIN EXOTIQUE'; *162* blank; *163-312* text of Part II; *313* 'Parte Terza | HOLSTIUS'; *314* blank; *315-357* text of Part III; *358* blank; *359* 'INDICE'; *360* 'QUESTO VOLUME È STATO IMPRESSO | NEL MESE DI MARZO DELL'ANNO MCMLXXIV | NELLE OFFICINE GRAFICHE VERONESI | DI ARNOLDO MONDADORI | STAMPATO IN ITALIA - PRINTED IN ITALY'; endpaper.

Cased in dark blue cloth with blue and white head bands and with white endpapers. Front: [at centre right:] [in gold] [publisher's device]. Back: blank. Spine: [in gold] [publisher's device] | [running down:] 'Patrick White | MAI UN PASSO AMICO'.

Glossy white paper dustjacket printed in light and dark green and black. Front: [in box:] 'Patrick White | MAI UN | PASSO AMICO | Premio Nobel 1973' | [at bottom right:] CLUB | DEGLI | EDITORI' | [publisher's device]. Back: blank. Spine: [in box:] [running down:] 'Patrick White | MAI UN PASSO AMICO | [at bottom:] [upright:] P 3' | [publisher's device]. Inside front flap: '*Mai un passo amico* | [blurb, 30 lines] | *Sopracoperta di Bruno Binosi*'. Inside back flap: '*Patrick White* | [biography, 41 lines] | Prezzo del volume L. 3000 (2830) | compreso un libro-bis'.

Published in March 1974. Price: 3000 (2850) lire.

Copies: NSL: ITA/WHI1/1 (lacks dustjacket); NSL: Mitchell Library A823/W587/28 (lacks dustjacket); NSL: Mitchell Library [PW]; Personal collection.

E.t3a Turkish First Edition First Issue (Istanbul: Milliyet Yayinlari, 1973)

PATRICK WHITE | [rule] | teyzemin | hikâyesi | [rule] | Türkçesi : | Kemal VARDARLI | [publisher's device]

19.5 x 11.4 cm. Unsigned: 192 leaves. pp.*8* 9-165 *166-168* 169-334 *335-336* 337-377 *378-384*.

1 blank; *2* blank; *3* 'TEYZEMIN HIKÂYESI'; *4* 'MĪLLĪYET YAYIN LTD. ŞTĪ YAYINLARI | Günün Kitaplari Dizisi : 6 | ° | Yayin hakki (Copyright) : Patrick White - Milliyet | Yayin Ltd. Şt. | ° | Orijinal adi : The Aunt's Story | ° | Grafik düzen: Ismet N. Islimyeli | ° | Birinci baski : Kasim 1973 | [at bottom] Bu kitap Yüksel Matbaasinda dizilmiş, Yelken Matbaasinda basilmiştir.'; *5* title page; *6* 'Bu kitabin bütün kişileri hayal ürünü- | dür, gerçek kişilerle hiç bir ilişkileri | yoktur.'; *7* 'BĪRĪNCĪ BÖLÜM | MEROE | [epigraph from] 'OLIVE SCHREINER'; *8* blank; 9-165 *166-168* 169-334 *335-336* 337-377 *378* text; *379-383* [advertisements]; *384* blank.

Perfectbound in red and white paper. Front: [publisher's device] | 'GÜNÜN KITAPLARI | teyzemin | hikâyesi | [in white] PATRICK WHITE | [illust. of a woman seated by a fern] [at bottom left:] NOBEL 1973'. Back: 'EN ÇOK SATAN KĪTAPLAR | (Best-Seller) |

LISTESINDEN SEÇMELER | teyzemin | hikâyesi | [in white] PATRICK WHITE | [in black] [biography, 19 lines] | [at left:] 15 Lira'. Spine: [in red] 'Milliyet | [in white] YAYINLARI | [in black] 6 | [running down:] TEYZEMIN HIKÂYESI PATRICK WHITE'.

Notes: The illust. on front cover is after that on the Compass paperback (see E1d above).

Copies: VSL: SLT 819.93 W582AS (1973); NSL: GRL E823.914/WHI (lacks original binding and dustjacket).

E.t3b Turkish First Edition Second Issue (Istanbul: Yayinlari Milliyet Yayin Ltd., 1973)

Notes: p.*4* 'Birinci baski : Kasim 1973 | İkinci baski Kasim 1973'.

E.t4 Turkish Second Edition (Istanbul: Yayinlari Milliyet Yayin Ltd., 1974)

PATRĪCK WHĪTE | (1973 NOBEL ARMAĞANI) | TEYZENĪN HIKÂYESĪ | (The Aunt's Story) | 2. Baski | Dilimize Çeviren | Gönül SUVEREN

20 x 14 cm. [1]^8 2-25^8 ($1 signed): 200 leaves. pp.*9* 10-390 *391-400*.

Endpaper; *1* blank; *2* blank; *3* [publisher's device] | 'ALTIN KĪTAPLAR YAYINEVI'; *4* blank; *5* title page; *6* 'Kapak resmi : ORAL ORHON | Dizgi ve Baski : ALTIN KĪTAPLAR Basimevi | [wavy rule] | TEYZENĪN HĪKÂYESĪ, ALTIN KĪTAPLAR YAYINEVĪ'nce | Nobel dizisi'nde ikinci kez Ocak 1974'te yayimlandi.'; *7-8* 'PATRĪCK WHĪTE | ve | 1973 NOBEL ARMAĞANI'; *9* 10-390 text; *391-392* 'ALTIN NOBEL DĪZISI' | [list of 62 titles]; *393-394* 'ALTIN KLÂSĪKER DĪZĪSI' | [list of 46 titles]; *395-397* 'MESHUR ROMANLAR SERISI' | [list of 111 titles]; *398* 'SERI 21 (Çagdas Yazarlar)' | [list of 17 titles]; *399* blank; *400* blank.

Cased in brown cloth. Front: [in silver] 'TEYZENIN HIKÂYESI'. Back and spine: blank.

White paper dustjacket. Front: [in white] '*PATRICK WHITE* | [in black] TEYZENĪN HĪKÂYESĪ | [col. illust. of a naked women. seated in a surreal garden] | ALTIN KĪTAPLAR / NOBEL ARMAĞANI'. Back: [in white] '*PATRICK WHITE* | [in black] TEYZENĪN HĪKÂYESĪ | [blurb, 31 lines] | [in green] kapak düzeni ve fotoğraf / oral or-hon Film ve baski : Renkler Matbaacilik 22 90 71'. Spine: 'patrick | white | [running down:] [in red] 'TEYZENĪN HĪKÂYESĪ' | [upright:] [publisher's device]. Inside front flap: blank. Inside back flap: 'Fiati 20 Lira'.

Price: 20 Lira.

Copies: VSL: SLT 819.93 W582AS.

E.t5 Spanish First Edition (Barcelona: Luis de Caralt, 1974)

PATRICK WHITE | EL PESO | DE LAS SOMBRAS | LUIS DE CARALT, EDITOR | Rosellón, 246 | BARCELONA

20.2 x 13.6 cm. [1]⁸ 2-19⁸ ($1 signed): 152 leaves. pp.*6* 7-134 *135-136* 137-259 *260-262* 263-296 *297-304*.

Endpaper; *1* [series device]; *2* blank; *3* title page; *4* '*Titulo de la obra original:* | *THE AUNT'S STORY* | © *Patrick White, 1948* | Traducción | de | Mª C. de AZPIAZU | Sobrecubierta | de | LUIS BALAGUER | RESERVADOS TODOS LOS DERECHOS | © LUIS DE CARALT, 1974 | Depósito legal: B. 44622-74 ISBN 84-217-1669-7'; *5* '*PRIMERA PARTE*'; *6* blank; 7-134 text of Part I; *135* '*SEGUNDA PARTE*'; *136* blank; 137-259 text of Part II; *260* blank; *261* '*TERCERA PARTE*'; *262* blank; 263-296 text of Part III; *297* 'INDICE'; *298* blank; *299* [at bottom right:] 'ESTE VOLUMEN | SE TERMINÓ DE IMPRIMIR | DURANTE EL MES DE NOVIEMBRE DE 1974 | EN LOS TALLERES GRÁFICOS | DE LA EDITORIAL CASAL I | VALL DE ANDORRA'; *300-304* blank; endpaper.

Cased in brown imitation cloth boards with red and yellow headbands and with white endpapers. Front and back: blank. Spine: [in gold on black panel:] 'PATRICK | WHITE | EL | PESO | DE LAS | SOMBRAS | [at bottom:] [cursive] *Luis* | *de* | *Caralt*'.

Glossy white paper dustjacket printed in full colour. Front: 'El peso de las | sombras | Patrick White' | [col. illust. of seated woman]. Back: [at bottom right:] 'T. G. Soler - Esplugas (Barna.)'. Spine: [running down:] 'Patrick | White / El peso | de las sombras | [at bottom:] [upright:] CARALT'. Inside front flap: [in red] 'EL PESO DE LAS SOMBRAS' | [description, 40 lines]. Inside back flap: [in red] [series device] 'EN PREPARACION | OBRAS DE' | [list of 15 authors follows].

Wraparound: 'PREMIO NOBEL'.

Published in November 1974.

Copies: NSL: Mitchell Library A823/W587/30 (lacks dustjacket); NSL: Mitchell Library [PW]; Personal collection.

E.t6 Japanese First Edition (Tokyo: Shufu no Tomosha, 1976)

409 p. Translator not cited. *The Aunt's Story* published along with selections of the work of Eyvind Johnson and Harry Martinson.

E.t7 Serbo-Croatian First Edition (Belgrade: Slovo Ljubve, 1979)

PATRIK VAJT | [in blue] PRIČA TEODORE GUDMAN | [publisher's device] | [rule] | SLOVO LJUBVE | Beograd | 1979.

20.6 x 14.5 cm. [1]⁸ 2-20⁸ ($2 signed): 160 leaves. pp.*4* 5-9 *10-18* 19-145 *146-150* 151-279 *280-284* 285-318 *319-320*.

Endpaper; *1* 'Despot Stefan Lazarević (1377-1427), | jedan od najprosvećenijih ljudi | srednjovekovne Srbije, | sin kneza Lazara | napisao je 1409, godine poslanicu | koja u akrostihu daje reči | *SLOVO LJUBVE.'* | [publisher's device]; *2* 'Biblioteka | DOBITNICI NOBELOVE NAGRADE | romani | Urednik | RADE VIJVODIČ'; *3* title page; *4* 'Naslov originala | PATRICK WHITE | THE AUNT'S STORY | S engleskog preleve | SNEŽANA STOJANOVIČ | ZLATICA | PUTINČANIN'; 5-9 *'PREDOGOVAR'* [by Snežana Stoja-nović and Zlatica Putinčanin]; *10* blank; *11* 'PRIČA TEODORE GUDMAN'; *12* blank; *13* 'For Betty Withycombe'; *14* 'Svi likovi u ovoi priči su izmišljeni I nemaju nikakve veze sa | stvarnim ličnostima.'; *15* 'I | MEROJ'; *16* blank; *17* [epigraph]; *18* blank; *19-145 146* text of Part I; *147* 'II | JARDIN EXOTIQUE'; *148* blank; *149* [epigraph]; *150* blank; 151-279 text of Part II; *280* blank; *281* 'III | HOLSTIUS'; *282* blank; *283* [epigraph]; *284* blank; 285-318 text of Part III; *319* 'SADRŽAJ'; *320* 'Patrik Vajt | PRIČA TEODORE GUDMAN | *Re-cenzent* | Rade Vojvodić | *Letitor* | Mirjana Vasiljević | *Korektor* | Ljiljana Tubin | *Zaštitni omot* | Gradimir Petrović | *Tehnićki urenik* | Lenka Kneževic – Zuborski | *Izdaje* | Izdavačka oganizacija | Slovo Ljubve | Beograd, Mutapova 12 | *Za izdavača* | Ljubiša Pantić | *Tiraž* | 5 000 | *Štampa* | ROGP »Kultura«, OOUR »Radiša Timotić« | Beograd, Dure Jakšića 9'; end-paper.

Cased in grey calico with white endpapers. Front: [in white] 'patrik | vajt | PRIČA | TEODORE GUDMAN'. Back: blank. Spine: [in white] 'NOBELOVA | NAGRADA | [running down:] Patrik Vajt : PRICA TEODORE GUDMAN | [at bottom:] [upright:] SLOVO LJUBVE'.

Green glossy paper dustjacket printed in full colour. Front: [in white] 'patrik | vajt | PRIČA | TEODORE GUDMAN' | [col. illust. of abstract head]. Back: blank. Spine: [in white] 'NOBELOVA | NAGRADA | [running down:] Patrik Vajt : PRICA TEODORE GUDMAN | [at bottom:] [upright:] SLOVO LJUBVE'. Inside front flap: [in white] 'Kom-plet XIII-XVIII. treće kolo' | [seven titles follow].

Print run: 5,000.

Copies: NSL: Mitchell Library [PW].

E.t8 Greek First Edition (Athens: Hestia, 1988)

Η ΙΣΤΟΡΙΑ ΤΗΣ ΘΕΙΑΣ

Notes: 371p. Translated by Seraphim Velentzas

Copies: NSL: Mitchell Library [PW].

E.t9 Swedish First Edition (Borås: Forum, 1991)

Patrick White | Tant Theodora | Översättning Ingegärd Martinell | Forum

23.4 x 16 cm. Unsigned: 152 leaves. pp.*10* 11-135 *136-138* 139-259 *260-262* 263-302 *303-304*.

Endpaper; *1* 'Tant Theodora'; *2* blank; *3* title page; *4* 'Tidigare utgivning | De fyra utkorade 1964 | Den oförstörbara mandalan 1969 | Livets träd 1970 | Målaren 1973 | Stormens öga 1976 | En frans an löv 1979 | Fallet Twyborn 1981 | Voss 1983 | Skavanker i spegeln 1984 |

Det kluvna minnet 1989 | [publisher's device] | Engelska originalets titel The Aunt's story | © Patrick White 1948, 1976 | Omslagsillustration Tom Roberts: Elaine (detajl) | Omslagstypografi Paul Eklund | Sättning Ytterlids, Falkenberg | Tryckning | Centraltryckeriet, Borås 1991 | Printed in Sweden | ISBN 91-37-10031-9'; *5* 'Till Betty Withycombe'; *6* blank; *7* 'Innehåll'; *8* blank; *9* 'Första delen* | Meroë' | [epigraph]; *10* blank; 11-135 text of Part I; *136* blank; *137* '*Andra delen* | Jardin exotique' | [epigraph]; *138* blank; 139-259 text of Part II; *260* blank; *261* 'Tredje delen* | Holstius' | [epigraph]; *262* blank; 263-296 text of Part III; 297-302 'Översättning av franska ord och fraser'; *303-304* blank; endpaper.

Cased in black paper-covered boards with black and red headbands and with white endpapers. Front and back: blank. Spine: [running down:] [in silver] 'PATRICK WHITE | TANT THEODORA | [upright] FORUM'.

Glossy paper dustjacket printed in full colour. Front: [in white] 'PATRICK | WHITE | [in red] TANT | THEODORA | [col. illust. of woman's head] | FORUM'. Back: [blurb, 26 lines] | 'FORUM | [rule] | ISBN 91-37-10031-9' | [barcode]. Spine: [running down:] [in white] 'PATRICK WHITE | TANT THEODORA | [upright:] FORUM'. Inside front flap: 'UR RECENSIONERNA AV | NÅGRA AV PATRICK WHITES | TIDIGARE BÖCKER : | [four titles follow] | *Ruth Halldén : Dagens Nyheter*'. Inside back flap: [photograph of author] | [biography, 13 lines] | 'Omslagsbild: Tom Roberts *Eileen 1892.* | Oil on canvas 49 x 36. Purchased 1892. Art Gallery of New South Wales.'.

Copies: NSL: Mitchell Library [PW].

E.t10 Hebrew First Edition (Tel Aviv: Am Oved, 1992)

[Sippura shel doda]

Notes: 335p. Trans. by Amatzya Porat. Not seen but see *Index Translationum*.

E.m1 Sound recording (Kew: Education Deptartment of Victoria, Visiting Teacher Service, [1981])
The Aunt's Story (8 audiocassettes).
Read by Brenda Swift.

E.m2 Sound recording (North Hobart: Hear-a-Book, [no date])
The Aunt's Story (8 audiocassettes).
Read by Diana Jeffrey. Also issued by the Royal Blind Society of New South in 1984 in two formats – 8 2-track audiocassettes and 2 4-track audiocassettes.

E.m3 Sound recording (North Sydney: Australian Listening Library, 1983)
The Aunt's Story (10 audiocassesttes)
Read by Flore Collis-George.

E.m4 Braille Edition (Annerley: Queensland Braille Writers Association, [1976])
From the Penguin edition of 1976.

F The Tree of Man (1955)

After the modest commercial success of *The Aunt's Story*, and the move to a small farm at Castle Hill, on the outskirts of Sydney, Patrick White had neither the inclination nor the time to write. However, by January 1950, he was reporting to his cousin, Peggy Garland, that 'For better or worse, I have begun another book. It is slow and painful.' (25 January 1950) The book was given the tentative title of 'A Life Sentence on Earth'. By March the writing had lapsed, mainly due to the demands of the farm. Throughout the rest of 1950 and 1951, writing was on White's mind, but a dark pessimism pervaded: 'I wish I could say I am writing. Too many things got in the way.' (1 July 1950); 'If only I could *wish* to write another book. But I don't.' (3 June 1951); 'There are moments when I do take interest in a book I have in my head … then I succumb to the feeling of: What is the use?' (15 August 1951) In April 1952 White wrote to Huebsch: 'A short time ago I began painfully to write another book, squeezing out an hour a day in which to do it, and then not every day … I suppose I have written roughly a quarter.' (3 April 1952)

By this time of White's second wind, the title had changed to the less pessimistic 'The Tree of Man'. Closer to the time of publication, White was at pains to have the source acknowledged. It was A.E. Housman's *A Shropshire Lad* (1896):

> There like the wind through woods in riot
>> Through him the gale of life blew high;
> The tree of man was never quiet:
>> Then 'twas the Roman, now 'tis I.

The writing proceeded fitfully throughout 1952 and 1953, and White wrote to Peggy Garland: 'I did hope to finish the *first* version of my book by Christmas, but I don't think I will manage it so soon. It sprawls out.' (15 November 1953) White must have been working relentlessly by this stage because only six months later he had almost finished the typing of the third and final draft. 'My chief and quite good excuse this time for not writing, is that I am hard at typing the book, have been for months, and cannot bring myself to give up a working hour for anything else.' (To Peggy Garland, 15 June 1954)

The typescript – 715 quarto pages – was submitted to The Viking Press in August 1954. Huebsch was travelling in Europe at this time and it was not till the 11th November that he sent the following telegram: 'VIKING CON-GRATULATES YOU ON BEAUTIFUL PROFOUNDLY IMPRESSIVE

FULFILMENT OF EXPECTATIONS'. Juliet O'Hea of Curtis Brown had also received a typescript of the novel to place with a London publisher, but one of her readers was unable to finish reading the book, and O'Hea herself wondered what it was about. It was submitted to Herbert Read, now a Director at Routledge. Read was supportive but could not convince his fellow directors of the merits of the novel. Routledge were getting out of fiction publishing and rejected *The Tree of Man*. The novel was also rejected by perhaps twenty other London publishers. Gollancz expressed an interest, even to the point of drawing up a contract, but White would not agree to reduce the length of the novel by some 25%, as Gollancz had wanted. O'Hea believed she had a typescript unsaleable in London.

At this point White raised the possibility of an Australian edition, but this was rejected by both O'Hea and Huebsch who pointed out that, for White to receive international acceptance, he must be published in both New York *and* London. It must be said that the realisation of an Australian edition was unlikely. White did not have the necessary contacts among Australian publishers, and Australian publishing did not have the necessary status or access to an effective international distribution network. The problem of the lack of a London publisher was solved by Huebsch who approached Frank Morley of Eyre & Spottiswoode and persuaded him to take on *The Tree of Man*.

The critical reception of the novel in the United States was almost entirely positive and enthusiastic, with James Stern leading the charge with an influential review on the front page of the *New York Times Book Review* (14 August 1955). The only negative review appeared in *Time*. The market reception was also good: 'they sold over 10,000 copies in the first fortnight.' (To Peggy Garland, 12 May 1955) Advance orders were such that *The Tree of Man* went into a second printing before publication. (See F1b)

The United Kingdom edition was published in April 1956 in a run of 20,000. There were three issues in April 1956 alone, and there was hope for an eventual sale of 40,000! Obviously, opinions at Eyre & Spottiswoode were buoyed by the novel's success in the United States. The critical opinion in Britain was positive but not so enthusiastic. There was a general view that *The Tree of Man* was an important book but that it could have done with some editorial pruning.

In Australia the critical reception was mixed. One of the most influential reviewers, A.D. Hope in the *Sydney Morning Herald* (16 June 1956, p.16) was particularly scathing, describing White's prose as 'pretentious and verbal sludge'.

A positive review by biographer and war correspondent, John Hetherington, was equally extreme, claiming that other novelists were to Patrick White as street fiddlers were to Yehudi Menuhin (*Age* 16 June 1956).

The impact of the reviews on sales was probably minimal. The Australian market appears to have been primed by newspaper reports of the novel's success in the United States. Supplies of *The Tree of Man* reached Australia late in June 1956 – two weeks after the Hope review. Eight thousand copies were sold in a matter of a few months. More than a year later White boasted to Keith Michell: '[A] Sydney bookseller told me the other day that *The Tree of Man* is very popular with truck drivers.' (9 October 1957) *The Tree of Man* also won the Australian Literary Society's Gold Medal for 1956.

White was active on his own behalf. As early as May he had visited David Moore, then at Angus & Robertson, with an advance copy of *The Tree of Man* and persuaded him to place a bulk order with London and to make the book the subject of a window display. He was also in touch with the newspapers, managing to have a short piece placed in Column Eight on the front page of the *Sydney Morning Herald* relating to a proposed Braille publication of *The Tree of Man*.

As usual White was sensitive to the physical appearance of his books. He approved of the book jacket design of the Viking edition but pointed out that 'an Australian critic … would be bound to pounce on the 'essential' tree and say 'that is not a <u>gum</u> tree, therefore, this is not an Australian novel', and condemn it.' (To Ben Huebsch, 16 June 1955) Because the Australian market was closed to American publishers, very few Australian critics or readers would have seen this American edition. White was also concerned about the sheer bulk of the book: 'I had not been prepared for such a Bible of a volume. Could not the paper be thinner?' (To Ben Huebsch, 16 June 1955) The Viking Press edition, however, was a handsome book, and White must have been pleased with it. He was not so pleased with the United Kingdom edition, particularly with the book jacket design. Apparently, Eyre & Spottiswoode had commissioned some gum trees from an amateur painter who worked at Australia House. The result was a drab mess, and, for *Voss*, White 'was determined not to leave the jacket to the publisher after what had happened to *The Tree of Man*.' (To Peggy Garland, 30 May 1957) This was the reason White first approached Sidney Nolan – to do the jacket design for the English edition of *Voss*.

The commercial and critical success of *The Tree of Man* extended into Europe with a major translation into German by Heinrich and Annemarie Böll.

European readers had been introduced to White's work through the French translation of *Happy Valley* (*Eden-Ville*) and the Italian translation of *The Aunt's Story* (*Mais Un Amico*), though these had limited influence. The German translation, however, had substance, being by a major German novelist (Böll himself became a Nobel Prize winner) and his wife. Over the next two decades this translation of *The Tree of Man* has gone through a number of issues in both hardback and paperback. It was also released through several of the influential German book clubs. Moreover, it won the Wupperthal Prize for translation in 1957. White did have misgivings about the Bölls' translation: as early as March 1957 he reported brawling with Böll 'who sounds as though he is trying to change what he is incapable of translating.' (To Frederick Glover, 24 March 1957), and he never saw the second part of the translation in proof. He was scathing about the title in German, *Zur Ruhe kam der Baum des Menschen nie* (a translation of the full line from Housman's *Shropshire Lad*: 'The tree of man is never quiet'). 'I suggested it might wrap itself round the jacket like a piece of string.' When the published translation arrived in the middle of 1957, Ile Krieger, a confidant to White, thought it excellent, but White was not mollified. *The Tree of Man* was also translated into Czech (1962), Swedish (1970), and Hungarian (1972), each translation adding lustre to White's European reputation. After the Nobel Prize, *The Tree of Man* was translated into a number of languages – Portuguese (1973), Spanish (1976), Russian (1976), Greek (1976), Rumanian (1981), Czech again (1984), Chinese (an extract in 1980, the whole in 1990), Vietnamese (1987) and Korean (1992).

The Tree of Man has also been published in other media. As early as 1955 White was admitting to Peggy Garland that he had 'a wild dream in which I see it done [in film] as I can see it.' (28 December 1955), and in 1958 the American actor Zachary Scott was interested in producing a film version. (To David Moore, 15 September 1958) The possibility of a film was again in the air in the mid-1980s (To Elizabeth Falkenberg, 1 June 1985), and White reported confidently to the same correspondent that Neil Armfield was going to direct *The Tree of Man*. (16 December 1989) But all these plans came to nothing. However, a radio version of *The Tree of Man*, co-written by Michael Le Moignan, was broadcast on ABC Radio in 42 episodes from 28 July 1983.

* * * * *

F1a U.S. First Edition (New York: Viking Press, 1955)

PATRICK WHITE | [floral ornament] | The | Tree | of | Man | A NOVEL | New York • 1955 | THE VIKING PRESS

21.8 x 14.5 cm. Unsigned: 256 leaves. pp.[*8*] *1-2* 3-98 *99-100* 101-200 *201-202* 203-367 *368-370* 371-499 *500-504*.

Endpaper; [*1*] blank; [*2*] blank; [*3*] [floral ornament] 'THE TREE OF MAN' | [floral ornament]; [*4*] 'BY THE SAME AUTHOR | THE AUNT'S STORY | THE LIVING AND THE DEAD | HAPPY VALLEY'; [*5*] title page; [*6*] 'COPYRIGHT © 1955 BY PATRICK WHITE | FIRST PUBLISHED BY THE VIKING PRESS IN AUGUST 1955 | PUBLISHED ON THE SAME DAY IN THE DOMINION OF CANADA | BY THE MACMILLAN COMPANY OF CANADA LIMITED | The lines of poetry on pages 389-90 are from | A.E. Housman's *A Shropshire Lad*, XXXI. | [publisher's device] | Library of Congress catalog card number: 55-7377 | PRINTED IN THE U.S.A. BY THE COLONIAL PRESS INC.'; [*7*] 'To | Manoly'; [*8*] blank; *1* [floral ornament] 'PART I' | [floral ornament]; *2* blank; 3-98 text of Part I; *99* [floral ornament] | 'PART II' | [floral ornament]; *100* blank; 101-200 text of Part II; *201* [floral ornament] | 'PART III' | [floral ornament]; *202* blank; 203-367 text of Part III; *368* blank; *369* [floral ornament] | 'PART IV' | [floral ornament]; *370* blank; 371-499 text of Part IV; *500-504* blank; endpaper.

Cased in light blue calico with fawn cloth spine, top edge in blue and with off-white endpapers. Front and back: blank. Spine: [in blue] 'PATRICK | WHITE | [floral ornament] | THE | TREE | OF | MAN | [floral ornament] | VIKING'.

White paper dustjacket with col. illust. of stylized tree, axe and book across front and spine. Front: [in white] '*THE TREE | OF MAN | A NOVEL BY | PATRICK WHITE*'. Back: [in brown] [ornamental rule] | 'The Tree of Man' | [blurb, 23 lines] | [ornamental rule]. Spine: [in white] '*THE | TREE | OF | MAN* | [in brown] *Patrick White* | [in red] *VIKING*'. Inside front flap: [in brown] '$4.50 | [in red] THE TREE OF MAN | [in brown] [blurb, 38 lines] | JACKET DESIGN BY GEORGE SALTER'. Inside back flap: [in red] 'PATRICK WHITE | [in brown] [biography, 9 lines] | His previous novels – totally different from | this one – were: | [in red] HAPPY VALLEY (1940) | [in brown] [quotation of three lines from] –JANE SPENCE SOUTHRON, *New York Times Book Review*. | [in red] THE LIVING AND THE DEAD (1941) | [in brown] [quotation of two lines from] –LOUIS B. SALOMON, *The Nation*. | [quotation of three lines from] –*Time*. | [in red] THE AUNT'S STORY (1948) | [in brown] [quotation of two lines from] –JAMES STERN, *New | York Times Book Review*. | [quotation of three lines from] –IRIS BARRY, *New York Herald | Tribune*. | [quotation of two lines from] –HAMILTON BASSO, | *The New Yorker*. | [in red] THE VIKING PRESS | *Publishers of the Viking Portable Library* | 18 East 48th Street, New York 17, N.Y. | [in brown] PRINTED IN U.S.A.'.

Published in August 1955. Price: US$4.50. The blurb on the dustjacket of the U.K. First Edition (see F2a below) claimed that the U.S. First Edition went through five impressions within three months.

Reviews: C.J. Rolo *Atlantic Monthly* July 1955, p.80 (180w); *Booklist* 15 September 1955, p.35; *Bookmark* November 1955, p.37; Riley Hughes *Catholic World* October 1955, p.65 (300w); Fanny Butcher *Chicago Sunday Tribune* 14 August 1955, p.3 (300w); Seymour Krum *Commonweal* 9 December 1955, p.265 (800w); *Kirkus* 1 June 1955, p.372 (310w); T.F. Smith *Library Journal* August 1955, p.1699 (110w); Stanley Cooperman *Nation* 5 November 1955, p.404 (550w); Taliaferro Boatwright *New York Herald Tribune Book Review* 14 August 1955, p.1 (800w); James Stern *New York Times Book Review* 14 August 1955, p.1 (1400w); *New*

Yorker 29 October 1955, p.163 (60w); Jane Voiles *San Francisco Chronicle* 26 August 1955, p.15 (750w); Walter Havighurst *Saturday Review* 13 August 1955, p.11 (650w); *Time* 15 August 1955, p.76 (650w).

Notes: The Viking edition (1955), the Eyre & Spottiswoode edition (1956), and the Jonathan Cape edition (1974) are all printed from the same setting, although the print dimensions are different. Presumably this was done by photolithography. Print dimensions (excluding headers and footers): 166 x 106 mm (Viking); 152 x 98 mm (Eyre & Spottiswoode); 166 x 106 mm (Jonathan Cape).

Copies: NSL: Mitchell Library [PW]; NSL: Mitchell Library A823/W587/48 (lacks dustjacket); NU: RB 1655.21; Personal collections (2 copies).

F1b U.S. First Edition Second Issue (New York: Viking Press, 1955)

Notes: p.[6] 'COPYRIGHT © 1955 BY PATRICK WHITE | FIRST PUBLISHED BY THE VIKING PRESS IN AUGUST 1955 | SECOND PRINTING BEFORE PUBLICATION'.

Copies: VSL: SLT 819.93 W582TR.

F1c U.S. First Edition Third Issue (New York: Viking Press, 1955)

Not seen, but referred to in the first U.K. edition (see F2a below).

F1d U.S. First Edition Fourth Issue (New York: Viking Press, 1955)

Not seen, but referred to in the first U.K. edition (see F2a below).

F1e U.S. First Edition Fifth Issue (New York: Viking Press, 1955)

Not seen, but referred to in the first U.K. edition (see F2a below).

F1f Canadian Subedition (Toronto: Macmillan, 1955)

Not seen, but referred to on p.[6] of F1a above.

F1g Viking Subedition (New York: Viking Press, 1974)

[floral ornament] THE | TREE OF | MAN | [rule] | PATRICK | WHITE | [floral orament] | [at bottom] THE | VIKING PRESS | NEW YORK

Notes: p.6 'Copyright © by Patrick White | All rights reserved | First published in 1955 by The Viking Press, Inc. | 625 Madison Avenue, New York, N.Y. 10022 | Published simultaneously in Canada by | The Macmillan Company of Canada Limited | SBN 670-72875-6 | Library of Congress catalog card number: 55-7377 | Printed in U.S.A.'. Cased in black calico boards. Lime green paper dustjacket printed in black. Price: US$12.50.

Copies: NSL: Mitchell Library [PW].

F2a U.K. First Edition (London: Eyre & Spottiswoode, 1956)

PATRICK WHITE | The Tree of Man | EYRE & SPOTTISWOODE | LONDON 1956

20.6 x 13.7 cm. [A]^{16} B-Q^{16}: 256 leaves. pp.[*8*] *1-2* 3-98 *99-100* 101-200 *201-202* 203-367 *368-370* 371-499 *500-504*.

Endpaper; [*1*] blank; [*2*] blank; [*3*] 'THE TREE OF MAN' | [blurb, 23 lines]; [*4*] blank; [*5*] title page; [*6*] 'The lines of poetry on pages 389-90 are from | A. E. Housman's *A Shropshire Lad*, XXXI. | [at bottom:] THIS BOOK IS PRINTED IN GREAT BRITAIN BY PHOTO- | LITHOGRAPHY FOR EYRE & SPOTTISWOODE (PUBLISHERS) | LTD., 15 BEDFORD STREET, LONDON, W.C.2, BY | BUTLER & TANNER LTD., FROME AND LONDON'; [*7*] 'To | Manoly'; [*8*] blank; *1* 'PART I'; *2* blank; 3-98 text of Part I; *99* 'PART II'; *100* blank; 101-200 text of Part II; *201* 'PART III'; *202* blank; 203-367 text of Part III; *368* blank; *369* 'PART IV'; *370* blank; 371-499 text of Part IV; *500-504* blank; endpaper.

Cased in dark blue cloth with off-white endpapers. Front and back: blank. Spine: [in gold] 'THE | TREE | OF | MAN | PATRICK | WHITE | EYRE & | SPOTTISWOODE'.

White paper dustjacket with col. illust. of a man in a forest of gumtrees across front and spine. It is signed Don Finley. Front: [in yellow] 'The | TREE of MAN | [in white] PATRICK WHITE'. Back: 'THE TREE OF MAN | by Patrick White | [quotation of seven lines] from the leading review by JAMES STERN in the | *New York Times* Book Review | [quotation of six lines from] ORVILLE PRESCOTT (*New York Times*) | [quotation of four lines from] *New York Herald-Tribune* | [quotation of three lines from] *New York Post* | [quotation of three lines from] *Cleveland Press* | [quotation of one line from] *Louisville Courier-Journal* | THE TREE OF MAN | is published at 18s. by | EYRE & SPOTTISWOODE · PUBLISHERS · LIMITED | 15 BEDFORD STREET, LONDON, W.C.2'. Spine: [in yellow] 'THE | TREE | OF | MAN | [in white] PATRICK | WHITE | EYRE & | SPOTTISWOODE'. Inside front flap: 'Patrick White | THE TREE OF MAN | [blurb, 32 lines] | [*Continued on back flap* | [at bottom right:] 18s. net'. Inside back flap: '*Continued from front flap*] | [blurb continues, 13 lines] | The title *The Tree of Man* is taken from a poem | by A.E. Housman. | [at bottom left:] APT, G8'.

Published 27 April 1956. Price: 18s. Run: 10,750. By 31 December 1959, 24,083 copies had been sold – 8,293 in the U.K. and 15,790 in the colonies, mainly Australia.

Reviews: *West Australian* 2 June 1956, p.27; Max Harris *Voice* v.7 no.7, p.29; P. Condy *Quadrant* Summer 1956/57, p.87-88; A.D. Hope *Sydney Morning Herald* 16 June 1956, p.15; *Books and Bookmen* 26 May 1956; John Hetherington *Age* 19 June 1956, p.1; Douglas Stewart *Bulletin* 18 July 1956, p.2 and 35; H.J. Oliver *Southerly* v.17 no.3, 1956, p.168-170; *Landfall* December 1956, p.350; M. Durack *Westerly* no.1, 1957, p.44.

Notes: This 'edition' is in fact a subedition, being a photolithographic reprint of the U.S. First Edition (see F1a above).

Copies: NSL: Mitchell Library [PW]; Personal collection; NU: RB1656.1 (lacks dustjacket); NSL: Mitchell Library A823/W587/4A1; VU: McL L/A-F White.

F2b U.K. First Edition Second Issue (London: Eyre & Spottiswoode, 1956)
Notes: p.[*6*] '*First impression April 1956* | *Second impression April 1956* | [at bottom:] THIS BOOK IS PRINTED IN GREAT BRITAIN BY PHOTO- | LITHOGRAPHY FOR EYRE & SPOTTISWOODE (PUBLISHERS [sic] | LTD.'. Published in April 1956. Price: 18s. Print run: 9,200.

F2c U.K. First Edition Third Issue (London: Eyre & Spottiswoode, 1956)
Notes: p.[*6*] '*First impression April 1956* | *Second impression April 1956* | *Third impression April 1956* | [at bottom:] THIS BOOK IS PRINTED IN GREAT BRITAIN BY PHOTO- | LITHOGRAPHY FOR EYRE & SPOTTISWOODE (PUBLISHERS [sic] | LTD.' The dustjacket has a number of variations on F2a: Inside front flap: [...] [at bottom left:] '*THIRD IMPRESSION*' [...]. Published in May 1956. Price: 18s. Print run: 10,000.

F2d U.K. First Edition Cape Subedition First Issue (London: Jonathan Cape, 1974)
PATRICK WHITE | THE | TREE OF MAN | [floral ornament] | [at bottom:] [publisher's device] | JONATHAN CAPE | THIRTY BEDFORD SQUARE LONDON

22 x 14 cm. Unsigned: 256 leaves. pp.[*8*] *1-2* 3-499 *500-504*.

Notes: p.*6* 'FIRST PUBLISHED 1955 | FIRST PUBLISHED IN GREAT BRITAIN 1956 | REISSUED 1974 | COPYRIGHT © 1955 BY PATRICK WHITE | JONATHAN CAPE LTD, 30 BEDFORD SQUARE, LONDON, WC1 | ISBN 0 224 01008 5 | The lines on pp. 389-90 are from A.E. Housman's | *A Shropshire Lad*, XXXI | PRINTED IN GREAT BRITAIN BY | LOWE AND BRYDONE (PRINTERS) LTD, THETFORD, NORFOLK | ON PAPER MADE BY JOHN DICKINSON AND CO. LTD | BOUND BY JAMES BURN, ESHER, SURREY'. Cased in imitation cloth boards. White glossy paper dustjacket with illust. of close-up of a tree trunk spreading across front, back and spine. Jacket photograph by Barry Pringle. Jacket design by M. Mohan. Published 13 June 1974. Price: £2.95. Print run: 3,000. ISBN 0224 01008 5.

Copies: NSL: Mitchell Library [PW]; VSL: LT 819.93 W582TR (1974); Personal collection.

F2e U.K. First Edition Cape Subedition Second Issue (London: Jonathan Cape, 1974)
Published 1974. Price: £2.95. Print run: 1,500.

Not seen, but known from the Jonathan Cape Archive held at the University of Reading.

F2f U.K. First Edition Cape Subedition Book Club Associates Issue (London: Book Club Associates, 1974)
Notes: p.*4* 'THIS EDITION PUBLISHED 1974 BY | BOOK CLUB ASSOCIATES | BY ARRANGEMENT WITH JONATHAN CAPE LTD | © 1955 BY PATRICK WHITE | The lines on pp. 389-90 are from A. E. Housman's | A Shropshire Lad, XXXI | [at bottom:] PRINTED IN GREAT BRITAIN BY | LOWE AND BRYDONE (PRINTERS) LTD, THETFORD, NORFOLK | ON PAPER MADE BY JOHN DICKINSON AND CO. LTD | BOUND BY JAMES BURN, ESHER, SURREY'. Cased in black cloth. White glossy paper dustjacket with illust. of close-up of a tree trunk spreading across front, back and spine. Jacket photograph by Barry Pringle. Jacket design by M. Mohan.

F3a Penguin Edition First Issue (Harmondsworth: Penguin, 1961)

PATRICK WHITE | [swelled rule] | THE TREE OF MAN | [at bottom:] PENGUIN BOOKS

17.9 x 11 cm. [A]^{16} B-P^{16} ($1 signed): 240 leaves. pp.*8* 9-98 *99-102* 103-195 *196-198* 199-355 *356-358* 359-479 *480* (the last page of each chapter is unnumbered).

1 'PENGUIN MODERN CLASSICS | 1657 | THE TREE OF MAN | PATRICK WHITE | [publisher's device] | [biography, 21 lines] | *Cover drawing by Sidney Nolan*'; *2* blank; *3* title page; *4* 'Penguin Books Ltd, Harmondsworth, Middlesex | AUSTRALIA: Penguin Books Pty Ltd, 762 Whitehorse Road, | Mitcham, Victoria | [short rule] | First published by Eyre & Spottiswoode 1956 | Published in Penguin Books 1961 | [short rule] | Copyright © Patrick White, 1956 | [short rule] | Made and printed in Great Britain | by Cox and Wyman Ltd, | London, Reading, and Fakenham | The lines of poetry on page 376 are from | A.E. Housman's *A Shropshire Lad*, XXXI' | [publisher's conditions, 7 lines]; *5* '*To Manoly*'; *6* blank; *7* 'PART ONE'; *8* blank; 9-98 *99* text of Part One; *100* blank; *101* 'PART TWO'; *102* blank; 103-195 *196* text of Part Two; *197* 'PART THREE'; *198* blank; 199-355 *356* text of Part Three; *357* 'PART FOUR'; *358* blank; 359-479 *480* text of Part Four.

Perfectbound in off-white paper printed in pale green, black and orange. Front: 'Patrick White | The Tree of Man | [b&w illust. of verandah of house] | PENGUIN MODERN CLASSICS [in orange] [publisher's device] 7/6'. Back: 'Patrick White | 'A monumental, moving epic' — *The Times* | [description, 12 lines] | [quotation of three lines from] Peter Green in the *Daily Telegraph*. | [quotation of three lines from] John Davenport in the *Observer*. | *For copyright reasons this edition is not for sale in the U.S.A. or Canada.* | [in orange] [publisher's device] [in black] PENGUIN MODERN CLASSICS'. Spine: [publisher's device] [running down:] 'Patrick White • The Tree of Man | [at bottom:] [upright:] 1657'. Inside front and back covers: blank.

Price: 7/6.

Copies: NSL: Mitchell Library A823/W587/4B1; NSL: Mitchell Library [PW]; VSL: SLT 819.93 W582T(1961).

F3b Penguin Edition Second Issue (Harmondsworth: Penguin, 1963)
Notes: p.*4* 'Published in Penguin Books 1961 | Reprinted 1963'. Price: 7/6.

F3c Penguin Edition Third Issue (Harmondsworth: Penguin, 1965)
Notes: p.*4* 'Published in Penguin Books 1961 | Reprinted 1963, 1965 | [short rule] | Copyright © Patrick White, 1956 | [short rule] | Made and printed in Great Britain | by Cox and Wyman Ltd, | London, Reading, and Fakenham | Set in Monotype Bembo'. Price: 7/6.

F3d Penguin Edition Fourth Issue (Harmondsworth: Penguin, 1967)
Notes: p.*4* 'Published in Penguin Books 1961 | Reprinted 1963, 1965, 1967 | [short rule] | Copyright © Patrick White, 1965 [sic] | [short rule] | Made and printed in Great Britain | by Cox and Wyman Ltd, | London, Reading, and Fakenham | Set in Monotype Bembo'. Price: AU$1.00.

F3e Penguin Edition Fifth Issue (Harmondsworth: Penguin, 1970)
Notes: p.*4* 'Published in Penguin Books 1961 | Reprinted 1963, 1965, 1967, 1970 | [rule] | Copyright © Patrick White, 1956 | [rule] | Made and printed in Great Britain | by Cox & Wyman Ltd, | London, Reading and Fakenham | Set in Montype Bembo'. Cover design by Sidney Nolan. Price: 50p or 10/-, AU$1.70, NZ$1.70, R1.20. ISBN 0 1400 1657 0.

F3f-g Penguin Edition Sixth to Seventh Issues (Harmondsworth: Penguin, 1971-1972)
Not seen.

F3h Penguin Edition Eighth Issue (Ringwood, Victoria: Penguin, 1973)
Notes: p.*4* 'Published in Penguin Books 1961 | Reprinted 1963, 1965, 1967, 1970, 1971, 1972, 1973 | [rule] | Copyright © Patrick White, 1956 | [rule] | Made and printed in Australia | at The Dominion Press, | Blackburn, Victoria | Set in Montype Bembo'. Cover drawing by Sidney Nolan. Some copies of this issue have a slightly different biography on p.*1*, in that it mentions the Nobel Prize. Price: 60p, AU$1.70, NZ$1.70, R1.45. ISBN 1400.1657 0.

F3i Penguin Edition Ninth Issue (Harmondsworth: Penguin, 1974)
Notes: p.*4* 'Published by Penguin Books 1961 | Reprinted 1963, 1965, 1967, 1970, 1971, 1972, 1973, 1974 | [rule] | Copyright © Patrick White, 1956 | | [rule] | Made and printed in Australia | at The Dominion Press, | Blackburn, Victoria | Set in Monotype Bembo'.

F3j Penguin Edition Tenth Issue (Harmondsworth: Penguin, 1975)
Notes: p.*4* 'Published by Penguin Books 1961 | Reprinted 1963, 1965, 1967, 1970, 1971, 1972, 1973, 1974, 1975 | [short rule] | Copyright © Patrick White, 1956 | [short rule] | Made and printed in Great Britain by | Cox & Wyman Ltd, | London, Reading and Fakenham | Set in Monotype Bembo'. Cover design by Sidney Nolan. Price: 95p, NZ$3.15. ISBN 01400 1657 0.

F3k Penguin Edition Eleventh Issue (Harmondsworth: Penguin, 1976)
Notes: p.*4* 'Published in Penguin Books 1961 | Reprinted 1963, 1965, 1967, 1970, 1971, 1972, 1973, 1974, 1975, 1976 | [...] | Made and printed in Great Britain by | Cox & Wyman Ltd, | London, Reading and Fakenham | Set in Monotype Bembo'. Price: 95p. Cover design by Sidney Nolan.

F3l Penguin Edition Twelfth Issue (Harmondsworth: Penguin, 1977)
Notes: p.*4* 'Published in Penguin Books 1961 | Reprinted 1963, 1965, 1967, 1970, 1971, 1973, 1974 (twice), 1975, 1976, 1977 | [...] | Made and printed in Great Britain by | Cox & Wyman Ltd, | London, Reading and Fakenham | Set in Monotype Bembo'. Price: [sticker] AU$2.95. Cover design by Sidney Nolan.

F3m-r Penguin Edition Thirteenth to Eighteenth Issues (Harmondsworth: Penguin, n.d)
Not seen.

F3s Penguin Edition Nineteenth Issue (Harmondsworth: Penguin, [1988])
PATRICK WHITE | [swelled rule] | THE TREE OF MAN | [publisher's device] | PEN-GUIN BOOKS

19.7 x 12.9 cm. Unsigned: 240 leaves. pp.*8* 9-98 *99-102* 103-195 *196-198* 199-355 *356-358* 359-479 *480* (the last page of each chapter is unnumbered).

Notes: p.*4* 'Published in Penguin Books 1961 | 19 20 | Copyright © Patrick White, 1955 | All rights reserved | Printed in England by Clays Ltd, St Ives plc | Set in Monotype Bembo'. Cover design by Neil Stuart. Cover illustration by Mel Odom. Price: £6.99, NZ$27.95, CAN$14.95. ISBN 0-14-001657-0.

F3t Penguin Edition Twentieth Issue (Harmondsworth: Penguin, [1992])
Notes: p.*4* 'Published in Penguin Books 1961 | 20 | Copyright © Patrick White, 1955 | All rights reserved | Printed in England by Clays Ltd, St Ives plc | Set in Monotype Bembo'. The cover shows a detail from *Home Leave* by Russell Drysdale in the Royal Collection, reproduced by gracious permission of H.M. Queen Elizabeth the Queen Mother. Published November 1992. Price: £6.99, AU$16.95, CAN$14.99, US$11.95. ISBN 0-14-018584-4'.

F3u Vintage Subedition First Issue (London: Vintage, 1994)
Notes: p.*4* 'Published by Vintage 1994 | 2 4 6 8 10 9 7 5 3 1 | Printed and bound in Great Britain by | Cox & Wyman, Reading, Berkshire'.

F3v Vintage Subedition Second Issue (London: London, n.d.)
Notes: p.*4* 'Published by Vintage 1994 | 2 4 6 8 10 9 7 5 3 | Printed and bound in Great Britain by | Cox & Wyman, Reading, Berkshire'.

F4 Pyramid Edition (New York: Pyramid Books, 1966)

THE TREE | OF MAN | Patrick White | [at bottom:] [publisher's device] | PYRAMID BOOKS • NEW YORK

17.8 x 10.6 cm. Unsigned: 256 leaves. pp.*1-6* 7-102 *103-104* 107-207 [105 is misnumbered '107'; 106 is not numbered; 107 is misnumbered '108'] *208-210* 211-355 *356* 357-380 *381-382* 383-512 *513* [i.e. 512].

1 'THE TREE OF MAN' | [blurb, 14 lines] | [quotation from] '—THE NEW YORK HERALD TRIBUNE'; *2* 'The Novels of | Patrick White | in Pyramid Editions | THE TREE OF MAN | VOSS | RIDERS IN THE CHARIOT'; *3* title page; *4* 'TO | *MANOLY* | THE TREE OF MAN | A PYRAMID BOOK | Published by arrangement with The Viking Press | The Viking Press edition published August, 1955 | Pyramid edition published May, 1966 | Copyright © 1955 by Patrick White | The lines of poetry on page 402 are from | A.E. Housman's *A Shropshire Lad*, XXXI. | Library of Congress catalog card number: 55-7377 | All rights reserved | Printed in the United States of America | PYRAMID BOOKS are published by Pyramid Publications, Inc. | 444 Madison Avenue, New York, New York 10022, U.S.A.'; *5* 'PART I'; *6* blank; 7-102, text of Part I; *103* 'PART II'; *104* blank; 107-207 text of Part II; *208* blank; *209* blank; *210* 'PART III'; 211-355 text of Part III; *356* blank;

357-380 text of Part III continues; *381* blank; *382* 'PART IV'; 383-512 text of Part IV; *513* [advertisements].

Perefectbound in orange-yellow and brown paper. Front: 'PYRAMID [publisher's device] N-1377 95c | [rule] | PATRICK WHITE | [rule] | One of the great novels of our | time. "Majestic and impressive." | —Orville Prescott, The New York Times | [rule] | THE TREE | OF MAN' | [illust. of house, tree and three figures]. Back: 'THE TREE | OF MAN | [quotation from] — NEW YORK TIMES BOOK REVIEW | PATRICK WHITE | [blurb, 5 lines] | [biography, 5 lines] | A PYRAMID BOOK 95c Cover: Frank Kalan Printed in U.S.A.' | [illust. of two kangaroos]. Spine: [at top:] 'N-1377 | 95c | [running down:] THE TREE OF MAN Patrick White | [at bottom:] [upright:] [publisher's device] | PYRAMID | BOOKS'.

Published in May 1966. Price: 95c.

Copies: NSL: Mitchell Library A823/W597/4C1; NSL: Mitchell Library [PW].

F5 Avon Edition (New York: Avon Books, 1975)

PATRICK | WHITE | The | Tree | of | Man | AVON | PUBLISHERS OF BARD, CAMELOT, DISCUS, EQUINOX AND FLARE BOOKS

17.8 x 10.4 cm. Unsigned: 256 leaves. pp.*6* 7-104 *105-106* 107-208 *209-210* 211-511 *512*.

1 'NOBEL PRIZE WINNER | PATRICK | WHITE | HIS TOWERING NOVEL OF STRUGGLE, | PASSION, AND TRIUMPH | The Tree of Man' | [quotations]; *2* '*Avon Books by* | Patrick White | THE EYE OF THE STORM 21527 $1.95 | THE TREE OF MAN 22665 $1.95'; *3* title page; *4* 'To | Manoly | The lines of poetry on pages 397-98 are from | A.E. Housman's A SHROPSHIRE LAD, XXXI. | AVON BOOKS | A division of | The Hearst Corporation | 959 Eighth Avenue | New York, New York 10019 | Copyright © 1955 by Patrick White. | Published by arrangement with The Viking Press, Inc. | Library of Congress Catalog Card Number: 55-7377. | ISBN: 0-380-00202-5 | All rights reserved, which includes the right | to reproduce this book or portions thereof in | any form whatsoever. For information address | The Viking Press, Inc., | 625 Madison Avenue, New York, New York 10022. | First Avon Printing, March, 1975. | AVON TRADEMARK REG, U.S. PAT. OFF. AND | FOREIGN COUNTRIES, REGISTERED TRADEMARK— | MARCA REGISTRADA, HECHO EN CHICAGO, U.S.A. | Printed in the U.S.A.'; *5* [floral device] | 'PART I' | [floral device]; *6* blank; 7-104 text of Part I; *105* [floral device] | 'PART II' | [floral ornament]; *106* blank; 107-208 text of Part II; *209* [floral device] | 'PART III' | [floral ornament]; *210* blank; 211-511 text of Part III; *512* 'THE BIG BESTSELLERS | ARE AVON BOOKS!'.

Perfectbound in glossy white paper. Front: 'AVON/22665/$1.95 [publisher's device] | [in green] NOBEL PRIZE WINNER | [in black] PATRICK | WHITE | Author of the nationwide | bestseller | THE EYE OF | THE STORM | [col. illust. of a man and woman's head] | [in green] The | Tree | of | Man | [in black] "A timeless work of art from which no | essential element of life has been omitted. | *The New York Times Book Review*'. Back: [blurb, 16 lines] | [quotation from] 'The *New York Times*' | [comment, 8 lines]. Spine: [publisher's device] 'AVON | [running down:] PATRICK WHITE / [in green] The Tree of Man 380.22665.195'.

Published in March 1975. Price: US$1.95.

Notes: Chapters 20 to 26 which comprise Part Four of the novel have been subsumed into Part Three in this edition, presumably without authority.

Copies: NSL Mitchell Library [PW].

F.t1a German First Edition First Issue (Köln and Berlin: Kiepenheuer & Witsch, 1957)

PATRICK WHITE | ZUR RUHE KAM DER BAUM | DES MEN-SCHEN NIE | ROMAN | KIEPENHEUER & WITSCH | KÖLN · BERLIN

21 x 12.8 cm. Unsigned: 268 leaves. pp.*10* 11-109 *110-112* 113-217 *218-220* 221-396 *397-400* 401-535 *536*.

Endpaper; *1* [publisher's device]; *2* blank; *3* 'ZUR RUHE KAM DER BAUM | DES MENSCHEN NIE'; *4* blank; *5* title page; *6* 'Titel der Originalausgabe: | THE TREE OF MAN | Aus dem Englischen von | Annemarie und Heinrich Böll | Schutzumschlag: | Werner Labbé | *1.-6. Tausend 1957* | *Alle deutschsprachigen Rechte bei* | *Verlag Kiepenheuer &* | *Witsch, Köln · Berlin* | *Gesamtherstellung: Bosch, Utrecht* | *Printed in Holland*'; *7* [epigraph from] 'A. E. HOUSMAN'; *8* blank; *9* 'ERSTER TEIL'; *10* blank; 11-109 *110* text of Part One; *111* 'ZWEITER TEIL'; *112* blank; 113-217 *218* text of Part Two; *219* 'DRITTER TEIL'; *220* blank; 221-396 *397* text of Part Three; *398* blank; *399* 'VIERTER TEIL'; *400* blank; 401-535 *536* text of Part Four; endpaper.

Cased in grey cloth. Front: [in red] 'ZUR RUHE | KAM DER BAUM | DES MENSCHEN | NIE'. Back: blank. Spine: [in red] 'PATRICK WHITE | *Zur Ruhe* | *kam der Baum* | *des Menschen* | *nie*' | [rule].

White paper dustjacket printed in black, green and red. Front: [background is stylised illust. of a tree] [in red] '*Patrick White* | [in white] ZUR RUHE | KAM | DER BAUM | DES | MEN-SCHEN | NIE | [in red] *Roman* | *Kiepenheuer & Witsch*'. Back: blank. Spine: [running down:] '*White / Baum des Menschen* | [upright:] *K&W*'. Inside front flap: 'PATRICK WHITE | *Zur Ruhe kam der Baum* | *des Menschen nie*' | [description, 37 lines]. Inside back flap: [description continues, 31 lines] | [biography, 12 lines] | 'KIEPENHEUER & WITSCH'.

Print run: 6,000.

Reviews: *Die Kiepe* v.5 no.2, 1957; Hubert Becher *Stimmen der Zeit* 1957, p.226-228; *Der Mittag* 1 January 1958; *Telegraf* 12 July 1959.

Copies: VSL: SLT 819.93 W582TRB (lacks dustjacket); VSL: SLT 819.93 W582TRB (lacks dustjacket); NSL: Mitchell Library; NSL: Mitchell Library [PW]; NU: Rare Books Collection.

F.t1b German First Edition Second Issue (Frankfurt am Main, Vienna and Zürich: Buchergilde Gutenberg, 1963)
Notes: p.533. Not seen, but referred to by *Gesamtverzeichnis des deutschsprachigen Schrifttums (GV) 1911-1965* (München: K.G. Saur, 1981), p.211; and Lawson, no.27.

F.t1c German First Edition Third Issue (Köln: Kiepenheuer & Witsch, 1973)
Notes: p.*6* 'Titel der Originalausgabe THE TREE OF MAN | Aus dem Englischen von Annemarie und Heinrich Böll | © 1957 by Verlag Kiepenheuer & Witsch, Köln | Schutzumschlag und Einband Hannes Jähn | Gesamtherstellung Mohndruck Reinhard Mohn OHG, Gütersloh | Printed in Germany 1973 | ISBN 3 462 00430 1'.

F.t1d German First Edition Fourth Issue (Münich: Deutscher Taschenbuch Verlag, 1973)
Patrick White: | Zur Ruhe kam der Baum des Menschen nie | Roman | Deutsche von Annemarie und Heinrich Böll | Deutscher | Taschenbuch | Verlag | [publisher's device]

18 x 10.9 cm. Unsigned: 272 leaves. pp.*8* 9-107 *108-110* 111-215 *216-218* 219-394 *395-398* 399-533 *534-544*.

Notes: p.*4* 'Ungekürzte Ausgabe | November 1973 | Deutscher Taschenbuch Verlag GmbH & Co. KG, | München | Alle deutschsprachigen Rechte bei Verlag | Kiepenheuer & Witsch, Köln | Titel der Originalausgabe: >The Tree of Man< | Umschlaggestaltung: Celestino Piatti | Gesamtherstellung: C.H.Beck'sche Buchdruckerei, | Nördlingen | Printed in Germany · ISBN 3-423-00992-6'. Perfectbound in glossy white paper printed in full colour. Published in November 1973. Price: DM7.80. Print run: 35,000.

F.t1e German First Edition Fifth Issue (Münich: Deutscher Taschenbuch Verlag, 1974)
Notes: Title, collation and binding are the same as for F.t1d above. On p.*4* 'Ungekürzte Ausgabe | 1. Auflage November 1973 | 2. Auflage April 1974: 36. bis 45. Tausend'. Published in April 1974. Print run: 10,000.

F.t1f German First Edition Sixth Issue (Münich: Deutscher Taschenbuch Verlag, n.d)
Not seen, but assumed.

F.t1g German First Edition Seventh Issue (Münich: Deutscher Taschenbuch Verlag, 1988)
Notes: pp.533. 4 Aufl. (dtv, 10875). ISBN 3-462-00430-1. DM 39.80; also see *Index Translationum*.

F.t2a German Second Edition First Issue (Stuttgart, Zürich and Salzburg: Europäischer Buchklub, 1960)

PATRICK WHITE | [in brown] ZUR RUHE KAM DER BAUM | DES MENSCHEN NIE | [in black] ROMAN | [in brown] EUROPÄISCHER BUCHKLUB | [in black] STUTTGART ZÜRICH SALZBURG

20.8 x 13 cm. [1]^8 2-32^8 ($1 signed): 256 leaves. pp.*1-6* 7-511 *512* (the last page of each chapter is unnumbered). Illust. with black and white drawings. Col. plates between pages 80-81, 96-97, 176-177, 336-337, 352-353, 448-449 and 464-465.

Endpaper; *1* 'ZUR RUHE KAM DER BAUM | DES MENSCHEN NIE'; *2* blank; *3* title page; *4* 'Aus dem Englischen übertragen von Annemarie und Heinrich Böll | Titel der Originalausgabe: „The Tree of Man" | *Illustrationen von Willie Widmann* | [at bottom:] SONDERAUSGABE EUROPÄISCHER BUCHKLUB | Stuttgart Zürich Salzburg | Alle deutschen Rechte beim Verlag Kiepenheuer & Witsch | in Köln-Marienburg | Gesamtherstellung: Druckhaus Neckartor, Stuttgart | Einbandgestaltung: Boris A Pfützner | Printed in Germany'; *5* [epigraph of four lines from] A. E. HOUSMAN'; *6* [illust.]; 7-508 *509* text; 510-511 *512* 'NACHWORT' [by Helmut M. Braem]; endpaper.

Cased in paper-covered boards decorated with vertical brown parallel lines and a grey leather spine. Front: [black panel with the signature of Patrick White]. Back: blank. Spine: [in gold on green panel:] 'WHITE | ZUR RUHE KAM | DER BAUM DES | MENSCHEN NIE'.

Copies: Personal collection; NSL: Mitchell Library [PW].

F.t2b German Second Edition Second Issue (Zürich: Buchklub ex Libris, 1960)
Notes: p.511. Not seen, but referred to by *Gesamtverzeichnis des deutschsprachigen Schrifttums (GV) 1911-1965* (München: K.G. Saur, 1981), p.210; and Lawson, no.24.

F.t2c German Second Edition Third Issue (Vienna, Darmstadt, Berlin: Deutsche Buchmeinschaft, 1963)
Notes: p.511. Not seen, but referred to by *Gesamtverzeichnis des deutschsprachigen Schrifttums (GV) 1911-1965* (München: K.G. Saur, 1981), p.211; and Lawson, no.28.

F.t3 Czech First Edition (Prague: Státne Nakladetelstvi Krásné Literatury a Uměni, 1962)

PATRICK WHITE | lidský strom | STÁTNI NAKLADATELSTVI | KRÁSNÉ LITERATURY | A | UMĚNI | PRAHA 1962

20.6 x 13.5 cm. Unsigned: 270 leaves. pp.*4* 5-105 *106* 107-212 *213-214* 215-393 *394* 395-533 *534* 535-538 *539-540*.

1 'SOUBODÁ SVĚTOVA PRÓZA | SVAZEK 143 | lidský strom'; *2* blank; *3* title page; *4* 'PŘELOŽIL JOSEF POSPIŠIL | © Eyre & Spottiswoode, London 1956 | Translation © Josef Pospišil, 1962'; 5-105 *106* text of Part I; 107-212 *213* text of Part II; *214* blank; 215-393 *394* text of Part III; 395-533 *534* text of Part IV; 535-538 *539* 'PATRICK WHITE | A

JEHO VIZE LIDSKÉHO OSUDU' [by Ian Milner]; 540 'SOUDOBÁ SVĚTOVA PRÓZA | SVAZEK 143 | ŘIDI DAGMAR STEINOVÁ | PATRICK WHITE | lidský strom | Z anglického originálu The Tree of Man, | vydaného nakladatelstvim Eyre & Spottiswoode, London 1956, | přeložil Josef Pospišil. Doslov napsal Ian Milner. | Obálku a vazbu navrhl Libor Fára. | Graficky upravila Hana Blažejová. | Vydalo Státni nakladatelstvi krásné literatury a uměni, n.p., | jako svou 1507. publikaci v redakci krásné literatury. | Praha 1962. | Odpovědná redaktorka Irena Wenigová. | Vytiskla Stráž, tiskařské závody, n.p., závod 4, Vimperk, | 33,04 autorských archů, 33,50 vydavatelských archů. | D 03*20180. | Vydáni prvni. | Naklad 8000 výtisků. | [in box:] 01-128-62 | 13/9 – Vázané 26,50 Kčs – 63/VIII–7'; endpaper.

Cased in light green calico with white endpapers. Front: [stylised] 'pw'. Back: blank. Spine: [running down:] 'PATRICK | WHITE | lidský strom'.

White glossy paper printed in green and black. Front: [background illust. of wooden door] 'lidský | strom | [running down:] [in green] PATRICK WHITE'. Back: [running down:] 'STÁTNI NAKLADATELSTVI KRÁSNÉ LITERATURY A UMĚNI'. Spine: [in white] 'PATRICK | WHITE | lidský strom'. Inside front flap: 'SOUBODÁ SVĚTOVÁ PRÓZA | SNKLU | lidský strom | PATRICK WHITE | Z angličtiny přeložil Josef Pospišil | [description, 19 lines] | [at bottom right:] 01-128-62 | 13/9 – Vázané 26,50 Kčs'. Inside back flap: 'PATRICK WHITE' | [biography, 25 lines] | [photograph of author].

Price: 26,50 Kčs. Print run: 8,000.

Copies: NSL: Mitchell Library [PW].

F.t4a Swedish First Edition First Issue (Stockholm: Albert Bonniers, 1970)

Patrick White | LIVETS TRÄD | ROMAN | *Albert Bonniers förlag* | *Stockholm*

21.7 x 14 cm. [1]^8 2-28^8 29^4 30^4 ($1 signed): 236 leaves. pp.*8* 9-95 *96-98* 99-191 *192-194* 195-349 *350-352* 353-471 *472*.

Endpaper; *1* 'LIVETS TRÄD'; *2* '*Av Patrick White har tidigare utgivits:* | De fyra utkorade 1964 | Den oförstörbara mandalan 1969'; *3* title page; *4* 'Lyrikcitaten på sid. 370-371 är hämtade ur | A. E. Housmans "A Shropshire Lad", XXXI. | Översättning av | MAGNUS K:SON LINDBERG | Engelska originalets titel: | The Tree of Man (London 1956) | © Patrick White 1956 | Printed in Sweden | Alb. Bonniers boktryckeri 1970 | Stockholm'; *5* '*Till Manoly*'; *6* blank; *7* 'DEL I'; *8* blank; 9-95 text of Part I; *96* blank; *97* 'DEL II'; *98* blank; 99-191 text of Part II; *192* blank; *193* 'DEL III'; *194* blank; 195-349 text of Part III; *350* blank; *351* 'DEL IV'; *352* blank; 353-471 *472* text of Part IV; endpaper.

Cased in yellow cloth with white endpapers. Front and back: blank. Spine: [running down:] 'PATRICK WHITE LIVETS TRÄD'.

Glossy white paper dustjacket printed in black and yellow. Front: 'PATRICK WHITE | LIVETS TRÄD | Roman | Bonniers'. Back: 'LIVETS TRÄD | [description, 32 lines] |

Omslag av Jan Biberg'. Spine: [running down:] 'PATRICK WHITE LIVETS TRÄD'. Inside front and back flaps: blank.

Copies: NSL: Mitchell Library A823/W587/4D1; NSL: Mitchell Library [PW]; Personal collection.

F.t4b Swedish First Edition Second Issue (Stockholm: Bokförlaget Aldus/Bonniers, 1973)

Notes: p.*4* 'ISBN 91-0-039077-1 | Engelska originalets titel: | The Tree of Man (London 1956) | Översättning av Magnus K:Son Lindberg | © Patrick White 1956 | Omslag av Herbert Lindgren | [rule] | Första svenska utgåva 1970 | Delfinserien 1973 | Lyrikcitaten på sid. 370-371 är hämtade ur | A. E. Housmans "A Shropshire Lad", XXXI. | | Printed in Sweden | Alb. Bonniers boktryckeri 1973 | Stockholm'. Perfectbound in white paper printed in full colour (col. illust. of tree and rural house).

F.t5 Hungarian First Edition (Budapest: Magvetó Kiadó, 1972)

PATRICK WHITE | [in red] Az élet fája | [in black] MAGVETÓ KIADÓ, BUDAPEST

18.6 x 12.7 cm. [1]-[2]^8 3-41^8: 328 leaves. pp.*4* 5-650 *651-656* (a portrait plate is inserted between pages *4* and 5).

Endpaper; *1* 'Patrick White | Az élet fája'; *2* 'VILÁGKÖNYVTÁR' | [in red] [rule] | [at bottom:] [publisher's device]; *3* title page; *4* 'Az angol eredetí címe | THE TREE OF MAN | Eyre & Spottiswoode, London 1956 | Fordította | VAJDA ENDRE | A fordítást az eredetivel összevetette | RÓNA ÉVA | Az elöszót írta | ZENTAI ÉVA | [at bottom:] © Patrick White, 1972'; 5-14 *15* '*ELÓSZO*'; *16* blank; *17* 'ELSÖ RÉSZ'; *18* blank; 19-139 text of Part I; *140* blank; *141* 'MÁSODIK RÉSZ'; *142* blank; 143-269 text of Part II; *270* blank; *271* 'HARMADIK RÉSZ'; *272* blank; 273-484 text of Part III; *485* 'NEGYEDIK RÉSZ'; *486* blank; 487-650 *651* text of Part IV; *652* blank; *653* blank; *654* 'Felelös kiadó a Magvetö Könyvkiadó igazgatója | Felelös szerkesztö Imre Katalin · Müszaki vezetö | Beck Péter · Tipográfus Romhányi Katalin · So- | rozattervezö Sebestyén Lajos · Védöboritó-grafika | Pécsi Gábor munkája · Kiadványszám 993 · 32,8 | (A5) iv terjedelemben, Garamond betütipusból, | 1972-ben · MA 2145 | 71-3084 Pécsi Szikra Nyomda – F. v.: Melles Rezsö'; *655* blank; *656* blank; endpaper.

Cased in blue cloth with white endpapers, light blue headpieces, a dark blue silk ribbon marker, and top edge in orange. Front: [publisher's device]. Back: [at top left:] '45,–'. Spine: [running up:] 'Patrick White · Az élet fája'.

White paper dustjacket with col. illust. of stylised tree on front. Front: 'Patrick | White | Az élet fája'. Back: 'A Magvetö Vilájkönyvtár sorozata | Elökészületben' | [list of 20 titles]. Spine: [running up:] 'Patrick White · Az élet fája'. Inside front flap: [blurb, 33 lines]. Inside back flap: [at top left:] '45,–'. On verso of dustjacket: '*A Világkönyvtár sorozatban megjelent müvek*' | [list of 88 titles in three columns].

Copies: VSL: SLT 819.93 W582TRE; NSL: Mitchell Library [PW]; NSL: Mitchell Library A823/W587/4F1 (lacks dustjacket); NSL: GRL E823.914/WHI (lacks dustjacket).

F.t6a Portuguese First Edition First Issue (Lisbon: Publicações Dom Quixote, 1973)

Patrick White | A ÁRVORE DO | HOMEM | PUBLICAÇÕES DOM QUIXOTE

20 x 12.2 cm. Unsigned: 328 leaves. pp.*10* 11-131 *132-134* 135-263 *264-266* 267-482 *483-484* 485-653 *654-656*.

1 [at bottom right:] [publisher's device]; *2* blank; *3* 'A ÁRVORE DO | HOMEM'; *4* 'AUTOR: | [biography, 33 lines] | *Bibliografia*' | [list, 13 lines]; *5* title page; *6* 'FICHA | © Patrick White, 1956. | Titulo original: The Tree of Man. | Editor original: Eyre & Spottiswoode, 1956. | Tradutor: Cardigos dos Reis. | Capa e orientação gráfica: Fernando Felgueiras. | Todos os direitos para a lingua portuguesa reservados | por Publicações Dom Quixote, | Rua Luciano Cordeiro, 119 —LISBOA'; *7* '*Dedicado a Manoly*'; *8* blank; *9* 'PRIMEIRA PARTE'; *10* blank; 11-131 text of Part I; *132* blank; *133* 'SEGUNDA PARTE'; *134* blank; 135-263 text of Part II; *264* blank; *265* 'TERCEIRA PARTE'; *266* blank; 267-482 text of Part III; *483* 'QUARTA PARTE'; *484* blank; 485-653 text of Part IV; *654* blank; *655* 'Colecção | Prémio Nobel' | [list of four titles]; *656* 'EDIÇÃO 3 E 323 | Este livro acabou de se imprimir | em 5 de Dezembro de 1973 | nas oficinas de | Guide-Artes Gráficas, Lda. | para | Publicações Dom Quixote | Rua Luciano Cordeiro, 119 —LISBOA'.

Perfectbound in light green paper card printed in dark green and black. Front: 'colecção | PRÉMIO NOBEL | Patrick White | A ÁRVORE | DO HOMEM | PUBLICAÇÕES DOM QUIXOTE'. Back: [photograph of the author] | [biography, 18 lines]. Spine: '3 | [running down:] A ÁRVORE | DO HOMEM | Patrick White' | [at bottom:] [upright:] [publisher's device].

Published in December 1973.

Copies: NSL: General Reference Library E823.914/WHI (lacks original binding and dustjacket); NSL: Mitchell Library A823/W587/37; NSL: Mitchell Library [PW]; Personal collection.

F.t6b Portuguese First Edition Second Issue (Lisbon: Circulo de Leitores, 1974)
Copies: not seen, but cited in the catalogue of the Biblioteca Nacional, Lisbon.

F.t6c Portuguese First Edition Third Issue (São Paolo: Circulo do Livro, 1981)
Notes: not seen, but referred to in *Index Translationum*.

F.t7 Greek First Edition (Athens: Zarbanos, 1976)

ΠΑΣΘΙϑ ϛΟΤΑΙΣ | ΣΟ | ΔΕΜΣΘΟ | ΣΟΤ | ΑΜΗΘΟΠΟΤ | ΛΕΣΑΥΘΑΡΓ : ϑ. ΧΑΚΑΜΟΠΟΤΚΟΤ | Β. ϑΑΣΡΑΜΓ | Δ.ϑ. ΦΑΘΒΑΜΟΡ | ΑΗΓΜΑ • 1976

21 x 14.7 cm. π^4 1-45^8 46^4 ($1 signed): 366 leaves. pp.[*8*] 1-726 *727-728*.

[*1*]-[*2*] blank; [*3*] 'ΠΑΣΘΙϑ | ϛΟΤΑΙΣ | ΒΘΑΒΕΙΟ | ΜΟΛΠΕΑ | 1973'; [*4*] blank; [*5*] 'ΣΟ | ΔΕΜΣΘΟ | ΣΟΤ | ΑΜΗΘΟΠΟΤ'; [*6*] blank; [*7*] title page; [*8*] 'ΡΣΟΠΘΟΣΟΣΤΠΟ | PAT-RICK WHITE | *THE TREE OF MAN* | Copyright 1956, by Patrick White | Copyright 1976, Δ.ϑ. Φαθβαμο'; 1-726 text; *727-728* blank.

Front: [illust. of man/tree] | [in green] 'ΣΟ | ΔΕΜ | ΣΘΟ | ΣΟΤ | ΑΜ | ΗΘΞ | ΠΟΤ | [in black] ΠΑΣΘΙϑ | ϛΟΤΑΙΣ | Δ.ϑ. Φαθβαμο|'. Back: [b&w photograph of the author within green box] | [at bottom right:] 'ΠΑΣΘΙϑ | ϛΟΤΑΙΣ'. Spine: 'ΠΑΣΘΙϑ | ϛΟΤΑΙΣ | [in green] ΣΟ | ΔΕΜ | ΣΘΟ | ΣΟΤ | ΑΜ | ΗΘΞ | ΠΟΤ | [in black] Δ.ϑ. Φαθβαμο|'. Inside front flap: [biography, 34 lines] | 'Δ.ϑ. ΦΑΘΒΑΜΟΡ | Βοτκ | 7 | Σγκ. 32.20.093 | φαι 32.49.728 | ϑΟΤΒΕΘΣΟΤΘΑ : ALIX STEINER-DEONNA | (ΡϛΕΔΙΟ)'. Inside back flap: [blurb, 43 lines].

Copies: VGRL Geelong Gr.F/WHI.

F.t8 Spanish First Edition (Barcelona: Plaza & Janes, 1976)

EL ARBOL | DEL HOMBRE | *por Patrick White* | [publisher's device] | PLAZA & JANES, S.A. | EDITORES

19.6 x 13.1 cm. [1]^8 2-40^8 ($1 signed): 320 leaves. pp.7 8-640 (first page of each chapter is not numbered).

Endpaper; *1* [series device]; *2* blank; *3* title page; *4* 'Título original: | THE TREE OF MAN | Traducción de | ALVARO CASTILLO | Portada de | ALVARO | Primera edición: Junio, 1976 | Copyright © Patrick White, 1956 | © 1976, PLAZA & JANES, S. A., Editores | Virgen de Guadalupe, 21-33. Esplugas de Llobregat (Barcelona) | Este libro se ha publicado originalmente en inglés con el título de | THE TREE OF MAN | [rule] | *Printed in Spain —* *Impreso en España* | ISBN: 84-0130189-0 — Depósito Legal: B. 24.818 – 1976 | GRAFI-CAS GUADA, S. A. — Virgen de Guadalupe, 33 | Esplugas de Llobregat (Barcelona)'; *5* 'A Manoly'; *6* blank; *7* 8-640 text; endpaper.

Cased in green paper-covered boards with white endpapers. Front and back: blank. Spine: [running down:] [in gold] '*PLAZA & JANES, S.A.* Editores | *E*[in white]*L* [in gold] *A*[in white]*RBOL DEL* [in gold] *H*[in white]*OMBRE* | [in gold] *por Patrick White*'.

White paper dustjacket printed with illust. in sandy tones across front and spine. Front: '*PATRICK WHITE* | [in white] el | árbol | del | hombre | [in black] Conmovedora epopeya, | que puede | considerarse | como el Génesis | australiano'. Back: [b&w photo of the author] | 'PATRICK WHITE' | [biography, 13 lines]. Spine: 'PATRICK | WHITE | [running down:] [in white] el árbol del hombre | [upright:] [in black] PLAZA & JANES'. Inside front flap: [in red] 'EN ESTA MISMA COLECCION' | [in black] [list of 7 titles follows]. Inside back flap: [in red] 'EN ESTA MISMA COLECCION' | [in black] [list of 9 titles follows].

Published in June 1976. ISBN 84-0130189-0.

Copies: NSL: Mitchell Library A823/W587/72 (lacks dustjacket); NSL: Mitchell Library [PW]; Personal collection.

F.t9 Spanish Second Edition (Barcelona: Plaza & Janes S.A. Editores, 1979)

[in gold] LOS | PREMIOS NOBEL | DE | LITERATURA | [line of stars] | *Patrick White* | *Eyvind Johnson* | [publisher's device] | PLAZA & JANES, S.A. EDITORES | [rule] | *1979*

18 x 12.5 cm. [1]^{16} 2-43^{16} 44^8 ($1 signed): 696 leaves. pp.*11* 12-13 *14-19* 20-746 *747-751* 752-1104 *1105-1107* 1108-1109 *1110-1113* 1114-1242 *1243-1245* 1246-1391 *1392*.

Endpaper; *1-2* blank; *3* [in gold] [publisher's device] | [in black] 'LOS PREMIOS NOBEL | DE LITERATURA | [horizontal brace] | VOL. XIV'; *4* blank; *5* title page; *6* 'PRIMERA EDICION | Febrero, 1979 | © de las obras de Patrick White: 1956, 1966, 1968, | 1974 by Patrick White | © de las obras de Eyvind Johnson: Eyvind Johnson, 1934, 1935 | © 1979 PLAZA & JANES, S.A., Editores | Virgen de Guadalupe, 21-33. Esplugas de Llobregat (Barcelona) | [rule] | *Printed in Spain — Impreso en España* | ISBN: 84-01-50314-0 — Depósito Legal: B. 4.340–1979'; *7* 'INDICE'; *8* blank; *9* 'PATRICK WHITE | PREMIO NOBEL 1973 | EL ARBOL DEL HOMBRE | LAS CACATUAS'; *10* blank; *11* 12-13 [biography]; *14* blank; *15* 'EL ARBOL DEL HOMBRE'; *16* blank; *17* '*A Manoly*'; *18* blank; *19* 20-746 text; *747* 'LAS CACATUAS'; *748* blank; *749* '*A Ronald Waters, por haber sobrevivado | a currenta y ocho años de amistad.*'; *750* blank; *751* 752-1104 text; *1105* 'EYVIND JOHNSON | PREMIO NOBEL 1974 | ERA EL AÑO 1914 | AQUI TIENES TU VIDA'; *1106* blank; *1107* 1108-1109 [biography]; *1110* blank; *1111* 'ERA EL AÑO 1914'; *1112* blank; *1113* 1114-1242 text; *1243* 'AQUI TIENES TU VIDA'; *1244* blank; *1245* 1246-1391 text; *1392* 'ESTE LIBRO SE IMPRIMIÓ EN LOS TALLERES | DE «GRÁFICAS GUADA, S.A.», | VIRGEN DE GUADALUPE, 33 | ESPLUGAS DE LLOBREGAT. | BARCELONA'; endpaper.

Cased in dark brown textured leather with red and yellow headbands, pink endpapers and a red silk ribbon marker. Front: [in gold] [publisher's device]. Back: blank. Spine: [in gold] 'LOS | PREMIOS | NOBEL | DE | LITERATURA | XIV | PLAZA & JANES'.

Copies: NSL: Mitchell Library [PW].

F.t10a Russian First Edition First Issue (n.p.: n.p., 1976)
Notes: not seen, but entry on Australian Bibliographic Network indicates a copy at NUN:S A823.9/WHI/1E.

F.t10b Russian First Edition Second Issue (Moscow: Progress, 1979)
Delo celoveceskoe.

Notes: pp.555. Trans. by N. Treneva. Referred to in *Index Translationum*.

Copies: ANL: N823.9 W587dr.

F.t11 Lithuanian First Edition (Vilnius: Vaga, 1980)

Gyvenimo medis.

Notes: pp.506. Translated by Lilija Vanagiene. Not seen, but referred to in *Index Transla-tionum*.

F.t12 Chinese Extract (Beijing: Foreign Languages Institute, 1980)

[*The Tree of Man*], chapters 1-4. In: *Waiguo Wenxue* [*Foreign Literatures*, a monthly published by the Foreign Languages Institute, Beijing], no. 4, 1980, (Special number on Australian Contemporary Literature). pp.7-24. Printed covers. 26 x 18.2 cm. pp.80. For a complete translation see F.t18 below.

Copies: NSL: Mitchell Library [PW].

F.t13 Romanian First Edition (Bucharest: Editura Univers, 1981)

PATRICK WHITE | COPACUL OMULUI | Traducere de *LEONTINA MOGA* | [publisher's device] Editura UNIVERS | Bucureşti, 1981

19.8 x 12.7 cm. Unsigned: 292 leaves. pp.*4* 5-581 *582-584* (the last page of each part is un-numbered).

1 'PATRICK WHITE | COPACUL OMULUI'; *2* 'Coperta de *Mǎriuca Brâncoveanu* | [at bottom:] PATRICK WHITE | *THE TREE OF MAN* | Penguin Books Ltd., Harmondsworth, | Middlesex, England | (c) Patrick White, 1956 | Toate drepturile asupra acestei versiuni | sînt rezervate Editurii Univers'; *3* title page; *4* blank; 5-581 *582* text; *583* 'Lector : DENISA COMǍNESCU | Tehnoredactor : NICOLAE ŞERBǍNESCU | [rule] | *Bun de tipar : 28.02.1981. Coli tipar 36,5.* | [rule] | [publisher's device] Tiparul executat sub comanda nr. 59 | la I.P. „Filaret", str. Fabrica de chibrituri | nr. 9-11, Bucureşti | Republicǎ Socialistǎ Românâ'; *584* blank.

Perfectbound in white paper printed in black, red, blue and dark olive. Front: [rule] | 'PATRICK WHITE | [rule] | COPACUL OMULUI' | [rule]. Back: [rule] | 'PATRICK WHITE | [rule] | COPACUL OMULUI | [rule] | EDITURA UNIVERS | [at bottom right:] [in white] Lei 17'. Spine: [running down:] [in white] 'PATRICK WHITE / COPACUL OMULUI'.

Published in February 1981. Price: Lei 17.

Copies: VSL: SLT 819.93 W582TRM; NSL: Mitchell Library [PW]; Personal collection.

F.t14 Estonian First Edition (Tallin: Eesti raamat, 1983)

Inimeste puu.

Notes: pp.464. Trans. by Vilma Jürisalu. Not seen, but referred to in *Index Translationum*.

F.t15 Czech Second Edition (Prague: Nakladatelstvi Svoboda, 1984)

• | [oxford rule] | PATRICK | WHITE | STROM ČLOVĚKA | 1984 | NAKLADATELSTVI SVOBODA | [oxford rule] | •

21 x 13.5 cm. Unsigned: 228 leaves. pp.*1-10* 11-92 *93-96* 97-182 *183-186* 187-326 *327-330* 331-440 *441-442* 443-448 *449-456* (last page of each chapter is unnumbered).

Endpaper; *1* '• | [oxford rule] | SVĚTOVÝ | SOCIÁLNI | ROMÁN | ÚSVIT'; *2* blank; *3* '• | [oxford rule] | PATRICK | WHITE | STROM | ČLOVĚKA | [oxford rule] | •'; *4* blank; *5* title page; *6* 'Přeložil Antonin Přidal | © Eyre & Spottiswoode, London 1956 | Translation © Antonin Přidal, 1984 | Epilogue © Antonin Přidal, 1984'; *7* '• | [oxford rule] | VE-NEVÁNO MANOLYMU'; *8* blank; *9* '• | [oxford rule] | PRVNI DIL'; *10* blank; 11-92 *93* text of Part I; *94* blank; *95* '• | [oxford rule] | DRUHÝ DIL'; *96* blank; 97-182 *183* text of Part II; *184* blank; *185* '• | [oxford rule] | TŘETI DIL'; *186* blank; 187-326 *327* text of Part III; *328* blank; *329* '• | [oxford rule] | ČTVRNY DIL'; *330* blank; 331-440 *441* text of Part IV; *442* blank; 443-448 *449* 'STVOŘENI ČLOVĚKA | V AUSTRALAKÉM BUSI'; *450* blank; *451* [publisher's device] | 'SVĚTOVÝ | SOCIÁLNI | ROMÁN | ÚSVIT | PAT-RICK WHITE / STROM ČLOVĚKA | z anlického originálu The Tree of Man, vydaného nakladatelstvim Eyre & Spottiswoode, Londýn 1956, přeložil a doslovem opatřil Antonin Přidal. | Přebal a vazbu navrhla Andréa Korbelářová. Vydáni prvni. Praha 1984. | Vydalo Nakladatelstvi Svoboda jako svou 5296. publikaci. Odpovědná redak- | torka Jarmila Svobodová. Výtvarná redaktorka Anna Kubů. Technická re- | daktorka Jaroslava Petráková. Vytisklo Rudé právo, tiskařské závody, Praha. | Náklad 20 000 výtisků. AA. 30,41, VA 31,24. Tematcká skupina 13/34. | Cena brož. výt. 30,20 Kčs, váz. výt. 36,– Kčs. | 73/605-22-815 Kčs 36,–'; *452-456* blank; endpaper.

Cased in tan calico boards with white endpapers. Front: [in brown] [illust. of summer sun]. Back: blank. Spine: [running down:] [in brown] 'PATRICK WHITE STROM ČLOVĚKA'.

Yellow glossy paper dustjacket printed in black, orange and white. Front: [illust. of bush scene] | [in white] 'Patrick | White | Strom | člověka'. Back: [illust. of bush scene] | [in white] 'NAKLADATELSTVI | SVOBODA | PRAHA | [publisher's device] | [at bottom:] 25–090–84 | 13/34 Kčs 36,–'. Spine: [running down:] 'PATRICK WHITE STROM ČLOVĚKA'. Inside front flap: [description, 28 lines]. Inside back flap: [blurb, 10 lines].

Price: 36 Kčs. Print run: 20,000.

Copies: NSL: Mitchell Library [PW].

F.t16 Polish First Edition (Warsaw: Państwowy Instytut Wydawniczy, 1985)

Drzewo człowiecze.

Notes: pp.572. Trans. by Maria Skibniewska. Not seen but referred to in *Index Translationum*.

F.t17 Vietnamese First Edition (Hanoi: Nha Xuat Ban Van Hoc, 1987)

VĂN HOC HIÊN ĐAI NƯỚC NGOÀI' | *VAN HOC ÒXTRAYLIA* | [rule] | PATRIC OAITO' | CÂY NGƯỜI | (hai tâp) | I | HOANG TÚY và MANH CHƯỜNG dieh | NHÀ XUẤT BAN VĂN HOC | Hà Nôi — 1987

[Vol.I:] pp.*4* 5-8 *9-12* 13-152 *153-154* 155-302 *303-304*.

[Vol.I:] *1* 'CÂY NGƯỜT'; *2* blank; *3* title page; *4* 'Dich tù nguyên ban tiêng Anh | THE TREE OF MAN | Nhà xuát ban Harmondsworth | Penguin, 1961'; 5-8 'Lờ'i gioi thiêu'; *9* 'TĂNG MANÔLY'; *10* blank; *11* 'PHAN MOT'; *12* blank; 13-152 text of Part I; *153* 'PHAN HAI'; *154* blank; 155-302 text of Part II; *303* [double rule] | 'Chiu trach nhiem xuat ban : | LY HAI CHAU | Bien tap noi dung : TRINH XUAN HOANH | Trinh bay sach : TRAN KHOAT | Trinh bay bia : VU DUY NGHIA | Sua ban in : VAN THO — KIM CHI | *** | CÂY NGUOI | *PATRIC OAITO* | NHA XUAT BAN VAN HOC | In 35 000 cuon kho 13 x 19 | Tai Nha in bao Nhun Dan Ha Noi | So in 44/87. So xuat ban 16/VH | Xong va gua luu chieu | ngay 10 thang 7 nam 1987' | [double rule]; *304* blank.

Sewn in off-white paper printed in black, brown and green. Front: 'patric oaito' | [in brown] CÂY NGƯỜT | [publisher's device] | [illust. of tree and horse]. Back: [b&w photograph of the author] | [biography, 26 lines] | 'HOP TAC XUAT BAN VOI OXTRAYLIA | GIA :'. Spine: [running down:] [in green] 'PATRIC OAITO [in brown] CÂY NGƯỜI | [upright:] [in black] vh | [in green] VAN HOC'.

Translated by Hoàng Túy and Minh Ching. Print run: 35,000.

Copies: NSL: Mitchell Library [PW] (Vol.I only).

F.t18 Chinese First Edition (Shang-hai: Shang-hai i wen ch'u pan she, 1990)

[Jen shu]

pp.702.

Translated by Hu Wen-chung and Li Yao. Titlepage verso: 'Patrick White | THE TREE OF MAN | [Chinese characters] Penguin Books 1973 [Chinese characters] | [seven lines of Chinese text] | [three lines of Chinese text] | [four lines of Chinese text] | three lines of text, giving production data, indicating a print run of 4,000] | ISBN 7—5327—0919—1 / I·484 | [two Chinese characters] 10.90 [one Chinese character].

Copies: NU East Asian Collection; Mitchell Library [PW].

F.t19 Korean First Edition (Seoul: Eulyoo Publishing Company, 1992)

[In-gan i-namu]

2 v. 20.3 x 15.3 cm. Unsigned. [Vol.I:] pp.[*2*] *1* 2 *3-9* 10-428 [*2*]; [Vol.II:] pp.[*2*] *1-3* 4-323 *324-327* 328-352 *353* 354 [*4*] (the first page of each chapter is not numbered).

Notes: [Vol.I:] p.[*2*] 'THE TREE OF MAN | Copyright © Patrick White, 1955 | The Korean language edition is published by | arrangement with The Commonwealth of Australia (represented by | the Australian Embassy to the Republic of Korea) | Korean Edition © 1992 by the Eulyoo Publishing Company, Ltd., Seoul, Korea | ISBN 89-324-7036-7'.

Perfectbound in glossy white paper covers with col. illust. after *Fig tree, Stanwell Park*, 1909, by Sydney Long on front; beige endpapers.

Translated by Yong-chi Kim. Price: 5,500KRW. Reported that 4,000 copies were published as part of a joint arrangement between the Korean publisher and Australia's Dept. of Foreign Affairs and trade. Apparently, the edition sold out in a few weeks. See Deborah Cameron *Sydney Morning Herald* 17 May 1993, p.8.

Copies: NSL: KOR/WHI/1; NSL: 823.3/W587/2.

F.m1 Abridged Edition (New York: Books Abridged Inc., n.d.)

[publisher's device] | The Sixth of June | LIONEL SHAPIRO | Waterfront | BUDD SCHULBERG | Reckless: Pride of the | Marines | ANDREW GEER | The Tree of Man | PATRICK WHITE | BOOKS ABRIDGED, INC. *New York*

21.5 x 14.3 cm. 224 leaves. pp.*1–6* 7–124 *125–126* 127–232 *233–234* 235–308 *309–310* 311–448.

Notes: p.*4*: 'The abridgements reprinted in this | book are used by permission of and | special arrangement with the publish- | ers holding the respective copyrights | COPYRIGHT 1955 | BY BOOKS ABRIDGED, INC. | All rights reserved, including the | right to reproduce this book or parts | thereof in any form | 19 | PRINTED IN | THE UNITED STATES OF AMERICA'. p.*309* 'THE | TREE | OF | MAN | A NOVEL BY | PATRICK WHITE | [publisher's device] AN ABRIDGEMENT'; 310 [biography]; 311–448 text; endpaper.

Copies: NU: Fisher Library 823.9108/132.

F.m2 Sound Recording (Adelaide: University of Adelaide, Department of Continuing Education, 1976)

The Tree of Man

Read by Brian Matthews.

F.m3 Sound Recording (North Sydney: Australian Listening Library, [1981]

The Tree of Man (16 audiocassettes).

Read by Wal Durbin from the Jonathan Cape edition of 1974.

F.m4 Sound Recording (Hove, South Australia: Visiting Teacher Service for Visually Impaired Children, Townsend School, 1987)

The Tree of Man (15 audiocassettes).

Not seen, but referred to on the National Bibliographic Database.

F.m5 Braille (Annerley: Queensland Braille Writing Association, [n.d.])

The Tree of Man (13 volumes of Interpoint Braille).

Not seen, but referred to on the National Bibliographic Database.

F.m6 Radio Production (Sydney: ABC Radio, 1983)

Notes: Produced by Michael Le Moignan. The first episode was broadcast on ABC Radio 2 on the 28 July 1983.

F.m7 Sound Recording (Burwood: Royal Blind Society of New South Wales, [n.d.])

The Tree of Man (4 audiocassettes, 4-track).

Read by Frank Knowles.

F.m8 Sound Recording (Wahroonga, N.S.W.: St Edmund's School for Blind and Visually Handicapped Students, [n.d.])

The Tree of Man (15 audiocassettes).

Read by Frank Kearns.

F.m9 Sound Recording (Melbourne: Royal Victorian Institute for the Blind, Tertiary Resource Centre, [n.d.])

The Tree of Man (4 audiocassettes, 4-track).

Read by Reg Macdonald.

G Voss (1957)

Patrick White first thought of an explorer novel in the early years of the war. The western desert and Nolan's desert paintings had worked on White's imagination, and in the late 1940s he had even identified the journeys of Ludwig Leichhardt as the basis for the story. 'Some years ago I got the idea for a book about a megalomaniac explorer … when I returned here after the War and began to look up old records, my idea seemed to fit the character of Leichhardt.' (To Ben Huebsch, 11 September 1956) White began to think about the novel again in the summer of 1954-1955 when hospitalised for a severe asthmatic attack. 'My only consolation is that the attacks are a great help creatively. Yesterday I was seeing quite clearly whole stretches of a novel I am planning to start after Christmas, and which had remained misty until now.' (To Ben Huebsch, 19 November 1954)

He began writing the book at this time and had almost finished the first draft by October 1955. He had begun the second draft by 29 December: 'I think it will be a long time before this one can be called finished. I shall have to re-write it at least once, probably twice.' (To Ben Huebsch, 25 October 1955) The second draft however was completed by the end of June 1956 and White determined that he would begin typing the final draft in August. By December the typescript of *Voss* was on its way 'by registered air mail' to White's agents in London and New York.

The novel was dedicated to Marie d'Estournelles de Constant [Marie Viton], whom White acknowledged in later years to have been a great encouragement during the dark years following the perceived failure of *The Aunt's Story*: 'it was her efforts as much as anything else that decided me to embark on *The Tree of Man*'. Viton was a reader at Gallimard, whom she persuaded to purchase the French translation rights to White's first three novels. Viton herself translated *Happy Valley* (which Gallimard published in 1951 under the title of *Eden-Ville*) and *The Living and the Dead* (never published). *The Aunt's Story* was not translated.

Late in January 1957 Huebsch wrote to White accepting *Voss* for The Viking Press. Proofs arrived from New York in March. The editor Marshall Best respected White's authority over the text but did make some suggestions: that hanging participles be cleaned up; that the use of 'that' and 'which' be made consistent; and that the excessive punctuation be thinned. White rejected these suggestions though he did allow some thinning out of commas. *Voss* was published by The Viking Press in August 1957.

White also received the welcome news that *Voss* had been chosen by the Book of the Month Club as their book for August. 'From the point of view of sales this is most satisfactory as the Book Club guarantees quite a considerable sum, which I shall halve with the publisher.' (To Peggy Garland, 30 May 1957) There was a suggestion – which White rejected – by the Book Club that the title be changed. 'A book grows with its title. If one starts to mess around with the latter afterwards, the whole thing begins to look a bit like a bad Hollywood film.' (To Ben Huebsch, 7 May 1957) Perhaps the Book Club nomination explains why *Voss* was printed simultaneously at three different locations in the United States (The Kingsport Press in Tennessee, The Colonial Press in Florida, and The Haddon Craftsmen in Pennsylvania).

'I don't think I have written since I received the copies of *Voss*, so I have not said how pleased I was with its appearance.' (To Ben Huebsch, 19 August 1957) As a rule White seems to have had confidence in The Viking Press as a designer of handsome trade editions. He did proffer some advice to Huebsch about the design of *Voss*'s jacket: 'I cut out the enclosed as it seemed to me to convey something of the climax of *Voss* … Perhaps Brueghel and the artist who does the jacket for V. may get together in some way.' (8 February 1957) Huebsch responded by suggesting that Brueghel's 'Triumph of Death' might be saved for a fresh edition of *Mein Kampf.*

White had signed the English agreement for *Voss* by March 1957. Eyre & Spottiswoode did not intend to publish until well into the next year (much to White's annoyance), but the Book Society chose it for its December selection, and so the publication was brought forward. Even so, Eyre & Spottiswoode still contrived not to have the book in Australia for the Christmas rush. The Society took 11,000 copies. Temple Smith was aware of White's attitude to editorial intervention and changed nothing in *Voss* except for some spelling corrections. The book was published in early December 1957 in a splash of publicity.

White had been disappointed with the jacket design on *The Tree of Man* and was determined to take the matter in hand. He approached Sidney Nolan whom he had admired for some years. 'You don't know me, but I have written several novels, of which the last, *The Tree of Man*, had a certain amount of success here and there. Another novel, *Voss*, is to be published in London within the next eighteen months by Eyre & Spottiswoode, who brought out *The Tree of Man* in such a filthy jacket. I have suggested they approach you …'. (To Sidney

Nolan, 7 March 1957) White provided a plot summary to Nolan and even pointed to the death of Palfreyman as a suitable subject. Nolan took the commission but in the end did not satisfy White. 'The jacket for *Voss* I do not like. S. sent me a preliminary drawing on a postcard which got the character to perfection—thin and prickly. Then the final version turned into that fat, amiable botanist.' (To Geoffrey Dutton, 13 December 1959) Apart from the E&S cased edition, Nolan's 'botanist', in a slightly modified form, has been used until quite recently on the Penguin paperback edition.

The critical reception in New York was positive but lukewarm, tending to put *Voss* aside and again to praise *The Tree of Man*. Sales were down. 'The reviews of *Voss* in the States have been mostly good, but it is not selling wildly … A strange development is an order of 1000 copies of *Voss* for the U.S. Army Libraries.' In London, in contrast, the reviews were exhilarating. In fact, *Voss* established White's reputation in London. Commercial success followed: 'I am told that *Voss* is selling well in England, though how well I could not say'. (To Ben Huebsch, 19 March 1958)

On top of the critical and commercial success of the English edition, White also won the inaugural W.H. Smith Award (1959) with a cash prize of £1,000: 'it was one in the eye for the Australian Professors of English who continue to accuse me of illiteracy'. White refused to go to England for the award ceremony; he was ill at the time. He also refused to make a sound recording or be involved in a telephone link-up, though he did complete a questionnaire, published in the W.H. Smith house magazine *The Newsbasket* (December 1959, p.18).

Although published in London in December 1957, stocks of *Voss* did not reach Australian shores till January. '[I] have signed agreements for German and Portuguese translations of *Voss*. I don't think it will ever arrive here, which I begin to find humiliating and exasperating'. (To Frederick Glover, 27 January 1958) The wait was made all the more frustrating by the promise of adverse criticism: 'I can feel the critics poised for their ritual murder.' (To the Moores, 12 January 1958) White must have felt let down. Australian criticism was very low-key. As David Marr states, the general editorial opinion seems to have been that *Voss* was a publishing event of no local importance. But *Voss* sold well in Australia: 'Here it has been at the top of the bestseller list in spite of the worst reviews.' (To Ben Huebsch, 19 March 1958) To cap this success *Voss* also won the Miles Franklin Prize for the best Australian novel of the year: 'As it was the first time awarded, the bull that went with it was most alarming'. (To the Moores, 5 April 1958) A few years later, during the fracas over the rejections of

'The Ham Funeral' for the Adelaide Festival, a journalist tried to show that people might buy White's books but they did not read them. The librarian at the Adelaide Circulating Library was quoted as saying 'No-one will read them. Each one comes out in a blaze of publicity. In the case of *Voss* the library purchased twenty-two copies. We get rid of them for 5/- a copy, and the last was reduced to 2/- a copy. (Marr p.391 : *Nation* 22 April 1961, p.5).

As shown above, foreign publishing houses were quick to pick up translation rights – White had signed agreements for German and Portuguese translations even before *Voss* had appeared in Australia. The German translation was a publishing event, and the first printing was of 5,000 copies. The success of *Voss* on top of that of *The Tree of Man* combined to guarantee White's status in the German-speaking world. The German translation of *Voss* was reissued as a paperback after White's Nobel Prize of 1973: the first two printings were of 20,000 and 10,000 copies respectively. Other translations consolidated White's world standing: Spanish (1962), Italian (1965), French (1967), Turkish (1973), Croatian (1974), Japanese (1975), Finnish (1977), Slovakian [Bratislava] (1977), Polish (1979), Czech (1980), Dutch (1982), Swedish (1983), Portuguese (1985), Hebrew (1990) and Chinese (1991). White was aghast when he received a copy of the Japanese translation for which he had not signed an agreement: 'there came a letter from the publisher to say that there had been no contract because, according to Japanese copyright law, a publisher can take anything after ten years. He hoped I understood!' (To Geoffrey Dutton, 31 August 1975)

Almost from the day of publication there have been efforts to produce a film version of *Voss*. When travelling in the United States in the late 1950s, White met with the actor Zachary Scott who was keen on both *The Tree of Man* and *Voss* as potential film projects. In England Keith Michell offered £3,000 for the film rights. Both offers came to nothing, but by 1968 Harry M. Miller, a show business entrepreneur, had purchased the film rights and had entered into an agreement with White. White retained control over the choice of director. He first suggested Satyajit Ray, but Ray was rejected by Miller as a maker of art movies. White's next suggestion was Ken Russell. Miller flew to London and came to an agreement with Russell. John McGrath, Russell's scriptwriter, thought *Voss* was an important novel and was a persuasive influence on Russell. McGrath visited Australia in June 1970, scouting locations. A year later White visited McGrath and Russell in London. He was a little disappointed with McGrath's script but was optimistic. Relations between McGrath and Russell were strained, and McGrath doubted the director's commitment. In the end

Russell admitted that he would not go to Australia because it was too far away and he did not like planes.

White's next choice was Joseph Losey who had directed *The Go-Between* (1970). Losey came out to Australia in February 1974 for talks. Losey took on the project. He approached Harold Pinter to do the script but settled for David Mercer. A German producer, Klaus Hellwig, became interested, and Losey, Mercer and film crew visited Australia in January 1977. The project foundered on Harry Miller's inability to raise financial backing. Miller's task was difficult due to Losey's reputation for losing money on his films and the resistance of the Australian film industry. Miller sold the film rights following financial difficulties in 1979. They were bought by Stuart Cooper, an American director, with the backing of Sidney Nolan. There was still talk of a film version in 1994.

More successful than *Voss* the film was *Voss* the opera. As early as 1972 Moya Henderson, then a Sacre Cœur nun, wrote to White proposing to compose an opera based on *Voss*. White was bemused but certainly not dismissive. After many years of study in Europe, Henderson in the end did not compose an opera, though she did set White's *Six Urban Songs*, first performed in 1986. In 1977 the Australian Opera (perhaps inspired by Henderson's initiative) came up with a new proposal for an opera: Jim Sharman would direct, Richard Meale would write the music, and David Malouf would do the libretto. White admired each of these artists. The team commenced work in July 1979, and by 1982 a fragment was ready to be performed at the Adelaide Festival. White critiqued Meale's work, wanting something harsher, grittier; but in the end he wrote: '*Voss* is yours to do what you will with it. I hope you have a tremendous success – a success I shall enjoy.' (To Richard Meale, 14 June 1982) *Voss* premiered at the Adelaide Festival on 1 March 1986 and then had a season at the Sydney Opera House: 'The *Voss* opera is a tremendous success – full houses and enthusiastic audiences … The novel should start selling again if Cody pulls his finger out.' (To Graham C. Greene, 25 June 1986) John Cody was the director of Jonathan Cape's Australasian subsidiary.

* * * * *

G1a U.S. First Edition (New York: Viking, 1957)

[in box of double rules:] [floral ornament] | VOSS | A NOVEL | [ornament] | BY | Patrick White | 1957 | The Viking Press | NEW YORK

20.9 x 13.9 cm. Unsigned: 224 leaves. pp.[6] *1-2* 3-442.

Endpaper; [*1*] [floral ornament] | 'VOSS'; [*2*] [floral ornament] 'BY THE SAME AUTHOR | The Tree of Man | The Aunt's Story | The Living and the Dead | Happy Valley'; [*3*] title page; [*4*] 'Copyright © 1957 by Patrick White | First published in 1957 | by The Viking Press, Inc. | 625 Madison Ave., New York 22 | Published in Canada by | The Macmillan Company of Canada Limited | Library of Congress catalog card number: 57-9493 | PRINTED IN THE UNITED STATES OF AMERICA BY | KINGSPORT PRESS, INC., KINGSPORT, TENNESSEE'; [*5*] [floral ornament] | 'For | Marie d'Estournelles de Constant'; [*6*] blank; *1* [floral ornament] | 'VOSS'; *2* blank; 3-442 text; endpaper.

Cased in blue calico with spine in light blue and with off-white endpapers. Front: [stamped in blind] [floral ornament] | 'VOSS'. Back: blank. Spine: [in dark blue panel:] [in light blue] [floral ornament] | [in silver] 'VOSS | [in light blue] [three lines of floral ornaments] | [outside panel:] [in dark blue] Patrick | White | [in dark blue panel:] [in light blue] [three lines of floral ornaments] | [outside panel:] [in dark blue] THE | VIKING | PRESS'.

White paper dustjacket printed in yellow and blue-green with illust. signed by 'Salter' of abstract landscape with fragments of handwritten letters across front and spine. Front: [in dark and light blue] '*VOSS* | [in orange] *A NOVEL BY* | [in black] PATRICK WHITE | [in orange] *Author of THE TREE OF MAN*'. Back: [at top right:] [b&w photograph of the author] | 'Photo by Hugh Clunies Ross, | courtesy *Sydney Morning Herald* | [at top left:] [in blue] Patrick | White | [in black] "... towers over most | other living novelists by | his ability to supply, | to lay bare the | conscious, romantic | yet private daydream, | the unlived life ..." | —JAMES STERN, | *New York Times Book Review* | *From the comments on* | [in blue] [shadow type] THE TREE OF MAN | [in black] [solid type] [quotation of two lines from] —EMERSON PRICE, *Cleveland Press* | [quotation of three lines from] —ORVILLE PRESCOTT, *New York Times* | [quotation of two lines from] —FANNY BUTCHER, *Chicago Tribune* | [quotation of two lines from] —GLENDY CULLIGAN, *Washington Post & Times-Herald*'. Spine: 'VOSS | *Patrick White* | [in blue] VIKING'. Inside front flap: BOOK-OF-THE-MONTH CLUB* SELECTION | *Trademark of Book-of-the-Month Club, Inc. | Reg. U.S. Pat. Off. and in Canada | [blurb, 44 lines] | JACKET DESIGN BY GEORGE SALTER'. Inside back flap: BOOK-OF-THE-MONTH | PATRICK WHITE | [biography, 37 lines] | [publisher's device] | THE VIKING PRESS | 625 Madison Avenue, New York 22, N. Y. | PRINTED IN THE U.S.A. | *593'.

Published in August 1957. Price: $5.

Reviews: *Kirkus* v.25, 15 June 1957, p.423 (320w); Donald Wasson *Library Journal* v.82, August 1957, p. 1909 (110w); Borden Deal *Saturday Review* v.40, 17 August 1957, p.13 (470w); Lewis Gannett *New York Herald Tribune Book Review* 18 August 1957, p.5 (700w); C. Hartley Grattan *New York Times Book Review* 18 August 1957, p.4 (1200w); *Time* v.70, 26 August 1957, p.84 (700w); Jean Holzhauer *Commonweal* v.66, 30 August 1957, p.550 (550w); *Booklist* v.54, September 1957, p.46; B.R. Redman *Chicago Sunday Tribune* 1 September 1957, p.4 (250w); Jane Voiles *San Francisco Chronicle* 6 September 1957, p.15 (650w); Phoebe Adams *Atlantic Monthly* v.200, October 1957, p.184 (320w); *New Yorker* v.33, 5 October 1957, p.197 (320w); *Bookmark* v.17, October 1957, p.12 (30w); Hilda Kirkwood *Canadian Forum* v.37, November 1957, p.190 (350w).

Notes: The copy in White's own collection is a presentation copy from the publisher in a half-leather binding. The University of Sydney copy has the ex libris of Colin Berckelman.

Extracts: 'The Death of Palfreyman', *Meanjin* v.16 no.3, September 1957; 'From *Voss*', *The American Pen*, v.8 no.1, Summer 1976, pp.1-5; [Untitled], *The Macmillan Anthology on Australian Literature* ed. by Ken L. Goodwin and Alan Lawson (South Melbourne: Macmillan, 1990), p.41-44; 'Death of an Explorer', *Sin, Sweat and Sorrow: the making of Capricornia Queensland 1840s-1940s* (Rockhampton: University of Central Queensland Press, Yapunya Imprint, 1993), p.20-21.

Copies: NU: RB 1657.4; NSL: Mitchell Library A823/W587/5B1 (lacks dustjacket); Personal collection; NSL: Mitchell Library [PW]; VU: McL L/A-F White.

G1b U.S. First Edition Another Issue (New York: Viking, 1957)
Notes: p.*4* 'Copyright © 1957 by Patrick White | © First published in 1957 | by The Viking Press, Inc. | 625 Madison Ave., New York 22 | Published in Canada by | The Macmillan Company of Canada Limited | Library of Congress catalog card number: 57-9493 | Printed in the U.S.A. by The Colonial Press Inc.'. The dustjacket is as for G1a except for the inside front flap: [at right] | '*Voss* $5.00 | [blurb, 44 lines] | *A Book-of-the-Month Club selection* | JACKET DESIGN BY GEORGE SALTER'; and inside back flap: 'PATRICK WHITE | [biography, 37 lines] | [publisher's device] | THE VIKING PRESS | 625 Madison Avenue, New York 22, N. Y. | PRINTED IN THE U.S.A.'.

G1c U.S. First Edition Another Issue (New York: Viking, 1957)
Notes: p. *4* 'Copyright © 1957 by Patrick White | First published in 1957 | by The Viking Press, Inc. | 625 Madison Ave., New York 22 | Published in Canada by | The Macmillan Company of Canada Limited | Library of Congress catalog card number: 57-9493 | Printed in the U.S.A. by The Haddon Craftsmen | Scranton, Pa.'.

G1d Canadian Subedition (Toronto: Macmillan, 1957)
Not seen, but referred to in the first edition (see G1a above). Published in August 1957. Price: $5.75.

G1e U.S. First Edition Viking Subedition (New York: Viking, 1974)
Notes: p.[*4*] 'Copyright © 1957 by Patrick White | All rights reserved | First published in 1957 by The Viking Press, Inc. | 625 Madison Avenue, New York, N.Y. 10022 | Published simultaneously in Canada by | The Macmillan Company of Canada Limited | SBN 670-74807-2 | Library of Congress catalog card number: 57-9493 | Printed in U.S.A.'. Cased in black calico with off-white endpapers. Pale green paper dustjacket. Published in January 1974. Price: $10. SBN 670-74807-2. A copy in a personal collection is inscribed to the author from Ben Huebsch.

G1f U.S. First Edition Avon Subedition (New York: Avon Books, 1975)
PATRICK | WHITE | *Voss* | [publisher's device] AVON | PUBLISHERS OF BARD, CAMELOT, DISCUS, EQUINOX AND FLARE BOOKS

17.8 x 10.4 cm. Unsigned: 224 leaves. pp.*4* 5-445 *446-448*.

Notes: p.*4* [floral ornament] | 'For | Marie d'Estournelles de Constant | AVON BOOKS | A division of | The Hearst Corporation | 959 Eighth Avenue | New York, New York 10019 | Copyright © 1957 by Patrick White. | Co-published by Avon Books and The Viking Press, Inc. | Library of Congress Catalog Card Number: 57-9493. | ISBN 0-380-00251-5 | All rights reserved, which includes the right to reproduce | this book or portion thereof in any form whatsoever. | For information address The Viking Press, Inc., | 625 Madison Avenue, New York, New York 10022. | First Avon Printing, February, 1975 | AVON TRADEMARK REG. U.S. PAT. OFF. AND | FOREIGN COUNTRIES, REGISTERED TRADEMARK– | MARCA REGISTRADA, HECHO EN CHICAGO, U.S.A. | Printed in the U.S.A.'. Perfectbound in white paper printed in full colour (illust. of a man's head). Published in February 1975. Price: US$1.95.

Copies: NSL: Mitchell Library [PW].

G2a U.K. First Edition (London: Eyre & Spottiswoode and The Book Society, 1957)

[swelled rule] | [hollow shadowed type] VOSS | [solid type] *A Novel* | [swelled rule] | PATRICK WHITE | EYRE & SPOTTISWOODE LTD | and THE BOOK SOCIETY LTD

20.5 x 14.1 cm. 1-15^{16} ($1,5 signed): 240 leaves. pp.*1-8* 9-478 *479-480*.

Endpaper; *1* [hollow shadowed type] 'VOSS'; *2* '*Also by Patrick White* | HAPPY VALLEY, 1939 | THE LIVING AND THE DEAD, 1941 | THE AUNT'S STORY, 1948 | THE TREE OF MAN, 1955'; *3* title page; *4* 'This edition issued on first publication by | THE BOOK SOCIETY LTD. | in association with | EYRE & SPOTTISWOODE (PUBLISHERS) LTD. | © *1957 Eyre & Spottiswoode (Publishers), Ltd.* | *Printed in Great Britain by Hazell Watson & Viney Ltd.* | *Aylesbury and Slough*'; *5* 'FOR | MARIE D'ESTOURNELLES | DE CONSTANT'; *6* blank; *7* [hollow shadowed type] 'VOSS'; *8* blank; *9-478* text; *479* blank; *480* blank; endpaper.

Cased in dark blue cloth with white endpapers. Front and back: blank. Spine: [in silver] 'VOSS | [thick rule] | PATRICK | WHITE | [at bottom:] E & S'.

Dull white paper dustjacket with illust. in grey-blue and dirty yellow with black line drawing by Sidney Nolan spreading across front, back and spine. Front: [painted in yellow on blue] 'VOSS' | [illust. of bearded man in hat before a row of huts which merge into a stylised landscape across spine and back]. Back: [painted in yellow on blue] 'PATRICK | WHITE'. Spine: [painted in yellow on blue] 'VOSS | PATRICK | WHITE | [at bottom:] [in black] EYRE & | SPOTTISWOODE'. Inside front flap: '*Book Society Choice* | [blurb, 50 lines] | [*continued on back flap* | [at left] 6/4137 [at right] 16s net'. Inside back flap: '*continued from front flap*] | [blurb continues, 8 lines] | REVIEWS OF | *The Tree of Man* | [quotation of two lines from] C. P. SNOW | [quotation of two lines from] JOHN METCALF *Sunday Times* | [quotation of four lines from] JOHN DAVENPORT *Observer* | [quotation of two lines from] PETER GREEN *Daily Telegraph* | [quotation of two lines from] GRAHAM GREENE | [quotation of three lines from] JAMES STERN *New York Times Book Review* | [quotation of three lines from] ORVILLE PRESCOTT *New York Times* | [quotation of one line from] GEOFFREY HUTTON *Melbourne Age* | [quotation of three lines from] *The West Australian* | [quotation of two lines from] *Johannesburg Sunday Times*'.

Wraparound of yellow paper. Front, back and spine: [in blue] 'Book Society Choice'.

Published 3 December 1957. Price: 16s (to Book Society members) and 18s. Print run: 21,000 (10,000 for general sale and 11,000 for The Book Club). By 31 December 1959, 32,381 copies had been sold – 11,542 in the U.K., 9,199 in the colonies, mainly Australia, and 11,640 'in quires' to The Book Club.

Reviews: Walter Allen *New Statesman* v.54, 7 December 1957, p.792 (850w); Patricia Hodgart *Manchester Guardian* 17 December 1957, p.4 (480w); *Age* 1 February 1958, (Literary Supplement) p.18; C. Kelly *Advertiser* (Adelaide) 1 February 1958, p.18; Kylie Tennant *Sydney Morning Herald* 8 February 1958; K.S. Prichard *Overland* no.13, Spring 1958, p.14; Douglas Stewart *Bulletin* 5 March 1958, p.2; Max Harris *Bulletin* 26 March 1958, p.46; *Observer* 22 February 1958, p.19-20; *Age* 12 April 1958, p.20; *Meanjin* v.17, Autumn 1958, p.94-100; *Australian Letters* v.1, April 1958, p.40-41; Mrs J.M. Forbes *Bulletin* 16 April 1958, p.46; H.J. Oliver *Southerly* v.19 no.1, 1958, p.46-49; Ian Turner *Overland* v.12, Winter 1958, p.36-37; *Quadrant* v.2, Spring 1958, p.4-5; *Prospect* v.1, June 1958, p.21-22.

Notes: One copy, now in a personal collection, has a paste-on on the front endpaper: 'With the Compliments of Eyre & Spottiswoode (Publishers) Ltd. [in ms] Received 19/11/57'. There is also a letter tipped in at front from Eyre & Spotiswoode to Colin Roderick, 14 November 1957.

> Dear Doctor Roderick,
> Miles Franklin Literary Prize:
> We have been asked by Mr Patrick White to submit a copy of his new novel, "Voss", for the above award.
> We were able to get a very few handbound copies in advance; these have to-day arrived and we have sent one off to you in the airmail post.
> I am writing now, however, to make certain that you know that this novel is about to be submitted, in order that we may avoid any difficulties being caused by possible delay in the arrival in Australia of the copies.
> Yours sincerely
> John Bright Holmes Director

The State Library of New South Wales, Mitchell Library has an uncorrected proof copy. Title page: [swelled rule] | [hollow shadow type] VOSS | [solid type] *A Novel* | [swelled rule] by PATRICK WHITE | EYRE & SPOTTISWOODE 1958 | [swelled rule] | 15, BEDFORD STREET • LONDON'. Sewn in brown paper covers. On front is paste-on: 'ROUGH UNCORRECTED | PROOF COPY | FOR YOUR PERSONAL READING | VOSS | by | PATRICK WHITE | • | EYRE & SPOTTISWOODE LTD.' On front in ms: 'December 2, 16s. Book Soc Choice'.

Sidney Nolan's original artwork which was the basis for the cover design is held in the Mitchell Library, State Library of New South Wales (ML 743). Ink and watercolour, 8.4 x 13.3 cm. Unsigned and undated. Presented by White, August 1974.

Copies: NU: 823.91A/W; NU: RB IMP 0073/12; NSL: Mitchell Library A823/W587/5A1 and 5B1; NSL: Mitchell Library [Miles Franklin Award Collection]; NSL: Mitchell Library [PW]; NSL: GRL N828.99943/W587/11 (lacks dustjacket); Personal collections (3 copies).

G2b U.K. First Edition Second Issue (London: Eyre & Spottiswoode, 1957)

[swelled rule] | [hollow shadowed type] VOSS | [solid type] *A Novel* | [swelled rule] | PATRICK WHITE | EYRE & SPOTTISWOODE 1957 | [swelled rule] | 15 BEDFORD STREET · LONDON

Copies: VSL: SLT 819.93 W582VO (lacks dustjacket); Personal collection (3 copies); NU: RB 1657.3; NSL: Mitchell Library [PW]; VU: McL L/A-F White.

G2c U.K. First Edition Third Issue (London: Eyre and Spottiswoode, 1958)
Notes: p.4 '*First published 1957 | Reprinted 1958 | 1-2 | 6/4137 | © 1957 Eyre & Spottiswoode (Publishers), Ltd. | Printed in Great Britain by Hazell Watson & Viney Ltd. | Aylesbury and Slough*'. Print run: 3,570.

G2d U.K. First Edition Fourth Issue (London: Eyre and Spottiswoode, 1958)
Notes: not seen but referred to in the Eyre & Spottiswoode archive, University of Reading. Print run: 5,000.

G2e U.K. First Edition Fifth Issue (London: Eyre and Spottiswoode, 1958)
Notes: p.4 '*First published 1957 | Reprinted three times 1958 | 1-4 | 6/4137*'. Print run: 4,895.

G2f U.K. First Edition Readers Union Issue (London: Readers Union / Eyre & Spottiswoode, 1959)

[swelled rule] | [hollow shadowed type] VOSS | [solid type] *A Novel* | [swelled rule] | PATRICK WHITE | [Readers Union device] | READERS UNION | EYRE & SPOTTISWOODE | [swelled rule] | LONDON 1959

Notes: p.4 '© Eyre & Spottiswoode (Publishers) Ltd 1957 | *This RU edition was produced in 1959 for sale to its | members only by Readers Union Ltd at 38 Wil- | liam IV Street, Charing Cross, London and at | Letchworth Garden City, Hertfordshire. Full details | of membership may be obtained from our London | address. The book is set in 11 point Georgian and | has been reprinted by Hazell Watson & Viney Ltd. | It was first published by Eyre & Spottiswoode Ltd.*'. Cased in beige linen cloth with off-white endpapers. The Readers Union device is on the spine. Yellow paper dustjacket, incorporating membership form and general order form. Price: 16s and 5s 9d (to members of the Readers Union).

G2g U.K. First Edition Sixth Issue (London: Eyre and Spottiswoode, 1962)

Notes: p.*4* '*First published 1957* | *Reprinted three times 1958* | *Reprinted 1962* | [at bottom:] 1·5 | 6/4137 | © *1957 Eyre & Spottiswoode (Publishers), Ltd.* | *Printed in Great Britain by John Dickens & Conner Ltd.* | *Northampton*'. Cased in dark blue cloth boards.

G2h U.K. First Edition Seventh Issue (London: Eyre & Spottiswoode, 1968)

Notes: p.*4* '*First published 1957* | *Reprinted three times 1958* | *Reprinted 1962* | *Reprinted 1968* | *1·6* | *SBN 413 41370 5* | © *1957 Eyre & Spottiswoode (Publishers), Ltd.* | *Printed in Great Britain by Redwood Press Limited, Trowbridge.*'. Cased in glossy printed paper-covered boards.

G2i U.K. First Edition Cape Subedition (London: Jonathan Cape, 1980)

[swelled rule] | [shadowed] VOSS | *A Novel* | [swelled rule] | PATRICK WHITE | [publisher's device] | JONATHAN CAPE | THIRTY BEDFORD SQUARE LONDON

20.3 x 13 cm. Unsigned: 239 leaves. pp.*8* 9-478.

Notes: p.*4* 'First published 1957 | © 1957 by Eyre & Spottiswoode (Publishers), Ltd | Reissued 1980 by Jonathan Cape Ltd | 30 Bedford Square, London WC1 | British Library Cataloguing in Publication Data | White, Patrick | Voss. | I. Title | 823'.9'1F PR6045.H19V/ | ISBN 0-224-01773-X | Printed in Great Britain by | The Anchor Press Ltd and bound by | Wm Brendon & Son Ltd, both of | Tiptree, Essex'. Cased in dark blue linen boards with beige endpapers. Royal blue paper dustjacket. Jacket design by Mon Mohan. A new issue of the 1957 Eyre & Spottiswoode edition. Published 27 March 1980. Price: £6.50 (price stickers show later prices of £7.50 and £8.50). Print run: 3,000. ISBN 0 224 01773 X.

G3a Penguin Edition First Issue (Harmondsworth: Penguin, 1960)

PATRICK WHITE | VOSS | [swelled rule] | PENGUIN BOOKS

18 x 11 cm. [1]¹⁶ 2-14¹⁶ ($1 signed): 224 leaves. pp.*6* 7-447 *448*.

1 'PENGUIN BOOKS | 1438 | VOSS | PATRICK WHITE' | [publisher's device]; *2* blank; *3* title page; *4* 'Penguin Books Ltd, Harmondsworth, Middlesex | AUSTRALIA: Penguin Books Pty Ltd, 762 Whitehorse Road, | Mitcham, Victoria | [rule] | First published by Eyre & Spottiswoode 1957 | Published in Penguin Books 1960 | [rule] | Copyright © Eyre & Spottiswoode (Publishers) Ltd, 1957 | [at bottom:] Made and printed in Great Britain | by Hazell Watson & Viney Ltd | Aylesbury and Slough'; *5* 'FOR | MARIE D'ESTOURNELLES | DE CONSTANT'; *6* blank; 7-447 *448* text.

Perfectbound in cream paper printed in orange and black. Front: [in orange] 'PENGUIN BOOKS | [in black] [rule] | VOSS | [black ink illust. of a man] | [at right:] [publisher's device] | PATRICK WHITE | [rule] | COMPLETE [in orange] 5/- [in black] UNABRIDGED'. Back: [in orange] 'PENGUIN BOOKS | [in black] [rule] | [b&w photograph of the author] | [at left:] [publisher's device] | [biography, 22 lines] | [rule] | NOT FOR SALE IN THE U.S.A. OR CANADA'. Spine: [running down:] 'Patrick White | [upright:] [in orange] [publisher's device] | [running down:] [in black] Voss | [at bottom:] [upright:] 1438'. Inside front cover: [blurb, 14 lines] | [quotation of two lines from] '–Walter Allen in the | *New Statesman* | [quotation of three lines from] –John Davenport in the *Ob-*

server | [quotation of three lines from] −Penelope Mortimer in | the *Sunday Times* | Cover drawing by Sidney Nolan | *For a complete list of books available* | *please write to Penguin Books* | *whose address can be found on the* | *back of the title page*'. Inside back cover: 'SOME RECENT | PENGUIN FICTION'.

Yellow paper wraparound. Front and back: 'Winner of the | [in yellow on black] W. H. Smith | [in black] £1000 | [in yellow on black] Literary Award'. Spine: [running down:] 'Patrick White • Voss'.

Notes: One copy has a sticker over the price on the front, giving the new price as 7/6. A number of copies have a variant binding which exhibits a number of differences, the most important being the price of 7/6 on the front.

Copies: NU: 823.91A; NU: RB 593.4/1; NSL: Mitchell Library [PW]; NSL: GRL Open Access 823.914/W587/21; Personal collection (3 copies); NSL: Mitchell Library A823/W587/5F1.

G3b Penguin Edition Second Issue (Harmondsworth: Penguin, 1962)
Notes: p.*1* 'PENGUIN MODERN CLASSICS'; *4* 'Published in Penguin Books 1960 | Reprinted 1962 | [rule] | Copyright © Eyre & Spottiswoode (Publishers) Ltd, 1957 | [at bottom:] Made and printed in Great Britain | by Hazell Watson & Viney Ltd | Aylesbury and Slough | Set in Linotype Granjon'. Perfectbound in cream paper printed in orange and black. Cover drawing by Sidney Nolan. Price: 7/6. Notes: One copy has a variant binding as follows: perfectbound in white paper covers printed in black, grey and orange on front, back and spine. Front: 'Patrick White | [in white] Voss | [illust.] | PENGUIN MODERN CLASSICS [in black on orange] [publisher's device] [in black] 5/-'.

G3c Penguin Edition Third Issue (Harmondsworth: Penguin, 1963)
Notes: p.*4* 'Published in Penguin Books 1960 | Reprinted 1962, 1963 | [rule] | Copyright © Eyre & Spottiswoode (Publishers) Ltd, 1957 | [rule] | Made and printed in Great Britain | by Hazell Watson & Viney Ltd | Aylesbury, Bucks | Set in Linotype Granjon'. Perfectbound in white paper covers printed in black, grey and orange on front, back and spine. Price: 7/6.

G3d Penguin Edition Fourth Issue (Harmondsworth: Penguin, 1966)
Notes: p.*4* 'Published in Penguin Books 1960 | Reprinted 1962, 1966 | [rule] | Copyright © Eyre & Spottiswoode (Publishers) Ltd, 1957 | [rule] | Made and printed in Great Britain | by Hazell Watson & Viney Ltd, | Aylesbury, Bucks | Set in Linotype Granjon'. Perfectbound in white paper covers printed in black and light green on front, back and spine. Price: 85c.

G3e Penguin Edition Fifth Issue (Harmondsworth: Penguin, 1968)
Notes: p.*4* 'Published in Penguin Books 1960 | Reprinted 1962, 1966, 1968 | [rule] | Copyright © Eyre & Spottiswoode (Publishers) Ltd, 1957 | [rule] | Made and printed in Great Britain | by Hazell Watson & Viney Ltd, | Aylesbury, Bucks | Set in Linotype Granjon'. Price: 7/-, AU$1.20, NZ$1.00, R0.85.

G3f Penguin Edition Sixth Issue (Harmondsworth: Penguin, 1970)
Notes: p.*4* 'Published in Penguin Books 1960 | Reprinted 1962, 1966, 1968, 1970 | [rule] |
Copyright © Eyre & Spottiswoode (Publishers) Ltd, 1957 | [rule] | Made and printed in
Great Britain | by Hazell Watson & Viney Ltd, | Aylesbury, Bucks | Set in Linotype Gran-
jon'. Perfectbound in paper covers printed in black, light green and red on front, back and
spine. Price: 50p or 10/-, AU$$1.70, NZ$1.70, R1.20. SBN 1400 1438 1.

G3g Penguin Edition Seventh Issue (Harmondsworth: Penguin, 1971)
Notes: p.*4* 'Published in Penguin Books 1960 | Reprinted 1962, 1966, 1968, 1970, 1971 |
[rule] | Copyright © Eyre & Spottiswoode (Publishers) Ltd, 1957 | [rule] | Made and printed
in Great Britain | by Hazell Watson & Viney Ltd, | Aylesbury, Bucks | Set in Linotype
Granjon'. Cover drawing by Sidney Nolan. Price: 50p, NZ$1.70, SA R1.20.

G3h Penguin Edition Eighth Issue (Harmondsworth: Penguin, 1972)
Notes: p.*4* 'Published in Penguin Books 1960 | Reprinted 1962, 1966, 1968, 1970, 1971,
1972 | [rule] | Copyright © Eyre & Spottiswoode (Publishers) Ltd, 1957 | [rule] | Made and
printed in Great Britain | by Hazell Watson & Viney Ltd, | Aylesbury, Bucks | Set in Lino-
type Granjon'. Cover drawing by Sidney Nolan.

G3i Penguin Edition Ninth Issue (Harmondsworth: Penguin, 1974)
Notes: p.*4* 'Published in Penguin Books 1960 | Reprinted 1962, 1966, 1968, 1970, 1971,
1972, 1974 | [rule] | Copyright © Eyre & Spottiswoode (Publishers) Ltd, 1957 | [rule] |
Made and printed in Australia | by Alexander Bros | Mentone, Victoria | Set in Linotype
Granjon'. Price: AU$1.70, NZ$1.70. ISBN 0 1400 1438 1.

G3j Penguin Edition Tenth Issue (Harmondsworth: Penguin, 1975)
Notes: p.*4* 'Published in Penguin Books 1960 | Reprinted 1962, 1966, 1968, 1970, 1971,
1972, 1973, 1975 | [rule] | Copyright © Patrick White, 1957 | [rule] | Made and printed in
Great Britain by | Hazell Watson & Viney Ltd, | Aylesbury, Bucks | Set in Linotype Gran-
jon'. Cover drawing by Sidney Nolan.

G3k Penguin Edition Eleventh Issue (Harmondsworth: Penguin, 1976)
Notes: p.*4* 'Published in Penguin Books 1960 | Reprinted 1962, 1966, 1968, 1970, 1971,
1972, 1973, 1975, 1976 | [rule] | Copyright © Patrick White, 1957 | [rule] | Made and
printed in Great Britain by | Hazell Watson & Viney Ltd, Aylesbury, Bucks | Set in Linotype
Granjon'. Cover drawing by Sidney Nolan. Price: £1.00, AU$2.95, NZ$3.25. ISBN 0 1400
1438 1.

G3l Penguin Edition Twelfth Issue (Harmondsworth: Penguin, 1977)
Notes: p.*4* 'Published in Penguin Books 1960 | Reprinted 1962, 1966, 1968, 1970, 1971,
1972, 1973, 1975, 1976, 1977 | [rule] | Copyright © Patrick White, 1957 | All rights re-
served | [rule] | Made and printed in Great Britain by | Hazell Watson & Viney Ltd, Ayles-
bury, Bucks | Set in Linotype Granjon'. Cover drawing by Sidney Nolan. Price: AU$5.50.

G3m Penguin Edition Thirteenth Issue (Harmondsworth: Penguin, 1979)
Notes: p.*4* 'Published in Penguin Books 1960 | Reprinted 1962, 1966, 1968, 1970, 1971, 1972, 1973, 1975, 1976, 1977, 1979 | [rule] | Copyright © Patrick White, 1957 | All rights reserved | [rule] | Made and printed in Great Britain by | Hazell Watson & Viney Ltd, Aylesbury, Bucks | Set in Linotype Granjon'. Cover drawing by Sidney Nolan. Price: £1.75, AU$4.95. ISBN 0 1400 1438 1.

G3n Penguin Edition Fourteenth Issue (Harmondsworth: Penguin, 1980)
Notes: p.*4* 'Published in Penguin Books 1960 | Reprinted 1962, 1966, 1968, 1970, 1971, 1972, 1973, 1975, 1976, 1977, 1979, 1980 | [rule] | Copyright © Patrick White, 1957 | All rights reserved | [rule] | Made and printed in Great Britain by | Hazell Watson & Viney Ltd, Aylesbury, Bucks | Set in Linotype Granjon'. Cover drawing by Sidney Nolan. Price: AU$5.50.

G3o Penguin Edition Fifteenth Issue (Harmondsworth: Penguin, 1981)
Notes: 19.5 x 12.8 cm. Perfectbound in white paper. Front: [in box:] [at top:] 'KING PENGUIN | [in grey rectangle:] | 'PATRICK WHITE | VOSS' | [col. illust.]. Back: [in box:] [at top:] 'KING PENGUIN | [blurb, 11 lines] | [quotations from] | Penelope Mortimer in the *Sunday Times* | *The New York Times Book Review* | Winner of the Nobel Prize for Literature | The cover shows a detail from 'Down on his Luck' by Frederick McCubbin, courtesy of | The Art Gallery of Western Australia, Perth' | [b&w photograph of the author] [at left:] [prices] [at right:] [ISBN]. Spine: [publisher's device] [runnning down:] 'PATRICK WHITE • VOSS' [ISBN].

G3p Penguin Edition Sixteenth Issue (Harmondsworth: Penguin, 1983)
Notes: p.*4* 'Published in Penguin Books 1960 | Reprinted 1962, 1966, 1968, 1970, 1971, 1972, 1973, 1975, | 1976, 1977, 1979, 1980 | Reissued as a King Penguin 1981 | Reprinted in Penguin Books 1983 | [rule] | Copyright © Patrick White, 1957 | All rights reserved | [rule] | Made and printed in Great Britain by | Hazell Watson & Viney Ltd, | Aylesbury, Bucks | Set in Linotype Granjon'. Cover design by Neil Stuart. Cover illustration by Mel Odom.

G3q Penguin Edition Seventeenth Issue (Harmondsworth: Penguin, 1983)
Not seen.

G3r Penguin Edition Eighteenth Issue (Harmondsworth: Penguin, 1986)
Notes: p.*4* 'Published in Penguin Books 1960 | Reprinted 1962, 1966, 1968, 1970, 1971, 1972, 1973, 1975, | 1976, 1977, 1979, 1980, 1981, 1983 (twice), 1986 | [short rule] | Copyright © Patrick White, 1957 | All rights reserved | [short rule] | Made and printed in Great Britain by | Hazell Watson & Viney Limited, | Member of the BPCC Group, | Aylesbury, Bucks | Set in Linotype Granjon'. Cover design by Neil Stuart. Cover illustration by Mel Odom. Price: £4.95, AU $6.95 (one copy has sticker indicating price of $8.95), NZ $11.95, CAN. $7.95, US$6.95. ISBN 0-14-001438-1.

G3s Penguin Edition Nineteenth Issue (Harmondsworth: Penguin, 1987)
Notes: p.*4* 'Published in Penguin Books 1960 | Reprinted 1962, 1966, 1968, 1970, 1971, 1972, 1973, 1975, | 1976, 1977, 1979, 1980, 1981, 1983 (twice), 1986, 1987 | [rule] | Copyright © Patrick White, 1957 | All rights reserved | [rule] | Made and printed in Great Britain by | Hazell Watson & Viney Limited, | Member of the BPCC Group, | Aylesbury, Bucks | Set in Linotype Granjon'. Price: AU$8.95.

G3t Penguin Edition Twentieth Issue (Harmondsworth: Penguin, [1988])
Notes: p.*4* 'Published in Penguin Books 1960 | 20 | Copyright © Patrick White, 1957 | All rights reserved | Made and printed in Great Britain by | BPCC Hazell Books Ltd | Member of BPCC Ltd | Aylesbury, Bucks, England | Set in Linotype Granjon'. Cover design has detail of 'Home Leave' by Russell Drysadale. Prices: £5.99, AU$14.99, NZ$21.95, CAN$10.95, US$7.95. ISBN 0-14-001438-1.

G3u Penguin Edition Twenty-first Issue (Harmondsworth: Penguin, [1993])
Notes: p.*4* 'Published in Penguin Books 1960 | 21 23 25 27 29 30 28 26 24 22 | Copyright © Patrick White, 1957 | All rights reserved | Printed in England by Clays Ltd, St Ives plc | Set in Linotype Granjon'. Published August 1993. Prices: £6.99, AU$15.95, NZ$23.95, CAN$12.95, US$9.95. ISBN 0 1400 1438 1.

G3v Vintage Subedition First Issue (London: Vintage, 1994)
Notes: not seen, but entry in *Australian Books in Print*. Published in September 1994. Price: AU$12.95.

G3w Vintage Subedition Second Issue (London: Vintage, n.d.)
Notes: p.*4* 'Published by Vintage 1994 | 2 4 6 8 10 9 7 5 3'.

G4 U.K. Second Edition (London: Longmans, 1965)

VOSS | Patrick White | *With Introduction and Notes by* | *H.P. Heseltine, B.A., M.A., Ph.D.* | [publisher's device] | Longmans

19 x 12.7 cm. [A]^{16} B-N^{16} ($1 and 5 signed 'F' and F*' respectively): 208 leaves. [6] 1-410 p.

Endpaper; [*1*] 'The Heritage of Literature Series | SECTION B NO.79 | VOSS'; [*2*] [series note]; [*3*] title page; [*4*] 'LONGMANS, GREEN & CO LTD | 48 Grosvenor Street, London W1 | *Associated companies, branches and representatives* | *throughout the world* | *first published by Eyre & Spottiswoode Ltd 1957* | *This edition © Longmans, Green & Co Ltd 1965* | *This edition first published by Longmans, Green & Co Ltd,* | *in association with Messrs Eyre & Spottiswoode Ltd* | Cover illustration by Sidney Nolan | *Printed in Great Britain by* | *Northumberland Press Limited* | *Gateshead on Tyne*'; [*5*] 'Contents'; [*6*] blank; 1-375 text; 376-378 'A GLOSSARY OF AUSTRALIAN TERMS AND | PLACE NAMES USED IN *VOSS*'; 379-380 'A GLOSSARY OF GERMAN WORDS | AND PHRASES USED IN *VOSS*'; 381-400 'INTRODUCTION' [by H.P. Heseltine]; 401-407 '*VOSS*: ISSUES AND PROBLEMS'; 408-410 'PATRICK WHITE: A SELECT BIBLIOGRAPHY'; endpaper.

Cased in grey imitation-cloth paper with beige endpapers. Front: [in white] 'VOSS | [in black] PATRICK WHITE | [illust.] | [publisher's device] [in white] MODERN CLASSICS'. Back: [in white] 'Longmans | Heritage of Literature Series | [in black] [list of ten themes] | B79'. Spine: [running down:] 'WHITE | [in white] VOSS' | [at bottom:] [upright] [publisher's device].

Published 8 June 1965. Price: 8s 6d.

Copies: ANL: A823A WHI; NU: 823.91A/W587/J9/2/1; NSL: Mitchell Library [PW]; NSL: Mitchell Library A823/W587/5H1.

G5 U.S. Second Edition (New York: Pyramid Books, 1968)

VOSS | PATRICK WHITE | PYRAMID BOOKS [publisher's device] NEW YORK

18 x 10.6 cm. Unsigned: 216 leaves. pp.*8* 9-430 *431-432*.

1 'VOSS | *The New York Times* said: | [quotation from] | C. HARTLEY GRATTAN | *The Saturday Review* said: | [quotation from] | JOHN BARKHAM'; *2* '*The Novels of Patrick White* | *in Pyramid Editions* | THE TREE OF MAN | VOSS | RIDERS IN THE CHARIOT'; *3* title page; *4* 'VOSS | A PYRAMID BOOK | Published by arrangement with The Viking Press, Inc. | Viking edition published August, 1957 | Pyramid edition published March, 1968 | Copyright © 1957 by Patrick White | Library of Congress catalog card number: 57-9493 | All Rights Reserved | Printed in the United States of America | PYRAMID BOOKS are published by Pyramid Publications, Inc. | 444 Madison Avenue, New York, New York 10022, U.S.A.; *5* '*for* | *Marie d'Estournelles de Constant*'; *6* blank; *7* 'VOSS'; *8* blank; 9-430 text; *431-432* [advertisements].

Perfectbound in white paper printed in full colour. Front: 'PYRAMID [publisher's device] N-1478 95c | [rule] | [in purple] PATRICK WHITE | [in black] [rule] | Book-of-the-Month Club Selection | A major novel of a fantastic journey | "Brilliant and sustained ... superb" | [rule] SATURDAY REVIEW | [in purple] VOSS' | [in black] [rule] | [col. illust. of figures in a rough landscape]. Back: [in purple] 'A MAN CALLED | VOSS | [in black] [blurb, 9 lines] | [rule] | [in purple] "This is a heroic and brilliant novel." –THE NEW YORKER | "The best novelist to come out of Australia." –HARPER'S | [in black] [rule] | [b&w photo of author] | [biography, 7 lines] | PYRAMID BOOKS 95C Cover: Frank Kalan Printed in U.S.A.'. Spine: 'N-1478 | 95c | [running down:] [in purple] VOSS [in black] Patrick White [upright:] [publisher's device] | PYRAMID | BOOKS'.

Published in March 1968. Price: 95c.

Copies: NSL: Mitchell Library [PW].

G.t1a German First Edition First Issue (Köln and Berlin: Kiepenheuer & Witsch, 1958)

PATRICK WHITE | VOSS | ROMAN | KIEPENHEUER & WITSCH | KÖLN • BERLIN

21 x 12.5 cm. Unsigned: 226 leaves. pp.*6* 7-450 *451-452*.

Endpaper; *1* [publisher's device]; *2* blank; *3* 'PATRICK WHITE • VOSS'; *4* blank; *5* title page; *6* 'Titel der Originalausgabe: Voss | Aus dem Englischen von John Stickforth | Schutzumschlag Werner Labbé | *1.-5. Tausend 1958* | *Alle deutschsprachigen Rechte bei* | *Verlag Kiepenheuer & Witsch, Köln • Berlin* | *Gesamtherstellung Kleins Druck= und Verlagsanstalt* | *Lengerich · Westfalen* | *Printed in Germany*'; 7-450 *451* text; *452* blank; endpaper.

Cased in tan cloth. Front: [in green] [three stylised leaves]. Back: blank. Spine: [in green] 'PATRICK WHITE | [rule] | VOSS'.

White paper dustjacket printed across front, back and spine in black, blue, light and dark green, and crimson; signed at bottom left on front: 'Werner Labbé'. Front: [in white] 'PATRICK WHITE | [in crimson] VOSS | [in white] ROMAN | Kiepenheuer & Witsch'. Back: blank. Spine: [running down:] [in white] 'PATRICK WHITE / VOSS'. Inside front flap: 'PATRICK WHITE | VOSS' | [blurb, 39 lines]. Inside back flap: [blurb continues from front flap, 41 lines] | 'KIEPENHEUER & WITSCH'.

Print run: 5,000.

Reviews: Christian Ferber *Die Welt* 4 October 1958; Hilde Spiel *Der Tagesspiegel* 30 November 1958; Hubert Becher *Stimmen der Zeit* v.164, 1959, p.399-400; Clara Menck *Frankfurter Allgemeine Zeitung* 10 January 1959; Richard Kaufmann *Süddeutsche Zeitung* 31 January/1 February 1959; Hulmut Kleffel *Christ und Welt* 21 May 1959.

Copies: VSL: SLT 819.93 W582VOS (2 copies, one of which lacks dustjacket); NSL: Mitchell Library A823/W587/5D1 (lacks dustjacket); Personal collection (presentation copy signed by the author to Greta and Stephen Feher, his Kirribilli friends, March 1960).

G.t1b German First Edition Second Issue (Köln and Berlin: Kiepenheuer & Witsch, 1958)

Not seen, but referred to in V. Wolf *Australian Literary Studies* v.11 no.1, 1983, p.108-119.

Print run: 3,000.

G.t1c German First Edition Third Issue (Reinbek bei Hamburg: Rowohlt, 1973)

Patrick White | Voss | Roman | [publisher's device] | Rowohlt

19.1 x 11.6 cm. Unsigned: 232 leaves. pp.*6* 7-222 [*2*] 223-450 *451-462*.

Notes: p.*4* '*Die Originalausgabe erschien bei Eyre & Spottiswoode,* | *London, unter dem Titel* «*Voss*» | *Aus dem Englischen übertragen von* JOHN STICKFORTH | *Umschlagentwurf Manfred Waller* | *Ungekürzte Ausgabe* | *Veröffentlicht im Rowohlt Taschenbuch Verlag GmbH,* | *Reinbek bei Hamburg, Dezember 1973* | *© 1957 by Patrick White* | *© 1958 by Verlag Kiepenheuer & Witsch, Köln* | *Gesamtherstellung Clausen & Bosse, Leck/Schleswig* | *Printed in Germany* | *ISBN 3 499 11760 6*'. Binding not seen. Print run: 20,000.

G.t1d German First Edition Fourth Issue (Reinbek bei Hamburg: Rowohlt, 1974)

Notes: p. *4 'Umschlagentwurf Manfred Waller* | 1.–20. Tausend Dezember 1973 | 21.–30. Tausend März 1974'. Perfectbound in off-white textured paper. Print run: 10,000.

G.t2a German Second Edition First Issue (Berlin, Darmstadt, Vienna: Deutsche Büch-Gemeinschaft, 1961)

Notes: p.511. Not seen, but referred to by *Gesamtverzeichnis des deutschsprachigen Schrifttums (GV) 1911-1965* (München: K.G. Saur, 1981), p.211; Lawson, no.37; and V. Wolf *Australian Literary Studies* v.11 no.1, 1983, p.108-119.

G.t2b German Second Edition Second Issue (Stüttgart, Hamburg, Münich: Deutscher Bücherbund, [1974])

PATRICK WHITE | [in red] VOSS | ROMAN | [publisher's device] | DEUTSCHER BÜCHERBUND | STUTTGART

23.1 x 14.2 cm. Unsigned: 256 leaves. pp.*4* 5-510 *511-512* (the last page of each chapter is unnumbered).

Endpaper; *1* 'PATRICK WHITE • VOSS'; *2* blank; *3* title page; *4* 'Titel der Originalausgabe: Voss | Aus dem Englischen von John Stickforth | Lizenzausgabe für die Mitglieder des | Deutschen Bücherbundes Stuttgart – Hamburg – München | Mit Genehmigung des Kiepenheuer & Witsch Verlages, Köln | Gesamtherstellung: Thomas F. Salzer KG, Wien | – 02102/2 –'; 5-510 *511* text; *512* blank; endpaper.

Cased in light blue cloth with white endpapers and red headbands. Front and back: blank. Spine: [running down:] [in white] 'Patrick White | [in purple] VOSS'.

Glossy white paper dustjacket printed across front, back and spine in full colour with illust. of bush scene at night. Front: [in white] 'Patrick White | [in green] VOSS'. Back: blank. Spine: [in white] 'Patrick White | [in green] VOSS'. Inside front flap: [description, 34 lines]. Inside back flap: [biography, 12 lines] | 'Buchausstattung: Rathin Chattopadhyay | Farbfoto: Hubertus Mall | -02102/2-'.

Price: DM 19.80.

Copies: NSL: GRL E823.914/WHI (lacks dustjacket); NSL: Mitchell Library A823/W587/44 (lacks dustjacket); NSL: Mitchell Library [PW]; Personal collection.

G.t3 German Third Edition (Leipzig: Reclam, 1987)

Patrick White | *VOSS* | *Roman* | [at bottom:] | *1987* | *Verlag Philipp Reclam jun. Leipzig*

17.7 x 10.8 cm. [1]^8 2-14^8 15-16^6 17-30^8 ($2 signed): 236 leaves. pp.*4* 5-461 *462* 463-467 *468* 469-470 *471-472*.

1 'WHITE · VOSS | [series device] | BELLETRISTIK'; *2* blank; *3* title page; *4* 'Aus dem Englischen | Übersetzung von John Stickforth | Mit einer Nachbemerkung von Bernhard Scheller | ISBN 3-379-00089-2 | Lizenzausgabe des Verlages Philipp Reclam jun. Leipzig für die DDR | mit freundlicher Genehmigung des Verlages Kiepenheuer & Witsch, | Köln | Text nach: Patrick White, Voss, Verlag Kiepenheuer & Witsch, Köln | 1958 | © Verlag Philipp Reclam jun. Leipzig 1987 (Nachbemerkung) | Reclams Universal-Bibliothek Band 1185 | 1. Auflage | Reihengestaltung : Lothar Reher | Lizenz Nr. 363. 340/79/87 · LSV 7331 · Vbg. 28,0 | Printed in the German Democratic Republic | Grafischer Grossbetrieb Völkerfreundschaft Dresden | Gesetzt aus Garamond-Antiqua | Bestellnummer: 6613320 | 00350'; *5-461* *462* text; *463-467* *468* 'Nachbemerkung'; *469-470* *471* 'Zeittafel'; *472* blank.

Perfectbound in beige paper covers. Front: [series device] | [oxford rule] | 'Patrick White | [rule] | Voss | [oxford rule] | [in black letter] <u>Reclam</u>'. Back: [biography, 13 lines] | [description, 14 lines] | *Belletristik* | 00350'. Spine: [running up:] '*1185* | *White · Voss*'. Inside front and back: blank.

Copies: ANL: N A823.3 W587vs.

G.t4a Spanish First Edition First Issue (Barcelona: Luis de Caralt, 1962)

PATRICK WHITE | TIERRA IGNOTA | [illust.] | LUIS DE CARALT | EDITOR | BARCELONA

20.3 x 14 cm. [1]^8 2-23^8 24^6: 190 leaves. pp.*5* 6-377 *378-380* (first page of each chapter is unnumbered).

Endpaper; *1* [series device]; *2* blank; *3* title page; *4* 'Titulo de la obra original: | *"VOSS"* | Versión española de | RAFAEL NADAL GUASP | Depósito Legal: B. 23.424 - 1962 | N.° Rgtro. 1163-58 | *ISBN 84-217-*1665-4 | RESERVADOS TODOS LOS DERECHOS | © LUIS DE CARALT, 1962 | IMPRESO EN ESPAÑA | Impreso en LIM - Juan Corrales, 46 - ESPLUGAS | DE LL. (Barna).'; *5* 6-377 text; *378-380* blank; endpaper.

Cased in red linen with endpapers vertically streaked in light green. Front: [stamped in gold] [illust. of a kangaroo]. Back: blank. Spine: [in gold on black panels] 'PATRICK | WHITE | TIERRA | IGNOTA | [in gold on red panel] *Luis | de | Caralt*'.

Glossy white paper dustjacket with col. illust. of skull against light and dark green and brown background across front and spine. Front: 'PATRICK WHITE | [in white] TIERRA | IGNOTA'. Back: [advertisement for Coleccion Gigante listing 98 titles] | [at bottom right:] 'T.G. Soler – Esplugas (Barna.)'. Spine: 'PATRICK | WHITE | TIERRA | IGNOTA | CARALT'. Inside front flap: 'TIERRA IGNOTA' | [blurb, 38 lines]. Inside back flap: [in blue] [series device] | [in black] 'LO MAS SELECTO DE LA | LITERATURA UNIVERSAL | [in blue] <u>EN PREPARACION</u> | OBRAS DE' | [in black] [list of 12 authors].

Copies: Personal collection; NSL: Mitchell Library 823.914/W587/41; VGRL: Geelong Sp.F/WHI.

G.t4b Spanish First Edition Second Issue (Madrid: Club Internacional del Libro, 1992)

Notes: pp.377. Not seen, but referred to in *Index Translationum*.

G.t5a Italian First Edition (Turin: Einaudi, 1965)

Patrick White | L'esploratore | Traduzione di Piero Jahier | Einaudi

22.5 x 14.1 cm. [1]^8 2-26^8 27^{10} ($1 signed): 218 leaves. pp.7 8-433 *434-436*.

Endpaper; *1* blank; *2* 'Titolo originale | *Voss* | © Eyre & Spottiswoode, London | © 1965 Giulio Einaudi editore s.p.a., Torino'; *3* title page; *4* blank; *5* 'L'esploratore | *Per Maria D'Estournelles De Constant*'; *6* blank; *7* 8-433 text; *434* [publisher's device] | '*Finito di Stampare in Torino il 5 luglio 1965*'; *435-436* blank; endpaper.

Cased in light green calico with white endpapers. Front and back: blank. Spine: [running down:] [in white] '*White* L'ESPLORATORE' | [upright:] [publisher's device].

White glossy paper dustjacket printed in full colour. Front: 'PATRICK WHITE | L'ESPLORATORE | [col. illust. of man] | EINAUDI'. Back: [b&w photograph of the author] | [blurb, 4 lines]. Spine: [running down:] '*White* L'ESPLORATORE' | [upright:] [publisher's device]. Inside front flap: [description, 42 lines] | 'In sopracoperto *Ritratto di P.M.* di Pablo Picasso (1901).'. Inside back flap: [description continues, 9 lines] | [biography, 15 lines].

Published in July 1965. Price: L24,000. ISBN 88-06-12625-3.

Reviews: Desmond O'Grady 'Patrick White's "Voss" in Italy' *Age* (Melbourne) 10 December 1966, p.22.

Copies: NSL: Mitchell Library [PW].

G.t5b Italian First Edition Second Issue (n.d.)
Not seen.

G.t5c Italian First Edition Third Issue (Turin: Einaudi, 1974)

Notes: p.*2* 'Titolo originale *Voss* | © 1957 Eyre & Spottiswoode, London | Copyright © 1965 Giulio Einaudi editore s.p.a., Torino Terza edizione'; p.*434* '*Finito di stampare il 10 novembre 1973 per conto della Giulio Einaudi editore s.p.a. | presso le Industrie Grafiche G. Zeppegno & C. s.a.s., Torino | Ristampa identica alla precedente del 27 agosto 1965* | C.L. 1262-5'. Cased in light green cloth. White glossy paper dustjacket printed in full colour; design from *Ritratto di P.M.* (1901) of Pablo Picasso.

Copies: VSL: SLT 819.93 W582VJ (lacks dustjacket); VGRL: Geelong It.F/WHI.

G.t6 Italian Second Edition ([Rome]: UTET, 1974)

Notes: not seen, but referred to in *Catalogo dei libri in commercio 1993: Autori* p.1914; pp.XXXII, 680. ISBN 88-02-02736-6. (Scrittori del mondo). Price: Lire 35,000.

G.t7 French First Edition (Paris: Gallimard, 1967)

PATRICK WHITE | Voss | TRADUIT DE L'ANGLAIS | PAR LOLA TRANEC | *nrf* | GALLIMARD

20.5 x 14 cm. Unsigned: 232 leaves. pp.*4* 5-461 *462-464*.

1 'DU MONDE ENTIER'; *2* blank; *3* title page; *4* '*Il a été tiré de cet ouvrage vingt-six exemplaires sur vélin pur fil* | *Lafuma-Navarre numérotés de 1 à 26.* | *Titre original :* | *VOSS* | *Tous droits de traduction, de reproduction et d'adaptation* | *réservés pour les pays, y compris l'U.R.S.S.* | © *Patrick White, 1957.* | © *Éditions Gallimard, 1967, pour la traduction rançaise* [sic].'; 5-461 *462* text; *463* 'DU MÊME AUTEUR | *nrf* | Eden-Ville | Le char des élus'; *464* 'ACHEVÉ D'IMPRIMER LE | 25 AVRIL 1967 SUR LES | PRESSES DE L'IMPRIMERIE | BUSSIÈRE, SAINT-AMAND (CHER) | – N° d'édit. 12529. – N° d'imp. 187. – | Dépôt légal : 2ᵉ trimestre 1967. | *Imprimé en France*'.

Sewn in white glossy card. Front: 'DU MONDE ENTIER | PATRICK WHITE | [in red] VOSS | [in black] ROMAN | TRADUIT DE L'ANGLAIS | PAR LOLA TRANEC | [series device] | [in red] *nrf* | [in black] GALLIMARD'. Back: 'PATRICK WHITE | [in red] VOSS | [in black] [blurb, 26 lines] | [in red] *nrf* | [at right:] [in black] 26,80 (+t.l.) | 27,50 FT.L.I.'. Spine: [in red] '*du monde* | *entier*' | [in black] PATRICK | WHITE | [in red] VOSS | [in black] *nrf* | GALLIMARD'. Inside front flap: [b&w photograph of the author] | [biography, 29 lines]. Inside back flap: '*dernières* | *publications*' | [list of ten titles by various authors].

Notes: White's own copy is a large paper copy (21.5 x 14.7 cm), numbered no.21. Its binding exhibits a number of variants. Sewn in off-white laid paper. Front: '[…] ENTIER | [in red] CDLXI | [in black] PATRICK […]'. Back: [in red] 'nrf | [in black] PUR FIL'. Inside front and back: blank.

Copies: VSL: SLT 819.93/W582VOT; Personal collection (2 copies); NSL: Mitchell Library A823/W587/5J1; NSL: Mitchell Library [PW].

G.t8a-e Turkish First Edition First to Fifth Issues (Istanbul: Altin Yayinevi, 1973-1974)

Not seen

G.t8f Turkish First Edition Sixth Issue (Istanbul: Altin Kitaplar Yayinevi, 1974)

PATRĪCK WHĪTE | 1973 NOBEL ARMAĞANI | ÇÖL | (Voss) | Türkçesi: | Ali SEDEN — Azize BERGĪN

20.3 x 13.5 cm. 1-33⁸ ($1 signed): 264 leaves. pp.*5* 6-7 *8-9* 10-528.

Endpaper; *1* [publisher's device] | 'ALTIN KĪTAPLAR YAYINEVĪ'; *2* 'ÇÖL. Meşhur Romanlar Serisinin 360. kitabi olarak Altin Kitaplar | Yayinevi tarafindan ilk kez Kasim 1973'de yayimlanmiştir.'; *3* title page; *4* '1.74.07 - 3 | Birinci Baski: Kasim 1973 | Ikinci Baski: Kasim 1973 | Üçüncü Baski: Aralik 1973 | Dördünkü Baski: Ocak 1974 | Beşinki Baski: Ocak 1974

| Altinci Baski: Şubat 1974 | Siralar Matbaasi – Istanbul'; *5* 6-7 'PATRĬCK WHĬTE | ve | 1973 NOBEL ARMAĞANI' [by Doğan Hizlan]; *8* blank; *9* 10-528 text; endpaper.

Cased in black cloth. Front: [stamped in gold] 'Çöl'. Back and spine: black.

White paper dustjacket printed on front, back and spine in orange, black and brown. Front: [in black] '*PATRICK WHITE* | [in orange] ÇÖL | ALTIN KĬTAPLAR / NOBEL ARMAĞANI'. Back: [in black] '*PATRICK WHITE* | [in orange] ÇÖL | [in black] [blurb and biography, 29 lines] | kapak düzeni ve fotograf / oral orhon BASKI ÇETIN OFSET 27 32 87'. Spine: [in yellow] 'patrick white | [running down:] ÇÖL'. Inside front and back flaps: blank.

Copies: VSL: SLT 819.93 W582VS; NSL: Mitchell Library [PW].

G.t9 Turkish Second Edition (Istanbul: Altin Kitaplar Yayinevi, 1983)

[on panel of horizontal lines:] PATRICK WHITE | ÇÖL | ÇÖL | ÇÖL | [at bottom right:] Türkçesi: | ALĬ SEDEN | AZĬZE BERGĬN

24 x 13.8 cm. 1-31⁸ 32⁴ ($1 signed): 252 leaves. pp.*6* 7-500 *501-504*.

Endpaper; *1* blank; *2* blank; *3* 'Altin Kitaplar | Yayinevi' [publisher's device]; *4* '■ | VOSS / ÇÖL | PATRICK WHITE | 1973 NOBEL ÖDÜLÜ | 2. BASKI - MAYIS 1983 | ■ | YAYIN HAKLARI: ALTIN KĬTAPLAR YAYINEVI'; *5* title page; *6* 'KAPAK RESMI : ŞAHIN | KAPAK FĬLMĬ : KOMBĬ GRAFĬK | DĬZGĬ - BASKĬ : ALTIN KĬTAPLAR MATBAASI'; 7-10 'Patrick White Üzerine' [by Doğan Hizlan]; 11-500 text; *502-504* blank; endpaper.

Cased in bright green vinyl.

White paper dustjacket with col. illust. of man with raised arms on front, and olive green ground on the back and spine. Front: [in green] [publisher's device] | [in black] 'NOBEL DĬZĬSĬ | [in white] *patrick white* | [in green outlined in white] ÇÖL'. Back: [in white on green] 'Patrick | White' | [at right:] [portrait of author] | [description and biography, 24 lines]. Spine: [in white on green] [publisher's device] | 'NOBEL DĬZĬSĬ | [running down:] [in yellow on green] *patrick white* | ÇÖL'.

Notes: Copy sighted has a sticker on the back of the dustjacket: [publisher's device] | 'Fiyati : 1100 TL. | K.D.V. dahil 1210.- TL'.

Copies: NSL: GRL TUR/WHI/1.

G.t10 Turkish Third Edition (Istanbul: Cem Yayinevi, 1990)

Patrick White | VOSS | Türkçesi: | NĬHAL YEĞĬNOBALI | [publisher's device] | kurucusu: | OĞUZ AKKAN | NURUOSMANĬYE CAD. KARDEŞLER HAN 1/3 CAĞALOĞLU - ĬSTANBUL

19.5 x 13.4 cm. Unsigned: 276 leaves. pp.*4* 5-552.

1 'VOSS'; *2* 'NOBEL DĬZĬSĬ | Cem Yayinevi ile Gözde Pazariama Ltd'nin ortak yapimi.'; *3* title page; *4* 'ÖZYURT MATBAACILIK | 1990 TEL.: 522 95 19'; 5-552 text.

Perfectbound in white paper covers. Front: [at right:] 'NOBEL 1973 | [Nobel medallion] | Patrick White | [in crimson] Voss | [at left:] [in blue] [publisher's device] | cem yayinevi' | [col illust.]. Back: [b&w photograph of the author] | [biography, 21 lines] | [at right:] [running down:] 'ISBN 975 - 406 - 220 -X'. Spine: [running up:] [in crimson] [publisher's device] 'PATRICK WHITE [in black] VOSS'.

Copies: NSL.

G.t11 Serbo-Croat First Edition (Zagreb: Znanje, 1974)

PATRICK WHITE | VOSS | S engleskoga preveo | JOSIP KATALINIĆ | ZNANJE ZAGREB 1974

19.3 x 12 cm. $[1]^8$ $2\text{-}26^8$ 27^4 χ^8 ($2 signed): 220 leaves. pp.*4* 5-438 *439-440*.

Endpaper; *1* 'PATRICK WHITE / VOSS' | [publisher's device]; *2* 'hit | BIBLIOTEKA MODERNE LITERATURE | Urednik | ZLATKO CRNKOVIĆ'; *3* title page; *4 'Naslov izvornika: | Patrick White | VOSS | Penguin Books, 1974 |* Priredio za tisak | ZLATKO CRNKOVIĆ | Kolaž na ovitku | ALFRED PAL'; 5-438 text; *439* 'NAKLADNI ZAVOD ZNANJE, ZAGREB | ZA IZDAVAČA: ING. BRUNO PEKOTA | KOREKTOR: ŠTEFICA KONJEVOD | TEHNIČKI UREDNIK: SREĆKO JOLIĆ | TISAK: ČGP »DELO«, LJUBLJANA, 1974 | U smislu člana 36. stava 1. točke 7. Zakona o oporezivanju proizvoda i uslaga | i na osnovi mišljenja Sekretarijata za prosvjetu i kulturu SRH broj 1885/1-1974. | oslobođeno od plaćanja poreza na promet.'; *440* blank; endpaper.

Cased in blue buckram with red headbands and white endpapers. Front: [at left:] 'hit | White | Voss'. Back: blank. Spine: 'hit | [running down:] White Voss'.

White glossy paper dustjacket printed in colour. Front: [at left:] 'hit | [centre:] Patrick | White | [at right:] Voss' | [col. illust. of man's face]. Back: [at top left:] [b&w photo of author] | 'Patrick White: VOSS | [description, 12 lines] | NAPISALI SU O KNJIGAMA IZ BIBLIOTEKE HIT' | [15 lines]. Spine: 'hit | [running down:] White Voss | [at bottom:] [upright:] [in white] Znanje'. Inside front flap: 'HIT | BIBLIOTEKA MODERNE | LITERATURE' | [15 titles]. Inside back flap: [another 17 titles].

Copies: NSL: Mitchell Library A823/W598/31 (lacks dustjacket); NSL: Mitchell Library [PW]; Personal collection.

G.t12 Japanese First Edition (Tokyo: The Simul Press, 1975)

[Bosu]

18.6 x 13.2 cm. Unsigned: 302 leaves. 2 v.: pp.[*2*] 1-279 *280* [*8*]; [*4*] *281* 282-583 *584* [6]. Translated by Michio Yaku.

Copies: NSL: Mitchell Library 823.914/DLL test; NSL: Mitchell Library [PW]; VGRL: N823.914/W587/20.

G.t13 Finnish First Edition (Helsinki: Kustannusosakeyhtiö Otava, 1977)

PATRICK WHITE | [rule] | KOHTI MANTAREEN SYDÄNTÄ | *Suomentanut Jussi Nousiainen* | [publisher's device] | HELSINGISSÄ | KUSTANNUSOSAKEYHTIÖ OTAVA

22.6 x 14.8 cm. [1]^8 2-27^8 ($1, 8 signed): 216 leaves. pp.*7* 8-426 *427-432*.

Endpaper; *1* 'KOHTI MANTAREEN SYDÄNTÄ'; *2* blank; *3* title page; *4* 'Englanninkielinen alkuteos | VOSS | Copyright © Patrick White, 1957 | ISBN 951-1-04455-9 | Kustannusosakeyhtiö Otavan painolaitokset | Keuruu 1977'; *5 'MARIE D'ESTOURNELLES DE CONSTANTILLE'*; *6* blank; *7* 8-426 text; *427-432* blank; endpaper.

Cased in black cloth with red endpapers. Front and back: blank. Spine: [running down:] [in red] 'PATRICK WHITE | [upright:] [in white] [rule] | KOHTI | MANTAREEN | SYDÄNTÄ' | [rule].

White glossy paper dustjacket printed in colour with illust. of men on horseback riding through a desert. Front: [in purple] 'PATRICK | WHITE | [rule] | [in white] KOHTI | MANTAREEN | SYDÄNTÄ | [at bottom left:] [running down:] OTAVA'. Back: [in white] [14 lines] | [at left:] '845 | Tilno 6432 | ISBN 951-1-04455-9 | OTAVA | [at right:] PÄÄLLYS: | KOSTI ANTIKAINEN'. Spine: [in purple] 'PATRICK | WHITE | [rule] | [in white] KOHTI | MANTAREEN | SYDÄNTÄ | OTAVA'. Inside front flap: 'Saatavissa myös | [rule] | Patrick White | MYRSKYN SILMÄ' | [description, 15 lines]. Inside back flap: '1974 nobelkirjailijan | [rule] | Eyvind Johnson | TULTA JA RUUSUJA' | [description, 16 lines].

Copies: NSL: Mitchell Library A823/W587/74 (lacks dustjacket); Personal collection.

G.t14 Czech First Edition (Bratislava: Vavrin, 1977)

[on verso:] EDÍCIA | VAVRÍN | SLOVENSKÝ | SPISOVATEĽ | 1977 | [on recto:] PATRICK | WHITE | VOSS

20.6 x 13.1 cm. Unsigned: 244 leaves. pp.*8* 9-468 *469-470* 471-477 *478* 479-482 *483-488*.

Endpaper; *1* [publisher's device]; *2* blank; *3* 'PATRICK | WHITE | VOSS'; *4-5* title pages; *6* 'Preložil | Eduard V. Tvarožek | Doslov napisal | a chronológiu zostavil Jozef Olexa | © Eyre and Spottiswoode 1957 | © Translation Eduard V. Tvarožek, 1977'; *7* 'Márii D'Estournelles de Constant'; *8* blank; 9-468 *469* text; *470* blank; 471-477 *478* 'Patrick White' [by Jozef Olexa]; 479-482 *483-484* 'Zivot a dielo'; *485* blank; *486* blank; *487* 'PATRICK | WHITE | VOSS | REDIGUJE HELENA DOBIÁŠOVÁ | Z anglického originálu Patrick White: Voss ktorý | vyšiel vo vydavateľstve Eyre & Spottiswoode, | London 1968, preložil Eduard V. Tvarožek. Doslov | napisal a chronológiu zostavil Jozef Olexa | Vydal Slovenský spisovateľ, Bratislava 1977, | v edicii Vavrin | Zodpovedná redaktorka Gabriela Hanáková | Korigovala Viera Tatarková | Prebal, väzbu a grafickú úpravu navrhol Jozef Gális | Technický redaktor Karol Dufek | Tem skup, 310/13 | Číslo Publikácie 2187 | Vydanie prvé | Náklad 22 000, AH 28.45, VH 29.07 | Vytlačila Pravda, tlačový kombinát KSS, | Tlačiarenské závody

Pravda, závod 01, Bratislava | Strán 488. Výmer SÚKK 1963/1-1976 | Viaz. Kčs 30.– | Broz. Kčs 24,60 | 13-72-052-77 | 605/22/85/6'; *488* blank; endpaper.

Cased in black linen with white endpapers. Front: [silver panel] | [in blind] [publisher's device]. Back: blank. Spine: [running down:] [in silver] 'WHITE'.

Silver glossy paper dustjacket. Front: 'PATRICK | WHITE | [at right:] [publisher's device] | [in red] VOSS' | [b&w illust. of bush scene at night] | [in red] [excerpt, 20 lines in 2 cols.]. Back: '72 - 052 - 77 | 13 Kčs 30.-' | [b&w photo of author] | [blurb, 20 lines in 2 cols.]. Spine: [running down:] 'WHITE'. Inside front flap: [in panel:] 'EDICIA | VAVRIN | VYCHADZA VO | VYDAVATELSTVE | SLOVENSKY | SPISOVATEL' | [list of 7 titles follows]. Inside back flap: [in panel:] 'PATRICK | WHITE | VOSS' | [description, 25 lines].

Price: Kčs 30.– (cased) and 24,60 (paper). Print run: 22,000.

Copies: NSL: Mitchell Library A823/W587/69 (rebound); NSL: Mitchell Library [PW].

G.t15 Polish First Edition (Warsaw: Państwowy Instytut Wydawniczy, 1979)

[at left:] Patrick White | [at right:] Voss | Prezełożyła | Maria Skibniewska | Państwowy Instytut Wydawniczy 1979

18.5 x 11.4 cm. [1]^{12} 2-17^{12} 18^{14} 19^{12} ($1 signed): 230 leaves. pp.*6* 7-457 *458-460*.

Endpaper; *1* 'White | Voss'; *2* [circle] 'Współczesna Proza Światowa' | [abstract illust. of footprints in sand]; *3* title page; *4* 'Tytuł oryginału | «Voss» | Opracowanie graficzne | Waldemar Świerzy | Układ typograficzny | Mieczysław Bancerowski | Copyright © Eyre & Spottiswoode (Publishers) Ltd, 1957 | © Copyright for the Polish edition by | Państwowy Instytut Wydawniczy, Warszawa 1979'; *5* 'Dedykowane | Marie d'Estournelles | de Constant'; *6* blank; 7-457 *458* text; *459* 'Współczesna | Proza | Światowa'; *460* 'PRINTED IN POLAND | Państwowy Instytut Wydawniczy, Warszawa 1979 r. | Wydanie pierwsze | Nakład 50 000 + 315 egz. Ark. wyd. 27,4. Ark. druk. 28,75 | Papier d. s. kl. IV, 63 g, 92 x 114/48 | oddano do składania we wrześniu 1878 r. | Skład wykonały : Zakłady Graficzne „Dom Słowa Polskiego" | Druk I oprawę wykonała : Drukarnia Wydawnicza w Krakowie | Nr zam. 1330/79 S-98 | Cena zł 80.–'; endpaper.

Cased in black vinyl with white endpapers. Front: blank. Back: [in blind] 'zł 80.–'. Spine: [running down:] [in white] 'Patrick White Voss' | [at bottom:] [upright:] [publisher's device].

Black glossy paper dustjacket printed in full colour with a stylised landscape on front. Front: [in white] [at left:] 'Patrick White | [circle] | [at right:] Voss | Państwowy | Instytut | Wydawniczy'. Back: blank. Spine: [in white] 'Patrick White Voss' | [at bottom:] [upright:] [publisher's device]. Inside front flap: [biography, 19 lines]. Inside back flap: [description, 22 lines] | 'zł 80.–'.

Price: zł 80. Print run: 50,000.

Copies: NSL: Mitchell Library A823/W587/68; NSL: Mitchell Library [PW].

G.t16 Polish Second Edition (Warsaw: Muza, 1993)

Notes: pp.573. ISBN 8 3707 9217 0. (Biblioteka bestellerow). Trans. by Maria Skibniewska. Not seen, but entry on the National Bibliographic Database; also see *Index Translationum*.

G.t17 Czech Second Edition (Prague: Svoboda, 1980)

[thick rule] | PATRICK WHITE | Poušť | Johanna | Vosse | SVOBODA | PRAHA 1980

20.4 x 13.2 cm. Unsigned: 216 leaves. pp.*6* 7-417 *418* 419-428 *429-432*.

Endpaper; *1* 'Poušť | Johanna | Vosse'; *2* blank; *3* title page; *4* 'Přeložil Antonín Přidal | © Eyre & Spottiswoode, Ltd., 1957 | Translation © Antonín Přidal, 1980 | Epilogue © Antonín Přidal, 1980'; *5* 'Věneváno | Marii d'Estournelles de Constant'; *6* blank; 7-417 *418* text; 419-428 *429* 'VOSS A TI DRUZI' [by Antonín Přidal] ; *430* blank; *431* 'PATRICK WHITE | Z anglického originálu Voss, | vydaného nakladatelstvim Penguin Books Ltd, | Harmondsworth, England, 1974, | přeložil a doslovem opatřil Antonín Přidal. | Obálku a vazbu navrhl Antonín Kalcovský. | Vydani I. Praha 1980. | Vydalo Nakladatelství Svoboda | jako svou 4621. publikaci. | Odpovědná redaktorka Jarmila Svobodová. | Výtvarný redaktor František Kraus. | Technická redaktorka Helena Tomková | Vytisklo Rudé právo, | tiskařské závody, Praha. | Náklad 85 000. AA 26,00, VA 27,26. | Tematická skupina 13/34. | Cena brož. výt. 29, – Kčs, | váz výt. 35, – Kčs. | 73/605 - 22 - 8.5 | 25 - 100 - 80 Kčs 35,– | Členská knižnice'; *432* blank; endpaper.

Cased in brown calico with dark brown endpapers. Front: [in dark brown] 'PATRICK WHITE | Poušť | Johanna | Vosse'. Back: blank. Spine: [running down:] [in dark brown] 'PATRICK WHITE / POUŠŤ JOHANNA VOSSE' | [at bottom:] [upright:] [publisher's device].

White glossy paper dustjacket printed in brown. Front: [in white] [rule] | [in yellow] 'PATRICK WHITE | [in white] Poušť | Johanna | Vosse | SVOBODA'. Back: [in white] '25 - 100 - 80 | 13/34 Kčs 35,—'. Spine: [running down:] [in yellow] 'PATRICK WHITE / [in white] POUŠŤ JOHANNA VOSSE' | [at bottom:] [upright:] [publisher's device]. Inside front flap: [in brown] [blurb, 38 lines]. Inside back flap: [blurb continues, 12 lines].

Price: Kčs 35 (cased) or 29 (paper). Print run: 85,000.

Copies: Personal collection (2 copies); NSL: Mitchell Library [PW].

G.t18 Dutch First Edition (Amsterdam: Uitgeverij de Arbeiderspers, 1982)

Patrick White *Voss* | Vertaald door Guido Golüke | Amsterdam • Uitgeverij De Arbeiderspers

20.6 x 13 cm. Unsigned: 270 leaves. pp.*6* 7-537 *538-540*.

Endpaper; *1* 'Voss'; *2* 'Grote ABC nr. 424'; *3* title page; *4* 'Copyright © 1957 Patrick White | Copyright Nederlandse vertaling © 1982 B. V. Uitgeverij | De Arbeiderspers, Amsterdam | Oorspronkelijke titel: *Voss* | Uitgave: Eyre & Spottiswoode (Publishers), Ltd. | Omslagfoto:

Gary Hansen uit | *Impressions of a continent* | Omslagontwerp: Frits Stoepman gvn | ISBN 90 295 5736 2'; *5* 'Voor Marie D'Estournelles de Constant'; *6* blank; 7-537 text; *538-540* blank; endpaper.

Cased in grey linen with white endpapers. Front and back: blank. Spine: [running down:] [in silver] 'Patrick White Voss' | [upright:] [publisher's device].

White glossy paper dustjacket printed in full colour. Front: 'Patrick | White | [in grey] VOSS' | [col. illust. of dessicated sheep's carcase]. Back: blank. Spine: [publisher's device] | 'Patrick | White | VOSS' | [detail from col. illust. on front]. Inside front flap: [description, 31 lines] | *'Vervolg op achterflap'*. Inside back flap: 'Vervolg van voorflap | [quotations, 19 lines] | ISBN 90 295 5736 2'.

Copies: NSL: Mitchell Library [PW].

G.t19 Swedish First Edition (Stockholm: Forum, 1983)

Patrick White | Voss | Översättning Ingegärd Martinell | Forum

21.9 x 13.8 cm. $[1]^{16}$ $2\text{-}16^{16}$ 17^8 ($[1]_1$ and 17_8 used as endpapers): 264 leaves. pp.*6* 7-521 *522-524* (endpapers not included in the pagination statement).

1-2 blank; *3* title page; *4* *'Tidigare utgivning* | De fyra utkorade 1964 | Den oförstörbara man-dalan 1969 | Livets träd 1970 | Målaren 1973 | Stormens öga 1976 | En frans av löv 1979 | Fallet Twyborn 1981 | [publisher's device] | Engelska originalets titel Voss | © Patrick White 1957 | Omslag Christer Jonson | Bonniers Grafiska Industrier AB 1983 | Printed in Sweden | ISBN 91-37-08202-7'; *5* 'Till Marie d'Estournelles | de Constant'; *6* blank; 7-521 *522* text; *523-524* blank.

Cased in fawn textured paper boards. Front and back: blank. Spine: [running down:] 'PATRICK WHITE VOSS'.

White glossy paper dustjacket printed in colour with illust. of a campfire across front, back and spine. Front: [in brown] 'Patrick White | [rule] | Voss'. Back: [description, 16 lines] | 'FORUM ISBN 91-37-08202-7'. Spine: [running down:] [in brown] 'PATRICK WHITE VOSS | [upright:] FORUM'. Inside front flap: [b&w photograph of the author] | [biography, 4 lines]. Inside back flap: 'PRESSRÖSTER OM TIDIGARE | BÖCKER AV PATRICK WHITE:' | [quotations, 30 lines].

Copies: NSL: Mitchell Library 823.914/W587/18; NSL: Mitchell Library [PW].

G.t20 Portuguese First Edition (Rio de Janeiro: Nova Fronteira, 1985)

Patrick White | Voss | *Tradução de* | PAULO HENRIQUES BRITTO | [pub-lisher's device] | EDITORA NOVA FRONTEIRA

21 x 14 cm. Unsigned: 240 leaves. pp.*6* 7-476 *477-480*.

1 'VOSS'; *2* blank; *3* title page; *4* 'Titulo Original: | Voss | © Eyre & Spottiswoode (Publish-ers) Ltd, 1957 | Direitos de edição de obra em lingua portuguesa, no Brasil, | adquiridos pela | EDITORA NOVE FRONTEIRA S/A | Rua Maria Andélica, 168 — Lagoa — CEP:

22.461 — Tel: 286-7822 | Endereço Telegráfico: NEOFRONT — Telex: 34695 ENFS BR | Rio de Janeiro, RJ | Revisão: VALDENIR PEIXOTO DA SILVA | ASTROGILDO ESTEVES FILHO | URANGA | CIP-Brasil. | Catalogação-na-forte | Sindicato Nacional dos Editores de Livros, RJ | [rule] | White, Patrick. | W586v Voss / Patrick White; tradução de Paulo | Henriques Britto. | Rio de Janeiro: Nova | Fronteira, 1985. | Tradução de: Voss | 1. Romance inglês. I. Titulo | [at left:] 84-0867 | [at right:] CDD-823 | CDU-820.31'; *5* 'A | MARIE D'ESTOURNELLES | DE CONSTANT'; *6* blank; *7-476* text; *477-478* blank; *479* 'ESTA OBRA FOI COMPOSTA PELA | GABARITO ARTE & TEXTO S/C | LTDA. E IMPRESSA NA EDITORA | VOZES LTDA., PARA A EDITORA | NOVA FRONTEIRA S.A., EM JA- | NEIRO DE MIL NOVECENTOS E OITENTA E CINCO. | [rule] | *Não encontrando este livro nas livrarias, pedir pelo Reembolso* | *Posal à EDITORA NOVA FRONTEIRA S.A. — Rua Maria* | *Angélica, 168 — Lagoa — CEP 22461 — Rio de Janeiro*'; *480* blank.

Sewn in white glossy paper card printed in colour. Front: 'Patrick White | [illust. of canyon] | [in red] VOSS | [illust. of man on horse] | [in black] Prêmio Nobel de Literatura (1973) | *"Um escritor de quem Tolstoi é o | único rival admissível."* | (Sunday Times) | [publisher's device] | EDITORA | NOVA | FRONTEIRA'. Back: [description, 21 lines] | [publisher's device] | 'EDITORA | NOVA | FRONTEIRA | [rule] | SEMPRE | UN BOM | LIVRO'. Spine: [running down:] 'Patrick | White | [in red] VOSS' | [publisher's device]. Inside front flap: 'VOSS' | [description, 36 lines]. Inside back flap: [description continues, 15 lines] | [biography, 12 lines] | [at bottom right:] 'Capa: Victor Burton | Desenho: "O abismo no Weatherboard", | de Robert Elwes.'.

Copies: NSL: Mitchell Library [PW].

G.t21 Macedonian First Edition (Skopje: Misla, 1986)

Notes: pp.535. Translated by Sveto Serafimov. Not seen, but referred to in *Index Translationum*.

G.t22 Hebrew First Edition (Tel Aviv: Zmora-Bitan, 1990)

[Voss]

21.6 x 13.8 cm. Unsigned: 220 leaves. pp.*6* 7-437 *438-440*.

Endpaper; *1* [one line]; *2* blank; *3* title page; *4* 'Patrick White | Voss | Copyright © Eyre & Spottiswoode | Publishers Ltd, 1957 | Hebrew Rights © 1990 by | Zmora-Bitan, Publishers | P.O.B. 22383, Tel-Aviv | Printed in Israel, 1990' | [12 lines]; *5* [one line]; *6* blank; 7-437 text; *438-440* blank; endpaper.

Notes: Trans. by Abrahan Birman and Chana Livnat, for which see *Index Translationum*.

Copies: NSL: Mitchell Library [PW].

G.t23 Chinese First Edition (Beijing: Wai kuo wen hsüen ch'u pan she, 1991)

[T'an hsien chia Wo-ssu]

pp.[*6*] 1-9 *10* 1-520 [*4*].

[*1*] blank; [*2*] [series device]; [*3*] blank; [*4*] blank; [*5*] title page; [*6*] 'Patrick White | VOSS | [rule] | Penguin Books, 1966 | [eight lines Chinese text] | TANXIANJIA WOSI | [rule] | [four lines of Chinese text] | [3 lines relating to production data, indicating a print run of 2,400] | [rule] | ISBN 7 – 5016 – 0089 – 9 / 1 · 89 [Chinese characters] 6.65 [Chinese character]; 1-9 [Introduction]; *10* blank; 1-520 text; [*4*] blank.

Perfectbound in white paper. Back: [series device: 'WAIGUO | 20 | WENXUE'] | [at bottom right:] isbn 7-5016-0089-9'.

Translated by Hu Wen-chung and Liu Shou-k'ang. See Y. Preston *Sydney Morning Herald* 28 July 1984, p.19. Print run: 2,400.

Copies: NU: East Asian 5988.

G.t24a Greek First Edition First Issue (Athens: Ekdoseis Kanake, 1990)

21 x 14 cm. Unsigned: 292 leaves. pp.*9* 10-15 *16-17* 18-31 *32-33* 34-580 *581-584* (the first page of each chapter is unnumbered).

Notes: See Vrasidas Karalis, 'Translating Patrick White's novels *Voss* and *The Vivisector* into Greek', *Southerly* v.63 no.1, 2003, p.133-141, and 'Some observations on the translation and interpretation of Patrick White's *Voss*', *Southerly* v.55 no.2, Winter 1995, p.6-22.

Copies: NSL: Mitchell Library [PW].

G.t24b Greek First Edition Second Issue (Athens: Ekdoseis Kanake, 1995)

ΠΑΤΡΙΚ ΓΟΥΑΙΤ | [in red] ΒΟΖ | ΣΠΟΥΔΗ ΣΤΗΝ ΠΕΡΙΠΕΤΕΙΑ | ΚΑΙ ΤΟΝ ΕΡΩΤΑ | [in black] Εισαγωγη–Μεταφραση | Βρασιδας Καραληζ | ΕΚΔΟΣΕΙΣ ΚΑΝΑΚΗ | ΑΘΗΝΑ 1995

Copies: VSL: SLT A823.3 W585VK.

G.t25 Malay First Edition (Kuala Lumpur: Dewan Bahasa dan Pustaka, Kementerian Pendidikan Malaysia, 1995)

Notes: pp.753. ISBN 9 8362 4760 2.

Not seen, but entry on the National Bibliographic Database.

G.t26 Russian First Edition

Not seen, but referred to by White in a letter to Hu Wenzhong, 19 November 1986 (National Library of Australia, MS 8553).

G.m1 Braille Edition (London: Royal National Institute for the Blind, 1961)

Voss (6 volumes of interpoint braille)

G.m2 Sound recording (North Hobart: Hear a Book, [1982])

Voss (15 audiocassettes)
Read by Ken Waters from the Eyre and Spottiswoode edition of 1957.

G.m3 Sound Recording (Melbourne: Royal Victorian Institute for the Blind, Tertiary Resource Centre, [n.d.])

Voss (3 audiocassettes, 4-track)
Read by Peggy Dunphy from the Penguin edition of 1960.

G.m4 Sound Recording (Enfield: Royal Blind Society of New South Wales, 1992)

Voss (4 audiocassettes, 4-track)
Read by David Baldwin from the Penguin edition of 1960.

G.m5 Radio Broadcast (ABC/National Library of Australia, 1996)

Voss
16 December 1996 to 24 January 1997
Abridged by Lesley Loughnan. Read by Robert Grubb. Produced by Rodney Wetherell.

H Riders in the Chariot (1961)

Riders in the Chariot required more research than White's previous novels. As early as February 1957, soon after submitting *Voss*, White was referring to his 'Jewish novel': '[It] will take a lot more thought and reading, and even then I may not have the courage to embark on anything so esoteric'. (To Ben Huebsch, 8 February 1957)

While reading and thinking White came up with the title, *Riders in the Chariot*, which he mentioned in a letter to Huebsch (2 September 1957). The chariot was a vision seen by each of the novel's 'voices', connecting their religious and artistic beliefs. White acknowledged a number of interconnecting influences, including the Biblical story of Elijah and a painting by Odilon Redon, seen by White in a Bond Street gallery in London in 1947.

White was ready to commence writing in February 1958 but put it off. For most of 1958 he and Manoly were travelling, first to Jerusalem, then on to Greece, England and the United States. He must have started writing immediately after his return to Australia in October 1958 because he was well into the book by December. (To Ben Huebsch, 17 December 1958) By May White had written 90,000 words and believed he was about three-quarters finished: 'When I say written though, a lot of it is very rough and will probably have to be re-written'. (To Ben Huebsch, 11 May 1959) By October he had almost finished the traumatic first draft. Less than twelve months later the second was finished. 'At last I have finished the second version. [...] About *Riders in the Chariot*: it does, I'm afraid, work out to about 230,000 [words]. I have tried it on Manoly and a Jewish friend [Klári Daniel]. [...] I don't think the Third version will take very long.' (To Ben Huebsch, 3 August 1960) It did not. By January 1961 he was about to send the typescript of *Riders in the Chariot* by airmail – '(first or second class depending on the sum involved!)'. (To Ben Huebsch, 3 January 1961) Manoly drove to town and posted one carbon copy to New York and one to London. 'The parcels crashed down into the bowels of the G.P.O. making me feel they had probably burst open at the start, and even if they hadn't, they were probably setting out on an ominous career'. (To Geoffrey Dutton, 5 January 1961) Only a few weeks later Huebsch telegrammed his acceptance: 'RIDERS IS A GREAT BOOK YOUR BEST CONGRATULATIONS'. In London, Temple Smith was equally impressed, although he was able to read only about 80 pages before he had to pass the typescript on to the Nolans. (Marr p.375)

White dedicated the book to Klári Daniel and Ben Huebsch: 'Klári has been my mentor [...] and you have been – you'. (To Ben Huebsch, 5 February 1961) Throughout the long gestation of *Riders in the Chariot*, Huebsch had acted as White's literary confidant. When the book was finally accepted by Viking the two men were obviously close. It was at this point that Huebsch asked White to address him as 'Ben'.

Riders in the Chariot was published in the United States in early October 1961. The United Kingdom edition came out a few weeks later. This was the first time that the publication of one of White's novels was well co-ordinated. The Viking Press edition was of the usual high production quality, and its dust-jacket design by George Salter has received qualified praise. A Nolan abstract landscape was used for the United Kingdom's edition jacket. White was well satisfied with Nolan's design: 'This painting is so much subtler and to the point when you actually see it; one would say it had actually been designed for the book, which in fact was not the case.' (To John Tasker, 30 October 1961) White had approached Sidney Nolan as early as November 1960 to do the jacket, but Nolan was then planning a trip to Africa. When Eyre & Spottiswoode received the typescript in the new year, Temple Smith hurried it over to the Nolans. Cynthia Nolan wrote to White that they loved the book and that Sid had already done some preliminary designs. (To Ben Huebsch, 5 February 1961) That is where the matter stood, much to White's frustration: 'You say in your letter that you are awaiting a photostat of the Sidney Nolan jacket from London. I am afraid you may continue to 'await' it, as Nolan has gone off to Egypt, and still no sign of a drawing of any sort'. (To Marshall Best of The Viking Press, 7 April 1961) It is interesting that even in the early 1960s there was a move towards uniform United States/United Kingdom editions. Temple Smith became so desperate that, with Nolan's permission, he went to his studio and took away a design, much against Cynthia Nolan's wishes. The original painted design is now in the State Library of New South Wales. White was also impressed with Nolan's design for the Penguin edition, 'which I am told is excellent in every way'. (To the Duttons, 18 November 1964)

The critical reception seems to have been uniformly positive, a fact which White keenly appreciated: '*Riders in the Chariot* keeps exploding at every letter delivery. I have now all the important American reviews. Most of them very good. I have even had, for the first time ever, a remarkably good review in the *Sydney Morning Herald*. (To John Tasker, 30 October 1961) However, as Marr points out, although the American reviews were full of praise, the editors had decided that White was a 'literary' author and had buried the reviews. Stern's glowing review appeared on page four of the *New York Times Book Review*. It was the English and Australian reception which was influential for *Riders in the Chariot*.

The commercial reception mirrored the pattern of the reviews: Eyre & Spottiswoode sold 24,000 copies – 9,000 in the United Kingdom, 9,500 in Australia, and almost 6,000 elsewhere in the English-speaking world. In 1961, White further consolidated his Australian success by winning his second Miles Franklin Award and was also awarded the Brotherhood Award by the American National Conference of Christians and Jews. In North America, only 8,000 copies of the Viking edition were sold. Marshall Best of Viking was obviously concerned about this relatively poor performance when he wrote to White, very carefully suggesting that more editorial intervention might result in a better book. White replied: 'The editing of novels – it sounds about as horrible as a packaged dinner'. (To Marshall Best, 16 October 1961; Marr p.382-383)

Translations of *Riders in the Chariot* followed routinely. White was excited when reporting to John Tasker that a French publisher was again showing interest: 'One of the most exciting recent bits of news is that Manés Sperber, a reader for Calmann-Levy [...] wants an option for all my available novels for that house. The French have been very cold since the failure of *Happy Valley* when published by Gallimard ten years ago. Now it looks as though I may get a hearing'. (To John Tasker, 31 October 1961; Marr p.393) Whatever happened, it was Gallimard who in 1965 published Suzanne Néttilard's translation entitled *Le char des élus*. Néttilard's method was to consult the author often, as is illustrated by her practice when translating *The Eye of the Storm* in the mid-1970s, so it can be assumed that White exercised considerable control over *Le char des élus*. Other translations were made into Swedish (1964), French (1965), Polish (1965), Spanish (1966), Finnish (1967), German (1969), Turkish (1973), Italian (1976), Yugoslavian (1979), and Hebrew (1980). The delay in producing a German translation is surprising given that translations of both *The Tree of Man* and *Voss* appeared within two years and one year respectively of publication in English. It is also surprising that there have been no translations of *Riders in the Chariot* since 1980.

* * * * *

H1a U.S. First Edition (New York: Viking, 1961)

Patrick White | [ornament] | RIDERS | IN THE | CHARIOT | 1961 | The Viking Press | NEW YORK

22 x 14.5 cm. Unsigned: 272 leaves. pp.[*10*] *1-2* 3-91 *92-94* 95-205 *206-208* 209-242 *243-244* 245-308 *309-310* 311-398 *399-400* 401-497 *498-500* 501-532 *533-534*.

Endpaper; [*1*] 'Riders in the Chariot'; [*2*] 'BY THE SAME AUTHOR | [ornament] | Voss | The Tree of Man | The Aunt's Story | The Living and the Dead | Happy Valley'; [*3*] title page; [*4*] 'Copyright © 1961 by Patrick White | All rights reserved | First published in 1961 by The Viking Press, Inc. | 625 Madison Avenue, New York 22, N.Y. | Published simultane-ously in Canada by | The Macmillan Company of Canada Limited | [publisher's device] | Library of Congress catalog card number: 61-13728 | Printed in the U.S.A. by The Colonial Press'; [*5*] '*For* | Klari Daniel | *and* | Ben Huebsch'; [*6*] blank; [*7*] 'The Prophets Isaiah and Ezekiel dined with me, and | I asked them how they dared so roundly to assert that | God spoke to them; and whether they did not think | at the time that they would be misunder-stood, & so be | the cause of imposition. | Isaiah answer'd: "I saw no God, nor heard any, in a | finite organical perception; but my senses discover'd the | infinite in everything, and as I was then perswaded, & | remain confirm'd, that the voice of honest indignation is | the voice of God, I cared not for the consequences, but wrote. ..." | I then asked Ezekiel why he eat dung, & lay so long on | his right & left side? he answer'd, "The desire of raising | other men into a perception of the infinite: this the | North American tribes practise, & is he honest who re- | sists his genius or conscience only for the sake of | present ease or gratification?" | –WILLIAM BLAKE'; [*8*] blank; [*9*] 'Riders in the Chariot'; [*10*] blank; *1* 'PART ONE' | [ornament]; *2* blank; 3-91 text of Part One; *92* blank; *93* 'PART TWO' | [ornament]; *94* blank; 95-205 text of Part Two; *206* blank; *207* 'PART THREE' | [ornament]; *208* blank; 209-242 text of Part Three; *243* 'PART FOUR' | [ornament]; *244* blank; 245-308 text of Part Four; *309* 'PART FIVE' | [ornament]; *310* blank; 311-398 text of Part Five; *399* 'PART SIX' | [ornament]; *400* blank; 401-497 text of Part Six; *498* blank; *499* 'PART SEVEN' | [ornament]; *500* blank; 501-532 text of Part Seven; *533* blank; *534* blank; endpaper.

Cased in dark blue cloth with pale blue top edge and white endpapers. Front: [in blind] '*P* | [ornament] | *W*'. Back: blank. Spine: [in gold] 'RIDERS | IN THE | CHARIOT | [orna-ment] | Patrick White | [at bottom:] THE | VIKING | PRESS'.

White paper dustjacket printed with illust. mainly in blue of figures and sun extending across front, back and spine. Front: [in white] 'PATRICK WHITE | [in yellow] *Riders* | *in the Chariot* | [in white] A NOVEL'. Back: [in black] 'PATRICK WHITE | "towers over most other living novelists by his | ability to supply, to lay bare the conscious, ro- | mantic yet pri-vate daydream..." | —JAMES STERN | *Riders in the Chariot* | "The most extraordinary novel I have read | in many years of 'new' novel reading | ...every word a masterpiece. What | a creative miracle!" | —LEO LERMAN'. Spine: [in white] 'PATRICK | WHITE | [in yellow] *Riders* | *in the* | *Chariot* | [in white] VIKING'. Inside front flap: [at top right:] '$5.95 | [in pink] RIDERS IN THE CHARIOT | [blurb, 40 lines] | JACKET DESIGN BY GEORGE SALTER'. Inside back flap: [in pink] 'ALSO BY PATRICK WHITE | [in blue] THE TREE OF MAN [in black] [quotation of four lines from] ORVILLE PRESCOTT, *The New York Times* | [in blue] VOSS [in black] [quotation of four lines from] BORDEN DEAL,

Saturday | *Review* | This book was a Book-of-the-Month Club se- | lection; winner of the W. H. Smith Annual | Literary Award and the Miles Franklin Award | in England. | [b&w photograph of the author] [running down:] BORIS COOK, SYDNEY | [upright:] [in blue] PATRICK WHITE [in black] [biography, 6 lines] | [in blue] THE VIKING PRESS | *Publishers of The Viking Portable Library* | 625 Madison Avenue, New York 22, N. Y. | PRINTED IN U.S.A.'.

Published in October 1961. Price $5.95. Print run: not known, but 8,000 copies sold.

Reviews: David Dempsey *Saturday Review* 7 October 1961, p.39-40 (750w); *Booklist* 15 December 1961, p.254; *Bookmark* v.21, December 1961, p.39 (50w); Fanny Butcher *Chicago Sunday Tribune* 8 October 1961, p.4 (350w); Melvin Maddocks *Christian Science Monitor* 12 October 1961, p.11 (550w); Oona Sullivan *Commonweal* 24 November 1961, p.235, p.11 (550w); Jeremy Brooks *Guardian* 27 October 1961, p.7 (550w); *Kirkus Review* v.29, 15 July 1961, p.640 (240w); F.W. Binns *Library Journal* 1 October 1961, p.3304 (130w); A. Alvarez *New Statesman* v.62, 3 November 1961, p.653 (2300w); Gouverneur Paulding *New York Herald Tribune Books* 8 October 1961, p.4 (700w); James Stern *New York Times Book Review* 8 October 1961, p.4 (1350w); Whitney Balliett *New Yorker* v.37, 9 December 1961, p.244 (1550w); McCready Huston *San Francisco Chronicle* 24 December 1961, p.16 (500w); Richard McLaughlin *Springfield Republican* 12 November 1961, p.2D (240w); *Time* 6 October 1961, p.100 (380w).

Notes: The copy in White's own collection is a presentation copy from the publisher in a half binding of red leather and marbled paper boards.

Copies: NSL: Mitchell Library A823/W587/6B1 (lacks dustjacket); NSL: Mitchell Library [PW]; VSL: SLT 819.93/W582R (lacks dustjacket); Personal collection (2 copies).

H1b Canadian Subedition (Toronto: Macmillan, 1961)
Not seen, but referred to in H1a above.

H1c U.S. First Edition Viking Subedition (New York: Viking, [1974])
Notes: Cased in black calico boards. Coarse red paper dustjacket.

Copies: NSL: Mitchell Library [PW].

H1d U.S. First Edition Avon Subedition (New York: Avon Books, 1975)

PATRICK | WHITE | Riders | *in the* | Chariot | [publisher's device] AVON | PUBLISHERS OF BARD, CAMELOT, DISCUS, EQUINOX AND FLARE BOOKS

17.6 x 10.3 cm. Unsigned: 272 leaves. pp.*8* 9-97 *98-100* 101-214 *215-216* 217-251 *252-254* 255-317 *318-320* 321-408 *409-410* 411-508 *509-510* 511-542 *543-544*.

Notes: p.*4* 'AVON BOOKS | A division of | The Hearst Corporation | 959 Eighth Avenue | New York, New York 10019 | Copyright © 1961 by Patrick White | Published by arrange- ment with The Viking Press, Inc. | Library of Congress Catalog Card Number: 61-13728 | All rights reserved, which includes the right | to reproduce this book or portions thereof in | any form whatsoever. For information address | The Viking Press, Inc. 625 Madison Avenue, New York, | New York 10022 | ISBN: 0-380-00467-4 | First Avon Printing, September, 1975 | AVON TRADEMARK REG. U.S. PAT. OFF. AND | FOREIGN COUNTRIES, REGISTERED TRADEMARK– | MARCA REGISTRADA, HECHO EN CHICAGO, U.S.A. | Printed in the U.S.A.'. Perfectbound in white paper printed in colour (col. illust. of woman's head). Published in September 1975. Price: US$2.25.

H2a U.K. First Edition (London: Eyre & Spottiswoode, 1961)

[hollow type] RIDERS | IN | THE | CHARIOT | [solid type] A NOVEL BY | PATRICK | WHITE | EYRE & SPOTTISWOODE | *22 Henrietta Street – London WC2*

20.5 x 13.8 cm. [A]^{16} B-Q^{16} R^4 S^{16} ($1 signed): 276 leaves. pp.*6* 7-99 *100* 101-217 *218* 219-255 *256* 257-552.

Endpaper; *1* 'RIDERS | IN THE CHARIOT | [blurb, 20 lines]; *2* [epigraph of 20 lines from] 'WILLIAM BLAKE'; *3* title page; *4* '*also by Patrick White* | THE LIVING AND THE DEAD | HAPPY VALLEY | THE AUNT'S STORY | THE TREE OF MAN | VOSS | *First published* 1961 | © 1961 *Patrick White* | *Printed in Great Britain* | *by the Shenval Press Ltd* | *London, Hertford and Harlow* | *Cat. No. 6/4253/2*'; *5* 'FOR | KLARI DANIEL | AND | BEN HUEBSCH'; *6* blank; 7-99 text of Part I; *100* blank; 101-217 text of Part II; *218* blank; 219-255 text of Part III; *256* blank; 257-324 text of Part IV; 325-418 text of Part V; 419-518 text of Part VI; 519-552 text of Part VII; endpaper.

Cased in brown calico with off-white endpapers. Front and back: blank. Spine: [in gold] [cursive] '*Riders* | *in the* | *Chariot* | [ornament] | *Patrick* | *White* | [at bottom:] *E & S*.

White paper dustjacket printed in brown featuring illust. of landscape by Sidney Nolan which extends across front, spine and back. Front: [in white] [cursive] 'Riders | in the Chariot | [rule] | [normal type] PATRICK WHITE'. Back: blank. Spine: [in white] 'RIDERS | IN THE | CHARIOT | [rule] | PATRICK | WHITE | [at bottom:] E & S'. Inside front flap: 'Riders in the Chariot | PATRICK WHITE | [blurb, 38 lines] | *The jacket illustration is taken from a painting* | *by Sidney Nolan* | [at bottom left:] 6/4253/2 [at bottom right:] 21S'. Inside back flap: blank.

Published 26 October 1961. Price: 21s. Remained in print until 1974. Print run: not known, but 24,000 copies sold.

Reviews: Max Harris *Nation* (Sydney) 21 October 1961, p.21-22; Chris Wallace-Crabbe *Bulletin* 25 November 1961, p.35-36; Alan Nicholls *Age* (Melbourne) 9 December 1961, Literary Supplement p.19; H.P. Heseltine *Meanjin* v.20, December 1961, p.474-475; G. Dutton *Australian Book Review* v.1, November 1961, p.1-3; O.N. Burgess *Australian Quarterly* v.34, March 1962, p.110-113; M. Aughterson *Prospect* v.5, 1962, p.28-30; J. McAuley *Quadrant* v.6, April 1962, p.79-81; David Bradley *Overland* v.23, April 1962, p.41-45; Marcel Aurrousseau *Meanjin* v.21, 1962, p.29-31; Colin Roderick *Southerly* v.2, 1962, p.62-77; [Miles Franklin Award Judges] *Bohemia* v.14, June 1962, p.3-4; M. McNally *Dissent* v.2, May-June 1962, p.24-25; Bernard Bergonzi *Spectator* 3 November 1962, p.628 (700w); *Times Literary Supplement* 15 December 1962, p.889 (5000w).

Notes: In a personal collection there is a corrected proof copy bound in plain red wrappers. In ms on front: 'Publication Oct 26 1961'. Corrections are not in White's hand. Second and third proof copies (both uncorrected) have been sighted in the same collection. They are sewn in plain blue paper wrappers. One of these was bought for $95 around 1990. A fourth proof copy, sewn in blue paper, is held by the State Library of Victoria (Call no. *LT A823.3 W582R). It was bought for $140 in 1994. A proof copy, with a note from *Times Literary Supplement* to Dan Davin, is held in the Baillieu Library, University of Melbourne (AX A823.3 White).

The original artwork by Sidney Nolan which was the basis for the dustjacket design is held in the Mitchell Library, State Library of New South Wales (ML 746). Dye on paper?, 25 x 30 cm. Unsigned, undated, unlabelled. Presented by Patrick White, August 1974.

Copies: NSL: Mitchell Library; NSL: Mitchell Library [PW]; NSL: Mitchell Library A823/W587/6A1 (lacks dustjacket); NU: RB 1661.11; NU: RB IMP 007304; Personal collection (3 copies); VU: McL L/A-F White; VU: Ducker A823.3 White.

H2b U.K. First Edition Jonathan Cape Subedition (London: Jonathan Cape, 1976)

PATRICK WHITE | [double rule] | Riders | in the Chariot | [publisher's device] | JONATHAN CAPE | THIRTY BEDFORD SQUARE LONDON

20.4 x 13 cm. Unsigned: 276 leaves. pp.*6* 7-99 *100* 101-217 *218* 219-255 *256* 257-552.

Notes: p.4 'FIRST PUBLISHED 1961 | THIS EDITION PUBLISHED BY JONATHAN CAPE LTD 1976 | © 1961 PATRICK WHITE | JONATHAN CAPE LTD, 30 BEDFORD SQUARE, LONDON, WC1 | ISBN 0 224 01192 8 | *For Klari Daniel | and | Ben Huebsch* | PRINTED IN GREAT BRITAIN BY | LOWE AND BRYDONE (PRINTERS) LTD, THETFORD, NORFOLK'. Cased in black linen boards. White textured paper dustjacket, printed in olive green and overprinted in white and black. Jacket design by Mon Mohan.

Published 8 April 1976. Price: £4.50. Print run: 3,000.

Copies: NU: 823.91/A/W587/J5/1; NSL: Mitchell Library [PW].

H3a Penguin Edition First Issue (Harmondsworth: Penguin, 1964)

Patrick White | Riders in the Chariot | [publisher's device] Penguin Books | in association with Eyre and Spottiswoode

18 x 11 cm. [1]^{12} 2^{12} 3-22^{10} 23-24^{12} : 248 leaves. pp.*6* 7-88 *89-90* 91-194 *195-196* 197-227 *228* 229-287 *288* 289-371 *372* 373-460 *461-462* 463-491 *492-496*.

1 'Penguin Books 2185 | Riders in the Chariot' | [biography, 29 lines]; *2* blank; *3* title page; *4* 'Penguin Books Ltd, Harmondsworth, | Middlesex, England | Penguin Books Pty Ltd, | Ringwood, Victoria, Australia | First published by Eyre & Spottiswoode 1961 | Published in Penguin Books 1964 | Copyright © Patrick White 1961 | Made and printed in Great Britain | by Hazell Watson & Viney Ltd | Aylesbury, Bucks | Set in Linotype Times' | [publisher's condition, 6 lines]; *5* '*For Klari Daniel and Ben Huebsch*'; *6* [epigraph from] 'WILLIAM

BLAKE'; 7-88 *89* text of Part One; *90* blank; 91-194 *195* text of Part Two; *196* blank; 197-227 *228* text of Part Three; 229-287 *288* text of Part Four; 289-371 *372* text of Part Five; 373-460 *461* text of Part Six; *462* blank; 463-491 *492* text of Part Seven; *493* '*Other Penguins by Patrick White are described | on the following pages*' | [at bottom:] [publisher's device]; *494* blank; *495* 'VOSS | [blurb, 10 lines] | [quotation of one line from] Walter Allen in the *New Statesman* | [quotation of two lines from] John Davenport in the *Observer* | [quotation of two lines from] Penelope Mortimer | in the *Sunday Times* | *Also available* | THE AUNT'S STORY | *Not for sale in the U.S.A. or Canada*'; *496* 'THE TREE OF MAN | 'A monumental, moving epic' — *The Times* | [blurb, 9 lines] [quotation of two lines from] Peter Green in the *Daily | Telegraph* | [quotation of two lines from] John Davenport in the *Observer* | *Not for sale in the U.S.A. or Canada* | *For a complete list of books available please write to Penguin Books* | *whose address can be found on the back of the title page*'.

Perfectbound in white paper. Front: [in orange] [publisher's device] 'a Penguin Book 7'6 | [thin rule] | Riders in the | Chariot | [thin rule] | Patrick White' | [col. illust. of a woman in a hat]. Back: [in black] [publisher's device] 'a Penguin Book | [thin rule] | [blurb, 4 lines] | [quotation of five lines from] – Maurice Edelman in | the *Sunday Times* | [quotation of three lines from] – A. Alvarez in the *New Statesman* | [quotation of four lines from] – Jeremy Brooks in | the *Guardian* | The cover is taken from a painting by Sidney Nolan | *For copyright reasons this edition is not for sale | in the U.S.A. or Canada* | [photograph of the author] | *Axel Poignant*'. Spine: [running down:] '[in white] Patrick White [in black] Riders in the Chariot [upright:] [publisher's device] | 2185'. Inside front and back covers: blank.

Price: AU$1.05.

Notes: There is at least one variant binding. Perfectbound in white paper. Front: [in orange] [publisher's device flanked by boomerangs] 'an Australian Penguin Book 10/6 | [rule] | Riders in the | Chariot | [rule] | Patrick White' | [col. illust.].

Copies: NSL: GRL N828.99943/W587/5 (lacks original binding); NSL: Mitchell Library A823/W587/6C1.

H3b Penguin Edition Australian Issue (Harmondsworth: Penguin, 1974)
Notes: p.*4* 'Published in Penguin Books 1964 | Reprinted 1974 | Copyright © Patrick White 1961 | Made and printed in Australia | at The Dominion Press, | Blackburn, Victoria | Set in Linotype Times'. Perfectbound in pale green paper covers with 'Penguin Modern Classics' on the front. Price: AU$2.20, NZ$2.20. ISBN 0 1400 2185 X.

H3c Penguin Edition Second Issue (Harmondsworth: Penguin, 1974)
Notes: p.*4* 'Published in Penguin Books 1964 | Reissued in Penguin Modern Classics 1974 | Copyright © Patrick White 1961 | Made and printed in Great Britain | by Hazell Watson & Viney Ltd, | Aylesbury, Bucks | Set in Linotype Times'. The cover shows an oil sketch by Sidney Nolan, by kind permission of the artist. Price: 60p, AU$2.10, NZ$2.10.

H3d Penguin Edition Third Issue (Harmondsworth: Penguin, 1975)
Notes: p.*4* 'Published in Penguin Books 1964 | Reissued in Penguin Modern Classics 1974 | Reprinted 1975 | Copyright © Patrick White, 1961 | Made and printed in Great Britain | by Hazell Watson & Viney Ltd, | Aylesbury, Bucks | Set in Linotype Times'. Perfectbound in

pale green paper covers. The cover shows an oil sketch by Sidney Nolan, by kind permission of the artist. Price: 90p, AU$3.05, NZ$3.05. ISBN 0 1400 2185 X.

H3e Penguin Edition Fifth Issue (Harmondsworth: Penguin, 1976)
Notes: p.*4* 'Published in Penguin Books 1964 | Reissued in Penguin Modern Classics 1974 | Reprinted 1975, 1976 | Copyright © Patrick White, 1961 | Made and printed in Great Britain | by Hazell Watson & Viney Ltd, | Aylesbury, Bucks | Set in Linotype Times'. Price: £1.00. ISBN 0 1400 2185 X.

H3f Penguin Edition Fifth Issue (Harmondsworth: Penguin, 1979)
Notes: 19.7 x 12.8 cm. Page *4* 'Published in Penguin Books 1964 | Reissued in Penguin Modern Classics 1974 | Reprinted 1975, 1976, 1979'. Perfectbound in white paper printed in black and violet. Cover design by Neil Stuart. Cover illustration (images of marbles, eyes and a fan) by Mel Odom.

H3g Penguin Edition Sixth Issue (Harmondsworth: Penguin, 1981)
Notes: p.*4* 'Published in Penguin Books 1964 | Reissued in Penguin Modern Classics 1974 | Reprinted 1975, 1976, 1979, 1981 | Copyright © Patrick White 1961 | All rights reserved | Made and printed in Great Britain | by Hazell Watson & Viney Ltd, Aylesbury, Bucks | Set in Linotype Times'. Perfectbound in pale green paper covers. The cover shows an oil sketch by Sidney Nolan, by kind permission of the artist. Price: £2.50, AU$5.95.

H3h Penguin Edition Seventh Issue (Harmondsworth: Penguin, 1984)
Notes: p.*4* 'Published in Penguin Books 1964 | Reissued in Penguin Modern Classics 1974 | Reprinted 1975, 1976, 1979, 1981, 1984 | Copyright © Patrick White 1961 | All rights reserved | Made and printed in Great Britain by | Hazell Watson & Viney Limited, | Member of the BPcc Group, | Aylesbury, Bucks | Set in Linotype Times'. Perfect bound in white paper card. Cover design by Neil Stuart. Cover illustration (a harnessed horse in soft pink, grey and yellow tones) by Mel Odom. Price: £3.95, AU$7.95, NZ$11.95, CAN$7.95, US$6.95. ISBN 0 1400 2185 X.

H3i Penguin Edition Eighth Issue (Harmondsworth: Penguin, [1992])
Notes: The cover shows *Sofala* (1947) by Russell Drysdale (oil on canvas on hardboard 71.7 x 93.1 cm) in the Art Gallery of New South Wales, purchased 1952'. Published in October 1992. Price: US$11.95, AU$14.95. ISBN 0 1401 8634 4.

H4 U.S. Second Edition Pyramid Edition (New York: Pyramid Books, 1966)

RIDERS | IN THE | CHARIOT | [rule] | PATRICK WHITE | [rule] | PYRAMID BOOKS [publisher's device] NEW YORK

17.9 x 10.4 cm. Unsigned: 264 leaves. pp.*8* 9-95 *96-98* 99-205 *206-208* 209-242 *243-244* *245-306* *307-308* 309-395 *396-398* 399-493 *494-496* 497-527 *528*.

1 'A GIANT NOVEL OF | FOUR EXTRAORDINARY PEOPLE | [blurb, 10 lines] | [quotation from] *New York Herald Tribune* | [quotation from] *The Manchester Guardian* | [quotation from] *The Library Journal*'; *2* 'The Novels of PATRICK WHITE | *in Pyramid Editions* | • | THE TREE OF MAN | VOSS | RIDERS IN THE CHARIOT'; *3* title page; *4* 'RIDERS IN THE CHARIOT | A PYRAMID BOOK | Published by arrangement with The Viking Press, Inc. | Viking Press edition published October, 1961 | Pyramid edition published July, 1966 | Copyright © 1961 by Patrick White | Library of Congress catalog card number: 61-13728 | All Rights Reserved | Printed in the United States of America | PYRAMID BOOKS are published by Pyramid Publications, Inc. | 444 Madison Avenue, New York, New York 10022, U.S.A.'; *5* 'For | Klari Daniel | *and* | Ben Huebsch'; *6* [epigraph from] 'WILLIAM BLAKE'; *7* 'PART ONE'; *8* blank; 9-95, text of Part One; *96* blank; *97* 'PART TWO'; *98* blank; 99-205 text of Part Two; *206* blank; *207* 'PART THREE'; *208* blank; 209-242 text of Part Three; *243* 'PART FOUR'; *244* blank; 245-306 text of Part Four; *307* 'PART FIVE'; *308* blank; 309-395 text of Part Five; *396* blank; *397* 'PART SIX'; *398* blank; 399-493 text of Part Six; *494* blank; *495* 'PART SEVEN'; *496* blank; 497-527 text of Part Seven; *528* [advertisement].

Perfectbound in white paper with col. illust. extending over front, spine and back. Front: [in white] 'PYRAMID [publisher's device] N-1451 95c | [thin rule] | PATRICK WHITE | [thin rule] | A major novel of narrative | greatness. "Brilliant and com- | passionate ... grand in design" | [rule] SATURDAY REVIEW | RIDERS | IN THE | CHARIOT' | [col. illust. of figures in receding landscape]. Back: [in white] 'RIDERS | IN THE | CHARIOT | [blurb, 9 lines] | "Astonishing ... vast | richness and vitality" | –THE SPECTATOR | [photograph of the author] | [in black] [biography, 7 lines] | [in white] A PYRAMID BOOK 95c Cover: Frank Kalan Printed in U.S.A.'. Spine: [in white] 'N-1451 | 95c | [running down:] RIDERS IN THE CHARIOT Patrick White | [upright:] [publisher's device] PYRAMID | BOOKS'.

Published in July 1966. Price: 95c.

Copies: Mitchell Library [PW].

H.t1a Swedish First Edition First Issue (Stockholm: Albert Bonniers Förlag, 1964)

PATRICK WHITE | De fyra utkorade | ROMAN | ALBERT BONNIERS FÖRLAG | STOCKHOLM

22.3 x 14.4 cm. [1]^8 2-32^8 33^6 ($1 signed): 262 leaves. pp.*6* 7-520 *521-524*.

1 'PATRICK WHITE • DE FYRA UTKORADE'; *2* blank; *3* title page; *4* '*Översättning av Torsten Blomkvist | Engelska originalets titel: | Riders in the Chariot (London 1961) | Copyright 1961 by Patrick White | Printed in Sweden | Alb. Bonniers boktryckeri 1964 | Stockholm*'; *5* [epigraph from] 'WILLIAM BLAKE'; *6* blank; 7-520 *521* text; *522-524* blank.

Sewn in buff-coloured paper card. Front and back: blank.

Blue-printed paper jacket, attached at spine. Front: [in white] 'PATRICK WHITE | [in yellow] De fyra | utkorade | [in white] ROMAN'. Back: [col. illust.]. Spine: [in white] 'PATRICK | WHITE | [in yellow] De fyra | utkorade'. Inside front flap: 'DE FYRA |

UTKORADE | [description, 30 lines] | *Forts. på bakre klaffen'*. Inside back flap: [description continues, 13 lines] | [biography, 7 lines] | 'BONNIERS | *Omslag av George Salter* | *Pris 36:50, inb. 44: —'*.

Copies: NSL: Mitchell Library A823/W587/6E1; NSL: Mitchell Library [PW].

H.t1b Swedish First Edition Second Issue (Stockholm: Bökorlaget Aldus/Bonniers, 1973)
Notes: p.*4* 'ISBN 91-0-034616-0 | Engelska originalets titel: Riders in the Chariot (1961) | Översättning av Torsten Blomkvist | Copyright © 1961 by Patrick White | Omslag av George Salter | Första utgåva 1964 | Delfinserien 1970 | Andra upplagen 1973 | Printed in Sweden | Alb. Bonniers boktryckeri 1973 | Stockholm'. Perfectbound in white paper printed in blue, green, yellow and red.

H.t2a French First Edition First Issue (Paris: Gallimard, 1965)

PATRICK WHITE | Le Char | des Élus | TRADUIT DE L'ANGLAIS | PAR SUZANNE NÉTILLARD | *nrf* | GALLIMARD

20.4 x 14 cm. [1]^{16} 2-16^{16} 17^{4} 18^{16} ($1 signed): 276 leaves. pp.*12* 13-102 *103-106* 107-219 *220-222* 223-256 *257-260* 261-324 *325-328* 329-416 *417-420* 421-547 *548* 549 *550-552*.

1-2 blank; *3* 'DU MONDE ENTIER'; *4* blank; *5* title page; *6* '*Il a été tiré de cet ouvrage vingt-six exemplaires | sur vélin pur fil Lafuma-Navarre numérotés de 1 à 26. | Titre original : |* RIDERS IN THE CHARIOT | *Tous droits d'adaptation, de reproduction et de traduction | réservés pour tous pays, y compris l'U. R. S. S. | First published 1961. | © 1961, Patrick White, printed in Great Britain | by the Shenval Press Ltd., London, Hertford and Harlow. | © 1965, Éditions Gallimard, pour la traduction française.*'; *7* [epigraph of 18 lines from] 'William Blake.'; *8* blank; *9* '*Pour Klari Daniel et Ben Huebsch.*'; *10* blank; *11* 'PREMIÈRE PARTIE'; *12* blank; 13-102 *103* text of Part I; *104* blank; *105* 'DEUXIÈME PARTIE'; *106* blank; 107-219 *220* text of Part II; *221* 'TROISIÈME PARTIE'; *222* blank; 223-256 *257* text of Part III; *258* blank; *259* 'QUATRIÈME PARTIE'; *260* blank; 261-324 *325* text of Part IV; *326* blank; *327* 'CINQUIÈME PARTIE'; *328* blank; 329-416 *417* text of Part V; *418* blank; *419* 'SIXIÈME PARTIE'; *420* blank; 421-547 *548* text of Part VI; 549 *550* 'TRADUCTION DES TERMES ÉTRANGERS'; *551* 'DU MÊME AUTEUR | [publisher's monogram] | EDEN-VILLE.'; *552* '*Cet ouvrage | a été achevé d'imprimer | sur les presses de l'Imprimerie Floch | à Mayenne, le 12 mars 1965. | Dépôt légal : 1er trimestre 1965. | N° d'édition : 10844. | (6290)*'.

Perfectbound in white glossy paper card. Front: 'DU MONDE ENTIER | PATRICK WHITE | [in red] LE CHAR | DES ÉLUS | [in black] ROMAN | TRADUIT DE L'ANGLAIS | PAR SUZANNE NÉTILLARD | [series device] | [in red] *nrf* | [in black] GALLIMARD'. Back: 'PATRICK WHITE | [in red] Le Char des élus | [in black] [description, 31 lines] | [in red] *nrf* | [in black] [at bottom right:] 31,10 F (+ t.l.) | 32 F T.L.I.'. Spine: [in red] '*du monde | entier* | [in black] PATRICK | WHITE | [in red] LE CHAR | DES ÉLUS | [in black] [publisher's monogram] | GALLIMARD'. Inside front flap: [biography, 33 lines]. Inside back flap: '*dernières | publications*' | [list of ten titles].

Wraparound of red paper. Front: [in white] 'PRIX NOBEL | de litérature | [in black] 1973'. Back: 'PATRICK WHITE | AVIS A MM. LES LIBRARIES'.

Published in March 1965. Price: 31,10 F.

Copies: NSL: Mitchell Library A823/W587/6D1 (rebound); NSL: Mitchell Library [PW].

H.t2b French First Edition Second Issue (Paris: Gallimard, 1973)

Notes: p.*552 'Cet ouvrage | a été achevé d'imprimer | sur les presses de l'Imprimerie Floch | à May-enne, le 19 novembre 1973. | Dépôt légal : 4ᵉ trimestre 1973. | Nᵒ d'édition : 18512. | Imprimé en France. | (12470) | 18512'*. Perfectbound in white glossy paper card.

Copies: VSL: SLT 819.93 W582RN; NSL: Mitchell Library A823/W587/6D1; NSL: Mitchell Library [PW]; Personal collection.

H.t3 Polish First Edition (Warszawa: Państwowy Instytut Wydawniczy, 1965)

PATRICK | WHITE | WÓZ | OGNISTY | Tom I [II] | Przelożlya Maria Skibniewska | [rule] | PAŃSTWOWY INSTYTUT WYDAWNICZY

19.6 x 12.5 cm. 2v.: (Vol.I:) [1]⁸ 2-18⁸ 19⁶ ($2 signed): 150 leaves; (Vol.II:) [1]⁸ 2-22⁸ 23² ($2 signed): 178 leaves. (Vol.I:) pp.*6* 7-297 *298-300*; (Vol.II:) pp.*4* 5-354 *355-356* (the last page of each chapter is unnumbered).

(Vol.I:) endpaper; *1* [publisher's device] | 'WHITE | WÓZ OGNISTY | * [**]'; *2* blank; *3* title page; *4* 'Tytuł originału | «RIDERS IN THE CHARIOT» | Poslowie HENRYKA KRZECZKOWSKIEGO | Slowniczek wyrazów żydowskich | opracowal | WITOLD TYLOCH | Okładke i obwolutę | projektowala | DANUTE STASZEWSKA | Copyright © 1961 Patrick White'; *5* [epigraph]; *6* blank; 7-297 *298* text; *299* 'Printed in Poland | Państwowy Instytut Wydawniczy, Warszawa 1965r. | Wydanie pierwsze | Nakład 10 000 + 290 egz. Ark. wyd. 15,3. Ark. druk. 18,75 | Papier druk. sat. kl. V, 60g, 82x104 / 32 z Fabryki Papieru w Kluczach | Oddano do składania 5.VIII.1964 r. | Podpisano do druku 6. I. 1965 r. | Druk ukoń-czono w lutym 1965 r. | Łódzka Drukarnia Dzielowa, Łódz, ul. Piotrkowska 86 | Zam. nr 368/A/64. N-10 | Cena t. I/II zł 40.–'*. (Vol.II:) [as for Vol.I except for the following] 5-342 *343* text; 344-351 *352* 'POSLOWIE' [by Henryk Krzeczkowski]; 353-354 *355* 'SLOWNICZEK WYRAZOW ŻYDOWSKICH'; *356* [as for p.*299* in vol.1].

Perfectbound in white paper. Front: 'PATRICK | WHITE | wóz ognisty | I [II]'. Back: 'Cena t. I/II zł 40.–'. Spine: [running down:] 'PATRICK WHITE • WÓZ OGNISTY | [upright:] [publisher's device] | I [II]'. Inside front flap: [double rule] | [biography, 34 lines] | [double rule]. Inside back flap: [double rule] | 'Nakładem Państwowego In- | stytutu Wy-dawniczego ukaza- | ly sie m. in. i sa w sprzeda- | ży nastepujace powieści :' | [list of four titles follows] | [double rule]. [Note: Vol.II has a negative image of the design on the binding of Vol.I].

Published in January 1965. Price: zł 40 per volume. Print run: 10,000.

Copies: NSL: Mitchell Library [PW].

H.t4 Spanish First Edition (Barcelona: Luis de Caralt, 1966)

PATRICK WHITE | EL CARRO | DE LOS | ELEGIDOS | [illust.] | LUIS DE CARALT | EDITOR | BARCELONA

20.4 x 14 cm. [1]⁸ 2-34⁸ ($1 signed): 272 leaves. pp.*9* 10-544.

Endpaper; *1* [series device]; *2* blank; *3* title page; *4* 'Titulo de la obra original: | RIDERS IN THE CHARIOT | Versión española | de | Carlos Puerto | Reservados todos los derechos | © Luis de Caralt, 1966 | Impreso en España | ISBN 84-217-1666-2 | Depósito Legal: B. 31.917 - 1966 N.° Registro: 9394 - 1965 | [rule] | Impreso en LIM - Juan Corrales, 46 - ESPLUGAS | DE LL. (Barna).'; *5* [epigraph]; *6* blank; *7* 'Para Klari Daniel y Ben Huebsch.'; *8* blank; *9* 10-544 text; endpaper.

Cased in red linen with endpapers streaked vertically with green lines. Front: [stamped in gold] [illust. of hand holding torch]. Back: blank. Spine: [in gold on black panel:] 'PATRIK [sic] | WHITE | EL | CARRO | DE LOS | ELEGIDOS | [in gold on red] *Luis* | *de* | *Caralt*'.

Glossy white dustjacket with col. illust. of a man's head against red and yellow background across front and spine. Front: 'PATRICK WHITE | EL | CARRO | DE LOS | ELEGIDOS'. Back: [advertisement for Coleccion Gigante]. Spine: 'PATRICK | WHITE | EL CARRO | DE LOS | ELEGIDOS | CARALT'. Inside front flap: [in blue] 'EL CARRO DE LOS ELEGIDOS' | [blurb, 38 lines] | [biography, 10 lines]. Inside back flap: [in blue] [series device] | [in black] 'LOS MAS SELECTO DE LA | LITERATURE UNIVERSAL | [in blue] <u>EN PREPARACION OBRAS DE</u>' | [list of 12 authors].

Published in October 1966. Price: 200 ptas. ISBN 8 4217 1666 2.

Notes: One of the copies in private hands has variant contents: p.*4* '[…] Puerto | Primera edición Octubre 1966 | Reservados […] España | Depósito Legal : B. 31.917 - 1966 N.° Registro : 9394 - 1965 | [rule] | Imprime : M. Pareja — Montaña, 16 — Barcelona'.

Copies: Personal collections (2 copies); NSL: Mitchell Library [PW].

H.t5 Spanish Second Edition (Barcelona: Orbis, 1985)
El carro de los elegidos.
Notes: pp.463. Translated by Carlos Puerto. Not seen, but referred to in *Index Translationum*.

H.t6 Finnish First Edition (Helsinki: Kustannusosakeyhtiö Otava, 1967)

PATRICK WHITE | Ne jotka | vaunuissa | ajavat I [II] | ROMAANI | Suomentanut Laura Tala | HELSINGISSÄ | KUSTANNUSOSAKEYHTIÖ | OTAVA

21 x 13.2 cm. 2v.: (Vol.I:) [1]⁸ 2-24⁸ 25⁴ ($1 signed): 196 leaves. pp.*9* 10-121 *122-125* 126-262 *263-265* 266-307 *308-311* 312-392; (Vol.II:) [1]⁸ 2-17⁸ 18⁴ ($1 signed): 140 leaves. pp.*7* 8-118 *119-121* 122-237 *238-241* 242-279 *280*.

(Vol.I:) endpaper; *1* 'Ne jotka vaunuissa ajavat I'; *2* blank; *3* title page; *4* 'Englanninkielinen alkuteos | *Riders in the Chariot* | © Patrick White 1961 | Kustannusosakeyhtiö Otava | Keuruu 1967'; *5* [epigraph from] '*William Blake* | (Suomentanut *Tuomas Anhava*)'; *6* blank; *7* 'I OSA'; *8* blank; *9* 10-392 text; endpaper. (Vol.II:) endpaper; *1* 'Ne jotka vaunuissa ajavat II'; *2* blank; *3* title page; *4* 'Englanninkielinen alkuteos | *Riders in the Chariot* | © Patrick White 1961 | Kustannusosakeyhtiö Otavan laakapaino | Helsinki 1967'; *5* 'V OSA'; *6* blank; *7* 8-279 text; *280* blank; endpaper.

Cased in blue cloth with beige endpapers. Front and back: blank. Spine: [running down:] [in white] 'Patrick White Ne jotka vaunuissa ajavat I [II]'.

White paper dustjacket printed in colour with illust. of tree across front, spine and back. Front: [in white] 'NE JOTKA | VAUNUISSA | AJAVAT | PATRICK WHITE | [in black] I [II] OTAVA'. Back: [blurb, 33 lines]. Inside front flap: [blurb continues, 26 lines] | 'OTAVA | *Päällys : Markuu Reunanen*'. Inside back flap: blank.

Copies: NSL: Mitchell Library A823/W587/6F1-2; Personal collection.

H.t7a German First Edition First Issue (Köln and Berlin: Kiepenheuer & Witsch, 1969)

Patrick White | *Die im feurigen Wagen* Roman | Kiepenheuer & Witsch

21 x 12.8 cm. Unsigned: 274 leaves. pp.*10* 11-545 *546-548*.

Endpaper; *1* [publisher's device]; *2* blank; *3* 'Die im feurigen Wagen'; *4* blank; *5* title page; *6* 'Titel der Originalausgabe | RIDERS IN THE CHARIOT | ©1961 by Patrick White | Aus dem Englischen von Curt und Maria Prerauer | Alle deutschsprachigen Rechte | bei Verlag Kiepenheuer & Witsch Köln Berlin | Gesamtherstellung Weiss & Zimmer AG Mönchengladbach | Schutzumschlag und Einband Hannes Jähn Köln | Printed in Germany 1969'; *7* 'Für Klari Daniel | und | Ben Huebsch'; *8* blank; *9* [epigraph]; *10* blank; 11-545 text; *546* blank; *547* 'Zur Uberstezung | [20 lines] | CURT UND MARIA PRERAUER'; *548* 'Von Patrick White erschienen | bei Kiepenheuer & Witsch | *Zur Ruhe kam der Baum* | *des Menschen nie* | Roman. Aus dem Englischen von | Annemarie und Heinrich Böll | *Voss* | Roman. Aus dem Englischen von | John Stickforth'; endpaper.

Cased in blue cloth stained orange on top edge and with light brown endpapers. Front and back: blank. Spine: [in yellow] 'PATRICK | WHITE | [in orange] Die im | feurigen | Wagen'.

White paper dustjacket with purple ground and fiery torch on front. Front: [at left:] 'Die | im | feurigen | Wagen | [at right:] Patrick | White | Roman | k&w'. Back: blank. Spine: 'Patrick | White | Die | im | feurigen | Wagen | k&w'. Inside front flap: [in red] [blurb, 41 lines]. Inside back flap: [in red] [blurb continues, 37 lines] | 'Kiepenheuer & Witsch'.

Print run: 2,200.

Reviews: Christian Ferber *Die Welt. Die Welt der Literatur* 22 May 1969; Gertrud Stolte-Adelt *Welt om Sonntag* 13 July 1969, p.17; Werner Wilk *Der Tagesspiegel* 10 August 1969; Ernestine Weber *Bücherei und Bildung* 21 August 1969, p.676-677; Wilhelm Krüger *General-Anzeiger* 28 August 1969; Helmut M. Braem *Frankfurter Allgemeine Zeitung* 20 September 1969; *Neue Zürcher Zeitung* 21 November 1969, p.85.

Notes: John B. Beston in *Southerly* v.33 no.4, 1973, p.426 claims that White had expressed a marked preference for the Prerauers' translation of *Riders in the Chariot* among the German versions of his novels.

Copies: Personal collection; NSL: Mitchell Library [PW].

H.t7b German First Edition Second Issue (Köln and Berlin: Kiepenheuer & Witsch, n.d.)
Notes: not seen, but referred to by Volker Wolf *Australian Literary Studies* v.11 no.1, 1983, p.108-119. Print run: 6,000.

H.t7c German First Edition Third Issue (Köln and Berlin: Kiepenheuer & Witsch, n.d.)
Notes: not seen, but referred to by Volker Wolf *Australian Literary Studies* v.11 no.1, 1983, p.108-119. Print run: 4,950.

H.t7d German First Edition Buchclub Subedition (Zürich: Buchclub ex Libris, 1973)
Notes: p.*6* 'Ungekürzte Lizenzausgabe für den | Buchclub Ex Libris Zürich 1973 | Titel der Originalausgabe | RIDERS IN THE CHARIOT | © 1961 by Patrick White | Aus dem Englischen von | Curt und Maria Prerauer | Alle deutschsprachigen Rechte | bei Verlag Kiepenheuer & Witsch Köln Berlin | Printed in Germany'. Cased in black linen with white laid endpapers.
Copies: NSL: Mitchell Library A823/W587/47.

H.t7e German First Edition Rowohlt Subedition (Reinbek bei Hamburg: Rowohlt, 1974)
Notes: p.*4 'Die Originalausgabe erschien bei The Viking Press, | New York, unter dem Titel «Riders in the Chariot» | Aus dem Englischen übertragen von* CURT *und* MARIA PRERAUER *| Umschlagentwurf Manfred Waller | Ungekürzte Ausgabe | Veröffentlicht im Rowohlt Taschenbuch Verlag GmbH, | Reinbek bei Hamburg, Januar 1974 | © 1961 by Patrick White | © 1969 by Verlag Kiepenheuer & Witsch, Köln | Gesamtherstellung Clausen & Bosse, Leck/Schleswig | Printed in Germany | ISBN 3 499 11761 4'*. Perfectbound in white textured card printed in black and red. Published in January 1974. Price: DM 8.80. Run: 20,000.
Copies: NSL: Mitchell Library A823/W587/46; NSL: Mitchell Library [PW].

H.t8 Turkish First Edition (Istanbul: Milliyet Yayinlari, 1973)

PATRICK WHITE | [rule] | ARABA ve SÜRÜCÜLERI | [rule] | Türkçesi: | Gülperi CANDAŞ – Ap KESKIN | [publisher's device] | Milliyet | YAYINLARI

19.5 x 11.2 cm. Unsigned: 344 leaves. pp.*8* 9-687 *688*.

1-2 blank; *3* 'ARABA VE SÜRÜCÜLERI'; *4* 'MĪLLĪYET YAYIN LTD. ŞTI. YAYINLARI | Günün Kitaplari Dizisi: 8 | • | Yayin hakki (Copyright): Patrick White –

Milliyet | Yayin Ltd. Şti. | • | Orijinal adi: Riders in the Chariot | • | Grafik düzen: | İsmet N. İslimyeli | • | Birinci baski: Kasim 1973 | Bu Kitap, ÖZAYDIN Matbaasinda dizilip basilmistir'; *5* title page; *6* blank; *7* 'BİRİNCİ BÖLÜM' | [epigraph from] 'William Blake'; *8* blank; 9-687 text; *688* text.

Perfectbound in white paper covers. Front: [publisher's device] 'GÜNÜN KİTAPLARI | ARABA ve | SÜRÜCÜLERI | [in white on red] PATRICK WHITE | [in red on yellow] NOBEL 1973'. Back: [in black on red] 'EN ÇOK SATAN KİTAPLAR | (Best-Seller) | LİSTESİNDEN SEÇMELER | ARABA ve SÜRÜCÜLERI | [in white on red] PATRICK WHITE | [b&w photograph of the author] | [biography, 19 lines] | [at left] 25 Lira'. Spine: [publisher's device] '8 | [running down:] ARABA VE SÜRÜCÜLERI | [in red] • | [in black] PATRICK WHITE'.

Price: 25 Lira.

Copies: NSL: GRL TUR/WHI/2; NSL: Mitchell Library [PW].

H.t9 Turkish Second Edition (Istanbul: Cem Yayinevi, 1973)
Arabadakiler.
Notes: pp.539. Trans. by Murat Belge. Not seen, but referred to in the *Index Translationum.*

H.t10 Italian First Edition (Turin: Einaudi, 1976)

Patrick White | I passaggeri del Carro | Traduzione di Camillo Pennati | Einaudi

21.8 x 13.5 cm. [1]⁸ 2-19¹⁶ 20⁴ ($1 signed): 300 leaves. pp.[*9*] 6-105 *106-109* 110-229 *230-233* 234-271 *272-275* 276-346 *347-349* 350-446 *447-449* 450-552 *553-555* 556-590 *591-596.*

[*1*] blank; [*2*] 'Titre originale *Riders in the Chariot* | Eyre & Spottiswoode, London | Copyright © Patrick White | Copyright © 1976 Giulio Einaudi editore s.p.a., Torino.'; [*3*] title page; [*4*] blank; [*5*] 'I passaggeri del Carro | *A Klari Daniel e Ben Huebsch*'; [*6*] blank; [*7*] 'Parte prima'; [*8*] blank; [*9*] 6-105 *106-109* 110-229 *230-233* 234-271 *272-275* 276-346 *347-349* 350-446 *447-449* 450-552 *553-555* 556-590 text; *591* 'Indice'; *592* blank; *593* [index]; *594* blank; *595* [publisher's device] | '*Finito di stampare il 31 gennaio 1976 per conto della Giulio Einaudi editore s.p.a.* | *presso l'officina Grafica Artigiana U. Panelli in Torino* | C.L. 4457-8'; *596* blank.

Sewn in white paper card. Front: '*PATRICK WHITE* | *I PASSAGGERI DEL CARRO* | [illust.] *EINAUDI*'. Back: [blurb, 27 lines] | [biography, 7 lines] | 'Lire 8000 (7547) | [at right:] [running down:] In copertina una fotografia di Christian Sunde. C.L. 4457-8'. Spine: [running down:] '*WHITE I PASSAGGERI DEL CARRO*' | [at bottom:] [upright:] [publisher's device].

Published in June 1976. Price: Lire 8000.

Copies: Personal collection; NSL: Michell Library [PW].

H.t11 Slovene First Edition (Ljubljana: Cankarjeva Založba, 1974)

PATRICK WHITE | [in brown] Na ognjenem | vozu | [in black] ROMAN | PRVA [DRUGA] KNJIGA

21.3 x 14.2 cm. 2v.: (Vol.I:) [1]^8 2-18^8 19^{10} ($2 signed): 154 leaves. Frontis., pp.*16* 17-125 *126-128* 129-262 *263-264* 265-306 *307-308*; (Vol.II:) [1]^8 2-24^8 ($2 signed): 192 leaves. pp.*7* 8-84 *85-86* 87-194 *195-196* 197-313 *314-316* 317-356 *357-359* 360-379 *380-384*.

(Vol.I:) endpaper; frontis.; *1* [in brown] 'Nobelova | nagrada | za literaturo | 1973' | [signature]; *2* blank; *3-5* 'PATRICK WHITE | je dobil | Nobelovo nagrado | za literaturo'; *6* blank; *7* [publisher's device] | 'CANKARJEVA ZALOŽBA | V LJUBLJANI | 1974'; *8* 'NOBELOVCI | 16 | Ureja | JANKO MODER | Patrick White | NA OGNJENEM VOZU | Prva knjiga | Prevedel in spremno besedo o avtorju napisal | JANKO MODER | Opremila | NADJA FURLAN | Založila | CANKARJEVA ZALOŽBA | V LJUBLJANI | Predstavnik | MILOŠ MIKELN | Natisnila tiskarna | ČGP »DELO« V LJUBLJANI | 1974 | Po mnenju Republiškega sekretariata za prosveto in kulturo SRS (št. 421-1/73 2 dne | 11. XII. 1973) je ta knjiga oproščena temeljnega davka od prometa proizvodov.'; *9* title page; *10* 'Isvirni naslov | RIDERS IN THE CHARIOT | © Patrick White c/o Curtis Brown Ltd. London | Prevedel JANKO MODER'; *11* '*POSCEVENO* | *KLARI DANIEL IN BENU HUEBSCHU*'; *12* blank; *13* [epigraph]; *14* blank; *15* 'PRVI DEL'; *16* blank; 17-125 text of Part I; *126* blank; *127* 'DRUGI DEL'; *128* blank; 129-262 text of Part II; *263* 'TRETJI DEL'; *264* blank; 265-306 text of Part III; *307* 'KAZALO'; *308* 'NOBELOVCI | 15 | Ureja | JANKO MODER | Patrick White | NA OGNJENEM VOZU | Prva knjiga | Prevedel | JANKO MODER | Opremila | NADJA FURLAN | Založila | CANKARJEVA ZALOŽBA | V LJUBLJANI | Predstavnik | MILOS MIKELN | Natisnila tiskarna | MLADINSKA KNJIGA V LJUBLJANI | 1974'; endpaper. (Vol.II:) endpaper; *1* [publisher's device] 'CANKARJEVA ZALOŽBA | V LJUBLJANI | 1974'; *2* 'NOBELOVCI | 16 | UREJA JANKO MODER'; *3* title page; *4* 'Izvirni naslov | RIDERS IN THE CHARIOT | © Patrick White c/o Curtis Brown Ltd. London | PREVEDEL JANKO MODER'; *5* 'CETRTI DEL'; *6* blank; *7* 8-356 text; *357* 'SPREMNA BESEDA | O AVTORJU'; *358* blank; *359* 360-379 [text of 'Spremna ...' by Janko Moder]; *380* blank; *381* 'WHITE PRI NAS'; *382* blank; *383* 'KAZALO'; *384* 'NOBELOVCI 16 | Ureja | JANKO MODER | Patrick White | NA OGNJENEM VOZU | Druga knjiga | Prevedel in spremno besedo o avtorju napisal | JANKO MODER | Opremila | NADJA FURLAN | založila | CANKARJEVA ZALOŽBA | V LJUBLJANI | Predstavnik | MILOŠS MIKELN | natisnila tiskarna | ČGP »DELO« V LJUBLJANI | 1974 | Po mnenju Republiškega sekretariata za prosveto in kulturo SRS (št 421-1/73 z dne | 11. XII. 1973) je ta knjiga oproščena temeljnega davka od prometa proizvodov.'; endpaper.

Cased in white bone vinyl with white endpapers. Front: [in gold] 'patrick white' | [signature of the author] | [design in gold incorporating a display W]. Back: [in gold] 'cankarjeva založba'. Spine: [running down:] [in gold] 'white'.

Copies: NSL: Mitchell Library [PW]; NSL: Mitchell Library A823/W587/32 and 32A.

H.t12 Hebrew First Edition (Tel Aviv: Zmora, Bitan, Modan, 1980)

21.8 x 14 cm. 2v.: (Vol.I:) Unsigned: 120 leaves. pp.*10* 11-96 *97-98* 99-201 *202-204* 205-237 *238-240*. (Vol.II:) Unsigned: 138 leaves. pp.[*6*] 241-300 *301-302* 303-384 *385-386* 387-477 *478-480* 481-510.

Notes: (Vol.I:) p.*4* 'RIDERS IN THE CHARIOT | by Partick [sic] White | Copyright © Patrick White, 1961 | © Hebrew Rights by | Zmora, Bitan, Modan — Publishers | P.O.B. 22383, Tel-Aviv | Printed in Israel, 1980'. Cased in glossy paper printed with four figures on front against grey ground.

Copies: NSL: Mitchell Library [PW].

H.m1 Braille First Edition (Burwood: Royal Blind Society of New South Wales, [n.d.])

Riders in the Chariot (12 volumes of Interpoint Braille).

Not seen, but referred to on the National Bibliographic Database.

H.m2 Braille Second Edition (Millswood: Braille Writing Association of South Australia, 1965)

Riders in the Chariot (16 volumes of Interline Braille).

H.m3 Sound Recording (Melbourne: Royal Victorian Institute for the Blind, Tertiary Resource Service, 1983)

Riders in the Chariot (4 audiocasettes, 4-track).

Read by Kathleen Baker from the Penguin edition of 1974.

H.m4 Sound Recording (Hove, South Australia: Visiting Teacher Service for Visually Impaired Children, 1987)

Riders in the Chariot (14 audiocasettes).

Read by Jack Higham from the U.K. First Edition.

H.m5 Sound Recording (Auckland: Royal New Zealand Foundation for the Blind, [198-?])

Riders in the Chariot (4 audiocassettes, 1204 min., 4-track).

I   The Burnt Ones (1964)

The earliest stories in this collection were written in 1962. Patrick White's motives for writing the stories were mixed. Certainly, at this time, he claimed: 'I am better able at the moment to work off my feelings in short stories ... I hadn't written one for about twenty years when I suddenly put 'Willy Wagtails' on paper'. (To the Duttons, 18 January 1962) Later in life White thought, 'most of my stories were written while travelling when I couldn't settle down to anything longer'. (To Hu Wenzhong, 13 March 1982) Another factor was that White had hit an impasse with *A Fringe of Leaves*.

Although some of the stories date from early 1962 it is not clear that White envisaged a collection at this time. However, he was certainly thinking of a collection a year later when he wrote to Geoffrey Dutton: 'I have a novella which will probably work out long enough for me to offer a volume of short things to Eyre & Spottiswoode'. (17 March 1963)

The novella was 'Dead Roses' which used material gathered at a 1962 Christmas house party at the Duttons' property on Kangaroo Island (S.A.). White was still re-writing 'Dead Roses' at the end of 1963. 'An Evening at Sissy Kamara's' was also written in 1963, especially for the collection. The other stories were written in 1962 and published throughout 1962 and early 1963 in a variety of literary magazines in both Australia (*Meanjin*, *Quadrant*, *Overland*, *Australian Letters*) and England (*London Magazine*). White also tackled the lucrative American magazine market with 'Miss Slattery and Her Demon Lover' and 'Being Kind to Titina'. The latter was accepted by *Harper's Bazaar* for a payment of $300. 'Miss Slattery' was hawked around, but, as White later wrote to Ben Huebsch, 'I think 'Miss Slattery' must have been turned down by almost every magazine in America'. (18 March 1964) The attempt on American magazines came to nothing when White arrived back from Kangaroo Island late in 1962 'to find *Harper's* proof of 'Being Kind to Titina' waiting for me. I started to correct and was shocked to find the guts had been cut out of it'. (To Eadith Haggard, 1 January 1963) White immediately pulled his story – it was later published in *Meanjin* for March 1962 – and returned the $300. 'Miss Slattery' was also withdrawn – it was then with the *New Yorker*. As far as White was concerned, the American magazine market – 'the reader of American magazines was a particular kind of moron' – was not worth bothering about.

The title of the collection, as explained by White to Ben Huebsch (16 December 1963), was a literal translation of the common Greek expression 'OI KAYMENOI' (= 'the poor unfortunates'). 'It is an expression of formal pity.'

By January 1964 the final draft of each of the stories was complete. The whole was then uniformly typed and submitted to Eyre & Spottiswoode and The Viking Press. By April both publishers had accepted, and White had finished marking the proofs by July. He was obviously quite sick of editorial interference and wrote to Marshall Best: 'I refuse to pander to the American reader'. (3 July 1964) *The Burnt Ones* was published in both London and New York in November 1964. The American reviews were good. However, magazine editors had defined White as a 'literary author' and so did not give prominence to the reviews. The English reviews were also good, 'except for a stinker in the *Sunday Times* and a very destructive one from Naipaul in the *Spectator*'. (To Peggy Garland, 25 October 1964) Sales in the United Kingdom and Australia were good; even though they were late arriving – 'The whole Sydney stock … sold out within twenty-four hours.' (To Marshall Best, 17 January 1965) – but in the United States it was a disaster. Only 1,700 copies were sold.

The Viking Press edition was again a high quality production. The jacket depicted a stylised sunburst on the front, designed by James and Ruth McCrea. The Eyre & Spottiswoode edition had a jacket with four painted portraits by Sidney Nolan. 'Yes, I think the jacket is marvellous in itself, but I can't feel it has a great connexion with the contents of the book. Still, it is so arresting I am sure it will sell a great many copies'. (To the Duttons, 18 November 1964) Both the London and New York jackets had on the back Axel Poignant's photograph of White in a sports jacket and Nolan's 'Galaxy' on the wall in the background.

Many of the stories in *The Burnt Ones* were republished in various forms. For example, there were several translations of both the collection and individual stories. White himself rewrote 'A Cheery Soul' as a playscript, and he thought 'Miss Slattery and Her Demon Lover' and 'Dead Roses' had potential as films. There was a Norwegian radio version of 'Willy Wagtails at Midnight' (To Elizabeth Harrower, 1 July 1976), and White was bemused by a request from Czech radio for permission to do 'Dead Roses' as a serial. (To the Duttons, 3 February 1968) The publishing histories of White's short stories are treated in Appendix 3 below.

* * * * *

I1a U.S. First Edition (New York: Viking, 1964)

The Burnt Ones | [swelled rule] | by Patrick White | *New York · The Viking Press*

21 x 14 cm. Unsigned: 160 leaves. pp.[*10*] *1-2* 3-79 *80* 81-125 *126* 127-143 *144* 145-275 *276* 277-308 *309-310*.

Endpaper; [*1*] 'The Burnt Ones'; [*2*] '*By the Same Author* | Riders in the Chariot | Voss | The Tree of Man | The Aunt's Story | The Living and the Dead | Happy Valley'; [*3*] title page; [*4*] 'Copyright © 1964 by Patrick White | All rights reserved | First published in 1964 by The Viking Press, Inc. | 625 Madison Avenue, New York, N.Y. 10022 | Published simultaneously in Canada by | The Macmillan Company of Canada Limited | Library of Congress catalog card number: 64-20679 | Printed in U.S.A. by The Colonial Press Inc. | [at bottom:] ACKNOWLEDGEMENTS | Thanks to the following magazines in which stories have appeared: | *Australian Letters* for "Willy-wagtails by Moonlight," "Miss Slat- | tery and Her Demon Lover," and "The Woman Who Wasn't Al- | lowed to Keep Cats"; *Overland* for "Clay"; *Quadrant* for "The | Letters"; *Meanjin* for "Being Kind to Titina" and "Down at the | Dump"; *The London Magazine* for "A Cheery Soul," "Clay," "The | Evening at Sissy Kamara's," and "Miss Slattery and Her Demon | Lover." [at right:] —P.W.'; [*5*] '*For Nin and Geoffrey Dutton*'; [*6*] blank; [*7*] '*oi kaumevoi...* | the burnt ones | (the poor unfortunates)'; [*8*] blank; [*9*] 'Contents'; [*10*] blank; *1* 'The Burnt Ones'; *2* blank; 3-66 text of 'Dead Roses'; 67-79 text of 'Willy-wagtails by Moonlight'; *80* blank; 81-104 text of 'A Glass of Tea'; 105-125 text of 'Clay'; *126* blank; 127-143 text of 'The Evening at Sissy Kamara's'; *144* blank; 145-180 text of 'A Cheery Soul'; 181-198 text of 'Being Kind to Titina'; 199-216 text of 'Miss Slattery and Her Demon Lover'; 217-232 text of 'The Letters'; 233-275 text of 'The Woman Who Wasn't Allowed to Keep Cats'; *276* blank; 277-308 text of 'Down at the Dump'; *309-310* blank; endpaper.

Cased in black paper-covered boards with spine in brown calico, top edge in red and with white endpapers. Front and back: blank. Spine: [in gold] 'The | Burnt | Ones | [rule] | Patrick | White | [at bottom:] VIKING'.

White paper dustjacket printed in three colours with illust. of stylised sunburst across front and spine. Front: 'THE | BURNT ONES | [at bottom:] BY | PATRICK WHITE'. Back: [b&w photograph of the author] | [in ochre] 'PATRICK WHITE | [in black] [quotation of three lines from] —ORVILLE PRESCOTT, *New York Times* | [quotation of three lines from] — ANGUS WILSON, *The Observer* (London) | [quotation of four lines from] —JOHN K. HUTCHENS, *New York Herald Tribune* | [quotation of two lines from] —A.J. BEELER, *Louisville Courier Journal* | [quotation of five lines from] —TED HUGHES, *The Listener* | THE VIKING PRESS · PUBLISHERS · NEW YORK'. Spine: 'THE | BURNT | ONES | [in white] PATRICK | WHITE | VIKING'. Inside front flap: [in ochre] '$4.95 | [in black] The Burnt Ones | [in ochre] By Patrick White | [blurb, 37 lines] | (Continued on back flap)'. Inside back flap: [in ochre] '(Continued from front flap) | [in black] [blurb continues, 14 lines] | [in ochre] PATRICK WHITE | [in black] [biography, 20 lines] | [in ochre] THE VIKING PRESS | *Publishers of the Viking Portable Library* | 625 Madison Ave., New York, N.Y. 10022 | [in black] PRINTED IN U.S.A. | JACKET DESIGNED BY JAMES AND RUTH MCCREA | PHOTOGRAPH OF PATRICK WHITE BY AXEL POIGNANT'.

Published in November 1964. Price: $4.95.

Reviews: Charles Higham *Bulletin* 12 December 1964; *Sewanee Review* v.73, Autumn 1965, p.736; *World Literature Today* v.39, Spring 1965, p.220.

Notes: In White's collection there is a presentation copy half bound in red leather and marbled paper boards.

Copies: NSL: Mitchell Library [PW]; Personal collection.

I1b Canadian Subedition (Toronto: Macmillan, 1964)
Notes: not seen, but assumed from statement on p.[*4*] of U.S. First Edition (see I1a above). Price: $6.25.

I2 U.K. First Edition (London: Eyre & Spottiswoode, 1964)

The Burnt Ones | [ornament] | Patrick White | EYRE & SPOTTISWOODE

20.3 x 13.4 cm. [A]^8 B-S^8 T^6 U^8 ($1 signed; T$_2$ signed 'T*'): 158 leaves. pp.*11* 12-314 *315-316* (the first page of each story is unnumbered).

Endpaper; *1* 'The Burnt Ones | [ornament] | This is the first collection of Patrick White's | stories to be published. It contains eleven | stories written since his last novel, | *Riders in the Chariot*.'; *2* blank; *3* title page; *4* '*First published in* 1964 | © *Patrick White*, 1964 | *Printed in Great Britain for* | *Eyre & Spottiswoode (Publishers) Ltd* | *by the Shenval Press* | *London, Hertford and Harlow*'; *5* 'OI KAYMENOI ... | the burnt ones (the poor unfortunates)'; *6* blank; *7* 'For Nin and Geoffrey Dutton'; *8* '*Acknowledgments* | My thanks to the following magazines in which stories | have appeared: 'Australian Letters' for *Willy-Wagtails* | *by Moonlight, Miss Slattery and her Demon Lover*, and | *The Woman who wasn't Allowed to Keep Cats*; 'Overland' | for *Clay*; 'Quadrant' for *The Letters*; 'Meanjin' for *Being* | *Kind to Titina* and *Down at the Dump*; 'The London | Magazine' for *A Cheery Soul, Clay, The Evening at Sissy | Kamara's*, and *Miss Slattery and Her Demon Lover*.| P. W.'; *9* '*Contents*'; *10* blank; *11* 12-314 text; *315* blank; *316* blank; endpaper.

Cased in black linen with white endpapers. Front and back: blank. Spine: [in gold] 'THE | BURNT | ONES | [ornament] | Patrick | White | E & S'.

Glossy white paper dustjacket. Front: 'The Burnt Ones | PATRICK WHITE' | [col. illust. of four painted portraits]. Back: [b&w photograph of the author] | 'PATRICK WHITE | Photograph by Axel Poignant'. Spine: 'PATRICK | WHITE | [running down:] The Burnt Ones | [upright:] E & S'. Inside front flap: [blurb, 39 lines] | '*The four paintings on the jacket are by* | *Sidney Nolan* | [at bottom right:] PRICE IN ...' [price clipped]. Inside back flap: 'Novels by | PATRICK WHITE | Riders in the Chariot | Voss | The Tree of Man | The Aunt's Story | The Living and the Dead | [at bottom:] PRINTED IN GREAT BRITAIN'.

Published 1 October 1964. Price: 25s. Remained in print until 1973.

Reviews: H. Kippax *Sydney Morning Herald* 24 October 1964, p.17; *Age* (Melbourne) 21 November 1964, Literary Supplement p.40; Jack Lindsay *Meanjin* v.22 no.4, 1964, p.372-376.

Notes: Advance copies have been seen in a private collection and at ADFA. They are sewn in a plain brown wrapper. Front: 'THE BURNT ONES | BY | PATRICK WHITE | ADVANCE COPY | Number of pages: 314 | Size of book: Large Crown 8vo | To be published: September 10, 1964 | Approximate price: 25 shillings | EYRE & SPOTTISWOODE | 22 HENRIETTA STREET • WC2'. One of these was bought for $150.

Copies: Personal collection; NU: RB IMP 007305; NSL: Mitchell Library A823/W587/8A1 (lacks dustjacket).

I3a Penguin Edition First Issue (Harmondsworth: Penguin, 1968)

Patrick White | The Burnt Ones | Penguin Books | in association with | Eyre & Spottiswoode

18.1 x 11.2 cm. [1]^{10} 2-16^{10} ($1 signed): 160 leaves. pp.*11* 12-76 *77* 78-89 *90* 91-113 *114* 115-135 *136* 137-152 *153* 154-189 *190* 191-207 *208* 209-225 *226* 227-241 *242* 243-284 *285* 286-316 *317-320*.

1 'Penguin Books 2776 | The Burnt Ones' | [biography, 24 lines] | [publisher's device]; *2* blank; *3* title page; *4* 'Penguin Books Ltd, Harmondsworth, | Middlesex, England | Penguin Books Australia Ltd, Ringwood, | Victoria, Australia | First published by Eyre & Spottiswoode 1964 | Published in Penguin Books 1968 | Copyright © Patrick White, 1964 | Made and printed in Great Britain by | Hazell Watson & Viney Ltd, | Aylesbury, Bucks | Set in Linotype Times' | [publisher's conditions, 8 lines]; *5* 'For Nin and Geoffrey Dutton'; *6* blank; *7* 'Contents'; *8* 'OI KAYMENOI ... | the burnt ones (the poor unfortunates)'; *9* 'Acknowledgements'; *10* blank; *11* 12-316 text; *317* 'More about Penguins'; *318* blank; *319* 'Riders in the Chariot | Patrick White | [19 lines] | *Also available* | The Aunt's Story | Not for sale in the U.S.A. or Canada'; *320* 'Patrick White in Penguins | Voss | [16 lines] | The Tree of Man | [14 lines] | Not for sale in the U.S.A. or Canada'.

Perfectbound in white paper printed in colour. Front: [publisher's device] [in orange] 'A PENGUIN BOOK | [in black] PATRICK WHITE | [in orange] THE BURNT ONES' | [illust. in black ink and yellow-brown wash]. Back: [in white on orange] [blurb, 22 lines] | 'Cover design by Jack Larkin | [in black] For copyright reasons this edition is not for sale in | the U.S.A. or Canada | United Kingdom 7/6 | Australia $1.30 | New Zealand $1.00 | South Africa R1.00'. Spine: [running down:] [in white on orange] Patrick White [in black on orange] The Burnt Ones | [upright:] [publisher's device] | 2776'.

Copies: NSL: Mitchell Libray A823/W587/8B1 (rebound so lacks original spine); NSL: Mitchell Library [PW]; VU: McL L/A-F White; VU: Ducker A823.3 White; Personal collection.

I3b Penguin Edition Australian Issue (Harmondsworth: Penguin, 1972)

Notes: p.*4* 'Published in Penguin Books 1968 | Reprinted 1972 | Copyright © Patrick White, 1964 | Made and printed in Australia at | The Dominion Press | North Blackburn, Victoria | Set in Linotype Times'. Perfectbound in white paper printed in orange and black. Cover design by Jack Larkin. Price: AU$1.50.

I3c Penguin Edition Second Issue (Harmondsworth: Penguin, 1974)
Not seen.

I3d Penguin Edition Third Issue (Harmondsworth: Penguin, 1975)
Notes: p.*4* 'Published in Penguin Books 1968 | Reprinted 1974, 1975 | Copyright © Patrick White, 1964 | Made and printed in Great Britain by | Hazell Watson & Viney Ltd, | Aylesbury, Bucks | Set in Linotype Times'. Perfectbound in white paper printed in orange and black. Cover design by Jack Larkin. Price: 75p, NZ$2.55. ISBN 0 14 | 00.2776 9.

I3e Penguin Edition Fourth Issue (Harmondsworth: Penguin, 1977)
Not seen.

I3f Penguin Edition Fifth Issue (Harmondsworth: Penguin, 1979)
Notes: p.*4* 'Published in Penguin Books 1968 | Reprinted 1974, 1975, 1977, 1979 | Copyright © Patrick White, 1964 | Made and printed in Great Britain by | Hazell Watson & Viney Ltd, | Aylesbury, Bucks | Set in Linotype Times'. Perfectbound in white paper printed in colour. Cover design by Jack Larkin. Price: £1.25, AU$3.95. ISBN 0 1400 2776 9.

I3g Penguin Edition Sixth Issue (Harmondsworth: Penguin, 1984)
Notes: 19.7 x 12.9 cm. Page *4* 'Published in Penguin Books 1968 | Reprinted 1974, 1975, 1977, 1979, 1984 | [...] Made and printed in Great Britain by | Hazell Watson & Viney Limited, | Member of the BPCC Group, | Aylesbury, Bucks | Set in Linotype Times'. Perfectbound in white glossy paper card. Cover design by Neil Stuart. Cover illustration (man with hair in flames) by Mel Odom. Price: £2.95, AU$[...], NZ$9.95, CAN $8.95, US$6.95. ISBN 0-14-002776-9.

I3h Penguin Edition Seventh Issue (Harmondsworth: Penguin, n.d.)
Notes: not seen, but assumed on the basis of I3i below.

I3i Penguin Edition Eighth Issue (Harmondsworth: Penguin, [1990])
Notes: 19.7 x 12.9 cm. Page *4* 'Published in Penguin Books 1968 | 10 9 8'. Cover design by Neil Stuart. Cover illustration (man with hair in flames) by Mel Odom. Price: £6.99, NZ$27.95, CAN$13.99.

I.t1 French First Edition (Paris: Gallimard, 1969)

PATRICK WHITE | Les échaudés | TRADUIT DE L'ANGLAIS | PAR YVONNE GUILLOUX | *nrf* | GALLIMARD

19.9 x 14.1 cm. 1-11^{16} 12^{12} 13^{16} ($1 signed; 12$_3$ is signed '12*'): 204 leaves. pp.*11* 12-89 *90-93* 94-107 *108-111* 112-138 *139-141* 142-165 *166-169* 170-188 *189-191* 192-233 *234-237* 238-257 *258-261* 262-281 *282-285* 286-303 *304-307* 308-357 *358-361* 362-400 *401-408*.

1-2 blank; *3* 'DU MONDE ENTIER'; *4* blank; *5* title page; *6* '*Il a été tiré de cet ouvrage vingt-six exemplaires | sur vélin pur fil Lafuma-Navarre numérotés de 1 à 26. | Titre original :* | THE BURNT ONES | *Tous droits de traduction, de reproduction et d'adaptation | réservés pour tous les pays, y compris l'U.R.S.S.* | © *Patrick White, 1964.* | © *Éditions Gallimard, 1969, pour la traduction française.*'; *7* '*A Nin et Geoffrey Dutton*'; *8* blank; *9* '*Roses fanées*'; *10* blank; *11* 12-89 text; *90* blank; *91* '*Hochequeues au clair de lune*'; *92* blank; *93* 94-107 text; *108* blank; *109* '*Un verre de thé*'; *110* blank; *111* 112-138 text; *139* '*Clay*'; *140* blank; *141* 142-165 text; *166* blank; *167* '*La soirée chez Sissy Kamara*'; *168* blank; *169* 170-188 text; *189* '*Une joyeuse créature*'; *190* blank; *191* 192-233 text; *234* blank; *235* '*Il faut être gentil avec Titina…*'; *236* blank; *237* 238-257 text; *258* blank; *259* '*Miss Slattery et son diable d'amant*'; *260* blank; *261* 262-281 text; *282* blank; *283* '*Les lettres*'; *284* blank; *285* 286-303 text; *304* blank; *305* '*La femme qui n'avait pas le droit | d'avoir des chats*'; *306* blank; *307* 308-357 text; *358* blank; *359* '*A la décharge*'; *360* blank; *361* 362-400 text; *401* [list of contents]; *402* blank; *403* 'DU MÊME AUTEUR | *nrf* | EDEN-VILLE | LE CHAR DES ÉLUS | VOSS'; *404* blank; *405* 'ACHEVÉ D'IMPRIMER LE | 20 MARS 1969 SUR LES | PRESSES DE L'IMPRIMERIE | BUSSIÈRE, SAINT-AMAND (CHER) | – N° d'édit. 14151. – N° d'imp. 148. – | Dépôt légal : Ier trimestre 1969. | *Imprimé en France*'; *406-408* blank.

Sewn in glossy white card. Front: 'DU MONDE ENTIER | PATRICK WHITE | [in red] LES ÉCHAUDÉS | [in black] NOUVELLES | TRADUITES DE L'ANGLAIS | PAR YVONNE GUILLOUX | [series device] | [in red] *nrf* | [in black] GALLIMARD'. Back: 'PATRICK WHITE | [in red] LES ÉCHAUDÉS | [in black] [blurb, 22 lines] | [in red] *nrf* | [in black] [at left:] HSC/26/10 | 69-IV | [at right:] 27 F'. Spine: [in red] '*du monde | entier* | [in black] PATRICK | WHITE | [in red] LES | ÉCHAUDÉS | [in black] *nrf* | GALLIMARD'. Inside front flap: [b&w photograph of the author] | [biography, 15 lines]. Inside back flap: '*dernières | publications*' | [list of twelve titles].

Notes: One copy in a personal collection is 'EXEMPLAIRE 2'. It has a glassine wrapper, is uncut and has a variant binding. Sewn in wove paper wrappers. 21.5 x 15 cm. Front: 'DU MONDE ENTIER | [in red] DLI | [in black] PATRICK WHITE | [in red] LES ÉCHAUDÉS | [in black] NOUVELLES | TRADUITES DE L'ANGLAIS | PAR YVONNE GUILLOUX | [series device] | [in red] *nrf* | [in black] GALLIMARD'. Back: [in red] '*nrf* | [at bottom right:] [in black] PUR FIL'. Spine: [in red] '*du monde | entier* | [in black] PATRICK | WHITE | [in red] LES | ÉCHAUDÉS | [in black] *nrf* | GALLIMARD'. Inside front and back flaps: blank.

Published in April 1969. Price: 27 FF (trade ed.), 81 FF (limited ed.).

Copies: VSL: SLT 819.93 W582BG; Personal collection (3 copies); NSL: Mitchell Library A823/W587/8C1 (rebound); ADFA (Copy no.21).

I.t2a Japanese Edition First Issue 'A Cheery Soul', 'Willy-wagtails by Moonlight' and 'Down at the Dump' (Tokyo: Kenkyusha, 1973)

[in black letter] <u>Kenkyusha Pocket English Series</u> | A CHEERY SOUL | & OTHER STORIES | *by* | PATRICK WHITE | *Edited, with Notes, by* | MIKIO HIRAMATSU | [publisher's device] | KENKYUSHA | TOKYO

17.2 x 11.5 cm. Unsigned: 89 leaves. Frontis., pp.*ii* iii-ix *x-xii* 1-160 *161-166*.

Notes: p.*ii* 'A CHEERY SOUL | WILLY-WAGTAILS BY MOONLIGHT | DOWN AT THE DUMP | from *The Burnt Ones* by PATRICK WHITE | published by EYRE & SPOTTISWOODE LTD., 1964 | By arrangement with MESSRS. CURTIS BROWN LTD., London | this edition of *A Cheery Soul & Other Stories* | is published for sale and distribution in Japan'. Perfectbound in pale green wrappers. White and green paper dustjacket. Price: ¥410.

Copies: NSL: Mitchell Library 823.914/W587/11 (lacks dustjacket); NSL: Mitchell Library A823/W587/23 (lacks dustjacket); NSL: Mitchell Library [PW].

I.t2b Japanese Edition Second Issue 'A Cheery Soul', 'Willy-wagtails by Moonlight' and 'Down at the Dump' (Tokyo: Kenkyusha, 1982)

Notes: p.*x* 'FOREWORD' [dated 1982]. Perfectbound in pale green wrappers. White and green paper dustjacket.

Copies: Private collection; NSL: Mitchell Library 823.914/W587/54 (lacks dustjacket).

I.t3 Danish First Edition (n.p.: Brøndums Forlag, 1974)

PATRICK WHITE | Kvinden der ikke måtte holde katte | og andre noveller | På dansk ved Mogens Boisen | BRØNDUMS FORLAG 1974

16.7 x 11.7 cm. Unsigned: 108 leaves. pp.*6* 7-9 *10-14* 15-112 *113-118* 119-143 *144-148* 149-210 *211-216*.

1-2 blank; *3* title page; *4* blank; *5* woodcut; *6* blank; 7-9 'PATRICK WHITE'; *10* blank; *11* 'VISNE ROSER'; *12* blank; *13* woodcut; *14* blank; 15-112 *113* text of 'Visne Roser'; *114* blank; *115* 'MISS SLATTERY | OG | HENDES DÆMONISKE ELSKER'; *116* blank; *117* woodcut; *118* blank; 119-143 *144* text of 'Miss Slattery ...'; *145* 'KVINDEN DER IKKE MÅTTE HOLDE KATTE'; *146* blank; *147* woodcut; *148* blank; 149-210 *211* text of 'Kvinden der ikke ...'; *212* blank; *213* 'KVINDEN DER IKKE MÅTTE HOLDE KATTE, med origi- | nalgrafik af Dan Sterup-Hansen, er trykt i 2000 eksemplarer, | hvoraf 1000 eksemplarer − forbeholdt Brøndums forlags abonnementsserie − er nummereret og signeret af kunstne- | ren. Teksten er trykt af Lennart Åkerlund og litografierne | af Hans Jørgen Brøndum. | Bogbind: Jørgen Larsen, Roskilde. Typografi: Bendt Kirke- | berg. | De tre noveller er overstat efter DEAD ROSES, MISS | SLATTERY AND HER DEMON LOVER og THE WOMAN | WHO WASN'T ALLOWED TO KEEP CATS fra novellesam- | lingen THE BURNT ONES, 1964. | © Copyright Brøndums forlag 1974.'; *214-216* blank.

Sewn in white paper card. Front, back and spine: blank.

Brown kraft paper. Front: [in olive green] [woodcut] | 'PATRICK WHITE | noveller'. Back: blank. Spine: [in olive green] [running down:] 'PATRICK WHITE | Kvinden der ikke måtte holde katte   og andre noveller   Brøndums forlag'.

Print run: 2,000.

Copies: NSL: Mitchell Library A823/W587/36.

I.t4 German Edition 'Down at the Dump' (Stuttgart: Philipp Reclam Jun., 1975)

PATRICK WHITE | Down at the Dump | Drunten auf der Müllkippe | ENGLISCH UND DEUTSCH | ÜBERSETZT UND MIT EINEM NACHWORT | VON HILARY HELTAY | HERAUSGEGEBEN VON WALTER PACHE | PHILIPP RECLAM JUN. STUTTGART

pp.*3* 4-81 *82* 83-99 *100* 101-103 *104*.

1 title page; *2* 'Der englische Text folgt der Ausgabe: Patrick White, The | Burnt Ones. Eyre & Spottiswoode, London 1964. | [at bottom:] Universel-Bibliothek Nr. 9808 | © 1964 by Patrick White. Deutschsprachige Rechte bei Philipp | Reclam jun. Stuttgart. © Philipp Reclam jun. Stuttgart 1975. | Schrift: Linotype Garamond-Antiqua. Printed in Germany 1975. | Herstellung: Reclam Stuttgart | ISBN 3-15-009808-4'; *3* 'Down at the Dump | Drunten auf der Müllkippe'; 4-81 text; *82* blank; 83-99 'Nachwort' [by Hilary Heltay]; *100* blank; 101-102 'Anmerkungen'; 103 'Literaturhinweise'; *104* 'Zweisprachige Ausgaben | IN RECLAMS UNIVERSAL-BIBLIOTHEK' | [list of nine titles].

Perfectbound in orange paper. Front: 'Patrick White | [rule] | Down at the Dump | Drunten | auf der Müllkippe | English/Deutsch | [rule] | Reclam'. Back: [at bottom:] [rule] | 'Universal-Bibliothek'. Spine: [running down:] 'White Down at the Dump · Drunten auf der Müllkippe 9808'.

Copies: Personal collection; NSL: Mitchell Library A823/W587/49.

I.t5 Spanish First Edition (Barcelona: Biblioteca Universal Caralt, 1976)

Patrick White | LOS CALCINADOS | [rule]

18 x 11.5 cm. [1]^8 2-20^8 χ1 ($1 signed): 161 leaves. pp.*6* 7-318 *319-322*.

1 [publisher's device] | [rule] | 'BIBLIOTECA UNIVERSAL CARALT'; *2* 'SERIE NOVELA'; *3* title page; *4* 'Primera edición : febrero de 1976 | RESERVADOS TODOS LOS DERECHOS | Titulo original : The Burnt Ones | Traducción : Domingo Manfredi Cano | Diseño cubierta : Balaguer | ISBN 84-217-4147-0 | N.° de registro : 11.603-74 | Depósito legal : B-48.375-1975 | © Patrick White, 1964 | © Luis de Caralt Editor S.A., Rosellón 246, Barcelona, 1976 | para la publicatión en lengua española | Impreso en España – Printed in Spain | Chimenos, S.A., Granollers (Barcelona)'; *5* '*Dedico este libro a* | *Nin y Geoffrey Dutton*'; *6* 'οι χαιμενοι ... | los calcinados | (los pobres desafortunados)'; 7-72 'ROSAS MUERTAS'; 73-85 'ESCUCHANDO PÁJAROS A LA LUZ DE LA LUNA'; 86-109 'UNA TAZA DE TÉ'; 110-131 'CLAY'; 132-149 'UNA VELADA CON SISSY KAMARA'; 150-187 'UN ALMA JUBILOSA'; 188-205 'SIENDO AMABLE CON TITINA'; 206-223 'MISS SLATTERY Y SU DEMONIO'; 224-240 'LAS CARTAS'; 241-284 'LA MUJER A QUIEN NO SE PERMITIA TENER GATOS'; 285-318 'ALLÁ EL VIEJO ALACÉN'; *319* 'INDICE'; *320* blank; *321-322* 'BIBLIOTECA UNIVERSAL CARALT'.

Perfectbound in white card printed in colour on front and back. Front: [background of burnt trees] 'PATRICK | WHITE | los | calcinados' | [at bottom right:] [publisher's device]. Back: [blurb, 7 lines] | [col. illust. of burnt trees] | [blurb continues, 22 lines] | 'T.G. Soler – Esplugas (Barna.)'. Spine: [publisher's device] | [running down:] 'LOS CALCINADOS | [device] Patrick White | [upright:] [at bottom:] 42 | CARALT'. Inside front cover: [inside box of three rules:] [publisher's device] | 'BIBLIOTECA UNIVERSAL CARALT' | [series blurb, 21 lines]. Inside back cover: [inside box:] 'En el lomo de los volúmenes | [publisher's device] | un simbolo identifica | la diversas series.'.

Published in February 1976.

Copies: Personal collection.

I.t6 Arabic Edition 'Clay' (1979)

[published in: *Foreign Literature* vol.6 no.1, July 1979]

20.6 x 16.1 cm. pp.*4* 5-238 *239-240*.

Notes: 'Clay'. Perfectbound and printed in red, green, light and dark blue.

Copies: NSL: Mitchell Library [PW].

I.t7 Chinese Edition 'Dead Roses' and 'The Letters' (1982)

[published in: *Shijie Wenxue* no.3, 1982]

20.3 x 14 cm. pp.*3* 4-320.

Notes: 'Dead Roses' and 'The Letters'. Perfectbound and printed in yellow and black. On p.319 is the following colophon: 'WORLD LITERATURE (BI-MONTHLY) | No.3, 1982'. Translator: Hu Wen-chung.

Copies: NSL: Mitchell Library [PW].

I.t8 Hungarian Edition 'Clay' and 'A Glass of Tea' (Budapest: Európa Könyvkiadó, 1988)

Jelzötüz | az éjszakában | XX. SZÁZADI | AUSZTRÁL | ELBESZÉLÖK | EURÓPA KÖNYVKIADÓ | BUDAPEST 1988

18.5 x 12.8 cm. Unsigned: 214 leaves. pp.*4* 5-418 *419-428* (the last page of each story is unnumbered).

Endpaper; *1* 'Jelzötüz | az éjszakában | XX. SZÁZADI | AUSZTRÁL | ELBESZÉLÖK'; *2* 'PUBLICATION SUBSIDISED | BY THE LITERARY ARTS BOARD | OF THE AUSTRALIAN COUNCIL'; *3* title page; *4* 'AUTHORS' COPYRIGHT © AUSTRALIAN ART COUNCIL | LITERATURE BOARD | EDITOR © KARIG SÁRA, 1988'; 5-409 *410* [stories, including: 151-179 *180* 'PATRICK WHITE | Clay' (trans. Udvarhelyi Hanna); 181-230 *231* 'PATRICK WHITE | Egy pohár tea' (trans.

Dezsényi Katalin)]; 411-418 *419* 'ÉLETRAJZI JEGYZETEK'; *420* blank; *421-427* 'TARTALOM'; *428* [colophon]; endpaper.

Cased in black cloth boards. Front: [in gold] 'Jelzötüz | az éjszakában'. Back: blank. Spine: [running down:] [in gold] 'Jelzötüz az éjszakában'.

White laminated paper dustjacket. Front: [in orange] 'Jelzötüz | [in brown] az éjszakában | [rule] | XX. századi | ausztrál | elbeszélök'. Back: blank. Spine: [running down:] [in brown] 'Jelzötüz az éjszakában'. Inside front flap: [in brown] [description, 26 lines]. Inside back flap: [in brown] [blurb, 11 lines] | '58, – Ft'.

White paper wraparound. Front: 'Megjelent Ausztrália | bicentenáriumára'.

Copies: NSL: Mitchell Library [PW].

I.t9 German Edition 'A Cheery Soul' (Frankfurt am Main: Fischer Taschenbuch Verlag, 1991)

[oxford rule] | Patrick White | Eine Seele von Mensch | *Short Story* | Aus dem Englischen von | Reinhild Böhnke | [publisher's device] | Fischer | Taschenbuch | Verlag

17.9 x 10.4 cm. Unsigned: 40 leaves. pp.*8* 9-76 *77-80*.

1 [oxford rule] | [publisher's device]; *2* [blurb, 22 lines]; *3* [biography, 19 lines]; *4* [oxford rule] | 'Erzähler-Bibliothek'; *5* title page; *6* 'Veröffentlicht im Fischer Taschenbuch Verlag GmbH, | Frankfurt am Main, Juni 1991 | Die Ausgabe erscheint | mit freundlicher Genehmigung des Autors | Der Text ist dem Erzählungsband >The Burnt Ones< | von Patrick White entnommen, der 1964 | bei Eyre & Spottiswoode, London, erschien | © Patrick White 1964 | Die deutsche Übersetzung von Reinhild Böhnke | erscheint mit freundlicher Genehmigung | des Verlags Volk und Welt, Berlin | © Verlag Volk und Welt, Berlin 1984 | Umschlaggestaltung: Hans-Georg Pospischil und | Hans Ulrich Scholpp | Illustration: Alfons Holtgreve | Gesamtherstellung: Clausen & Bosse, Leck | Printed in Germany | ISBN 3-596-10710-5'; *7* [oxford rule] | 'Eine Seele von Mensch'; *8* [oxford rule]; 9-76 text; *77* blank; *78-80* [advertisements].

Perfectbound in white paper covers printed in brown. Front: 'FISCHER | [illust.] | [in black on green] PATRICK WHITE | [in black on orange] EINE SEELE VON MENSCH | [in black on yellow] SHORT STORY'. Back: [in black on green] [publisher's device] | [in black] [blurb, 9 lines] | 'ERZÄHLER-BIBLIOTHEK'. Spine: [running up:] [in black on green] 'PATRICK WHITE [in black on orange] EINE SEELE VON MENSCH [in black] 10710 | [at bottom:] [upright:] 980' | [publisher's device].

Published in June 1991. Price: 9.80.

Copies: VSL: SLT A823.3/W585BB; NSL: Mitchell Library 823.914/W587/38.

I.t10   German First Edition (Frankfurt am Main: S. Fischer Verlag, 1992)

Patrick White | DIE VERBRANNTEN | [rule] | *Erzählungen* | *Aus dem Englischen von* | *Reinhard Kaiser u. a.* | *S. Fischer*

20.8 x 12.9 cm.   Unsigned: 200 leaves.   pp.*10* 11-92 *93-94* 95-109 *110* 111-139 *140* 141-167 *168* 169-189 *190* 191-235 *236* 237-257 *258* 259-279 *280* 281-353 *354* 355-393 *394-400*.

Endpaper; *1* [publisher's device]; *2* blank; *3* title page; *4* 'Die Erzählung *Wippsterze im Mondenlicht* | wurde von Joachim Kalka übersetzt, | *Eine Glas Tee* von Frank Auerbach, | *Eine Seele von Mensch* von Reinhild Böhnke, | *Drunten auf der Müllkippe* von Hilary Heltay. | Die englische Originalausgabe erschien 1964 unter dem Titel | *The Burnt Ones* bei Eyre & Spottiswoode, London | Copyright © Patrick White, 1964 | Deutsche Ausgabe: | © S. Fischer Verlag, Frankfurt am Main 1992 | Die Übersetzung von *Willy-Wagtails by Moonlight* | (*Wippsterze im Mondenlicht*) erscheint mit freundlicher Genehmigung | des Fischer Taschenbuch Verlags GmbH, Frankfurt am Main; | die Übersetzung von *A Glass of Tea* (*Ein Glas Tee*) | mit freundlicher Genehmigung von Frank Auerbach; | die Übersetzung von *A Cheery Soul* (*Eine Seele von Mensch*) | mit freundlicher Genehmigung des Verlags Volk und Welt, Berlin; | die Übersetzung von *Down at the Dump* | (*Drunten auf der Müllkippe*) mit freundlicher Genehmigung | des Verlags Philipp Reclam jun., Stuttgart. | Umschlaggestaltung: Buchholz/Hinsch/Walch | Satz: Utesch Satztechnik GmbH, Hamburg | Druck und Einband: F. Spiegel Buch GmbH, Ulm | Printed in Germany | ISBN 3-10-091203-9'; *5* '*FÜR NIN UND GEOFFREY DUTTON*'; *6* blank; *7* '*INHALT*'; *8* blank; *9* 'OI KAYMENOI | Die Verbrannten (Die armen Unglücklichen)'; *10* blank; 11-393 *394* text; *395* blank; *396-399* [advertisements]; *400* blank; endpaper.

Casebound in black cloth with grey endpapers and with red headband and marker. Front: [in white] [illust. after painting by Fred Williams which appears on the dustjacket]. Back: blank. Spine: [running down:] [in red on a white rectangle:] '*Patrick White* | DIE VERBRANNTEN' | [upright:] [in red on black] [publisher's device]. Inside front and back covers: blank.

Glossy black paper dustjacket. Front: [in white] 'Patrick White | [in red] *DIE* | *VERBRANNTEN* | [col. illust. of *After the Fire* (1968) by Fred Williams] | [in white] S. Fischer'. Back: [in white] '>Die Verbrannten<, | die berühmt gewordene erste Erzählungssammlung | des australischen Nobelpreisträgers Patrick White, | erscheint hier erstmals vollständig in | deutscher Übersetzung. | [quotation of three lines from] *(Sunday Telegraph)* | ISBN 3-10-091203-9 | [barcode] | DM 39,80'. Spine: [running down:] [in white] 'Patrick White | [in red] DIE VERBRANNTEN'. Inside front flap: [in white] [blurb, 37 lines]. Inside back flap: [b&w photograph of the author] | [running down:] [at right:] 'Foto: Jerry Bauer | [biography, 24 lines] | Umschlaggestaltung: Buchholz/Hinsch/Walch | Fred Williams, >After the Fire<, 1968, Gouache, clac, | charcoal on paper. Australian National Gallery'.

Price: DM 39,80.

Copies: VSL: SLT A823.3 W585BK; NSL: Mitchell Library [PW].

I.t11   German Edition 'Dead Roses' (Frankfurt am Main: S. Fischer, 1995)

Patrick White | Welke Rosen | Erzählung | Aus dem Englischen von Reinhard Kaiser | [at bottom:] S. Fischer

22 x 12.9 cm. Unsigned: 56 leaves. pp.*6* 7-110 *111-112.*

Endpaper; *1* [publisher's device]; *2* blank; *3* title page; *4* [see photocopy]; *5* 'WELKE ROSEN'; *6* blank; 7-110 *111* text; *112* blank; endpaper.

Cased in paper-covered boards with black endpapers. Front: [in white] [against a background of black and red roses] 'Patrick White | [in black] Welke Rosen | Erzählung | Fischer Bibliothek'. Back: [in white] [blurb, 22 lines] | 'Fischer Bibliothek | ISBN 3-10-091205-5'. Spine: [runningup:] [in white] 'Patrick White Welke Rosen'.

Copies: ANL: N A823.3 W587de.

I.m1   Braille Edition (Enfield: Royal Blind Society of New South Wales, 1965)

The Burnt Ones (7 volumes of interline Braille).

Transcribed from the Penguin edition of 1964.

J   Four Plays (1965)

In the late 1950s a number of people expressed an interest in Patrick White's play, 'The Ham Funeral', first written around 1947. White submitted the play for the 1962 Adelaide Festival, but it was rejected by the Festival's governors. The story of the controversy is recounted below in Appendix 2, but the staging of 'The Ham Funeral' was the beginning of a short, intense and traumatic period of play-writing for White. By 1964 White was again writing novels but book collections of short stories (*The Burnt Ones*) and plays (*Four Plays*) had resulted from this period of diversion.

Between 1960 and 1964 White revived one play, wrote three others, wrote a number of short stories and novellas, and attempted an original opera libretto. A number of reasons for this diversification have been posited, including the resuscitation of a suppressed interest in the theatre, a new contact with theatre people both at home and abroad, a psychic release following the arduous creation of *Riders in the Chariot*, perhaps an unconscious attempt to raise his literary status by diversifying his output, and more probably the desire to find new ways to say the 'unsayable things'.

It is not known when White conceived the notion of a collection of his plays, but by December 1964 Eyre & Spottiswoode was planning one. (To James Stern, 14 December 1964)

Of the four plays: 'The Ham Funeral' was written in London in 1947 and first performed by the Adelaide University Theatre Guild on 15 November 1961 (Director: John Tasker); 'A Season at Sarsaparilla' was written in the middle of 1961 and first performed by the Adelaide University Theatre Guild for the Adelaide Festival on 14 September 1962 (Director: John Tasker); 'A Cheery Soul', based on a short story of the same title, was written in mid-1962 and first performed by the Union Theatre Repertory Company, Melbourne on 19 November 1963 (Director: John Sumner); and 'Night on Bald Mountain' was written late in 1962 and first performed by the Adelaide University Theatre Guild on 9 March 1964 (Director: John Tasker). For detailed accounts of writing, performance, publishing and recepiton history for each of White plays, see Appendix 2 below.

Four Plays was only cursorily reviewed and had limited commercial success. The Viking Press did not produce their own edition but instead issued 495 copies of the United Kingdom edition with minor changes to the title page, the binding and the dustjacket. The United Kingdom edition, published by Eyre &

Spottiswoode, earnt for White only £350 in royalties – perhaps indicating sales of fewer than 2,000. This edition was a modest production wrapped in a jacket with a striking and colourful abstract design by Desmond Digby.

Penguin Books declined to issue a paperback edition of *Four Plays* but in Australia, Sun Books, started up by Geoffrey Dutton and Brian Stonier, published at least six issues between 1967 and 1978. (To Geoffrey Dutton, 17 October 1965) The Sun Books issues were photolithographic reprints of the United Kingdom edition except for some minor changes and the omission of the plates. This same edition was then published by Currency Press as the first volume of White's *Collected Plays* (1985).

* * * * *

J1 U.K. First Edition (London: Eyre & Spottiswoode, 1965)

[rule] | Four plays by | Patrick White | [rule] | EYRE & SPOTTISWOODE, LONDON

20.6 x 13.7 cm. [A]⁸ B-X⁸ Y¹⁰ ($1 signed; Y₂ signed 'Y*'): 178 leaves. pp.*11* 12-74 *75* 76-177 *178-179* 180-264 *265* 266-356; 16 p. of plates.

Endpaper; *1* 'FOUR PLAYS BY | PATRICK WHITE'; *2* 'ALSO BY PATRICK WHITE | *novels* | THE LIVING AND THE DEAD | HAPPY VALLEY | THE AUNT'S STORY | THE TREE OF MAN | VOSS | RIDERS IN THE CHARIOT | *stories* | THE BURNT ONES'; *3* title page; *4* '*First published in 1965 by | Eyre & Spottiswoode (Publishers) Ltd | 22 Henrietta Street, London WC2 | © Patrick White 1961, 1962, 1963, 1964, 1965 | Printed in Great Britain by | The Shenval Press, London, Hertford and Harlow*'; *5* '*for* | FREDERICK GLOVER'; *6* blank; *7* 'CONTENTS'; *8* blank; *9* 'ILLUSTRATIONS'; *10* blank; *11* 'The Ham Funeral'; *12* 'CHARACTERS'; *13* '*First produced by the Adelaide University Theatre Guild | November 15, 1961* | CAST'; *14* 'SCENE'; 15-74 text of 'The Ham Funeral'; *75* 'The Season at Sarsaparilla | A Charade of Suburbia | in Two Acts'; 76 'CHARACTERS'; *77* '*First produced by the Adelaide University Theatre Guild | September 14, 1962* | CAST'; 78 'SCENE'; 79-177 text of 'A Season at Sarsaparilla'; *178* blank; *179* 'A Cheery Soul | A Comedy in Three Acts'; 180 'CHARACTERS'; 181 '*First produced by the Union Theatre Repertory Company, Melbourne | November 19, 1963* | CAST'; 182 'SCENES'; 183-264 text of 'A Cheery Soul'; *265* 'Night on Bald Mountain | A Play in Three Acts'; 266 'CHARACTERS'; 267 '*First produced by the Adelaide University Theatre Guild, | March 9, 1964* | CAST'; 268 'SCENES'; 269-356 text of 'Night on Bald Mountain'; endpaper.

Cased in black paper-covered boards with white endpapers. Front and back: blank. Spine: [in silver] [rule] 'Four | Plays | by | Patrick | White | [rule] | [at bottom:] E&S'.

White paper dustjacket with col. illust. in an abstract style on front, spine and back. Front: [in red] 'FOUR | PLAYS | [in black] Patrick White'. Back: blank. Spine: [in black] 'FOUR | PLAYS | [running down:] [in white] Patrick White | [upright:] [in black] E&S'. Inside front flap: 'THE HAM | FUNERAL | THE SEASON AT | SARSAPARILLA | A CHEERY SOUL | NIGHT ON BALD | MOUNTAIN | [blurb, 26 lines] | *(continued on back flap)* | [rule] PRICE IN U.K. | 35 s net'. Inside back flap: '(*continued from front flap*) | [blurb continues, 12 lines] | [rule] | Books by Patrick White | *NOVELS* | Riders in the Chariot | Voss | The Tree of Man | The Aunt's Story | The Living and the Dead | *SHORT STORIES* | The Burnt Ones | [rule] | *Jacket design by Desmond Digby* | PRINTED IN GREAT BRITAIN'.

Published 8 June 1965. Price: 35s. Print run: approx. 2,000 (of which 500 sent to the United States).

Reviews: T.G. Rosenthal *Australian Book Review* v.4, September 1965, p.196-197; Charles Osborne *London Magazine* v.5 no.6, September 1965, p.95-100; P. Griffith *Advertiser* (Adelaide) 13 November 1965, p.16; H. Kippax *Sydney Morning Herald* 23 October 1965, p.19; K. Macartney *Meanjin* v.24 no.4, December 1965, p.528-530; L. Kramer *Bulletin* 11 December 1965, p.52-53; T. Herring *Southerly* v.25 no.4, 1965, p.219-233; *Spectator* 24 September 1965, p.384; E. James *Australian* 15 January 1966, p.15; J.F. Burrows *Australian Literary Studies* v.2 no.3, June 1966, p.155-170; R. Flantz *Overland* no.35, November 1966, p.53-54; N. Horrocks *Library Journal* v.91 no.11, 1 June 1966, p.2870; R. Cook *Harper's Magazine* v.233, September 1966, p.114; C. Pieterse *Journal of Commonwealth Literature* no.2, 1966, p.170-171.

Notes: ADFA has an 'Advance Copy' sewn in brown paper. Front: 'FOUR PLAYS | BY | PATRICK WHITE | ADVANCE COPY | Number of Pages 356 | Size of book: L.Crown 8vo | Illustrations: 8 pages half-tones | To be published: September 1965 | Approximate price: 35 shillings net | EYRE AND SPOTTISWOODE | 22 HENRIETTA STREET • WC2'.

Copies: Personal collection; NU: RB IMP 007306; NSL: Mitchell Library [PW]; NSL: GRL N828.99942/W587/1A (lacks dustjacket); NSL: Mitchell Library A822/W587/1A1 (lacks dustjacket); VU: McL L/A-D White.

J2a U.S. Subedition (New York: Viking, 1966)

Notes: p.*4* '*Copyright* © *1965 Patrick White* | *All rights reserved* | *Published in* 1966 *by The Viking Press, Inc.* | *625 Madison Avenue, New York, N.Y.* 10022 | *Published simultaneously in Canada by* | *The Macmillan Company of Canada Limited* | *Library of Congress catalog card number :* 66-19168 | *Printed in Great Britain*'. Cased in a dusty pink linen with white endpapers. Dustjacket as for J1a except that 'E&S' on the spine has been punched out to show 'VIKING' on the spine of the binding. The State Library of Victoria (La Trobe Library) copy has the Viking binding with altered dustjacket, but retains the Eyre & Spottiswoode title page. According to Marr (p.703), only 495 copies were sold in the United States.

J2b Canadian Subedition (Toronto: Macmillan Company of Canada, 1966)
Not seen. but assumed from the reference on p.*4* of the U.S. Subedition (see J2a above).

J2c U.S. Subedition Second Issue (San Francisco, Tri-Ocean, 1967)
Not seen, but referred to by Lawson, no.61.

126

J3a Australian Subedition First Issue (Melbourne: Sun Books, 1967)

Four plays by | Patrick White | Sun Books · Melbourne | in association with Eyre & Spottiswoode, London

17.9 x 11.3 cm. [A]^{10} B-X^8 Y^{10} ($1 signed; Y$_2$ signed 'Y*'): 186 leaves. pp.[*5*] 2-10 *11* 12-74 *75* 76-177 *178-179* 180-264 *265* 266-356.

Notes: p.[*4*] '*for* | FREDERICK GLOVER | Sun Books Pty Ltd, Melbourne, Victoria, Australia | First published by Eyre & Spottiswoode (Publishers) Ltd 1965 | Published in Sun Books 1967 | Copyright © Patrick White 1961, 1962, 1963, 1964, 1965 | National Library of Australia registry number Aus 67-748 | Reproduced and printed in Hong Kong by | The Continental Printing Co. Ltd | Set in Monotype Bembo & Fournier'; p.2-10 'INTRODUCTION | H. G. Kippax'. Perfectbound in white paper printed in purple, blue and green on front and back. Cover design by Brian Sadgrove. There are no plates in this or subsequent paperback issues. Price: AU$1.65.

Copies: Personal collection; NSL: GRL N828.99942/W587/1B; NSL: Mitchell Library A822/W587/1B1.

J3b Australian Subedition Second Issue (Melbourne: Sun Books, 1972)
Notes: p.*4* 'Published in Sun Books 1967. | [...] | Reproduced and printed in Hong Kong | Set in Monotype Bembo & Fournier'.

J3c-d Australian Subedition Third to Fourth Issues (Melbourne: Sun Books, 1973-1974)
Not seen.

J3e Australian Subedition Fifth Issue (Melbourne: Sun Books, 1977)
Notes: p.*4* 'Published in Sun Books 1967 | Reprinted 1972, 1973, 1974, 1977 | [...] | Reproduced and printed in Hong Kong | Set in Monotype Bembo & Fournier'. Perfectbound in white and mauve covers. Cover design by Cato Hibberd Hornblow Hawksby Design. Price: AU$3.95. ISBN 0 7251 0034 6.

J3f Australian Subedition Sixth Issue (Melbourne: Sun Books, 1978)
Notes: p.*4* 'Published in Sun Books 1967. | Reprinted 1972, 1973, 1974, 1977, 1978 | [...] | Reproduced and printed in Hong Kong | Set in Monotype Bembo & Fournier'. Perfectbound in white and mauve covers. Cover design by Cato Hibberd Hornblow Hawksby Design. Price: AU$3.95.

J3g Australian Subedition Seventh Issue (Sydney: Currency Press, 1985)

[rule] | PATRICK | WHITE | [rule] | COLLECTED PLAYS | Volume I | [publisher's device] | Currency Press · SYDNEY

20.2 x 12.8 cm. Unsigned: 182 leaves. pp.*9* 10-74 *75* 76-177 *178-179* 180-264 *265* 266-361 *362-364*; illust.

Notes: p.*4* 'AUSTRALIAN DRAMATISTS SERIES | General Editor: Katharine Brisbane | First published in 1965 as | Four Plays by Patrick White by | Eyre & Spottiswoode, London. | This edition published in 1985 by | Currency Press Pty Ltd, | PO Box 452 Paddington, | N.S.W. 2021, Australia. | [...] | Cover design by Kevin Chan | Printed by Colorcraft Ltd, Hong Kong'; p.357-361 'BIBLIOGRAPHICAL NOTE' [by May-Brit Akerholt]. Sewn in glossy black paper card. Cover design includes William Dobell's *The Dead Landlord*; photo by Henry Jolles. Photograph of White by Gerrit Fokkema. Published in October 1985. Price: AU$19.95. Remained in print until 1997. The text of the plays is reprinted from J1. For volume 2 of the *Collected Plays* see AA1 below.

J4 Australian Second Edition 'The Season at Sarsaparilla' (Sydney: Currency Press, 1984)

THE | SEASON | AT | SARSAPARILLA | BY | PATRICK WHITE | [publisher's device] | Current Theatre Series | published by Currency Press, Sydney, in association | with the State Theatre Company of South Australia

21 x 14.8 cm. Unsigned: 56 leaves. pp.*4* 5-52 [*8*] 53-103 *104*.

1 title page; *2* 'CHARACTERS'; *3* '*First produced by the Adelaide University Theatre Guild,*| *September 14, 1962* | CAST'; *4* 'SCENE' | [description, 23 lines]; 5-52 text; [*1*] 'THE SEASON AT SARSAPARILLA | By Patrick White | Cast | [...] | This production opened at the Playhouse on 24 November 1984'; [*2-8*] [details of the 1984 production]; 53-103 text continues; *104* blank.

Saddle-stapled with white paper card covers printed in red with illust. of suburban roofs at right on front. Front: 'THE | SEASON | AT | SARSAPARILLA | BY | PATRICK WHITE' | [at bottom:] [logo of State Theatre Company]. Back: [in box:] 'CURRENT THEATRE SERIES | THE SEASON AT SARSAPARILLA | [blurb, 23 lines] | Cover design by Geoffrey Gifford | ISBN 0 86819 107 3 | [logo] | [at right:] [running down:] Patrick White THE SEASON AT SARSAPARILLA CURRENCY'. Inside front cover: 'CURRENT THEATRE SERIES | First published in 1965 by | Eyre & Spottiswoode, London. | This edition published in 1984 by | Currency Press Pty Ltd, | PO Box 452, Paddington, NSW, 2021, | Australia, in association with the | State Theatre Company of South Australia. | Copyright © Patrick White 1961 | [publisher's conditions, 7 lines] | [author's condition, 7 lines] | All applications for performance or public | reading should be made to the author's | agents, Curtis Brown (Aust.) Pty Ltd, | PO Box 19, Paddington, NSW, 2021, | Australia. | National Library of Australia card number | and ISBN 0 86819 107 8 | Printed by Bridge Printery, Sydney'. Inside back cover: blank.

Copies: Personal collection; NSL: Mitchell Library 822.914/W587/3; NSL: Mitchell Library [PW].

J5 Australian Second Edition 'Night on Bald Mountain' (Sydney: Currency Press, 1996)

NIGHT ON BALD | MOUNTAIN | Patrick White | [publisher's device] | The Australian Playhouse Series | Currency Press. Sydney | in association with | State Theatre Company of South Australia

21 x 14 cm. Unsigned: leaves. pp.[7] 2-50 i-xxiv 51-98.

Contents: [1] title page; [2] 'CURRENT THEATRE SERIES | First published in 1965 as | *Four Plays by Patrick White* | by Eyre and Spottiswoode. | London. | Copyright © Patrick White, 1965 | [copyright statement, 18 lines] | National Library of Australia | Cataloguing-in-Publication data | [7 lines] | Set by Currency, Paddington. | Printed by Bridge Printery.'; [3] 'Contents'; [4] blank; [5] '*Night on Bald Mountain* was first produced by the | Adelaide University Theatre Guild on 9th March 1964 | with the following cast: | [cast, 8 lines] | Directed by John Tasker | Designed by Wendy Dickson'; [6] [Characters and setting]; [7] 2-50 text; i-xxiv [program of the 1996 production by the State Theatre Company of South Australia and Company B Belvoir]; 51-98 text continues.

Perfectbound in white paper card with illust. of stage curtain across front and back. Front: [in white] 'NIGHT ON BALD MOUNTAIN | PATRICK WHITE | *THE* AUSTRALIAN | *PLAYHOUSE* '. Back: [in white] 'NIGHT ON BALD MOUNTAIN | PATRICK WHITE | [description, 8 lines] | [biography, 13 lines] | *THE* AUSTRALIAN *PLAYHOUSE* | STATE THEATRE COMPANY OF SOUTH AUSTRALIA | [rule] | Published by Currency Press ISBN 0 86819 469 7' | [rule]. Spine: [in white] [running down:] 'Patrick White   Night on Bald Mountain   Currency / The Australian Playhouse'.

Published in June 1996. Price: AU$13.95. ISBN 0 86819 469 7.

Copies: VSL: LT A822.3 W582N; VU: McL L/A-D White.

J.m1 Braille Edition (Annerley: Queensland Braille Writing Association, 1984)

Four Plays (10 volumes of Braille).

Transcribed from the Sun Books edition of 1978.

K The Solid Mandala (1966)

The Solid Mandala was originally conceived as a novella, but by June 1964 Patrick White was hinting to Ben Huebsch that he was about to write the last of the Sarsaparilla novels (that is, those novels and plays that refer to White's fictional town of Sarsaparilla, derived from Castle Hill). (12 June 1964) White and Lascaris had bought a new house at 20 Martin Road in Centennial Park, Sydney and so were preparing – both physically and emotionally – to leave Dogwoods. White finished the first draft in only a few months; in fact he finished only a few weeks after moving into 20 Martin Road. Even for White the writing of this first draft was very quick. 'My new novel has been obsessing me for months, with the result that it has poured out rather chaotic, and the process of oxywelding will probably take longer and be more painful than usual'. (To Peggy Garland, 25 October 1964)

After putting the manuscript aside until the new year, White, on coming back to it, commented: 'It must have written itself.' (To the Duttons, 18 January 1965) The 'oxywelding' of the second draft went well until in February White had a severe bout of asthma, which he thought, might have been brought on by his struggle with the novel. Towards the end of March the second draft was complete. (To Geoffrey Dutton, 21 March 1965) Again he put the book aside for a month and then typed the final draft in May and June. 'It has turned out shorter than I had anticipated (about 300 quarto pages of type) because my handwriting seems to have developed a spread with age'. (To Marshall Best, 6 June 1965)

The typescript was sent to London and New York on 21 June. It was dedicated to David and Gwen Moore who were delighted. Marshall Best of Viking accepted *The Solid Mandala* in July: 'I think it is the most concentrated and most intensely felt of all your books.' (Best to PW, 15 July 1965) White, however, thought he was losing ground in New York: 'After their great enthusiasm for *The Solid Mandala* the Americans are playing a bit safe over their percentages. However I realise I am not much of a proposition to an American publisher'. (To Geoffrey Dutton, 1 August 1965) Eyre & Spottiswoode also accepted the book and advanced £1,500 – White's largest advance to that time. E&S also wanted to change the title but of course White would not budge: 'The title is the book and the book the title'. (To Juliet O'Hea, 21 July 1965) It is not known when White first thought of the title, although it was usually in the early stages of the writing. The mandala was a Jungian symbol, and White was reading Jung at this time.

The Solid Mandala was published in New York in February 1966 and in London and Australia a few months later. The more conservative approach of Viking resulted in a smaller print run and less publicity. The reception was predictable: '[the reviews] were only so-so and our sales have been disappointing'. (Marshall Best to Juliet O'Hea, 9 June 1966) Marr reveals that Viking sold only about 5,700 copies of *The Solid Mandala*, a figure significantly down on sales of *Riders in the Chariot* (7,000). Neither *The Burnt Ones* nor *The Solid Mandala* earned White's advance from Viking.

White's perception was that the American reviews had been good, except for the routine 'stinker' in *Time*. It was clear to him, however, that New York reviews were not enthusiastic, and the *New Yorker* had not carried a review at all. The English and Australian reviews were good and sales of 12,700 were significantly better than sales in the United States, although down on the 24,000 copies of *Riders in the Chariot*.

The Viking Press edition came out in the high quality house style. The jacket, designed by Enrico Arno, was on textured paper depicting a hand holding several glass marbles. It is interesting that the blurb on the front of the jacket refers back to *The Tree of Man* in an effort to again bring White's name to the attention of the American literary market. There is no record of White's opinion of the book or jacket design, but he did take a closer interest in the English edition. He had Eyre & Spottiswoode commission Desmond Digby who came up with a design of a large red sphere against a blue-green sky.

Publishers were not helped in their efforts to sell his novels by White's 1967 new year resolution not to accept any more literary prizes. Management at *Encyclopædia Britannica* could not believe that he would refuse a $10,000 prize which went with the Britannica Award for Literature for 1966. More controversially, White also withdrew *The Solid Mandala* from the Miles Franklin Award: 'I hadn't entered *The Solid Mandala* because some of the books which have won the prize in the last few years have taken any glory out of it.' (To Juliet O'Hea, 7 May 1967) He was astonished then to find that he had won the award after Eyre & Spottiswoode had entered it without his permission. He insisted that they withdraw it, and then he contacted the Award's trustees and told them he would refuse to accept the award. Eventually, Peter Mather's *The Trap* was given the award.

White was fed up with Eyre & Spottiswoode: they were slow to publish (they intended to hold *The Solid Mandala* back for a year!); Temple Smith, the publisher with whom White had most sympathy, had gone to Secker & Warburg; Juliet O'Hea found that their accounts were in a mess; and their promotion of White's books was considered unacceptable. 'I already refer to them as my ex-publishers but until I have another book to offer I'm not going to bother thinking about someone else'. (To Juliet O'Hea, 7 May 1967)

A number of translations of *The Solid Mandala* were produced: Polish (1968), Swedish (1969), Norwegian (1970), French (1970), Italian (1973), Spanish (1973), Rumanian (1974), German (1978) and Hebrew (1987). It is not clear how much White was consulted about these translations. One who did consult was Ingegärd Martinell who was preparing the Swedish translation. White replied patiently to her enquiries about lamb's fry, mutton flaps, and shower teas with care and precision. Dealing with translations was a happy chore; White wondered about the mistakes made by translators who did not ask questions.

* * * * *

K1a U.S. First Edition (New York: Viking Press, 1966)

The Solid Mandala | [ornamental rule] | [rule] | [ornamental rule] | A NOVEL BY | *Patrick White* | NEW YORK • THE VIKING PRESS

21.2 x 14.4 cm. Unsigned: 160 leaves. pp.[*10*] *1-3* 4-13 *14-17* 18-204 *205-207* 208-285 *286-289* 290-309 *310* p.

Endpaper; [*1*] 'THE SOLID MANDALA' | [at bottom:] [publisher's device]; [*2*] '*Also by Patrick White* | THE BURNT ONES | RIDERS IN THE CHARIOT | VOSS | THE TREE OF MAN | THE AUNT'S STORY | THE LIVING AND THE DEAD | HAPPY VALLEY'; [*3*] title page; [*4*] [at bottom:] 'Copyright © 1966 by Patrick White | All rights reserved | First published in 1966 by The Viking Press, Inc. | 625 Madison Avenue, New York, N.Y. 10022 | Published simultaneously in Canada by | The Macmillan Company of Canada Limited | Library of Congress catalog card number: 66-10984 | Printed in U.S.A. by H. Wolff Book Mfg. Co.'; [*5*] '*For Gwen and David Moore*'; [*6*] blank; [*7*] 'CONTENTS | *One* [leaf ornament] *In the Bus* [leaf ornament] 1 | *Two* [leaf ornament] *Waldo* [leaf ornament] 15 | *Three* [leaf ornament] *Arthur* [leaf ornament] 205 | *Four* [leaf ornament] *Mrs. Poulter and the Zeitgeist* [leaf ornament] 287'; [*8*] blank; [*9*] '*There is another world, but it is in this one.* | —Paul Eluard | *It is not outside, it is inside: wholly within.* | —Meister Eckhart | *... yet still I long* | *for my twin in the sun ...* | —Patrick Anderson | *It was an old and rather poor church; many of the ikons* | *were without settings; but such churches are the best for* | *praying in.* | —Dostoevski'; [*10*] blank; *1* 'One | [ornamental rule] | [rule] | [ornamental rule] | *In the Bus*'; *2* blank; *3* 4-13 text of Part One; *14* blank; *15* '*Two* | [ornamental rule] | [rule] | [ornamental rule] | *Waldo*'; *16* blank; *17* 18-204 text of Part Two; *205* '*Three* | [ornamental rule] | [rule] | [ornamental rule] | *Arthur*'; *206* blank; *207* 208-285 text of Part Three; *286* blank; *287* '*Four* |

[ornamental rule] | [rule] | [ornamental rule] | *Mrs. Poulter and the Zeitgeist*; *288* blank; *289*
290-309 text of Part Four; *310* blank; endpaper.

Cased in light blue paper-covered boards with dark blue cloth spine and white endpapers.
Front and back: blank. Spine: [in gold] *'The | Solid | Mandala* | [in light blue] [ornamental
rule] | [rule] | [ornamental rule] | [in gold] *Patrick | White* | [at bottom:] VIKING'.

Textured cream-coloured paper dustjacket printed with col. illust. of a hand holding glass
marbles extending across front and spine. Front: [in yellow] 'PATRICK WHITE | [in
white] The Solid | Mandala | [in black] A novel of twin brothers | by the author of THE
TREE OF MAN'. Back: [b&w photograph of the author] | [at right:] [running down:]
'BORIS COOK | [upright:] On Patrick White | [quotation of four lines from] – GILBERT
HIGHET | [quotation of two lines from] – ANGUS WILSON | [quotation of three lines from] –
ORVILLE PRESCOTT | [quotation of three lines from] – JOHN K. HUTCHENS | THE
VIKING PRESS · PUBLISHERS · NEW YORK'. Spine: [in yellow] 'PATRICK |
WHITE | [running down:] [in white] The Solid Mandala | [upright:] [in black] VIKING'.
Inside front flap: [at top right:] '$5.00 | [in blue] THE SOLID MANDALA | [in black]
[blurb, 44 lines] | [in blue] THE VIKING PRESS · NEW YORK'. Inside back flap: [in
blue] 'PATRICK WHITE | [in black] [biography, 43 lines] | [in blue] THE VIKING
PRESS | *Publishers of the Viking Portable Library* | 625 Madison Avenue, New York, N.Y.
10022 | PRINTED IN U.S.A. | [running down:] *Jacket design by Enrico Arno*'.

Published in February 1966. Price: $5.

Reviews: William Ready *Library Journal* v.91, 15 January 1966, p.282 (180w); [Alwyn Lee]
Time v.87, 11 February 1966, p.58 (600w); Bernard McCabe *Saturday Review* v.49, 12 Feb-
ruary 1966, p.36 (410w); J.D. Scott *New York Times Book Review* 13 February 1966, p.49
(600w); *Newsweek* v.67, 14 February 1966, p.96A (550w); J.L. Quinn *Best Sellers* v.25, 15
February 1966, p.430 (850w); E.P.J. Corbett *America* v.114, 19 February 1966, p.270 (440w);
Roderick Cook *Harper's Weekly* v.232, March 1966, p.151 (220w); Bernard Bergonzi *New
York Review of Books* v.6, 17 March 1966, p.20 (800w); Michael O'Malley *Critic* v.24, April
1966, p.67 (1450w); Marilyn Gardner *Christian Science Monitor* 21 April 1966, p.7 (190w);
Julian Moynahan *Book Week* 24 April 1966, p.13 (600w); *Virginia Quarterly Review* v.42,
Summer 1966, p.xc (150w); *Choice* July 1966, p.413 (110w); J. Bradley *Critic* v.7 Au-
gust/September 1966, p.54; W. Keeney *Southern Review* (Louisiana) Autumn 1966, p.1050.

Notes: In White's collection there is a presentation copy half bound in dark blue leather and
marbled paper boards.

Copies: Personal collection (2 copies); NSL: Mitchell Library A823/W587/9A1 (lacks dustjacket); NSL: Mitchell Library [PW].

K1b Canadian Subedition (Toronto: Macmillan, 1966)
Notes: not seen, but assumed from statement on p.[*4*] of K1a above. Price: $6.25.

K1c U.S. First Edition Viking Subedition (New York: Viking, 1973)
Notes: p.[*4*] 'Copyright © 1966 by Patrick White | All rights reserved | First published in
1966 by The Viking Press, Inc. | 625 Madison Avenue, New York, N.Y. 10022 | Published

simultaneously in Canada by | The Macmillan Company of Canada Limited | SBN 670-65632-1 | Library of Congress catalog card number: 66—10984 | Printed in U.S.A'. Cased in black calico boards. Textured light brown paper dustjacket.

K2a U.K. First Edition First Issue (London: Eyre & Spottiswoode, 1966)

The | Solid Mandala | A novel by | PATRICK WHITE | Eyre & Spottiswoode | London

20.6 x 13.7 cm. Unsigned: 160 leaves. pp.*10* 11-316 *317-320*.

Endpaper; *1* 'The Solid Mandala' | [blurb, 11 lines]; *2* 'Also by Patrick White | NOVELS | *Riders in the Chariot* | *Voss* | *The Tree of Man* | *The Aunt's Story* | *The Living and the Dead* | SHORT STORIES | *The Burnt Ones* | PLAYS | *Four Plays*'; *3* title page; *4* '© PATRICK WHITE 1966 | *First published 1966 in Great Britain by* | *Eyre & Spottiswoode (Publishers) Ltd* | *167 Fleet Street, London, E C 4* | *Printed in Great Britain by* | *Northumberland Press Limited,* *Gateshead*'; *5* [four epigraphs]; *6* blank; *7* 'For GWEN and DAVID MOORE'; *8* blank; *9* 'CONTENTS | I In the Bus *page* 11 | II Waldo *page* 23 | III Arthur *page* 215 | IV Mrs Poulter and the Zeitgeist *page* 296'; *10* blank; 11-316 *317* text; *318-320* blank; endpaper.

Cased in crimson calico with grey-green endpapers. Front and back: blank. Spine: [in gold] '*The* | *Solid* | *Mandala* | [rule] | PATRICK | WHITE | [at bottom:] E & S'.

White laminated paper dustjacket printed with col. illust. of large red sphere against a blue-green sky extending across front, spine and back. Front: [in white] [cursive] '*Patrick White* | [roman] THE SOLID MANDALA'. Back: blank. Spine: [in black] [cursive] 'Patrick | White | [running down:] [roman] THE SOLID MANDALA | [at bottom:] [upright:] E & S'. Inside front flap: 'PATRICK WHITE | The Solid Mandala | [blurb, 31 lines] | *Jacket design by Desmond Digby* | PRICE IN U.K. | 25s net'. Inside back flap: 'Also by Patrick White | *NOVELS* | Riders in the Chariot | Voss | The Tree of Man | The Aunt's Story | The Living and the Dead | *SHORT STORIES* | The Burnt Ones | *PLAYS* | Four Plays | [at bottom:] PRINTED IN GREAT BRITAIN'.

Published 12 May 1966. Price: 25s. Remained in print until 1973.

Reviews: H.P. Heseltine *Australian Book Review* v.5, March 1966, p.84-85 (2130w); T.G. Rosenthal *Australian* 2 April 1966, p.10 (2090w); M. Dunleavy *Canberra Times* 9 April 1966, p.11 (1665w); J. McLaren *Overland* no.34, May 1966, p.49-50 (810w); H. Kippax *Sydney Morning Herald* 14 May 1966, p.15 (600w); C. Higham *Bulletin* 14 May 1966, p.54-55; F. King *Sunday Telegraph* (London) 15 May 1966, p.12; Irving Wardle *Observer* 15 May 1966, p.26; K. Dick *Spectator* v.216, 20 May 1966, p.639; Karl Miller *New Statesman* v.71, 27 May 1966, p.780 (1000w); J. Barbour *Nation* (Australia) no.195, 28 May 1966, p.21-22 (1455w); N. Jillett *Age Literary Review* 28 May 1966, p.21 (1200w); T. Tanner *London Magazine* v.6, June 1966, p.112; Anthony Burgess *Listener* v.75, 2 June 1966, p.804; *Times Literary Supplement* 9 June 1966, p.509 (1650w); J.K. Ewers *Western Australian Teachers Journal* v.56, 1966, p.219; "Scrutarius" *Walkabout* v.32, October 1966, p.47; A.A. Phillips *Meanjin* v.25 no.1, 1966, p.31-33 (1125w); *Guardian Weekly* 15 December 1966, p.10; *Punch* v.251, 28 December 1966, p.970.

Notes: An advance copy has been seen in a personal collection. It is bound in a plain blue paper wrapper. Front: 'THE SOLID MANDALA | [oxford rule] | Patrick White | [oxford rule] | ADVANCE COPY | Eyre & Spottiswoode • Publishers • Ltd | Large Crown 8vo pp 320 About 25s net | Probable publication April 1966'. The ADFA copy has the signatures of Gwen and David Moore, the dedicatees, on the dedication page.

Copies: NSL: Mitchell Library A823/W587/9B1 (lacks dustjacket); NSL: Mitchell Library [PW]; NU: 823.91A/W587/J4/1/20; NU: RB IMP 007308; VSL: SLT 819.93/W582S; Personal collections (3 copies); ADFA; VU: McL L/A-F White.

K2b U.K. First Edition Jonathan Cape Subedition (London: Jonathan Cape, 1976)

PATRICK WHITE | *The Solid Mandala* | [at bottom:] [publisher's device] | JONATHAN CAPE | THIRTY BEDFORD SQUARE LONDON

20.4 x 13 cm. Unsigned: 160 leaves. pp.*10* 11-316 *317-320* p.

Notes: p.*4* 'FIRST PUBLISHED IN GREAT BRITAIN 1966 | THIS EDITION PUBLISHED BY JONATHAN CAPE LTD 1976 | © PATRICK WHITE 1966 | JONATHAN CAPE LTD, 30 BEDFORD SQUARE, LONDON WC1 | ISBN 0 224 01247 9 | [at bottom:] PRINTED IN GREAT BRITAIN BY | LOWE AND BRYDONE (PRINTERS) LTD, THETFORD, NORFOLK'. Cased in black imitation-cloth boards with white endpapers. White textured paper dustjacket printed on front, spine and back in light brown, overprinted in white and black lettering. Jacket design by Mon Mohan. Published 8 April 1976. Price: £3.50. Print run: 3,000.

K3a Penguin Edition First Issue (Harmondsworth: Penguin, 1969)

Patrick White | The Solid Mandala | Penguin Books | in association with Eyre & Spottiswoode

18 x 11 cm. [1]^{10} 2-16^{10} ($1 signed): 160 leaves. pp.*10* 11-315 *316-320*.

1 'Penguin Books | The Solid Mandala' | [biography, 24 lines]; *2* blank; *3* title page; *4* 'Penguin Books Ltd, Harmondsworth, | Middlesex, England | Penguin Books Australia Ltd, Ringwood, | Victoria, Australia | First published by Eyre & Spottiswoode 1966 | Published in Penguin Books 1969 | Copyright © Patrick White, 1966 | Made and printed in Great Britain | by Hazell Watson & Viney Ltd, Aylesbury, Bucks | Set in Linotype Times' | [publisher's conditions, 8 lines]; *5* 'For *Gwen* and *David Moore*'; *6* blank; *7* '*There is another world, but it is in this one.* | Paul Eluard | *It is not outside, it is inside: wholly within.* | Meister Eckhart | *… yet still I long | for my twin in the sun …* | Patrick Anderson | *It was an old and rather poor church; many of the | ikons were without settings; but such churches are | the best for praying in.* | Dostoyevsky'; *8* blank; *9* 'Contents'; *10* blank; 11-315 *316* text; *317* 'More about Penguins'; *318* blank; *319* '*Patrick White in Penguins* | Voss | [blurb, 11 lines] | [quotation of three lines from] John Davenport in *The Observer* | The Tree of Man | [blurb, 8 lines] [quotation of two lines from] Peter Green | in the *Daily Telegraph* | [quotation of three lines from] John Davenport in *The Observer* | *Not for sale in the U.S.A. or Canada*'; *320* 'Riders in the Chariot | Patrick White | [blurb, 4 lines] [quotation of five lines from] Maurice Edelman in | the *Sunday*

Times | [quotation of three lines from] A. Alvarez in the *New Statesman* | [quotation of five lines from] Jeremy Brooks in the *Guardian* | *Also available* | The Burnt Ones | The Living and the Dead | *Not for sale in the U.S.A. or Canada'*.

Perfectbound in white paper. Front: [in black] 'Patrick White [publisher's device] | [in brown] The Solid Mandala' | [illust. in black featuring a man's head surrounded by rainbow and circular images]. Back: [blurb, 14 lines] [at top right:] [publisher's device] | [in brown] 'Cover illustration by Phillippe Poncet de la Grave | For copyright reasons this edition is not for sale in U.S.A. or Canada | [in black] [at bottom left:] United Kingdom 40p 8/- | Australia $1.35 | New Zealand $1.10 | South Africa R0.97'. Spine: [running down:] 'Patrick White [in white] The Solid Mandala | [upright:] 2975' [publisher's device].

Price: 40p or 8/-, AU$1.35, NZ$1.10, SA R0.97.

Copies: NSL: Mitchell Library A823/W587/9D1 (rebound and so lacks original spine); NSL: Mitchell Library [PW]; NSL: GRL N828.99943/W587/6 (rebound) .

K3b Penguin Edition Second Issue (Harmondsworth: Penguin, 1972)
Notes: p.*4* 'Published in Penguin Books 1969 | Reprinted 1972 | Copyright © Patrick White, 1966 | Made and printed in Australia at | The Dominion Press | North Blackburn, Victoria | Set in Linotype Times'. Perfectbound in white paper. Cover design (two men, one holding a marble in his open palm) by David Wire. Price: AU$1.50.

K3c Penguin Edition Third Issue (Harmondsworth: Penguin, 1974)
Notes: p.*4* 'Published in Penguin Books 1969 | Reprinted 1972, 1974 | Copyright © Patrick White, 1966 | Made and printed in Australia at | The Dominion Press | North Blackburn, Victoria | Set in Linotype Times'. Perfectbound in white paper. Cover design (two men, one holding a marble in his open palm) by David Wire.

K3d Penguin Edition Fourth Issue (Harmondsworth: Penguin, 1975)
Notes: p.*4* 'Published in Penguin Books 1969 | Reprinted 1974, 1975 | Copyright © Patrick White, 1966 | Made and printed in Great Britain | by Hazell Watson & Viney Ltd, Aylesbury, Bucks | Set Linotype Times'. Perfectbound in white paper. Cover design (two men, one holding a marble in his open palm) by David Wire. Price: 80p, NZ$2.75. ISBN 0 1400 2975 3.

K3e Penguin Edition Fifth Issue (Harmondsworth: Penguin, 1977)
Notes: not seen, but assumed on the basis of K3f below.

K3f Penguin Edition Sixth Issue (Ringwood, Vic.: Penguin, 1981)
Notes: p.*4* 'Published in Penguin Books 1969 | Reprinted 1974, 1975, 1977, 1981 | Copyright © Patrick White, 1966 | All rights reserved | Made and printed in Australia at | The Dominion Press, Blackburn, Victoria | Set in Linotype Times'. Perfectbound in white paper printed with a black ground. The cover shows a detail from *Lovers and Shell* by David

Strachan reproduced by permission of the Ballarat Fine Art Gallery. Price: AU$5.95, £1.95. ISBN 0 1400 2975 3.

K3g Penguin Edition Seventh Issue (Harmondsworth: Penguin, 1983)
Notes: 19.6 x 12.8 cm. Page *4* 'Published in Penguin Books 1969 | Reprinted 1974, 1975, 1977, 1983 | Copyright © Patrick White, 1966 | All rights reserved | Made and printed in Great Britain by | Hazell Watson & Viney Ltd, Aylesbury, Bucks | Set in Lynotype Times'. Perfectbound in white paper printed in black and violet. Cover design by Neil Stuart. Cover illustration (images of marbles, eyes and a fan) by Mel Odom. Price: £2.95, AU$6.95, CAN$5.95, US$4.95. ISBN 0 1400 2975 3.

K3h Penguin Edition Eighth Issue (Harmondsworth: Penguin, 1985)
Notes: p.*4* 'Published in Penguin Books 1969 | Reprinted 1974, 1975, 1977, 1983, 1985'. Perfectbound in white paper printed in black and violet. Cover design by Neil Stuart. Cover illustration (images of marbles, eyes and a fan) by Mel Odom. Price: AU$7.95.

K3i Penguin Edition Ninth Issue (Harmondsworth: Penguin, 1993)
Notes: not seen, but entry in *Australian Books in Print*. Published July 1993. Price: $14.95.

K4 U.S. Second Edition (New York: Avon Books, 1975)

PATRICK | WHITE | The | Solid | Mandala | [publisher's device] AVON | PUBLISHERS OF BARD, CAMELOT, DISCUS, EQUINOX AND FLARE BOOKS

17.7 x 10.5 cm. Unsigned: 160 leaves. pp.[*8*] *1-2* 3-13 *14-16* 17-206 *207-208* 209-288 *289-290* 291-312.

[*1*] 'NOBEL PRIZE WINNER | PATRICK | WHITE | HIS COMMANDING NOVEL OF | INTERWOVEN PASSIONS AND | INTERTWINED DESTINIES | The Solid Mandala | [quotation from] | *The New Republic* | [quotation from] *John K. Hutchens* | [quotation from] *San Francisco Chronicle*'; [*2*] '*Avon Books by* | Patrick White | THE EYE OF THE STORM 2127 $1.95 | THE TREE OF MAN 22665 $1.95 | VOSS 22384 $ 1.95 | THE VIVISECTOR 24158 $2.25'; [*3*] title page; [*4*] 'AVON BOOKS | A division of | The Hearst Corporation | 959 Eighth Avenue | New York, New York 10019 | Copyright © 1966 by Patrick White. | Published by arrangement with The Viking Press, Inc. | Library of Congress Catalog Card Number: 66-10984 | [publisher's conditions, 5 lines] | First Avon Printing, July, 1975 | ISBN: 0-380-00375-9 | AVON TRADEMARK REG. U.S. PAT. OFF. AND | FOREIGN COUNTRIES, REGITERED TRADEMARK— | MARCA REGISTRADA, HECHO EN CHICAGO, U.S.A. | Printed in the U.S.A.; [*5*] '*For Gwen and David Moore*'; [*6*] blank; [*7*] 'CONTENTS'; [*8*] [epigraphs]; *1* [ornament] | 'ONE | [rule] | IN THE BUS'; *2* blank; 3-13 text of Part One; *14* blank; *15* [ornament] 'TWO | [rule] | WALDO'; *16* blank; 17-206 text of Part Two; *207* [ornament] | 'THREE | [rule] |

ARTHUR'; *208* blank; 209-288 text of Part Three; *289* [ornament] | 'FOUR | [rule] | MRS. POULTER AND | THE ZEITGEIST'; *290* blank; 291-312 text of Part Four.

Perfectbound in white paper printed in black and violet. Front: 'AVON/24852/$1.95 [publisher's device] | [in violet] NOBEL PRIZE WINNER | [in black] PATRICK | WHITE | Author of the nationwide | bestseller | THE EYE OF | THE STORM | [col. illust. of two men's heads] | [in violet] The | Solid | Mandala | [in black] "Exhilarating ... totally convincing ... | wonderfully fresh and human ... every page | is vibrant with live people in live contact." | *Saturday Review*'. Back: [blurb, 14 lines] | [5-line quotation from] '*Christian Science Monitor*' | [comment, 8 lines]. Spine: [publisher's device] | 'AVON | [running down:] PATRICK WHITE / [in violet] The Solid Mandala [in black] 380-24851-195'.

Published in July 1975. Price: US$1.95.

Copies: NSL: Mitchell Library [PW].

K.t1 Polish First Edition (Warsaw: Państwowy Instytut Wydawniczy, 1968)

Patrick White | Węzeł | [series device] | Przełożyła | Maria Skibniewska | 1968 | Państwowy Instytut Wydawniczy

18.5 x 12.2 cm. [1]⁸ 2-23⁸ 24² ($2 signed): 186 leaves. pp.*6* 7-369 *370-372*.

Endpaper; *1* 'White | Węzeł'; *2* [in green] [biography, 26 lines]; *3* title page; *4* 'Tytuł oryginału | «THE SOLID MANDALA» | Okładkę, obwolutę i strony tytułowe | projektowała | JOLANTA BARĄCZ | © *Patrick White 1966* | Printed in Poland | Państwowy Instytut Wydawniczy, Warszawa 1968 r. | Wydanie pierwsze | Nakład 20 000 + 288 egz. Ark. wyd. 18. Ark. druk. 23,25 | Papier druk. sat. kl. V, 70 g, z form. 75X100/32 | z Fabryki Papieru w Częstochowie | Oddano do składania 10. II. 1968 r. | Podpisano do druku 8. VIII. 1968 r. | Druk ukończono we wrześniu 1968 r. | Łódzka Drukarnia Dziełowa, Łódź, ul. Rewolucji 1905 r. nr 45 | Nr zam. 116/A/68. N-40. Cena zł 30.–'; *5* 'W AUTOBUSIE'; *6* blank; 7-369 *370* text; *371* 'SPIS RZECZY'; *372* 'WSPÓLCZESNA PROZA ŚWIATOWA | w tej serii w roku 1968 ukaża się:' | [list of 12 titles]; endpaper.

Cased in grey cloth with dark green endpapers. Front: [in green] 'Patrick White | Węzeł'. Back: [in green] 'CENA ZŁ 30.–'. Spine: [running down:] [in green] 'Patrick White Węzeł' | [upright:] [publisher's device].

White paper dustjacket printed with dark green ground and man with raised club across front, back and spine. Front: [in white] 'PAŃSTWOWY INSTYTUT WYDAWNICZY | Patrick White | Węzeł' | [publisher's device]. Back: blank. Spine: [running down:] [in white] 'Patrick White Węzeł' | [at bottom:] [upright:] [publisher's device]. Inside front flap: 'CENA ZŁ 30.– '. Inside back flap: blank.

Published in August 1968. Price: zł 30. Print run: 20,000.

Copies: NSL: Mitchell Library A823/W587/9C1 (lacks dustjacket); NSL: Mitchell Library A823/W587/9C2 (lacks dustjacket); NSL: Mitchell Library [PW]; Personal collection.

K.t2 Swedish First Edition (Stockholm: Albert Bonniers Förlag, 1969)

PATRICK WHITE | *Den oförstörbara* | *mandalan* | ROMAN | ALBERT
BONNIERS FÖRLAG | STOCKHOLM

21.5 x 13.3 cm. [1]^8 2-17^8 18^4 19^8 ($1 signed): 148 leaves. pp.*10* 11-292 *293-296*.

1 'Den oförstörbara mandalan'; *2 'Av Patrick White har tidigare utgivits:* | De fyra utkorade
1964'; *3* title page; *4 'Översättning av* | INGEGÄRD MARTINELL | *Engelska originalets
titel:* | *The Solid Mandala (London 1966)* | © *Patrick White 1966* | *Printed in Sweden* | *Alb.
Bonniers boktryckeri 1969* | *Stockholm'*; *5* [epigraphs]; *6* blank; *7* 'INNEHÅLL'; *8* blank; *9 'Till*
| GWEN *och* DAVID MOORE'; *10* blank; 11-292 *293* text; *294-296* blank.

Sewn in white paper printed in brown and black. Front: [background of house in bush at
night] [in white] [within a stylised moon] 'Patrick White | Den oförstörbara | mandalan | [at
bottom:] Roman   Bonniers'. Back: [stylised moon] | [in white] [description, 28 lines] |
'BONNIERS Omslag av Jean Biberg Pris 42: 50'. Spine: [in white] 'Patrick White Den
oförstörbara Mandalan'.

Price: 42:50.

Copies: NSL: Mitchell Lirbary A823/W587/9E1 (rebound); NSL: Mitchell Library [PW];
Personal collection.

K.t3 Norwegian First Edition (Oslo: Gyldendal, 1970)

PATRICK WHITE | *Den uknuselige mandala* | ROMAN | OVERSATT
AV | AKSEL BULL NJÅ | GYLDENDAL NORSK FORLAG | OSLO
1970

22 x 13.4 cm. [1]^8 2-19^8 '20a'^{2} '20b'^{4} ($1 signed): 158 leaves. pp.*8* 9-312 *313-316*.

1 'Den uknuselige mandala'; *2* blank; *3* title page; *4* 'Originalens titel: | « The Solid Mandala » |
© PATRICK WHITE 1966 | Printed in Norway | Reistad & Sønn, Oslo 1970 | *Tilegnet* |
GWEN OG DAVID MOORE'; *5* [epigraphs]; *6* blank; *7* 'INNHOLD'; *8* blank; 9-312 *313*
text; *314-316* blank.

Sewn in glossy white paper printed in red, purple and orange. Front: [in purple] '*Patrick
White* | [oxford rule] | *Den uknuselige* | *mandala* | *gyldendal norsk forlag*' | [abstract illust. of
two men]. Back: [photograph of the author]. Spine: [running down:] [in purple] 'Patrick
White | Den uknuselige mandala | gyldendal'. Inside front flap: [in purple] 'Den uknuselige
mandala' | [rule] | [description, 52 lines]. Inside back flap: [in purple] [rule] | [biography, 37
lines] | [rule] | 'GYLDENDAL NORSK FORLAG'.

Copies: NSL: Mitchell Library A823/W587/9G1 (rebound); NSL: Mitchell Library [PW];
Personal collection.

K.t4 French First Edition (Paris: Gallimard, 1970)

PATRICK WHITE | Le mystérieux | Mandala | TRADUIT DE
L'ANGLAIS | PAR ANDRÉE R. PICARD | *nrf* | GALLIMARD

20.6 x 14.2 cm. Unsigned: 184 leaves. pp.*12* 13-360 *361-368*.

1-2 blank; *3* 'DU MONDE ENTIER'; *4* blank; *5* title page; *6* '*Titre original :* | THE SOLID MANDALA | *Tous droits de traduction, de reproduction et d'adaptation* | *réservés pour tous les pays, y compris l'U.R.S.S.* | © *Patrick White, 1966.* | © *Éditions Gallimard, 1970, pour la traduction française.*'; *7* '*A Gwenn et David Moore*'; *8* blank; *9* [epigraphs]; *10* blank; *11* 'I | *Dans l'autobus*'; *12* blank; 13-360 *361* text; *362* blank; *363* [list of contents]; *364* blank; *365* 'DU MÊME AUTEUR | *nrf* | EDEN-VILLE. | LE CHAR DES ÉLUS. | VOSS. | LES ÉCHAUDÉS.'; *366* blank; *367* '*Cet ouvrage* | *a été achevé d'imprimer* | *sur les presses de l'Imprimerie Floch* | *à Mayenne le 23 octobre 1970.* | *Dépôt légal : 4ᵉ trimestre 1970.* | *Nᵒ d'édition :* *15387.* | *Imprimé en France.* | *(9739)*'; *368* blank.

Perfectbound in glossy white paper card. Front: 'DU MONDE ENTIER | PATRICK WHITE | [in red] LE MYSTÉRIEUX | MANDALA | [in black] ROMAN | TRADUIT DE L'ANGLAIS | PAR ANDRÉE R. PICARD | [series device] | [in red] *nrf* | [in black] GALLIMARD'. Back: 'PATRICK WHITE | [in red] Le Mystérieux Mandala | [in black] [blurb, 18 lines] | [in red] *nrf* | [in black] [at left:] 27/50 | 70-X'. Spine: [in red] 'du monde | entier | [in black] PATRICK | WHITE | [in red] LE MYSTÉRIEUX | MANDALA | [in black] *nrf* | GALLIMARD'. Inside front flap: [b&w photograph of the author] | [biography, 18 lines]. Inside back flap: '*dernières* | *publications*' | [list of 10 titles].

Copies: VSL: SLT 819.93 W582SPI; Personal collection (2 copies); NSL: Mitchell Library [PW]; NSL:Mitchell Library A823/W587/9F1 (rebound).

K.t5 Italian First Edition (Milan: Valentino Bompiani, 1973)

PATRICK WHITE | Màndala solido | Bompiani

20.8 x 12.2 cm. Unsigned: 180 leaves. pp.*8* 9-21 *22* 23-355 *356-360*.

Endpaper; *1* 'Màndala solido'; *2* blank; *3* title page; *4* 'Titolo originale: | THE SOLID MANDALA | Copyright © 1966 by Patrick White | (Prima edizione in Gran Bretagna, 1966) | Traduzione dall'inglese di | ANDREA D'ANNA | © 1973, Casa editrice Valentino Bompiani & C. S.p.A. | Via Pisacane, 26 - Milano | CL 04-1330-5'; *5* [epigraphs]; *6* blank; *7* 'a Gwen e David Moore'; *8* blank; 9-21 *22* 23-355 text; *356* blank; *357* 'INDICE'; *358* blank; *359* [index]; *360* '*FINITO DI STAMPARE* | *NEL MESE DI NOVEMBRE 1973* | *DA « LA VARESINA GRAFICA » AZZATE (VA)*'; endpaper.

Cased in green glossy paper-covered boards with green headbands and white endpapers. Front: [in white] 'Patrick White | [in pink] [rule] | Màndala solido'. Back: blank. Spine: [running down:] [in white] 'Patrick White • Màndala solido • Bompiani'.

Glossy white paper dustjacket printed in green and pink. Front: [in white] 'Patrick White | [in pink] [rule] | Màndala solido'. Back: [in white] [blurb, 36 lines] | [at right] [running down:] [at top:] CL 04-1330-5 [at bottom:] C.D.U. 86'. Spine: [running down:] [in white] 'Patrick White • Màndala solido • Bompiani'. Inside front flap: [biography, 47 lines]. Inside back flap: [biography continues, 16 lines] | [at bottom:] 'L. 4.000 | (3774)'.

Price: L.4000.

Copies: NU: 823.91A/W587/J4/TI1; NSL: Mitchell Library [PW]; Personal collection.

K.t6 Romanian First Edition (Bucharest: Editura Univers, 1974)

[shadowed] PATRICK WHITE | BILA VRĂJITĂ | [roman] Traducere şi cuvînt înainte | de *Anda Teodorescu* | EDITURA UNIVERS | Bucureşti — 1974

20 x 13 cm. [1]⁸ 2-20⁸ ($2 signed): 160 leaves. pp.*4* 5-10 *11-12* 13-316 *317-320*.

1 'PATRICK WHITE • BILA VRĂJITĂ'; *2* *'The Solid Mandala* | A novel by | Patrick White | Eyre & Spottiswoode | London | © by Patrick White, 1966 | Toate drepturile asupra acestei | versiuni sînt rezervate Editurii UNIVERS'; *3* title page; *4* Coperta de *Dan Ionescu*'; 5-10 *11* 'CUVÎNT ÎNAINTE' [by Anda Teodorescu]; *12* blank; 13-316 *317* text; *318* blank; *319* 'CUPRINS'; *320* 'Lector: MARIA VONGHIZAS | Tehnoredactor: ELENA BABI | [rule] | *Tiraj 32 130. Bun de tipar: 15.XI.1974.* | *Coli tipar 20.* | [rule] [publisher's device] || Tiparul executat sub comanda | nr. 40 600 la Combinatul Poligrafic | „Casa Scînteii", Piata Scînteii nr. 1 | Bucureşti, | Republica Socialistă România'.

Sewn in white paper printed in brown, red, green, yellow and lilac. Front: [in white] 'BILA VRĂJITĂ | [in red] PATRICK WHITE | [running down:] [in brown] PREMIUL | NOBEL 1973 | [at bottom:] [upright:] [in yellow] [publisher's device] [in white] *univers*'. Back: [in white] [blurb, 13 lines] | 'Lei 11'. Spine: [running down:] [in white] 'Patrick White • Bila vrăjită'.

Copies: NSL: Mitchell Library A823/W587/29; NSL: Mitchell Library [PW]; Personal collection.

K.t7 Spanish First Edition (Barcelona: Barral Editores, 1973)

PATRICK WHITE | LAS ESFERAS | DEL MANDALA | [publisher's device] | BREVE | BIBLIOTECA DE LITERATURAS | BARRAL EDITORES | 1973

19.5 x 13.2 cm. [1]⁸ 2-23⁸ 24⁴ ($1 signed): 188 leaves. pp.*10* 11-249 *250* 251-343 *344* 345-369 *370-376*.

1-2 blank; *3* 'LAS ESFERAS DEL MANDALA'; *4* blank; *5* title page; *6* 'Título de la edición original: | *The Solid Mandala* | (Eyre & Spottiswoode-Londres, 1966) | Traducción de: | *Silvia Pupato* | y | *Román Garciá-Azcárate* | Primera edición: diciembre, 1973 | © Patrick White, 1966 | © de los derechos en lengua castellana y | de la traducción española: BARRAL EDITORES, S.A. | BARCELONA, 1972 | ISBN 84 - 211 - 0286 - 9 | Depósito Legal: B. 49.905 - 1973 Printed in Spain'; *7* [epigraphs]; *8* blank; *9* 'Para GWEN y DAVID MOORE'; *10* blank; 11-24 'I. EN EL AUTOBUS'; 25-249 'II. WALDO'; *250* blank; 251-343 'III. ARTHUR'; *344* blank; 345-369 'IV. MRS. POULTER Y EL ZEITGIST'; *370* blank; *371* 'INDICE'; *372* blank; *373* 'Impreso en el mes de diciembre | de 1973 en los talleres gráficos | de Linomonograph S. A., | Riera S. Miguel, 9 | Barcelona'; *374-376* blank.

Perfectbound in white paper. Front: [in box:] 'PATRICK WHITE | LAS ESFERAS | DEL MANDALA | [in another box:] [publisher's device] BARRAL | [illust. of medieval woodcut representing two wrestlers] | PREMIO NOBEL DE LITERATURA 1973'. Back: [in box:] [wrestlers] | [in another box:] '*Cubierta de Julio Vivas* | [blurb, 16 lines] | [in another box:] SERIES DE RESPUESTA 86 | BREVE BIBLIOTHECA DE LITERATURAS | [publisher's device] BARRAL EDITORES'. Spine: [running up:] [in white on grey]

'PATRICK WHITE   LAS ESFERAS DEL MANDALA | [at bottom:] [upright:] 86' | [publisher's device]. Inside front flap: [b&w photograph of the author] | [biography, 16 lines] | 'Bibliografía:' | [8 lines]. Inside back flap: '*TITULOS PUBLICADOS*'.

Black paper wraparound. Front: [in silver] ¿Quién es realmente | Patrick White, el Premio | Nobel de Literatura de 1973? | esta es su novela más importante'. Back: [same text as on front].

Published in December 1973.

Copies: VSL: SLT 819.93 W582SP; NSL: Mitchell library A823/W587/25.

K.t8 German First Edition (Düsseldorf: Claassen Verlag, 1978)

Patrick | White | Die ungleichen | Brüder | Roman | Deutsch | von | Matthias Büttner | claassen

22 x 14.2 cm. Unsigned: 198 leaves. pp.*10* 11-25 *26* 27-393 *394-396*.

Endpaper; *1* 'Patrick White | Die ungleichen Brüder'; *2* blank; *3* title page; *4* 'Der Titel der 1966 bei Eyre & Spottiswoode, London, | erschienenen Originalausgabe lautet: | THE SOLID MANDALA | Copyright © 1966 by Patrrick White | 1. Auflage 1978 | Copyright © 1978 by claassen Verlag GmbH, Düsseldorf | Alle rechte der Verbreitung in deutscher Sprache, | auch durch Film, Funk, Fernsehen, fotomechanische Wiedergabe, Tonträger jeder Art | und auszugsweisen Nachdruck, sind vorbehalten. | Gesetzt aus der Garamond der Linotype GmbH | Satz: Industriedruck AG, Essen | Druck und Bindearbeiten: Ueberreuter, Wien | ISBN 3 546 49619 1'; *5* 'Für Gwen und David Moore'; *6* blank; *7* [epigraphs]; *8* blank; *9* 'Inhaltsverzeichnis'; *10* blank; 11-25 *26* 27-393 text; *394* 'Nobelpreis für Literatur 1973: | Patrick White | Im Auge des Sturms | 520 Seiten, gebunden | [quotation of four lines from] *Welt am Sonntag* | Der Maler | 569 Seiten, gebunden | [quotation of eight lines from] *Horst Bienek in Deutsche Zeitung*'; *395* 'Iris Murdoch | Uhrwerk der Liebe'; *396* 'Nadine Gordimer | Der Besitzer'; endpaper.

Cased in tan cloth with white headbands and white endpapers. Front and back: blank. Spine: [in white on a dark brown panel:] 'Patrick White | DIE UN- | GLEICHEN | BRÜDER | claassen'.

Glossy brown paper dustjacket. Front: [in white] 'Patrick White | [light/dark blue rule] | DIE UN- | GLEICHEN | BRÜDER | Roman claassen | [light/dark blue rule] | [quotation of four lines from] *Aus der Begründung zur Verleihung des | Nobelpreises für Literatur 1973*'. Back: [light/dark blue rule] | [in white] [quotation of 16 lines from] '*The Spectator* | 245 09619'. Spine: [in white] 'Patrick White | [light/dark blue rule] | DIE UN- | GLEICHEN | BRÜDER | [in light brown] claassen'. Inside front flap: [in white] [description, 35 lines]. Inside back flap: [quotation, 7 lines] | [black & white photograph of the author] | [biography, 4 lines] | 'Von Patrick White sind im claassen | Verlag bereits erschienen: | *Der Maler*, Roman, 580 S., Ln. | *Im Auge des Sturms*, Roman, 599 S., Ln. | Schutzumschlag: | Ursula und Peter J. Kahrl, | Ertscheid'. Inside dustjacket: [list of book titles in eight columns].

Published in May 1978. Price: DM 38.00. Print run: 8,000. ISBN 3-546-49619-1.

Reviews: Horst Bienek *Süddeutsche Zeitung* 20-21 May 1978; *Ruhr-Nachrichten* 6 June; Hans Jansen *Westdeutsche Allgemeine Zeitung* 19 June 1978; Ingeborg Brandt *Welt am Sonntag* 11 June 1978; Heina Albers *Hamburger Abendblatt* 1 July 1978; Han Büttow *Die Welt* 1 July 1978; Tina Weiland *Kieler Nachrichten* 5 July 1978; Elisabeth Kaiser *Deutsche Zeitung. Christ und Welt* 7 July 1978; Helmut Winter *Frankfurter Allgemeine Zeitung* 29 July 1978; Otto F. Beer *Der Tagesspiegel* 30 July 1978; Geno Hartlaub *Deutsches Allgemeine Sonntagsblatt* 13 August 1978; Wolfgang Wagner *Hannoversche Allgemeine Zeitung* 9 September 1978; Otto F. Beer *Rheinischer Merkur* 6 October 1978; Ekkehard Faude *Bücherkommentare* November-December; Sabine Korsukewitz *Schwäbische Zeitung* 12 December 1978; Andreas Seiler-Franklin *Neue Zürcher Zeitung* 12 December 1978; Hedwig Rohde *Saarbrücker Zeitung* 8 June 1979.

Copies: NU: 823.91A/W587/J4TG/1; NSL: Mitchell Library A823/W587/75 (lacks dust-jacket); NSL: Mitchell Library [PW].

K.t9 Hebrew First Edition (Tel Aviv: Zmora-Bitan, 1987)

[Gulat ha-Mandala]

Notes: pp.295. Trans. by G. Ariokh. Also see *Index Translationum*.

Copies: NSL: Mitchell Library [PW].

K.t10 Romanian Second Edition (Bucharest: Editura Orpheus, 1993)

[Bila vrajita]

Notes: pp.340. Trans. by Anda Teodorescu. Not seen, but referred to in *Index Translationum*.

K.m1 Braille First Edition (Victoria Park: Association for the Blind of Western Australia, [n.d.])

The Solid Mandala (4 volumes of Interpoint Braille)

Not seen, but referred to on the National Bibliographic Database.

L The Vivisector (1970)

The original idea for *The Vivisector* was the result of a sad letter from the aging
Roy de Maistre, received by Patrick White in January 1967. After thinking
about the novel for a month White commenced writing on the 14th February.
Almost immediately he suffered a major asthmatic attack and was hospitalised.

It is not clear when White adopted the title, *The Vivisector*, but as early as
May 1967 he was asking Maie Casey to bring back anti-vivisectionist literature
from London.

He wrote to Maie Casey that 'The end of *The Vivisector* is in sight' (26 November 1967), though it was not till the 20th February in the new year that the
first draft was finished. In April 1968 White wrote to Marshall Best: 'I have
started on the second version, and the chaotic opening, which had been worry-
ing me, is now coming good.' (7 April 1968) White estimated that the book
would be about 224,000 words and that the redrafting would take several years.
For the time being White and Lascaris were going overseas: it was not till November of that year that they returned, and White got the manuscript from the
bank safety deposit box. 'Fortunately, it is more or less what I intended, and now
I am busy writing the second version.' (To Eleanor Arrighi, 24 November 1968)

In February White's sister, Suzanne, died unexpectedly. White was shaken
and determined to finish the second draft as soon as possible. 'Since this warning
I have been working as hard as possible, to finish at least the second version of
The Vivisector in case I pop off too. Someone else could edit the Second Version
if necessary … I am a few sheets off the end of the Second Version.' (To Cynthia Nolan, 30 March 1969). This appears to be an extraordinary concession by
White who was always secretive and jealous of his work in progress. The second
draft was completed on Good Friday, April 1969. 'I'm working hard now, but
sometimes spend the whole day typing and re-typing the same couple of pages:
very exhausting and depressing' (To Geoffrey Dutton, 14 June 1969), but the
final draft took only twelve weeks. It came out at 562 typed pages and was
mailed to New York and London on 8th September. (Marr p.487)

The book was dedicated to the Nolans who had for several years provided a
sounding board for White's speculations about art and creativity.

Following the farce of the 1967 Miles Franklin Award (for which see the
introduction to the previous chapter on *The Solid Mandala*), it was common
knowledge among London publishers that White was looking for a new publisher. He was courted by a number, including Macmillan, Collins, and even

Angus & Robertson, but it was Jonathan Cape who prevailed. White had lunched with Tom Maschler and was pleased with the latter's sympathy with contemporary literature. White had also met with Graham C. Greene – the novelist's nephew and a principal at Cape. Greene was pessimistic following the austerity of the meeting, but White had more or less made up his mind. Juliet O'Hea was in complete agreement. Cape's offer for *The Vivisector* was generous – a £5,000 advance and royalties starting at 15%. White accepted the offer immediately. (To Juliet O'Hea, 11 December 1969)

White makes no reference to the physical qualities of the Viking edition of *The Vivisector*. It was well produced in the usual house style; its jacket was modest, presenting only a photographic enlargement of brushstrokes on an artist's canvas. The Cape edition was more adventurous in utilising a commissioned painting by Tom Adams. It was praised by White as having just the 'right touch of Bacon-ish horror' (To Colwell, Jonathan Cape, 15 March 1970), although on another occasion (To Miss Forbes, G. Heywood Hill Ltd, London, 22 June 1970, ADFA: G22) he complained 'I am disappointed in the jacket: something went wrong between the drawing I saw and the final version. The Viking jacket is far more appropriate this time'. It seems that Cape were very careful in their handling of White, even to the extent that they sent proofs of the blurbs to him: 'Thank you for the draft blurb, which I tore into considerably, as you will see. I think my version may whet the curiosity slightly more than yours'. (To Juliet Page, 4 February 1970) It is notable that White exercised some control over both the text and the physical presentation of the book.

The Viking Press had accepted *The Vivisector* as early as October 1969 – Marshall Best had written White that he was 'deeply shaken and terrified' (To Juliet O'Hea, 5 October 1969) – but in the new year White was complaining mildly that '[t]he Viking tempo has slackened off since the days when Ben Huebsch and Harold Guinzburg were living just around the corner'. (To Geoffrey Dutton, 4 January 1970) *The Vivisector* was published in the United States on the 8th July 1970 and in the United Kingdom and Australia in mid-October.

The critical reception of *The Vivisector* in the United States was sympathetic but muted. The book was not a commercial success, selling only 4,000 of Viking's first issue of 13,000 (*Letters* p.367-8). In London, Cape made the publication of *The Vivisector* into a literary event. The book received mixed reviews but made a critical impact. The first issue of 12,000 was quickly sold, and a few weeks later another 10,000 were sold in Australia.

The Vivisector was republished in paperback versions in both the United States and the United Kingdom. Penguin produced eight issues between 1973 and 1992 before selling the rights to Random House who produced the Vintage issue in 1994. An Australian issue was produced in 1973, presumably to fill the local demand created by White's Nobel Prize. Avon published a paperback edition in the United States in 1975.

The Vivisector was translated into a number of European languages, including Swedish (1970), Norwegian (1971), German (1972), Polish (1973), French (1979) and Dutch (1980). White had varying degrees of influence over these translations. The most significant – the Swedish translation of 1970 by Magnus Lindberg – was certainly based on a close correspondence between the author and translator.

* * * * *

L1a U.S. First Edition First Issue (New York: Viking, 1970)

[ornament] *The Vivisector* | [rule] | PATRICK WHITE | NEW YORK · THE VIKING PRESS

22.8 x 14.9 cm. Unsigned: 288 leaves. pp.[*8*] *1-2* 3-567 *568*.

Endpaper; [*1*] *'The Vivisector'*; [*2*] *'Also by Patrick White* | *Novels* | Happy Valley | The Living and the Dead | The Aunt's Story | The Tree of Man | Voss | Riders in the Chariot | The Solid Mandala | *Stories* | The Burnt Ones | *Plays* | Four Plays'; [*3*] title page; [*4*] 'Copyright © 1970 by Patrick White | All rights reserved | First published in 1970 by The Viking Press, Inc. | 625 Madison Avenue, New York, N.Y. 10022 | Published simultaneously in Canada by | The Macmillan Company of Canada Limited | SBN 670-74739-4 | Library of Congress catalog card number: 72-104137 | Printed in U.S.A.'; [*5*] *'For Cynthia and Sidney Nolan'*; [*6*] blank; [*7*] 'As I see it, painting and religious experience are the same thing, and | what we are all searching for is the understanding and realisation of | infinity. | BEN NICHOLSON | Cruelty has a Human Heart, | And Jealousy a Human Face; | Terror the Human Form Divine, | And Secrecy the Human Dress. | The Human Dress is forged in Iron, | The Human Form a fiery Forge, | The Human Face a Furnace seal'd, | The Human Heart its hungry Gorge. | WILLIAM BLAKE | They love truth when it reveals itself, and they hate it when | it reveals themselves. | SAINT AUGUSTINE | He becomes beyond all others the great Invalid, the great Crim- | inal, the great Accursed One—and the Supreme Knower. For he | reaches the unknown. | RIMBAUD'; [*8*] blank; *1* *'The Vivisector'*; *2* blank; 3-567 text; *568* blank; endpaper.

Cased in grey paper-covered boards with aqua-blue cloth spine, blue and white headbands and off-white endpapers. Front and back: blank. Spine: [running down:] 'PATRICK WHITE | [upright:] [in yellow] [ornamental rule] | VIKING | [ornamental rule] | [running down:] [in black] *The Vivisector*'.

White glossy paper dustjacket with illust. in pale blue monotone of a photographic enlargement of brushstrokes on an artist's canvas on front. Front: [in yellow] 'THE | [in orange]

VIVISECTOR | [in white] A NOVEL BY | PATRICK | WHITE'. Back: [in box of single orange rules:] [in black] 'On Patrick White' | [quotation of 16 lines from] [in orange] — Orville Prescott | [in black] [quotation of three lines from] [in orange] —Anthony Burgess | [in black] On THE VIVISECTOR | [quotation of six lines from] [in orange] —James Stern | [in black] THE VIKING PRESS · PUBLISHERS · NEW YORK | SBN 670-74739-4'. Spine: [running down:] [in orange] 'THE VIVISECTOR | [in blue] PATRICK WHITE | [upright:] [in orange] [publisher's device] | [in black] VIKING'. Inside front flap: [at top right:] '$8.95 | [in orange] THE | VIVISECTOR | [in black] [blurb, 35 lines] | [in orange] JACKET DESIGN BY MEL WILLIAMSON | [in black] 0770'. Inside back flap: [biography, 7 lines] | [in orange] 'THE VIKING PRESS | *Publishers of The Viking Portable Library* | *and Viking Compass paperbacks* | 625 Madison Avenue, New York, N.Y. 10022 | PRINTED IN U.S.A.'.

Published in July 1970. Price: $8.95. Print run: 13,000.

Reviews: J.A. Phillips *Best Sellers* 1 August 1970, p.176 (550w); L.J. Davis *Book World* 2 August 1970, p.2 (600w); John Thompson *Harper's Magazine* v.241, September 1970, p.94 (900w); Jody Haberland *Library Journal* v.95, August 1970, p.2724 (160w); David Pryce-Jones *New York Times Book Review* 8 November 1970, p.50 (800w); *Kirkus Reviews* 1 May 1970, p.529; *New Leader* v.53, 7 September 1970, p.22; *National Observer* v.9, 17 August 1970, p.17; *Books & Bookmen* December 1970, p.28; S. Lipski 'How the U.S. press treated *The Vivisector*' *Australian* 29 August 1970, p.18; *Hudson Review* Spring 1971, p.177.

Notes: In White's own collection there is a presentation copy, half-bound in dark blue leather, blue marbled paper boards, gilt-edge and with light blue endpapers. Inside this copy a Christmas greeting card 'From The Viking Press, with Grossman Publishers' (n.d.). ML [PW]

Extracts: [Untitled], *Marmalade's Book of Cats: Australian writing and art* (Manly: Marmalade Press, 1993), p.95.

Copies: NSL: Mitchell Library A823/W587/13B1 (lacks dustjacket); NSL: Mitchell Library [PW]; Personal collection (2 copies); VU: McL L/A-F White.

L1b Canadian Subedition (Toronto: Macmillan, 1970)
Not seen, but assumed based on statement on p.[4] of L1a above.

L1c U.S. First Edition Viking Subedition (New York: Viking, 1973)
Notes: p.[4] 'Copyright © 1970 by Patrick White | All rights reserved | First published in 1970 by The Viking Press, Inc. | 625 Madison Avenue, New York, N.Y. 10022 | Published simultaneously in Canada by | The Macmillan Company of Canada Limited | SBN 670-74739-4 | Library of Congress catalog card number: 72-104137 | Printed in the U.S.A.'. Cased in black linen with off-white endpapers. Brown coarse-textured paper. Published in January 1974.

L2 U.K. First Edition (London: Jonathan Cape, 1970)

PATRICK WHITE | THE VIVISECTOR | [at bottom:] [publisher's device] | JONATHAN CAPE | THIRTY BEDFORD SQUARE | LONDON

20.2 x 13.2 cm. [A]^{16} B-T^{16} U^{18} (U$_9$ signed U*): 322 leaves. pp.*6 7-642 643-644*.

Endpaper; *1* 'THE VIVISECTOR'; *2 'by the same author:* | *Novels* | RIDERS IN THE CHARIOT | VOSS | THE TREE OF MAN | THE AUNT'S STORY | THE LIVING AND THE DEAD | THE SOLID MANDALA | *Short Stories* | THE BURNT ONES | *Plays* | FOUR PLAYS'; *3* title page; *4* 'FIRST PUBLISHED 1970 | © 1970 BY PATRICK WHITE | JONATHAN CAPE LTD | 30 BEDFORD SQUARE, LONDON WC1 | SBN 224 61915 2 | [at bottom:] PRINTED AND BOUND BY | BUTLER & TANNER LTD, FROME AND LONDON'; *5* 'For Cynthia and Sidney Nolan'; *6* [epigraphs]; *7-642* text; *643* blank; *644* blank; endpaper.

Cased in terracotta paper-covered boards with graphite on top edge and off-white endpapers. Front and back: blank. Spine: [in gold] 'PATRICK | WHITE | [ornamental rule] | THE | VIVISECTOR' | [at bottom:] [publisher's device].

White, lightly textured paper with col. illust. in surrealist style signed by 'Tom Adams' across front, spine and back. Front: [painted] 'the vivisector | [printed in white] PATRICK WHITE'. Back: blank. Spine: [in white] 'PATRICK | WHITE | [painted] *the* | *vivisector*' | [at bottom:] [publisher's device]. Inside front flap: [blurb, 45 lines] | [at bottom right:] '40s net | [rule] | IN UK ONLY | [rule] | £2.00 net'. Inside back flap: 'PATRICK WHITE | [biography, 20 lines] | [at bottom:] SBN 224 61915 2 | Jacket painting by Tom Adams | © Jonathan Cape Ltd, 1970'.

Published 22 October 1970. Price: 40s. Print run: 18,000 (publisher's records indicate there may have been an over-run of 1,500).

Reviews: T.G. Rosenthal *New Statesman* v.80, 23 October 1970, p.536 (2100w); *Times Literary Supplement* 23 October 1970, p.1213 (1200w); P. Cosgrave *Spectator* v.225, 1970, p.525; D. Mahon *Listener* v.84, 1970, p.635-636; *Guardian Weekly* 7 November 1970, p.18; *Observer* 25 October 1970, p.34; J.B. Beston *Makar* v.4 no.4, 1970, p.15-18; R.N. Coe *Meanjin* v.29 no.4, 1970, p.526-529; C. Semmler *Australian Book Review* v.9, October, 1970, p.22; B. Kiernan *Australian* 17 October 1970, p.22; E. Williams *Sydney Morning Herald* 17 October 1970, p.19; K. England *Advertiser* (Adelaide) 24 October 1970, p.16; D.J. O'Hearn *Age* (Melbourne) 31 October 1970, p.16; O. Webster *Bulletin* 31 October 1970, p.52-53; D. Green *Canberra Times* 7 November 1970, p.14; J. Barbour *Nation* (Sydney) 28 November 1970, p.21-22; J.B. Beston *Westerly* no.4, December 1970, p.58-61 (2460w); V. Osborne *Sydney Morning Herald* 19 December 1970, p.19; K. England *Advertiser* (Adelaide) 12 December 1970, p.18; M. Clark *Age* (Melbourne) 26 December 1970, p.12; J. McLaren *Overland* no.46, Summer 1970, p.37-38 (1360w); L. Cantrell *Meanjin* v.30 no.1, 1971, p.125-129 (1340w); T. Herring *Southerly* v.31 no.1, 1971, p.3-16 (5800w); J.B. Beston *Australian Literary Studies* v.5 no.2, 1971, p.168-175 (2400w); P. Adams *Australian Book Review* February, p.57, 1971 (150w); E. Perkins *LINQ* v.1 no.1, 1971, p.43-46.

Notes: Uncorrected proof copies have been sighted in a personal collection and at ADFA. On p.*1* is '40s October'. It is sewn in yellow paper with paste-on on front: 'THE

VIVISECTOR | [rule] | PATRICK WHITE | [ornament] | Jonathan Cape Ltd'. On inside back flap of dustjacket is: 'PROOF ONLY | provisional publication | date: | October 8, 1970'. A second uncorrected proof copy in the same collection has a paste-on on the title page: [in ts] 'N.Z. Price $4.75 | Dispatch Date U.K. 6th August | Cataloguing Advertising. | [stamp] PLEASE RETURN URGENTLY | TO | [printed] ANTIPODES PUBLISHING CO. LTD. | [rule] | P.O. BOX 1467, WELLINGTON'. A third uncorrected proof copy, sewn in yellow paper, is held by the State Library of Victoria (Call no. *LT A823.3 W585VI). The private copy was bought for $100 in 1994. The ADFA first edition was Dorothy Green's review copy, with her annotations on dustjacket and endpapers.

Copies: NSL: Mitchell Library A823/W587/13A1 (lacks dustjacket); NSL: Mitchell Library [PW]; NSL: GRL N828.99943/W587/10 (lacks original binding and dustjacket); NSL: JRF/066957; Personal collection; ADFA.

L3a Penguin Edition First Issue (Harmondsworth: Penguin, 1973)

Patrick White | The Vivisector | Penguin Books

18 x 11 cm.. Unsigned: 312 leaves. pp.*8* 9-616 *617-624* (last page of each chapter is not numbered).

1 'Penguin Books | The Vivisector' | [biography, 24 lines] | [publisher's device]; *2* blank; *3* title page; *4* 'Penguin Books Ltd, Harmondsworth, | Middlesex, England | Penguin Books Australia Ltd, Ringwood, | Victoria, Australia | First published by Jonathan Cape 1970 | Published in Penguin Books 1973 | Copyright © Patrick White, 1970 | Made and printed in Great Britain by | Richard Clay (The Chaucer Press), Ltd, Bungay, Suffolk | Set in Linotype Pilgrim' | [publisher's conditions, 8 lines]; *5* 'For Cynthia and Sidney Nolan'; *6* blank; *7* [epigraphs]; *8* blank; 9-616 *617* text; *618* blank; *619* 'More about Penguins | and Pelicans'; *620* blank; *621* 'The Boy in the Bush | D.H. Lawrence and M.L. Skinner'; *622* 'The Tree of Man'; *623* 'Voss'; *624* 'The Penguin Book of Australian Verse | Edited with an Introduction by Harry Heseltine'.

Perfectbound in black, pale green and cream paper covers. Front: [in pale green] [publisher's device] 'Penguin Modern Classics | Patrick White | [thin rule] | [in white] The Vivisector' | [col. illust. of surgical instruments, etc.]. Back: [in white on pale green] [at top right] [publisher's device] | 'Penguin Modern Classics | Patrick White | [in black] [thin rule] | The Vivisector | [blurb, 15 lines] | The cover shows a detail from 'Still Life with | Self Portrait' by John Brack, by kind permission | of the artist | For copyright reasons this edition is not for | sale in the U.S.A. or Canada | [at bottom left:] United Kingdom 60p | Australia $2.10 (recommended) | New Zealand $2.10 | [at bottom right:] Fiction | Literature | ISBN 0 14 | 00.3693 8'. Spine: [publisher's device] [running down:] [in white] 'Patrick White [in black] The Vivisector ISBN 0 14 | 00.3693 8'.

Price: 60p, AU$2.10, NZ$2.10. ISBN 0 1400 3693 8.

Copies: NSL: Mitchell Library A823/W587/16 (rebound and so lacks original spine); NSL: Mitchell Library [PW].

L3b Penguin Edition Australian Issue (Harmondsworth: Penguin, 1973)
Notes: 18 x 11 cm. p.*4* 'Published in Penguin Books 1973 | Copyright © Patrick White, 1970 | Made and printed in Australia by | Alexander Brothers Ltd, Mentone, Victoria | Set in Linotype Pilgrim'. Perfectbound in black, pale green and cream paper covers. The cover shows a detail from 'Still Life with Self Portrait' by John Brack, by kind permission of the artist. Price: 60p, AU$1.95, NZ$1.95. ISBN 0 1400 3693 8.

L3c Penguin Edition Second Issue (Harmondsworth: Penguin, 1974)
Notes: p.*4* 'Published in Penguin Books 1973 | Reprinted 1974 | Copyright © Patrick White, 1970 | Made and printed in Australia at | The Dominion Press, North Blackburn, Victoria | Set in Linotype Pilgrim'. Perfectbound in black, pale green and cream paper covers. The cover shows a detail from 'Still Life with Self Portrait' by John Brack, by kind permission of the artist. Price: 60p, AU$1.95, NZ$1.95.

L3d Penguin Edition Third Issue (Harmondsworth: Penguin, 1977)
Notes: p.*4* 'Published in Penguin Books 1973 | Reprinted 1974, 1977 | Copyright © Patrick White, 1970 | Made and printed in Great Britain by | Richard Clay (The Chaucer Press) Ltd, Bungay, Suffolk | Set in Linotype Pilgrim'. Perfectbound in black, pale green and cream paper covers. The cover shows a detail from 'Still Life with Self Portrait' by John Brack, by kind permission of the artist.

L3e Penguin Edition Fourth Issue (Harmondsworth: Penguin, 1982)
Not seen.

L3f Penguin Edition Fifth Issue (Harmondsworth: Penguin, 1985)
Notes: 19.6 x 13.8 cm. Page *4* 'Published in Penguin Books 1973 | Reprinted 1974, 1977, 1982, 1985 | Copyright © Patrick White, 1970 | All rights reserved | Made and printed in Great Britain by | Richard Clay (The Chaucer Press) Ltd, Bungay, Suffolk | Set in Linotype Pilgrim'. Perfectbound in white and pale green card. The cover shows a detail from 'Still Life with Self Portrait' by John Brack, by kind permission of the artist. Price: £4.95, AU$8.95, NZ$13.50, CAN$7.95. ISBN 0-14-003693-8.

L3g Penguin Edition Sixth Issue (Harmondsworth: Penguin, n.d.)
Not seen.

L3h Penguin Edition Seventh Issue (Harmondsworth: Penguin, [c1988])
Notes: p.*4* 'Published in Penguin Books 1973 | 10 9 8 7 | Copyright © Patrick White, 1970 | All rights reserved | Printed in England by Clays Ltd, St Ives plc | Set in Linotype Pilgrim'. Perfectbound in white and pale green wrappers. Front: [col. illust. of detail of John Brack's *Still Life with Self Portrait*] | [at top right] [publisher's device] | [in white box:] 'PATRICK WHITE | [rule] | *The Vivisector*'. The cover shows a detail from *Still Life with Self Portrait* by John Brack, by kind permission of the artist. Price: £7.99, US$11.95. ISBN 0 1401 8527 5.

L3i Penguin Edition Eighth Issue (Harmondsworth: Penguin, [1992])

Notes: p.*4* 'Published in Penguin Books 1973 | 10 9 8 | [...] | Printed in England by Clays Ltd, St Ives plc | Set in Linotype Pilgrim'. Published in March 1992. Price: AU$15.95, US$11.95. ISBN 0 1401 8527 5.

L3j Vintage Subedition (London: Vintage, 1994)

Notes: 19.8 x 12.9 cm. Page *4* 'Published by Vintage 1994 | 2 4 6 8 10 9 7 5 3 1 | [...] | Printed and bound in Great Britain by | Cox & Wyman, Reading, Berkshire'. Perfectbound in paper covers. Published in September 1994. Price: $12.95.

L4 U.S. Second Edition (New York: Avon Books, 1975)

PATRICK WHITE | The | Vivisector | [at bottom:] [publisher's device] AVON | PUBLISHERS OF BARD, CAMELOT, DISCUS, EQUINOX AND FLARE BOOKS

17.8 x 10.7 cm. Unsigned: 304 leaves. pp.*8* 9-247 *248* 249-527 *528* 529-603 *604-608*.

1 'NOBEL PRIZE WINNER | PATRICK | WHITE | HIS MAGNIFICENT NOVEL OF | THE PASSIONS OF ART | AND HUMAN LIFE | "Splendid ... intense ... emotionally explosive." | *Harper's* | [quotation from] *The New York Times Books Review* | [quotation from] *San Francisco Chronicle*'; *2* 'Avon Books by | Patrick White | THE EYE OF THE STORM 21527 $1.95 | THE TREE OF MAN 22665 $1.95 | VOSS 22384 $1.95'; *3* title page; *4* 'AVON BOOKS | A division of | The Hearst Corporation | 959 Eighth Avenue | New York, New York 10019 | Copyright © 1970 by Patrick White. | Co-published by Avon Books and The Viking Press, Inc. | Library of Congress Catalog Card Number: 72-104137. | ISBN: 0-380-00324-4 | [publisher's conditions, 5 lines] | First Avon Printing, May, 1975. | AVON TRADEMARK REG. U.S. PAT. OFF. AND | FOREIGN COUNTRIES, REGISTERED TRADEMARK – | MARCA REGISTRADA, HECHO EN CHICAGO, U.S.A. | Printed in the U.S.A.'; *5* '*For Cynthia and Sidney Nolan*'; *6* blank; *7* [epigraphs]; *8* blank; 9-247 text of chapters 1-4; *248* blank; 249-527 text of chapters 5-8; *528* blank; 529-603 text of chapters 9-10; *604-608* [advertisements].

Perfectbound in white paper printed in black and brown. Front: 'AVON/24158/$2.25 [publisher's device] | [in brown] NOBEL PRIZE WINNER | [in black] PATRICK | WHITE | Author of the nationwide | bestseller | THE EYE OF | THE STORM | [col. illust. of a man's head before an abstract canvas] | [in brown] The | Vivisector | [in black] "SUPERB ... A powerful vision of human life poised | somewhere between heaven and hell ... He is | among the foremost novelists writing in English." | *Christian Science Monitor*'. Back: [blurb, 14 lines] | [quotation of six lines from] '*San Francisco Chronicle*' | [comment, 8 lines]. Spine: [publisher's device] | 'AVON | [running down:] PATRICK WHITE / [in brown] The Vivisector | [at bottom:] [in black] 380.24158.225'.

Published in May 1975. Price: US$2.25.

Copies: NSL: Mitchell Library [PW].

L.t1 Swedish First Edition (Stockholm: Bonniers, 1970)

Patrick | White | [double rule] | Målaren | ROMAN | Bonniers

21.8 x 13.9 cm. [1]^8 2-30^8 (in sixteens) 31-32^9 (in eighteens) 33-34^8 (in sixteens) ($1 signed: 31$_2$ signed '31‡'): 274 leaves. pp.*6* 7-547 *548*.

Endpaper; *1* 'Målaren'; *2* '*Av Patrick White har tidigare utgivits:* | De fyra utkorade 1964 | Den oförstörbara mandalan 1969 | Livets träd 1970'; *3* title page; *4* '*Till Cynthia och Sidney Nolan* | ISBN 91-0-038959-5 | Översättning av | MAGNUS K:SON LINDBERG | Engelska originalets titel: | The Vivisector (New York 1970) | © Patrick White 1970 | Printed in Sweden | Alb. Bonniers boktryckeri | Stockholm'; *5* [epigraphs]; *6* blank; 7-547 *548* text; endpaper.

Cased in green linen with white endpapers. Front and back: blank. Spine: [running down:] 'Patrick White Målaren'.

White glossy paper dustjacket. Front: [on background of brushstrokes and two green eyes:] 'Målaren | Patrick | White | Roman | Bonniers'. Back: 'Målaren | [blurb, 17 lines] | [quotation of seven lines from] Ingmar Björksten i *Patrick White – epikern från Australien* | [at left:] Omslag av Jean Biberg [at right:] ISBN 91-0-038959-5'. Spine: [running down:] 'Patrick White Målaren'. Inside front and back flaps: blank.

Copies: NSL: Mitchell Library A823/W587/19; NSL: Mitchell Library [PW]; Personal collection.

L.t2 Norwegian First Edition (Oslo: Gyldendal, 1971)

PATRICK WHITE | *Vivisektoren* | OVERSATT AV | OLAV ANGELL | GYLDENDAL NORSK FORLAG | OSLO 1971

21.1 x 13 cm. [1]^{16} 2-19^{16} 20^4 ($1 signed): 308 leaves. pp.*6* 7-614 *615-616*.

Endpaper; *1* '*Vivisektoren*'; *2* blank; *3* title page; *4* 'Originalens titel: | The Vivisector | © 1970 by PATRICK WHITE | Printed in Norway | Reistad & Sønn, Oslo | Omslag: Peter Haars | ISBN 82 05 00017 4 (h.) | ISBN 82 05 00018 2 (ib.) | *CYNTHIA OG SIDNEY NOLAN* | *tilegnet* | Utgitt med støtte av | Norsk kulturfond'; *5* [epigraphs]; *6* blank; 7-614 *615* text; *616* blank; endpaper.

Cased in orange cloth with off-white endpapers and maroon top edge. Front: [illust. in red of abstract depiction of a man's head]. Back: blank. Spine: [running down:] [in red] 'PATRICK WHITE | VIVISEKTOREN'.

Mottled green paper wrappers. Front: [at left:] 'GYLDENDAL | NORSK FORLAG | PATRICK WHITE | [vertical rule] [at right:] VIVI- | SEKTOREN | ROMAN' | [illust. in black, brown and tan of a man's head]. Back: 'ISBN 80 05 00017 4 (h.) | ISBN 82 05 00018 2 (ib.)' | [photograph of the author]. Spine: [running down:] 'PATRICK | WHITE | VIVI- | SEKTOREN | [upright] Gyldendal'. Inside front flap: 'VIVISEKTOREN' | [description, 36 lines]. Inside back flap: [quotation of three lines] | [blurb, 5 lines] | [rule] | 'DEN UKNUSELIGE | MANDALA | Oversatt av Aksel Bull Njå | [quotation of 20 lines from] Thor Edvin Dahl i Aftenposten | Gyldendal Norsk Forlag | REISTAD & SØNN, OSLO'.

Note: A paperback issue of this edition uses the cased issue's dustjacket as the binding: sewn in speckled tan paper and printed in black, brown and tan.

Copies: VSL: SLT 819.93 W582VA (cased); NSL: Mitchell Library A823/W587/13C1 (sewn); NSL: Mitchell Library [PW] (sewn); NSL: GRL E823.914/WHI (cased) (lacks dustjacket).

L.t3a   German First Edition First Issue (Hamburg and Düsseldorf: Claassen Verlag, 1972)

Patrick | White | Der Maler | – The Vivisector – | Roman | Deutsch | von | Willhelm Borgers | und | Erwin Bootz | Claassen | Verlag

22 x 14 cm. Unsigned: 286 leaves. pp.*7* 8-569 *570-572* (the first page of each chapter is un-numbered).

Endpaper; *1* 'Patrick | White | Der Maler'; *2* blank; *3* title page; *4* 'Titel der 1970 bei Jonathan Cape Ltd., London, | erschienen Originalausgabe : | THE VIVISECTOR | © 1970 by Patrick White | 1. Auflage 1972 | Copyright © 1972 by Claassen Verlag GmbH, | Hamburg und Düsseldorf | Alle rechter der Verbreitung in deutscher Sprache, | auch durch Film, Funk, Fernsehen, | fotomechanische Wiedergabe, Tonträger jeder Art | und auszugsweisen Nachdruck, sind Vorbehalten | Gesetzt aus der 9/11 Punkt Times der Monotype Corp. | Gesamtherstellung : Thomas F. Salzer KG, Wien | Printed in Austria | ISBN 3 546 49621 3'; *5* 'Für Cynthia | und | Sidney Nolan'; *6* [epigraphs]; *7* 8-569 text; *570* 'Heinrich Mann'; *571* 'Marie Luise Kaschnitz | Nicht nur von hier und von heute'; *572* 'Dolf Sternberger | Heinrich Heine'; endpaper.

Cased in white linen with white endpapers. Front and back: blank. Spine: [on inlaid blue panel:] 'White | Der Maler | Claassen'.

White glossy paper dustjacket printed in full colour. Front: [painted] 'Der | Maler | [printed] THE VIVISECTOR | PATRICK WHITE | ROMAN CLAASSEN'. Back: [biography, 4 lines] | [at bottom:] '245 09621'. Spine: 'PATRICK | WHITE | DER | MALER | CLAASSEN'. Inside front flap: [blurb, 39 lines] | [rule] | 'Schutzumschlag : Werner Rebhuhn'. Inside back flap: [blurb continues, 38 lines].

Reviews: *Frankfurter Neue Presse* 27 September 1972; Johannes Kleinstück *Die Welt* 28 September 1972; Elisabeth Kaiser *Stuttgarter Zeitung* 28 October 1972; Elisabeth Kaiser *Saarbrücker Zeitung* 29 November 1972; Martha Nowak *Tagesanzeiger* 9 February 1973; *Mannheimer Morgen* 3-4 March 1973; Helmut Winter *Frankfurter Allgemeine Zeitung* 22 March 1973; Gerd Mahr *Rheinischer Merkur* 26 October 1973; Sabine Schultze *Rhein-Neckar-Zeitung* 8 December 1973.

Copies: Personal collection.

L.t3b German First Edition Second Issue (Stüttgart, Hamburg, Münich: Deutscher Bucherbund, 1974)

Notes: pp.569. DM 17.80. 2 Aufl.

L.t3c German First Edition Third Issue (Frankfurt am Main: Fischer Taschenbuch, 1974)
Notes: 17.9 x 10.5 cm.; p.*4* 'Fischer Taschenbuch Verlag | Juli 1974 | Ungekürtze Ausgabe | Umschlagentwurf: Christoph Laies | Titel der Originalausgabe >The Vivisector< | Deutsch von Wilhelm Borgers und Erwin Bootz | Fischer Taschenbuch Verlag GmbH, Frankfurt am Main | Lizenzausgabe mit freundlicher Genehmigung des | Claassen Verlages GmbH, Hamburg und Düsseldorf | © 1972 by Claassen Verlag GmbH, Hamburg und Düsseldorf | >The Vivisector< © 1970 by Patrick White | Gesamtherstellung: Ebner, Ulm | Printed in Germany | ISBN 3 436 01929 1'. Perfectbound in white textured paper printed in full colour. Published in July 1974. Price: DM 8.80.

L.t3d German First Edition Fourth Issue (Zurich: Buchclub Ex Libris, 1974)
Notes: 22 x 14 cm.; p.*4* 'Titel der 1970 bei Jonathan Cape Ltd., London, | erschienen Originalausgabe : | THE VIVISECTOR | © 1970 by Patrick White | Ungekürzte Lizenzausgabe für den | Buchclub Ex Libris Zürich 1974 | Copyright © 1972 by Claassen Verlag GmbH, | Hamburg und Düsseldorf | Alle rechter der Verbreitung in deutscher Sprache, | auch durch Film, Funk, Fernsehen, | fotomechanische Wiedergabe, Tonträger jeder Art | und auszugsweisen Nachdruck, sind Vorbehalten | Gesetzt aus der 9/11 Punkt Times der Monotype Corp. | Printed in Austria'. Cased in blue linen with white headband and white endpapers. Dustjacket not seen.

L.t3e German First Edition Fifth Issue (Münich, Zurich: Piper, 1989)
Notes: p.[*4*] 'Die Originalausgabe erschien 1970 unter dem Titel | »The Vivisector« | bei Jonathan Cape Ltd., London. | Weitere Werke sind in der Piper Serie | in Vorbereitung. | ISBN 3-492-11094-0 | August 1989 | R.Piper GmbH & Co. KG, München | Lizenzausgabe mit Genehmigung | der claassen Verlag GmbH, Düsseldorf | Originalausgabe © Patrick White, 1970 | Deutsche Ausgabe © claassen Verlag GmbH, | Düsseldorf 1972 | Umschlag: Federico Luci, | unter Verwendung des Gamäldes »Atelierszene« (1981) | von Markus Oehlen | © VG Bild-Kunst, Bonn 1989 | Satz: Thoams F. Salzer KG, Wien | Druck und Bindung: Clausen & Bosse, Leck | Printed in Germany'. Perfectbound in white paper covers. Published in August 1989. Price: DM 19.80. ISBN 3-492-11094-0. (Serie Piper, 1094).

L.t4 Polish First Edition (Warsaw: Państwowy Instytut Wydawniczy, 1973)

[rule] | Patrick White [series device] | [rule] | Wiwisekcja | [rule] | Przełożyła Maria Skibniewska | PAŃSTWOWY INSTYTUT WYDAWNICZY 1973

18.5 x 12.3 cm. [1]^8 2-46^8 ($2 signed): 368 leaves. pp.*6* 7-731 *732-736* (the last page of each chapter is unnumbered).

1 [at bottom right:] 'White | Wiwisecja'; *2* [biography, 38 lines]; *3* title page; *4* 'Tytuł oryginału | The Vivisector | Okładkę, obwolutę i stronę tytulową | projektowal Jerzy Jaworowski | © 1970 by Patrick White'; *5* [epigraphs]; *6* blank; 7-731 *732* text; *733* [running down:] [at left:] 'WSPÓLCZESNA PROZA SWIATOWA | [upright:] TYTUŁY ROKU 1973' | [list, 13 titles]; *734* [running down:] [at left:]'WSPÓLCZESNA PROZA SWIATOWA | [upright:] DO NABYCIA WE WSZYSTKICH | KSIĘGARNIACH :' | [list, 15 titles]; *735* [another 8 titles]; *736* 'PRINTED IN POLAND | Państwowy Instytut Wydawniczy, Warszawa 1973 r. | Wydanie pierwsze. | Nakład 15.000 + 290 egz. Ark. wyd. 37,8. Ark. druk. 46. | Papier sat. kl. IV, 65 g f. 75x100/32. | Oddano do składania 10.X.1972 r. | Podpisano do druku w maju 1973 r. | Druk ukończono we wrześniu 1973 r. | Wroclawska Drukarnia Dzielowa | Nr zam. 811/A. — R-6 | Cena zł 60.—'.

Cased in grey cloth with orange endpapers. Front: blank. Back: [at top right:] 'zł 60.—'. Spine: [running down:] 'Patrick White · Wiwisekcja' | [upright:] [publisher's device].

Blue paper dustjacket. Front: 'PAŃSTWOWY INSTYTUT WYDAWNICZY | [rule] | Patrick White [series device] | [rule] | Wiwisekcja' | [abstract col. illust. of two people wrestling]. Back: [col. illust.] [at top right:] 'zł 60.—'. Spine: [running down:] 'Patrick White Wiwisekcja' | [upright:] [publisher's device]. Inside front and back flaps: blank.

Price: zł 60. Print run: 15,000.

Copies: VSL: SLT 819.93 W582VIS (lacks dustjacket); NSL: Mitchell Library A823/W587/20 (lacks dustjacket); NSL Mitchell Library [PW].

L.t5 French First Edition (Paris: Gallimard, 1979)

PATRICK WHITE | Le vivisecteur | * [* *] | TRADUIT DE L'ANGLAIS | PAR GEORGES MAGNANE | *nrf* | GALLIMARD

21.5 x 14.9 cm. 2 v.: (Vol.I:) Unsigned: 168 leaves. pp.*10* 11-328 *329-336*. (Vol.II:) Unsigned: 168 leaves. pp.*6* 7-333 *334-336* (the last page of each chapter is unnumbered).

(Vol.I:) *1-2* blank; *3* 'DU MONDE ENTIER'; *4* blank; *5* title page; *6* '*Titre original :* | THE VIVISECTOR | *Tous droits de traduction, de reproduction et d'adaptation* | *réservés pour tous les pays.* | © *Patrick White, 1970* | © *Éditions Gallimard, 1979, pour la traduction française.*'; *7* '*A Cynthia et Sydney Nolan*'; *8* blank; *9* [epigraphs]; *10* blank; 11-328 *329* text; *330* blank; *331* 'DU MÊME AUTEUR | *nrf* | EDEN-VILLE | LE CHAR DES ÉLUS | VOSS | LES ÉCHAUDÉS | LE MYSTÉRIEUX MANDALA | L'ŒIL DU CYCLONE, I et II'; *332* blank; *333* 'L'impression de ce livre | a été réalisée sur les presses | des Imprimeries Aubin | à Poitiers/Ligugé | [printer's device] | pour les Editions Gallimard'; *334* blank; *335* 'Achevé d'imprimer le 5 avril 1979 | N° d'édition 24981. — N° d'impression, L 11408 | Dépôt légal 2ᵉ trimestre 1979 | *Imprimé en France*'; *336* '24981'. (Vol.II:) *1-2* blank; *3* 'DU MONDE ENTIER'; *4* blank; *5* title page; *6* '*Titre original :* | THE VIVISECTOR | *Tous droits de traduction, de reproduction et d'adaptation* | *réservés pour tous les pays.* | © *Patrick White, 1970* | © Éditions Gallimard, 1979, pour la traduction française.'; 7-333 *334* text; *335* 'DU MÊME AUTEUR | *nrf* | EDEN-VILLE | LE CHAR DES ÉLUS | VOSS | LES ÉCHAUDÉS | LE MYSTÉRIEUX MANDALA | L'ŒIL DU CYCLONE, I et II'; *336* 'L'impression de ce livre | a été réalisée sur les presses | des Imprimeries Aubin | à Poitiers/Ligugé | [printer's device] | pour les Editions Gallimard | Achevé d'imprimer le 5 avril 1979 | N° d'édition 24982. — N° d'impression, L 11409 | Dépôt légal 2ᵉ trimestre 1979 | *Imprimé en France* | 24982'.

Perfectbound in white glossy paper card. Front: 'DU MONDE ENTIER | PATRICK WHITE | [in red] Le vivisecteur | [in black] * [* *] | ROMAN | TRADUIT DE L'ANGLAIS | PAR GEORGES MAGNANE | [series device] | [in red] *nrf* | [in black] GALLIMARD'. Back: 'Patrick White | [in red] Le Vivisecteur | [in black] [description, 24 lines] | [biography, 7 lines] | [in red] *nrf* | [in black] [at bottom right:] 79-IV'. Spine: [in red] 'du monde | entier | [in black] PATRICK | WHITE | [in red] LE | VIVISECTEUR | [in black] * [**] | *nrf* | GALLIMARD'.

Copies: VSL: SLT 819.93 W582VM (vols.1-2); NSL: Mitchell Library A823/W587/66 (vol.2 only); NSL: Mitchell Library [PW].

L.t6   Dutch First Edition (Amsterdam: Uitgeverij de Arbeiderspers, 1980)

Patrick White | De vivisector | VERTAALD DOOR KOOS SCHUUR | [publisher's device] | AMSTERDAM | UITGEVERIJ DE ARBEIDERSPERS

22 x 14 cm. Unsigned: 338 leaves. pp.*8* 9-676.

Endpaper; *1* 'De vivisector'; *2* blank; *3* title page; *4* 'Copyright © 1970 Patrick White | Copyright Nederlandse Vertaling © 1980 B.V. Uitgeverij De | Arbeiderspers, Amsterdam | Oorsponkelijke titel: *The vivisector* | Uitgave: Jonathan Cape Ltd, London 1970 | Omslag: Ann Kelland | Omslagontwerp: Barbara van Dongen Torman | ISBN 90 295 5735 4'; *5* '*Voor Cynthia en Sydney Nolan*'; *6* blank; *7* [epigraphs]; *8* blank; 9-676 text; endpaper.

Cased in red silk with off-white endpapers. Front and back: blank. Spine: [running down:] [in gold] 'PATRICK WHITE | DE VIVISECTOR' | [publisher's device].

White glossy paper dustjacket. Front: 'PATRICK | WHITE [in puce] DE | VIVISECTOR' | [col. illust. of reclining figure with palette for head]. Back: blank. Spine: [running down:] [in white] 'PATRICK WHITE | DE VIVISECTOR' | [upright:] [publisher's device]. Inside front flap: [blurb, 36 lines] | '*vervolg op achterflap*'. Inside back flap: '*vervolg van voorflap* | [quotation of five lines from] – *Frankfurter Allgemeine Zeitung* | [quotation of six lines from] – *le Monde* | ISBN 90 295 5735 4'.

Wraparound: [in puce] 'NOBELPRIJS 'Duizeling- | wekkend! Patrick White in | topvorm.' – Encounter'.

Copies: Personal collection.

L.t7 Polish Second Edition (Warsaw: Muza, 1993)

[in white] [series device] | PATRICK | WHITE | [rule] | Wiwisekcja | [rule] | Przelozyla | [rule] | MARIA SKIBNIEWSKA | [publisher's device]

19.7 x 13 cm. Unsigned: 400 leaves. pp.*6* 7-799 *800*.

Endpaper; *1* [in white] 'WHITE | [rule] | Wiwisekcja'; *2* blank; *3* title page; *4* 'Tytul oryginalu : *The Vivisector* | Projekt obwoluty: *Maciej Sadowski* | Redakcja: *Barbara Gruszka* | Redakcja graficzno-techniczna: *Mariusz Jastak* | Korekta: *Janina Slominska* | © for this Polish edition by MUZA S.A., Warszawa 1993 | ISBN 83-7079-178-6 | MUZA S.A. | Warszawa 1993'; *5* [epigraphs]; *6* blank; 7-799 text; *800* 'MUZA S.A. | 00-590 Warszawa | ul.Marszalkowska 8 (II p) | tel. 29 50 83, 21 50 58 | Warszawa 1993 | Wydanie II (poprawione) | Sklad i lamanie : MUZA S.A. | Druk i oprawa: Mladinska Knjiga, Lublana (Slowenia)'; endpaper.

Cased in black cloth with black endpapers. Front: [in blind] [series device] | 'WHITE'. Back: blank. Spine: [in blind] [series device] [publisher's device].

Glossy white paper dustjacket printed in full colour. Front: [in white] [series device] | 'PATRICK | WHITE | [rule] | Wiwisekcja' | [rule] | [col. illust. of man's head]. Back: [in white] [series device] | [rule] | 'Biblioteka | Bestsellerów | [rule] | [publisher's device] | [rule] | [biography, 4 lines] | ISBN 83-7079-178-6'. Spine: [in white] [series device] | [running down:] 'PATRICK WHITE Wiwisekcja' | [upright:] [publisher's device]. Inside front flap: [in white] [series device] | [rule] | 'Biblioteka | Bestsellerów' | [rule] | [blurb, 21 lines]. Inside back flap: [in white] [series device] | [rule] | 'Biblioteka Bestsellerów | [rule] | Kolejny tytul | serii:' | [Irving Stone's Pasja zycia].

Copies: NSL: Mitchell Library.

M The Eye of the Storm (1973)

The Eye of the Storm is centred on the death of the aristocratic Mrs Elizabeth Hunter, based squarely on Patrick White's own mother, Ruth. Even as Ruth lay dying in 1964, White knew he would write a novel about her death, and early in 1970 he wrote to Geoffrey Dutton: 'but rather than coax out [short] stories before they are ready to come naturally, I shall probably start a long novel which has been nagging at me in the most astonishing way the last couple of weeks'. (4 January 1970)

White commenced writing on the Australia Day weekend of 1970 and had fixed on the title from the very beginning, judging from enquiries he made of Maie Casey: 'Have you had any experience of hurricanes, land, sea, or air? I am particularly interested in how far up they reach, and how they would affect flying; also the *eye* of the hurricane: whether a ship can sail along within the eye and miss most of the storms'. (To Maie Casey, 1 February 1970).

White worked quickly on the first draft and thought he was about two-thirds finished when he was interrupted in July by the public unpleasantness towards John McGrath, the prospective assistant director of *Voss*. (McGrath came to Australia to scout for film locations and was greeted by a very hostile media: see Marr p.498-499.) White returned to *The Eye of the Storm* in September and completed the first draft in January 1971. 'Now I'm going to make the MS into a parcel which I won't open till we get back from Europe.' (To Geoffrey Dutton, 1 February 1971) White and Lascaris left for Europe in April and returned in October. Having got the manuscript back from the bank safety deposit box, White read *The Eye of the Storm* through and got down to the second draft immediately: 'I am now writing the second version and am glad to have had that to take my mind off other things since we got back.' (To Ronald Waters, 21 November 1971) By February 1972 about two-thirds of the second draft was complete: 'hating it at present; every word is a stone to be lifted painfully'. (To Geoffrey Dutton, 13 February 1972) 'I shall be glad when I can put the whole thing in the bank, and go to sleep for a couple of months ... (The bank is the only solution, I've found: otherwise, instead of staying clear, one keeps picking it up and having another look)'. (To the Nolans, 27 February 1972) By the end of April the second draft was finished and the manuscript went into a bank deposit box. White retrieved it in early July and began typing the final draft. This was a terrible physical chore: 'As I type a book my hand develops a dying fall which makes the fingers (or the two I use) linger on the wrong letters over and over again … I am almost three-quarters through *The Eye*'. (To Cynthia Nolan, 8 October 1972) By the 14th November it was finished. White had hurried so that Tom Maschler could read it while visiting Australia.

Even as White put the finishing touches to the final draft he was disturbed by the publication of another book called *In the Eye of the Storm* – on the guerillas in Angola. He even considered changing the title: 'An alternative is *The Darker Purpose*, or better perhaps *Darker Purposes*. It comes from the opening of *Lear*.' (To the Duttons, 12 November 1972)

Maschler read the typescript and liked it; he also assured White that the title could stay. In discussing publication with Juliet O'Hea, White was keen for *The Eye of the Storm* to come out first in London. He realised that he owed much to Viking but thought that United States reviews were poor, that sales were low, and that the American publisher had lost its panache. Moreover, he was not sure how sympathetic Viking people were towards him now. (To Juliet O'Hea, 9 December 1972) O'Hea made some enquiries and reported back to White: '… everyone at Viking would be totally desolate if you were ever to leave them.' (O'Hea to White, 10 January 1973) White sent a copy of the typescript to Viking and received Alan Williams' acceptance only a few weeks later: 'HAVE JUST EMERGED SHAKEN AND AWED FROM THE VORTEX THAT IS ELIZABETH HUNTER. HEARTFELT CONGRATULATIONS.' (Alan Williams to White, 14 February 1975) White had also sent a copy of the manuscript to Maie Casey, whom he hoped would accept the dedication. She did.

The Eye of the Storm was published in London in September 1973. Advance copies were rushed to Sweden in anticipation of the Nobel Prize announcement, but supplies bound for Australia were held up on strike-bound docks. The London reviews were mixed: Paul Bailey (*Observer* 4 September 1973) was extremely negative, but good reviews appeared in the *New Statesman* and the *Guardian*. Sales, however, were good from the beginning and spectacular following the announcement on the 18th October that White had won the Nobel Prize for Literature.

In the United States *The Eye of the Storm* was published in January 1974. The critical reception was still mixed but at least White was back on the front pages. (Marr p.545-6) Alan Williams had doubled the print run to 18,000 on the strength of the Nobel Prize, and the advance for the paperback rights was the largest White had ever received. By March Viking had sold 25,000 copies and were reprinting. The first editions in both the United States and the United Kingdom were quickly followed by re-issues, book club issues and paperback editions. Translations also proliferated: German (1973, 1974), Finnish (1974), Italian (1974), Japanese (1974), Turkish (1974), Spanish (1974), Swedish (1975), Polish (1976), Czech (1978), French (1978), Croatian (1979), Bulgarian (1984), Chinese (1986) and Hebrew (2001).

White apparently made no comment on the design of either the English or American editions. Both were handsome trade productions. The Cape edition had a design (an abstract waterscape featuring black swans against a swirling background) by Desmond Digby, who had done a number of dustjackets and theatre set designs for White since the early 1960s. The Viking Press edition jacket was a tame affair consisting of the author's name (in black) and the book's title (in green) on beige paper.

* * * * *

M1a U.K. First Edition (London: Jonathan Cape, 1973)

PATRICK WHITE | [rule] | THE EYE | OF | THE STORM | [publisher's device] | [at bottom:] JONATHAN CAPE | THIRTY BEDFORD SQUARE LONDON

20.4 x 13.5 cm. A-P^{16} R-U^{16} ($1,5 signed): 304 leaves. pp.*9* 10-608.

Endpaper; *1* 'THE EYE OF THE STORM'; *2 'by the same author'* | *Novels* | RIDERS IN THE CHARIOT | VOSS | THE TREE OF MAN | THE AUNT'S STORY | THE LIVING AND THE DEAD | THE SOLID MANDALA | THE VIVISECTOR | *Short Stories* | THE BURNT ONES | *Plays* | FOUR PLAYS'; *3* title page; *4* 'FIRST PUBLISHED 1973 | © 1973 BY PATRICK WHITE | JONATHAN CAPE LTD, 30 BEDFORD SQUARE, LONDON WC1 | ISBN 0 224 00902 8 | [at bottom:] PRINTED IN GREAT BRITAIN | BY EBENEZER BAYLIS AND SON LTD | THE TRINITY PRESS, WORCESTER, AND LONDON | ON PAPER MADE BY JOHN DICKINSON AND CO. LTD | BOUND BY G. AND J. KITCAT LTD, LONDON'; *5* 'TO MAIE CASEY'; *6* blank; *7* 'I was given by chance this human body so | difficult to wear' | *Nō play* | He felt what could have been a tremor of | heaven's own perverse love. | *Kawabata* | Men and boughs break; | Praise life while you walk and wake; | It is only lent. | *David Campbell*'; *8* blank; *9* 10-608 text; endpaper.

Cased in dark blue immitation cloth with pale blue top edge and light yellow endpapers. Front and back: blank. Spine: [in gold] 'THE EYE | OF THE | STORM | [ornament] | PATRICK | WHITE' | [publisher's device].

White, lightly textured paper dustjacket with col. illust. depicting abstract beach- or riverscape featuring black swans against a swirling background across front, spine and back. Front: [in black] 'THE EYE | OF THE | STORM | [in white] Patrick White'. Back: blank. Spine: [in white] 'THE EYE OF | THE STORM | Patrick White' | [in black] [publisher's device]. Inside front flap: [blurb, 42 lines] | [at bottom right:] '£2.95 net | [rule] | IN UK ONLY'. Inside back flap: 'Patrick White | THE VIVISECTOR | [quotation of six lines from] *New Statesman* | [quotation of five lines from] *Sunday Times* | [quotation of seven lines from] *Observer* | [quotation of ten lines from] *London Magazine* | [quotation of six lines from] *Encoun-*

ter | [at bottom:] ISBN 0 224 00902 8 | Jacket painting by Desmond Digby | © Jonathan Cape Ltd 1973'.

Published 16 September 1973. Price: £2.95. Print run: 23,000.

Reviews: William Walsh *New Statesman* v.86, 7 September 1973, p.320 (1050w); *Times Literary Supplement* 21 September 1973, p.1072 (2400w); *Contemporary Review* October 1973, p.213; *Guardian Weekly* 15 September 1973, p.21; *Kirkus Reviews* v.41, 1 November 1973, p.1229; T. O'Keefe *Listener* v.90, 27 September 1973, p.427; *Observer* 9 September 1973, p.17; *Publishers Weekly* 19 November 1973, p.57; Peter Ackroyd *Spectator* v.231, 8 September 1973, p.312; G. Dutton *Australian Book Review* v.12, November 1973, p.121-122 (3600w); A. Mitchell *Advertiser* (Adelaide) 6 October 1973, p.20 (900w); C. Harrison-Ford *Australian* 29 September 1973, p.18 (1000w); B. Kiernan *Australian* 6 October 1973, p.13 (1400w); C. Flower *Bulletin* 20 October 1973, p.52-53 (810w); M. Pettigrove *Canberra Times* 5 October 1973, p.11 (2200w); K. Tennant *Sydney Morning Herald* 6 October 1973, p.22 (810w); D. Rowbotham *Courier-Mail* (Brisbane) 10 November 1973, p.16; C. Semmler *Sydney Morning Herald* 8 December 1973, p.13 (45w); V. Brady *Westerly* no.4, December 1973, p.60-70 (6000w); B. Kiernan *Age* (Melbourne) 6 October 1973, p.13; E. Kynaston *Nation Review* 12-18 October 1973, p.1647; R. Beston *Hemisphere* v.17, December 1973, p.35; D. Green *Meanjin* v.32 no.4, 1973, p.395-405; J. McLaren *Overland* no.57, 1973, Summer, p.59-60 (1500w); *Economist* v.249, 10 November 1973, Autumn Survey p.4 (270w); Jonathan Raban *Encounter* v.41, December 1973, p.80 (370w); *Bonniers Litterära Magasin* v.42, 1973, p221-223; L. Kramer *Quadrant* v.18, January/February 1974, p.65-68 (2500w); P. Beaton *Southerly* v.34 no.3, 1974, p.219-232.

Notes: An uncorrected proof copy has been sighted in a private collection. It has a paste-on on p.*1*: 'THE EYE OF THE STORM | Patrick White | [blurb, 25 lines] | approx £2.50 September 1973'. Stamp: 'Max Taylor PO Box 158 Strathfield 2135 Phone 76-5236 929-0566 (messages)'. In MS on title page: 'OK BR/R/AUST/ABC cataloguer | Max Taylor 12/73'. Insert: 'Compliments of the Australian Publishing Co. P/L of Hornsby'. Refers to a letter of 23.11.73 and recommends Australian retail price of $6.75. In MS: 'Our | Eye of the Storm John Deas | 14/2/74'. This copy appears to be an advance copy sent from the publisher to the Australian Publishing Co. and then onto a 'cataloguer' for placement in various advertising venues. It then passed into private hands. Other uncorrected proof copies are held at the State Library of New South Wales, Mitchell Library and ADFA. One of the ADFA proof copies is the review copy sent to Dorothy Green.

Copies: NSL: Mitchell Library A823/W587/15A1 (lacks dustjacket); NSL: Mitchell Library [PW]; NSL: JFR/066949; NSL: GRL N823.914/W587/2 (lacks dustjacket); NU: 823.91/A/W587/J2/1; VU: AX A823.3 White; Personal collection.

M1b U.K. First Edition Second Issue (London: Book Club Associates, 1973)

PATRICK WHITE | [rule] | THE EYE | OF | THE STORM | [at bottom:] BOOK CLUB ASSOCIATES | LONDON

Notes: p.*4* 'THIS EDITION PUBLISHED 1973 BY | BOOK CLUB ASSOCIATES | BY ARRANGEMENT WITH JONATHAN CAPE LTD. | © 1973 BY PATRICK WHITE | [at bottom:] | PRINTED IN GREAT BRITAIN | BY EBENEZER BAYLIS AND SON LTD | THE TRINITY PRESS, WORCESTER, AND LONDON | ON PAPER

MADE BY JOHN DICKINSON AND CO. LTD | BOUND BY G. AND J. KITCAT LTD, LONDON'. Cased in dark blue calico with white endpapers. Front and back: blank. Spine: [in gold] 'THE EYE | OF THE | STORM | [ornament] | PATRICK | WHITE' | [at bottom:] [Book Club Associates device]. Published in October 1973. £2.95. Print run: 6,000.

M1c First U.K. Edition Third Issue (London: Jonathan Cape, 1974)
Notes: p.*4* 'FIRST PUBLISHED 1973 | REPRINTED 1973, 1974 | © 1973 BY PAT-RICK WHITE | JONATHAN CAPE, 30 BEDFORD SQUARE, LONDON WC1 | ISBN 0 224 00902 8 | PRINTED PHOTOLITHO IN GREAT BRITAIN | BY EBE-NEZER BAYLIS AND SON LTD | THE TRINITY PRESS, WORCESTER, AND LONDON | ON PAPER MADE BY JOHN DICKINSON AND CO. LTD | BOUND BY G. AND J. KITCAT LTD, LONDON'. Published 22 February 1974. Price: £2.95. Print run: 3,250.

M2a U.S. First Edition (New York: Viking, 1974)

PATRICK WHITE | THE EYE | OF THE | STORM | THE VIKING PRESS NEW YORK

22 x 14.5 cm. Unsigned: 304 leaves. pp.*9* 10-608 p.

Endpaper; *1* 'THE EYE OF THE STORM'; *2* '*Also by Patrick White* | *Novels* | Happy Valley | The Living and the Dead | The Aunt's Story | The Tree of Man | Voss | Riders in the Chariot | The Solid Mandala | The Vivisector | *Stories* | The Burnt Ones | *Plays* | Four Plays'; *3* title page; *4* 'Copyright © 1973 by Patrick White | All rights reserved | Published in 1974 by The Viking Press, Inc. | 625 Madison Avenue, New York, N.Y. 10022 | Published simultaneously in Canada by | The Macmillan Company of Canada Limited | SBN 670-30374-7 | Library of Congress catalog card number: 73-3501 | Printed in U.S.A.'; *5* 'TO MAIE CASEY'; *6* [three epigraphs]; *7* 'THE EYE OF THE STORM'; *8* blank; *9* 10-608 text; endpaper.

Cased in dark grey paper-covered boards with spine in aqua-blue linen cloth, light blue top edge and off-white fibrous endpapers. Front and back: blank. Spine: [in metallic pink] [running down:] 'THE EYE OF THE STORM | [in silver] [upright:] PATRICK | WHITE | VIKING'.

Beige paper dustjacket. Front: 'PATRICK | WHITE | [in green] [thick rule] | THE EYE | OF THE | STORM | THE NEW NOVEL BY THE | NOBEL LAUREATE FOR 1973'. Back: [in green] '"... indisputably | possessed of genius."* | [rule] | [in black] [quotation of three lines from] –*FRANCIS KING, *The Sunday Telegraph* | [in green] [rule] | [in black] [quotation of five lines from] –WILLIAM TREVOR, *The Guardian* | [in green] [rule] | [in black] [quotation of six lines from] –NINA BAWDEN, *Daily Telegraph* | [in green] [rule] | [in black] [quotation of five lines from] –MAURICE WIGGIN, *The Sunday Times* | [in green] [rule] | [in black] THE VIKING PRESS PUBLISHERS NEW YORK | SBN 670-30374-7'. Spine: [running down:] [in green] 'PATRICK | WHITE | [upright:] [in black] VIKING | [running down:] [in green] THE EYE OF | THE STORM'. Inside front flap: '$8.95 | [quotation from the novel, 8 lines] | [in green] [rule] | [in black] [blurb, 30 lines] | *(Continued on back flap)* | 0174'. Inside back flap: '*(Continued from front flap)* | [blurb continues, 8 lines] | [biography, 18 lines] | *Jacket design by Mel Williamson* | [in green] [publisher's device] | [in black] THE VIKING PRESS | *Publishers of The Viking Portable Library* | *and Viking Compass paperbacks* | 625 Madison Avenue, New York, N.Y. 10022 | PRINTED IN U.S.A.'.

Published in January 1974. Price: US$8.95. Print run: 18,000.

Reviews: Arnold Asrelsky *Library Journal* v.98, 1 December 1973, p.3579 (140w); Peter Wolfe *New Republic* v.170, 5/12 January 1974, p.17 (1700w); Shirley Hazzard *New York Times Book Review* 6 January 1974, p.1 (2950w); A.F. Bellette *Ariel* v.5 no.3, 1974, p.128-130; June Goodwin *Christian Science Monitor* 9 January 1974, p.F6 (1000w); Martha Duffy *Time* v.103, 14 January 1974, p.67 (700w); *Newsweek* v.83, 21 January 1974, p.93 (800w); Edward Weeks *Atlantic Monthly* v.233, February 1974, p.233 (650w); D.K. Mano *National Review* v.26, 15 February 1974, p.214 (850w); E.B. Gallagher *Best Sellers* v.33, 15 February 1974, p.514 (250w); John Skow *Harper's Magazine* v.248, March 1974, p.92 (700w); A. Broyard *New York Times* 2 January 1974, p.2; J.B. Breslin *America* v.130, 2 March 1974, p.158 (700w); George Steiner *New Yorker* v.50, 4 March 1974, p.109 (1900w); Christopher Ricks *New York Review of Books* v.21, 4 April 1974, p.19 (2950w); Robert Phillips *Commonweal* v.100, 17 May 1974, p.269 (1150w); Judith Grant *Canadian Forum* v.54, May/June 1974, p.16 (900w); *Choice* April 1974, p.263; *Books & Bookmen* February 1974, p.85; *Book World* 20 January 1974, p.3; *Hudson Review* v.27, Summer 1974, p.283; *National Observer* v.13, 26 January 1974, p.21; *New York Times* 2 January 1974, p.35; *Prairie Schooner* Fall 1974, p.268; *Village Voice* v.19, 7 February 1974, p.23; 'White bursts on N.Y.' *Sydney Morning Herald* 4 January 1974, p.12.

Notes: A copy in White's own collection is a presentation copy half-bound in dark blue leather and blue marbled paper boards. The U.S. First Edition is essentially a reprint of the U.K. First Edition.

Copies: NSL: Mitchell Library A823/W587/24 (lacks dustjacket); NSL: Mitchell Library [PW]; VU: McL L/A-F White; Personal collection.

M2b Canadian Subedition (Toronto: Macmillan, 1974)
Notes: Not seen, but assumed from the statement on p.*4* of U.S. First Edition (see M2a above).

M2c-f U.S. First Edition Second to Fifth Issues (New York: Viking, 1974)
Notes: not seen, but assumed given Sixth Issue (see M2g below).

M2g U.S. First Edition Sixth Issue (New York: Viking, 1974)
Notes: p.*4* 'Sixth printing May 1974'. It is thought that this issue was remaindered in Australia.

M3a Penguin Edition First Issue (Harmondsworth: Penguin, 1975)

Patrick White | The Eye of the Storm | Penguin Books

18 x 10.9 cm. [A]^16 B-I^16 K^8 L-T^16 ($1 signed): 296 leaves. pp.*8* 9-588 *589-592* (the last page of each chapter is not numbered).

1 'Penguin Books | The Eye of the Storm' | [biography, 21 lines] | [publisher's device]; *2* blank; *3* title page; *4* 'Penguin Books Ltd, | Harmondsworth, Middlesex, England | Penguin Books Australia Ltd, | Ringwood, Victoria, Australia | Penguin Books (N.Z.) Ltd, | 182-190 Wairau Road, Auckland 10, New Zealand | First Published by Jonathan Cape 1973 | Published in Penguin Books 1975 | Copyright © Patrick White, 1973 | Made and printed in Great Britain by | Cox & Wyman Ltd London, Reading and Fakenham | Set in Monotype Garamond' | [publisher's conditions, 8 lines]; *5* 'To Maie Casey'; *6* blank; *7* [epigraphs]; *8* blank; 9-588 *589* text; *590* blank; *591* 'More About Penguins | and Pelicans'; *592* blank.

Perfectbound in black paper covers. Front: [in white] 'PATRICK WHITE [publisher's device] | Winner of the | 1973 Nobel Prize for Literature | THE EYE OF THE STORM' | [col. illust. of lightning over city at night]. Back : [at top right:] [publisher's device] | [blurb, 6 lines] | [quotation of six lines from] '— *Daily Telegraph* | [quotation of four lines from] — *New Statesman* | In *The Eye of the Storm* Patrick White, | Nobel Prize winner for Literature in 1973, | plots the tides of love, hate, comedy, | tragedy, impotence and longing that fester | beneath family relationships. | Cover photograph by Adam Woolfitt/Susan Griggs Agency | United Kingdom £2.50 | Australia $5.95 (recommended) | [at bottom left:] Fiction | ISBN 0 14 | 00.3963 5'. Spine: [in white] [running down:] 'PATRICK WHITE THE EYE OF THE STORM ISBN 0 14 | 00.3963 5' | [upright:] [publisher's device].

Notes: A number of copies have a variant binding which includes a copyright statement on the back cover: '[...] Griggs Agency | For copyright reasons this edition is not for sale in the U.S.A. or Canada | United Kingdom £2.50 | Australia $5.95 (recommended) | [at bottom right:] Fiction | ISBN 0 14 | 00.3963 5'.

Copies: NSL: Mitchell Library A823/W587/50; NSL: Mitchell Library [PW]; Personal collection; VSL: SLT A823.3 W585E (1975); NU: 823.91A/W587/J2/2.

M3b Penguin Edition Second Issue (Harmondsworth: Penguin, 1976)
Not seen.

M3c Penguin Edition Third Issue (Harmondsworth: Penguin, 1977)
Notes: 18 x 11 cm. p.*4* 'Published in Penguin Books 1975 | Reprinted 1976, 1977 | [...] | Made and printed in Great Britain by | Cox & Wyman Ltd, London, Reading and Fakenham | Set in Monotype Garamond'. Cover design of lightning over city at night. Price: £1.25, [sticker] AU$2.95

M3d-e Penguin Edition Fourth to Fifth Issues (Harmondsworth: Penguin, 1978-1980)
Not seen.

M3f Penguin Edition Sixth Issue (Harmondsworth: Penguin, 1982)
Notes: p.*4* 'Published in Penguin Books 1975 | Reprinted 1976, 1977, 1978, 1980, 1982 | Copyright © Patrick White, 1973 | All rights reserved | Set, printed and bound in Great Britain by | Cox & Wyman Ltd, Reading | Set in Monotype Garamond'. Price: £2.95.

M3g-i Penguin Edition Seventh to Ninth Issues (Harmondsworth: Penguin, n.d.)
Not seen

M3j Penguin Edition Tenth Issue (Harmondsworth: Penguin, [1992])
Notes: 19.6 x 12.8 cm.; p.*4* 'Published in Penguin Books 1975 | 10 | Copyright © Patrick
White, 1973 | All rights reserved | Printed in England by Clays Ltd, St Ives plc | Set in
Monotype Garamond'. Perfectbound in pale green paper covers. The cover shows a detail
from *The Storm* by Walter Withers in the Art Gallery of New South Wales, Sydney. Published in December 1992. Price: £6.99, CAN$14.99, US$11.95, AU$15.95. ISBN 0-14-
018605-0.

M4a U.S. Second Edition First Issue (New York: Avon, 1975)
Not seen. See M4f below for details of this edition, said to be first printed in January 1975.

M4b-e U.S. Second Edition Second to Fifth Issues (New York: Avon, 1975)
Not seen.

M4f U.S. Second Edition Sixth Issue (New York: Avon, 1975)

PATRICK | WHITE | *The* | Eye | *of the* | Storm | [publisher's device]
AVON | PUBLISHERS OF BARD, CAMELOT, DISCUS, EQUINOX
AND FLARE BOOKS

17.8 x 10.5 cm. Unsigned: 272 leaves. pp.*10* 11-544.

1 'Nobel Laureate | PATRICK | WHITE | In awarding Patrick White the Nobel Prize for |
Literature, the Royal Swedish Academy acclaimed | his "unbroken creative power, an ever
deeper | restlessness and seeking urge, an onslaught against | vital problems that have never
ceased to engage | him, and a wrestling with the language in order to | extract all its power
and all its nuances, to the | verge of the unattainable." | The following pages contain a sam-
pling of the extraordinary critical acclaim accorded | The | Eye | of the | Storm'; *2-3* [12 quo-
tations]; *4* blank; *5* title page; *6* 'AVON BOOKS | A division of | The Hearst Corporation |
959 Eighth Avenue | New York, New York 10019 | Copyright © 1973 by Patrick White. |
Published by arrangement with the Viking Press, Inc. | Library of Congress Catalog Card
Number: 73-3501. | ISBN: 0-380-00214-0 | All rights reserved, which includes the right | to
reproduce this book or portions thereof in | any form whatsoever. For information address |
The Viking Press, Inc., | 625 Madison Avenue, New York, New York 10022. | First Avon
Printing, January, 1975. | Sixth Printing | AVON TRADEMARK REG. U.S. PAT. OFF.
AND | FOREIGN COUNTRIES REGISTERED TRADEMARK— | MARCA REG-
ISTRADA, HECHO EN CHICAGO, U.S.A. | Printed in the U.S.A.'; *7* 'To Maie Ca-
sey'; *8* blank; *9* [epigraphs]; *10* blank; 11-544 text.

Perfectbound in silver-coated white paper. Front: 'AVON/21527/$1.95 [publisher's device] |
[in crimson] NOBEL PRIZE WINNER | [in black] PATRICK | WHITE | THE NA-
TIONWIDE | BESTSELLER | [in crimson] *The* | [illust. of a woman's head] | Eye | *of the*
| Storm | "Deep entertainment ... satisfaction ... | every kind of love, licit and illicit ... | a
writer who has mastered his craft ..." | *Los Angeles Times*'. Back: [blurb, 11 lines] | [quotation

of 10 lines from] '*The New York Times Book Review* | SELECTED BY THE LITERARY GUILD | [running down:] [at bottom right:] Printed in U.S.A.'. Spine: [publisher's device] | 'AVON | [running down:] PATRICK WHITE / [in crimson] *The* Eye *of the* Storm 380.21527.195'.

Copies: NSL: Mitchell Library A823/W587/53; NSL Mitchell Library [PW].

M.t1 German First Edition (Düsseldorf: Claassen-Verlags; Zürich: Coron-Verlag; Paris: Les Editions Rombaldi, [1973])

[from front cover of binding] [in gold] Patrick White | [in black] Im Auge des Sturms | [in blind] NOBELPREIS | FÜR | LITERATUR | [in gold] [crown]

22.7 x 16 cm. Unsigned: 332 leaves. pp.*8* 9-11 *12-14* 15-17 *18-20* 21-37 *38-46* 47-113 *114-116* 117-159 *160-162* 163-214 *215-216* 217-230 *231-232* 233-253 *254-256* 257-319 *320-322* 323-403 *404-406* 407-484 *485-486* 487-509 *510-512* 513-572 *573-574* 575-598 *599-600* 601-660 *661-664*; illust.

Endpaper; frontis.; *1* [in red] 'NOBELPREIS | [in black] FÜR LITERATUR | [in red] 1973'; *2* blank; *3* [in box of red ornamental rules:] 'DIE SAMMLUNG | [in red] NOBEL-PREIS FÜR LITERATUR | [in black] STEHT UNTER DER | SCHIRMHERR-SCHAFT | DER SCHWEDISCHEN AKADEMIE | UND DER NOBELSTIFTUNG | STOCKHOLM'; *4* [black and white portrait of the author]; *5* 'DIESE AUSGABE VON | [in red] PATRICK WHITE | [in black] IM AUGE DES STURMS | [in red] NOBEL-PREIS 1973 | AUSTRALIEN | [in black] IST EINE AUF DEN | KREIS DER NOBEL-PREISFREUNDE | BESCHRÄNKTE AUFLAGE | UND ERSCHEINT MIT GENEHMIGUNG DES | CLAASSEN-VERLAGES DÜSSELDORF IM | [in red] CORON-VERLAG ZÜRICH'; *6* blank; *7* [in red] 'KLEINE GESCHICHTE | [in black] DER ZUERKENNUNG | DES NOBELPREISES AN | [in red] PATRICK WHITE | [in black] VON | [in red] DR. KJELL STRÖMBERG | [in black] EHEMALIGEM KULTURATTACHÉ AN DER | SCHWEDISCHEN BOTSCHAFT IN PARIS'; *8* blank; 9-11 text; *12* blank; *13* [in red] 'VERLEIHUNGSREDE | [in black] VON | [in red] ARTUR LUNDQVIST | [in black] PRÄSIDENT DES NOBELPREISKOMITEES | DER SCHWEDISCHEN AKADEMIE | ANLÄSSLICH DER FEIERLICHEN ÜBERREICHUNG | DES NOBELPREISES FÜR LITERATUR | AN | [in red] PAT-RICK WHITE | [in black] AM | 10.12.1973'; *14* blank; 15-17 text; *18* blank; *19* [in red] 'LEBEN UND WERK | [in black] VON | [in red] PATRICK WHITE | [in black] VON | HELMUT M. BRAEM'; *20* blank; 21-37 text; *38* blank; *39* 'IM AUGE DES STURMS'; *40* blank; *41* 'PATRICK WHITE | [in red] IM AUGE DES STURMS | [in black] RO-MAN'; *42* blank; *43* 'Für | Maie Casey'; *44* [epigraphs]; *45* [illust.]; *46* blank; 47-113 *114-116* 117-159 *160-162* 163-214 *215-216* 217-230 *231-232* 233-253 *254-256* 257-319 *320-322* 323-403 *404-406* 407-484 *485-486* 487-509 *510-512* 513-572 *573-574* 575-598 *599-600* 601-654 text; 655-660 'BIBLIOGRAPHIE'; *661* 'INHALT'; *662* blank; *663* 'Diese Ausgabe von | Patrick White | » Im Auge des Sturms « | ist für den Kreis der Nobelpreis-freunde bestimmt | und trägt in der Reihe des literarischen Nobelpresies | die laufende Nummer | 68 | Die sammlung wird in Zusammenarbeit mit | Les Editions Rombaldi, Paris, herausgegeben und erscheint im Coron-Verlag, Zürich | Bei der französischen Ausgabe ha-ben mitgewirkt: Für die literarische Direktion : Christobal de Ascerado | Für die kunstlerische Leitung : Gerard Angiolini | unter Mitwirkung für allgemeine Nobelpreisfragen und Bibliographie von | Werner Martin, Osnabrück | Übersetzung der Begleittexte : Erika Gebühr und Ulrich K. Dreikandt | Die Illustrationen fertigte : Heinz Jost, Bern | Otmar Frick, Reutlingen | © der Begleittexte: Les Editions Rombaldi, Paris | © Deutsche Übersetzung der Begleittexte und »Leber und Werk« : Coron-Verlag, Zürich | © des Romans von P. White : Claassen-Verlag, Düsseldorf | Druck : Hanseatische Druckanstalt GmbH, Hamburg | Papier : Peter Temming AG, Glückstadt | Bindearbeiten : W. Sigloch, Künzelsau'; *664* blank; endpaper.

Cased in white silk with white endpapers. Front: [in gold] 'Patrick White | [in black] Im Auge des Sturms | [in blind] NOBELPREIS | FÜR | LITERATUR' | [in gold] [crown]. Back: blank. Spine: [in gold] 'Patrick White | [in black] Im Auge | des Sturms | [at bottom:] [in gold] Nobelpreis | für | Literatur | 1973'.

Copies: NSL: Mitchell Library [PW].

M.t2a German Second Edition First Issue (Düsseldorf: Claassen Verlag, 1974)

Patrick | White | Im Auge | des Sturms | Roman | Deutsch | von | Matthias Büttner | Claassen

22 x 14.1 cm. Unsigned: 300 leaves. pp.7 8-599 *600* (the first page of each chapter is unnumbered).

Endpaper; *1* 'Patrick | White | Im Auge | des Sturms'; *2* blank; *3* title page; *4* 'Titel der 1973 bei Jonathan Cape Ltd., London, | erschienenen Originalausgabe: | THE EYE OF THE STORM | © 1973 by Patrick White | [at bottom:] 1. Auflage 1974 | Copyright © 1974 by Claassen Verlag GmbH, | Düsseldorf | Alle Rechte der Verbreitung in deutscher Sprache, | auch durch Film, Funk, Fernsehen, | fotomechanische Wiedergabe, Tonträger jeder Art | und auszugsweisen Nachdruck, sind vorbehalten | Gesetzt aus der 9/11 Punkt Garamond | Gesamtherstellung : Druckerei Gebr. Rasch & Co., Bramsche | ISBN 3 546 49622 1 '; *5* 'Für | Maie Casey'; *6* [epigraphs]; *7* 8-599 text; *600* 'Patrick White | Der Maler | 580 Seiten, Leinen | [quotation of eight lines from] Horst Bienek in Deutsche Zeitung | Ingmar Björkstén | Patrick White - die Stimme Australiens | 160 Seiten, Leinen | [quotation of nine lines from] Hessischer Rundfunk | Claassen Verlag · 4 Düsseldorf 1 · Postfach 9229'; endpaper.

Cased in blue cloth with white laid endpapers. Front and back: blank. Spine: [in blue on white panel:] 'White | Im Auge | des Sturms | Claassen'.

White paper dustjacket printed in blue and black. Front: 'PATRICK WHITE | [in yellow] Im | Auge | des | Sturms | [in white] Der neue | Roman | des Nobel- | preisträgers | [in yellow] Claassen'. Back: [in white] '»*Im Auge des Sturms* | ist eine ausserordentliche Leistung. | Es hat die Tiefe | und die Reichhaltigkeit eines Meisterwerks.« | THE SPECTATOR | »Patrick White erhielt den Nobelpreis für Literatur | für seine epische, psychologische | Erzählkunst, | durch die der Literatur | ein neuer Erdteil zugeführt worden ist.« | *Aus der Begründung zur Verleihung | des Nobelpreises für Literatur 1973 | an Patrick White* | »Patrick White ist nicht ein Autor, | der die Welt zu verändern gedenkt — | wohl aber einer, | der eine ganze Menge von ihr enthüllt, | und oft genug Bereiche, | die noch verblüffend unbekannt erscheinen.« | *Christian Ferber, DIE WELT* | 245 09622'. Spine: [running down:] [in white] 'WHITE Im Auge | des Sturms | [at bottom:] [upright:] Claassen'. Inside front flap:

[blurb, 41 lines]. Inside back flap: 'Von Patrick White ist im Claassen | Verlag bereits erschienen | *Der Maler*, Roman, 580 S., Ln. | [quotation of 29 lines from] *Westdeutscher Rundfunk*' | [biography, 5 lines].

Published in September 1974. Price: DM 34.00. Print run: 10,000. ISBN 3-546-49622-1.

Reviews: Helmut Winter *Frankfurter Allgemeine Zeitung* 5 September 1974; *Frankfurter Neue Presse* 6 September 1974; Georg Böse *Der Tagesspiegel* 22 September 1974; Horst Bienek *Die Zeit* 27 September 1974; Rainer Taeni *Deutsche Zeitung* 11 October 1974; Barbara Höpping *Rheinischer Merkur* 11 October 1974; Georg Böse *Augsburger Allgemeine* 24 October 1974; *Ruhr-Nachrichten. Essener Tageblatt* 15 November 1974; Ingeborg Brandt *Welt am Sonntag* 27 November 1974; Werner Hesse *Die Rheinpfalz. Unterhaardter Rundschau* 27 November 1974; *Neue Zürcher Zeitung* 29 November 1974, p.87; Hedwig Rohde *Deutsches Allgemeines Sonntagsblatt* 1 December 1974, p.21; Rudolf Grimm *General-Anzeiger* 10 January 1975; Rainer Taeni *Kölner Stadt-Anzeiger* 18 January 1975; Heinz Albers *Hamburger Abendblatt* 31 January 1975; *Deutsche Wochen-Zeitung* 14 February 1975; Margaret Studer *Tagesanzeiger* 30 May 1975.

Copies: VSL: SLT 819.93 W582EB; NSL: Mitchell Library 823/W587/43; NSL: Mitchell Library [PW]; NU: 823.91/W587/J2/TG (lacks dustjacket); NSL: Mitchell Library A823/W587/27 (lacks dustjacket); Personal collection.

M.t2b German Second Edition Second Issue (Zurich: Buchclub Ex Libris, 1975)
Notes: p.*4* 'Ungekürtze Lizenzausgabe für den | Buchclub Ex Libris Zürich 1975'.

M.t2c German Second Edition Third Issue (Münich, Zurich: Piper, 1992)
Notes: pp.599. DM 19.80. Print run: 6,000. ISBN 3-492-11128-9. (Serie Piper, 1128); also see *Index Translationum*.

M.t3 Finnish First Edition (Helsinki: Kustannusosakeyhtiö Otava, 1974)

[on verso:] PATRICK WHITE | [on recto:] MYRSKYN SILMÄ | [at left:] SUOMENTANUT JUSSI NOUSIAINEN | [rule] | HELSINGISSÄ KUSTANNUSOSAKEYHTIÖ OTAVA | [publisher's device]

22.5 x 15 cm. [1]^8 2-30^8 ($1 signed): 240 leaves. pp.*9* 10-474 *475-480* (the first page of each chapter is unnumbered).

Endpaper; *1* 'MYRSKYN SILMÄ'; *2-3* title pages; *4* 'Englanninkielinen alkuteos | The Eye of Storm [sic] | © 1973 by Patrick White | ISBN 951-1-01467-6 | Kustannusosakeyhtiö Otavan painolaitokset | Keuruu 1974'; *5* '*Maie Caseylle*'; *6* blank; *7* [epigraphs]; *8* blank; *9* 10-474 text; *475-480* blank; endpaper.

Cased in black paper-covered boards with red endpapers. Front and back: blank. Spine: [running down:] [in white] 'PATRICK WHITE [in red] myrskyn silmä'.

White paper wrappers printed in black with col. illust. of woman in wheelchair across front and spine. Front: [in white] 'myrskyn silmä [in grey] OTAVA | PATRICK | WHITE'. Back: [at bottom:] [publisher's device] | 'ISBN 951-1-01467-6'. Spine: [running down:] [in white] 'PATRICK WHITE [in red] myrskyn silmä'. Inside front flap: '582 | PATRICK

WHITE | MYRSKYN SILMÄ | [blurb, 44 lines] | *jatkuu takaliepees* | [running down:] [at left] PÄÄLLYS: KOSTI ANTIKAINEN'. Inside back flap: [blurb continues, 5 lines] | [biography, 40 lines].

Notes: One copy sighted has a variant dustjacket: Back: [in white] '1973 NOBEL-KIRJAILIJAN | PÄÄTEOS, LUKUKOKEMUS | JOKA EI HEVIN UNDHDU | [rule] | [in red] PATRICK WHITE | MYRSKYN SILMÄ | [in white] [blurb, 10 lines] | PÄÄLLYS : KOSTI ANTIKAINEN | 845 | Tilno 4822 | ISBN 951-1-01467-6'. Inside front flap: 'Otavan julkaisemia | Nobel-kirjailijoiden teoksia' | [list of titles by Nobel Laureates]. Inside back flap: [list continues].

Copies: Personal collection (2 copies); NSL: Mitchell Library A823/W587/26 (lacks dustjacket); NSL: Mitchell Library [PW]; NSL: GRL E823.914/WHI.

M.t4 Italian First Edition (Milan: Bompiani, 1974)

PATRICK WHITE | L'occhio dell'uragano | Bompiani

20.5 x 12 cm. Unsigned: 154 leaves. pp.*6* 7-583 *584-608*.

1 'L'occhio dell'uragano'; *2* [at bottom:] 'Dello stesso autore presso l'editore Bompiani: | Màndala solido'; *3* title page; *4* 'Titolo originale: | THE EYE OF THE STORM | Copyright © 1973 by Patrick White | (Prima edizione in Gran Bretagna: Jonathan Cape Ltd, 1973) | Traduzione dall'inglese di | PAOLA BOTTALLA NORDIO, LOREDANA DA SCHIO, RODOLFO DELMONTE | Coordinamento: BERNARD HICKEY | [at bottom:] © 1974, Casa editrice Valentino Bompiani & C. S.p.A. | Via Pisacane, 26 - Milano | CL 04-1459-X'; *5* 'a Maie Casey'; *6* [epigraphs]; 7-583 text; *584* blank; 585-592 'NOTA | ALL'EDIZIONE ITALIANA | di | Bernard Hickey'; *593* 'INDICE'; *594* blank; *595* [index]; *596* blank; *597-601* 'LETTERATURA MODERNA' | [190 titles]; *602-605* 'I DELFINI' | [176 titles]; *606* blank; *607* '*Finito di stampare | nel mese di giugno 1974 | dalla Edigraf s.r.l. - Segrate (Milano)*'; *608* blank.

Perfectbound in glossy blue paper card. Front: [in white] 'Patrick | White | [in light blue] L'occhio | dell'uragano | [in white] *Romanzo* | Bompiani'. Back: [in white] [blurb, 41 lines] | [running down:] [at top right:] 'CL 04-1459-X | [at bottom right:] C.D.U. 86'. Spine: [running down:] [in white] 'Patrick White • L'occhio dell'uragano • Bompiani'. Inside front flap: [in white] [biography, 48 lines]. Inside back flap: [in white] 'Letteraria Bompiani | [36 titles] | [at bottom left:] L. 4.800 | [at bottom right:] (4528)'.

Price: L4800.

Copies: VSL: SLT 819.93 W582EBO; NSL: Mitchell Library A823/W587/40 and 40A; NSL: Mitchell Library [PW]; Personal collection.

M.t5 Japanese First Edition (Tokyo: Mikasa Shobo, 1974)

[Taif no-me]

19.5 x 13.3 cm. Unsigned: leaves. pp.*6* 7-269 *270-274*.

Cased in grey sculpted paper boards with buff endpapers and brown silk ribbon. White glossy paper dustjacket with illust. of stylised landscape in pastel tones. Yellow paper wraparound.

Translated by Hiroo Mukai. Price: ¥ 890. Published by Mikaso-Shobo by arrangement through Charles E. Tuttle Co., Tokyo (p.*271*). ISBN 0097-005124-8937.

Copies: Personal collection; NSL: Mitchell Library [PW]; ANL: OJ 5988 5043.

M.t6 Turkish First Edition (Istanbul: Hürriyet Yayinlari, 1974)

Patrick White | [in red] FIRTINANIN | GÖZÜ | [in black] (The Eye of the Storm) | Çeviren : | NES'E OLCAYTU | [publisher's device] Nuruosmaniye Caddesi, No 3, Cagaloglu — ISTANBUL

20.3 x 14.1 cm. [1]^8 2-33^8 ($1 signed): 264 leaves. pp.*9* 10-528.

Endpaper; *1-2* blank; *3* 'FIRTINANIN GÖZÜ'; *4* [rule] | 'HÜRRIYET YAYINLARI : 69 | DEV ROMANLAR : 17 | [rule] | FIRTINANIN GÖZÜ | Patrick White | [rule] | Yayin Hakki (Copyright) : Hürriyet Yayinlari ve Patrick White | Birinci baski : Subat, 1974 | Dizgi - baski : Dizerkonca Matbaasi | Kapak baskisi : Tem Ofset | Cilt : Aytaç Kirma ve Cilt Atelyesi'; *5* title page; *6* 'DEV ROMANLAR'; *7* [epigraphs]; *8* 'MAIE CASEY'YE'; *9* 10-528 text; endpaper.

Cased in blue cloth with grey endpapers. Front and back: blank. Spine: [running down:] [in gold] 'FIRTINANIN GÖZÜ || Patrick | White | [at bottom:] [upright:] 69' | [publisher's device].

Red paper dustjacket. Front: [in red] '1973 NOBEL ÖDÜLÜ | [in purple] FIRTINANIN GÖZÜ | [in white] Patrick | White' | [at bottom left:] [publisher's device]. Back: [in yellow] [blurb, 26 lines] | [at bottom right:] '30 lira'. Spine: 'DEV ROMANLAR | 18 | [running down:] [in white] FIRTINANIN GÖZÜ || [in purple] Patrick | White | [at bottom:] [upright:] 69' | [publisher's device]. Inside front flap: [blurb and biography, 44 lines]. Inside back flap: [in red] 'DEV ROMANLAR DIZISI'.

Price: 30 lira.

Copies: Personal collection.

M.t7 Spanish First Edition (Barcelona: Luis de Caralt, 1974)

PATRICK WHITE | EL FOCO | DE LA TEMPESTAD | LUIS DE CARALT | EDITOR | Ganduxer, 77 | BARCELONA

20 x 13.7 cm. [1]^8 2-35^8: 280 leaves. pp.*6* 7-555 *556-560*.

Endpaper; *1* [series device]; *2* blank; *3* title page; *4* '*Titulo de la obra original:* | *THE EYE OF THE STORM* | © *1973 by Patrick White* | Traducción | de | MANUEL BARTOLOMÉ LÓPEZ | RESERVADOS TODOS LOS DERECHOS | © LUIS DE CARALT, 1974 | Depósito Legal: B. 33.495 - 1974 [at right:] ISBN 84-217-1668-9'; *5* 'A MAIE CASEY'; *6* blank; 7-555 text; *556* blank; *557* [at bottom right:] 'ESTE VOLUMEN | SE TERMINÓ DE IMPRIMIR | DURANTE EL MES DE SEPTIEMBRE DE 1974 | EN LOS TALLERES GRÁFICOS | DE LA EDITORIAL CASAL I VALL | DE ANDORRA'; *558-560* blank; endpaper.

Cased in brown imitation-cloth boards with white endpapers. Front and back: blank. Spine: [in gold on black panels:] 'PATRICK | WHITE | EL | FOCO | DE LA | TEMPESTAD | [at bottom:] [cursive] *Luis | de | Caralt*'.

White glossy paper dustjacket. Front: [hollow type] 'PATRICK | WHITE | [solid type] [in blue] EL FOCO DE LA | TEMPESTAD' | [black & white illust. of stylised eye]. Back: [at bottom right:] 'T.G. Soler - Esplugas (Barna.)'. Spine: [hollow type] 'PATRICK | WHITE | [solid type] [in blue] EL | FOCO | DE LA | TEMPESTAD | [in black] CARALT'. Inside front flap: [in blue] 'EL FOCO DE LA TEMPESTAD' | [blurb, 40 lines]. Inside back flap: [in blue] [series device] | 'LO MAS SELECTO DE LA | LITERATURA UNIVERSAL'.

Copies: NSL: Mitchell Library 823.914/W587/44 (lacks dustjacket); NSL: Mitchell Library [PW]; NSL: Mitchell Library A823/W587/33; Personal collection.

M.t8 Swedish First Edition (Stockholm: Forum, 1975)

Patrick White | Stormens öga | Forum

21.8 x 13.8 cm. [1]^8 2-32^8 ($1 signed): 256 leaves. pp.*6* 7-509 *510-512*.

Endpaper; *1* 'Stormens öga'; *2* '*Av Patrick White har tidigare på svenska utgivits:* | *Livets träd* | *De fyra utkorade* | *Den oförstörbara mandalan* | *Målaren*'; *3* title page; *4* '*Till Maie Casey* | Engelska originalets titel The Eye of the Storm (London 1973) | Översättning MAGNUS K:SON LINDBERG | Copyright © 1973 by Patrick White | Omslag av Christer Jonson | ISBN 91-37-05880-0 | Printed in Sweden | Tryckt hos Schmidts Boktryckeri AB, Helsingborg 1975'; *5* [epigraphs]; *6* blank; 7-509 *510* text; *511* 'Ingmar Björkstén | Patrick White | epikern från Australien'; *512* blank; endpaper.

Cased in green paper-covered boards. Front and back: blank. Spine: [in white] 'Patrick White Stormens öga'.

White glossy paper dustjacket with illust. of modernist painting of elderly women against a predominantly green landscape. Front: [in white] 'Patrick White | Stormens öga | [at bottom right:] Forum'. Back: [blurb, 2 lines]. Spine: [running down:] [in white] 'Patrick White | Stormens öga | [at bottom:] [upright:] Forum'. Inside front flap: [b&w photograph of the author] | '"For en episk och psykologisk | berättarkonst som infört en ny | världsdel i litteraturen." | Svenska Akademiens motivering för | Nobelpriset i litteratur till Patrick White | 1973. | [at bottom:] FORUM ISBN 91-37-05880-0'. Inside front flap: [blurb, 14 lines] | [quotation of 18 lines from] 'Ingmar Björkstén | i *Patrick White - epikern | från Australien*'.

Copies: NSL: Mitchell Library A823/W587/73 (lacks dustjacket); NSL: Mitchell Library [PW]; Personal collection.

M.t9 Polish First Edition (Warsaw: Państwowy Instytut Wydawniczy, 1976)

[at left:] Patrick White | [circle] | Współczesna | Proza | Światowa | [at right:] Oko | cyklonu | Przełożyła | Maria Skibniewska | [at bottom:] Państwowy Instytut Wydawniczy 1976

17.8 x 11.7 cm. [1]^8 2-45^8 46^6 ($2 signed): 366 leaves. pp.*8* 9-731 *732*.

1 'White | Oko cyklonu'; *2* [illust.]; *3* title page; *4* 'Tytuł oryginału | The Eye of the Storm | Opracowanie graficzne | Waldemar Świerzy | © 1973 by Patrick White | PRINTED IN POLAND | Państwowy Instytut Wydawniczy, Warszawa 1976 r. | Wydanie pierwsze | Nakład 30 000 + 290 egz. Ark. wyd. 38,2. Ark. druk. 45,75 | Papier druk. sat. kl. IV, 65 g, 75X100/32 | Oddano do składania 25 listopada 1975 r. | Podpisano do druku w maju 1976 r.

| Druk ukończono w maju 1976 r. | Wrocławskie Zakłady Graficzne — Zakład Główny | Nr. zam. 1794/A J-119 | Cena zł 75.—'; *5* 'Dedykowane | *Maie Casey*'; *6* blank; *7* [epigraphs]; *8* blank; 9-731 *732* text.

Sewn in glossy card printed in full colour. Front: [background illust. of a hand with ring across front, spine and back] [in white] 'Patrick White | [at right:] Oko cyklonu | [at bottom right:] Państwowy | Instytut | Wydawniczy'. Back: blank. Spine: [running down:] [in white] 'Patrick White Oko cyklonu' | [at bottom:] [upright:] [publisher's device]. Inside front flap: [description, 33 lines]. Inside back flap: [biography, 9 lines] | 'zł 75.—'.

Published in May 1975. Price: zł 75. Print run: 30,000.

Copies: NSL: Mitchell Library A823/W587/64 (rebound); NSL: Mitchell Library [PW]; Personal collection.

M.t10 Czech First Edition (Prague: Odeon, 1978)

p*atrick* | white | [in orange] [abstract illust.] | [in black] o*ko* | *urugánu* | o*deon*

20.5 x 13.5 cm. Unsigned: 280 leaves. pp.*10* 11-553 *554* 555-557 *558-560*.

Endpaper; *1* [in orange] 'k*lub* | *čtenáru* | [in black] / *odeon* /'; *2* blank; *3* [in orange] 'p*atrick* | white | [in black] o*ko* | *uragánu*'; *4* blank; *5* title page; *6* 'Přeložil | MIREK ČEJKA | © 1973 by Patrick White'; *7* [in orange] '*věnováno* | m*aie* caseyové'; *8* blank; *9* [epigraphs]; *10* blank; 11-553 *554* text; 555-557 *558* '/ o *dile a tvůrči osobnosti* p*atricka* w*hitea* /' [by Mirek Cejka]; *559* blank; *560* 'KLUB ČTENÁŘŮ | Svazek 420 | [in orange] p*atrick* | white | o*ko* | *uragánu* | Z anglického originálu | The Eye of the Storm | (Jonathan Cape, London 1973) | přeložil a doslov napsal Mirek Čejka. | Obálku, vazbu a grafickou úpravu | navrhl Pavel Hrach. | Vydal Odeon, | nakladatelstvi krásné literatury | a uměni, n.p., jako svou 3618. publikaci | v redakci krásné literatury. | Praha 1978. | Odpovědná redaktorka Eva Kondrysová. | Ze sazby mono-foto vytiskl ofsetem | TISK, knižni výroba, n.p., | závod 3, Česky Těšin. | 34,12 autorských archů, | 34,71 vydavatelských archů. | 605 22 856. Vydáni prvni. | Náklad 82 000 výtisků. | 01-036-78. 13/34. | Cena váz. 36 Kčs.'; endpaper.

Cased in fawn cloth with white endpapers. Front: [in orange] [abstract illust.]. Back: blank. Spine: [running down:] [in orange] 'o*ko uragánu* [abstract illust.] p*atrick* | white'.

Buff coloured paper dustjacket. Front: 'p*atrick* | white | [in orange] o*ko urugánu* | klub | čtenárů | |odeon|'. Back: [at top left:] '01-036-78 | 13/34 | 36 kčs' | [at bottom left:] [publisher's device]. Spine: [running down:] 'o*ku urugánu* [in orange] [abstract illust.] [in black] p*atrick* | white'. Inside front flap: 'p*atrick* | white | o*ku* | *urugánu* | *Z angli čtiny přeložil Mirek Čejka*' | [blurb, 33 lines]. Inside back flap: [biography, 40 lines].

Price: 36 kčs. Print run: 82,000.

Copies: NSL: Mitchell Library A823/W587/67; NSL: Mitchell Library [PW]; Personal collection.

M.t11 French First Edition (Paris: Gallimard, 1978)

PATRICK WHITE | L'oeil du cyclone | I [II] | TRADUIT DE L'ANGLAIS | PAR SUZANNE NÉTILLARD | [publisher's mongram] | GALLIMARD

20.4 x 14.1 cm. 2 v.: (Vol.I:) Unsigned: 160 leaves. pp.[*8*] 11-318 *319-322*. (Vol.II:) Unsigned: 200 leaves. pp.[*4*] 7-399 *400-402*.

(Vol.I:) [*1*] 'DU MONDE ENTIER'; [*2*] blank; [*3*] title page; [*4*] '*Titre original :* | THE EYE OF THE STORM | *Tous droits de traduction, de reproduction et d'adaptation* | *réservés pour tous les pays.* | © *Patrick White, 1973.* | © *Éditions Gallimard, 1978, pour la traduction française.*'; [*5*] 'A MAIE CASEY'; [*6*] blank; [*7*] [epigraphs]; [*8*] blank; 11-318 *319* text; *320* blank; *321* 'DU MÊME AUTEUR | [publisher's monogram] | EDEN-VILLE | LE CHAR DES ÉLUS | VOSS | LES ÉCHAUDÉS | LE MYSTÉRIEUX MANDALA'; *322* '*Cet ouvrage* | *a été achevé d'imprimer* | *sur les presses de l'Imprimerie Floch* | *à Mayenne le 9 janvier 1978.* | *Dépôt légal : 1ᵉʳ trimestre 1978.* | *Nᵒ d'édition : 22952.* | *Imprimé en France.* | *(15083)* | [at bottom left:] 22952'. (Vol.II:) [as for Vol. I except for:] p.7-399 *400* text; *401* 'DU MÊME AUTEUR | [publisher's monogram] | EDEN-VILLE | LE CHAR DES ÉLUS | VOSS | LES ÉCHAUDÉS | LE MYSTÉRIEUX MANDALA'; *402* '*Cet ouvrage* | *a été achevé d'imprimer* | *sur les presses de l'Imprimerie Floch* | *à Mayenne le 9 janvier 1978.* | *Dépôt légal : 1ᵉʳ trimestre 1978.* | *Nᵒ d'édition : 22953.* | *Imprimé en France.* | *(15084)* | [at bottom left:] 22953'.

Both volumes are perfectbound in white glossy card. Front: 'DU MONDE ENTIER | PATRICK WHITE | [in red] L'ŒIL | DU CYCLONE | [in black] I [II] | ROMAN | TRADUIT DE L'ANGLAIS | PAR SUZANNE NÉTILLARD | [series device] | [in red] [publisher's monogram] | [in black] GALLIMARD'. Back: 'PATRICK WHITE | [in red] L'œil du cyclone | [in black] [description, 26 lines] | [biography, 7 lines] | [in red] [publisher's monogram] | [in black] [at bottom right:] 78.1'. Spine: [in red] '*du monde* | *entier* | [in black] PATRICK | WHITE | [in red] L'ŒIL | DU CYCLONE | [in black] I [II] | [publisher's monogram] | GALLIMARD'.

Copies: VSL: SLT 819.93 W582EN (2 vols.); NSL: Mitchell Library 823.914/W587/10; NSL: Mitchell Library [PW]; NSL: FRE/WHI/1.

M.t12 Serbo-Croat First Edition (Zagreb: August Cesarec, 1979)

PATRICK WHITE | OKO | OLUJE | [publisher's device] | AUGUST CESAREC | ZAGREB 1979

19.7 x 12 cm. [1]⁸ 2-33⁸ 34⁴ ($1 signed): 268 leaves. pp.*8* 9-535 *536*.

Endpaper; 1 'PATRICK WHITE / OKO OLUJE'; 2 'BIBLIOTEKA BESTSELER | Urednik | DRAGAN MILKOVIĆ | Naslov izvornika | PATRICK WHITE | THE EYE OF THE STORM | Cox & Wyman Ltd London, 1975 | Prijevod | LJILJANA FILIPOVIĆ | Likovna oprema | NENAD DOGAN'; 3 title page; 4 blank; 5 '*Posvećeno Maie Casey*'; 6 blank; 7 [epigraphs]; 8 blank; 9-535 text; 536 'IZDAVAČKO PODUZEĆE: AUGUST CESAREC | ZAGREB, BRAĆE OREŠKI 18 | ZA IZDAVAČA: DRAGAN MILKOVIĆ | KOREKTOR: VESNA MAGJER | TEHNIČKI UREDNOK: FRANJO PROFETA | TISAK: NIŠRO *VJESNIK OOUR TMG*'; endpaper.

Cased in orange linen cloth with white endpapers. Front: 'Patrick White | OKO | OLUJE | BESTSELER'. Back: blank. Spine: [running down:] 'Patrick White OKO OLUJE' | [at bottom:] [upright:] [publisher's device].

White paper dustjacket printed with black ground and full colour illustration. Front: [in white] 'Patrick White | OKO | OLUJE | BESTSELER'. Back: blank. Spine: [in white] 'Patrick White OKO OLUJE' | [at bottom:] [upright:] [publisher's device]. Inside front flap: [in

white] 'Patrick White | OKO OLUJE' | [biography and blurb, 36 lines]. Inside back flap: [in white] 'DOSAD IZAŠLO U BIBLIOTECI | BESTSELER' | [16 titles follow].
Copies: VGRL: Geelong Cro.F/WHI.

M.t13 Bulgarian First Edition (Sofija: Narodna Kultura, 1984)

Okoto na burjata.
Notes: pp.659. Translated by Julijan Konstantinov. Also see *Index Translationum*.
Copies: NSL: Mitchell Library [PW].

M.t14 Chinese First Edition (Kwei-lin Shih: Li-jiang Zh'u Pan She [Hangzhou University], 1986)

[Feng Pao Yen]
Notes: pp.710. Translated by Zhu Jiong-giang, et al. Issued in both cased and papeback bindings.
Copies: NSL: Mitchell Library [PW]; ANL: OC 5988 5043 [NUCOM].

M.t15 Hebrew First Edition (Lod: Zmora-Bitan, n.d.)

[En-ha seara]
Notes: 652p. trans. by G. Ariokh. Not seen but see *Index Translationum*.

M.m1 Braille (London: Royal National Institute for the Blind, n.d.)
The Eye of the Storm (8 volumes of Interpoint Braille).
Copies: ANL Braille 2751.

M.m2 Sound Recording (Burwood: Royal Blind Society of New South Wales, n.d.)
The Eye of the Storm (4 audiocassettes, 4-track).
Read by John Dease.
Not seen, but see entry on the National Bibliographic Database.

M.m3 Sound Recording (Toronto: Canadian National Institute for the Blind, 1978)
The Eye of the Storm (17 audiocassettes, 25.5 hours).
Read by Carmen Matthews.
Copies: Ottawa Public Library (not seen).

M.m4 Sound Recording (Melbourne: Royal Victorian Institute for the Blind, Tertiary Resource Service, 1985)
The Eye of the Storm (4 audiocassettes, 4-track).
Read by Peggy Dunphy from the Cape edition of 1973.
Not seen, but see entry on the National Bibliographic Database.

N The Cockatoos (1974)

The Cockatoos comprises six short stories composed at various times. 'A Woman's Hand' was conceived as one of three novellas to be published as a group by Geoffrey Dutton's Sun Books as *Praises*. It was composed late in 1965 and published in *Australian Letters* in August 1966. Marr claims that White was still redrafting early in 1973. 'The Full Belly' was composed in mid-1966. 'The Night the Prowler' was first composed while White was travelling in Europe in late 1967 although the final draft was not completed until early in 1970. 'Five-Twenty' was composed around September 1967 and was published in *Southerly* in 1968. 'Sicilian Vespers' was first composed in Greece in October 1971 although White was still drafting the story early in 1973. 'The Cockatoos' was composed early in 1973 as White was gathering his other stories into the collection. For a fuller history of individual stories, including their publication subsequent to *The Cockatoos*, see Appendix 3 below.

The idea for a collection of novellas came to White as early as August 1965 when he began 'A Woman's Hand', the first of a group of three novellas planned for Dutton's Sun Books. Nothing, however, came of this venture. By October 1971, after getting 'Sicilian Vespers' down on paper, White thought he had enough for a volume of short pieces. Early in 1973 when he was putting the finishing touches to the collection, the final – title – story came to him. The dry months of summer had forced the cockatoos out of the bush and into the city looking for food. A number had turned up at Martin Road and were encouraged by Lascaris who put sunflower seeds out on the lawn. White was delighted with them and wrote a new story entitled 'The Cockatoos', 'from which I think the book should take its title, as I can see a beautiful jacket'. (To Tom Maschler, 29 April 1973)

By August 1973 *The Cockatoos* was finished, and a typescript was sent to London. White, however, held off sending it to New York, waiting till *The Eye of the Storm* was launched. (To Marshall Best, 5 August 1973) A few months later White was still waiting for his London publisher's response. Finally, it came: 'I am glad to get your reactions to *The Cockatoos*. I had begun to grow very despondent.' (To Tom Maschler, 23 October 1973)

White got proofs in the new year and an advance copy – 'jacket and all' – in March. The book was published in London in June and in New York in January 1975.

White was very pleased with the appearance of the London edition, especially with the jacket design by Desmond Digby – a painting in white, blue and yellow of a flight of cockatoos across front, spine and back (To Tom Maschler, 13 December 1973).

The critical reception was extensive and on the whole favourable. Sales however were modest – although a second issue of the American edition came out within a month – and there have been only four paperback issues and two translations of the whole collection.

* * * * *

N1a First U.K. Edition First Issue (London: Jonathan Cape, 1974)

PATRICK WHITE | THE | COCKATOOS | Shorter Novels and Stories | [at bottom:] [publisher's device] | JONATHAN CAPE | THIRTY BEDFORD SQUARE LONDON

20.4 x 13 cm. [A]^{16} B-H^{16} I^{12} K^{16}: 156 leaves. pp.*8* 9-307 *308-312*.

Endpaper; *1* 'THE COCKATOOS'; *2* '*by the same author* | *Novels* | RIDERS IN THE CHARIOT | VOSS | THE TREE OF MAN | THE AUNT'S STORY | THE LIVING AND THE DEAD | THE SOLID MANDALA | THE VIVISECTOR | THE EYE OF THE STORM | *Short Stories* | THE BURNT ONES | *Plays* | FOUR PLAYS'; *3* title page; *4* 'First published 1974 | © 1966, 1968, 1974 by Patrick White | Jonathan Cape Ltd, 30 Bedford Square, London WC1 | ISBN 0 224 00992 3 | My thanks to the following publications in which stories have appeared: | *Australian Letters* and Macmillan's *Winter's Tales* for 'A Woman's Hand'; | Angus and Robertson's *Coast to Coast* for 'The Full Belly'; and *Southerly* | *Magazine*, University of Sydney, for 'Five-Twenty'. | [at bottom:] PRINTED IN GREAT BRITAIN BY | BUTLER & TANNER LTD | FROME AND LONDON'; *5* '*Contents*'; *6* blank; *7* 'To Ronald Waters | for having survived | forty-eight years | of friendship'; *8* blank; 9-94 text of 'A Woman's Hand'; 95-119 text of 'The Full Belly'; 120-168 text of 'The Night the Prowler'; 169-196 text of 'Five-Twenty'; 197-258 text of 'Sicilian Vespers'; 259-307 text of 'The Cockatoos'; *308-310* blank; endpaper.

Cased in dark green imitation cloth with beige endpapers and top edge in pale blue. Front and back: blank. Spine: [in gold] 'THE | COCKATOOS | [ornament] | PATRICK | WHITE' | [at bottom:] [publisher's device].

White, lightly-textured paper with col. illust. of a flight of cockatoos across front, back and spine. Front: 'PATRICK | WHITE | [in yellow/white] The | Cockatoos'. Back: blank. Spine: 'PATRICK | WHITE | [in yellow/white] The | Cockatoos' | [at bottom:] [publisher's device]. Inside front flap: [blurb, 41 lines] | 'Patrick White was awarded the 1973 | Nobel Prize for Literature 'for an epic, | psychological narrative art which has | introduced a new continent into literature'. | [at right:] £2.50 net | [rule] | IN UK ONLY'. Inside back flap: 'Patrick White | [rule] | THE EYE OF THE STORM | [quotation of 13 lines from] *Daily Telegraph* | [quotation of seven lines from] *Sunday Telegraph* | THE VIVISECTOR | [quotation of five lines from] *Sunday Times* | [quotation of three lines from] *New Statesman* | THE

TREE OF MAN | [quotation of four lines from] *New York Times.* | ISBN 0 224 00992 3 | Jacket painting by Desmond Digby | © Jonathan Cape Ltd 1974'.

Published 13 June 1974. Price: £2.50. Print run: 15,000 – 9,000 for the U.K., 6,000 for Australia.

Reviews: Russell Davies *Observer* (London) 16 June 1974, p.33; *Times Literary Supplement* 28 June 1974, p.687 (1800w); Valentine Cunningham *New Statesman* v.88, 5 July 1974, p.23 (360w); R. Wade *Contemporary Review* v.225, October 1974, p.213-216; *Kirkus Reviews* v.42, 1 November 1974, p.1175; Peter Ackroyd *The Spectator* v.232, 22 June 1974, p.771; *Publishers Weekly* v.206, 25 November 1974, p.40; L. Kramer *Sydney Morning Herald* 22 June 1974, p.13 (1600w); M. Dick *Sydney Morning Herald* 7 December 1974, p.16 (44w); J. Docker *National Times* 4-9 November 1974, p.22; G. Fawcett *Books and Bookmen* v.21 no.3, December 1974, p.58-59; K. England *Advertiser* (Adelaide) 17 August 1974, p.20 (1600w); B. Kiernan *Age* (Melbourne) 15 June 1974, p.13 (1000w); C. Harrison-Ford *Australian* 22 June 1974, p.24 (1200w); *Canberra Times* 24 January 1975, p.8; *Courier-Mail* (Brisbane) 25 January 1975, p.17; J.S. Ryan *Hemisphere* v.19 no.2, February 1975, p.26-31; A.J. Hassall *Southerly* v.35 no.1, 1975, p.3-13; B. Kiernan *Meanjin* v.34 no.1, 1975, p.37; B. Boucher *Advertiser* (Adelaide) 17 June 1978, p.24 (50w); D. Green *National Times* 22 July 1978, p.28 (1700w).

Notes: Uncorrected proof copies have been sighted at ADFA and in a personal collection. The title page exhibits two stylised cockatoos which are not present in the published version. It is sewn in paper with paste-on on front: 'THE COCKATOOS | BY | PATRICK WHITE | [rule] | JONATHAN CAPE'. ADFA has a second, different, uncorrected proof copy with dustjacket; on inside front flap: [running up:] 'PROOF ONLY PROVISIONAL PUBLICATION DATE JUNE 13th 1974'.

For the screenplay version of 'The Night the Prowler' (1978), see Appendix 3 below.

Copies: NSL: Mitchell Library A823/W587/18 (lacks dustjacket); NSL: Mitchell Library [PW]; NSL: JFR/066948; NSL: GRL N823.914/W587/3 (lacks dustjacket); VSL: LT A823.3 W585C; Personal collection; NU: RB 1674.1.

N1b U.K. First Edition Second Issue (London: Jonathan Cape, 1974)
Notes: p.*4* 'First published 1974 | Reprinted 1974'.
Copies: ADFA.

N2a U.S. First Edition (New York: Viking, 1975)

[floral ornament] | THE | COCKATOOS | [thick rule] | STORIES BY | PATRICK | WHITE | [floral ornament] | [at bottom:] THE | VIKING PRESS | [rule] | NEW YORK

20.8 x 13.8 cm. Unsigned: 156 leaves. pp.[*10*] 9-307 *308-310*.

Endpaper; [*1*] 'THE COCKATOOS' | [publisher's device]; [*2*] [floral ornament] | *'by the same author* | [rule] | *Novels* | RIDERS IN THE CHARIOT | VOSS | THE TREE OF MAN | THE AUNT'S STORY | THE LIVING AND THE DEAD | THE SOLID MANDALA | THE VIVISECTOR | THE EYE OF THE STORM | *Short Stories* | THE BURNT ONES | *Plays* | FOUR PLAYS'; [*3*] title page; [*4*] 'Copyright © 1966, 1968, 1974 by Patrick White | All rights reserved | Published in 1975 by The Viking Press, Inc. | 625 Madison Avenue, New York, N.Y. 10022 | Published simultaneously in Canada by | The Macmillan Company of Canada Limited | Printed in U.S.A. | Library of Congress Cataloging in Publication Data: | White, Patrick, 1912- | The cockatoos. | CONTENTS: A women's hand.- The full belly.- The night the | prowler. [etc.] | I. Title. | PZ3.W58469Co3 [PR9619.3.W5] 823 74-3792 | ISBN 0-670-22648-3 | My thanks to the following publications, in which stories have appeared: | *Australian Letters* and Macmillan's *Winter's Tales* for 'A Woman's Hand'; | Angus and Robertson's *Coast to Coast* for 'The Full Belly'; and *Southerly* | *Magazine* for 'Five-Twenty'.'; [5] 'To Ronald Waters | for having survived | forty-eight years | of friendship'; [6] blank; [7] '*Contents*'; [8] blank; [9] 'THE COCKATOOS'; [10] blank; 9-307 text; *308-310* blank; endpaper.

Cased in black calico with pale blue top edge and pale blue endpapers. Front and back: blank. Spine: [in metallic blue] [running down:] 'THE COCKATOOS [horizontal rule] PATRICK WHITE | [upright:] VIKING'.

White textured paper dustjacket printed in pale aqua. Front: [in blue] 'THE | COCKATOOS | [in black] [thick rule] New Stories by | [in blue] PATRICK | WHITE | [in black] *Author of* | *The Eye of the Storm*'. Back: [in blue] '*THE COCKATOOS* take flight abroad— | some advance word from English critics: | [rule] | [in black] [quotation of eight lines from] −*The Times* | [in blue] [rule] | [quotation of three lines from] −ISOBEL MURRAY, *The Financial Times* | [in blue] [rule] | [in black] [quotation of five lines from] −PETER ACKROYD, *The Spectator* | [in blue] [rule] | [in green] [quotation of five lines from] − ELIZABETH BERRIDGE, *Daily Telegraph* | [in blue] [rule] | [in black] [quotation of four lines from] −CHRISTOPHER WORDSWORTH, *The Guardian* | [in blue] [rule] | [in black] THE VIKING PRESS *Publishers* NEW YORK | SBN 670-22648-3'. Spine: [running down:] 'PATRICK | WHITE || THE | COCKATOOS | [at bottom:] [upright:] [in black] [publisher's device] | *Viking*'. Inside front flap: '$8.95 | [blurb, 25 lines] | *Jacket design by Mel Williamson* | 0175'. Inside back flap: [b&w photograph of the author] | [running down:] [at right:] 'DR. EVA PAVLOVIC | [upright:] | [biography, 15 lines] | [in blue] THE VIKING PRESS | *Publishers of The Viking Portable Library* | *and Viking Compass paperbacks* | 625 Madison Avenue, New York, N.Y. 10022 | PRINTED IN U.S.A.'.
Published in January 1975. Price: $8.95.

Reviews: W.J. Harding *Library Journal* v.99, 1 December 1974, p.3148 (120w); *Booklist* v.71, 1 January 1975, p.444; Eudora Welty *New York Times Book Review* 19 January 1975, p.4 (1500w); Bruce Allen *Saturday Review* v.2, 25 January 1975, p.34 (2200w); J.A. Avant *New Republic* v.172, 22 March 1975, p.23 (2900w); J.B. Breslin *America* v.132, 22 March 1975, p.216 (800w); *Choice* v.12, May 1975, p.397 (170w); N.J. Loprete *Best Sellers* v.35, September 1975, p.151 (170w); J. Mellors *Listener* v.93, 9 January 1975, p.61-62; A. Broyard *New York Times* 14 January 1975, p.31; *Hudson Review* v.28, Summer 1975, p.309; *Psychology Today* v.9, June 1975, p.22; *Sewanee Review* v.83, July 1975, p.R72.

Notes: A copy in White's own collection is a presentation copy half-bound in dark red leather and marbled paper boards. ADFA has an advance copy, which is the Cape edition (see N1a above) with information about the Viking edition pasted on the front cover.

Copies: Personal collection; NSL: Mitchell Library [PW].

N2b First U.S. Edition Second Issue (New York: Viking, 1975)

Notes: p.*4* 'Printed in the U.S.A. | Second printing February 1975'. Cased in black linen boards with light blue endpapers. White textured paper dustjacket printed in pale aqua, and overprinted on front, spine, back and back flap in dark blue. Jacket design by Mel Williamson.

Price: US$8.95.

Copies: NSL: Mitchell Library A823/W587/38 (lacks dustjacket); NSL: Mitchell Library [PW].

N3a Penguin Edition First Issue (Harmondsworth: Penguin, 1978)

Patrick White | The Cockatoos | Shorter Novels and Stories | Penguin Books

18 x 11 cm. [1]^{12} 2-12^{12}: 144 leaves. pp.*9* 10-86 *87* 88-109 *110* 111-154 *155* 156-180 *181* 182-238 *239* 240-284 *285-288* (the first page of each story is not numbered).

1 'Penguin Books | The Cockatoos' | [biography, 20 lines]; *2* blank; *3* title page; *4* 'Penguin Books Ltd, Harmondsworth, | Middlesex, England | Penguin Books, 625 Madison Avenue, | New York, New York 10022, U.S.A. | Penguin Books Australia Ltd, Ringwood, | Victoria, Australia | Penguin Books Canada Ltd, 2801 John Street, | Markham, Ontario, Canada L3R 1B4 | Penguin Books (N.Z.) Ltd, 182-190 Wairau Road, | Auckland 10, New Zealand | First published by Jonathan Cape 1974 | Published in Penguin Books 1978 | Copyright © Patrick White, 1966, 1968, 1974 | [acknowledgements, 5 lines] | Made and printed in Great Britain by | Hazell Watson & Viney Ltd | Aylesbury, Bucks | Set in Intertype Times' | [publisher's conditions, 8 lines]; *5* 'To Ronald Waters | for having survived | forty-eight years | of friendship'; *6* blank; *7* 'Contents'; *8* blank; *9* 10-86 'A Woman's Hand'; *87* 88-109 'The Full Belly'; *110* 111-154 'The Night the Prowler'; *155* 156-180 'Five Twenty'; *181* 182-238 'Sicilian Vespers'; *239* 240-284 'The Cockatoos'; *285* 'More about Penguins | and Pelicans'; *286* blank; *287* 'Patrick White | Riders in the Chariot | [comment, 5 lines] | The Aunt's Story | [comment, 5 lines] | The Solid Mandala | [comment, 5 lines] | The Living and the Dead | [comment, 4 lines] | The Burnt Ones' | [comment, 4 lines]; *288* 'Patrick White | A Fringe of Leaves | [comment, 5 lines] | The Tree of Man | [comment, 7 lines] | Voss | [comment, 4 lines] | The Vivisector | [comment, 6 lines] | The Eye of the Storm' | [comment, 4 lines]. Perfectbound in white paper printed in full colour. Front: [at right:] [publisher's device] | [in white on black] 'THE | COCKATOOS | Shorter Novels and Stories by Nobel Prize Winner | PATRICK WHITE' | [illust. of a painting depicting cockatoos in a landscape]. Back: [at top right:] [publisher's device] | [in white on black] [blurb, 7 lines] | [quotation from] 'Elizabeth Berridge | in the *Daily Telegraph* | [quotation from] Francis King | in the *Sunday Telegraph* | [quotation from] Peter Ackroyd in the *Spectator* | The cover shows a detail from | 'Irrigation Lake, Wimmera' by Arthur Boyd. | Reproduced with the permission of the | National Gallery of Victoria, Melbourne | [at bottom left:] United Kingdom 90p | Australia $2.50 (recommended) | [at bottom right:] Fiction | ISBN 0 14 | 00.4463 9'. Spine: [running

down:] [in black on white] 'PATRICK WHITE   THE COCKATOOS | ISBN 0 14 | 00.4463 9' | [upright:] [publisher's device].
Price: 90p, AU$2.50.

Copies: NSL: Mitchell Library A823/W587/58; NSL: Mitchell Library [PW]; NU: 823.91A/W587/E2/2.

N3b Penguin Edition Second Issue (Harmondsworth: Penguin, 1979)
Notes: p.*4* 'Published in Penguin Books 1978 | Reprinted 1979 | Copyright © Patrick White, 1966, 1968, 1974 | [acknowledgements, 5 lines] | Made and printed in Great Britain by | Hazell Watson & Viney Ltd | Aylesbury, Bucks | Set in Intertype Times'. Price: AU$3.95.

N3c Penguin Edition Third Issue (Harmondsworth: Penguin, 1983)
Notes: 19.8 x 12.8 cm.; p.*4* 'Published by Penguin Books 1978 | Reprinted 1979, 1983 | Copyright © Patrick White, 1966, 1968, 1974 | All rights reserved | Made and printed in Great Britain by | Hazell Watson & Viney Ltd, Aylesbury, Bucks | Set in Intertype Times'. Perfectbound in white paper. Cover design by Neil Stuart. Cover illustration (cockatoos in flight) by Mel Odom. Price: £2.50, AU$5.95, CAN$5.95, US$4.95. ISBN 0 1400 4463 9.

N3d Penguin Edition Fourth Issue (Harmondsworth: Penguin, 1985)
Notes: p.*4* 'Published in Penguin Books 1978 | Reprinted 1979, 1983, 1985'. Cover design by Neil Stuart. Cover illustration (cockatoos in flight) by Mel Odom. Price: AU$7.95.

N3e Penguin Edition Fifth Issue (Harmondsworth: Penguin, [1991])
Notes: p.*4* 'Published in Penguin Books 1978 | 10 9 8 7 6 5 | Copyright © Patrick White, 1966, 1968, 1974 | All rights reserved | Printed in England by Clays Ltd, St Ives plc | Set in Intertype Times'. Perfectbound in white paper card. The cover shows a detail from *Irrigation Lake, Wimmera* by Arthur Boyd b.1920, Australian, in the National Gallery | of Victoria, resin and tempera on masonite, 81.3 x 121.9 cm, puchased 1950. Price: £5.99, CAN$10.95, AU$14.95. ISBN 0-14-018582-8.

N3f Penguin Edition Sixth Issue (Harmondsworth: Penguin, [1993])
Notes: p.4 'Published in Penguin Books 1978 | 10 9 8 7 6'. The cover shows a detail from *Irrigation Lake, Wimmera* by Arthur Boyd b.1920, Australian, in the National Gallery | of Victoria, resin and tempera on masonite, 81.3 x 121.9 cm, puchased 1950. Published in March 1993. Price: AU$14.95, US$1095.

N.t1   Spanish First Edition (Barcelona: Plaza & Janes S.A. Editores, 1976)

LAS CACATUAS | *por Patrick White* | [publisher's device] | PLAZA & JANES. S.A. | EDITORES

19.5 x 12.9 cm. [1]⁸ 2-23⁸: 184 leaves. pp.*9* 10-103 *104-107* 108-133 *134-137* 138-192 *193-195* 196-227 *228-231* 232-302 *303-305* 306-360 *361-368*.

Endpaper; *1* [series device] | 'NOVELISTAS | DEL | DIA'; *2* blank; *3* title page; *4* 'Titulo original: | THE COCKATOOS | Traducción de | ALVARO CASTILLO | Portada de | ALVARO | Primera edición: Enero, 1976 | © 1966, 1968, 1974 by Patrick White | © 1976, PLAZA & JANES, S. A., Editores | Virgen de Guadalupe, 21-33. Esplugas de Llobregat (Barcelona) | Este libro se ha publicado originalmente en inglés con el titulo de | THE COCKATOOS | (ISBN: 0 224 00992 3. Jonathan Cape. Londres. Ed. original.) | [rule] | *Printed in Spain — Empreso en España* | ISBN: 84-01-30175-0 — Depósito Legal: B. 1.263 - 1976'; *5* '*A Ronald Waters, por haber sobrevivido a cua-* | *renta y ocho años de amistad.*'; *6* blank; *7* 'UNA MANO DE MUJER'; *8* blank; *9* 10-103 text; *104* blank; *105* 'LA BARRIGA LLENA'; *106* blank; *107* 108-133 text; *134* blank; *135* 'LA NOCHE DEL MERODEADOR'; *136* blank; *137* 138-192 text; *193* 'LAS CINCO Y VEINTE'; *194* blank; *195* 196-227 text; *228* blank; *229* 'VISPERAS SICILIANAS'; *230* blank; *231* 232-302 text; *303* 'LAS CACATÚAS'; *304* blank; *305* 306-360 text; *361* 'INDICE'; *362* blank; *363* [index]; *364* blank; *365* 'Este libro se imprimió en los talleres | de GRÁFICAS GUADA, S. A. | Virgen de Guadalupe, 33 | Esplugas de Llobregat. | Barcelona'; *366-368* blank; endpaper.

Cased in green imitation-cloth boards with white endpapers. Front and back: blank. Spine: [running down:] [in gold] '*PLAZA & JANES, S.A.* Editores | *L*[in white]*AS* [in gold] *C*[in white]*ACATÚAS* | [in gold] por Patrick White'.

Glossy white paper dustjacket printed in full colour. Front: [against background of seated man with shotgun] [diagonally] '*Patrick White* | [in red] *LAS CACATUAS*'. Back: [black & white photograph of the author] | 'PATRICK WHITE' | [description 12 lines]. Spine: 'PATRICK | WHITE | [running down:] [in red] *LAS CACATUAS* | [at bottom:] [upright:] [in black] PLAZA & JANES'. Inside front flap: [in pink] 'EN ESTA MISMA COLECCION'. Inside back flap: [in pink] 'EN ESTA MISMA COLECCION'.

Green paper wraparound. Front: [in white on green] 'Magistral colección de novelas | cortas y cuentos del Premio | Nobel de Literatura 1973'.

Copies: NSL: Mitchell Library 823.914/W587/24 (lacks dustjacket); NSL: Mitchell Library [PW]; Personal collection.

N.t2 Spanish Second Edition (Barcelona: Plaza & Janes S.A. Editores, 1979)

See F.t9 above.

N.t3 Estonian Edition 'The Night the Prowler' and 'The Cockatoos' (Tallinn, Estonia: Kirjastus «Perioodika», 1979)

PATRICK WHITE | HIILIJA ÖÖ | KAKADUUD | Inglise keelest tõlkinud | Enn Soosar | «Loomingu» Raamatukogu 1979 2/3 | Kirjastus «Perioodika» | Tallinn

19.9 x 14.2 cm. [1]^8 2-6^8 ($1 signed): 48 leaves. pp.*1-4* 5-43 *44* 45-90 *91-96*.

1 [hollow type] 'LR | [solid type] «LOOMINGU» RAAMATUKOGU | 1979 2/3 (1102/1103)'; *2* blank; *3* title page; *4* [at top right:] 'T (Austraalia) | [rule] | W 56 | [centre] Tõlgitud raamatust | The Cockatoos | Stories by Patrick White | The Viking Press | New York [1975] | Copyright © 1966, 1968, 1974 by Patrick White | © Tõlge eesti keelde ja järelsõna. Kirjastus «Perioodika», | «Loomingu» Raamatukogu, 1979'; 5-43 'HIILIJA ÖÖ'; *44* blank; 45-84 'KAKADUUD'; 85-90 *91* 'JÄRELSÕNA'; *92* blank; *93* 'SISUKORD'; *94* '«LOOMINGU» RAAMATUKOGUS 1979. AASTAL | ILMUNUD:'; *95* 'Toimetaja J. Ojamaa. | Toimetuse aadress: 200 001 Tallinn, Harju tn. 1, | tel. 449-254; 440-782. | Trük- kida antud 12. I 1979. | Trükiarv 24 000. | Kaama Tselluloosi- ja Paberikombinaadi ofsetpa- ber nr. 2, 60x84 1/16 | Trükipoognaid 6,0. | Formaadile 60x90 kohaldatud trükipoognaid 5,58. | Arvestuspoognaid 5,66. | Tellimus nr. 4149. | EKP Keskkomitee Kirjastuse trükikoda, | Tallinn. Pärnu mnt. 67-a. | Hind 20 kop.' | [six lines of cyrillic text]; *96* blank.

Saddle-stapled with black paper wrappers. Front: [in white on black] [at top left:] '«Loom- ingu» | Raamatukogu | 1979 | [rule] | 2/3 | [at top right:] XXIII aastakäik | [centre:] LR | [rule] | [at left:] PATRICK | WHITE | [at right:] HIILIJA ÖÖ | KAKADUUD' | [illust. of the author]. Back: [in white on black] 'Hind 20 kop. | 78 175'. Spine: blank.

Copies: NSL: Mitchell Library A823/W587/65.

N.t4 Bulgarian First Edition (Varna: Georgi Bakalov, 1986)

Kakadu

Notes: pp.192. Translated by Spas Nikolov. Also see *Index Translationum*.

Copies: NSL: Mitchell Library [PW].

N.t5 Russian First Edition 'A Woman's Hand' (Moscow: Isvestija, 1986)

Zenskaja ruka

Notes: pp.222. Translated by R. Oblonskaja. Also see *Index Translationum*.

Copies: VU: Baill A823.3 White.

N.m1 Sound Recording (North Hobart: Hear-a-Book, 1978)

The Cockatoos (9 audiocasettes).

Read by Peg Radcliffe.

O A Fringe of Leaves (1976)

A Fringe of Leaves was created by Patrick White over a period of some fifteen years, from 1961 to 1975. The initial idea was very much influenced by Sidney Nolan, who had visited Fraser Island, off the Queensland coast, with Barrett Reid in 1947. (Fraser Island was named after Eliza Fraser, a woman who lived with the local Indigenous Badtjala people for some time following the shipwreck of the *Stirling Castle* in 1836.) Nolan and Reid stayed for several weeks, painting, writing and taking photographs. Years later, in London, Nolan painted a second series of Eliza Fraser paintings. These were exhibited in 1957 in the Nolan retrospective at the Whitechapel Gallery. White viewed these and met up with Nolan in Florida in 1958. At the time, they discussed the story of the marooned Eliza.

The next stage of the gestation was in 1961 when White visited Fraser Island, apparently with the purpose of researching a novel. As he wrote to Peggy Garland, 'I now know what I want to know.' (22 June 1961) Shortly after, he wrote to Geoffrey Dutton: 'Today I did a dreadful thing. I started another novel, and am in that state of hope, fear, and frustration.' (28 September 1961) Towards the end of 1961, White outlined the plot of *A Fringe of Leaves* to Ben Huebsch: 'This Victorian lady was stripped of everything, until she was reduced to wearing a vine round the waist – hence the "fringe of leaves" – to hide her wedding ring and anything else she had'. (To Ben Huebsch, 3 November 1961) The writing process is difficult to track through White's letters but years later he indicated that he had got about two-thirds of the way into the novel before he abandoned it. (To Frederick Glover, 15 January 1967)

At the beginning of 1963 *A Fringe of Leaves* was revived when Stefan Haag of the Elizabethan Theatre Trust suggested to White that he might write the libretto for an opera to open the new Opera House in Sydney. White had a vision of *A Fringe of Leaves* as an opera, with sets by Nolan, libretto by himself, and music by the young composer, Peter Sculthorpe. There exists in the Aboriginal Treaty Committee Papers (National Library of Australia MS 6856) a single leaf from an exercise book containing about thirty lines from the libretto being developed by White. Nothing came of this project, mainly because of artistic differences between White and Sculthorpe. It should be noted, however, that Sculthorpe produced a number of works which make reference to the Eliza Fraser story, including *Eliza Fraser Sings*, with words by Barbara Blackman (1978), *Mangrove* (1979), and *Great Sandy Island* (1998).

Over the next few years White ocasionally went back to the manuscript – 'I sometimes take out the MS of *A Fringe of Leaves* and look at it. It still attracts me, and I may come back to her one day.' (To Geoffrey Dutton, 5 January 1969) By mid-1973, White was planning to return to the novel, but first he wanted to see the Great Barrier Reef and be 'immersed in the seascapes and light before embarking on the Mrs Fraser novel – if I do.' (To Geoffrey Dutton, 15 July 1973) In August White and Lascaris went on a cruise in the Whitsundays.

After the Nobel Prize, *A Fringe of Leaves* became a method by which White was able to order his life. The other motivation was White's mortality. 'Today I started on *A Fringe of Leaves* which I want to finish before I am finished'. (To Tom Maschler, 2 January 1974) He began from scratch and worked steadily throughout 1974, reporting to Maschler in September that he was very close to finishing the first draft. (22 September 1974) Having put the manuscript aside for a few weeks, White returned to it in November 1974. Early in 1975 about one-third of the second draft was complete, and White was proceeding with some urgency: '… I think to myself, supposing I die? The publisher may get hold of it, and in spite of the clause in my will, give it to some hack who will turn it into something quite different from what I intended.' (To Geoffrey Dutton, 13 January 1975) White hoped that the second draft would be finished before the spring, and on the 13th April he wrote to Ninette Dutton: 'I am getting towards the end of my second version'. The third draft was also completed quickly, by the 14th September. The book was dedicated to Desmond Digby.

'I sent the typescript to Juliet [O'Hea] about a week ago, so I imagine it will have arrived by now. Yesterday I sent a copy to Sid Nolan … I have not yet sent a copy of the book to New York'. (To Tom Maschler, 30 September 1975) Jonathan Cape had accepted *A Fringe of Leaves* by November (To Brett Whiteley, 4 November 1975), and it was only then that a copy of the typescript was sent to Viking in New York. By January 1976 Viking also had accepted the book, although both Marshall Best and Alan Williams annoyed White by queries relating to punctuation and colonial place names: 'If the American reader has to be told about Van Diemens Land and Moreton Bay, can't you say something on the jacket about their being the Tasmania and Brisbane of today'. (11 January 1976)

As usual White was alert to the possibilities of the dustjacket and finicky about its design. Given that Sidney Nolan had first introduced White to Eliza Fraser, it was appropriate that Nolan was invited to do the design. 'Sid Nolan has said he will do a jacket for *A Fringe of Leaves*, but that may mean going to his studio and carrying off something'. (To Tom Maschler, 31 August 1975) Maschler did see Nolan and it was decided that 'Mrs Fraser and Convict, 1962-1964' would be used, though White was unhappy about other aspects of the design. 'Why they have to make a fuss about its not wrapping over when most jackets don't wrap over is something I don't understand. A lot of them have abstracts of reviews of previous books printed on the book. Desmond [Digby] has had trouble with that art director at Cape; amongst other things he always wants lettering which we don't feel goes with the designs. They sent me a dreadful blurb this time which I had to rewrite entirely, but of course that won't prevent them sticking on some embarassing bits of their own. Still, I have found Cape much more understanding and co-operative than other publishers.' (To Cynthia Nolan, 20 March 1976) The resulting jacket was blank on the back, although quotations from reviews of earlier books did appear on the inside back flap.

White was less happy about the vulgar jacket design for the Viking edition. 'Thank you for the [advance] copy of *A Fringe of Leaves*. The jacket – well, your letter prepared me for the worse: I expected something of a boob show ... What I don't like is the cluster of African huts and the ship standing practically on end on the book. Why won't you let me have plain lettering like any other writer one respects? I don't believe many people buy books for awful jackets. They put me off'. (To Alan Williams, 26 December 1976) The published book was equally reviled: 'That jacket asks for a bad review. Why must you subject me to this indignity when others are allowed lettering? I detect a whiff of JACKIE [Kennedy-Onassis], who could well be your downfall'. (To Alan Williams, 20 February 1977)

The Cape edition was published in September 1976, and the Viking edition in January 1977. Reviews in England and Australia were positive, although White thought them under-whelming. (To Peggy Garland, 18 September 1976) In the United States reviews were respectful, but White had almost given away the American critics: 'Thank you for the reviews. I only glanced very quickly and then threw them away.' (To Alan Williams, 20 February 1977)

David Marr (p.569) quotes White as claiming that *A Fringe of Leaves* had an 'astonishing reception' (To Peggy Garland, 9 October 1976) and sold well. In both the United Kingdom and the United States the first editions were quickly followed up by Book Club and paperback editions, and a number of translations, including Hebrew (1978), Swedish (1979), Polish (1980), French (1981), Slovakian (1981), German (1982) and Czech (1983), followed over the next decade.

* * * * * *

O1a U.K. First Edition First Issue (London: Jonathan Cape, 1976)

PATRICK WHITE | [rule] | A FRINGE | OF LEAVES | [publisher's device] | JONATHAN CAPE | THIRTY BEDFORD SQUARE LONDON

20.5 x 13.2 cm. Unsigned: 204 leaves. pp.*8* 9-405 *406-408*.

Endpaper; *1* 'A FRINGE OF LEAVES'; *2* '*by the same author* | *Novels* | RIDERS IN THE CHARIOT | VOSS | THE TREE OF MAN | THE AUNT'S STORY | THE LIVING AND THE DEAD | THE SOLID MANDALA | THE VIVISECTOR | THE EYE OF THE STORM | *Short Stories* | THE BURNT ONES | THE COCKATOOS | *Plays* | FOUR PLAYS'; *3* title page; *4* 'FIRST PUBLISHED 1976 | © 1976 BY PATRICK WHITE | JONATHAN CAPE LTD, 30 BEDFORD SQUARE, LONDON WC1 | ISBN 0 224 01290 8 | BRITISH LIBRARY CATALOGUING IN PUBLICATION DATA | WHITE, PATRICK | A FRINGE OF LEAVES | ISBN 0-224-01290-8 | I. TITLE | 823'.9'1F PR6045. H19F7 | PRINTED IN GREAT BRITAIN BY | COX & WYMAN LTD | LONDON, FAKENHAM AND READING'; *5* 'TO DESMOND DIGBY'; *6* blank; *7* 'A perfect Woman, nobly planned, | To warn, to comfort, and command. | *William Wordsworth* | RAT-WIFE   Humbly begging pardon — are your worships troubled | with any gnawing things in the house? | ALMERS   Here? No, I don't think so. | RAT-WIFE   If you had, it would be such a pleasure to rid your | worships' house of them. | RITA   Yes, yes, we understand, But we have nothing of the | sort here. | *Henrik Ibsen* | If there is some true good in a man, it can only be | unknown to himself. | *Simone Weil* | Love is your last chance. There is really nothing else | on earth to keep you there. | *Louis Aragon*'; *8* blank; 9-405 text; *406-408* blank; endpaper.

Cased in blue imitation-cloth with blue on top edge and pale yellow endpapers. Front and back: blank. Spine: [in gold] 'A | FRINGE | OF | LEAVES | [ornament] | PATRICK | WHITE' | [publisher's device].

White paper dustjacket printed on front, back and spine in blue. Front: [in white] 'Patrick White | [in orange] A Fringe of Leaves' | [col. illust. by Sidney Nolan of beachscape with man and woman in left foreground]. Back: blank. Spine: [in white] 'Patrick | White | [in orange] A | Fringe | of | Leaves' | [in white] [publisher's device]. Inside front flap: [blurb, 39 lines] | [at bottom right:] '£4.50 net | [rule] | IN UK ONLY'. Inside back flap: 'Patrick White | *The Cockatoos* | [quotation of eight lines from] *Daily Telegraph* | *The Eye of the Storm* [quotation of seven lines from] *Sunday Telegraph* | *The Vivisector* | [quotation of three lines from] *Sunday Times* | *The Tree of Man* | [quotation of four lines from] *New York Times* | *The Solid Mandala* | [quotation of two lines from] *Guardian* | *Riders in the Chariot* | [quotation of two lines from] *Sunday Times* | ISBN 0 224 01290 8 | Jacket painting by Sidney Nolan'.

Published 9 September 1976. Price: £4.50. Print run: 25,000.

Reviews: Julian Barnes *New Statesman* v.92, 10 September 1976, p.348 (400w); Randolph Stow *Times Literary Supplement* 10 September 1976, p.1097 (700w); *America* v.135, 2 October 1976, p.196; *Books & Bookmen* v.22, October 1976, p.64; *Kirkus Reviews* v.44, 1 November 1976, p.1187; *Listener* v.96, 30 September 1976, p.409; *Observer* 12 September 1976, p.28; *Publishers Weekly* v.210, 1 November 1976, p.65; *Spectator* v.237, 11 September 1976, p.24; P.T. Plowman *Bulletin* (Sydney) 25 September 1976, p.62 (385w); E. Perkins *LINQ* v.5 no.2,

1976, p91-98 (1485w); K. England *Advertiser* (Adelaide) 25 September 1976, p.25 (690w); A.A. Phillips *Age* (Melbourne) 9 October 1976, p.22 (1050w); T. Shapcott *Australian* 25 September 1976, Weekend Supplement p.9, (1100w); D. Green *Nation Review* 22-28 October 1976, p.20 (1610w); J. McLaren *Overland* no.65, 1976, p.71-72 (1450w); J.D. Pringle *Sydney Morning Herald* 25 September 1976, p.15 (960w); W. Blaxland *Sydney Morning Herald* 11 December 1976, p.13 (40w); C. Semmler *Sydney Morning Herald* 11 December 1976, p.13 (50w); *Publishers Weekly* v.212, 21 November 1977, p.63.

Notes: The University of Sydney has a proof copy (RB IMP 007311) with White's corrections in red throughout. Sewn in brown paper with a date of 5th March 1976. The provisional publishing date was 9th September 1976. A second – uncorrected – proof copy has been sighted in a personal collection. It is sewn in brown paper. Front: 'A FRINGE OF LEAVES | by | PATRICK WHITE | JONATHAN CAPE | *5th March 1976*'. A third – uncorrected – proof copy has been sighted in a personal collection. It contains a letter from Cape to Professor Colin Roderick, dated 11 June 1976. A fourth – uncorrected – proof copy is to be found at ADFA. ADFA also has an advance copy of the printed book, sent to Dorothy Green for review; it contains copious annotations.

Copies: VSL: SLT A823.3/W585FR (lacks final leaf); NSL: Mitchell Library A823/W587/51 (lacks dustjacket); NSL: Mitchell Library [PW]; NU: 823.91/A/W587/J7/1; Personal collection (2 copies); ADFA; VU: McL L/A-F White.

O1b U.K. First Edition Book Club Issue (London: The Book Club, 1977)
PATRICK WHITE | [rule] | A FRINGE | OF LEAVES | [at bottom:] THE BOOK CLUB | LONDON
20.3 x 12.3 cm. Unsigned: 204 leaves. pp.*8* 9-405 *406-408*.
Notes: p.*4* 'First published 1976 | © 1976 by Patrick White | The Book Club | 125 Charing Cross Road | London WC2H 0EB | This edition 1977 by arrangement with | Jonathan Cape | [at bottom:] Printed and bound in Great Britain by | REDWOOD BURN LIMITED | Trowbridge & Esher'. Cased in red paper-covered boards with white endpapers. Glossy white paper dustjacket printed with col. illust. of a woman on a beach across front and spine. Jacket design by Lysbeth Liverton. Published in August 1977. Price: £4.50.

O2a U.S. First Edition First Issue (New York: Viking, 1977)
A | FRINGE OF | LEAVES | Patrick White | THE VIKING PRESS NEW YORK
22.1 x 15 cm. Unsigned: 208 leaves. pp.[*16*] 9-405 *406-408*.

Endpaper; [*1*] blank; [*2*] blank; [*3*] [publisher's device]; [*4*] blank; [*5*] 'A FRINGE OF LEAVES'; [*6*] blank; [*7*] '*by the same author* | *Novels* | RIDERS IN THE CHARIOT | VOSS | THE TREE OF MAN | THE AUNT'S STORY | THE LIVING AND THE DEAD | THE SOLID MANDALA | THE VIVISECTOR | THE EYE OF THE STORM | *Short Stories* | THE BURNT ONES | THE COCKATOOS | *Plays* | FOUR PLAYS'; [*8*] blank; [*9*] title page; [*10*] 'Copyright © Patrick White, 1976 | All rights reserved | Published in 1977 by The Viking Press | 625 Madison Avenue, New York, N.Y. 10022 | Published simultaneously in Canada by | The Macmillan Company of Canada Limited |

[rule] | Library of Congress Cataloging in Publication Data | White, Patrick, 1912- | A fringe of leaves. | I. Title. | PZ3.W5846Fr3 (PR9619.3.W5) 823 76-18961 | ISBN 0-670-33073-6 | [rule] | Printed in the United States of America'; [*11*] 'TO DESMOND DIGBY'; [*12*] blank; [*13*] [epigraphs]; [*14*] blank; [*15*] 'A FRINGE OF LEAVES'; [*16*] blank; 9-405 text; *406-408* blank; endpaper.

Cased in blue paper-covered boards with spine in olive green cloth and off-white endpapers. Front and back: blank. Spine: [running down:] [in metallic blue] 'A FRINGE OF LEAVES | [upright:] [in white] Patrick | White | [in metallic blue] VIKING'.

White paper dustjacket printed in green on back and spine and with col. illust. of gentle-woman in jungle scene on front. Front: [in yellow] 'PATRICK WHITE | [in white] A FRINGE OF LEAVES | a novel'. Back: [quotation of two lines from] '–PETER S. PRESCOTT, *Newsweek* | [quotation of four lines from] –ROBIE MACAULEY, *The New York Times Book Review* | [quotation of two lines from] –BRUCE ALLEN, *The Chicago Tribune* | [quotation of five lines from] –JANE LARKIN CRAIN, *Saturday Review* | [quotation of four lines from] –PAUL THEROUX, *The Times* (London) | THE VIKING PRESS/*Publishers*/NEW YORK | [at bottom right:] SBN 670-33073-6'. Spine: [running down:] [in white] 'A FRINGE | OF LEAVES || [in black] PATRICK | WHITE | [upright:] [in white] VIKING'. Inside front flap: [at top right:] '$10.00 | [blurb, 41 lines] | *Jacket painting by Cornelia Gray* | [at bottom right:] 0177'. Inside back flap: [biography, 25 lines] | [in blue] [publisher's device] | [in black] 'THE VIKING PRESS | 625 Madison Avenue | New York, N.Y. 10022 | PRINTED IN THE U.S.A.'.

Published in January 1977. Price: $10.

Reviews: Evan Connell *Harper's Bazaar* v.254, February 1977, p.92 (1400w); G.J. Soete *Library Journal* v.101, 1 December 1977, p.2512 (120w); Robie Macauley *New York Times Book Review* 20 January 1977, p.3 (1000w); George Steiner *New Yorker* v.53, 23 May 1977, p.131 (1150w); P.S. Prescott *Newsweek* v.89, 24 January 1977, p.71 (600w); J.L. Crain *Saturday Review* v.4, 22 January 1977, p.40 (200w); *Antioch Review* v.35, Spring 1977, p.322; *Booklist* v.73, 1 February 1977, p.794; *Book World* 27 February 1977, p.69; *Contemporary Review* v.220, January 1977, p.45; *Guardian Weekly* v.116, 2 January 1977, p.14; *Hudson Review* v.30, Summer 1977, p.308; *National Observer* v.16, 12 February 1977, p.21; *New York Times* 18 January 1977, p.35 *Wall Street Journal* 3 March 1977, p.14; J.A. Keane *Best Sellers* v.37, May 1977, p.41 (240w); *Sewanee Review* v.85, July 1977, p.509; *World Literature Today* v.51, Spring 1977, p.330; J.S. Grant *Canadian Forum* v.57, August 1977, p.39 (750w); *Choice* v.14, April 1977, p.206 (160w); Lynn Dickerson *Christian Century* vol.94, 27 April 1977, p.410 (400w).

Notes: This 'edition' is a photolithographic reprint of the U.K. First Edition (see O1a above).

Copies: Personal collection.

O2b Canadian Subedition (Toronto: Macmillan Canada, 1977)
Not seen, but assumed from the statement on p.[*10*] of the U.S. First Edition (see O2a above).

O2c U.S. First Edition Second Issue (New York: Viking, 1977)

Notes: p.[*10*] 'Printed in the United States of America | *Second printing February 1977*'. A copy in White's own collection is half-bound in dark green half leather with marbled paper boards. Published in February 1977. Price: $10.

Copies: NSL Mitchell Library A823/W587/52 (lacks dustjacket); NSL Michell Library [PW].

O3 U.S. Second Edition (New York: Viking, 1977)

A | FRINGE OF | LEAVES | Patrick White | THE VIKING PRESS NEW YORK

21.5 x 14.2 cm. Unsigned: 160 leaves. pp.[*14*] *1* 2-303 *304-306*.

Endpaper; [*1*] blank; [*2*] blank; [*3*] [publisher's device]; [*4*] blank; [*5*] 'A FRINGE OF LEAVES'; [*6*] blank; [*7*] title page; [*8*] 'Copyright © Patrick White, 1976 | All rights reserved | Published in 1977 by The Viking Press | 625 Madison Avenue, New York, N.Y. 10022 | Published simultaneously in Canada by | The Macmillan Company of Canada Limited | Printed in the United States of America'; [*9*] 'TO DESMOND DIGBY'; [*10*] blank; [*11*] [four epigraphs]; [*12*] blank; [*13*] 'A FRINGE OF LEAVES'; [*14*] blank; *1* 2-303 text; *304-306* blank; endpaper.

Cased in olive-green paper-covered boards with white endpapers. Front and back: blank. Spine: [running down:] [in blue] 'A FRINGE OF LEAVES | [upright:] [in white] Patrick | White | [in blue] VIKING'.

Dustjacket is as for O2a except for the following: Back: [illust. of ship sinking] | [quotation of 13 lines from] –PAUL THEROUX, *The Times* (London)'. Spine: [running down:] [in white] A FRINGE | OF LEAVES || [in black] PATRICK | WHITE | [upright:] [in white] VIKING'. Inside front flap: [blurb, 41 lines] | *Jacket painting by Cornelia Gray* | [at bottom right:] *Book Club* | *Edition*'. Inside back flap: [biography, 25 lines] | 'PRINTED IN THE U.S.A. | 1116'.

Copies: Personal collection.

O4a Penguin Edition First Issue (Harmondsworth: Penguin, 1977)

Patrick White | A Fringe of Leaves | Penguin Books

18.1 x 11.2 cm. Unsigned: 184 leaves. pp.*6* 7-365 *366-368* (last page in each chapter is unnumbered).

1 'Penguin Books | A Fringe of Leaves' | [biography, 21 lines]; *2* blank; *3* title page; *4* 'Penguin Books Ltd, Harmondsworth, | Middlesex, England | Penguin Books, 625 Madison Avenue, | New York, New York 10022, U.S.A. | Penguin Books Australia Ltd, Ringwood, | Victoria, Australia | Penguin Books Canada Ltd, 2801 John Street, | Markham, Ontario, Canada L3R 1B4 | Penguin Books (N.Z.) Ltd, 182-190 Wairau Road, | Auckland 10, New Zealand | First published by Jonathan Cape 1976 | Published in Penguin Books 1977 | Copyright © Patrick White, 1976 | All rights reserved | Made and printed in Great Britain by | Richard Clay (The Chaucer Press) Ltd, Bungay, Suffolk | Set in Monotype Times |

[publisher's conditions, 8 lines]; *5* 'To Desmond Digby'; *6* [epigraphs]; *7-365 366* text; *367* 'More about Penguins and Pelicans'; *368* blank.

Perfectbound in black paper printed in white. Front: [at top right:] [publisher's device] | [in white] 'A FRINGE | OF LEAVES | A powerful historical novel by Nobel Prize Winner | PATRICK | WHITE' | [col. illust. of two figures]. Back: [at top right:] [publisher's device] | [in white] [description, 17 lines] | [quotation of five lines from] '– *Daily Telegraph* | [quotation of three lines from] – *Guardian* | Cover painting by Sidney Nolan | [at centre:] United Kingdom 95p | [at right:] Fiction | ISBN 0 14 | 00.4409 4'. Spine: [running down:] [in white] 'PATRICK WHITE A FRINGE OF LEAVES ISBN 0 14 | 00.4409 4' | [upright:] [publisher's device].

Price: 95p., AU$2.50.

Copies: NU: 823.91/W587/J7/4; NSL: Mitchell Library [PW]; NSL: Mitchell Library A823/W587/62 (rebound); Personal collection (3 copies).

O4b Penguin Edition Second Issue (Harmondsworth: Penguin, 1979)
Not seen.

O4c Penguin Edition Third Issue (Harmondsworth: Penguin, 1981)
Notes: 18 x 11 cm.; *p.4* 'Published in Penguin Books 1977 | Reprinted 1979, 1981 | Copyright © Patrick White, 1976 | All rights reserved | Made and printed in Great Britain by | Richard Clay (The Chaucer Press) Ltd, Bungay, Suffolk | Set in Monotype Times'. Cover painting by Sidney Nolan. Price: £1.95, AU$5.95. ISBN 0 1400 4409 4.

O4d Penguin Edition Fourth Issue (Harmondsworth: Penguin, 1982)
Notes: *p.4* 'Printed in Penguin Books 1977 | Reprinted 1979, 1981, 1982 | Copyright © Patrick White, 1976 | All rights reserved | Made and printed in Great Britain by | Richard Clay (The Chaucer Press) Ltd, Bungay, Suffolk | Set in Monotype Times'.

O4e Penguin Edition Fifth Issue (Harmondsworth: Penguin, 1982)
Notes: *p.4* 'Printed in Penguin Books 1977 | Reprinted 1979, 1981, 1982 (twice) | Copyright © Patrick White, 1976 | All rights reserved | Made and printed in Great Britain by | Richard Clay (The Chaucer Press) Ltd, Bungay, Suffolk | Set in Monotype Times'.

O4f Penguin Edition Sixth Issue (Harmondsworth: Penguin, 1983)
Not seen.

O4g Penguin Edition Seventh Issue (Harmondsworth: Penguin, 1985)
Notes: *p.4* 'Published by Penguin Books 1977 | Reprinted 1979, 1981, 1982 (twice), 1983, 1985 | Copyright © Patrick White, 1976 | All rights reserved | Made and printed in Great Britain by | Richard Clay (The Chaucer Press) Ltd, Bungay, Suffolk | Set in Monotype Times'. Perfectbound in white paper. Cover design by Neil Stuart. Cover painting [painting looking through leaves] by Mel Odom.

O4h Penguin Edition Eighth Issue (Harmondsworth: Penguin, n.d.)
Not seen.

O4i Penguin Edition Ninth Issue (Harmondsworth: Penguin, n.d.)
Notes: p.*4* 'Published by Penguin Books 1977 | 10 9'. Perfectbound in white paper. Cover design by Neil Stuart. Cover painting [women looking through leaves] by Mel Odom.

O4j Penguin Edition Tenth Issue (Harmondsworth: Penguin, [1988])
Notes: p.*4* 'Published by Penguin Books 1977 | 10'.

O4k-m Penguin Edition Eleventh to Thirteenth Issues (Harmondsworth: Penguin, n.d.)
Not seen.

O4n Penguin Edition Fourteenth Issue (Harmondsworth: Penguin, [1993])
Notes: p.*4* 'Published in Penguin Books 1977 | 20 19 18 17 16 15 14 | [...] | Printed in England by Clays Ltd, St Ives plc | Set in Monotype Times'. Perfectbound in white paper card with cover illustration containing a detail from Robert Dowling's *Mrs Adolphus Seales with Black Jimmie on Merrang Station* (1856). Published March 1993. Price: £7.99, US$11.95, AU$14.95, CAN$13.99. ISBN 0 1401 8610 7.

O5 U.S. Third Edition (New York: Avon Books, 1978)

A | Fringe | of | Leaves | PATRICK | WHITE | [at bottom:] [publisher's device] | AVON | PUBLISHERS OF BARD, CAMELOT AND DISCUS BOOKS

17.3 x 10.3 cm. Unsigned: 192 leaves. pp.[*8*] 1-373 *374-376*.

[*1*] 'Nobel Laureate | PATRICK WHITE | HIS NEW NOVEL OF PASSION | AND SURVIVAL | A Fringe of Leaves | [quotation from] *Los Angeles Times* | [quotation from] *The New York Times* | [quotation from] *Publisher's Weekly*'; [*2*] '*Other Avon books by* | Patrick White | THE AUNT'S STORY   26740 $1.95 | THE EYE OF THE STORM   21527 $1.95 | RIDERS IN THE CHARIOT   25403 $1.95 | THE SOLID MANDALA 24851 $1.95 | THE TREE OF MAN   22665 $1.95 | THE VIVISECTOR   24158 $2.25 | VOSS   22384 $1.95'; [*3*] title-page; [*4*] 'AVON BOOKS | A division of | The Hearst Corporation | 959 Eighth Avenue | New York, New York 10019 | Copyright © Patrick White, 1976 | Published by arrangement with The Viking Press. | Library of Congress Catalog Card Number: 76-18961 | ISBN: 0-380-01826-8 | All rights reserved, which includes the right | to reproduce this book or portions thereof in | any form whatsoever. For information address | The Viking Press, 625 Madison Avenue, | New York, New York 10022 | First Avon Printing January, 1978 | AVON TRADEMARK REG. U.S. PAT. OFF. AND

IN | OTHER COUNTRIES, MARCA REGISTRADA, | HECHO EN U.S.A. | Printed in the U.S.A.'; [*5*] 'TO DESMOND DIGBY'; [*6*] blank; [*7*] [epigraphs]; [*8*] blank; 1-373 text; *374* 'NOBEL PRIZE WINNER | Saul Bellow | Humboldt's Gift | [quotations from] CHICAGO TRIBUNE | NEWSWEEK | BOSTON GLOBE'; *375* 'THE BIG BESTSELLERS | ARE AVON BOOKS' | [list of 20 titles by various authors] | [coupon]; *376* 'A Wide-Canvas American Epic! | THE SMASHING COAST-TO-COAST BESTSELLER | VOYAGE | A NOVEL OF 1896 | STERLING HAYDEN | [quotation from] Chicago Daily News | [quotation from] San Francisco Examiner'.

Perfectbound in white paper printed in bright blue. Front: [col. illust. representing a woman's head against a background of foliage] | [running down:] [at top left:] 'AVON /36160/$1.95 | [publisher's device] | [in white] A Fringe of | Leaves | THE STORY OF A | WOMAN'S AWAKENING TO | PRIMAL DESIRE IN A SAVAGE EDEN | PATRICK WHITE | NOBEL PRIZE WINNER | "A PASSIONATE BOOK... | THAT RIVALS THE FINEST HE HAS DONE." | Chicago Tribune'. Back: [in white] '"A | CELEBRATION | OF A | STRONG, | WARM, | INDOMITABLE | WOMAN" | *Cosmopolitan* | [blurb, 10 lines] | "A VASTLY ENJOYABLE NOVEL, | and also a rather intense experience of human | endurance; it requires a period of time to recover, | when one has finished reading it, and that is | something that happens only with the greatest fiction." | *Paul Theroux, The London Times* | SELECTED BY THE LITERARY GUILD'. Spine: [in white] [running up:] 'PATRICK WHITE / A Fringe of Leaves'. Inside front and back: blank.

Copies: NU: 823.91A/W587/J7/2; NSL: Mitchell Library [PW].

O.t1 Hebrew First Edition (Tel Aviv: Am Oved, 1978)

[Gedile alim]

Notes: pp.373. Translated by Amazia Porat. Also see *Index Translationum*.

Copies: NSL: Mitchell Library [PW].

O.t2a Swedish First Edition First Issue (Helsingborg: Forum, 1979)

Patrick White | En frans av löv | Översättning av Roland Adlerberth | Forum

21.7 x 13.6 cm. [1]^8 2-26^8: 208 leaves. pp.*6* 7-412 *413-416*.

Endpaper; *1* 'En frans av löv'; *2* blank; *3* title page; *4* [publisher's device] | 'Originalets titel : A Fringe of Leaves | © 1976 by Patrick White | Omslag av Christer Jonsson | ISBN 91-37-07071-1 | Printed in Sweden by | Schmidts Boktryckeri AB, Helsingborg 1979'; *5* [epigraphs]; *6* blank; 7-412 *413* text; *414-416* blank; endpaper.

Cased in black cloth with white endpapers. Front and back: blank. Spine: [running down:] [in silver] 'PATRICK WHITE EN FRANS AV LÖV'.

Glossy paper dustjacket with col. illust. of painting of a woman on a beach across front, spine and back. Front: [in mauve] 'PATRICK WHITE | EN FRANS AV LÖV | [at bottom:] [in yellow] FORUM'. Back: [in white] [blurb, 9 lines] | 'FORUM | ISBN 91-37-07071-1'.

Spine: [running down:] [in white] 'PATRICK WHITE EN FRANS AV LÖV'. Inside front flap: [description, 38 lines]. Inside back flap: [photograph] | [biography, 7 lines]. Copies: NSL: Mitchell Library 823.914/W587/4 (lacks dustjacket); NSL: Mitchell Library [PW].

O.t2b Swedish First Edition Second Issue (Stockholm: MånPocket, 1983)

[En frans av löv]

Notes: pp.412. Trans. by Roland Adlerberth. Not seen, but referred to in *Index Translationum*.

O.t3 Polish First Edition (Warsaw: Państwowy Instytut Wydawniczy, 1980)

[at left:] 'Patrick | White | [at right:] Przepaska | z liści | Przełożyla | Maria Skibniewska | Państwowy Instytut Wydawniczy 1980

18.5 x 11.4 cm. [1] 2-14^{12} 15^4 [16]^{12} [17]^{12}: 196 leaves. pp.*8* 9-388 *389-392*.

Endpaper; *1* 'White | Przepaska z liści'; *2* 'Współczesna Proza Światowa' | [b&w illust. of a stylised tornado]; *3* title page; *4* 'Tytuł oryginalu | A Fringe of Leaves | Opracowanie graficzne | Waldemar Świerzy | Uklad typograficzny | Mieczysław Bancerowski | © 1976 by Patrick White | © Copyright for the Polish edition by | Państwowy Instytut Wydawniczy, Warszawa 1980 | ISBN 83-06-00183-4'; *5* 'Dedykowane | Desmondowi Digby'; *6* blank; *7* [epigraphs]; *8* blank; 9-388 *389* text; *390* blank; *391* 'Wspolczesna | Proza | Swiatowa | [list of 14 titles]; *392* 'PRINTED IN POLAND | Państwowy Instytut Wydawniczy, Warszawa 1980 | Wydanie pierwsze | Nakład 30 000+315 egz. Ark. wyd. 23,1. Ark. druk. 24,5 | Papier d. s. kl. IV. 63 g 92 x 114 | Oddano do składania w maju 1979 r. | Skład wykonaly Zakłady Graficzne „Dom Slowa Polskiego" | Druk i oprawe wykonała Drukarnia Wydawnicza w Krakowie | Nr zam. 2301/80. C-48 | Cena zł 80,-'; endpaper.

Cased in black paper-covered boards. Front and back: blank. Spine: [running down:] [in white] 'Patrick White Przepaska z liści' | [upright:] [publisher's device].

Black paper dustjacket. Front: [in white] [at left:] 'Patrick White | [at right:] Przepaska z liści | [at bottom:] Państwowy | Instytut | Wydawniczy'. Back: blank. Spine: [running down:] [in white] 'Patrick White Przepaska z liści'. Inside front flap: [biography, 8 lines]. Inside back flap: [description, 25 lines] | 'zł 80.–'.

Published in May 1979. Price: zl 80. Print run: 30,000.

Copies: VSL: SLT A823.3 W582FS; NSL: Mitchell Library [PW]; NSL: Mitchell Library 823.914/W587/46.

O.t4 Polish Second Edition (Warsaw: Muza SA, 1995)

[in white on black] PATRICK | WHITE | PRZEPASKA Z LIŚCI | [in black] *przelożyla* | MARIA SKIBNIEWSKA | MUZA SA | Warszawa 1995

16.5 x 10.5 cm. Unsigned: 232 leaves. pp.*8* 9-462 *463-464* (each chapter begins on a recto; if previous chapter ends on a recto, the intervening verso is unnumbered).

1 [in white on black] 'PATRICK | WHITE | PRZEPASKA Z LIŚCI'; *2* blank; *3* title page; *4* 'Tytul oryginalu : *A Fringe of Leaves* | Projekt okladki : *Maciej Sadowski* | Redakcja technic-zna : *Mariusz Jaśtak* | Korekta : *Mariola Stańczak* | W projekcie okladki wykorzystano : Ty-cjan | *Alegoria trzech okresów zycia* | (fragment) | © published by Jonathan Cape | © Patrick White 1976 | © for the Polish translation by Rafal Skibiński | © for this Polish edition by MUZA SA, Warszawa 1995 | ISBN 83-7079-343-6 | MUZA SA | Warszawa 1995'; *5* 'De-dykowane | Desmondowi Digby'; *6* blank; *7* [epigraphs]; *8* blank; *9-462* *463* text; *464* [at bottom:] 'MUZA SA | ul. Marszalkowska 8 | 00-590 Warszawa | tel. 621 50 57, 621 50 58 | Sklad i lamanie : MUZA SA | Przygotowanie do druku : P.U.P. ARSPOL, Bydgoszcz | Druk i oprawa : Zaklady Graficzne im. KEN SA, Bydgoszcz'.

Perfectbound in white textured card. Front: [at top left:] [publisher's device] | [in light green] 'PATRICK | WHITE | [in white] PRZEPASKA Z LIŚCI'. Back: [publisher's device] | [blurb, 17 lines] | 'ISBN 83-7079-343-6'. Spine: [running down:] 'PATRICK WHITE PRZEPASKA Z LIŚCI' | [at bottom:] [upright:] [publisher's device].

Copies:. NSL: Mitchell Library [PW].

O.t5a French First Edition First Issue (Paris: Gallimard, 1981)

PATRICK WHITE | UNE CEINTURE | DE FEUILLES | *Traduit de l'anglais* | *par Jean Lambert* | *nrf* | GALLIMARD

20.6 x 14 cm. Unsigned: 216 leaves. pp.*8* 9-426 *427-432* (the last page of each chapter is unnumbered).

1 blank; *2* '*Œuvres de Patrick White* | *nrf* | EDEN-VILLE | LE CHAR DES ÉLUS | VOSS | LES ÉCHAUDÉS | LE MYSTÉRIEUX MANDALA | L'OEIL DU CYCLONE | LE VIVISECTEUR'; *3* 'DU MONDE ENTIER'; *4* blank; *5* title page; *6* '*Titre original :* | A FRINGE OF LEAVES | *Tous droits de traduction, de reproduction, et d'adaptation* | *réservés pour tous les pays.* | *© Patrick White, 1976.* | *© Éditions Gallimard, 1981, pour la traduction fran-çaise.*'; *7* '*A Desmond Digby*'; *8* [epigraphs]; 9-426 *427* text; *428* blank; *429* '*Cet ouvrage* | *repro-duit* | *par procédé photomécanique* | *a été achevé d'imprimer* | *dans les ateliers de la S.E.P.C.* | *à Saint-Amand (Cher), le 11 mai 1981.* | *Dépôt légal : 2ᵉ trimestre 1981.* | *N° d'édition : 28109.* | *Imprimé en France.* | *(138)*'; *430* blank; *431* blank; *432* '28109'.

Perfectbound in white glossy paper. Front: 'DU MONDE ENTIER | PATRICK WHITE | [in red] Une ceinture | de feuilles | [in black] ROMAN | TRADUIT DE L'ANGLAIS | PAR JEAN LAMBERT | [series device] | [in red] [publisher's device] | [in black] GALLIMARD'. Back: 'PATRICK WHITE | [in red] Une ceinture de feuilles | [descrip-tion and biography, 31 lines] | [in red] [publisher's device] | [at bottom right:] [in black] 81-V | A 22470'. Spine: [in red] 'du monde | entier | [in black] PATRICK | WHITE | [in red] UNE CEINTURE | DE FEUILLES | [in black] [publisher's device] | GALLIMARD'.

White paper wraparound. Front: [in white] 'PRIX NOBEL'. Back: [in black] 'Patrick WHITE | UNE CEINTURE DES FEUILLES | DISTRIBUTION SODIS | 128, avenue du Maréchal-de Lattre-de-Tassigny | 77400 Lagny | A22470'.

Copies: VSL: SLT A823.3 W585FRL; NSL: Mitchell Library 823.914/W587/14; NSL: Mitchell Library [PW].

O.t5b   French First Edition Second Issue (Paris: Gallimard Collection L'Imaginaire, 1985)

Notes: p.*431* 'O*uvrage reproduit | par procédé photomécanique. | Impression S.E.P.C. | à Saint-Amand (Cher), le 14 février 1985. | Dépôt légal : février 1985. | Numéro d'imprimeur : 183. |* ISBN 2-07-070315-0. / Imprimé en France.'; *432* [at bottom left:] '35101'. Perfectbound in glossy white card. Price: 45 FF. ISBN 2-07-070315-0.

O.t6 Slovak First Edition (Bratislava: Edícia Eva Smena, 1981)

[on verso:] SMENA [black & white illust.] | [on recto:] [at left:] edícia | Eva | [at right:] Patrick White | STRAPCE | LÍSTIA [black & white illust.]

20.6 x 13.5 cm. Unsigned: 164 leaves. pp.*10* 11-323 *324-328*.

Endpaper; *1* [at left:] 'edícia | Eva | SMENA | [at right:] Patrick White | STRAPCE LÍSTIA'; *2-3* [black & white illust.]; *4-5* title page; *6* [at left:] 'TRANSLATION © MICHAL BREZNICKÝ 1981 | [at right:] © PATRICK WHITE | A Fringe of Leaves | Jonathan Cape, | London 1976 | Preložil | Michal Breznický | [rule] | [at left:] *EVA | edícia | svetovej | prózy | o ženách | pre ženy* | [at right:] SMENA | 1981'; *7* '*DESMONDOVI DIGBYMU*'; *8* blank; *9* [epigraphs]; *10* blank; 11-323 text; *324* blank; *325* [biography, 42 lines]; *326* blank; *327* [at left:] 'edícia | Eva | SMENA | [at right:] Patrick White | STRAPCE | LÍSTIA | [at centre:] Z anglického originálu A Fringe of Lea- | ves, Jonathan Cappe [sic], London 1976, pre- | ložil Michal Breznický. Presbal, väzba | a grafická úprava Milan Veselý. Vydala | Smena, vydavatelstvo SÚV SZM, Brati- | slava, ako svoju 2757. publikáciu. Edícia | Eva, zväzok 77, vydanie prvé. Rok vyda- | nia 1981. Zodpovedná redak- torka edície | a publikácie Viera Juričková. Výtvarná | redaktorka L'ubica Štuková. Tech- nická | redaktorka Zdenka Remeňová. Jazyko- | vá redaktorka Eva Kleknerová. AH | 23,39 (text 22,40; ilustr. 0,99). VH | 23,76. Vytlačila Pravda, tlačový Kombi- | nát KSS-TZP, záved 01, Bratislava. 73- | 061-81. 13/3-4. Cena viaz. 33,– kčs'; *328* blank; endpaper.

Cased in white linen with green printed endpapers. Front: [at left:] [in brown] 'edícia | Eva | SMENA | [at right:] [in black] Patrick White | STRAPCE | LÍSTIA' | [black & white il- lust.]. Back: blank. Spine: [running down:] 'Patrick White'.

Glossy white paper dustjacket printed in black, brown, tan and green. Front: [a left:] [in tan] 'edícia | Eva | [in brown] SMENA | [at right:] [in green] Patrick White | STRAPCE | LÍSTIA' | [col. illust.]. Back: [col. illust.] | [in tan] '73-061-81 | 13/3-4 | Cena viaz. 33,– Kčs'. Spine: [running down:] 'Patrick White'. Inside front flap: [blurb, 42 lines]. Inside back flap: [blurb continues, 41 lines].

Price: 33 kčs.

Copies: NSL: Mitchell Library [PW].

O.t7 Bulgarian First Edition (Plovdiv: Hr. G. Danov, 1981)
[Pojas ot lista]

Notes: pp.432. Trans. by Dimitár Stefanov. Not seen, but referred to in *Index Translationum*.

O.t8a German First Edition First Issue (Düsseldorf: Claassen Verlag, 1982)

Patrick White | [rule] | DER LENDENSCHURZ | [rule] | Roman | Deutsch von | Kurt Heinrich Hansen | claassen

21.8 x 14 cm. Unsigned: 208 leaves. pp.*8* 9-412 *413-416*.

Endpaper; *1* 'Patrick White | DER LENDENSCHURZ'; *2* blank; *3* title page; *4* 'Der Titel der 1976 bei Jonathan Cape Ltd., London, erschienenen Originalausgabe | lautet: A FRINGE OF LEAVES | Copyright © 1976 by Patrick White | 1. Auflage 1982 | Copyright © 1982 by claassen Verlag GmbH, Düsseldorf | Alle Rechte der Verbreitung in deutscher Sprache, auch durch Film, Funk, Fernse- | hen, fotomechanische Wiedergabe, Tonträger jeder Art, auszugsweisen Nachdruck | oder Einspeicherung und Rückgewinnung in Daten- verarbeitungsanlagen aller Art, sind vorbehalten. | Gesetzt aus der Garamond der Fa. Hell | Satz: Bauer & Bökeler Filmsatz GmbH, Denkendorf | Papier: Papierfabrik Schleipen GmbH, Bad Dürkheim | Druck und Bindearbeiten: Ebner Ulm | Printed in Germany | ISBN 3546 496183'; *5* 'Für Desmond Digby'; *6* blank; *7* [epigraphs]; *8* blank; 9-412 text; *413* 'Patrick White | Die ungleichen Brüder | Roman. 396 Seiten, gebunden | [quotation of four lines from] *The Spectator* | Im Auge des Sturms | Roman. 520 Seiten, gebunden | [quotation of four lines from] *Welt am Sonntag* | Der Maler | Roman. 580 Seiten, gebunden | [quotation of nine lines from] *Horst Bienek in Deutsche Zeitung* | claassen Verlag, Postfach 9229, 4000 Düsseldorf 1'; *414* 'Margaret Atwood' | [advertisements for three titles]; *415* 'Iris Murdoch' | [advertisements for four titles]; *416* 'Paul Theroux' | [advertisements for two titles]; endpaper.

Cased in brown cloth. Front and back: blank. Spine: [in beige] 'PATRICK | WHITE | [rule] | DER LENDEN- | SCHURZ | [at bottom:] | claassen'.

White paper dustjacket printed with col. illust. of female wooden statue across front and spine. Front: [in white] 'PATRICK | WHITE | [in green] DER LENDEN- | SCHURZ | [in yellow] ROMAN | [in red] claassen'. Back: [blurb, 11 lines] | '245 09618'. Spine: [in white] 'PATRICK | WHITE | [in yellow] [rule] | [in white] DER LENDENSCHURZ | [in yellow] claassen'. Inside front flap: [description, 45 lines]. Inside back flap: [b&w photo- graph] | [biography, 4 lines] | 'Von Patrick White sind im claassen | Verlag bereits erschie- nen: | *Der Maler*, Roman, 580 S., Ln. | *Im Auge des Sturms*, Roman, 599 S., Ln. | *Die unglei- chen Brüder*, Roman, 393 S., geb. | Schutzumschlag und Foto: | Peter J. Kahrl, Etscheid'.

Price: DM 39.80. ISBN 3-546-49618-3.

Copies: VSL: SLT A823.3 W582FH; NSL: Mitchell Library [PW].

O.t8b German First Edition Second Issue (Münich: Piper, 1990)

Notes: p.*4* 'Die Originalausgabe erschien 1976 unter dem Titel | »A Fringe of Leaves« | bei Jonathan Cape Ltd., London. | Von Patrick White liegt | in der Serie Piper bereits vor: | Der Maler (1094) | Weitere Werke sind in Vorbereitung. | ISBN 3-492-11126-2 | August 1990 | R. Piper GmbH & Co. KG, München | Lizenzausgabe mit Genehmigung | der claassen Verlag GmbH, Düsseldorf | Originalausgabe © Patrick White, 1976 | Deutsche Ausgabe © claassen Verlag GmbH, | Düsseldorf 1982 | Unschlag: Federico Luci, | unter Verwendung des Gemäldes »Fantasia« | von L. Alvarez de Lugo | Satz: Thomas F. Salzer KG, Wien |

Druck und Bindung: Clausen & Bosse, Leck | Printed in Germany'. Perfectbound in white paper printed with fawn ground and col. illust. on front. Published in August 1990. Price: DM 17.80. ISBN 3-492-1126-2.

O.t9   German Second Edition (Frankfurt am Main: Büchergilde Gutenberg, 1988)

Patrick White | Der Lendenschurz | Roman | Deutsch von Kurt Heinrich Hansen | Büchergilde Gutenberg | Frankfurt am Main

20.8 x 12.8 cm. Unsigned: 212 leaves. pp.*6* 7-420 *421-424* (the last page of each chapter is unnumbered).

Endpaper; *1* 'Patrick White | Der Lendenschurz'; *2* blank; *3* title page; *4* 'Für Desmond Digby'; *5* [epigraphs]; *6* blank; 7-420 *421* text; *422* blank; *423* 'Der Titel der 1976 bei Jonathan Cape Ltd., London, erschienenen Originalaus- | gabe lautet : >A FRINGE OF LEAVES<. Copyright © 1976 by Patrick White | Lizenzausgabe für die Büchergilde Gutenberg, Frankfurt am Main, mit | freundlicher Genehmigung der claassen Verlags GmbH, Düsseldorf | Copyright © 1982 by claassen Verlag GmbH, Düsseldorf | Alle rechte der Verbreitung in deutscher Sprache, auch durch Film, Funk, | Fernsehen, fotomechanische Wiedergabe | Tonträger jeder Art, auszugsweisen | Nachdruck oder Einspeicherung und Rückgewinnung in Datenverarbei- | tungsanlagen aller Art, sind Verbehalten. | Schutzumschlag und Einband Hennes Maier, Frankfurt am Main | Schrift Borgis Baskerville | Satz und Druch Richard Wenzel, Goldbach | Bindung Grossbuchbinderei Monheim GmbH, Monheim | Printed in Germany 1988 ISBN 3 7632 3493 4'; *424* blank; endpaper.

Cased in red cloth with white laid endpapers. Front and back: blank. Spine: [in white] *'Patrick* | *White* | [rule] | *Der* | *Lenden-* | *schurz* | [rule] | *BÜCHERGILDE* | *GUTENBERG'*.

White paper dustjacket printed in colour across front, spine and back. Front: *'Patrick* | *White* | [rule] | *Der* | *Lenden-* | *schurz* | *BÜCHERGILDE* | *GUTENBERG'*. Back: blank. Spine: [in white] *'Patrick* | *White* | [rule] | *Der* | *Lenden-* | *schurz* | [rule] | *BÜCHERGILDE* | *GUTENBERG'*. Inside front flap: [description, 32 lines]. Inside back flap: [blurb, 13 lines] | [biography, 13 lines].

Notes: this is a separate edition to the first German edition, published in 1982 (see O.t8a above).

Copies: NSL: Mitchell Library [PW].

O.t10a Czech First Edition (Praha: Odeon, 1983)

[on verso:] PATRICK WHITE | Odeon | [on recto:] sukně z listí

20.5 x 12.8 cm. Unsigned: 204 leaves. pp.*10* 11-396 *397-398* 399-406 *407-408*.

Endpaper; *1* 'ssp | SOUDOBÁ | SVĚTOVÁ | ODEON'; *2* blank; *3* [at left:] 'PATRICK WHITE | [at right:] SUKNĚ | Z LISTÍ'; *4-5* title page; *6* 'PŘELOŽIL ANTONÍN PŘIDAL | © 1976 by Patrick White'; *7* 'VENOVÁNO | DESMONDU DIGBYMU'; *8* blank; *9* [epigraphs]; *10* blank; 11-396 *397* text; *398* blank; 399-406 *407* 'IZOLDA A

TRISTAN V AUSTRALSKÉM BUSI'; *408* 'PATRICK WHITE / SUKNÊ Z LISTÍ | ssp || SOUDOBÁ | SVĚTOVÁ | PRÓZA || ŘÍDÍ | EDUARD HODOUŠEK | SVAZEK 365 | Z anglického originálu A Fringe of Leaves | (Jonathan Cape, London 1976) | přeložil a doslov napsal Antonín Přidal. | Obálku, vazbu a grafickou úpravu navrhl Miloslav Fulín. | Na obálce použito fotografie Ivana Doležala, | na vazbě kresby Vladimíra Tesaře. | Vydal Odeon, nakladatelství krásné literatury a uměni, n. p., | jako svou 4081. publikaci v redakci krásné literatury. Praha 1983. | Odpovědná redaktorka Eva Kondrysová. | Vytiskla Stráž, tiskařské závody, n. p., Plzeň, závod ve Vimperku. | Autorských archů 22,20, vydavatelských archů 22,65. | Vydání první. Náklad 23 250 výtisků. 605 22 846. | 01-007-83. 13/34. | Cena váz. 27 Kčs.'; endpaper.

Cased in light green paper-covered boards with off-white endpapers. Front: [in white] 'ssp' | [in black] [stylised line drawing]. Back: blank. Spine: [running down:] 'sukně z listí || PATRICK | WHITE || [in white] SOUDOBÁ | SVĚTOVÁ PRÓZA'.

White paper dustjacket with black ground on front and spine, and a map of southeastern Australia on back. Front: [in light green/white] 'sukně | z listí | [in white] PATRICK WHITE | [illust.] | [at bottom right:] ODEON'. Back: blank. Spine: [in light green] 'sukně z listí || PATRICK | WHITE.' Inside front flap: 'PATRICK | WHITE | SUKNĚ Z LISTÍ | z angličtiny přeložil | Antonin Přidal' | [blurb, 39 lines]. Inside back flap: [portrait of author] | [biography, 36 lines] | '01-007-83 13/34 Cena váz. 27 kčs.'.

Price: 27 kčs. Print run: 23,250.

Copies: NSL: CZE/WHI/1.

O.t10b Czechoslovakian Second Edition (Prague: Odeon/Klub Čtenárů, 1986)

[Sukně z listí]

Notes: 342 p. Trans. by Antonín Přidal

Copies: NSL: Mitchell Library [PW].

O.t11a Chinese First Edition (Beijing: Zhongguo Wenxue, 1993)

[Shuye qun]

Notes: pp.469. ISBN 7 507 10209 2. Perfectbound in paper. Trans. by Li Yao.

Copies: not seen, but see entry on the National Bibliographic Database.

O.t11b Chinese First Edition Second Issue (Beijing: Zhongguo Wenxue, 1994)

[Shuye qun]

Notes: pp.469. ISBN 7 507 10209 2.

Copies: VU: EA 5988.5 W504

O.m1 Braille (Victoria Park: Association for the Blind of Western Australia, 1983)

A Fringe of Leaves (13 vols. of Braille)

Copies: not seen, but see entry on the National Bibliographic Database.

O.m2 Sound Recording (North Hobart: Hear-a-Book, 1983)

A Fringe of Leaves (13 audiocassettes).

Read by Anne Fraser.

O.m3 (Melbourne: Royal Victorian Institute for the Blind, Tertiary Resource Service, 1985)

A Fringe of Leaves (3 audiocassettes, 4-track).

Read by Katherine Mundy.

P   The Night the Prowler (1978)

The short story, *The Night the Prowler*, was first composed while White was travelling in Europe in late 1967, although the final draft was not completed until early in 1970. It was published in *The Cockatoos* (1974). White first made the suggestion that the story might be made into a film to theatre producer Jim Sharman, late in 1975. Sharman asked for a screenplay, and a few weeks later White reported to Geoffrey Dutton that 'This is pouring out of me'. (Marr p.562) White and Sharman met again in Marseilles in July 1976, when Sharman reported that he had found a producer. Sharman also raised the $400,000 to finance the project: the New South Wales Film Corporation contributed $350,000. Shooting commenced in October 1977, and the film premièred at the Sydney Film Festival in June 1978. It was released commercially in the middle of 1979.

* * * * *

P1 First Edition (Sydney: Penguin Books Australia; London: Jonathan Cape, 1978)

<u>*THE NIGHT THE PROWLER*</u> | *short story and screenplay* | Patrick White | Penguin Books Australia | and Jonathan Cape

19.6 x 13 cm. Unsigned: 80 leaves. pp.*6* 7-57 *58-62* 63-158 *159-160*; 8 p. of plates.

1 'Penguin Books | The Night the Prowler' | [biography, 18 lines]; *2* blank; *3* title page; *4* 'Penguin Books Ltd, | Harmondsworth, Middlesex, England | Penguin Books, | 625 Madison Avenue, New York, N.Y. 10022, U.S.A. | Penguin Books Australia Ltd, | Ringwood, Victoria, Australia | Penguin Books Canada Ltd, | 2801 John Street, Markham, Ontario, Canada | Penguin Books (N.Z.) Ltd, | 182-190 Wairau Road, Auckland 10, New Zealand | "The Night the Prowler" (short story) first published in the | collection *The Cockatoos*, Jonathan Cape 1974 | *The Cockatoos* published in Penguin Books 1978 | Screenplay first published in this edition, | jointly by Penguin Books Australia and Jonathan Cape 1978 | Short story copyright © Patrick White, 1974 | Screenplay copyright © Patrick White, 1976 | Film stills copyright © Chariot Films Pty Ltd, 1977 | Set in Granjon by The Dova Type Shop, Melbourne | Made and printed in Australia | at The Dominion Press, Blackburn, Victoria | [publisher's conditions, 9 lines] | White, Patrick Victor Martindale, 1912- | The night the prowler. | Originally published in The cockatoos, shorter | novels and stories, London: Jonathan Cape, | 1974 | Simultaneously published, London: Jonathan | Cape. | ISBN 0 224 01668 7 (Cape) | ISBN 0 14 005082 5 | 1. The night the prowler (Motion picture). | I. Title. | A823.3'; *5* '*THE NIGHT THE PROWLER* | *short story*'; *6* blank; 7-57 text for short story; *58* blank; *59* 'The Night the Prowler | *The Night the Prowler*, adapted by Patrick White | from his short story, has been made into a film | presented by the New South Wales Film Corporation. | Directed by Jim Sharman, *The Night the Prowler* | stars Ruth Cracknell as Doris Bannister, John Frawley | as Humphrey Bannister, and Kerry Walker as Felicity. | John

Derum appears as John Galbraith, Maggie | Kirkpatrick as Mrs Bannister's friend Madge, and | Terry Camilleri as the prowler.'; *60* blank; *61* '*THE NIGHT THE PROWLER* | *screen-play*'; *62* blank; 63-64 'Characters'; [8 p. of b & w photographs] 65-158 text of screenplay; *159* blank; *160* blank.

Perfectbound in white paper printed with col. illust. of film still on front, black on the back and orange on the spine. Front: [at top right:] [publisher's device] | [in white] 'THE NIGHT | THE PROWLER | [in orange] NOW A MAJOR MOTION PICTURE | [at bottom:] [in black] Patrick White'. Back: [at top right:] [publisher's device] | [in white] [quotation of four lines from] '*Nation Review* | *The Night the Prowler*, presented by the New | South Wales Film Corporation, was directed by | Jim Sharman and stars Ruth Cracknell and | John Frawley as Doris and Humphrey | Bannister, and Kerry Walker as Felicity. John | Derum appears as John Galbraith, Maggie | Kirkpatrick as Mrs Bannister's friend Madge, | and Terry Camilleri as the prowler. | [at bottom left:] Penguin Books Australia and Jonathan Cape | Australia $2.95 (recommended) | [at bottom right:] Fiction | Drama | ISBN 0 14 | 00.5082 5'. Spine: [running down:] [in white] 'Patrick White [in black] The Night The Prowler ISBN 0 14 | 00.5082 5' | [upright:] [publisher's device].

Price: AU$2.95. ISBN 0 1400 5082 5.

Copies: NSL: Mitchell Library A823/W587/63; NU: 823.91A/W587/J10/1; NSL: Mitchell Library [PW]; VSL: SLT 819.93/W582N (2 copies); McL L/A-F White.

P.t1 Serbian First Edition (Belgrade: Rad, 1977)

Noć lupeža

107 p.

Trans. by Marija Herman-Sekulič. Print run: 9,500.

P.m1 Film (Sydney: Chariot Films Pty Ltd, 1978)

Notes: *The Night the Prowler* premièred at the Sydney Film Festival in June 1978. It was re-leased commercially in Sydney in June 1979. It also screened at the London Film Festival in July 1979 where it received mixed reviews (Derek Malcolm *Guardian Weekly* 22 July 1979, p.21; Tom Milne *Observer* 18 November 1979, p.14). Motion picture, 35 mm, approx. 90 minutes. Producer: Anthony Buckley. Director: Jim Sharman. Script: Patrick White. Cinematography: David Sanderson. Cast: Ruth Cracknell, John Frawley, Kerry Walker, John Derum, Maggie Fitzpatrick, Terry Camilleri. This film has been issued as a videocassette by Chariot Films (Sydney, 1978) and Australian Video (Adelaide, *c*1980). It was also broadcast by SBS Television on 2 April 1994.

P.m2 Sound Recording (Hobart: Hear-a-Book, 1983)

The Night the Prowler (2 audiocassettes).

Read by Peg Radcliffe.

Q Big Toys (1978)

Big Toys was written in November and December 1976, in the afterglow of the very successful Sydney revival of *The Season at Sarsaparilla*. In a general sense, *Big Toys* reflects White's interest in urban politics and corruption. In the more specific sense, the play was something of a vehicle for Kate Fitzpatrick. White had been very taken with Fitzpatrick's performance as Nola Boyle in *The Season*. *Big Toys* was not well received by the critics, but it was a popular success: 'There has been a bit of gnashing of teeth from the audiences, but at least the theatre is packed every night, sometimes chairs in the aisles'. (To Betty Withycombe, August 1977)

* * * * *

Q1 Australian First Edition (Sydney: Currency Press, 1978)

Big Toys | [rule] | Patrick White | [publisher's device] | CURRENCY PRESS • SYDNEY

21 x 13.2 cm. Unsigned: 40 leaves. pp.*i–vii* viii-xiv [*4*] *1* 2-61 *62*, illust.

Endpaper; *i* [biography, 33 lines] | *ii* 'By the same author | *Four plays* | *The Ham Funeral* | *The Season at Sarsaparilla* | *A Cheery Soul* | *Night on Bald Mountain* | Novels | *Happy Valley* | *The Living and the Dead* | *The Aunt's Story* | *The Tree of Man* | *Voss* | *Riders in the Chariot* | *The Solid Mandala* | *The Vivisector* | *The Eye of the Storm* | *A Fringe of Leaves* | Stories | *The Burnt Ones* | *The Cockatoos*'; *iii* title page; *iv* 'CURRENCY PLAYS | General Editor: Katharine Brisbane | First published in 1978 | by Currency Press Pty Ltd, | 87 Jersey Road, Woollahra, | N.S.W. 2025, Australia. | Copyright © Patrick White 1978 | [author's conditions, 8 lines] | All applications for performance or | public reading should be made to | Curtis Browne (Australia) Pty Ltd, | P.O. Box 19, Paddington, | N.S.W. 2021, Australia. | [publisher's conditions, 10 lines] | National Library of Australia card number | and ISBN 086819 019 5 | Setting by Filmset Limited, Hong Kong | Printed by Hedges and Bell Pty Ltd, Melbourne.; *v* 'To all those involved in the | original production'; *vi* [b&w photograph] '*Kate Fitzpatrick as Mag in the Old Tote Theatre | Company production. Photo: Robert McFarlane.*'; vii-xiv 'Preface' [by Katharine Brisbane]; *xv-xviii* [b&w photographs]; *1* 'Big Toys' | [rule]; *2* '*Big Toys* was first performed at the Parade Theatre, | Sydney, by the Old Tote Theatre Company on 27th July | 1977 with the following cast: | MAG BOSANQUET   Kate Fitzpatrick | TERRY LEGGE   Max Cullen | RITCHIE BOSANQUET   Arthur Dignam | Setting designed by Brian Thompson | Fashions designed by Victoria Alexander | Directed by Jim Sharman'; 3-58 text; 59-61 'OTHER CURRENCY PUBLICATIONS'; *62* blank; endpaper.

Cased in purple linen cloth stamped in gold down spine. Front and back: blank. Spine: [running down:] 'PATRICK WHITE   BIG TOYS   Currency'.

Glossy white paper dustjacket. Front: [b&w photograph of actress] | [in white] 'PATRICK | WHITE [in mauve] BIG | TOYS'. Back : [b&w photograph of the author] | [at top left:] [in white] [publisher's device] | [at left:] [blurb, 26 lines] | 'Cover: Kate Fitzpatrick as | Mag

Bosanquet in the Old | Tote Theatre Company | production, 1977. | Photo: Brett Hilder. | Patrick White. Photo: | Brett Hilder'. Spine: [running down:] [in white] 'Patrick White Big Toys Currency'. Inside front and back flaps: blank.

Price: AU$6.95 (hbk) and AU$3.95 (pbk). Remained in print until 1985.

Reviews: G. Dutton *Australian* 10-11 February 1979, Weekend Supp. p.8 (355w); H. Hewitt *Canberra Times* 5 May 1979, p.17 (180w); P. Corris *National Times* 10 February 1979, p.29.

Notes: This edition was also issued in a paperback that uses the dustjacket design.

Copies: Personal collection (2 copies); NSL Mitchell Library A822/W587/3; NU: 822.91/A/W587/J1/1;NSL: Mitchell Library [PW].

Q2 Australian Second Edition (Sydney: Currency Press, 1993)

BIG TOYS | by | Patrick White | [publisher's device] | Current Theatre Series | Published by Currency Press, Sydney | in association with Playbox Centre of Monash University

20.1 x 12.5 cm. Unsigned: 32 leaves. pp.[*9*] 6-22 *23* 24-28 *i-ii* iii-viii *ix* x *xi-xii* 29-39 *40* 41-58 *59-60*.

[*1*] blank; [*2*] blank; [*3*] 'Big Toys'; [*4*] blank; [*5*] title page; [*6*] 'CURRENT THEATRE SERIES | First published in 1978 by | Currency Press Pty Ltd | This edition published in 1993 | by Currency Press, PO Box 452, Paddington 2021, | Australa in association with Playbox Theatre Centre | of Monash University. | Copyright © The estate of Patrick White, 1993 *Big* | *Toys.* | [copyright statement, 14 lines] | National Library of Australia | Cataloguing-in-Publication data | [5 lines] | Printed by Bridge Printery, Sydney.'; [*7*] 'Contents | [...] | *Big Toys* was first performed at the Parade Theatre, Sydney, by the | Old Tote Theatre Company on 27 July 1977 with the following | cast: | MAG BOSANQUET Kate Fitzpatrick | TERRY LEGGE Max Cullen | RITCHIE BOSANQUET Arthur Dignam | Directed by Jim Sharman | Fashions designed by Victoria Alexander | Set designed by Brian Thompson'; [*8*] 'CHARACTERS | [...] | SETTING'; [*9*] 6-22 *23* 24-28 text; *i* 'PATRICK WHITE | [in white] BIG TOYS | SEASON | Playbox 93'; *ii* iii-viii *ix* x *xi-xii* [details of the 1993 production of *Big Toys*]; 29-58 text continues; *59-60* blank.

Perfectbound in glossy white paper card. Front: 'PATRICK WHITE | [in red] BIG TOYS | [in white] SEASON | Playbox 93'. Back: [in single rule box:] 'Current Theatre Series | BIG TOYS. [description, 6 lines] | PATRICK WHITE [biography, 9 lines] | PLAYBOX THEATRE CENTRE OF MONASH UNIVERSITY [description, 10 lines] | CURRENCY'S CURRENT THEATRE SERIES [description, 8 lines] | Cover: CATO Design [at right:] ISBN 0 86819 352 6'. Spine: [running down:] 'Patrick White BIG TOYS Currency'. Inside front and back covers: blank.

Published in June 1993. Price: AU$12.95. ISBN 0 8681 9352 6.

Copies: NSL: Mitchell Library 822.914/W587/6; VU: McL L/A-D White.

Q3 U.S. First Edition (n.p.: Limehouse Editions, 1985)

Notes: Not seen but description sighted on www.amazon.com, 7 August 1997. Published in June 1985. Price: US$7.95. ISBN 0 8791 0238 1.

Q.t1 Hungarian First Edition (Budapest, 1980)

NAGYVILÁG | VILÁGIRODALMI FOLYÓIRAT | XXV. évfolyam 8. szám, 1980. augusztus

Notes: [Big Toys] p.1189-1223 *1224* 'Patrick White | ÓRIAS JÁTÉKOK'. [Translated by Karig Sara]. Inside front cover: black & white photograph of Kate Fitzpatrick in the Sydney production of Big Toys. Page 1188: black & white photograph of the set of Sydney production. Inside back cover: black & white photograph of the author. Colophon (p.1264): 'Budapest (Hungary). ISSN 0547-1613'. Price: 'Ára: 16,– t'.

Copies: Personal collection.

Q.m1 Video Recording (Sydney: ABC, 1980)

Big Toys (video cassette, 85 min.).

Notes: Directed by Chris Thompson; Executive Producer Alan Burke; Editor Neil Thumpston.

R The Twyborn Affair (1979)

The idea for *The Twyborn Affair* came to Patrick White whilst in Melbourne at the beginning of 1975 to accept the honour of Australian of the Year. He visited the National Gallery of Victoria with Barry Jones MHR, and Jones related the story of Herbert Dyce Murphy, who was depicted in E. Phillips Fox's painting 'In the Arbour'. White obtained further details from Stephen Murray-Smith, who had made contact with Dyce Murphy, then living on the Mornington Peninsula in Victoria. (For more on Dyce Murphy, see Moira Watson, 'Herbert Dyce Murphy: the fact and the fiction', *Australian Book Review* no.137, December 1991-January 1992, p.4-7.) White also went back to the Monaro Plains to research his time there as a jackaroo. Finally he got down to work in the early days of 1977: 'When the festivities are over I expect to start the novel which has been in my head for over a year. It was working so hard in me this morning it got me out of bed at 4 o'clock.' (To Alan Williams, 26 December 1976)

The European section of *The Twyborn Affair* was completed by April: 'I'm about half way through the first version of the novel, which is the point where X goes down to the Monaro.' It is interesting that while White no longer thought of the main character as Dyce Murphy, he refers to 'X'; either the character had no name(s) or White was unwilling to reveal it.

In April White again went to the Monaro in preparation for writing the Australian section of the novel. It was about this time that he wrote to Betty Withycombe to retrieve his Monaro letters of the 1930s. Betty returned all of White's letters – about four hundred of them, neatly arranged for deposit with the Bodleian Library, Oxford. He read a few of the early letters, and then left them in the dining room for some time. Eventually, he burnt them.

The first draft of the novel was finished in October 1977. He put it away for some months, being distracted by the filming and editing of *The Night the Prowler* and the festive season. He began the second draft in the new year. In March he wrote, 'I am back peacefully with *The Twyborn Affair*. ... I'm about a third of the way through the second version ... After that I shall type and tinker some more before it is ready. So please don't expect it too soon. Probably another year.' (To Grahame C. Greene, 12 March 1978) By August he was typing the final draft: 'I shall probably finish about February unless some dreadful diversion, illness – or even death, holds me up!' (To Geoffrey Dutton, 27 August 1978) In fact, White finished the final draft in November 1978, spurred on by the visiting Greene, who shrewdly pointed out that White would save the postage if he could hand the typescript over to Greene while he was in the country. By December Cape had accepted *The Twyborn Affair*. A second copy of the typescript was given to Jim Sharman, who White hoped would accept the dedication: 'I was worried what it would do to your reputation … but I realised you don't have a reputation.' (Marr p.587)

White had again delayed sending the typescript to The Viking Press in New York, because he wanted London to have a head start. Alan Williams accepted the book for publication with enthusiasm. (Marr p.587)

White was concerned about the look of his book. He had arranged for Luciana Arrighi to do the jacket illustration for the English edition: 'I do very much wonder how the jacket will turn out. It has been an anxious time, for myself, and even more so, Luciana. I see so many awful jackets nowadays. Here the bookshop windows all suggest American airports.' (To Grahame C. Greene, 13 June 1979)

The Twyborn Affair was launched in London in November 1979 and in New York in March 1980. It was shortlisted for the Booker Prize but White had it removed. Criticism was entirely favourable. In Australia it was a bestseller: 'I'm glad you liked *The Twyborn Affair*. Its reception in Australia has been extraordinary. In the beginning reviewers didn't know quite what they ought to say. Then some of them started coming out in the book's favour and it's a bestseller, only just below the latest Forsyth.' (To James Stern, 22 December 1979) In the United States the critical reception was also favourable – although White believed the reviews to be full of inaccuracies – but sales were still modest.

The Twyborn Affair has been translated into a number of languages, including Swedish (1981), French (1983), Serbo-Croat (1984), Hebrew (n.d.) and Yugoslav (1984). In corresponding with the French translator White keenly appreciated that *The Twyborn Affair* would present technical difficulties: 'I shall be ready to answer any of the questions you may have to ask about *The Twyborn Affair* … I feel you will have to follow your own instincts in most cases in the translation.' (To Jean Lambert, 29 January 1981) White was more dismissive of the German translation by Kurt Heinrich Hansen: 'The man Claassen engaged to translate the remainder of my <u>fiction</u> lives in Hamburg. Can't remember his name offhand.' (To Elizabeth Falkenberg, 15 October 1982)

Apparently, there was an attempt to produce *The Twyborn Affair* as a film. David Malouf drafted a film script. Jim Sharman was to direct but was unable to raise the necessary finance. (To Luciana Arrighi, 24 December 1986)

* * * * *

R1 First U.K. Edition (London: Jonathan Cape, 1979)

THE | TWYBORN | AFFAIR | [rule] | A Novel | by | PATRICK WHITE | [at bottom:] [publisher's device] | JONATHAN CAPE | THIRTY BEDFORD SQUARE LONDON

20.4 x 13 cm. [A]¹⁶ B-M¹⁶ N⁸ O¹⁶ ($1 signed): 216 leaves. pp.*1-10* 11-130 *131-132* 133-302 *303-304* 305-432.

Endpaper; *1* 'THE TWYBORN AFFAIR'; *2* '*by the same author* | *Novels* | RIDERS IN THE CHARIOT | VOSS | THE TREE OF MAN | THE AUNT'S STORY | THE LIVING AND THE DEAD | THE SOLID MANDALA | THE VIVISECTOR | THE EYE OF THE STORM | A FRINGE OF LEAVES | *Short Stories* | THE BURNT ONES | THE COCKATOOS | *Plays* | FOUR PLAYS'; *3* title page; *4* 'First published 1979 | © 1979 by Patrick White | Jonathan Cape Ltd, 30 Bedford Square | London WC1 | British Library Cataloguing in Publication Data | White, Patrick | The Twyborn Affair. | I. Title | 823'.9'1F PR9619.3 W5T/ | ISBN 0-224-01733-0 | [at bottom:] Printed in Great Britain by | The Anchor Press Ltd and bound by | Wm Brendon & Son Ltd, both of Tiptree, Essex'; *5* 'TO JIM SHARMAN'; *6* blank; *7* 'What else should our lives be but a series of beginnings, of painful | settings out into the unknown, pushing off from the edges of | consciousness into the mystery of what we have not yet become. | *David Malouf.* | My suspicion is that in Heaven the Blessed are of the opinion that | the advantages of that locale have been overrated by theologians | who were never actually there. Perhaps even in Hell the damned | are not always satisfied. | *Jorge Luis Borges* | Sometimes you'll see someone with nothing on but a bandaid. | *Diane Arbus*'; *8* blank; *9* 'Part I'; *10* blank; 11-130 text of Part I; *131* '*Part II*'; *132* blank; 133-302 text of Part II; *303* '*Part III*'; *304* blank; 305-432 text of Part III; endpaper.

Cased in dark brown imitation-cloth with brown top edge and buff endpapers. Front and back: blank. Spine: [in gold] 'THE | TWYBORN | AFFAIR | [ornament] | PATRICK | WHITE' | [at bottom:] [publisher's device].

White, lightly textured paper dustjacket printed in purple on front, back and spine. Front: [in gold] '*The* | Twyborn | Affair | [in black outlined in gold] PATRICK | WHITE' | [black line illust. featuring a bust]. Back: [in black] 'Also by Patrick White | [rule] | *THE COCKATOOS* | [quotation of six lines from] *Daily Telegraph* | *THE EYE OF THE STORM* | [quotation of five lines from] *Sunday Telegraph* | *THE VIVISECTOR* | [quotation of two lines from] *Sunday Times* | *THE TREE OF MAN* | [quotation of three lines from] *New York Times* | *THE SOLID MANDALA* | [quotation of two lines from] *Guardian* | *RIDERS IN THE CHARIOT* | [quotation of four lines from] *Sunday Times* | *A FRINGE OF LEAVES* | [quotation of five lines from] *Guardian*'. Spine: [in gold] '*The* | Twyborn | Affair | [in black] PATRICK | WHITE' | [cont. of illust. from front] | [at bottom:] [publisher's device]. Inside front flap: [blurb, 38 lines] | [at bottom right:] '£5.95 net | [rule] | IN UK ONLY'. Inside back flap: 'Patrick White was awarded the Nobel | Prize for Literature in 1973. Among the | remarkable novels which have brought | him world acclaim are *Voss, The Tree of* | *Man* and *A Fringe of Leaves.* | [at bottom:] ISBN 0 224 01733 0 | Jacket drawing by Luciana Arrighi | Jacket design by Mon Mohan | © Jonathan Cape Ltd 1979'.

Published 29 September 1979. £5.95. Print run: 25,000.

Reviews: Angus Wilson *Observer* 9 December 1979, p.35; William Walsh *Times Literary Supplement* 30 November 1979; *Books & Bookmen* v.25, November 1979, p.47; *Guardian Weekly* 19 August 1979, p.23; *Listener* v.102, 29 November 1979, p.761; *New Statesmen* v.98, 28 September 1979, p.470; *Spectator* v.243, 29 September 1979, p.24; Neil Jillett *Age* (Melbourne) 29 November 1979, p.27 (1775w); Jim Davidson *National Times* 24 November 1979, p.54-55; Jean Bedford *National Times* 24 November 1979, p.55; P. Corris *National Times* 15 December 1979, p.34 (60w); G. Tout-Smith *Overland* no.78, December 1979, p.65-67; J. McLaren *Australian Book Review* no.16, November 1979, p.8-9; K. England *Advertiser* (Adelaide) 3 November 1979, p.25 (760w); G.A. Wilkes *Australian* 10-11 November 1979, Weekend Supplement, p.12; G. Dutton *Bulletin* v.100, 27 November 1979, p.86+ (1140w); M. Clark *Sydney Morning Herald* 13 October 1979, p.20 (980w); R. Hall *Sydney Morning Herald* 15 December 1979, p.18 (60w); B. Jefferis *Sydney Morning Herald* 15 December 1979, p.18 (60w); N. Phelan *Sydney Morning Herald* 15 December 1979, p.18 (55w); E. Riddell *Sydney Morning Herald* 15 December 1979, p.18 (55w); H. Daniel *Age* (Melbourne) 26 January 1980, p.24 (100w); P. Pierce *Meanjin* v.39, July 1980, p.260-263 (1610w); R. Nevin *National Times* 7-13 December 1980 (60w); L. Kramer *Quadrant* v.24, July 1980, p.66-67.

Notes: One copy in private hands has a dedication from the author to Sir Ralph Richardson dated 31 October 1979. An uncorrected proof copy has been sighted in a personal collection; it is sewn bound in a plain brown paper wrapper (Front: 'TWYBORN AFFAIR | PATRICK WHITE | [publisher's devices] | UNCORRECTED PROOF') and was bought for $100. Another uncorrected proof, sewn in red paper, is held by the State Library of Victoria (Call no. *LT A823.3 W585T). It was bought for $100 in 1994. ADFA's copy was a review copy sent to Dorthy Green; it has numerous annotations.

Copies: NSL (ML) A823/W587/78 (lacks dustjacket); NSL (ML) [PW]; NSL JFR/066956; NU: 823.91/A/W587/J7/1; private collections (3); ADFA; VU: McL L/A-F White.

R2a U.S. First Edition First Issue (New York: Viking, 1980)

The Twyborn Affair | [illust. of a knot] *Patrick White* | THE VIKING PRESS NEW YORK

23.5 x 15.5 cm. Unsigned: 216 leaves. pp.*10* 11-130 *131-132* 133-302 *303-304* 305-432.

Endpaper; *1* 'THE TWYBORN AFFAIR'; *2* '*by the same author* | *Novels* | RIDERS IN THE CHARIOT | VOSS | THE TREE OF MAN | THE AUNT'S STORY | THE LIVING AND THE DEAD | THE SOLID MANDALA | THE VIVISECTOR | THE EYE OF THE STORM | A FRINGE OF LEAVES | *Short Stories* | THE BURNT ONES | THE COCKATOOS | *Plays* | FOUR PLAYS'; *3* title page; *4* [publisher's device] | 'Copyright © Patrick White, 1979 | All rights reserved | First published in 1980 by The Viking Press | 625 Madison Avenue, New York, N.Y. 10022 | Published simultaneously in Canada by | Penguin Books Canada Limited | LIBRARY OF CONGRESS CATALOGING IN PUBLICATION DATA | White, Patrick, 1912- | The Twyborn affair. | I. Title | PZ3.W58469Tw 1980 [PR9619.3.W5] 823 79-26242 | ISBN 0-670-73789-5 | Printed in the United States of America | Set in Bembo'; *5* 'TO JIM SHARMAN'; *6* blank; *7* [epigraphs]; *8* blank; *9* '*Part One*' | [illust.of a knot]; *10* blank; 11-130 text of Part One; *131* '*Part*

Two' | [illust. of a knot]; *132* blank; 133-302 text of Part Two; *303 'Part Three'* | [illust. of a knot]; *304* blank; 305-432 text of Part Three; endpaper.

Cased in buff paper-covered boards with black linen spine and off-white endpapers. Front: [at bottom right:] [stamped in blind] 'PW'. Back: blank. Spine: [in gold] [running down:] '*The* | *Twyborn Affair* || [ornament] || *Patrick* | *White* | [upright:] VIKING'.

Glossy white paper printed in yellow on front, back and spine. Front: [in red] [hollow type] 'PATRICK | WHITE | [in black] [solid type] The | Twyborn | Affair | [illust. of a butterfly in red and brown] | [in red] [hollow type] A NOVEL'. Back: [in black] 'The | Twyborn | Affair | [in red] BY NOBEL LAUREATE | [hollow type] PATRICK | WHITE | [illust. of butterfly in red and brown] | [in black] [solid type] [quotation of four lines from] —Angus Wilson | *The Observer* | [quotation of four lines from] —William Walsh | *Times Literary Supplement* | THE VIKING PRESS PUBLISHERS NEW YORK | ISBN 0-670-73789-5'. Spine: [running down:] [in red] [hollow type] 'PATRICK | WHITE || [in black] [solid type] The | Twyborn Affair | [at bottom:] [upright:] [in red] VIKING'. Inside front flap: '$14.95 | [blurb, 35 lines] | [in red] *Jacket design by Mel Brofman* | [in black] 0480'. Inside back flap: 'JOHN STOCKDALE | [b&w photograph of the author] | [biography, 24 lines] | [in red] THE VIKING PRESS | 625 Madison Avenue | New York, N.Y. 10022 | PRINTED IN U.S.A.'.

Published 22 April 1980. Price: US$14.95.

Reviews: *Atlantic Monthly* v.245, May 1980, p.102; *Books in Canada* v.9, June 1980, p.10; *Booklist* v.76, 1 March 1980, p.930; *Books of the Times* v.3, June 1980, p.253, *Best Sellers* v.40, June 1980, p89; *Book World* v.10, 18 May 1980, p.3; *Christian Science Monitor* v.72, 7 May 1980, p.17; *Choice* v.18, October 1980, p.251; *Critic* v.38, 15 June 1980, p.5; *Encounter* v.54, January 1980, p.58; *Kirkus Reviews* v.48, 15 February 1980, p.245; *Library Journal* v.107, 15 February 1980, p.532; *New Leader* v.63, 2 June 1980, p.17; *Newsweek* v.95, 7 April 1980, p.88C; *New Yorker* v.56, 28 April 1980, p.142; *New York Review of Books* v.27, 17 April 1980, p.25; *New York Times Book Review* v.85, 27 April 1980, p.3; *New Republic* v.182, 3 May 1980, p.37; *Publishers Weekly* v.217, 7 March 1980, p.69; *Sewanee Review* v.88, October 1980, p.R92; *Wall Street Journal* 18 June 1980, p.22; *World Literature Today* v.55, Winter 1981, p.173.

Notes: A presentation copy in White's collection is half-bound in black leather with marbled paper boards, head in black and dark grey endpapers. Uncorrected proof copies have been sighted in the Mitchell Library (823.914/W587/50), at ADFA and in a private collection. Each is sewn in a blue paper wrapper. Front: '*The Twyborn Affair* | [knot ornament] | *Patrick White* | [in box:] PUB. DATE ___ PRICE ___ | UNREVISED AND UNPUBLISHED PROOFS. CONFIDENTIAL | Please do not quote for publication until verified | with finished book. This copy is not for | distribution to the public. | THE VIKING PRESS'. Page *1* has: 'THE TWYBORN AFFAIR | Patrick White | Fiction | April $10.95 | 432 pages 6x9 | LC: 79-3619 | ISBN: 0-670-73785-5' | [blurb, 25 lines] | [biography, 6 lines]. The Mitchell Library copy was bought for $90.

Copies: NSL (ML) 823.914/W587/2 (lacks dustjacket); NSL (ML) [PW]; Private collections (2 copies).

R2b Canadian Subedition (Toronto: Penguin, 1980)

Not seen, but assumed from the statement on p.*4* of the U.S. First Edition (see R2a above).

R3a Penguin First Edition First Issue (Harmondsworth: Penguin, 1981)

The Twyborn Affair | [illust. of a knot] | *Patrick White* | [at bottom:] [publisher's device]

18.2 x 11.2 cm. Unsigned: 216 leaves. pp.*10* 11-130 *131-132* 133-302 *303-304* 305-432.

1 'THE TWYBORN AFFAIR'; *2* '*by the same author* | *Novels* | RIDERS IN THE CHARIOT | VOSS | THE TREE OF MAN | THE AUNT'S STORY | THE LIVING AND THE DEAD | THE SOLID MANDALA | THE VIVISECTOR | THE EYE OF THE STORM | A FRINGE OF LEAVES | *Short Stories* | THE BURNT ONES | THE COCKATOOS | *Plays* | FOUR PLAYS'; *3* title page; *4* 'Penguin Books Australia Ltd, | 487 Maroondah Highway, P.O. Box 257 | Ringwood, Victoria, 3134, Australia | Penguin Books Ltd, | Harmondsworth, Middlesex, England | Penguin Books, | 625 Madison Avenue, New York, N.Y. 10022, U.S.A. | Penguin Books Canada Ltd, | 2801 John Street, Markham, Ontario, Canada | Penguin Books (N.Z.) Ltd, | 182-190 Wairau Road, Auckland 10, New Zealand | First published in the United Kingdom by Jonathan Cape, 1979 | First published in the United States by The Viking Press, 1980 | Published by Penguin Books Australia, 1981 | Copyright © Patrick White, 1979 | Typeset in the USA in Bembo | Offset from the Viking Press edition, 1980 | Made and printed in Australia by Hedges & Bell | All rights reserved [publisher's conditions, 11 lines] | CIP | White, Patrick, 1912 | The Twyborn affair. | First published: London: | Jonathan Cape, 1979. | ISBN 0 14 005544 4 | I. Title. | A823'.3'; *5* 'TO JIM SHARMAN'; *6* blank; *7* [epigraphs]; *8* blank; *9* '*Part One*' | [knot]; *10* blank; 11-130 text of Part One; *131* blank; *132* '*Part Two*' | [knot]; 133-302 text of Part Two; *303* '*Part Three*' | [knot]; *304* blank; 305-432 text of Part Three.

Perfectbound in white paper covers printed in black. Front: [at top right:] [publisher's device] | [in white] 'THE | TWYBORN | AFFAIR | A new novel by the Nobel Prize Winner | PATRICK WHITE' | [col. illust. featuring a woman's head and bust]. Back: [at right:] [publisher's device] | [in white] [blurb, 12 lines] | [quotation of one line from] '—Angus Wilson in the *Observer* | [quotation of three lines from] —William Walsh in the *Times Literary Supplement* | The cover shows a | detail from *Woman in a Hamburger* | by William Dobell. (Private collection) | [at bottom left:] Australia $5.95 (recommended) | [at bottom right:] Fiction | ISBN 0 14 | 00 6027 8'. Spine: [running down:] [in white] 'PATRICK WHITE THE TWYBORN AFFAIR | ISBN 0 14 | 00 6027 8' | [upright:] [publisher's device].

Notes: p.*4* 'Offset from the Viking Press edition, 1980'.

Copies: NSL: Mitchell Library 823.914/W587/3; NSL: Mitchell Library [PW]; Private collection.

R3b Penguin First Edition Second Issue (Harmondsworth: Penguin, [1985])
19.8 x 13 cm.
Notes: 19.8 x 13 cm.; p.*4* 'Printed in the United States of America by | Offset Paperback
Mfrs., Inc., Dallas, Pennsylvania | Set in Bembo'. Cover design by Neil Stuart. Cover illustra-
tion by Mel Odom. Published 1985. US$4.95. ISBN 0 1400 5544 4.

R3c Penguin First Edition Third Issue (Harmondsworth: Penguin, 1988)
Notes: p.*4* 'Reprinted 1985, 1988 | [...] | Printed and bound in Great Britain by | Cox &
Wyman Ltd, Reading | Set in Bembo'. Price: £4.95, AUS$11.95, NZ$18.99, CAN$9.95,
US$6.95. ISBN 0 1400 5544 4.

R3e Penguin First Edition Fourth Issue (Harmondsworth: Penguin, [1993])
Notes: 'The cover shows *A Sergeant of the Light Horse*, 1920 by George Lambert [...] National
Gallery of Victoria'. Price: AU$16.95.

R4 Penguin Second Edition (Harmondsworth: Penguin, 1981)

PATRICK WHITE | THE | TWYBORN | AFFAIR | [publisher's
device] | A KING PENGUIN | PUBLISHED BY PENGUIN
BOOKS

19.8 x 13 cm. Unsigned: 192 leaves. pp.*8* 9-110 *111-114* 115-262 *263-266* 267-378 *379-384*.

Notes: p.*4* 'Filmset, printed and bound in Great Britain by | Hazell Watson & Viney Ltd,
Aylesbury, Bucks | Set in Garamond'. On the front cover is 'Bondi Beach' by Elioth Gruner,
reproduced by kind permission of the Art Gallery of New South Wales. On the back cover is
a photograph of Patrick White by Axel Poignant. Published November 1981. £2.95,
AUS$6.95. ISBN 0 1400.6073 1.

R.t1 Swedish First Edition (Stockholm: Forum, 1981)

Patrick White | Fallet Twyborn | Översättning Ingegärd Martinell | Forum

22 x 14 cm. [1]¹⁶ 2-15¹⁶ 16⁶ ($1,16 signed): 246 leaves. pp.*8* 9-143 *144-146* 147-334 *335-
336* 337-486 *487-492*.

Endpaper; *1* 'Fallet Twyborn'; *2* blank; *3* title page; *4* '*Till Jim Sharman* | *Tidigare utgivning* |
De fyra utkorade 1964 | Den oförstörbara mandalan 1969 | Livets träd 1970 | Målaren 1973 |
Stormens öga 1976 | En frans av löv 1979 | [publisher's device] | Originalets titel | The Twy-
born Affair | © 1979 by Patrick White | Omslag Christer Jonson | Sättning Fälths i Värnamo
| Otava, Keuruu, Finland 1981 | Printed in Finland | ISBN 91-37-07401-6'; *5* [epigraphs]; *6*
blank; *7* '*Första delen*'; *8* blank; 9-143 text of Part I; *144* blank; *145* '*Andra delen*'; *146* blank;
147-334 text of Part II; *335* '*Tredje delen*'; *336* blank; 337-482 text of Part III; 482-486 *487*
'Översättning av de franska orden och uttrycken'; *488-492* blank; endpaper.

Cased in white linen with yellow headbands and white endpapers. Front and back: blank.
Spine: [running down:] [in yellow] 'PATRICK WHITE Fallet Twyborn'.

Glossy white paper dustjacket printed in full colour. Front: 'PATRICK WHITE | Fallet Twyborn | [col. illust. of a man running] | FORUM'. Back: [blurb, 9 lines] | [col. illust.] | 'FORUM | ISBN 91-37-07401-6'. Spine: [running down:] 'PATRICK WHITE Fallet Twyborn'. Inside front flap: [quotations]. Inside back flap: [b&w photograph of the author] | [biography, 6 lines].

Copies: Private collection.

R.t2 French First Edition (Paris: Gallimard, 1983)

PATRICK WHITE | LES INCARNATIONS | D'EDDIE TWYBORN | *Traduit de l'anglais* | *par Jean Lambert* | *nrf* | GALLIMARD

20.6 x 13.9 cm. Unsigned: 240 leaves. pp.[*14*] 13-142 *143-146* 147-327 *328-330* 331-470 *471-478*.

[*1-3*] blank; [*4*] 'DU MÊME AUTEUR | *Aux Éditions Gallimard* | EDEN-VILLE | LE CHAR DES ÉLUS | VOSS | LES ÉCHAUDÉS | LE MYSTÉRIEUX MANDALA | L'ŒIL DU CYCLONE | LE VIVISECTEUR | UNE CEINTURE DE FEUILLES'; [*5*] '*Du monde entier*'; [*6*] blank; [*7*] title page; [*8*] '*Titre original :* | THE TWYBORN AFFAIR | © *Patrick White, 1979.* | © *Éditions Gallimard, 1983, pour la traduction française.*'; [*9*] '*A Jim Sharman*'; [*10*] blank; [*11*] [epigraphs]; [*12*] blank; [*13*] '*Première partie*'; [*14*] blank; 13-470 *471* text; *472* blank; *473* '*Composé par SEP 2000 à Paris* | *et achevé d'imprimer* | *par l'Imprimerie Floch à Mayenne* | *le 16 février 1983.* | *Dépôt légal : février 1983.* | *Numéro d'imprimeur : 20648.* | ISBN 2-07-020653-X / *Imprimé en France*'; *474-477* blank; *478* [at bottom left:] '31546'.

Perfectbound in a glossy white paper card. Front: 'DU MONDE ENTIER | PATRICK WHITE | [in red] Les incarnations | d'Eddie Twyborn | [in black] ROMAN | TRADUIT DE L'ANGLAIS | PAR JEAN LAMBERT | [series device] | [in red] *nrf* | [in black] GALLIMARD'. Back: 'PATRICK WHITE | [in red] Les incarnations | d'Eddie Twyborn | [in black] [blurb, 27 lines] | [biography, 3 lines] | [in red] *nrf* | [in black] [ornament] 83-111 A 20653 ISBN 2-07-020653-X 140 FF tc'. Spine: [in red] '*du monde* | *entier* | [in black] PATRICK | WHTE | [in red] LES INCARNATIONS | D'EDDIE TWYBORN | [in black] *nrf* | GALLIMARD'.

Price: 140 FF.

Copies: VSL: SLT 819.93/W582TL; NSL: Mitchell Library [PW]; Private collection.

R.t3 Serbo-Croat First Edition (Zagreb: August Cesarec, 1984)

PATRICK WHITE | TWYBORNOVA | STVAR | [publisher's device] | AUGUST CESAREC ZAGREB

19.4 x 11.8 cm. [1]⁸ 2-25⁸ 26¹⁰ ($2 signed): 210 leaves. pp.6 7-125 *126* 127-289 *290* 291-418 *419-420*.

Endpaper; *1* 'PATRICK WHITE/TWYBORNOVA STVAR'; *2* 'BIBLIOTEKA BESTSELER | Naslov izvornika | Patrick White | THE TWYBORN AFFAIR | Jonathan Cape Ltd, London 1979 | First published 1979 | Copyright © 1979 by Patrick White | Prijevod | INES ZUPANOV | Odgovorni urednik | DRAGAN MILKOVIC | Glavni urednik | ZDRAVKO ZIDOVEC'; *3* title page; *4* 'Posveceno Jimu Sharmanu'; *5* [epigraphs]; *6* blank; 7-125 text of Part I; *126* blank; 127-289 text of Part II; *290* blank; 291-418 text of Part III; *419* '[publisher's device] | Â̓UGUST C̓ESAREC Z̓AGREB | 1984 | Izdavac | ITRO AUGUST CESAREC | OOUR Izdavacka djelatnost | Zagreb, Prilaz JA 57 | Tisak | Štamparski zavod OGNJEN PRICA | Zagreb, Savska cesta 31 | Naklada | 8.000 | Za izda-vaca | DRAGAN MILKOVIC | Lektor | MARILKA KRAJNOVIC | Korektor | MIRENA PEHNEC | Likovna oprema | NENAD DOGAN | Tehnicki urednik | FRANJO PROFETA'; *420* blank; endpaper.

Cased in grey imitation-cloth with white endpapers. Front: [in white] [at top left:] 'BESTSELER | [at bottom:] Patrick White | TWYBORNOVA | STVAR'. Back: blank. Spine: [in white] [running down:] 'Patrick White | TWYBORNOVA STVAR' | [upright:] [publisher's device].

Black paper dustjacket printed in full colour. Front: [in white] [at top left:] 'BESTSELER | [at bottom:] Patrick White | TWYBORNOVA | STVAR'. Back: [in white] [at left:] 'Pat-rick White | TWYBORNOVA STVAR | [biography, 19 lines] | BESTSELER' | [at right:] [b&w photograph of the author] | [blurb, 12 lines]. Spine: [in white] [running down:] 'Pat-rick White | TWYBORNOVA STVAR' | [upright:] [publisher's device]. Inside back flap: [in white] 'IZAŠLO BIBLIOTECI BESTSELER' | [list of 41 titles follows]. Inside back flap: [in white] 'USKORO U BIBLIOTECI BESTSELER | [list of 7 titles follows] design NENAD DOGAN foto SANJA BACHRACH'.

Print run: 8,000.

Copies: VGRL: Geelong Cro.F/WHI.

R.t4a   German First Edition First Issue (Düsseldorf: Claassen Verlag, 1986)

Patrick White | DIE | TWYBORN | AFFÄRE | *Roman* | Deutsch von | Kurt Heinrich Hansen | claassen

22 x 14.2 cm. Unsigned: 248 leaves. pp.*10* 11-146 *147-148* 149-340 *341-342* 343-491 *492-496*.

Endpaper; *1* 'Patrick White | Die Twyborn Affäre'; *2* blank; *3* title page; *4* 'Die Originalaus-gabe erschien 1979 unter dem Titel | The Twyborn Affair | bei Jonathan Cape Ltd., London | 1. Auflage 1986 | Copyright © 1986 by claassen Verlag GmbH, Düsseldorf | »The Twy-born Affair« Copyright © 1979 by Patrick White | Alle deutschen Rechte vorbehalten | Ge-setzt aus der Garamond der Fa. Berthold | Satz: Dörlemann-Satz, Lemförde | Papier: Papier-fabrik Schleipen GmbH, Bad Dürkheim | Druck und Bindearbeiten: Pustet, Grafischer Be-trieb, Regensburg | Printed in Germany | ISBN 3 546 49617 5'; *5* 'Für Jim Sharman'; *6* blank; *7* [epigraphs]; *8* blank; *9* 'Teil I'; *10* blank; 11-146 *147-148* 149-340 *341-342* 343-491 text; *492-496* [advertisements]; endpaper.

Cased in grey paper-covered boards with white endpapers. Front and back: blank. Spine: [on grey panel:] '*Patrick White* | [hollow type] DIE | TWYBORN | AFFÄRE | [at bottom:] [solid type] claassen'.

Grey paper dustjacket. Front: '*Patrick White* | [hollow type] DIE | TWYBORN | AFFÄRE | [solid type] *Roman / claassen*' | [col. illust. of women seated at table overlooking seascape]. Back: [b&w photograph of the author] | '*Patrick White* | [quotation of ten lines from] *Angus Wilson* | 245 09617'. Spine: '*Patrick White* | [hollow type] DIE | TWYBORN | AFFÄRE | [at bottom:] [solid type] claassen'. Inside front flap: [quotation of 43 lines from] '*Angus Wilson*'. Inside back flap: [biography, 13 lines] | 'Bei claassen erschienen die Romane: »Der Maler« (1972), »Im Auge des Sturms« (1974), »Die ungleichen Brüder« (1978) und »Der Lendenschurz« (1982). | Schutzumschlag: | Klaus Detjen, Hamburg'.

Price: DM 39.80. ISBN 3-546-49617-5.

Copies: VSL: SLT A823.3/W582TH; NSL: Mitchell Library [PW].

R.t4b German First Edition Second Issue (Munich, Zurich: Piper, 1991)
Notes: pp.491. DM 16.80. Print run: 10,000. ISBN 3-492-11127-0. (Serie Piper, 1127). Trans. by Kurt Heinrich Hansen. See also *Index Translationum*.

R.m1 Sound Recording (North Hobart: Hear-a-Book, 1984)
The Twyborn Affair (11 audiocasettes).
Read by Mary Marshall from the Jonathan Cape edition of 1979.

R.m2 Braille Edition (Canberra: Canberra Braille Transcribers, 1989)
The Twyborn Affair (10 volumes of Braille).
Transcribed from the Cape edition of 1979.

R.m3 Sound Recording (Enfield: Royal Blind Society of New South Wales, 1992)
The Twyborn Affair (5 audiocassettes).
Read by John Burton from the Jonathan Cape edition of 1979.

R.m4 Extract (Melbourne: Oxford University Press, 1993)
Australian Gay and Lesbian Writing: an Anthology ed. by Robert Dessaix (Melbourne: Oxford University Press, 1993), p.252-273. [Seated beside the fire […] dreams, or nightmares.]

S Flaws in the Glass (1981)

Over the years Patrick White was little interested in assisting literary historians with biographical studies. He was also opposed to the idea that he would ever write an autobiography. He kept few personal papers and often exhorted his friends to burn his letters. In 1967 he commented to Maie Casey: 'It's an odd thing [i.e. narrating in the first person], but I can never do that. Immediately I become inhibited. So I could never think of writing an autobiography'. (26 November 1967) However, White had participated in a considerable number of biographical pieces – notes on the early dustjackets, 'The prodigal son', an anonymous piece in *Meanjin* (June 1956), an interview in *Southerly* (1973), the Nobel Prize biography. When writing *The Twyborn Affair* White came to realise that perhaps he should write a memoir (he resolutely denied it was an autobiography) for a variety of reasons – to announce his homosexuality, to confront his flaws, to examine the influences on his creative motivation.

By January 1980 White had prepared a sketch which was published in the literary supplement of the hundredth anniversary issue of the *Bulletin* (edited by Geoffrey Dutton). 'This portrait began as a doodle, and grew and grew, so that I don't feel I shall be able to waste it.' (To Shirley Hazzard, 9 December 1979) By March, the first draft was finished: 'Yesterday I finished <u>shaping</u> my self-portrait. Shall probably have to fiddle with it for years, but at least it is down on paper.' (To David Moore, 22 March 1980) By August the second draft was almost finished: 'I'm nearing the end of a second version of my self-portrait *Flaws in the Glass*'. (To Randolph Stow, 24 August 1980) As usual he took a month off before returning to type the final draft. Having worked on the final draft for seven weeks, White collapsed early in December. Although the illness was not serious, White was badly shaken. 'What made me particularly depressed was not having finished my self-portrait and perhaps no time to do it. I am now bashing away again and hope to finish in a couple of weeks.' (To the Sterns, 28 December 1980) He finished *Flaws in the Glass* on New Year's Day, 1981.

The manuscript was probably submitted to Jonathan Cape towards the end of January 1981. Cape knew they had a sensation on their hands and moved quickly towards publication. Their editorial department was concerned about a number of issues, especially the treatment of the Kerrs ('amiable, rorty old, farting John Kerr'), but White refused to alter a word. In fact, he added a less than flattering postscript. 'Lots of correspondence with Cape about *Flaws in the*

Glass. There are bits which worry them, but I have said those bits must stay if it is to be published at all'. (To Peggy Garland, 12 April 1981)

Flaws in the Glass was published in London in October 1981 and in New York in February 1982. However, even before publication, review copies were creating a sensation. Charles Osborne, who received a review copy from the *Financial Times*, immediately rang Sidney Nolan about the section on the Nolans. Nolan took legal advice and attempted to have publication stopped. In the end he was advised against suing White. Nolan took his own revenge; it was both graphic and bitter. (See Marr p.607)

Although White thought that the press – both English and Australian – behaved badly, in fact reviews were good. Sales were also good – *Flaws in the Glass* was White's best seller – though again White took a cynical view, putting *Flaws in the Glass*'s success down to the fact that 'people wanted to have a perv'.

* * * * *

S1a U.K. First Edition (London: Jonathan Cape, 1981)

PATRICK WHITE | [rule] | *Flaws | in the | Glass* | [rule] | A SELF-PORTRAIT | [at bottom:] [publisher's device] | JONATHAN CAPE | THIRTY BEDFORD SQUARE LONDON

22.2 x 14.4 cm. Unsigned: 136 leaves. pp.[*10*] 1-155 *156* 157-217 *218* 219-257 *258* 259-260 *261-262*, plates of b&w photographs between pages 54-55, 86-87, 118-119, 150-151, 214-215 and 230-231.

Endpaper; [*1*] '*Flaws in the Glass*'; [*2*] '*by the same author | Novels* | RIDERS IN THE CHARIOT | VOSS | THE TREE OF MAN | THE AUNT'S STORY | THE LIVING AND THE DEAD | THE SOLID MANDALA | THE VIVISECTOR | THE EYE OF THE STORM | A FRINGE OF LEAVES | THE TWYBORN AFFAIR | *Short Stories* | THE BURNT ONES | THE COCKATOOS | *Plays* | FOUR PLAYS'; [*3*] title page; [*4*] 'First published 1981 | Copyright © 1981 by Patrick White | Jonathan Cape Ltd, 30 Bedford Square, London, WCI | British Library Cataloguing in Publication Data | White, Patrick | Flaws in the glass. | 1. White, Patrick – Biography | 2. Authors, Australian – 20th century – Biography | I. Title | 823 PR9619.3.W5Z/ | ISBN 0-224-02924-X | [at bottom:] Photoset in Great Britain by | Rowland Phototypesetting Limited, | Bury St Edmunds, Suffolk and printed by | Butler & Tanner Ltd, | Frome and London'; [*5*] 'to Manoly | again'; [*6*] blank; [*7*] '*Contents*'; [*8*] 'The author and publisher are grateful to the | following for permission to reproduce photo- | graphs: Brett Hilder, 1; Axel Poignant, 17; Ern | Macquillan, 22; J. Wong from Colorific!, 25; | Will Young, 26, 27; and Elly Polymeropoulou, | 28.'; [*9*] '*Illustrations*'; [*10*] [illustrations continued]; 1-155 text of 'Flaws in the Glass'; *156* blank; 157-217 text of 'Journeys'; *218* blank; 219-257 text of 'Episodes and Epitaphs'; *258* blank; 259-260 text of 'Notes'; *261* blank; *262* blank; endpaper.

Cased in blue linen with off-white endpapers. Front and back: blank. Spine: [in gold] '*Flaws | in the | Glass* | [ornament] | PATRICK | WHITE' | [at bottom:] [publisher's device].

216

White, lightly textured paper dustjacket printed in blue on front, back and spine. Front: [in white] '*Patrick White* | [in black] [rule] | [in black outlined in gold] FLAWS | [short rule] *in the* [short rule] | GLASS | [in black] [rule] | [in white] [hollow type] *A Self-Portrait*' | [in black] [illust. of acorns and oak leaves]. Back: [b&w photograph of the author]. Spine: [in white] '*Patrick* | *White* | [in black] [rule] | [in black outlined in gold] FLAWS | *in the* | GLASS | [in black] [rule] | [in white] [hollow type] *A Self-* | *Portrait*' | [in black] [publisher's device]. Inside front flap: [blurb, 38 lines] | [at bottom right:] '£7.95 net | [rule] | IN UK ONLY'. Inside back flap: '*The Novels of* | PATRICK WHITE | *The Twyborn Affair* | [quotation of six lines from] *Observer* | *A Fringe of Leaves* | [quotation of six lines from] *Guardian* | *The Eye of the Storm* | [quotation of six lines from] *Sunday Telegraph* | *The Vivisector* | [quotation of three lines from] *Sunday Times* | *The Solid Mandala* | [quotation of two lines from] *Guardian* | *Riders in the Chariot* | [quotation of two lines from] *Sunday Times* | ISBN 0 224 02924 X | Author's photograph by J. Wong from | Colorific! © Colorific! 1981 | Jacket design by Mon Mohan | © Jonathan Cape Ltd 1981'.

Published in October 1981. Price: £7.95. Print run: 15,000.

Reviews: Robert Drewe *Bulletin* 20 October 1981, pp.26-30; Ronald Conway *Australian* 24-25 October 1981, Magazine p.8; Michael Davie *Age* (Melbourne) 17 October 1981, p.25; Hal Porter *Age* (Melbourne) 24 October 1981, p.23; J.D. Pringle *Sydney Morning Herald* 17 October 1981, p.49; *Booklist* 1 December 1981, p.479; *Economist* v.281, 31 October 1981, p.101; *Guardian Weekly* 8 November 1981, p.22; *Guardian Weekly* 27 December 1981, p.22; *Kirkus Review* v.49, 15 December 1981, p.1574; *Listener* v.106, 10 December 1981, p.722; *New Statesman* v.102, 30 October 1981, p.30; *Observer* 1 November 1981, p.32; *Observer* 6 December 1981, p.25; *Publishers Weekly* v.220, 18 December 1981, p.65; *Spectator* 7 November 1981, p.34; *Spectator* 28 November 1981, p.20; Davin Dan *Times Literary Supplement* 20 November 1981, p.1273; Dorothy Green *National Times* 8-14 November 1981, p.54; *Times Educational Supplement* 24 September 1982, p.31; *British Book News* March 1982, p.182; Andrew Field *Age Monthly Review* February 1982, p.3-4; *Guardian Weekly* 7 March 1982, p.18; *British Book News* June 1983, p.341; *Books & Bookmen* July 1983, p.19; *Age* (Melbourne) 2 July 1983, Saturday Extra p.8; George Turner *Overland* no.87, May 1983.

Notes: A copy in White's own collection is a presentation copy from the publisher half-bound in dark red leather and red linen boards. Uncorrected proof copies have been sighted in a personal collection and at ADFA. They are sewn in a plain green wrapper. Front: 'PATRICK WHITE | [rule] | *Flaws* | *in the* | *Glass* | [rule] | A SELF PORTRAIT | Trimmed page size: 216 x 138 mm | Extent: 272 pp and 12 pp halftone illustrations | Provisional U.K. Published Price: £7.95 | Provisional U.K. Publication Date: October 15 1981 | [publisher's devices] | UNCORRECTED PROOF'. One copy was bought for $75. ADFA also has Dorothy Green's copy, used for her review and therefore heavily annotated.

Extracts: *Changing Places: Australian Writers in Europe 1960s–1990s* (St Lucia: University of Queensland Press, 1994), p.20-31.

Copies: NSL: Mitchell Library [PW]; NSL: Mitchell Library 823.914/W587/5; NU: 823.91/A/W587/J13/1; Personal collection; VSL: LT A823.3/W585F (lacks dustjacket); VU: McL L/A-F White.

S1b U.K. First Edition Second Issue (London: Jonathan Cape, 1981)
Notes: not seen but referred to in Jonathan Cape archive, University of Reading. Published in
October 1981. Price: £7.95. Print run: 6,000.

S1c U.K. First Edition Third Issue (London: Jonathan Cape, 1982)
Notes: p.[*4*] 'First published 1981 | Reprinted 1981, 1982 | Copyright © 1981 Patrick White
| Jonathan Cape Ltd, 30 Bedford Square, London WC1'. Published in January 1982. Price:
£8.50. Print run: 3,000.

S2a U.S. First Edition (New York: Viking, 1982)

Patrick White | [rule] | FLAWS | IN THE | GLASS | [rule] | *A Self-
Portrait* | THE VIKING PRESS NEW YORK

22 x 14 cm. Unsigned: 136 leaves. pp.[*10*] 1-155 *156* 157-217 *218* 219-257 *258* 259-260
261-262; plates of b&w photographs between pages 54-55, 86-87, 118-119, 150-151, 214-
215 and 230-231.

Endpaper; [*1*] [publisher's device]; [*2*] blank; [*3*] 'FLAWS | IN THE | GLASS'; [*4*] 'by the
same author | *Novels* | RIDERS IN THE CHARIOT | VOSS | THE TREE OF MAN |
THE AUNT'S STORY | THE LIVING AND THE DEAD | THE SOLID MANDALA
| THE VIVISECTOR | THE EYE OF THE STORM | THE FRINGE OF LEAVES |
THE TWYBORN AFFAIR | *Short Stories* | THE BURNT ONES | THE COCKATOOS
| *Plays* | FOUR PLAYS'; [*5*] title page; [*6*] 'Copyright © 1981 by Patrick White | All rights
reserved | Published in 1982 by The Viking Press | 625 Madison Avenue, New York, N.Y.
10022 | Published simultaneously in Canada by | Penguin Books Canada Limited | [ac-
knowledgments, four lines] | LIBRARY OF CONGRESS CATALOGING IN
PUBLICATION DATA | White, Patrick, 1912- | Flaws in the glass. | 1. White, Patrick,
1912- – Biography. | 2. Novelists, Australian – 20th century - Biography. | I. Title. |
PR9619.3.W5Z465 1982 823 [B] 81-52220 | ISBN 0-670-31759-4 AACR2 | Printed in
the United States of America | Set in Linotron Garamond'; [*7*] 'to Manoly | again'; [*8*] blank;
[*9*] '*Contents* | Flaws in the Glass 1 | Journeys 157 | Episodes and Epitaphs 219 | Notes
259'; [*8*] blank; [*9*] '*Illustrations*'; [*10*] [list of illustrations continues]; 1-155 text of 'Flaws in
the Glass'; *156* blank; 157-217 text of 'Journeys'; *218* blank; 219-257 text of 'Episodes and
Epitaphs'; *258* blank; 259-260 text of 'Notes'; *261-262* blank; endpaper.

Cased in dark grey paper-covered boards with white calico spine and white endpapers. Front
and back: blank. Spine: [in red] '*Patrick* | *White* | [running down:] FLAWS IN THE
GLASS | [upright] VIKING'.

Glossy white paper dustjacket. Front: [in box:] [in red on beige] 'PATRICK WHITE | [in
silver on beige] FLAWS | IN THE | GLASS | [in red on beige] A SELF-PORTRAIT'.
Back: [in box:] [in red on beige] [quotation from the book, 17 lines] [at bottom right:] 'ISBN
0-670-31759-4'. Spine: [running down:] 'FLAWS IN THE GLASS | [in red] PATRICK
WHITE VIKING'. Inside front flap: [at top right:] '$14.95 | [blurb, 42 lines] | [at bottom
right:] 0282'. Inside back flap: [b&w photograph of the author] [running down:] [at right:]
'JOHN STOCKDALE | [biography, 10 lines] | Jacket design by R. Adelson | [publisher's

device] | THE VIKING PRESS | 625 Madison Avenue | New York, N.Y. 10022 | Printed in U.S.A.'.

Published in February 1982. Price: $14.95.

Reviews: *Atlantic Monthly* v.249, March 1982, p.83; *Books in Canada* v.11, May 1982, p.83; *Best Sellers* v.42, April 1982, p.24; *Book World* v.12, 31 January 1982, p.8; *Library Journal* v.107, 15 January 1982, p.179; *Newsweek* v.99, 1 March 1982, p.71; *New Yorker* v.58, 7 June 1982, p.145; Nadine Gordimer *New York Review of Books* v.29, 15 April 1982, p.14-15; *New York Times Book Review* 7 February 1982, p.9; *Prairie Schooner* v.56, Fall 1982, p.92; *Saturday Review* v.9, February 1982, p.62 and March 1982, p.81; *World Literature Today* v.56, Summer 1982, p.569.

Notes: A copy in White's own collection is a presentation copy from the publisher, bound in pale blue leather; there is a Christmas card inside: 'from Alan and all at Viking'. An uncorrected proof copy has been sighted in a personal collection. It is sewn in plain yellow wrappers. Front: 'PATRICK WHITE | *Flaws* | *in the* | *Glass* | [rule] | A SELF-PORTRAIT | [in box:] | PUB. DATE [in ms] 2/82 PRICE [in ms] $13.95'.

Copies: NSL: Mitchell Library [PW]; Personal collection.

S2b Canadian Subedition (Toronto: Penguin, 1982)
Not seen, but assumed from the statement on p.[6] of the U.S. First Edition (see S2a above).

S3a Penguin Edition First Issue (Harmondsworth: Penguin, 1983)

Patrick White | FLAWS IN | THE GLASS | *A Self-portrait* | [publisher's device] | PENGUIN BOOKS

19.8 x 12.9 cm. Unsigned: 136 leaves. pp.[*10*] 1-155 *156* 157-217 *218* 219-257 *258* 259-260 *261-262*; 12 p. of plates.

[*1*] 'PENGUIN BOOKS | FLAWS IN THE GLASS' | [biography and comment, 20 lines]; [*2*] blank; [*3*] title page; [*4*] 'Penguin Books Ltd, Harmondsworth, Middlesex, England | Penguin Books, 625 Madison Avenue, New York 10022, U.S.A. | Penguin Books Australia Ltd, Ringwood, Victoria, Australia | Penguin Books Canada Ltd, 2801 John Street, Markham, Ontario, Canada L3R 1B4 | Penguin Books (N.Z.) Ltd, 182-190 Wairau Road, Auckland 10, New Zealand | First published in Great Britain by Jonathan Cape Ltd 1981 | First published in the United States of America by The Viking Press 1982 | Published in Penguin Books 1983 | Copyright © Patrick White, 1981 | All rights reserved | Grateful acknowledgment is made to the following for permission to reproduce | photographs: Brett Hilder, photograph 1; Axel Poignant, photograph 17; Ern | Macquillan, photograph 22; J. Wong from Colorific!, photograph 25; Will Young, | photographs 26 and 27; and Elly Polymeropoulou, photograph 28. | Made and printed in Great Britain | by Richard Clay (The Chaucer Press) Ltd, | Bungay, Suffolk.' | [publisher's conditions, 9 lines]; [*5*] 'to Manoly | again'; [*6*] blank; [*7*] 'CONTENTS'; [*8*] blank; [*9*] 'ILLUSTRATONS'; [*10*] blank; 1-155 text of 'Flaws in the Glass'; *156* blank; 157-217 text of 'Journeys'; *218* blank; 219-257 text of 'Episodes and

Epitaphs'; *258* blank; 259-260 text of 'Notes'; *261* [publisher's device] | 'MORE ABOUT PENGUINS | AND PELICANS | [information follows, 18 lines]; *262* blank.

Perfectbound in white paper covers. Front: [in black on pale blue] '*PATRICK WHITE* | [in white] *Flaws* | [rule] | *in the* | [rule] | *Glass* | [in black] *a self-portrait*' | [publisher's device]. Back: [in black on pale blue] [comment, 8 lines] | [quotation of two lines from] 'David | Lodge in the *Sunday Times* | [quotation of four lines from] Angus Wilson in the *Observer* | [quotation of four lines from] *Australian Book Review* | Patrick White won the Nobel Prize for Literature | [at bottom left:] U.K. £2.50 | AUST. $6.95 | (recommended) | CAN. $5.95 | U.S.A. $5.95 | [at bottom right:] [publisher's device] | Autobiography | ISBN 0 14 | 00.6293 9'. Spine: [in white on orange] [running down:] '*PATRICK WHITE* [in black] *Flaws in the Glass* | ISBN 0 14 | 00.6293 9' | [upright:] [publisher's device].

Price: £2.50, AU$6.95, CAN$5.95, US$5.95.

Copies: NSL: Mitchell Library 823.914/W587/9; NSL: Mitchell Library [PW]; Private collection (2 copies).

S3b Penguin Edition Second Issue (Harmondsworth: Penguin, 1984)
Notes: p.*4* 'Published in Penguin Books 1983 | Reprinted 1984 | [...] | Made and printed in Great Britain'. Price: AU$7.95.

S3c Penguin Edition Third Issue (Harmondsworth: Penguin, 1985)
Notes: p.*4* 'Published in Penguin Books 1983 | Reprinted 1984, 1985 | [...] | Made and printed in Great Britain | by Richard Clay (The Chaucer Press) Ltd, | Bungay, Suffolk'. Price: AU$9.95.

S3d Penguin Edition Fourth Issue (Harmondsworth: Penguin, n.d.)
Not seen.

S3e Penguin Edition Fifth Issue (Harmondsworth: Penguin, 1992)
Notes: p. *4* 'Published in Penguin Books 1983 | 5 7 9 10 8 6 | [...] | Printed in Great Britain Clays Ltd, St Ives plc'. Perfectbound in white and pale green paper covers. Cover photograph of Patrick White by Cecil Beaton, reproduced by courtesy of Sotheby's, London. Published in May 1992. Price: £6.99, CAN$12.99, AU$16.95. ISBN 0 1401 8574 7.

S.t1 Swedish First Edition (Stockholm: Forum, 1984)

Patrick White | Skavanker i spegeln | Ett självporträtt | [at bottom:] Översättning Ingegärd Martinell | Forum

21.8 x 13.8 cm. Unsigned: 166 leaves. pp.*10* 11-193 *194-196* 197-267 *268-270* 271-328 *329-332* p., plates of b&w photographs between pages 60-61, 92-93, 124-125, 156-157, 221-222 and 252-253.

Endpaper; *1* 'Skavanker i spegeln'; *2* blank; *3* title page; *4* '*Tidigare utgivning* | De fyra ut-korade 1964 | Den oförstörbara mandalan 1969 | Livets träd 1970 | Målaren 1973 | Stormens öga 1975 | En frans av löv 1979 | Fallet Twyborn 1981 | Voss 1983 | [at bottom:] [publisher's device] | Engelska originalets titel | Flaws in the glass. A self-portrait | © Patrick White 1981 | Omslag Christer Jonson | Sättning och trychning Beta Grafiska i Lund 1984 | Printed in Sweden | ISBN 91-37-08517-4'; *5* '*till Manoly* | *igen*'; *6* blank; *7* 'Innehåll'; *8* blank; *9* 'Skavanker i spegeln'; *10* blank; 11-193 text; *194* blank; *195* 'Resor'; *196* blank; 197-267 text; *268* blank; *269* 'Episoder och epitafer'; *270* blank; 271-316 text; 317-320 'Noter och an-märkningar'; 321-322 'Bildförteckning'; 323-324 'Verkregister'; 325-328 *329* 'Personregister'; *330-332* blank; endpaper.

Cased in white paper-covered boards with off-white endpapers. Front and back: blank. Spine: [running down:] 'Patrick White · Skavanker i spegeln'.

Glossy white wrappers dustjacket. Front: [in grey] 'Patrick White | Skavanker i spegeln | [in red] Ett självporträtt. | [col. illust. of retouched portrait of the author in a picture frame] | [in grey] FORUM'. Back: [biography, 23 lines] | 'FORUM | ISBN 91-37-08517-4'. Spine: [in grey] 'Patrick White Skavanker i spegeln. | [upright:] FORUM'. Inside front flap: [biogra-phy, 6 lines]. Inside back flap: 'UR RECENSIONERNA AV | NÅGRA AV PATRICK WHITES | TIDIGARE BÖCKER: | *En frans av löv* | [quotation of eight lines from] *Artur Lundkvist i Dagens Nyheter* | *Finns i pocket* | *Fallet Twyborn* | [quotation of five lines from] *Ruth Halldén i Dagens Nyheter* | [quotation of five lines from] *Ingmar Björkstén* | *i Svenska Dagbladet* | *Voss* | [quotation of two lines from] *Tommy Hammarström i Expressen* | [quotation of two lines from] *Ulf Gyllenhak i Sydsvenska Dagbladet* | [quotation of three lines from] *Heidi von Born i Allt om böcker*'.

Copies: Personal collection; NSL: Mitchell Library [PW]; NSL: Mitchell Library 823.914/W587/17.

S.t2 French First Edition (Paris: Gallimard, 1985)

PATRICK WHITE | DÉFAUTS | DANS LE MIROIR | UN AUTOPORTRAIT | *Traduit de l'anglais* | *par Jean Lambert* | *nrf* | GALLIMARD

20.4 x 13.9 cm. Unsigned: leaves. pp.*10* 11-201 *202* 203-322 *323-324* 325-326 *327-336*.

1-3 blank; *4* 'DU MÊME AUTEUR | *Aux Éditions Gallimard* | EDEN-VILLE | LE CHAR DES ÉLUS | VOSS | LES ÉCHAUDÉS | LE MYSTÉRIEUX MANDALA | L'ŒIL DU CYCLONE | LE VIVISECTEUR | UNE CEINTURE DE FEUILLES | LES INCARNATIONS D'EDDIE TWYBORN'; *5* '*Du monde entier*'; *6* blank; *7* title page; *8* '*Titre original :* | FLAWS IN THE GLASS — A SELF-PORTRAIT | © *Patrick White, 1981* | © *Éditions Gallimard, 1985, pour la traduction française.*'; *9* '*à Manoly*'; *10* blank; 11-201 *202* text of 'Défauts dans le miroir'; 203-276 text of 'Voyages'; 277-322 *323* text of 'Épisodes et épitaphs'; *324* blank; 325-326 *327* text of 'Notes'; *328* blank; *329* contents; *330* blank; *331* '*Composition SEP 2000 à Paris.* | *Impression S.E.P.C.* | *à Saint-Armand (Cher), le 15 février 1985.* | *Dépôt légal : février 1985.* | *Numéro d'imprimeur : 271.* | ISBN 2-07-026567.6./Imprimé en France.'; *332-335* blank; *336* [at bottom left:] '35124'.

Perfectbound in a glossy cream-coloured paper card. Front: 'DU MONDE ENTIER | PATRICK WHITE | [in red] Défauts | dans le miroir | *Un autoportrait* | [in black] TRADUIT DE L'ANGLAIS | PAR JEAN LAMBERT | [series device] | [in red] *nrf* | [in black] GALLIMARD'. Back: 'PATRICK WHITE | [in red] Défauts dans le miroir | [in black] [blurb, 32 lines] | [biography, 3 lines] | [barcode] [ornament] 85-111 A26567 ISBN 2-07-026567-6   120 FF tc'. Spine: [in red] '*du monde* | *entier* | [in black] PATRICK | WHITE | [in red] DÉFAUTS | DANS | LE MIROIR | [in black] *nrf* | GALLIMARD'. Inside front and back: blank.

Copies: VSL: SLT A823.3/W585FL; NSL: Mitchell Library 823.914/W587/27; NSL: Mitchell Library [PW].

S.t3 Chinese First Edition (Beijing, 1990)

[Ching chung hsia tzu]

pp.380. Translated by Li Yao.

Notes: White's copy is inscribed on flyleaf: 'To Patrick White | with best wishes and thanks! | Li Yao | Aug. 20, 1990'. Publication assisted by the Australia Council. Extracts translated and published in: *Waiguo Wenxue* (*Foreign Literatures*), a monthly publication by the Foreign Languages Institute, Beijing. No.4, 1982, pp.29-32.

Copies: NSL: Mitchell Library [PW].

S.t4 German First Edition (Frankfurt am Main: S. Fischer, 1994)

Patrick White | RISSE IM SPIEGEL | [rule] | Ein Selbstporträt | Aus dem Englischen von | Reinhard Kaiser | S. Fischer

21 x 13 cm. Unsigned: 176 leaves. pp.6 7-215 *216* 217-297 *298* 299-348 *349* 350 *351-352*; 12 pages of plates between pages 192 and 193.

Endpaper; *1* [publisher's device]; *2* blank; *3* title page; *4* '*WIEDER FÜR MANOLY* | Die englische Originalausgabe erschien 1982 | unter dem Titel >Flaws in the Glass. | A Self-Portrait< bei Jonathan Cape Ltd., London. | Copyright © 1981 Patrick White | Deutsche Ausgabe: | © 1994 S. Fischer Verlag GmbH, Frankfurt am Main | Schutzumschlag: Raphie Ergar | Satz: Fotosatz Reinhard Amann, Aichstetten | Druck und Bindung: Wilhelm Röck, Weinsberg | Printed in Germany 1994 | ISBN 3-10-091204-7'; *5* '*INHALT*'; *6* blank; 7-215 *216* 'RISSE IM SPIEGEL'; 217-297 *298* 'REISEN'; 299-348 *349* 'EPISODEN UND EPITAPHE'; 350 *351* '*ANMERKUNGEN*'; *352* '*WERKVERZEICHNIS*'; endpaper.

Cased in purplish grey cloth with grey endpapers. Front: [in white] [illust. of broken mirror]. Back: blank. Spine: [running up:] [in blue on white panel] '*Patrick White* | RISSE IM SPIEGEL' | [upright] [in blue] [publisher's device].

Glossy white dustjacket printed with col. illust of man's reflection on front. Front: 'PATRICK WHITE | [rule] | RISSE | IM | SPIEGEL | [rule] | EIN SELBSTPORTRÄT | S. FISCHER'. Back: [blurb, 8 lines] | [quotation of three lines from] '*David Lodge*, >Sunday Times< | [at bottom:] ISBN 3-10-091204-7'. Spine: [running up:] 'PATRICK WHITE

RISSE IM SPIEGEL' | [at bottom:] [upright] [publisher's device]. Inside front flap: [description, 34 lines]. Inside back flap: [black & white photograph of the author] [running up:] 'Foto © Brett Hilder | [biography, 12 lines] | Umschlaggestaltung: Raphie Etgar'.

Price: DM 44.

Copies: ANL: N A823.3 W587.

S.t5 Russian First Edition

Notes: Not seen, but referred to by White in a letter to Hu Wen-chung, 19 November 1986 (National Library of Australia, MS 8553).

S.m1 Braille Edition (South Yarra, Vic.: Braille and Talking Book Library, 1984)

Flaws in the Glass (8 vols. of Braille).

Transcribed from the Cape edition of 1981.

S.m2 Sound Recording (Enfield: Royal Blind Society of New South Wales, 1985)

Flaws in the Glass (2 audiocassettes, 4-track).

Read by Richard Morecroft and Hugh Wade from the Penguin edition of 1982.

S.m3 Sound Recording (North Sydney: Australian Listening Library, [n.d.])

Flaws in the Glass (8 audiocassettes).

Read by Dorothy Aherne.

S.m4 Sound Recording (North Hobart: Hear-a-Book, 1982)

Flaws in the Glass (10 audiocassettes).

Read by Harper Wilson from the Cape edition of 1981.

S.m5 Extracts (St Lucia: University of Queenland Press, 1994)

Notes: See *Patrick White: Selected Writings* ed. by Alan Lawson (St Lucia: University of Queensland Press, 1994), p.224-267 (Y1 below).

T Signal Driver (1983)

Signal Driver was commissioned by Jim Sharman, when art director of the Adelaide Festival. White completed the first draft by the end of April 1981. By May, Sharman had chosen Neil Armfield as director. The play was a feature of the Adelaide Festival 1982.

* * * * *

T1a Australian First Edition First Issue (Sydney: Currency Press, 1983)

Signal Driver | A Morality Play for the Times | [rule] | Patrick White | [publisher's device] | CURRENCY PRESS • SYDNEY

20.2 x 12.6 cm. Unsigned: 36 leaves. pp. *vii* viii-ix *x-xii 1-5* 6-50 *51-60*.

i [biography, 34 lines]; *ii* 'By the same author | Plays | *Four plays* | *The Ham Funeral* | *The Season at Sarsaparilla* | *A Cheery Soul* | *Night on Bald Mountain* | *Big Toys* | Novels | *Happy Valley* | *The Living and the Dead* | *The Aunt's Story* | *The Tree of Man* | *Voss* | *Riders in the Chariot* | *The Solid Mandala* | *The Vivisector* | *The Eye of the Storm* | *A Fringe of Leaves* | *The Twyborn Affair* | Short Stories | *The Burnt Ones* | *The Cockatoos* | Self-portrait | *Flaws in the Glass*'; *iii* title page; *iv* 'CURRENCY PLAYS | General Editor: Katharine Brisbane | First published in 1983 by | Currency Press Pty Ltd, | 87 Jersey Road, Woollahra, | N.S.W. 2025, Australia. | Copyright © Patrick White 1983 | Introduction copyright © Neil Armfield 1983 | Music copyright © Carl Vine 1983 | [author's condition, 8 lines] | All applications for performance | or public reading should be made to | Curtis Brown (Australia) Pty Ltd, | P.O. Box 19 Paddington, | N.S.W. 2021, Australia. | [publisher's conditions, 9 lines] | National Library of Australia card number | and ISBN 0 86819 068 3 | Cover design by Kevin Chan | Typeset and printed by Colorcraft Ltd, Hong Kong'; *v* 'To Neil Armfield'; *vi* [b&w photograph]; *vii* viii-ix 'Aurora Australis' [by Neil Armfield, dated Avignon, 1982]; *x-xii* [b&w photographs]; *1* 'SIGNAL DRIVER'; *2* [b&w photographs]; *3* '*Signal Driver* was first performed by the Lighthouse | Company at the Playhouse, Adelaide, on 5 March 1982 as | part of the Adelaide Festival, with the following cast: | [list of cast] | Designed by Stephen Curtis | Music by Carl Vine | Directed by Neil Armfield'; *4* 'CHARACTERS | [list] | SETTING' | [description, 11 lines]; *5* 6-50 text; *51-60* 'MUSIC TO THE PLAY'.

Perfectbound in white paper card. Front: [in red] 'SIGNAL DRIVER | [in black] Introduced by Neil Armfield | Music by Carl Vine | [in white on red] Patrick White' | [b&w photograph]. Back: [blurb, 10 lines] | [in white on red] 'Cover: Peter Cummins and Kerry Walker as the two Beings in the | Lighthouse production. Photo by David Wilson. | Back cover: Patrick White. Photo by News Ltd.' | [b&w photograph of the author]. Spine: 'Patrick White Signal Driver Currency'.

Published in May 1983. Price: AU$12.95. ISBN 0 8681 9068 3. Remained in print until 1995, when price was AU$13.95.

Reviews: Barry Oakley *Sydney Morning Herald* 16 June 1983, p.38; *Age* (Melbourne) 1 October 1983, Saturday Extra p.18.

Copies: Personal collection; NSL: E822.914/W587/3; NSL: Mitchell Library 823.914/W587/ 1.

T1b Australian First Edition Second Issue (Sydney: Currency Press, 1993)

Notes: not seen, but entry in *Australian Books in Print*. Published in July 1993. Price: AU$14.95.

T2 U.S. First Edition (n.p.: Applause Theatre Book Publishers, 1985)

Notes: not seen, but referred to on <www.amazon.co.uk> 4 August 1997. Published in June 1985. Price: $7.95. ISBN 0 87910 239 X.

U Netherwood (1983)

While in Adelaide for rehearsals of *Signal Driver* in February 1982, White several times referred to the plight of the intellectually disabled in the general community. He commenced writing *Netherwood* when he returned to Sydney in March, but the play was delayed several months because of illness. It was not completed until October of that year. (To Elizabeth Falkenberg, 15 October 1982) Jim Sharman chose *Netherwood* – about de-institutionalised mental patients – for the Adelaide Festival of 1983 (he felt the new play should be given preference over a revival of *The Ham Funeral*). White attended rehearsals in Adelaide in April 1983 and also returned for the opening night in June.

* * * * *

U1 Australian First Edition (Sydney: Currency Press, 1983)

NETHERWOOD | Patrick White | [publisher's device] | Current Theatre Series | published by Currency Press, Sydney | in association with the State Theatre Company of South Australia

21 x 14.8 cm. Unsigned: 28 leaves. pp.*2* 3-26 [*4*] 27-52.

1 title page; *2* 'CURRENT THEATRE SERIES | First published in 1983 by | Currency Press Pty Ltd | P.O. Box 452, Paddington, | N.S.W. 2021, Australia, | in association with the State Theatre | Company of South Australia. | Copyright © Patrick White 1983 | [author's condition, 8 lines] | All applications for performance | or public reading should be made to | Curtis Brown (Australia) Pty Ltd, | P.O. Box 19 Paddington, | N.S.W. 2021, Australia. | [publisher's conditions, 9 lines] | National Library of Australia card number | and ISBN 0 86819 071 3 | Typeset and printed by Bridge Printery, | Sydney'; *3* '*Netherwood* was first performed by Lighthouse The State | Theatre Company of South Australia at the Playhouse, | Adelaide, on 11 June 1983 with the following cast: | [list of cast members] | Designed by Ken Wilby | Musical direction by Alan John | Directed by Jim Sharman'; [*4*] 'CHARACTERS | [list] | SETTING' | [description, 29 lines]; 5-26 text; [*1-4*] [cast and credits]; 27-52 text continues.

Saddle-stapled with white paper card wrapper printed in black with eyes of author on front. Front: [in white] 'NETHERWOOD | by Patrick White'. Back: [in box:] 'LIGHTHOUSE CURRENCY | Current Theatre Series | [blurb, 5 lines] | [biography, 10 lines] | LIGHTHOUSE, the acting ensemble of the State Theatre | Company of South Australia, has its home at the Playhouse of the | Adelaide Festival Centre and was formed under the artistic | direction of Jim Sharman in 1982. *Netherwood* was written for | the Lighthouse Company and was premiered on 11 June 1983. | [acknowledgments, 4 lines] | Cover design by Mark Thomson | ISBN 0 86819 071 3 | [outside box:] [running down:] Patrick White NETHERWOOD Currency'. Inside front and back: blank.

Published in June 1983. Price: AU$3.50. ISBN 0 8681 9071 3. Remained in print until 1997, when price was AU$10.95.

Reviews: Barry Oakley *Sydney Morning Herald* 16 July 1983, p.38; *Age* (Melbourne) 1 October 1983, Saturday Extra, p.18.

Notes: A copy in private hands has manuscript annotations to the text in White's hand.

Copies: NSL: Mitchell Library 822.914/W587/2; NSL: Mitchell Library [PW]; NSL: N822.914/W587/2; Personal collection (2 copies).

V Memoirs of Many in One (1986)

The inspiration for *Memoirs of Many in One* lies in Patrick White's own old age: the novel is essentially a study of old age and senility, and White himself is very much one of the characters. The placement of himself so firmly in the novel was probably only possible after White had written *Flaws in the Glass*.

Some parts of the novel were reworked from 'The Binoculars and Helen Nell', abandoned some fifteen years earlier. He began writing in July 1984: 'I only wish I could get back to my own work – a fiction I started some weeks ago, about a senile character who is myself in my various roles and sexes. It gives me great scope.' (To Ronald Waters, 16 August 1984) White worked on the novel for about three months, working quickly, thinking, perhaps only half-seriously, that senility was imminent. 'I should really spend years on it but my own senility might overtake me.' (To Kerry Walker, 17 July 1984). What did intervene was a trip to New Zealand (to present the Media Peace Prize) and the collapse of several vertabrae in his back. By early January 1985 White was able to return to work, and the second draft was finished in four months. Instead of typing the third draft himself, White had his agent Barbara Mobbs arrange the typing. White then reworked the typescript. It was sent to London in June 1985.

While the book was being prepared by Cape and Viking, White had an idea for a frontispiece to *Memoirs of Many in One*: 'She is me, so I thought I'd have a photo of me as Patrick on the back flap'. (*Starting Again, a Time in the Life of William Yang* (Sydney, 1989, p.92). Before the photographs could be taken, White was hospitalised. William Yang took the photographs of White in the hospital and then overlaid images of cats, archangels and Greek icons. (For these photographs see William Yang's *Patrick White: the late years* Sydney: Macmillan, 1995). However, as Yang explained to White, the corpse looked like Patrick White, not Alex Demirjian Gray. A second shoot was arranged. Kerry Walker did the make-up, and the venue was to be Manoly's bedroom (much to his annoyance). Only a few shots of Alex as corpse were required, then several of Alex in shadow. In the afternoon several shots of Patrick as Patrick were taken – one of which appeared on the back of the dustjacket for the Cape edition of *Memoirs of Many in One*. In the end White was not happy with the photographs of himself as Alex. Furthermore, many of his friends advised him not to use the photographs. He agreed, and the photographs from the second shoot have never been published.

If White was prepared to take advice from those closest to him, he was still *not* prepared to make concessions to his publishers. Both Cape and Viking wanted to credit White as author, but White insisted that the (transparent) conceit that he was merely the editor be maintained. Furthermore, he was appalled at Viking describing him as a 'Nobelist' on the dustjacket. Viking apologised.

Memoirs of Many in One was published in London on 1 April 1986 and in New York in October. The critics were puzzled, amused, angry and delighted, but the book sold well. White himself was bemused by the critics: 'Some of [the reviews] were rather quaint. Particularly the lady who says: 'Alex is presumably based on Mr Lascaris −' Poor Manoly! I felt like writing and telling her Alex is 100% P.W.' (To Graham C. Greene, 25 June 1986)

As usual, White was keen to liaise with his translators and made several suggestions regarding the French translation of *Memoirs of Many in One*: '*Triple Mémoires* doesn't seem to me to convey the book. How would you translate *Splinters of the Ego* into French? Or would it be possible to suggest a company of actors which make up the central character? Would *Comédiens du Moi* sound just silly?' (To Jean Lambert, 14 May 1987) The French translation appeared as *Mémoires éclatés, d'Alex Xenophon Demirjian Gray*. The novel has also appeared in German (1988) and Swedish (1989).

* * * * *

V1a U.K. First Edition (London: Jonathan Cape, 1986)

Memoirs of | *Many in One* | by Alex Xenophon Demirjian Gray | edited by | PATRICK WHITE | [publisher's device] | JONATHAN CAPE | THIRTY-TWO BEDFORD SQUARE LONDON

20.3 x 13.3 cm. Unsigned: 96 leaves. pp.*8* 9-192.

Endpaper; *1* 'MEMOIRS OF | MANY IN ONE'; *2* '*by the same author*' | *Novels* | THE LIVING AND THE DEAD | THE AUNT'S STORY | THE TREE OF MAN | VOSS | RIDERS IN THE CHARIOT | THE SOLID MANDALA | THE VIVISECTOR | THE EYE OF THE STORM | A FRINGE OF LEAVES | THE TWYBORN AFFAIR | *Short Stories* | THE BURNT ONES | THE COCKATOOS | *Plays* | THE HAM FUNERAL | THE SEASON AT SARSAPARILLA | A CHEERY SOUL | NIGHT ON BALD MOUNTAIN | BIG TOYS | SIGNAL DRIVER | NETHERWOOD | *Autobiography* | FLAWS IN THE GLASS'; *3* title page; *4* 'First published 1986 | Copyright © 1986 by Patrick White | Jonathan Cape Ltd, 32 Bedford Square, London WC1B 3EL | British Library Cataloguing in Publication Data | White, Patrick | Memoirs of many in one. | I. Title | 823 [F] PR9619.3.W / | ISBN 0-224-02371-3 | [at bottom:] Printed by Butler and Tanner Ltd, Frome and London'; *5* 'TO THE FLYING NUN'; *6* blank; *7* [family tree showing three generations of the Gray family]; *8* blank; 9-16 text of '*Editor's Introduction*'; 17-59 text of '*Memoirs of Alex Xenophon Demirjian Gray*'; 60-63 '*Editor's Intrusion*'; 64-122 text of

'*Memoirs (contd)*'; 123-124 text of '*Editor's Remarks*'; 125-140 text of '*Alex Gray's Theatrical Tour of Outback Australia*'; 141-145 text of '*Editor's Remarks*'; 145-178 text; 179-192 text of '*Epilogue*'; endpaper.

Cased in black paper-covered boards with white endpapers. Front and back: blank. Spine: [running down:] [in gold] 'Memoirs of Many in One *edited by Patrick White | by Alex Xenophon Demirjian Gray*' | [upright:] [publisher's device].

White lightly textured paper dustjacket printed in green on front, spine and back. Front: [in gold] [rule] | [in black] [rule] | [in black outlined with gold] 'Memoirs | of Many | in One | [in grey] BY ALEX XENOPHON DEMIRJIAN GRAY | EDITED BY | [in white] *Patrick | White*' | [in black] [rule] | [in gold] [rule]. Back: [b&w photograph of the author] | 'ISBN 0-224-02371-3' | [barcode]. Spine: [in gold] [rule] | [in black] [rule] | [running down:] [in gold] 'Memoirs of Many in One | BY ALEX XENOPHON DEMIRJIAN GRAY || [in grey] EDITED BY | [in white] *Patrick White*' | [upright:] [in black] [publisher's device] | [rule] | [in gold] [rule]. Inside front flap: [blurb, 40 lines] | '£8.95 | [rule] | IN UK ONLY'. Inside back flap: 'Also by Patrick White | Winner of the 1973 Nobel Prize for | Literature | *Novels* | The Living and the Dead | The Aunt's Story | The Tree of Man | Voss | Riders in the Chariot | The Solid Mandala | The Vivisector | The Eye of the Storm | A Fringe of Leaves | The Twyborn Affair | *Short Stories* | The Burnt Ones | The Cockatoos | *Plays* | The Ham Funeral | The Season at Sarsaparilla | A Cheery Soul | Night on Bald Mountain | Big Toys | Signal Driver | Netherwood | *Autobiography* | Flaws In The Glass | [at bottom:] Author's photograph by William Yang | Jacket design by Mon Mohan | © Jonathan Cape Ltd 1986'.

Black paper wraparound. Front and back: [in white] 'The New Novel by Patrick White | NOBEL PRIZE WINNER 1973'.

Published in April 1986. Price: £8.95. Print run: 15,000.

Reviews: A.S. Byatt *Times Literary Supplement* 4 April 1986, p.357 (900w); Bethwyn Brown *West Australian* 19 April 1986, p.33; Leonie Kramer *Quadrant* v.30 no.9, September 1986, p.66-67; Laurie Clancy *Overland* no.104, September 1986, p.72; Veronica Fen *Canberra Times* 12 May 1986, p.B2; Andrew Riemer *Southerly* v.46 no.2, June 1986, p.239-244; David Rowbotham *Courier Mail* 5 April 1986, p.6; David Malouf *Weekend Australian Magazine* 5-6 April 1986, p.13; Chris Wallace-Crabbe *Australian Book Review* no.82, July 1986, p.7-8; Susan McKernan *Bulletin* 15 April 1986, p.117-118; David English *Age* 5 April 1986, p. 13; R. Bates *British Book News* July 1986, p.426; Axel Clark *Scripsi* v.4 no.2, November 1986, p.1-5; *Campaign Australia* no.126, 1986, p.34; P. Horn *London Review of Books* v.8 no.8, 1986, p.15; Elizabeth Jolley *Fremantle Arts Review* v.1 no.5, May 1986, p.15; B. Maddox *Listener* 3 April 1986, p.28; B. Martin *Spectator* 12 April 1986, p.32-33; J. Neville *London Magazine* v.26 nos. 1-2, 1986, p.143-145; M. Seymour *Books and Bookmen* no.366, 1986, p.28; David J. Tacey *Meridian* v.5 no.1, May 1986, p.89-91; W.L. Webb *Guardian* 13 April 1986, p.21; Gillian Wilce *New Statesman* 25 April 1986, p.26 (200w); Thomas Shapcott *Sydney Morning Herald* 5 April 1986, p.48; Craig Munro *Age Monthly Review* February 1987, p.4-5; Ann Nugent *Blast* no.1, Autumn 1987, p.2-3; Humphrey McQueen *The Good Reading Guide* (Melbourne: McPhee-Gribble, 1989) p.271; Andrew Riemer *The Good Reading Guide* (Melbourne: McPhee-Gribble, 1989) p.271-272.

Notes: *Memoirs of Many in One* is the only one of White's novels which survives in an original manuscript. It was donated by White in 1988 to a London anti-apartheid organisation, the Canon Collins Education Trust for Southern Africa, an organisation concerned with the education of black children. The Trust put the manuscript up for auction at Sotheby's in 1991; it was jointly purchased by the National Library of Australia and the State Library of New South Wales for £12,650. (See Terry Ingram, 'Sotheby's underestimates Aust addiction to fiction', *Australian Financial Review* 25 July 1991, and William Fraser, 'Rare glance over White's shoulder', *Sydney Morning Herald* 25 September 1991). The original 220-page manuscript – a first or second draft, written in blue ballpoint pen on both sides of lined foolscap paper, with White's draft introduction and changes and additions in red ballpoint pen – now resides in the State Library of New South Wales (ML MSS 5497). Microfilm copies are available at that library and the National Library, and selected pages are also available through the website of the State Library of New South Wales. It has been posited by Paul Brunton of the State Library of New South Wales, that the manuscript is in fact an elaborate hoax, got up by White as a joke on the academic community. Brunton argues that the manuscript was produced after the publication of the novel, and that the 'corrections' compound the hoax. David Marr, believing White was not normally such a subtle prankster, argues that the manuscript is a genuine draft of the novel. For the Brunton thesis see William Fraser, 'Patrick White's last laugh', *Sydney Morning Herald Good Weekend* 16 May 1992, p.18-24, and John Stapleton, 'The Patrick White hoax: a novel theory', *Sydney Morning Herald* 17 May 1994, p.4.

Two uncorrected proof copies (with annotations throughout) have been sighted in personal collections. They are sewn in a plain paper wrapper. Front: 'Trimmed page size: 198 x 129 mm | Extent: 192 pp + frontispieces not included in this proof | Provisional U.K. Published Price: £8.95 | Provisional U.K. Publication Date: 6th March 1986 | [publisher's devices] | UNCORRECTED PROOF'. On p.*1* is: 'These are uncorrected bound proofs. Please check any quotations or attributions against the bound copy of the book.' One copy was bought for $75. A third uncorrected proof, sewn in red paper, is held in the State Library of Victoria (Call no. *LT 819.93 W582G). A fourth uncorrected copy held in private hands has the same corrections plus a further overlay of marginal annotations.

Copies: Personal collection (2 copies); NSL: Mitchell Library 823.914/W587/22 (lacks dustjacket); VU: McL L/A-F White.

V1b U.K. First Edition Australian Issue (London: Jonathan Cape, 1986)
Notes: p.*4* 'First published 1986 | Copyright © 1986 by Patrick White | Jonathan Cape Ltd, 32 Bedford Square, London WC1B 3EL | British Library Cataloguing in Publication Data | White, Patrick | Memoirs of many in one. | I. Title | 823 [F] PR9619.3.W / | ISBN 0-224-02371-3 | [at bottom:] Printed at Griffin Press Limited, Marion Road, South Australia.'. Cased in green calico with off-white endpapers. Front and back: blank. Spine: [in gold] [running down:] 'Memoirs of Many in One *edited by Patrick White* | *by Alex Xenophon Demirjian Gray*'. White lightly textured paper dustjacket printed in green on front, spine and back. Published April 1986. Print run: 20,000.

Copies: NSL: Mitchell Library 823.9154/W587/22; NSL: Mitchell Library [PW]; Personal collection (2 copies).

V2a U.S. First Edition (New York: Viking, 1986)

Memoirs of | *Many in One* | by Alex Xenophon Demirjian Gray | edited by | PATRICK WHITE | [publisher's device] | Viking

20.3 x 13.4 cm. Unsigned: 96 leaves. pp.*8* 9-192.

Endpaper; *1* 'MEMOIRS OF | MANY IN ONE'; *2 'by the same author'* | [list of 14 titles]; *3* title page; *4* 'VIKING | Viking Penguin Inc. | 40 West 23rd Street, | New York, New York 10010, U.S.A. | First American edition | Published in 1986 | Copyright © Patrick White, 1986 | All rights reserved | LIBRARY OF CONGRESS CATALOGING IN PUBLICATION DATA | White, Patrick, 1912- | Memoirs of many in one, by Alex Xenophon Demirjian | Gray. | I. Title. | PR9619.3.W5M4 1986 823 85-41086 | ISBN 0-670-81320-6 | Printed in the United States of America by | R.R. Donnelley & Sons Company, Harrisonburg, Virginia | Set in Bembo 8pt.'; *5* 'TO THE FLYING NUN'; *6* blank; *7* [family tree]; *8* blank; 9-16 '*Editor's Introduction*'; 17-192 text; endpaper.

Cased in pale blue paper-covered boards with blue calico spine and dusty blue endpapers. Front and back: blank. Spine: [in gold] [running down:] 'Patrick White || Memoirs of Many in One | VIKING'.

Glossy white paper dustjacket in dark green on back and spine and with col. illust. of a painted woman's face. Front: [in green] 'PATRICK WHITE | [at bottom:] [double rule] | [in mauve] MEMOIRS | [rule] | OF MANY IN ONE | [rule] | BY ALEX XENOPHON DEMIRJIAN GRAY' | [double rule]. Back: [in green] [double rule] | 'Praise from England for | Patrick White's *Memoirs of Many in One* | [rule] | [in white] [quotation of three lines from] —*Financial Times* | [quotation of three lines from] —*The Guardian* | [quotation of four lines from] —*The Spectator* | [quotation of one line from] —*New Statesman* | [quotation of four lines from] —*Sunday Times* | [quotation of one lines from] —*Sunday Telegraph* | [in green] [double rule] | [barcode] | ISBN 0-670-81320-6'. Spine: [in green] [running down:] 'PATRICK | WHITE | [upright:] [double rule] | [running down:] [in mauve] MEMOIRS OF MANY IN ONE | [upright:] [in green] [double rule] [at bottom:] [in white] [publisher's device] | VIKING'. Inside front flap: 'ISBN 0-670-81320-6 FPT>15.95' | [blurb, 35 lines]. Inside back flap: [b&w photograph of the author] | [running down:] 'John Stockdale | [biography, 10 lines] | Jacket design by Neil Stuart | Illustration on front of jacket by Ralph Masiello | [at left:] [publisher's device] | VIKING | [at right:] VIKING PENGUIN INC. | 40 West 23rd Street | New York, N.Y. 10010 | Printed in U.S.A.'.

Published in October 1986. Price: $15.95.

Reviews: *Publishers Weekly* 15 August 1986; David W. Henderson *Library Journal* v.111, 1 September 1986, p.217 (150w); John Bemrose *Macleans* 20 October 1986; Jonathan Baumbach *New York Times Book Review* 26 October 1986, p.12 (1100w); Rupert Schieder *Books Canada* v.16 no.2, March 1987, p. 36 (950w); K. Garebian *Canadian Forum* April 1989, p.29-31; Peter Wolfe *Antipodes* v.1 no.1, March 1987, p.44; S. Whaley *Globe & Mail* (Toronto) 25 October 1986, pE21.

Notes: A copy in White's own collection is a presentation copy from the publisher bound in black leather. An advance copy has been sighted in a personal collection. It is sewn in a plain paper wrapper. Front: '*Memoirs of* | *Many in One* | by Alex Xenophon Demirjian Gray | edited by | PATRICK WHITE | [...] | PUB. DATE [in ms] 10/86   PRICE [in ms] $15.95'. Bought for $50.

Copies: NSL: Mitchell Library [PW]; Personal collection.

V2b Canadian Subedition (Toronto: Irwin Publishing, 1986)

Notes: p.*4* 'Copyright © 1986 Patrick White | Canadian Cataloguing in Publication Data | White, Patrick, 1912- | Memoirs of many in one | ISBN 0-7725-1650-2 | I. Title. | PR9619.3.W5M4 1986 823 C86-094114-0 | [publisher's conditions, 7 lines] | 1 2 3 4 5 6 7 8   93 92 91 90 89 88 87 86 | Published by Irwin Publishing Inc.'. Cased in pale blue paper-covered boards with blue calico spine and dusty blue endpapers. Glossy white paper dustjacket in dark green on back and spine and with col. illust. of a painted woman's face. Price: $19.95 CAN.

Copies: NSL: Mitchell Library [PW].

V3 Penguin Edition (Harmondsworth: Penguin, 1987)

Memoirs of | Many in One | *By Alex Xenophon Demirjian Gray* | EDITED BY | PATRICK WHITE | [at bottom:] [publisher's device] | PENGUIN BOOKS

19.1 x 12.2 cm. Unsigned: 96 leaves. pp.*8* 9-192.

1 'PENGUIN BOOKS | MEMOIRS OF MANY IN ONE' | [biography]; *2* blank; *3* title page; *4* 'Penguin Books Ltd [... publisher's addresses] | First published in Great Britain by Jonathan Cape 1986 | First published in the U.S.A. by Viking 1986 | Published in Penguin Books 1987 | Copyright © Patrick White, 1986 | All rights reserved | Made and printed in Great Britain by | Richard Clay Ltd, Bungay, Suffolk | Typset in Bembo | [publisher's conditions, 'x' lines]; *5* 'TO THE FLYING NUN'; *6* blank; *7* [family tree]; *8* blank; 9-192 text.

Perfectbound in glossy white paper covers with col. illust. on front and back. Front: 'ALEX XENOPHON DEMIRJIAN GRAY | [in violet] MEMOIRS OF | MANY IN ONE | [in black] [double rule] EDITED BY [double rule] | PATRICK WHITE | 'ONE OF THE GREAT MAGICIANS OF FICTION' | —ANGUS WILSON IN THE *OBSERVER*' | [col. illust. of a woman's mask and a decorative fan] | [at bottom right:] [publisher's device]. Back: [in box:] [in violet] 'MEMOIRS OF | MANY IN ONE | [in black] [double rule] | EDITED BY | [double rule] | PATRICK WHITE | [blurb, 12 lines] | [quotation from] David Leavitt, author of *The Lost Language of Cranes* | [quotation from] *Daily Telegraph* | [quotation from] *The New York Times Book Review* | Cover illustration by Lee Stannard | [at bottom left:] [publisher's device] | A PENGUIN BOOK | Fiction | [list of prices] | [at bottom right] ISBN 0-14-009426-1   90000 | [barcode] | 9 980140094268'. Spine: [in black and white on orange] 'MEMOIRS OF MANY IN ONE   EDITED BY PATRICK WHITE' [at bottom:] [ISBN] [publisher's device]. Inside front and back covers: blank.

Copies: NU 823.91A/W587J14/2; NSL Mitchell Library [PW].

V.t1 French First Edition (Paris: Gallimard, 1988)

PATRICK WHITE | MÉMOIRES | ÉCLATÉS | D'ALEX XENOPHON | DEMIRJIAN GRAY | roman | *Traduit de l'anglais* | *par Jean Lambert* | *nrf* | GALLIMARD

20.5 x 14 cm. Unsigned: 108 leaves. pp.*12* 13-210 *211-216* (the last page of each section is unnumbered).

1-3 blank; *4* 'DU MÊME AUTEUR | *Aux Éditions Gallimard* | EDEN-VILLE | LE CHAR DES ÉLUS | VOSS | LES ÉCHAUDÉS | LE MYSTÉRIEUX MANDALA | L'ŒIL DU CYCLONE | LE VIVISECTEUR | UNE CEINTURE DE FEUILLES | LES INCARNATIONS D'EDDIE TWYBORN | DÉFAUTS DANS LE MIROIR. Un autoportrait.'; *5* '*Du monde entier*'; *6* blank; *7* title page; *8* '*Titre original:* | MEMOIRS OF MANY IN ONE | BY ALEX XENOPHON DEMIRJIAN GRAY | EDITED BY PATRICK WHITE | © *Patrick White, 1986.* | © *Éditions Gallimard, 1988, pour la traduction française.*'; *9* '*A la nonne volante.*'; *10* blank; *11* [genealogy]; *12* blank; *13-210 211* text; *212* blank; *213* [contents]; *214* blank; *215* '*Composé et achevé d'imprimer* | *par la Société Nouvelle Firmin-Didot* | *à Mesnil-sur-l'Estrée, le 20 octobre 1988.* | *Dépôt légal : octobre 1988.* | *Numéro d'imprimeur : 9261.* | ISBN 2-07-071362-8 / Imprimé en France'; *216* [at bottom left:] '44711'.

Sewn in glossy cream card. Front: 'DU MONDE ENTIER | PATRICK WHITE | [in red] MÉMOIRES | ÉCLATÉS | D'ALEX XENOPHON | DEMIRJIAN GRAY | [in black] | ROMAN | TRADUIT DE L'ANGLAIS | PAR JEAN LAMBERT | [series device] | [in red] *nrf* | [in black] GALLIMARD'. Back: 'PATRICK WHITE | [in red] Mémoires éclatés | d'Alex Xenophon Demirjian Gray | [in black] [description, 26 lines] | [biography, 3 lines] | [barcode] 88-XI A71362 ISBN 2-07-071362-8 98 FF tc'. Spine: [in red] '*du* | *monde* | *en-tier* | [in black] PATRICK | WHITE | [in red] MÉMOIRES | ÉCLATÉS | D'ALEX | XENOPHON | DEMIRJIAN | GRAY | [in black] *nrf* | GALLIMARD'.

Published in November 1988. Price: 98 FF. ISBN 2-07-071362-8.

Copies: Personal collection.

V.t2 German First Edition (Düsseldorf: Claassen Verlag, 1988)

Dolly Formosa | *und die* | *Auserwählten* | [rule] | *Die Memoiren der* | *Alex Xeno-phon Demirjian Gray* | [rule] | Herausgegeben von Patrick White | Deutsch von Frank Heibert | claassen

21 x 13.5 cm. Unsigned: 120 leaves. pp.*8* 9-72 *73-74* 75-144 *145-146* 147-223 *224* 225-238 *239-240*.

Endpaper; *1* '*Dolly Formosa und die Auserwählten*'; *2* blank; *3* title page; *4* 'Die Originalausgabe erschien 1986 unter dem Titel | »Memoirs of Many in One | by Alex Xenophon Demirjian Gray | edited by Patrick White« | im Verlag Jonathan Cape Ltd., London | [cataloguing data, 7 lines] | Copyright © 1988 by claassen Verlag GmbH, Düsseldorf | »Memoirs of Many in One« Copyright © 1986 by Patrick White | Alle deutschen Rechte vorbehalten | Gesetzt aus der Garamont Amsterdam | Satz: Dörlemann-Satz, Lemförde | Papier: Papierfabrik

Schleipen GmbH, Bad Durkheim | Druck und Bindearbeiten: Franz Spiegel Buch GmbH, Ulm-Jungingen | Printed in Germany | ISBN 3-546-49616-7'; *5 'Der fliegenden Nonne gewidmet'*; *6* blank; *7* [genealogy]; *8* blank; 9-16 *17 'Einführung des Herausgebers'*; *18* blank; *19-66 67 'Die Memoiren der Alex Xenophon Demirjian Gray'*; *68* blank; 69-72 *73 'Einmischung des Herausgebers'*; *74* blank; 75-144 *145 'Memoiren (Forts.)'*; *146* blank; 147-163 *164 'Alex Grays Theatralische Tournee | durchs australische Outback'*; 165-207 *208 'Bemerkungen des Herausgebens'*; 209-223 *224 'Epilog'*; 225-238 *239* 'NACHWORT | *Alex im Wunderland* [by Frank Heibert]; *240* blank; endpaper.

Cased in brown cloth with white endpapers. Front and back: blank. Spine: [running down:] [in yellow] '*DOLLY FORMOSA UND DIE AUSERWÄHLTEN* | Herausgegeben von *PATRICK WHITE* | [at bottom:] [upright:] [in white] *claassen*'.

Glossy brown paper dustjacket printed with full col. illust. on front. Front: [in yellow] '*DOLLY FORMOSA* | *UND DIE* | *AUSERWÄHLTEN* | [in white] Die Memoiren der | *Alex Xenophon Demirjian Gray* | [in yellow] Herausgegeben von | *PATRICK WHITE* | [at bottom right:] [running down:] [in white] *claassen*'. Back: [in white] [blurb, 7 lines] | '245 09616'. Spine: [running down:] [in yellow] '*DOLLY FORMOSA UND DIE AUSERWÄHLTEN* | Herausgegeben von *PATRICK WHITE* | [at bottom:] [upright:] [in white] *claassen*'. Inside front flap: [in white] [description, 41 lines]. Inside back flap: [in white] [blurb, 10 lines] | [biography, 19 lines] | 'Schutzumschlag: Klaus Detjen, Hamburg, unter | Verwendung eines Gemäldes von Gérard Beringer.'.

Price: DM 39.80. ISBN 3-546-49616-7.

Copies: NSL: Mitchell Library [PW].

V.t3 Swedish First Edition (Oslo: Forum, 1989)

Det kluvna minnet | Alex Xenophon Demirjian Grays memoarer | *sammanställda av* | Patrick White | Översättning Ingegärd Martinell | Forum

23.4 x 16 cm. Unsigned: 88 leaves. pp.*8* 9-175 *176*.

Endpaper; *1* 'Det kluvna minnet'; *2* blank; *3* title page; *4 'Tidigare utgivning* | De fyra utkorade 1964 | Den oförstörbara mandalan 1969 | Livets träd 1970 | Målaren 1973 | Stormens öga 1976 | En frans av löv 1979 | Fallet Twyborn 1981 | Voss 1983 | Skavanker i spegeln 1984 | Citaten s.121-23 är hämtade ur | C. A. Hagbergs översättning av | Antonius och Kleopatra | [publisher's device] | Engelska originalets titel Memoirs of many in one | by Alex Xenophon Demirjian Gray. Edited by Patrick White | © Patrick White 1986 | Svensk utgåva enligt avtal med Lennart Sane Agency | Omslagillustration Christer Jonson | Omslagtypgrafi Paul Eklund | Sättning GL-grafiska AB, Klippan | Printed in Norway by | Norbok a.s., Oslo | Gjøvik 1989 | ISBN 91-37-09455-6'; *5* 'Till den flygande nunnan'; *6* blank; *7* [genealogy]; *8* blank; 9-16 'Redaktörens förord'; 17-55 'Alex Xenophon Demirjian Grays memoarer'; 56-59 'Redaktören lägger sig i'; 60-112 'Memoarer (forts.)'; 113-114 'Redaktörens kommentar'; 115-128 'Alex Grays teaterturne i landsorten'; 129-132 'Redaktörens kommentar'; 133-163 'Memoarer (fort.)'; 164-175 *176* 'Epilog'; endpaper.

Cased in black paper-covered boards with white endpapers. Front and back: blank. Spine: [in gold] 'Patrick White Det kluvna minnet | [at bottom:] [upright:] FORUM'.

White glossy paper dustjacket. Front: 'Det kluvna minnet | [rule] | Alex Xenophon Demirjian Grays memoarer | [rule] | SAMMANSTÄLLDA AV | [in purple] | Patrick White | [in black] [rule] | [illust.] | ROMAN | [rule] | FORUM'. Back: [blurb, 15 lines] | 'FORUM ISBN 91-37-09455-6'. Spine: [in purple] 'Patrick White [in black] Det kluvna minnet | [at bottom:] [upright:] FORUM'. Inside front flap: 'UR RECENSIONERA AV | NÅGRA AV PATRICK WHITES | TIDIGARE BÖCKER:'. Inside back flap: [b&w photograph of the author] [biography, 15 lines].

Copies: NSL: Mitchell Library [PW].

W Three Uneasy Pieces (1987)

In the middle of 1986 Patrick White was approached by the editors of *Scripsi* for something for a special issue to be published by Penguin in 1987. White wrote the prose poems in the spring of 1986, and *Scripsi* received them in September. White was afraid the pieces would come out in 1988, breaking his self-imposed boycott on publishing new material in Australia's Bicentennial year. He withdrew the pieces in November and offered them to Bruce Pascoe who brought them out in paperback before Christmas. Cape republished in 1988 but *Three Uneasy Pieces* was never offered to The Viking Press because of a dispute between White and Curtis Brown. The paperback was issued by Penguin in 1990. The only translation to date is into French (1994).

* * * * *

W1 First Australian Edition (Fairfield, Victoria: Pascoe Publishing, 1987)

Patrick | White | three | uneasy | pieces

21 x 13.8 cm. Unsigned: 32 leaves. pp.*10* 11-12 *13-14* 15-23 *24-26* 27-59 *60-64*.

1 'three | uneasy | pieces'; *2* blank; *3* title page; *4* 'First published 1987 | by Pascoe Publishing Pty Ltd | P.O. Box 51, Fairfield 3078 | Australia | © Patrick White 1987 | All rights reserved. No part of | this publication may be reproduced or | transmitted in any form or by any | means without permission | Three Uneasy Pieces | ISBN 0 947087 13 3 | Printed in Australia by | The Book Printer, Maryborough | Typeset in Palatino by Bookset | Cover graphics Stephen Pascoe'; *5* '*To Thea Waddell*' ; *6* blank; *7* [b&w photograph of author and Manoly Lascaris] 'THREE POTATOES | and Two Guest Stars | [running down at left of photograph:] *Photo © William Yang*'; *8* blank; *9* 'The | Screaming | Potato'; *10* blank; 11-12 text; *13* 'Dancing With | Both Feet | on the Ground'; *14* blank; 15-23 text; *24* blank; *25* 'The Age | of a Wart'; *26* blank; 27-59 text; *60* blank; *61* [advertisement for *The Babe is Wise*]; *62-64* blank.

Cased in red paper-covered boards without endpapers. Front and back: blank. Spine: [running down:] [in white] 'Three Uneasy Pieces Patrick White'.

Glossy white paper dustjacket. Front: [in red] 'Patrick | White | [in black] three | uneasy | pieces' | [publisher's device]. Back: 'Patrick White, the most influential force | in Australian writing, presents these | *Three Uneasy Pieces.* | *I have seen her holding a skinned potato* | *perhaps admiring her artistry or wondering* | *whether to gouge the eyes.* | As we get older the potato eyes, warts and melanomas of our soul shrivel. *As the world* | *darkens, the evil in me is dying.* | *Three Uneasy Pieces* follows the progress of | the wart. Superb writing as we would expect, | new shades and tones which might surprise. | [at bottom:] [publisher's device] ISBN 0 947087 13 3'. Spine: [running down:] [in black] 'Three Uneasy Pieces' [in red] Patrick White'. Inside front and back flaps: blank.

Notes: This edition was also issued in paperback; perfectbound in white paper covers.

Published in December 1987. Price: AU$14.95 (hb); AU$7.95 (pb). Remained in print until 1997.

Reviews: Barrett Reid *Age* 26 December 1987; Don Anderson *Sydney Morning Herald* 26 December 1987, p.34; Ninette Dutton *Overland* no.111, June 1988, p.17-18; Katharine England *Advertiser Magazine* 23 January 1988, p.8; Carolyn Bliss *Antipodes* Spring 1988; Anthony Burgess *Weekend Australian* 20-21 February 1988.

Copies: NSL: Mitchell Library; NSL: Mitchell Library [PW]; Personal collection (2 copies); VSL: SLT 819.93 W582W; VU: McL L/A-F White.

W2 Jonathan Cape Edition (London: Jonathan Cape, 1988)

THREE | UNEASY | PIECES | *Patrick White* | [publisher's device] | JONATHAN CAPE | THIRTY-TWO BEDFORD SQUARE LONDON

22.2 x 14 cm. Unsigned: 32 leaves. pp.[*12*] 11-12 *13-14* 15-24 *25-26* 27-59 *60-62*.
Endpaper; [*1*] blank; [*2*] blank; [*3*] 'THREE | UNEASY | PIECES'; [*4*] *'by the same author* | *Novels* | THE LIVING AND THE DEAD | THE AUNT'S STORY | THE TREE OF MAN | VOSS | RIDERS IN THE CHARIOT | THE SOLID MANDALA | THE VIVISECTOR | THE EYE OF THE STORM | A FRINGE OF LEAVES | THE TWYBORN AFFAIR | MEMOIRS OF MANY IN ONE | *Short Stories* | THE BURNT ONES | THE COCKATOOS | *Plays* | THE HAM FUNERAL | THE SEASON AT SARSAPARILLA | A CHEERY SOUL | NIGHT ON BALD MOUNTAIN | BIG TOYS | SIGNAL DRIVER | NETHERWOOD | *Autobiography* | FLAWS IN THE GLASS'; [*5*] title page; [*6*] 'First published in Great Britain 1988 | Jonathan Cape Ltd, | 32 Bedford Square, London, WC1B 3EL | Copyright © Patrick White 1987 | A CIP catalogue record for this book | is available from the British Library | ISBN 0 224 02594 5 | [at bottom:] Printed in Great Britain by | Mackays of Chatham PLC, Chatham, Kent; [*7*] *'To Thea Waddell'* ; [*8*] blank; [*9*] [b&w photograph of author and companion in kitchen] | [running down:] *'Photo © William Yang* | [upright] THREE POTATOES | and two Guest Stars'; [*10*] blank; [*11*] [rule] | *'The Screaming* | *Potato'* | [rule]; [*12*] blank; 11-12 text; *13* [rule] | *'Dancing with Both Feet* | *on the Ground'* | [rule]; *14* blank; 15-24 text; *25* [rule] | *'The Age of* | *a Wart'* | [rule]; *26* blank; 27-59 text; *60-62* blank; endpaper.
Cased in black cloth with white endpapers. Front and back: blank. Spine: [running down:] [in gold] 'PATRICK WHITE   THREE UNEASY PIECES' | [at bottom:] [upright:] [publisher's device].
White paper dustjacket printed in glossy black on front, back and spine. Front: [in white] 'PATRICK | WHITE | [in yellow] THREE | UNEASY | PIECES'. Back: [in white] "This is direct, simple, and very moving. It has | to be read.' ANTHONY BURGESS | [at bottom:] ISBN 0-224-02594-5' | [barcode]. Spine: [running down:] [in white] 'PATRICK WHITE   [in yellow] THREE UNEASY PIECES' | [in white] [upright:] [publisher's device]. Inside front flap: [blurb, 33 lines] | '£7.95 net | [rule] | IN UK ONLY'. Inside back flap: [biography, 5 lines] | 'MEMOIRS OF MANY IN ONE | [quotation of two lines from] Gillian | Wilce, *New Statesman* | [quotation of three lines from] Nicholas Best, *Financial Times* | [quotation of two lines from] Nicholas Shrimpton, *Sunday* | *Times* | [quotation of five

lines from] Brian Martin, *Spectator* | [quotation of one line from] Selina Hastings, *Daily Telegraph* | [at bottom:] Jacket design © Jonathan Cape Ltd 1988'.

Published 27 October 1988. Price: £7.95, CAN$19.95. Print run: 3,500.

Reviews: Lucy Ellmann *Guardian Weekly* 27 November 1988, p.28; Robert L. Ross *World Literature Written in English* v.28 no.2, Autumn 1988, p.267-268.

Notes: This is an offset reprint of the Australian First Edition (see W1 above). An uncorrected proof copy has been sighted in a personal collection. It is sewn in a plain paper wrapper. Front: 'Trimmed size 216 x 138 mm | Extent 60 pp | Provisional U.K. Published Price: £7.95 | Provisional U.K. Publication Date: 27 October 1988 | [publisher's devices] | UNCORRECTED PROOF'. Bought for £20. A second uncorrected proof copy with the dustjacket was sighted in the same collection. A third uncorrected proof, sewn in red paper, is held in the State Library of Victoria (Call no. *LT 819.93 W582W).

Copies: NSL: Mitchell Library 823.914/W587/29 (lacks dustjacket); NSL: Mitchell Library [PW]; Personal collection (2 copies).

W3 Penguin Edition (London: Penguin, 1990)

THREE | UNEASY | PIECES | *Patrick White* | [publisher's device] | PENGUIN BOOKS

19.8 x 13 cm. Unsigned: 32 leaves. pp.*10* 11-59 *60-64*.

1 'PENGUIN BOOKS | THREE UNEASY PIECES' | [biography, 23 lines]; *2* blank; *3* title page; *4* 'PENGUIN BOOKS | Published by the Penguin Group, | 27 Wrights Lane, London W8 5TZ, England | Viking Penguin Inc., 40 West 23rd Street, New York, New York 10010, USA | Penguin Books Australia Ltd, Ringwood, Victoria, Australia | Penguin Books Canada Ltd, 2801 John Street, Markham, Ontario, Canada L3R 1B4 | Penguin Books (NZ) Ltd, 182-190 Wairau Road, Auckland 10, New Zealand | Penguin Books Ltd, Registered Offices: Harmondsworth, Middlesex, England | First published in Great Britain by Jonathan Cape 1988 | Published in Penguin Books 1990 | 1 3 5 7 9 10 8 6 4 2 | Copyright © Patrick White, 1987 | All rights reserved | Made and printed in Great Britain by | Richard Clay Ltd, Bungay, Suffolk' | [publisher's conditions, 9 lines]; *5* '*To Thea Waddell*' ; *6* blank; *7* [b&w photograph of author and companion in kitchen] | 'THREE POTATOES | and two Guest Stars'; *8* blank; *9* [rule] | '*The Screaming* | *Potato*' | [rule]; *10* blank; 11-12 text; *13* [rule] | '*Dancing with Both Feet* | *on the Ground*' | [rule]; 15-24 text; *25* [rule] | '*The Age of* | *a Wart*' | [rule]; *26* blank; 27-59 text; *60* blank; *61* 'For the best in Paperbacks, look for the' [publisher's device] | [list of addresses]; *62* blank; *63* 'BY THE SAME AUTHOR | Voss | [comment, 11 lines] | The Twyborn Affair | [comment, 8 lines] | A Fringe of Leaves' | [comment, 7 lines]; *64* 'BY THE SAME AUTHOR | Memoirs of Many in One | [comment, 14 lines] | *Also published:*' | [list of nine titles].

Perfectbound in white paper covers printed in purple, black and cream. Front: 'PATRICK | WHITE | WINNER OF THE NOBEL PRIZE FOR LITERATURE | [thick rule] | THREE | UNEASY | PIECES | [thick rule] | THE SCREAMING POTATO | DANCING WITH BOTH FEET ON THE GROUND | THE AGE OF A WART' | [at bottom:] [publisher's device]. Back: [quotation of 11 lines from] '– *Observer* | [quotation of three lines from] – Anthony Burgess in | the *Independent* | [quotation of four lines from] – *Evening Standard* | [quotation of two lines from] – *Yorkshire Post* | [at bottom left:] [pub-

lisher's device] | A PENGUIN BOOK | Fiction | U.K. £3.99 | N.Z. $15.95 | (incl. GST) | CAN. $9.95 | [at bottom right:] ISBN 0-14-012588-4' | [barcode].
Price: £3.99, NZ$15.95, CAN$9.95. ISBN 0-14-012588-4.
Copies: NSL: Mitchell Library 823.914/39; NSL: Mitchell Library [PW].

W.t1 French First Edition (Paris: Arléa, 1994)

PATRICK WHITE | Prix Nobel de Littérature | HISTOIRES PEU ORDINAIRES | *traduit de l'anglais par Jacqueline Délia* | arléa

20.5 x 12.5 cm. Unsigned: 48 leaves. pp.*8* 9-65 *66-68* 69-72 *73-74* 75-91 *92-96*.
1-2 blank; *3* 'HISTOIRES PEU ORDINAIRES'; *4* '«L'ÉTRANGÈRE» | COLLECTION DIRIGÉE PAR JACQUELINE DÉLIA | DÉJA PARUS : | [list of ten titles] | ISSN 0998-4585 | ISBN 2-86959-197-7 | © Mars 1994 – L'Étrangère pour la traduction française | Titre original: Three uneasy pieces'; *5* title page; *6* '*Titre original:* | Three uneasy pieces'; *7* 'L'ÂGE 'D'UNE VERRUE'; *8* blank; 9-65 text; *66* blank; *67* 'LE CRI DÉCHIRANT | DE LA POMME DE TERRE'; *68* blank; 69-72 text; *73* 'DANSER LES DEUX PIEDS | PAR TERRE'; *74* blank; 75-91 text; *92* blank; *93* 'TRANSCODÉ | ET ACHEVÉ D'IMPRIMER | EN FÉVRIER 1994 | SUR LES PRESSES DE | L'IMPRIMERIE HÉRISSEY | A ÉVREUX (EURE) | Numéro d'édition : 00198 | Numéro d'impression : 64383 | Dépôt légal : Mars 1994 | *Imprimé en France*'; *94-96* blank.
Perfectbound in glossy white card. Front: [at top right:] [publisher's device] | [in white] 'Patrick White | [rule] | Prix Nobel de Littérature | [rule] | HISTOIRES | [rule] | PEU | [rule] | ORDINAIRES | [rule] | [illust. of men and women dancing] | [in black] *arléa*'. Back: [in box of single blue rules:] [in blue] 'HISTOIRES | PEU ORDINAIRES | [in black] *Traduit de l'anglais (Australie)* | [blurb, 25 lines] | [at bottom left:] Couverture: | *G-P Seurat* | *Chahut (détail)* | Diffusion Le Seuil | 27 rue Jacob. 75006 Paris | 69 F TTC | [at bottom right:] [barcode] | [running down:] [device] GROU-RADENEZ & JOLY – PARIS 6'. Spine: [running down:] 'Patrick White HISTOIRES PEU ORDINAIRES' | [at bottom:] [upright:] [publisher's device].
Reviews: Gérard Meudal *Libération* (Paris) 24 mars 1994.
Copies: NSL: Mitchell Library [PW].

W.m1 Sound Recording (Victoria Park: Association for the Blind of Western Australia, 1990)

Not seen, but entry on the National Bibliographic Database. One audiocassette. Read by Jay Townsend from the Jonathan Cape edition (1988).

W.m2 Extract (St Lucia: University of Queensland Press, 1994)

Notes: 'Dancing with Both Feet on the Ground' is reprinted in *Patrick White: Selected Writings* ed. Alan Lawson (St Lucia: University of Queensland Press, 1994), p.183-188 (see Y1 below).

X Patrick White Speaks (1989)

After a severe illness in the winter of 1988, Patrick White, with the help of his literary agent Barbara Mobbs, began to sort through his papers. A number of typescript polemical speeches came to light, which Paul Brennan of Primavera Press arranged to publish. In his usual self-effacing manner, White wrote to David Marr, 'My God, how did I spout all that over the years?' (Marr p.638)

* * * * *

X1a Australian First Edition (Sydney, Primavera Press, 1989)

PATRICK | WHITE | SPEAKS | *Primavera Press* | SYDNEY

22 x 14.5 cm. Unsigned: 104 leaves. pp.*12* 13-208 (numerous pages are unnumbered); 16 pages of plates.

Endpaper; *1* 'What interests me most about this book is its consistency | with the novels — the moral stance is firm from the beginning. | As novelist and citizen, Patrick White is the voice of our | country's conscience. He begs us to search our hearts. | Dorothy Green | poet & critic'; *2* blank; *3* 'PATRICK | WHITE | SPEAKS'; *4* blank; *5* title page; *6* '*Primavera Press* | PO Box 575 | Leichhardt NSW | Australia 2040 | telephone (02) 569 1452 | Publisher — *Paul Brennan* | Editors — Christine Flynn and Paul Brennan | Text copyright © Patrick White 1989 | Introductions copyright © Primavera Press 1989 | All rights reserved. [publisher's conditions, 6 lines] | Inquiries should be addressed to the publisher. | National Library of Australia | Cataloguing-in-Publication entry: | [rule] | White, Patrick, 1912- | Patrick White Speaks. | Bibliography. | ISBN 0 9589494 7 6. | ISBN 0 9589494 6 8 (pbk.). | I. Title. | A825'.3 | [rule] | MANUFACTURED WHOLLY WITHIN AUSTRALIA'; *7* '*Editors' Note*'; *8* 'Contents'; *9* 'Contents' [cont.]; *10* '*Illustrations*'; *11* 'PATRICK | WHITE | SPEAKS'; *12* [biography, 17 lines] | [introduction to first piece, 5 lines]; 13-197 text; *198* blank; 199-201 '*Notes*'; 202-203 '*Editions of Patrick White's Works*'; 204-207 'Also from PRIMAVERA PRESS' [advertisements follow]; 208 'Colophon | This book has been set in Garth Graphic type, designed by Renée le Winter and | Constance Blanchard in 1979 for the Compugraphic Organisation, and named after the | co-founder of Compugraphic, William W. Garth. It is a distinctive old-style face with a | calligraphic look. | The type in this book was set by Tensor typesetters, Rozelle. Their MCS 8400 phototypesetter read 5.25 inch floppy discs with IBM files, that had been converted | with the assistance of Gary Mitchell at Logic Group (Aust.) in Annandale from Apple | IIGS 3.5 inch discs via Macintosh files. The manuscript was keyed in by Christine | Flynn using Appleworks software and an Apple IIGS. Text design is by the publisher. | The typeface on the jacket is Century Old Style, designed by Morris Fuller Benton | in 1906 for the American Typefounders. Jacket design is by Harry C. Pears of Typeface | Research. The paper is Gloplus 100 gsm supplied by The Paper House. Printed by | Griffin Press, Netley, South Australia.'; endpaper.

Cased in plum cloth with pink endpapers. Front and back: blank. Spine: [running down:] [in white] 'Patrick White Speaks   PRIMAVERA PRESS'.

White glossy paper dustjacket printed with pink fleck on front, back, spine and inside both flaps. Front: [in red through violet] 'Patrick | White | Speaks | [in black] PRIMAVERA

PRESS' | [in red] [ornamental rule]. Back: [sepia photograph of the author]. Spine: [running down:] [in red] 'Patrick White Speaks [in black] PRIMAVERA PRESS'. Inside front and back flaps: blank.

Published in July 1989. Price: AU$29.95 (hbk), $16.95 (pbk). ISBN 0 9589 4946 8.

Reviews: Veronica Brady *Fremantle Arts Review* v.4 no.10, October 1989, p.14-15; Jim McClelland *Sydney Morning Herald* 19 August 1989, p.80; Peter Pierce *Bulletin* 19 September 1989 p.118-119; Paul Carter *Australian Book Review* no.114, September 1989, p.12-13; Janine Haines *Australian Magazine* 26-27 August 1989, p.7; Ralph Summy *Social Alternatives* v.8 no.3, October 1989, p.71-72; Cath Filmer-Davies *Courier Mail* 7 October 1989, p.7; David McCooey *West Australian* 26 August 1989, p.8; Katharine England *Advertiser* 29 July 1989, p.14; Jeff Doyle *Canberra Times* 24 March 1990, p.B4; Laurie Clancy *Age* (Melbourne) 17 February 1990, Saturday Extra p.10; Ann Nugent *Age Monthly Review* v.9 no.10 February 1990, p.5-6; Carolyn Bliss *Australian and New Zealand Studies in Canada* no.4, Fall 1990, pp.1-14.

Notes: A paperback version of this edition was issued at the same time. The design on the paper covers was the same as the dustjacket of the hardback edition. An uncorrected proof copy has been sighted in a personal collection. It is sewn in plain white card and is uncut. It has a ms annotation: 'Paul Brennan to Nicholas Pounder 22.6.89'. The contract between the publishers (Paul Brennan and Christine Flynn) and Patrick White is held at the National Library of Australia (Manuscript Collection MS 8116 Folder 35). It provides for the following royalties: 10% on hardback copies; 5% on copies 1 to 5,000; 7.5% on copies 5,001 to 20,000; 10% on all copies over 20,000; and 10% on remainders. Also held in MS 8116 are copies of many typescript copies of White's speeches; these derive from White himself.

Copies: NSL: Mitchell Library 825.914/W587/1; NSL: Mitchell Library [PW]; Personal collection (2 copies).

X1b U.K. Subedition (London, Jonathan Cape, 1990)

PATRICK | WHITE | SPEAKS | [publisher's device] | JONATHAN CAPE | LONDON

22.2 x 14 cm. Unsigned: 100 leaves. pp.[*10*] 13-197 *198* 199-201 *202*; 16 pages of plates. Endpaper; [*1*] 'PATRICK | WHITE | SPEAKS'; [*2*] '*by the same author* | *novels* | the living and the dead | the aunt's story | the tree of man | voss | riders in the chariot | the solid mandala | the vivisector | the eye of the storm | a fringe of leaves | the twyborn affair | memoirs of many in one | *short stories* | THE BURNT ONES | THE COCKATOOS | THREE UNEASY PIECES | *plays* | THE HAM FUNERAL | THE SEASON AT SARSAPARILLA | A CHEERY SOUL | NIGHT ON BALD MOUNTAIN | BIG TOYS | SIGNAL DRIVER | NETHERWOOD | *autobiography* | FLAWS IN THE GLASS'; [*3*] title page; [*4*] 'First published in Great Britain 1990 | Jonathan Cape Ltd, 20 Vauxhall Bridge Road, London SW1V 2SA | Text © Patrick White 1989 | Introduction © Primavera Press 1989 | Patrick White has asserted his right | to be identified as the author of this work | A CIP catalogue record for this book | is available from the British Library | ISBN 0-224-02788-3 | Printed in Great Britain by | Mackays of Chatham PLC, Chatham, Kent'; [*5*] 'Contents'; [*6*] 'Contents' [cont.]; [*7*] 'Illustrations'; [*8*] 'Illustrations' [cont.]; [*9*] '*Editors' Note*'; [*10*] [biography, 17 lines] | [introduction to first piece, 5 lines]; 13-197 text; *198* blank; 199-201 '*Notes*';

202 blank; endpaper.

Cased in sandy cloth. Front and back: blank. Spine: [running down:] [in gold] 'PATRICK WHITE SPEAKS' | [upright:] [publisher's device].

White glossy paper dustjacket with photograph of the author on front. Front: [in dark green] 'PATRICK | WHITE | [in red] SPEAKS'. Back: [at bottom:] 'ISBN 0-224-02788-3' | [barcode]. Spine: [running down:] [in green] 'PATRICK WHITE [in red] SPEAKS' | [at bottom:] [upright:] [publisher's device]. Inside front flap: [blurb, 26 lines] | '£12.95 net | [rule] | IN UK ONLY'. Inside back flap: [biography, 5 lines] | [at bottom:] 'Jacket design by Hilary Turner | © Jonathan Cape Ltd 1990'.

Price: £12.95.

Copies: NSL: Mitchell Library 824.914/W857/1; NSL: Mitchell Library [PW]; Personal collection.

X1c Penguin Subedition (London, Penguin, 1992)

PATRICK WHITE SPEAKS | [rule] | [at bottom:] [publisher's device] | PENGUIN BOOKS

19.7 x 12.8 cm. Unsigned: 104 leaves. pp.[*8*] 13-201 *202-212*.

[*1*] 'PENGUIN BOOKS | PATRICK WHITE SPEAKS' | [biography, 29 lines]; [*2*] blank; [*3*] title page; [*4*] 'PENGUIN BOOKS | Published by the Penguin Group | Penguin Books Ltd, 27 Wrights Lane, London W8 5TZ, England | Penguin Books USA Inc., 375 Hudson Street, New York, New York 10014, USA | Penguin Books Australia Ltd, Ringwood, Victoria, Australia | Penguin Books Canada Ltd, 10 Alcorn Avenue, Toronto, Ontario, Canada M4V 3B2 | Penguin Books (NZ) Ltd, 182-190 Wairau Road, Auckland 10, New Zealand | Penguin Books Ltd, Registered Offices: Harmondsworth, Middlesex, England | First published in Great Britain by Jonathan Cape 1990 | Published in Penguin Books 1992 | 10 9 8 7 6 5 4 3 2 1 | Text copyright © Patrick White, 1989 | Introductions copyright © Primavera Press, 1989 | All rights reserved | The moral right of the author has been asserted | Printed in England by Clays Ltd, St Ives plc' | [publisher's conditions, 6 lines]; [*5*] 'Contents'; [*6*] 'Contents' [cont.]; [*7*] '*Editors' Note*'; [*8*] [biography, 17 lines] | [introduction to the first piece, 22 lines]; 13-201 text; *202* blank; *203-212* [advertisements for titles by White and other authors].

Perfectbound in white paper covers printed in grey on front and orange on spine. Front: [in white] 'Patrick White Speaks | The collected essays, articles and speeches | of the Nobel Prize winning novelist | [b&w photograph of the author] | Patrick White' [publisher's device]. Back: [in black] [blurb, 15 lines] | [quotation of two lines from] '– *Yorkshire Post* | [quotation of four lines from] – *20/20* | [quotation of two lines from] | – *Independent* | Cover photograph by Axel Poignant | [at left:] [publisher's device] A PENGUIN BOOK | Politics | Biography/Autobiography | U.K. £6.99 | [at right:] ISBN 0-14-015933-9' | [barcode]. Spine: [running down:] [in black] 'Patrick White Speaks [in white] Patrick White | [at bottom:] ISBN 0 14 | 01.5933 9' | [upright:] [publisher's device]. Inside front and back: blank.

Price: £6.99. ISBN 0-14-015933-9.

Notes: This subedition does not include the plates.

Copies: NSL: Mitchell Library [PW]; Personal collection.

Y Selected Writings (1994)

This selection of writings was compiled by Professor Alan Lawson and is important for the inclusion of a number of previously uncollected pieces.

* * * * *

Y1 Australian First Edition (St Lucia: University of Queensland Press, 1994)

PATRICK | WHITE | SELECTED WRITINGS | EDITED BY ALAN LAWSON | University of Queensland Press

19.8 x 12.9 cm. Unsigned: 168 leaves. pp.*v* vi *vii–ix* x-xxii *1-3* 4-10 *11* 12-29 *30* 31-119 *120-123* 124-188 *189-191* 192-194 *195-196* 197 *198* 199-207 *208-210* 211 *212-213* 214-281 *282-284* 285 *286* 287-297 *298* 299-304 *305-314*.

i 'PATRICK WHITE'; *ii* 'UQP AUSTRALIAN AUTHORS'; *iii* title page; *iv* 'First published 1994 by the University of Queensland Press | Box 42, St Lucia, Queensland 4067 Australia | © Estate of Patrick White 1994 | Compilation, introduction and notes © Alan Lawson 1994 | [publisher's conditions, 5 lines] | Typeset by University of Queensland Press | Printed in Australia by McPherson's Printing Group, Victoria | Distributed in the USA and Canada by | International Specialized Book Services, Inc., | 5804 N.E. Hassalo Street, Portland, Oregon 97213-3640 | [cataloguing data, 9 lines] | ISBN 0 7022 2625 4'; *v* vi 'Contents'; *vii* 'Acknowledgements'; *viii* blank; *ix* x-xxii 'Introduction'; *1* '1 | *A Way with Words:* | *Selected Short Fiction*'; *2* 'EDITOR'S NOTE'; *3* 4-10 'Uncollected Story | THE TWITCHING COLONEL'; *11* 12-29 'The Burnt Ones | CLAY'; *30* 31-119 'The Cockatoos | A WOMAN'S HAND'; *120* blank; *121* '2 | *Sex and Humour:* | *Selected Short Fiction*'; *122* 'EDITOR'S NOTE'; *123* 124-133 'Uncollected Story | ON THE BALCONY'; *134* 135-160 'The Burnt Ones | WILLY WAGTAILS BY MOONLIGHT'; *161* 162-182 'Uncollected Story | FÊTE GALANTE'; *183* 184-188 'Three Uneasy Pieces | DANCING WITH BOTH FEET ON THE GROUND'; *189* '3 | *Poet*'; *190* 'EDITOR'S NOTE'; *191* 192-194 'Uncollected Poems'; *195* '4 | *Stage-Struck:* | *Theatre Pieces*'; *196* 197 'EDITOR'S NOTE'; *198* blank; 199-207 text; *208* blank; *209* '5 | Writing Life | Life Writing'; *210* 211 'EDITOR'S NOTE'; *212* blank; *213* 214-223 'Selected Private Letters'; *224* 225-267 [Extracts from] 'Flaws in the Glass'; *268* 269-281 'Selected Interviews and Talks on Writing'; *282* blank; *283* '6 | *Public Man:* | *Essays,* | *Letters, and Speeches*'; *284* 285 'EDITOR'S NOTE'; *286* blank; 287-297 text; *298* 299-305 'Selected Bibliography'; *306-314* [advertisements].

Perfectbound in paper card. Front: [black and white photograph of the author] | [in yellow] 'PATRICK | WHITE | [in white] SELECTED WRITINGS | EDITED BY ALAN LAWSON | UQP'. Back: [in white] 'UQP AUSTRALIAN AUTHORS | [blurb, 18 lines] | [biography of Alan Lawson, 10 lines] | Series General Editor: Laurie Hergenhan, | Professor of Australian Literature, University of Queensland | *Cover design by Christopher McVinish,* *using a photograph of Patrick White* | *kindly lent by David Marr* | [at left:] UQP PAPERBACKS | Australian Literature' | [at right:] [barcode]. Spine: [running down:] [in yellow] 'PATRICK WHITE [in white] EDITED BY ALAN LAWSON | [upright:] UQP'.

Published in January 1994. Price: $AU21.85 (pbk). ISBN 0702226254.

Reviews: Elizabeth Riddell *Sydney Morning Herald* 16 July 1994, p.9A; Tony Maniaty *Weekend Australian* 2-3 July 1994, Review 6; Judy Smallman *Australian Book Review* no.163, August 1994, p.63; Glen Thomas *Social Alternatives* v.13 nos.3-4, October 1994, p.55-57; David A. Myers *Imago: new writing* v.7 no.1, March 1995, p.86-87; R. Brown *Australian Studies* no.9, November 1995, pp.136-138; Cleo Lloyd da Silva *Antipodes* v.9 no.2, December 1995, p.173-174.

Copies: VSL: LT A828.308 W585P.

Z Letters (1994)

Even in the 1950s Patrick White was requesting that his correspondents should destroy all his letters. White himself kept no copies of his own letters (with a few notorious exceptions in relation to his most famous bust-ups) and destroyed all incoming letters. Moreover, White destroyed collections of his letters if they were returned to him. For example, when White was researching *The Twyborn Affair*, he asked his cousin Betty Withycombe to return some of the letters from his jackaroo days. Withycombe returned all 400 letters, neatly boxed in preparation for lodging with the Bodleian Library, Oxford. White burnt them all, without ever telling his cousin.

When David Marr began researching White's biography, White gave him permission to copy letters found in private hands. Marr located more than 2,000 letters before the publication of *Patrick White: A Life* in 1991, and a further 1,000 before publication of *Patrick White: Letters* in 1994.

* * * * *

Z1a Australian First Edition (Sydney: Random House Australia, 1994)

PATRICK WHITE | LETTERS | Edited by David Marr | RANDOM HOUSE [publisher's device] | AUSTRALIA

24 x 15.8 cm. Unsigned: 344 leaves. pp.*viii* ix *x* 1-677 *678*; illust.; 22 pages of plates.

Endpapers; *i* 'PATRICK WHITE | LETTERS'; *ii* [illust. of White by 'Spooner']; *iii* title page; *iv* 'By the same author | Barwick | The Ivanov Trail | Patrick White: A Life | Random House Australia | [4 lines] | First published 1994 | Copyright © David Marr and the Estate of Patrick White 1994 | [9 lines] | ISBN 0 09 182992 5. | [3 lines] | Design by Helen Semmler | Typeset in Goudy Old Style and Berkeley Old Style | by Midland Typesetters Pty Ltd | Printed by Griffin Paperbacks, Adelaide'; *v* 'To | Peggy Garland | who showed me the first bundle | and said, | 'You may be interested.''; *vi* [quotation of 5 lines from] '*The Ham Funeral*'; *vii-viii* '*Contents*'; ix 'Note | [19 lines] | D.E.M. | 6 August 1994'; *x* blank; 1-622 text; 623-625 '*Notes* | WHITE AND HIS LETTERS'; 626 'ABBREVIATIONS'; 627-630 'ACKNOWLEDGEMENTS'; 630-631 'ILLUSTRATIONS AND PHOTOGRAPHS'; 632-646 'THE CAST OF CORRESPONDENTS'; 647-677 '*Index*'; *678* blank; endpapers.

Cased in black paper-covered boards. Front and back: blank. Spine: [in white] [running down:] 'PATRICK WHITE | LETTERS || *David Marr*' [upright:] [publisher's device].

Glossy black paper dustjacket. Front: [in white] 'PATRICK WHITE | LETTERS | [illust. of White by Brett Whiteley] | [in orange] *Edited by* | *David Marr*'. Back: [in white] "Letters are the devil, | and I always hope that | any I have written | have been destroyed...' | *Patrick White* | RANDOM HOUSE [publisher's device] | AUSTRALIA | [barcode] | Aust RRP $49.95'. Spine: [in white] [running down:] 'PATRICK WHITE | LETTERS || [in orange] *David Marr*' | [upright:] [publisher's device]. Inside front flap: [in white] [blurb, 41 lines].

Inside back flap: [photograph of David Marr] | [in white] [biography of Marr, 17 lines] | '*Front cover illustration*: 'Flaws in the Glass (Portrait of | Patrick White)' 1981 | 87cm x 94cm oil and mixed medium on board | Courtesy of the estate of Brett Whiteley | *Jacket design*: Helen Semmler'.

Price: AU$49.95. ISBN 0091829925 (hbk); 009183063X (pbk).

Previews: William Fraser *Sydney Morning Herald* 10 September 1994.

Reviews: Brian Matthews *Age* (Melbourne) 1 October 1994, Saturday Extra p.8; Michael Davie *Sydney Morning Herald* 1 October 1994, Spectrum 11A; *Weekend Australian* 1-2 October 1994, Review p.5; Brian Kiernan *Weekend Australian* 1-2 October 1994, Review 5; Gavin Simpson *West Australian* 7 October 1994, Today 8; Elizabeth Riddell *Bulletin with Newsweek* 11 October 1994; Andrew Field *Courier Mail* 22 October 1994, Weekend 6; L. van Nunen *Time Australia* 31 October 1994; Christine Slade *Canberra Times* 29 October 1994, p.C10; Michael Heyward *Australian Book Review* no.166, November 1994, p.6-7; Andrew Riemer *The Independent Monthly* November 1994, p.72-74; Peter Coleman *Sydney Review* no.69, October 1994, p.10 and *Adelaide Review* no.133, November 1994, p.29-30; Bruce Williams *Eureka Street* v.4 no.10, December 1994, p.30-32; Alison Croggon *Voices* v.4 no.4, Summer 1994-95, p.99-102; C. Lloyd da Silva *CRNLE Reviews Journal* 1995, pp.128-131; Hilary Corke *Spectator* 21 January 1995, p.41; *Economist* 18 February 1995, p.88-89; Clement Semmler *Quadrant* March 1995, p.79-81; Allan Ashbolt *Editions* no.22, March 1995; David Tacey *Times Literary Supplement* 3 March 1995, p.23; Tim Winton *London Review of Books* 22 June 1995, p.18-19; Alan Ross *London Magazine* v.35 nos.1-2, April-May 1995, p.128-130; David Coad *World Literature Today* Summer 1995, p.642; Genevieve Stuttaford *Publishers Weekly* 1 April 1996 p.60-61; Janice E. Braun *Library Journal* 15 June 1996 p.66; Bruce Pennington *Lambda Book Report* September 1996, p.20; Thomas L. Erskine *Magill Book Reviews* 1 March 1997.

Extracts: *Age* 24 September 1994, Extra 6, and 26 September 1994, p.11; *Sydney Morning Herald* 26 September 1994, p.11, and 17 October 1994, p.9; *Courier Mail* 15 October 1994, Weekend 3; *Patrick White: Selected Writings* ed. by Alan Lawson (St Lucia: University of Queensland Press, 1994), p.213-223; *With Fond Regards: private lives through letters* (Canberra, National Library of Australia, 1995).

Copies: VU: MEANJ A823.3 White; VU: McL L/A-F White; Personal collection.

Z1b U.K. Subedition (London: Jonathan Cape, 1994)
Not seen, but a record appears on the National Bibliographic Database. ISBN 0224035169.

Z1c U.S. Subedition (Chicago: University of Chicago Press, 1996)
Not seen, but entry sighted on <www.amazon.com> 7 August 1997. 9.34 x 6.47 cm. Price: US$35.00. ISBN 0 2268 9503 3.

Z.m1 Sound Recording (South Yarra, Vic.: Louis Braille Books, 1996)
Letters (23 audiocassettes, 34 hours 24 minutes).
Read by Paul Karo from the Random House edition of 1994.

AA   Collected Plays Volume 2 (1994)

Currency Press issued the first volume of Patrick White's *Collected Plays* in 1985, but this publication was essentially another issue of the original *Four Plays*, first published in 1965. The second volume of *Collected Plays* collects White's later plays, including *Big Toys* (first published 1978), *Netherwood* (first published 1983), and *Signal Driver* (first published 1983). *Collected Plays Volume 2* is important for the first publication of *Shepherd on the Rocks*.

* * * * *

AA1   Australian First Edition (Sydney: Currency Press, 1994)

[rule] | PATRICK | WHITE | [rule] | COLLECTED PLAYS | Volume II | [publisher's device] | CURRENCY PRESS • SYDNEY

20.5 x 13 cm. Unsigned: 118 leaves. pp.*i–iv* v *vi* vii-xi *xii 1* 2-3 *4* 5-52 *53* 54-55 *56* 57-96 *97* 98-99 *100-101* 102-168 *169* 170-172 *173-174* 175-231 *232* 233-234 *235-236*; illust.

i [biography, 32 lines]; *ii* 'Also by Patrick White'; *iii* title page; *iv* 'AUSTRALIAN DRAMATISTS | General Editor: Katharine Brisbane | *Big Toys* first published by Currency Press 1978, *Netherwood* | first published by Currency Press 1983, *Signal Driver* first | published by Currency Press 1983. | This edition first published in 1994 by | Currency Press Pty Ltd, | PO Box 452 Paddington, | N.S.W. 2021, Australia. | [...] | Cover design by Kevin Chan | Artwork by The Master Typographer | Typeset in Baskerville by The Master Typographer, Sydney | Printed by Ligare Pty. Ltd., Sydney'; v 'CONTENTS'; *vi* blank; vii-xi 'INTRODUCTION' [by Pamela Payne]; *xii* blank; *1* 2-3 *4* 5-52 'BIG TOYS'; *53* 54-55 *56* 57-96 'SIGNAL DRIVER'; *97* 98-99 *100-101* 102-168 'NETHERWOOD'; *169* 170-172 *173-174* 175-231 'SHEPHERD ON THE ROCKS'; *232* blank; 233-234 'A SELECT BIBLIOGRAPHY'; *235-236* blank.

Sewn in glossy black paper card. Front: 'AUSTRALIAN DRAMATISTS | [in white] Patrick | White | [in black] COLLECTED PLAYS VOLUME II | [in white] Big Toys | [rule] | Signal Driver | [rule] | Netherwood | [rule] | Shepherd on the Rocks' | [col. illust.]. Back: [in white] [biography, 11 lines] | [black & white photograph of the author] | 'Cover: Brett Whiteley, *Patrick White as a Headland* (1980). Reproduced by permission of | the executors of the estate of Brett Whiteley. | Photo by Peter Smart. | Above: Patrick White. | Photo by Milton Wordley-Rapport.' | [at right] [barcode]. Spine: [running down:] [in white] 'Patrick | White || [in black] COLLECTED PLAYS VOLUME II | [upright] [in white] Currency'.

Published in May 1994. Price: AU$19.95. ISBN 0 86819 305 4.

Reviews: N. Fletcher *Australasian Drama Studies* v.28, 1994, pp.190-193; Peter Fitzpatrick *Australian Book Review* no.165, October 1994; Alexandra Cromwell *Antipodes* v.9 no., June 1995, p.51-52.

Notes: This is the first publication of 'Shepherd on the Rocks'.

Copies: VSL: SLT A822.3 W585P.

Appendix 1: Poetry

Apart from Patrick White's published poetry – essentially the two collections, *Thirteen Poems* (c1929) and *The Ploughman and Other Poems* (1935) plus a few occasional pieces – a few unpublished poems have also survived. In the Manuscript Collection of the National Library of Australia (MS 8649) there is a canvas notebook containing some thirty poems. The notebook dates from around August 1934 and was apparently given by White to his cousin, Elizabeth (Betty) Withycombe. Given that 28 of the thirty poems were subsequently published in *The Ploughman*, the notebook is something of a preliminary draft of that work. The two unpublished poems were 'Soirée' and 'Interpretation'. Bertram Rota Ltd offered the notebook to the Library in 1989: the asking price was £5,000.

Surviving in the Duke of Baena (Pepé Mamblas) papers, also in the Manuscript Collection in the National Library of Australia (MS 7712), are another two poems which appear never to have been published. They are 'Déjeuner à Guéthary' and an untitled piece which begins 'Those who have discarded truth for the lie of living …', both dated 28 August 1937, St-Jean-de-Luz.

'A Rustic Eclogue'
First published: *Thirteen Poems.*

'Long Ago: a Reminiscence'
First published: *Thirteen Poems.*

'Trees in Winter'
First published: *Thirteen Poems.*

'Shadow Play'
First published: *Thirteen Poems.*

'Susan'
First published: *Thirteen Poems.*

The Window'
First published: *Thirteen Poems.*

'The Death of Arabella Cheyne'
First published: *Thirteen Poems.*

'In Nihil Ibimus'
First published: *Thirteen Poems.*

'Requiem'
First published: *Thirteen Poems.*

'The Birds'
First published: *Thirteen Poems.*

'Orchard Row'
First published: *Thirteen Poems.*

'Seraphita'
First published: *Thirteen Poems.*

'St. Jacques, Dieppe'
First published: *Thirteen Poems.*

'Meeting Again'
Composed: January 1934.
First published: *London Mercury* v.30, June 1934, p.104.
Later published: *The Ploughman and Other Poems.*

'The Ploughman'
Composed: December 1933.

First published: *London Mercury* v.30, June 1934, p.105.
Later published: *Literary Digest* (New York) v.118, 11 August 1934, p.31; *The Best Poems of 1935* ed. Thomas Moult (London, 1935), p.24-25; *The Ploughman and Other Poems*.

'Lines Written on Leaving the Scilly Islands'
Composed: 3 January 1933.
First published: *The Ploughman and Other Poems*.

'If I Could Tell You'
Composed: 3 January 1933.
First published: *The Ploughman and Other Poems*.

'Isles of Scilly'
Composed: 18 December 1932.
First published: *The Ploughman and Other Poems*.

'Futility'
Composed: 25 December 1932.
First published: *The Ploughman and Other Poems*.

'After Rain'
Composed: August 1933.
First published: *The Ploughman and Other Poems*.

'When Thoughts are Still and Formless'
Composed: August 1933.
First published: *The Ploughman and Other Poems*.
Later published: *Poets of Australia* ed. George Mackaness (Sydney, 1946), p.462-463, also in the second edition published as *An Anthology of Australian Verse* ed. George Mackaness (Sydney, 1952), p.379.

'Rain in Summer'
Composed: July 1933.
First published: *The Ploughman and Other Poems*.
Later published: *Poets of Australia* ed. George Mackaness (Sydney, 1946), p.463, also in the second edition published as *An Anthology of Australian Verse* ed. George Mackaness (Sydney, 1952), p.379-380.

'If You Would See'
Composed: July 1933.
First published: *The Ploughman and Other Poems*.

'I Walked in the Garden'
Composed: July 1933.
First published: *The Ploughman and Other Poems*.

'Lovely, Lovely You May Be'
Composed: October 1933.
First published: *The Ploughman and Other Poems*.

'He Looked for Love'
Composed: October 1933.
First published: *The Ploughman and Other Poems*.

'Lines Written After an Encounter With Death in a Country Lane'
Composed: December 1933.
First published: *The Ploughman and Other Poems*.

'Bitter Were the Tears She Wept'
Composed: December 1933.
First published: *The Ploughman and Other Poems*.

'Lament in Winter'
Composed: December 1933.
First published: *The Ploughman and Other Poems*.

'Resurrection'
Composed: December 1933.
First published: *The Ploughman and Other Poems*.

'They Held out Their Hands to Me'
Composed: October 1933.
First published: *The Ploughman and Other Poems*.

'O Cold, Cold Rain'
Composed: November 1933.
First published: *The Ploughman and Other Poems*.

'Second Life'
Composed: November 1933.
First published: *The Ploughman and Other Poems*.

'Alone'
Composed: January 1934.
First published: *The Ploughman and Other Poems*.

'Godstow Abbey'
Composed: January 1934.
First published: *The Ploughman and Other Poems*.

'The Bells'
Composed: February 1934.
First published: *The Ploughman and Other Poems*.

'The Bridge'
Composed: February 1934.
First published: *The Ploughman and Other Poems*.

'Trio'
Composed: February 1934.
First published: *The Ploughman and Other Poems*.

'Wisdom for the Wise'
Composed: March 1934.
First published: *The Ploughman and Other Poems*.

'October'
Composed: October 1934.
First published: *The Ploughman and Other Poems*.

'Early Autumn'
Composed: October 1934.
First published: *The Ploughman and Other Poems*.

'Dirge'
Composed: September 1934.
First published: *The Ploughman and Other Poems*.

'Oram's Grave'
Composed: 1934.
First published: *The Ploughman and Other Poems*.

'Interlude'
Composed: September 1934.
First published: *The Ploughman and Other Poems*.

'Morning Soliloquy'
Composed: August 1934.
First published: *The Ploughman and Other Poems*.

'To a Gull Blown Inland by the Storm'
Composed: August 1934.
First published: *The Ploughman and*

Other Poems.

'The House Behind the Barricades'
First published: *New Verse* no.30,
Summer 1938, p.9.
Later published: *The Year's Poetry 1938*
comp. Denys Kilham Roberts and
Geoffrey Grigson (London, 1938),
p.114-115; *Patrick White: Selected
Writings* ed. Alan Lawson (1994),
p.191.
Note: In the National Library of Australia (Manuscript Collection, MS
7712) there is a copy of *The Year's Poetry 1938* with the following inscription in White's hand: 'To Pepé with
best wishes from one of the authors
Christmas '38. Patrick'.

'Lines from Egypt'
Composed: In Egypt during the war.
First published: *Australia* 1 September
1941, p.43.
Later published: *Patrick White: Selected
Writings* ed. Alan Lawson (1994),
p.192.

'Defending the Right to Offend'
First published: *Overland* no.100, September 1985, p.36.
Later published: *Patrick White: Selected
Writings* ed. Alan Lawson (1994),
p.194.

'Nine Thoughts from Sydney'
Composed: 1970.
First published: *Patrick White Speaks*
(1989), p.24-25; *The Sydney Review*
August 1989, p.12.
Later published: *Patrick White: Selected
Writings* ed. Alan Lawson (1994),
p.192-194.

'Six Urban Songs'

Composed: c1963.
First published: Programme notes for
Moya Henderson's song cycle, Sydney
Symphony Orchestra, 12, 14 and 15
April 1986 (see Marr p.694, n.39).
Henderson's autograph score (37 p.) is
held at the Australian Music Centre,
Sydney. The piece was dedicated to
White on the occasion of his seventieth birthday. Facsimiles of the autograph score are held by a number of
libraries.
Notes: White and Peter Sculthorpe
had collaborated on this song cycle in
1964, but after the relationship broke
down the manuscript was returned to
White who presumably destroyed it.
Sculthorpe, however, had made a surreptitious copy (in the lavatory while
feigning diarrhœa) and it was a descendent of this copy that was used by
Henderson.

[Eliza Fraser]
Composed: c1964.
First published: Peter Sculthorpe *Sun
Music: journeys and reflections from a
composer's life* (Sydney: ABC Books,
1999), p.78-79.
Notes: Peter Sculthorpe was commissioned by the Elizabethan Theatre
Trust to write an opera about Eliza
Fraser, with the libretto by Patrick
White. White produced a preliminary
libretto, but the collaboration broke
down. Sculthorpe had clearly retained
some of White's libretto, which he
published in 1999. Sculthorpe also
used White's initial vision as inspiration for a number of works, including
Eliza Fraser Sings (1978), based on
words by Barbara Blackman, *Mangrove* (1979) and the *Great Sandy Island* (1998).

Appendix 2: Plays and Screenplays

The following checklist does not include those plays and screenplays written by White but never performed and now lost. David Marr refers to a number of lost works: 'Love's Awakening', written in 1923, White's second year at Tudor House; a play written by White after his arrival in London in July 1935; 'Juliana', based on *The Aspern Papers* and written during the war years; and 'Don Juan and Don Joan', written in Athens in early 1963. Two works – 'Monkey Puzzle', a screenplay written in 1977-78 and 'Last Words', a screenplay written in 1979 – were never produced, but are now known from scripts held in the State Library of New South Wales (ML MSS 7008), acquired from Sydney bookseller Nicholas Pounder in 2000.

Bread and Butter Women. Comedy in three acts

Composed: Oxford, c early 1933.　　　　Première: 23 January 1935.
Venue: Bryant's Playhouse, Sydney [St Peter's Church Hall, Darlinghurst].
Run: 7 weeks (one night per week).
Publication: Not published.　　　　Manuscript: Not extant.
Preview: *Sydney Sunday Sun and Guardian* 16 December 1934, Colour section p.2.
Reviews: *Playbox* March 1935, p.13; *Sydney Mail* 30 January 1935, p.17; *Sydney Morning Herald* 24 January 1935, p.8; *Smith's Weekly* 16 February 1935, p.23.
Notes: For a description of Beryl Bryant and Bryant's Playhouse, and the circumstances of the production of White's plays, see Marr p.131-132.

The School for Friends. Comedy in one act

Composed: c early 1937.　　　　Première: April 1937.
Venue: Bryant's Playhouse, Sydney [St Peter's Church Hall, Darlinghurst].
Run: 4 performances, 2 in April and two in June 1937.
Publication: Not published.　　　　Manuscript: Not extant.
Reviews: T.W. Whitelock *Everyone's* 9 June 1937, p.42.
Notes: For a description of Beryl Bryant and Bryant's Playhouse, and the circumstances of the production of White's plays, see Marr p.131-132.

Peter Plover's Party

Composed: c early 1937.　　　　Première: 26 January 1938.
Venue: Little Theatre, London.
Run: Ran for over 400 performances.
Publication: In: *Sketches from 'Nine Sharp'* (French's Acting Edition, no.1093), (London: Samuel French, 1938), pp.[41] 42-45. (See Joy Hooton 'A Patrick White

Sketch' *Australian Literary Studies* v.12 no.3, 1986, p.410); *Patrick White: Selected Writings* ed. Alan Lawson (1994), p.199-200.

Manuscript: Not extant.

Reviews: *Times* (London) 27 January 1938, p.10; *Punch* 16 February 1938, p.189; *Home* (Sydney) May 1938, p.82; *Sydney Morning Herald* 26 March 1938, p.6.

Notes: Short sketch in a popular and very successful revue, written by Herbert Farjeon with music by Walter Leigh and design by Hedley Briggs. Farjeon had seen White's sketch at the Arts Theatre Club and bought it for his revue (Marr p.167, after Ronald Waters' account. See also 'Copyright Reserved' which ran in September 1937 and was reviewed in *Sketch* 29 September 1937, p.626). 'It was one of the most exciting evenings I have spent. […] On the night I arrived at the theatre with my nose hanging on by a couple of shreds of red flesh and feeling as if I had dressed for a wake. But the moment I entered the theatre I knew this was going to be an evening, and it was – everything went with a swing – it is the most elegant revue I have seen, and I am sure it will be the talk of the town.' (To Pepé Mamblas, 27 January 1938)

Revivals: A note in French's Acting Edition gives the fee at 5s for each representation of the sketch. Even in the early 1950s, White was receiving some royalties on 'Peter Plover's Party' which was still popular in amateur revue (Marr p.273).

Return to Abyssinia. Comedy

Composed: 1939.   Première: March 1947.
Venue: Bolton's Theatre, London.   Run: 11-30 March 1947.

Publication: Not published, but for a synopsis see *The Story of Bolton's Theatre First Season* (London, 1947).

Manuscript: White wrote to Ingmar Björkstén (*Letters* 27 May 1973) that as far as he knew there was no extant copy of the play. J.R. Dyce in *Patrick White as Playwright* (St Lucia, Qld.: University of Queensland Press, 1974) details a very extensive but unsuccessful search for the manuscript of this play (pp.135-136).

Reviews: *Times* 13 March 1947, p.10; *Observer* 16 March 1947, p.2; *Stage* 13 March 1947, p.5; *What's On* 21 March 1947; *Daily Mail* 12 March 1947, p.3.

Notes: *Return to Abyssinia* was to have premièred at Bolton's Theatre in 1939, but the war began and the performance was cancelled. White had plans to sell the play in New York in early 1940. The 1947 production was a moderate success. (See *Australian Literary Studies*, vol.7 no.4, October 1976.)

La Grande Amoureuse

Composed: 1939.   Première: May 1940.
Publication: *Patrick White: Selected Writings* ed. Alan Lawson (1994), p.201-202.
Manuscript: See Appendix 7.

254

Notes: A sketch for the revue, *The Swinging Gate*. This work is only known from the copy in the Lord Chamberlain's Papers. The May 1940 première date may have been speculative as nothing further – venue, run, reviews – is known about this work.

The Ham Funeral. A Tragi-farce in two acts

Composed: Summer 1947. White had been influenced by William Dobell's painting, *The Dead Landlord*, painted in London before the war.
Première: 15 November 1961.
Company: Adelaide University Theatre Guild (in association with the Australian Elizabethan Theatre Trust).
Venue: University Union Hall.   Run: 15 to 25 November 1961.
Program: *The World Premiere of The Ham Funeral by Patrick White* (Adelaide, November 1961). pp.6. Contents include: 'About the play' by Patrick White; cast and credits; a programme for 1962; 'About the author' by Geoffrey Dutton; and 'About "The Dead Landlord"' by Bill Dobell. A poster was produced for the occasion, designed by 'Ostoja' [Kotkowski] after William Dobell's 'The Dead Landlord'; the poster measures 50.5 x 37.5 cm and is printed in black and red (ADFA: G22 Folio 1/1) – reproduced in J.R. Dyce *Patrick White as Playwright* (St Lucia, Qld.: University of Queensland Press, 1974), p.140.
Manuscript: See Appendix 7.
Publication: *Four Plays* (1965); *Collected Plays* (1985).
Translation: White, in a letter to Frederick Glover (19 March 1962), referred to a German translation of *The Ham Funeral* by Curt and Maria Prerauer, but this was apparently never performed and never published.
Reviews: H. Kippax, *Nation* (Sydney) 2 December 1961, p.18; *Bulletin* 25 November 1961, p.31; R. Covell *Sydney Morning Herald* 18 November 1961, p.11; M. Harris *Nation* (Sydney) 16 December 1961, p.18; H. Tidemann *Advertiser* (Adelaide) 16 November 1961, p.10; J.J. Bray *Meanjin* v.21, 1962, p.32-34.
Notes: Directed by John Tasker. Designed by S. Ostoja Kotkowski. See also John Tasker 'Notes on 'The Ham Funeral'' in *Meanjin* v.23, September 1964, p.299-302.

Revival
Opening: 6 July 1962.
Company: Australian Elizabethan Theatre Company.
Venue: Palace Theatre, Sydney.   Run: 2½ weeks.
Program: Program was sold by Nicholas Pounder in the mid-1990s.
Manuscript: See Appendix 7.
Reviews: *Sydney Morning Herald* 12 July 1962, p.6; N. Kessell *Sun* (Sydney) 12 July1962, p.34; *Mirror* (Sydney) 12 July1962, p.9; David McNicoll *Telegraph* (Sydney) 12 July1962, p.47; Nola Dekyvere *Sunday Telegraph* 15 July1962, p.51; H. Kip-

pax *Nation* (Sydney) 28 July1962, p.18.
Notes: Produced by John Tasker. Cast: Zoe Caldwell as The Girl.

Revival
Opening: October 1962.
Company: Twelfth Night Theatre Company (Brisbane).

Revival
Opening: June 1968.
Company: Rockhampton Little Theatre.

Revival
Company: Sydney Theatre Company.
Opening: 14 November 1989.   Venue: Wharf Theatre, Sydney.
Program: Program was sold by Nicholas Pounder in the mid-1990s.
Reviews: M. Prerauer *Weekend Australian* 11-12 November 1989, p.7; A. Bennie *Sydney Morning Herald* 11 November 1989, p.89.
Notes: Directed by Neil Armfield. Music by Carl Vine. Cast: Robyn Nevin, Max Cullen, Kerry Walker, Tyler Coppin. The production was considered to be a hit. For photographs of the cast see William Yang *Patrick White* (1995). ABC FM made a direct broadcast of this production on 28 November 1989 (see Ron Blair 'Vintage White' *24 Hours* November 1989, p.6-7).

The Season at Sarsaparilla. A Charade of suburbia in two acts

Composed: May-June 1961. Written in reaction to the rejection of *The Ham Funeral* by the Governors of the Adelaide Festival. 'My final reaction has been to sit down on May Day and start a new play, the first for fourteen years. The last two days it has been pouring out in almost an alarming way, and will probably shock more than the *Funeral*, as this one is purely Australian, and at the same time has burst right out of the prescribed four walls of Australian socialist realism.' (To Geoffrey Dutton, 2 May 1961)
Première: 14 September 1962.
Company: Adelaide University Theatre Guild.
Venue: University Union Hall.
Run: 14 to 22 September; eight nights and one matinée.
Program: *The World Premiere of "The Season at Sarsaparilla" by Patrick White* (Adelaide, September 1962). pp.6. Contents include: 'Patrick White' by Max Harris, the cast and production details, and Guild details; the title page includes a detail from a painting by John Brack. (Copies: NSL: Mitchell Library Q792.92/4)
Manuscript: See Appendix 7.
Publication: *Four Plays* (1965); *The Season at Sarsaparilla* (1984); *Collected Plays* (1985).

Translation: White, in a letter to Frederick Glover (19 March 1962), referred to a German translation of *The Season at Sarsaparilla* by Curt and Maria Prerauer, but this was apparently never performed and never published.

Reviews: H. Kippax *Nation* (Sydney) 22 September 1962, p.15-17; A.A. Phillips *Overland* no.25, Summer 1962-1963, p.33-34; David Bradley *Meanjin* v.21 no.4; 'Life in "Sarsaparilla"', *Australian Women's Weekly* 19 September 1962.

Notes: Directed by John Tasker. Cast: Zoe Caldwell. Set designed by Desmond Digby. The nine performances were attended by more than 4,000 people.

Revival

Company: Union Theatre Repertory Company.

Opening: 16 October 1962.

Venue: University Union Theatre.　　　　Run: 4 weeks.

Manuscript: See Appendix 7.

Program: *The University of Melbourne in association with The Australian Elizabethan Theatre Trust presents The Union Theatre Repertory Company [...] 114th Production "The Season at Sarsaparilla" by Patrick White* (Melbourne, October 1962). pp.16. Contents: title page; 'About the play' by John Sumner; 'About the playwright' by Chris Wallace-Crabbe; cast; staff of the company; 'Future plans'; and a membership application form.

Reviews: Geoffrey Hutton *Herald* (Melbourne) 19 October 1962; *Age* (Melbourne) 17 October 1962, Review p.5.

Notes: Directed by John Sumner. Cast: Zoe Caldwell. The production was a success, taking about £5,000 in the four weeks. For the Director's perspective see John Sumner *Recollections of Play: a Life in Australian Theatre* (Melbourne University Press, 1993), pp.136-139.

Revival

Opening: May 1963.　　　　Venue: Theatre Royal, Sydney.

Run: Five weeks.

Program: Program was sold by Nicholas Pounder in the mid-1990s. It contained a note by H.G. Kippax, and pictorial wrappers illustrated by cartoonist Les Tanner.

Reviews: Ron Saw and Frank Harris *Mirror* (Sydney) 23 May 1963; David McNicoll *Sunday Telegrah* (Sydney) 26 May and 7 July 1963; Harry Kippax *Nation* (Sydney) 1 June 1963, p.18-19.

Notes: Directed by John Tasker. Set designs by Desmond Digby. This production was a box office failure.

Revival

Company: Old Tote Theatre Company.　　　　Opening: 3 November 1976.

Venue: Drama Theatre, Sydney Opera House.

Program: Program and two handbills were sold by Nicholas Pounder in the mid-1990s.

Preview: Janet Hawley *Australian* (Sydney) 3 November 1976, p.10.
Reviews: John Tasker *Theatre Australia* November-December 1976, p.17; David Marr *Bulletin* 13 November 1976; Barry Lowe *National Times* 22-27 November 1976, p.48.
Notes: Directed by Jim Sharman. Designed by Wendy Dickson. Assistant director: Ian Tasker. Cast: Kate Fitzpatrick, Max Cullen, Bill Hunter, Robyn Nevin.

Revival
Opening: 1977.
Company: Twelfth Night Theatre Company (Brisbane).

Revival
White refused Knox Grammar School permission to perform *The Season at Sarsaparilla* because it was an amateur production. See *Sydney Morning Herald* 11 April 1981, p.3.

Revival
Company: State Theatre Company of South Australia.
Opening: 1984.
Venue: The Playhouse, Adelaide Festival Centre.
Notes: Directed by Neil Armfield. For photographs of the set for this production, see May-Brit Akerholt, *Patrick White* (Amsterdam: Rodopi, 1988).

Revival
Opening: 24 November 1984.
Venue: Playhouse (Arts Centre), Melbourne.
Notes: Directed by Neil Armfield. Designed by Stephen Curtis and Amanda Lovejoy.
Source: May-Brit Akerholt, *Patrick White* (Amsterdam: Rodopi, 1988).

Revival
Company: State Theatre Company of Western Australia.
Opening: 21 July 1992.
Venue: Hole in the Wall Theatre, Subiaco Theatre Centre.
Previews: Anglea Wellington *West Australian* 16 July 1992, p.36.
Run: 21 July to 15 August 1992.
Notes: Directed by Leith Taylor. Cast: Diane Jeffries, Andy King, Polly Low and Steven Shaw.

A Cheery Soul

Composed: May-July 1962. The play was based on a short story, for which see Appendix 3: Short Stories. Even as White wrote the short story he envisaged the actress Nita Pannell in the role of Miss Docker. In June 1962 he sent galley proofs of the story to Pannell in an effort to persuade her to do the role. The play was written in the winter of 1962. It was turned down by the Adelaide University Theatre Guild, but in November, when in Melbourne for *The Season at Sarsaparilla*, White convinced John Sumner to produce the play.

Première: 19 November 1963.

Company: The Union Theatre Repertory Company.

Venue: University Union Theatre.

Run: Four weeks.

Program: *The University of Melbourne in association with The Australian Elizabethan Theatre Trust presents The Union Theatre Repertory Company [...] 128th Production "A Cheery Soul" by Patrick White* (Melbourne, November 1963). pp.16. Contents: title page; 'About the playwright' by Chris Wallace-Crabbe; 'About the play' by John Sumner; cast; staff of the company; and a membership application form.

Manuscript: See Appendix 7.

Publication: *Four Plays* (1965).

Reviews: *Sun* (Melbourne) 20 November 1963, p.18; *Sydney Morning Herald* 20 November 1963, p.14; *Jewish Herald* 22 November 1963, p.15; *Age* (Melbourne) 21 November 1963, p.5; *Sunday Telegraph* (Sydney) 24 November 1963; J. Merralls *Nation* (Sydney) 25 January 1964, p.19-20; Keith Macartney *Meanjin* v.23, March 1964, p.93-95.

Notes: Directed by John Sumner. Set designs by Desmond Digby. The production was a box office failure, losing more than £4,000. White recalled in a letter to Ninette Dutton (11 February 1979) that on one night there were only seven people in the audience. Years later, John Sumner claimed that only about 2,500 attended, out of a possible 11,454. For the Director's perspective see John Sumner *Recollections of Play: a Life in Australian Theatre* (Melbourne University Press, 1993), pp.144-147.

Revival

Opening: 17 January 1979.

Company: Sydney Theatre Company.

Venue: Drama Theatre, Sydney Opera House.

Run: 17 January to 13 February 1979.

Manuscript: See Appendix 7.

Reviews: H. Kippax *Sydney Morning Herald* 19 January 1979, p.8.

Notes: Directed by Jim Sharman. Designed by: Brian Thompson. Costumes: Anna Senior. Cast: Robyn Nevin, Peter Carroll, Pat Bishop, Maggie Kirkpatrick et al. The production was a success, averaging 85% capacity audiences. For photographs of the set for this production, see May-Brit Akerholt, *Patrick White* (Amsterdam: Rodopi, 1988).

Revival
Opening: 4 June 1992.
Company: Royal Queensland Theatre Company.
Venue: Suncorp Theatre, Brisbane.   Run: 4 to 20 June 1992.
Reviews: Sue Gough *Bulletin* 23 June 1992, p.103-104; Des Partridge *Courier* (Brisbane) 5 June 1992, p.16.
Notes: Directed by Neil Armfield. Designer: Bill Haycock. Cast: Carole Skinner, Jennifer Flowers et al. This production was taken to the Adelaide Festival 1994.

Revival
Opening: 24 February 1994.
Company: Royal Queensland Theatre Company.
Venue: Her Majesty's Theatre, Adelaide.
Run: 24 February to 2 March 1994.
Program: *18th Biennial Adelaide Festival 1994.*
Reviews: Peter Goers *Advertiser* (Adelaide) 11 March 1994, p.12.

Revival
Opening: 7 May 1996.
Company: Melbourne Theatre Company.
Venue: The Playhouse, Victorian Arts Centre, Melbourne.
Run: Previewed on 3 May. Ran from 7 May to 1 June 1996.
Program: *Robyn Nevin as A Cheery Soul by Patrick White* (Melbourne Theatre Company, 1996). pp.24. Contents: cast and credits; notes about White, his contribution to Australian theatre, A Cheery Soul; and biographies.
Previews: Steven Carroll *Age* (Melbourne) Entertainment Guide 3 May 1996, p.12.
Reviews: *Sydney Morning Herald* 28 June 1996; Helen Thomson *Age* (Melbourne) 9 May 1996, p.A17.
Notes: Directed by Neil Armfield. Designer: Dale Ferguson. Composer: John Rodgers. Cast: Robyn Nevin as Miss Docker.

Night on Bald Mountain

Composed: Late 1962. White wrote the play between returning home from the Melbourne season of *The Season at Sarsaparilla* in November and Christmas 1962. 'The title deliberately pinched from Moussorgsky. If it comes off, it will be the first Australian tragedy.' (To Peggy Garland, 11 November 1962) Although considered for the Adelaide Festival 1962, it was eventually knocked back by the Governors. Again, it was staged by the University Theatre Guild.
Première: 9 March 1964.
Company: Adelaide University Guild Theatre.
Venue: University Union Hall.   Run: 9 to 26 March 1964.
Program: *The World Premiere of "Night on Bald Mountain" by Patrick White* (Adelaide,

March 1964). 1 folded sheet. (Copies: NSL: Mitchell Library Q792.92/5). A program and handbill are also held by the State Library of New South Wales (ML MSS 7290).

Publication: *Four Plays* (1965); *Collected Plays* (1985); *Night on Bald Mountain* (1996).

Translation: By Renate Völkner; had a season at the Stadltheater Hildesheim, c1980 (see *Letters* p.531).

Manuscript: See Appendix 7.

Reviews: M. Armstrong *Bulletin* (Sydney) 28 March 1964, p.43; P. Griffith *Advertiser* (Adelaide) 10 March 1964, p.6; H. Kippax *Nation* (Sydney) 21 March 1964, p.19; Roger Covell *Sydney Morning Herald* 11 March 1964, p.12; Martin Long *Telegraph* (Sydney) 11 March 1964, p.2; H.A. Standish *Herald* (Melbourne) 10 March 1964, p.14; Howard Palmer *Sun* (Melbourne) 11 March 1964, p.28; G. Dutton *Nation* (Sydney) 4 April 1964, p.15; Bryn Davies *Nation* (Sydney) 18 April 1964, p.17; Mary Finnin, 'Adelaide en Fête', *Twentieth Century* v.19, 1964, p.52-58; 'Culture in Australia – Adelaide's Festival', *Current Affairs Bulletin* v.33 no.12, 27 April 1964, p.182-186.

Notes: Directed by John Tasker. Cast: Nita Pannell, Joan Bruce, Alexander Archdale. Set designs by Wendy Dickson. The production was considered a success.

Revival

Venue: Stadltheater Hildesheim.

Translation: Renate Völkner.

Run: c1980

Notes: See *Letters*, p.531.

Revival

Opening: 8 June 1996.

Company: State Theatre Company of South Australia and Company B Belvoir.

Venue: The Playhouse, Adelaide Festival Centre.

Run: 8 to 29 June 1996.

Previews: J. Litson, 'Stage White' *Australian Magazine* 1-2 June 1996, p.18-21; T. Lloyd [Preview and interview with Neil Armfield] *The Advertiser* (Arts Monthly) June 1996, p.3.

Reviews: T. Lloyd *Advertiser* (Adelaide) 8 June 1996, p.9; Peter Ward *Australian* 11 June 1996, p.12.

Notes: Directed by Neil Armfield. Designed by Anna Borghesi. Music by Carl Vine. Cast: Ralph Cotterill, Essie Davis, Gillian Jones, Barry Otto, Keith Robinson, Steve Rodgers, Carole Skinner.

Revival

Opening: 6 July 1996.

Company: State Theatre Company of South Australia and Company B Belvoir.

Venue: Belvoir Street Theatre, Sydney.

Run: Previewed 5 July. Ran from 6 July to 4 August 1996.

Reviews: David Marr *Sydney Morning Herald* 9 July 1996, p.16; John McCallum *Weekend Australian* 13-14 July 1996.
Notes: Directed by Neil Armfield.

Big Toys: A Play in three acts

Composed: For the play's composition, production and reception see Q above.
Company: Old Tote Theatre Company.   Première: 27 July 1977.
Venue: Parade Theatre, Anzac Parade, Kensington.
Run: 27 July to 13 September 1977.
Program: Program and handbill were sold by Nicholas Pounder in the mid-1990s.
Publication: *Big Toys* (1978); *Collected Plays vol. 2* (1994).
Translation: By Ursula Grüzmacher-Tabori for the Staatstheater Saarbrücken season opening 7 September 1979 (See *Letters* p.531).
Manuscript: See Appendix 7.
Reviews: D. Malouf *Quadrant* September 1977, p.26-27; Dorothy Hewett *Theatre Australia* August 1977; K. Brisbane *National Times* 1-6 August 1977, p.26; H.G. Kippax *Sydney Morning Herald* 30 July 1977, p.6.
Notes: Directed by Jim Sharman. Set designed by Brian Thomson. Cast: Max Cullen, Arthur Dignam, Kate Fitzpatrick. For photographs of backstage festivities, see William Yang, *Patrick White: The Late Years* (Sydney: Macmillan, 1995). For photographs of the set for this production, see May-Brit Akerholt, *Patrick White* (Amsterdam: Rodopi, 1988).

Revival
Opening: 1 October 1977.
Company: Old Tote Theatre Company.
Venue: Comedy Theatre, Melbourne.
Run: 1 October to 5 November 1977.
Program: *Big Toys* (Melbourne, 1977). pp.[20].
Reviews: Sally White *Age* (Melbourne) 3 October 1977, p.2.
Note: 'I came to Melbourne yesterday for the opening of Big Toys … The theatre was full right up to the end of the Sydney run although a lot of people hated the play. Down here we are in a much larger theatre and Melbourne will not feel so involved with goings-on which are far more Sydney; it is impossible to tell how it will go. I heard a fair amount of teeth-sucking round me last night, even a few snores.' (To Shirley Hazzard and Francis Steegmuller, 2 October 1977)

Revival
Said to have been taken to Canberra at this time (see Marr p.576), but not confirmed.

Revival
In a letter to Elizabeth Falkenberg, dated 20 July 1978, White refers to a rehearsal of *Big Toys* in Brisbane (National Library of Australia, MS 8234) – not confirmed.

Revival
In a letter to Elizabeth Falkenberg, dated 20 July 1978, White refers to a performance of *Big Toys* at the English Theatre in Vienna (National Library of Australia, MS 8234) – not confirmed.

Revival
In a letter to Elizabeth Falkenberg, dated 6 April 1980, White refers to a performance of *Big Toys* at Saarbrücken as being 'received with polite applause' (National Library of Australia, MS 8234) – not confirmed.

Television
Screening: Produced for the ABC TV's Australian Theatre Festival and broadcast at 8.30pm on 24 August 1980.
Previews: Jane McCredie *Age* (Melbourne) 21 August 1980, Green Guide p.3; Brian Courtis *Age* (Melbourne) 22 August 1980, p.2.
Reviews: Dennis Prior *Age* (Melbourne) 29 August 1980.
Notes: Directed by Chris Thompson. Set designs by Quentin Hole. Cast: Diane Cilento, Max Cullen, John Gaden.

Revival
Opening: 1 June 1993.
Company: Playbox Theatre Centre (Melbourne).
Venue: Merlyn Theatre, The C.U.B. Malthouse.
Run: 1 to 19 June 1993. Throughout June 1993 this production went on tour to Geelong, Ballarat, Monash University (Frankston and Clayton campuses), and Warragul.
Program: *Big Toys* (1993). pp.[12]. There is also a small poster issued for this production.
Reviews: M. Robertson *Age* (Melbourne) 12 June 1993, Saturday Extra p.11; L. Radic *Age* (Melbourne) 4 June; H. Thomson *Australian* 4 June 1993; F. Scott-Newman *Bulletin* 29 June 1993.
Notes: Directed by Malcolm Robertson. Cast: Julie Nihill, Geoff Paine, Carillo Gantner.

The Night the Prowler [film]

Première: 2 June 1978.   Venue: State Theatre, Sydney
Manuscript: See Appendix 7.
Publication: *The Night the Prowler* (1978).
Preview: L. Scott *Sydney Morning Herald* 2 June 1978, p.4.

Reviews: Martha DuBose *Sydney Morning Herald* 5 June 1978, p.7; Geraldine Pascall, *Australian* 5 June 1978, p.8.

Notes: Based on a short story published in *The Cockatoos* (1974). Screenplay by Patrick White. Directed by Jim Sharman. Cinematography by David Sanderson. Designs by Luciana Arrighi. Premièred at the 25th Sydney Film Festival. The total budget was $420,000, of which the New South Wales Film Corporation invested $350,000.

Signal Driver. A Morality play for the times

Composed: For the play's composition, production and reception see T above.
Company: Lighthouse. The State Theatre Company of South Australia.
Première: 5 March 1982.
Venue: Festival Centre Playhouse, Adelaide.
Run: 5, 6 and 15-20 March 1982.
Program: Programme for the *Adelaide Festival 5-21. Mar. 82* describes the production of *Signal Driver* on p.10. The play programme (1 folded sheet ([7] p.), illust., 21 cm), held at NSL: Mitchell Library (Call no. Q822.914/W587/1). A poster was sold by Nicholas Pounder in the mid-1990s.
Publication: *Signal Driver* (1983); *Collected Plays vol. 2* (1994).
Reviews: Brian Kiernan *Sydney Morning Herald* 6 March 1982, p.46; P. Ward *Australian* 8 March 1982; H.G. Kippax *Sydney Morning Herald* 8 March 1982, p.41.
Notes: Directed by Neil Armfield. Set designs by Stephen Curtis. Music by Carl Vine. Cast: Peter Cummins, Kerry Walker, John Wood, Melissa Jaffer. For photographs of backstage festivities see William Yang, *Patrick White* (1995). For photographs of the set for this production, see May-Brit Akerholt, *Patrick White* (Amsterdam: Rodopi, 1988).

Revival
Opening: August 1983.
Company: Queensland Theatre Company.   Venue: S.G.I.O. Theatre, Brisbane.
Program: Not seen, but see entry in Nicholas Pounder *Catalogue* #897 for a programme of 8 pp.
Notes: Directed by Neil Armfield. Set designs by Mike Bridges. Cast: George Spartels, Sheila Bradley, Elizabeth Alexander, Errol O'Neill.

Revival
Opening: Previews on 9, 10 and 12 September 1983. Opening night 13 September 1983.
Company: Melbourne Theatre Company in association with The Queensland Theatre Company.
Venue: Athenaeum Theatre, Melbourne.
Run: 9 September to 15 October 1983.

Program: *Signal Driver by Patrick White* (Melbourne, 1983). pp.20. Contents: MTC Board of Management; Queensland Theatre Company; the author; photographs from the Queensland Theatre Company production, 1983; cast; biographies; MTC staff; coming attractions; sponsor acknowledgments.
Reviews: Leonard Radic *Age* (Melbourne) 15 September 1983, p.14.
Notes: Produced by Neil Armfield. Set designs by Mike Bridges. Music by Carl Vine. Cast: Elizabeth Alexander, Errol O'Neill, Sheila Bradley and George Spartels. For photographs of the set for this production, see May-Brit Akerholt, *Patrick White* (Amsterdam: Rodopi, 1988).

Revival
Opening: 25 May 1985.
Company: Company B, Belvoir Street Theatre.
Venue: Belvoir Street Theatre, Sydney.
Run: 25 May to 23 June 1985.
Program: Program and three-colour poster (100 x 74 cms) designed by Martin Sharp were sold by Nicholas Pounder in the mid-1990s.
Reviews: H. Kippax *Sydney Morning Herald* 27 May 1985, p.10.
Notes: Directed by Neil Armfield. Set designs by Stephen Curtis. Music by Carl Vine. Cast: Richard Healey, Val Levkowicz, John Gaden, Kerry Walker. For photographs of the set for this production, see May-Brit Akerholt, *Patrick White* (Amsterdam: Rodopi, 1988). Considered not to have been a success.

Revival
Opening: 1985(?)
Company: [Perth Festival] – not confirmed.

Netherwood

Composed: For the play's composition, production and reception see U above.
Company: Lighthouse. The State Theatre Company of South Australia.
Première: 11 June 1983.
Venue: The Playhouse, Adelaide Festival Centre.
Publication: *Netherwood* (1983); *Collected Plays vol. 2* (1994). A handbill was sold by Nicholas Pounder in the mid-1990s.
Reviews: P. Farrell *Advertiser* (Adelaide) 13 June 1983; M. Morley *National Times* 17 June 1983; H.G. Kippax *Sydney Morning Herald* 14 June 1983; P. Ward *Australian* 13 June 1983.
Notes: Directed by Jim Sharman. Set designs by Ken Wilby. Musical direction by Alan John. For photographs of the set for this production, see May-Brit Akerholt, *Patrick White* (Amsterdam: Rodopi, 1988).

Revival
Opening: 1984.
Company: Lighthouse Company.   Venue: Seymour Centre, Sydney.
Reviews: J. Moses *Australian* 23 January 1984.
Notes: Directed by Neil Armfield. For photographs of backstage festivities see William Yang *Patrick White* (1995).

Shepherd on the Rocks

Composed: May 1985 to early 1987. 'A couple of days ago I had an idea for another play drop into my head from the past – a Thirties Scandal which I shall have to set in Australia to avoid trouble.' (To Elizabeth Falkenberg, 1 June 1985) Originally titled *The Budgiwank Experiment, Shepherd on the Rocks* is loosely based on the remarkable story of the Rev. Harold Davidson, who was defrocked for his questionable missionary activities; see Alan Jenkins, *The Thirties* (London, 1976). By the end of January 1986, the play was almost finished: 'I am stuck in the last scene. It will come with a rush eventually'. (To Grahame C. Greene, 14 February 1986) The play was accepted for the Adelaide Festival 1987. White attended rehearsals in April 1987 and returned for the opening night. 'Shepherd on the Rocks brought in the public. As far as I am concerned, it was a great success: design, music, acting, direction all that I could have wished.' (To Moya Henderson, 10 June 1987)
Première: 9 May 1987.
Company: State Theatre Company of South Australia.
Venue: Playhouse, Adelaide.
Program: Program was sold by Nicholas Pounder in the mid-1990s.
Publication: *Collected Plays vol. 2* (1994).
Reviews: J. Waites *Advertiser* (Adelaide) 2 May 1987, p.1; S. Harris *Advertiser* (Adelaide) 11 May 1987; Ken Healey *Sydney Morning Herald* 12 May 1987; M. Bramwell *The Adelaide Review* no.39, June 1987, p.12+; B. Hoad *Bulletin* 19 May 1987; H. Musa *Canberra Times* 10 April 1987; P. Ward *Australian* 11 May 1987.
Notes: Directed by Neil Armfield. Set designs by Brian Thompson. Music by Carl Vine. Considered but not produced by the Sydney Theatre Company's 1989 season; see Martin Portus, 'The Victims of a Messiah Complex' *Sydney Morning Herald* 30 April 1989, p.74.

Appendix 3: Short Stories

'The Twitching Colonel'
Composed: London, winter 1936-1937.
First published: *London Mercury* 35, April 1937, p.602-609.
Later published: *Patrick White: Selected Writings* ed. Alan Lawson (1994), p.3-10.

'Cocotte'
Composed: Not known.
First published: *Horizon: A Review of Literature and Art* 1(5), May 1940, p.364-366.

'After Alep'
Composed: Before November 1944.
First published: *Bugle Blast: An Anthology from the Services* Third series, ed. Jack Aistrop and Reginald Moore (London, 1945), p.147-155.

'On the Balcony'
Composed: Athens, 1945.
First Published: *Harper's Bazaar* August 1957, p.112, 166, 168-169.
Later published: *Patrick White: Selected Writings* ed. Alan Lawson (1994), p.123-133.

'Being Kind to Titina'
Composed: January 1962.
First published: *Meanjin* v.21 no.1, March 1962, p.5-19.
Review: J.F. Burrows, 'The Short Stories of Patrick White' *Southerly* v.24 no.2, 1964, p.116-125; Clement Semmler, 'Sarsaparilla in Soloferno' *Australian Book Review* v.1 no.8, June 1962, p.94-95.

Later published: *The Burnt Ones* (1964).
Comments: This story was also offered in the United States and was being considered by *Harper's Bazaar*; White withdrew the story after the *New Yorker* made substantial editorial changes to 'Miss Slattery and Her Demon Lover'.

'A Cheery Soul'
Composed: By May 1962.
First published: *London Magazine* v.2 no.6, September 1962, p.6-36; *A Cheery Soul and Other Stories* (1973) (See I.t2a).
Review: J.F. Burrows, 'The Short Stories of Patrick White' *Southerly* v.24 no.2, 1964, p.116-125.
Later published: *The Burnt Ones* (1964).
Translation: [German] *Eine Seele von Mensch* trans. Reinhild Boehnke (Frankfurt am Main, 1991). pp.76. ISBN 3-596-10710-5. DM 9.80. (Fischer-Taschenbücher, 10710) (See I.t9).
Comments: The whole issue of *London Magazine* in which White's story appeared was devoted to Australian art and literature.

'The Letters'
Composed: By June 1962.
First Published: *Quadrant* v.6 no.2, April 1962, p.5-17.
Review: J.F. Burrows, 'The Short Stories of Patrick White' *Southerly* v.24 no.2, 1964, p.116-125; Clement Semmler, 'Sarsaparilla in Soloferno'

Australian Book Review v.1 no.8, June 1962, p.94-95.
Later published: *A Century of Australian Short Stories* ed. Cecil Hadgraft and Richard Wilson (Melbourne, 1963), p.312-325; *Voices* ed. Robert Rubens (London, 1963), p.242-260; *The Burnt Ones* (1964); *The Illustrated Treasury of Australian Stories* selected by Geoffrey Dutton (Melbourne, 1986), p.141-152.
Translation: [Chinese] *Shijie Wenxue* [*World Literature*] v.3, 1982, p.77-94. Translated by Hu Wen-chung.

'The Woman Who Wasn't Allowed to Keep Cats'
Composed: December 1962.
First published: *Australian Letters* v.5 no.2, December 1962, p.30-57.
Review: J.F. Burrows, 'The Short Stories of Patrick White' *Southerly* v.24 no.2, 1964, p.116-125.
Later published: *The Burnt Ones* (1964).

'Willy Wagtails at Midnight'
Composed: c January 1962.
First published: *Australian Letters* v.4 no.3, March 1962, p.35-43.
Reviews: J.F. Burrows, 'The Short Stories of Patrick White' *Southerly* v.24 no.2, 1964, p.116-125; Clement Semmler, 'Sarsaparilla in Soloferno' *Australian Book Review* v.1 no.8, June 1962, p.94-95.
Later published: *The Burnt Ones* (1964); *The Vital Decade: Ten Years of Australian Art and Letters* selected by Geoffrey Dutton and Max Harris (Melbourne, 1968), p.214-220; *A Cheery Soul and Other Stories* (1973) (See I.t2a-b); *Modern Stories in English*

ed. W.H. New and H.J. Rosengarten (New York, 1975); *The Treasury of English Short Stories* ed. N. Sullivan (Garden City, NY, 1985); *Prose Writing for Australians: An Anthology of Feature Articles and Short Stories* ed. Alan Mahar and John Powers (Melbourne, 1985), p.268-277; *Relations: Australian Short Stories* ed. Carmel Bird (Wantirna South, Vic., 1991), p.112-122 – published in the United States as *Australian Short Stories* (Boston, 1991); *Patrick White: Selected Writings* ed. Alan Lawson (1994), p.134-144.
Translation: [Hungarian] *Nagyvilág* v.2, 1966, p.179-185 (trans. Éva Zentai); [German] 'Wippsterze im Mondenlicht' in: *Australien Erzählt* ed. Volker Wolf, trans. Joachim Kalka (Frankfurt am Main: Fischer Taschenbüch Verlag, 1991), p.155-169.

'Clay'
Composed: October 1962.
First published: *Overland* v.26, April 1963, p.5-13.
Review: J.F. Burrows, 'The Short Stories of Patrick White' *Southerly* v.24 no.2, 1964, p.116-125.
Later published: *London Magazine* v.3 no.4, July 1963, p.6-23; *The Burnt Ones* (1964); *Australian Writing Today* ed. Charles Higham (Harmondsworth, 1968), p.108-128; *Classic Australian Short Stories* comp. J. Waten and S. Murray-Smith (Melbourne, 1974), p.216-234; *The Faber Book of Contemporary Australian Short Stories* ed. Murray Bail (London, 1988), p.118-138; *Patrick White: Selected Writings* ed. Alan Lawson (1994),

p.11-29; *The Oxford Book of Australian Short Stories* selected by Michael Wilding (Melbourne, 1994), p.135-151 – reprinted in paperback 1995.
Translation: [Arabic] [*Foreign Literature*] v.1 no.6, July 1979, p.111-137 (trans. by Mahmoud Fallaha); [Hungarian] in: *Jelzötuuz az* no.20, 1988 (trans. by Hanha Udvarhelyi).

'Dead Roses'
Composed: January to November 1963.
First published: *The Burnt Ones* (1964).
Later published: *An Australian Selection* comp. J. Barnes (Sydney, 1974), p.215-275.
Translation: [German] *Welke Rosen: Erzaehlung* trans. Reinhard Kaiser (Frankfurt am Main: S. Fischer, 1995). pp.110. ISBN 3-10-091205-5. DM 20.00; [Chinese] *Shijie Wenxue* [*World Literature*] no.3, 1982, p.4-77 (trans. Hu Wen-chung).
Comments: Based on events at a house party at the Duttons' Kangaroo Island property held in December 1962.

'A Glass of Tea'
Composed: Mid-1962.
First published: *The Burnt Ones* (1964).
Later published: *Short Stories of Australia: The Moderns* ed. Beatrice Davis (Sydney, 1967), p.260-281; *An Australian Selection* comp. J. Barnes (Sydney, 1974), p.193-214.
Translation: [Chinese] *Waiguo Wenxue* [*Foreign Languages*] no.4, 1982, p.17-28; [Hungarian] in: *Jelzötüz az éjszakában, XX Századi Ausz-*

trál Elbeszélök (Budapest: Európan Könyvkiadó, 1988), p.181-212.

'The Evening at Sissy Kamara's'
Composed: Early 1963.
First published: *The Burnt Ones* (1964).
Later published: *London Magazine* v.4 no.3, June 1965, p. 5-18.
Comments: In the 'Acknowledgments' in *The Burnt Ones*, White acknowledges permission from the *London Magazine* to publish this story, suggesting that the story had been accepted by the magazine before the collection had been accepted by Eyre & Spottiswoode.

'Miss Slattery and Her Demon Lover'
Composed: By January 1963.
First published: *Australian Letters* v.5 no.3, April 1963, p.27-37.
Review: J.F. Burrows, 'The Short Stories of Patrick White' *Southerly* v.24 no.2, 1964, p.116-125.
Later published: *London Magazine* v.3 no.8, November 1963, p.7-21; *The Burnt Ones* (1964); *The Vital Decade: Ten Years of Australian Art and Letters* selected by Geoffrey Dutton and Max Harris (Melbourne, 1968), p.221-229; *Australian Writing Today* ed. Charles Higham (Harmondsworth, 1968), p.91-107; *The Penguin Best Australian Short Stories* ed. Mary Lord (Melbourne, 1991), p.195-211; *Patrick White: Selected Writings* ed. Alan Lawson (1994), p.144-160; *Australian Love Stories* ed. Kerryn Goldsworthy (Melbourne, 1996), p.162-179.
Translation: [German] in: *Air Mail from Down Under / Zeitgenössische Literatur Australiens. The Ozlit Collection.*

Vol.1 Short Stories ed. Rudi Kraussman and Michael Wilding (Vienna, Sydney: Gangan Books, 1990), p.124-144 (trans. Olaf Reinhardt).
Comments: This story was also accepted by the *New Yorker*, but White withdrew it after heavy editorial intervention.

'Down at the Dump'
Composed: Early 1963.
First published: *Meanjin* v.22 no.2, June 1963, p.153-179.
Review: J.F. Burrows, 'The Short Stories of Patrick White' *Southerly* v.24 no.2, 1964, p.116-125.
Later published: *The Burnt Ones* (1964); *Modern Australian Writing* ed. Geoffrey Dutton (London, 1966), p.37-71 – reprinted in 1967 and also available in Braille; *On Native Grounds* ed. C.B. Christesen (Sydney, 1969), p.247-269; *Commonwealth Short Stories* ed. Anne Rutherford and Donald Hannah (London, 1971), p.13-40; *The Faber Book of Contemporary Australian Short Stories* ed. Murray Bail (London, 1988), p.87-117; *The Penguin Book of Australian Short Stories* ed. Harry Heseltine (Ringwood, Vic., 1976), p.190-219 – reprinted 1978, 1980 and also available as a sound recording and in Braille; republished by the Penguin Group as *Favourite Australian Short Stories* (Melbourne, 1995); *Australian Short Stories* selected by Kerryn Goldsworthy (Melbourne, 1983), p.230-259 – reprinted 1986 and re-issued 1989 by Houghton-Mifflin Australia, and reprinted 1990, and republished by Jacaranda Wiley Ltd 1992; *The Australian Short Story* ed. Laurie Hergenhan (St Lucia, Qld,

1986), p.164-191 – reprinted 1987, 1989, second edition 1992.
Translation: [German] *Down at the Dump / Drunten auf der Muellkippe* trans. Hilary Heltay (Stuttgart: Reclam, 1975). pp.103. ISBN 3-15-009808-4. DM 1.60; [Japanese] [*Australian Literature, Short Story Masterpieces*] (Tokyo: The Simul Press, 1982), p.182-222 (trans. by Miki Hiramatsu).
Comments: White made some minor changes at the request of Clem Christesen; the original text was restored in *The Burnt Ones* (1964).

'A Woman's Hand'
Composed: Mid-1965.
First published: *Australian Letters* v.7 no.3, August 1966, p.13-40.
Later published: *Winter's Tales 13* ed. A.D. Maclean (London, 1967), p.154-240; *The Cockatoos* (1974); *Best for Winter: A Selection from Twenty-Five Years of Winter's Tales* ed. A.D. Maclean (New York, 1979); *A Woman's Hand* (illust. by Judy Deykin). Large print edition. (Lewes, Sussex: Large Print Books, 1987). pp.179. ISBN 1 85 290005 9. Published in the United States in 1989 by Guild Quality Large Print; price: US$19.95; *Patrick White: Selected Writings* ed. Alan Lawson (1994), p.30-119.
Translation: [Russian] *Zhenskaia Vuka* (Moscow: Izvestica, 1986) (trans. R. Oblonskoi).
Reviews: G. Lehmann, 'A Flight of Peacocks', *Bulletin* (Sydney) v.88, 15 October 1966, p.57 (1210w).

Appendix Three – Short Stories

'The Full Belly'
Composed: Mid-1966.
First published: *Coast to Coast 1965-66* ed. Clement Semmler (Sydney, 1966), p.225-242.
Later published: *We Took Our Orders and Are Dead* ed. Shirley Cass and others (Sydney, 1971), p.196-223; *The Cockatoos* (1974).
Reviews: G. Lehmann, 'Sex and Sunday suits', *Bulletin* v.89, 21 January 1967, p.29; M. Wilding, [Review of *Coast to Coast, 1965-1966*] *London Magazine* v.7 no.3, 1967, p.122.

'The Night the Prowler'
Composed: While travelling in Europe, mid-1968.
First published: *The Cockatoos* (1974).
Translation: [Estonian] 'Hiilija öö', *Loomingu Raamatukogu* v.2 no.3, 1979 (trans. by Enn Soosar).

'Five-Twenty'
Composed: Mid-1967.
First published: *Southerly* v.28 no.1, 1968, p.3-25.
Later Published: *Coast to Coast 1967-68* ed. A.A. Phillips (Sydney, 1968), p.103-123; *The Cockatoos* (1974); *Oxford Book of Short Stories* ed. V.S. Pritchett (Oxford, 1981) – an American edition was also published in 1981, reprinted in 1988, and also available in Braille and as a sound recording; *The Art of the Tale: An International Anthology of Short Stories 1945-1985* ed. Daniel Halpern (New York, 1986), p.756-773 – reprinted by Penguin in paperback in 1987.
Translation: [Japanese] [Anthology of Twentieth-Century Writers] (Tokyo: Shueisha, 1990), p.1265-1290. ISBN 4-08-129005-9.

'Sicilian Vespers'
Composed: While travelling in Europe, October 1971.
First published: *The Cockatoos* (1974).

'The Cockatoos'
Composed: Early 1974.
First published: *The Cockatoos* (1974).
Later published: *The Arbor House Treasury of Nobel Prize Winners* ed. M.H. Greenburg and C.G. Waugh (New York, 1983).
Translation: [Estonian] 'Hiilija öö', *Loomingu Raamatukogu* v.2 no.3, 1979 (trans. by Enn Soosar).

'Fête Galante'
Composed: While travelling in Europe, September 1976.
First published: *Meanjin* v.36, 1977, p.3-24.
Later published: *Patrick White: Selected Writings* ed. Alan Lawson (1994), p.161-182.

Appendix 4: Musical Adaptations

During the early 1960s Patrick White was experimenting with a number of different literary forms, including plays, poetry, short stories, and even a screenplay entitled 'Triple Sec'. He was also interested in having his words set to music, either as opera or song.

Late in 1963, the Elizabethan Theatre Trust commissioned composer Peter Sculthorpe to write an opera using a libretto by Patrick White. White and Sculthorpe collaborated for a short period of time on a work about Eliza Fraser, the 1836 castaway after whom Fraser Island is named. Eventually, the collaboration broke down but not before White had given Sculthorpe a number of poetical sketches, including 'Six Urban Songs', later set to music by Moya Henderson, as well as work related to the Fraser story (see Appendix 1 above).

Again, early in the 1980s and apparently motivated by the imminent public performance of the opera Voss, White again toyed with the idea of writing a libretto. He completed a lengthy sketch for a work entitled 'Births, deaths and lotteries', but a number of composers shied away from the collaboration with White. Carl Vine, however, who had written the music for a number of White's plays, did set White's sketch to music in his *Aria* (1984). For a surviving typescript of White's sketch see Appendix 7 MS/17.

CONYNGHAM, Barry

From Voss

London: Universal Edition, [1980].
Score, 11 pages, 23.0 x 31.0 cm.
11 minutes.
From Voss is taken from a larger work for orchestra, solo female voice, piano, trombone, viola, harp, cor anglais, percussion and cello.

HENDERSON, Moya

Six Urban Songs

a) Sydney: Australian Music Centre, 1983.
Score, 72 pages.
Mezzo soprano and orchestra.
25 minutes.
Note: 'dedicated to Patrick White in honour of his 70th birthday'. Performed by the Sydeny Symphony Orchestra on 12, 14 and 15 April 1986. The six songs include

'Night and Dreams', 'Song of the Housewives', 'To Watch the River', 'Rhinestones', 'Sick Song' and 'God'.

b) Sydney: Australian Music Centre, 1985.
Score, 36 pages.
Mezzo soprano and piano.

VINE, Carl

Aria

Sydney: Australian Music Centre, 1984.
Score, 27 leaves, 30.0 x 43.0 cm.
Reprinted: London: Chester Music, 1988.
The text for *Aria* was written by Patrick White c1982 as an experiment for a larger operatic collaboration, entitled 'Births, deaths and lotteries'. The work was commissioned by Flederman and written for that group with the English soprano, Jane Manning, to whom the work is dedicated. *Aria* was last performed by Jane Manning and Flederman at the BBC Late Night Proms Concerts in 1988. For the above information and a complete copy of the libretto, see Carl Vine's website at www.carlvine.au.nu, sighted 20 March 2004.

Richard MEALE

Voss (opera)

1. Performance

a) Adelaide: Festival Theatre, 1982.
A fragment from Richard Meale's *Voss* (Garden Scene from Act I) was performed by the Sydney Symphony Orchestra (Conductor: Ronald Zollman) at the Festival Theatre on the night of 6 March 1982 as part of the Adelaide Festival. See Festival *Programme* p.95-97. Previewed in the *Sydney Morning Herald* 1 March 1986, p.3.

b) Adelaide: Festival Theatre, 1986.
Richard Meale's *Voss* premièred on 1 March 1986 at the Festival Theatre during the Adelaide Festival. Subsequent performances were on 3, 6 and 8 March. It was performed by the Adelaide Symphony Orchestra (Conductor: Stuart Challender) with a cast of Geoffrey Chard, Marilyn Richardson, and principal artists from the Australian Opera. The opera was directed by Jim Sharman, designed by Luciana Arrighi, and with libretto by David Malouf. Duration was approx. 3 hours, including intervals. (See: *1986 Adelaide Festival 1-23 March [Programme]*, p.6-7). A performance program has not been sighted, but one was sold by Nicholas Pounder, Sydney, in the mid-1990s. Reviewed by J. Carmody *National Times* 7-13 March 1986.

c) Sydney: Opera House, June 1986.
Richard Meale's *Voss* opened the Sydney Opera House's 1986 winter season. It premièred on 5 June 1986, with subsequent performances on 7, 12, 18, 21, 23, 26 and 28 (matinee) June. It was performed by the Sydney Symphony Orchestra (Conductor: Stuart Challender) with a cast of Geoffrey Chard, Marilyn Richardson, and principal artists from the Australian Opera. The opera was directed by Jim Sharman, designed by Brian Thomson (sets) and Luciana Arrighi (costumes), choreography by Chrissie Koltai, and with libretto by David Malouf. Duration was approx. 3 hours, including intervals. Previewed (with interview with Jim Sharman) in *Sydney Morning Herald* 31 May 1986, p.48. Reviews: Roger Covell *Sydney Morning Herald* 7 June 1986; J. Carmody *National Times* 13-19 June 1986, p.31; Maria Prerauer *Australian* 9 June 1986, p.10; J. Sykes *24 Hours* v.11 no.2, 1986, p.12-14; R. Aldritch *Campaign Australian* no.127, 1986, p.38-39.

d) Melbourne: Victorian Arts Centre, March 1987.
Richard Meale's *Voss* opened in Melbourne at the State Theatre on 14 March 1987. Previewed (with interviews with Jim Sharman and Richard Meale) in the *Age* 14 March 1987, Saturday Extra, p.9.

e) Sydney: Opera House, October 1990.
Opened 8 October 1990. Performed by the Sydney Symphony Orchestra (Conductor: Dobbs Franks) with a cast of Eilene Hanna, Christopher Doig, and artists from the Australian Opera. Directed by Jim Sharman, rehearsed by Brian Fitzgerald, designed by Brian Thomson (sets) and Luciana Arrighi (costumes). An opera program was sold by Nicholas Pounder, Sydney, in the mid-1990s. Reviews: Maria Prerauer *Australian* 10 October 1990, p.12; Brian Hoad *Bulletin* 23 October 1990, p.111; Fred Blanks *Sydney Morning Herald* 10 October 1990, p.14; Kames Waites *The Sydney Review* no.26, November 1990, p.16.

2. Score
Sydney: Australian Music Centre, [1987].
Voss: opera in two acts from the novel by Patrick White. Libretto by David Malouf. Music by Richard Meale. (Sydney: Australian Music Centre, [1987]). Facsimile of the composer's score.

3. Sound recording
Sydney: Philips, 1987.
Front: [in white] 'PHILIPS | [in gold] Digital Classics | *RICHARD MEALE* | [painted] *VOSS* | *GEOFFREY CHARD* • *MARILYN RICHARDSON* | [rule] | *THE AUSTRALIAN OPERA CHORUS* | *SYDNEY SYMPHONY ORCHESTRA* | [rule] | *STUART CHALLENDER* | *SPONSORED BY* | ANZ Group | *WORLD PREMIERE RECORDING*'.

Box (32 x 32 x 2.5 cm) containing 2 x 12-inch sound disks (125 minutes): 33 1/3 rpm, stereo. This recording is also available in compact disk and audiocasette tape.
Reviews: 'The Transformation of Voss – now music has been made of it' *This Australia* Summer 1987p.67-68.
Notes: Recorded in the Sydney studios of the ABC, November 1986 to January 1987. Libretto by David Malouf from the novel by Patrick White. Performers include Stuart Challender (conductor), The Sydney Symphony Orchestra, The Australian Opera Chorus, Geoffrey Chard and Marilyn Richardson. For a description of the recording sessions see Andrew Saw, *Sydney Morning Herald* 2 December 1986, p.18.

4. Video recording
Sydney: The Australian Opera in association with the Australian Broadcasting Commission, 1988.
Front: [in white] [logo] 'ABC [at right:] VIDEO ARTS | THE AUSTRALIAN OPERA [at right:] Stereo | [painted] Voss | [in red] [at right] by RICHARD MEALE | from the novel by | PATRICK WHITE | Libretto by | DAVID MALOUF | Conducted by | STUART CHALLENDER | [in white in red box:] WORLD PREMIERE | VIDEO RECORDING | FOR GENERAL EXHIBITION'. Back: [logo] 'ABC | [at right] VIDEO ARTS | [at right:] Stereo | THE AUSTRALIAN OPERA • ESSO NIGHT AT THE OPERA | [quotation of two lines from] The Bulletin | [quotation of two lines from] The Australian | Featuring: | GEOFFREY CHARD and MARILYN RICHARDSON | Conductor | STUART CHALLENDER | Director | JIM SHARMAN | STATE ORCHESTRA OF VICTORIA | PRODUCED FOR TELEVISION IN ASSOCIATION WITH THE AUSTRALIAN | BROADCASTING CORPORATION | Executive Producer and Director: Peter Butler | Sound Producer: David Harvey | Duration: Approx. 120 minutes | Recorded live at the Victorian Arts Centre, March 26, 1987 | © The Australian Opera 1990'.
1 videocassette (VHS). Approx. 120 minutes. Leaflet.
Notes: Opera in two acts. Sung in English with English subtitles. This video recording has been re-released several times: (Melbourne: ABC, [1988]); (Sydney: CEL Arts, [1988]); (Sydney: ABC Video, [1991]).

SPIERS, Colin

The Day of Death and Dreams

Sydney: Australian Music Centre, 1989.
Score, 35 pages.
Tenor and piano.
18 minutes 30 seconds.
Notes: Words by Patrick White, from *The Tree of Man*.

WOOD, Steve
The Tree of Man
Sydney: Australian Music Centre, 2002.
Score, 5 pages.
Tenor and piano.
3 minutes.
Notes: Words by Patrick White and Steve Wood.

Appendix 5: Miscellaneous Writings

Patrick White's miscellaneous and occasional pieces numbers only a few more than one hundred separate items. This is a very small number for a modern author, indicative of the fact that White was a wealthy man independent of his literary success, thus allowing him some freedom from the need to rely on a secondary income from the frequent publication of short pieces.

The following reference numbering system indicates the miscellaneous nature of the piece, the year of publication, and a running number within that year.

Misc 1922/1. [Letter] *Sunday Times* (Sydney) 29 January 1922.

Misc 1922/2. [Letter] *Sunday Times* (Sydney) 22 October 1922.

Misc 1924/1. 'The Tramp' *The Tudorian* 1924.

Misc 1941/1. [Letter to 'Andrea'] *Sydney Sun and Guardian* 10 August 1941, p.18.

Misc 1942/1. 'The Sewing Machine of Tobruk' *Australia* 1 January 1942, p.65.

Misc 1942/2. Stanley Kunitz and Howard Haycraft (eds.), 'Patrick White' [Interview]. In: *Twentieth Century Authors* (New York, 1942), p.1509-1510.

Misc 1945/1. 'Across the Wire' [A special report by White] (1945). Public Record Office AIR 20/5845 123974 (Marr p.677).

Misc 1946/1. [Letter] *Sydney Morning Herald* 30 October 1946. Reprinted in *Letters* (1994).

Misc 1955/1. S.J. Kunitz and V. Colby (eds.), 'Patrick White' [Interview]. In: *Twentieth Century Authors*. 1st Supplement (New York, 1955), p.1074.

Misc 1956/1. [Letter] *Sydney Morning Herald* 2 June 1956.

Misc 1956/2. 'Writes in "Stained Glass"' [Interview with Kylie Tennant] *Sydney Morning Herald* 22 September 1956, p.10.

Misc 1956/3. [Letter] *People* 12 December 1956, p.48.

Misc 1957/1. [Promotion for *Voss*, which includes extracts from letters from White to his publisher Ben Huebsch], *Book of the Month Magazine*, July 1957.

Misc 1957/2. 'Talk with Patrick White' [Interview with Ian Moffitt] *New York Times Book Review* 18

August 1957, p.18. Reprinted in *Sydney Morning Herald* 24 August 1957, p.2.

Misc 1958/1. [Interview] *Sydney Morning Herald* 4 April 1958, p.1. Misc 1958/2. 'Responsibility and the Human' [Review of A. Thomas *The Director* and L. Hornblow *The Loveseekers*] *Sydney Morning Herald* 9 August 1958, p.12.

Misc 1958/3. 'The Prodigal Son' *Australian Letters* v.1 no.3, April 1958, p.37-40. Reprinted: *The Writer in the Modern World* ed. H.P. Heseltine and S. Tick (Melbourne, 1962), p.115-118; *The Vital Decade* ed. Geoffrey Dutton and Max Harris (Melbourne, 1968), p.156-158; *Patrick White Speaks* (1989), p.13-17; *The Macmillan Anthology of Australian Literature* ed. Ken L. Goodwin and Alan Lawson (South Melbourne, 1990), p.374-376; *Patrick White: Selected Writings* ed. Alan Lawson (1994), p.268-271.

Misc 1959/1. 'The Writing Business' [Interview with Peter Hastings] *Observer* (Sydney) 21 March 1959, p.176.

Misc 1959/2. [Questionnaire] *The Newsbasket* (London) December 1959, p.18.

Misc 1961/1. 'Patrick White's new novel', *Australian Letters* v.3 no.3, March 1961, pp.39-52.

Misc 1961/2. [Letter] *Sunday Mirror* 29 July 1961, p.1.

Misc 1961/3. 'Famous Author "Hates Writing"' [Interview with Pat Griffith] *Advertiser* (Adelaide) 18 November 1961, p.17.

Misc 1961/4. 'Australian Myths Debunked' [Interview with Ian Moffitt] *Sunday Mirror* (Sydney) 3 December 1961, p.13.

Misc 1962/1. 'Trust and the "Funeral"' [Letter] *Nation* 13 January 1962, p.17.

Misc 1962/2. 'An Australian Enigma: Conversation with Patrick White' [Interview with Brian Davies] *Melbourne University Magazine* Spring 1962, p.69-71.

Misc 1962/3. 'What Books did you Know and Like Most in your Childhood' *Australian Book Review*, Children's Book and Educational Supplement, 1962, p.4.

Misc 1962/4. 'Gerry Lewers has Left Us' [Obituary] *Sydney Morning Herald* 18 August 1962, p.12.

Misc 1963/1. 'The Marriage of Stan and Amy' [Extract]. In: *Australian Idiom: An Anthology of Contemporary Prose and Poetry* ed. H.P. Heseltine (Melbourne, 1963).

Misc 1963/2. 'Novelist Patrick White' [Interview] *Literary Letter* March 1963, p.1-4.

Misc 1963/4. 'Patrick White 1912- – life at Castle Hill' [Interview with John Hetherington]. In: *Forty-two Faces: profiles of living Australian writers* (Melbourne, 1963).

Misc 1964/1. 'Patrick White's Opera' [Letter] *Bulletin* 27 June 1964, p.17.

Misc 1964/2. 1876 [in red] B.W. Huebsch [in black] 1964 | A record of a meeting of his friends at the | Grolier Club, New York City, on December 9, 1964 | PRIVATELY PRINTED. pp.*7* 8-31 *32*. Notes: p.32 [publisher's device] | 'Photograph by Lotte Jacobi | Set in Emerson types by Westcott & Thomson | 750 copies (not for sale) printed in U.S.A. | on Curtis Rag paper by The Meriden Gravure Co. | Design: M.B. Glick'. For a letter from Patrick White see p.30-31.

Misc 1965/1. 'Staging of "Night on Bald Mountain"' [Letter] *Sydney Morning Herald* 7 January 1965, p.2.

Misc 1965/2. 'A social occasion', [Extract from *The Solid Mandala*] *Meanjin* v.24 no.1, 1965, pp.18-24.

Misc 1966/1. 'A Visit to Sir Osbert' [Letter] *Bulletin* v.88, 22 January 1966, p.26.

Misc 1967/1. 'The Miles Franklin Award' [Letter] *Australian Book Review* v.6 no.8, June 1967, p.132.

Misc 1967/2. [Letter re: Britannica Award] *Sydney Morning Herald* 13 December 1967, p.2.

Misc 1968/1. 'Theatre' [Letter] *Sydney Morning Herald* 16 March 1968, p.2.

Misc 1968/2. 'Noted Citizens Attack South Africa' [Brief collective interview] *Sydney Morning Herald* 20 March 1968, p.11.

Misc 1968/3. [Letter] *Nation* 11 May 1968, p.15.

Misc 1968/4. 'Awards for Literature' [Letter] *Sydney Morning Herald* 26 November 1968, p.2.

Misc 1968/5. 'Britannica Awards' [Letter] *Sydney Morning Herald* 30 November 1968, p.2.

Misc 1969/1. [Extract from *Riders in the Chariot*]. In: *In the Making* (Melbourne, 1969), p.219-220.

Misc 1969/2. 'Patrick White' [Interview with Craig McGregor]. In: *In the Making* (Melbourne, 1969), p.218-221. Reprinted: *Patrick White Speaks* (1989), p.19-23; *Critical Essays on Patrick White* ed. Peter Wolfe (Boston, 1990), p.218-221; and *Patrick White: Selected Writings* ed. Alan Lawson (1994), p.271-275.

Misc 1969/3. '39 Sign Publicly to Defy Service Act' [Brief interview] *Sydney Morning Herald* 10 December 1969, p.9.

Misc 1970/1. [Extract from *The Tree of Man*]. In: *Authors and Areas of Australia* (Austin, Texas, 1970), p.69.

Misc 1970/2. 'Profile of a Great Man's Profile' [Interview with David Rowbotham] *Courier-Mail* (Brisbane) 30 March 1970, p.2.

Misc 1970/3. 'White' [Interview with Elizabeth Riddell] *Australian* 1 August 1970, p.15. Reprinted as 'A Morning at Mr White's'. In: *The Armchair Australian* ed. James Hall (Sydney, 1970), p.102-106.

Misc 1970/4. 'Moratorium Proceeding as Planned' [Letter] *Australian* 16 September 1970, p.14.

Misc 1972/1. 'Patrick White v "Great God Sport"' [Interview with ABC TV interviewer] *Sydney Morning Herald* 18 March 1972, p.1.

Misc 1972/2. 'Bread and Games' [Letter] *Sydney Morning Herald* 4 July 1972, p.2.

Misc 1972/3. 'Patrick White's Story' [Interview with Ashley Owen (Brian Dale)] *Australian Financial Review* 11 July 1972, p.2-3.

Misc 1972/4. 'Black Bans by Builders' Labourers' [Letter] *Sydney Morning Herald* 21 August 1972, p.6.

Misc 1972/5. 'Why Knock Mavis and Bazza?' [Letter] *Sydney Morning Herald* 7 November 1972, p.6.

Misc 1972/6. [Letter calling for change of government] *Australian, Canberra Times, Sydney Morning Herald, Age* (Melbourne), *Advertiser* (Adelaide), *Courier-Mail* (Brisbane), *Newcastle Morning Herald, Mercury* (Hobart) 23 November 1972.

Misc 1972/7. 'Centennial Park Rally, June 18, 1972. Grass Roots Conservation' *Wildlife in Australia* v.9 no.4, December 1972, p.116.

Misc 1973/1. 'Australian Writers in Profile: 11. A Conversation with Patrick White' [Interview with Thelma Herring and G.A. Wilkes] *Southerly* v.33 no.2, 1973, p.132-143.

Misc 1973/2. 'Civilisation, Money and Concrete' delivered as a speech in August 1973; first published in *Patrick White Speaks* (1989), p.35-36.

Misc 1973/3. 'The Wit and Wisdom of Patrick White' [Interview with Maria Prerauer] *Sunday Telegraph* (Sydney) 12 August 1973, p.71 and 75.

Misc 1973/4. [Interview with Tara McCarthy] Canadian Broadcasting Commission, September 1973.

Misc 1973/5. [Interview] *Listener* 25 October 1973.

Misc 1973/6. 'The Oasis of the Backyard' *Sydney Morning Herald* 5 November 1973, p.6.

Misc 1973/7. Letter to J.F. Cope (Speaker, House of Representatives). Australia. House of Representatives, *Debates* 29 November 1973, p.4081.

Misc 1973/8. [Interview], ABC Radio 2, 9 December 1973.

Misc 1973/9. 'Wheat Sale' [Letter] *Advertiser* (Adelaide) 26 December 1973, p.6.

Misc 1973/10. Ingmar Bjorkstén, *Patrick White: epikern fran Australien* (Stockholm: Forum, 1973). Includes a lengthy interview with Patrick White. Translated into German as *Patrick White: die Stimme Australiens* (Düsseldorf: Claassen Verlag, 1973) and into English as *Patrick White: A General Introduction* (St Lucia: University of Queensland, 1976).

Misc 1974/1. [Cover title:] Reimpression de | LES PRIX NOBEL | EN 1973 | BIOGRAPHY | PATRICK WHITE | COPYRIGHT © THE NOBEL FOUNDATION 1974. pp.[2] 221-223 [*224*]. Stapled with blue paper cover. Front: title page. Back: 'Printed in Sweden | Stockholm 1974. Kungl. Boktryckeriet P.A. Norstedt &

Söner'. Reprinted in *Patrick White Speaks* (1989), p.39-44.

Misc 1974/2. 'Setting Out Blue Prints for a Better Year' *Sydney Morning Herald* 3 January 1974, p.9.

Misc 1974/3. 'Australian of the Year'. Reprinted in *Patrick White Speaks* (1989), p.47-48.

Misc 1974/4. 'Patrick White Names Three 'Mavericks'' *Sydney Morning Herald* 26 January 1974, p.1.

Misc 1974/5. 'Patrick White Names the Men Who Matter' *Advertiser* (Adelaide) 26 January 1974, p.1.

Misc 1974/6. 'With Whitlam' given in a speech in May 1974 at the Sydney Opera House. Reprinted in *Patrick White Speaks* (1989), p.51-53.

Misc 1974/7. 'Text of the speech made by Patrick White at Centennial Park meeting on 18th June, 1972' and 'Speech made by Patrick White at Melbourne Town Hall on 25th January, 1974 when accepting award as Australian of the Year, 1973', *Abbey's Broadsheet* no.2, [1974]. 1 leaf (28.5 x 21.5 cm). (Copies: NSL: Mitchell Library). Reprinted in *Patrick White Speaks* (1989) as 'A Living Living-Room', p.27-28, and 'Mad Hatter's Party', p.31-33.

Misc 1974/8. 'White Seeks Protest by Canberra' *Advertiser* (Adelaide) 14 February 1974, p.1.

Misc 1974/9. [Letter] *Time* 25
March 1974, p.2.

Misc 1974/10. 'Patrick White's
Tribute to the Whitlam Government'
Meanjin v.33 no.2, 1974, p.220-221.
Reprinted in *Patrick White Speaks*
(1989).

Misc 1974/11. 'Poor Henry Lawson'
Grenfell Record June 1974. Reprinted
in *Patrick White Speaks* (1989), p.55-
57, and *Patrick White: Selected
Writings* ed. Alan Lawson (1994),
p.276-277.

Misc 1974/12. 'A Day with Patrick
White' [Interview with Ingmar
Bjorkstén for *Veckojournalen*, trans. by
J.S. Martin] *Nation Review* v.4
no.36, 21-27 June 1974, p.1179.

Misc 1974/13. 'Soviet Dissidents'
[Letter] *Canberra Times* 5 July 1974,
p.2.

Misc 1974/14. 'Saigon Prisoners'
[Letter] *Bulletin* v.96, 20 July 1974
p.5-6.

Misc 1974/15. [Letter] *Australian*
(Adelaide) 2 October 1974, p.8.

Misc 1974/16. 'The Perils of Art in
Sydney Town' *Sydney Morning
Herald* 2 November 1974, p.16.

Misc 1975/1. [Letter] *Armidale and
District Historical Society. Journal and
Proceedings* no.18, January 1975, p.19.

Misc 1975/2. 'Awareness and the
Environs' [Letter] *Australian*
(Adelaide) 28 May 1975, p.8.

Misc 1975/3. 'White Hits at Mining'
Advertiser (Adelaide) 28 May 1975,
p.1.

Misc 1976/1. 'Kerr and the
Consequences' given as a speech at
the Sydney Town Hall, 11 November
1976. First published in *Kerr and the
Consequences* (Camberwell, Vic.:
Widescope International Publishers,
1976), and reprinted in *Patrick White
Speaks* (1989), p.59-60.

Misc 1976/2. 'The Cynthia I Knew'
[Tribute] *Australian* 7 December
1976, p.7.

Misc 1977/1. 'Citizens for
Democracy' given as a speech at the
University of Queensland, 7 March
1977. Also given in Sydney, 8 March
1977, in an amended form. Reprinted
in *Patrick White Speaks* (1989), p.63-
67, and *Patrick White: Selected
Writings* ed. Alan Lawson (1994),
p.287-290.

Misc 1978/1. 'A Noble Pair' given as
a speech in Canberra, 13 January
1978. Broadcast by ABC Radio, 14
January 1978. Reprinted in *Patrick
White Speaks* (1989), p.69-71.

Misc 1978/2. 'Patrick White: A
Revealing Profile' [Interview with
David Leitch] *National Times* 27
March-1 April 1978, p.30-35.

Misc 1978/3. [Letter on Henry Lawson] *Sydney Morning Herald* 17 May 1978, p.6. Reprinted in *Patrick White: Selected Writings* ed. Alan Lawson (1994), p.291.

Misc 1979/1. 'A Very Literary Luncheon' *National Times* 30 June 1979, p.26-27, 30-31.

Misc 1980/1. 'Flaws in the Glass: Sketches from a Self-portrait' [Extract] *Bulletin* 29 January 1980, p.146-154.

Misc 1980/2. [Letter on White's right to comment on Australian society] *Sydney Morning Herald* 1 April 1980.

Misc 1980/3. 'The Private Patrick White' [Interview with Andrew Clark] *New York Times* 27 April 1980, p.BR8.

Misc 1980/4. 'Patrick White Replies: Nowra's Vision of Australia' [Letter] *Sydney Morning Herald* 6 September 1980, p.19, and reprinted in *Patrick White: Selected Writings* ed. Alan Lawson (1994), p.207. Written to the editor in response to Kippax's review of Louis Nowra's *Inside the Island*. The *Sydney Morning Herald* did not publish the letter and so it was placed as an advertisement for the Nimrod Theatre.

Misc 1980/5. 'Libraries for Living' [Speech] *Australian* 20-21 September 1980, Magazine p.13; and *Age*

(Melbourne) 20 September 1980, p.24; *Sydney Morning Herald* 20 September 1980, p.11; *Australian Library News* v.10, September 1980, p.11. Reprinted in *Patrick White Speaks* (1989), p.73-78.

Misc 1980/6. 'Patrick White: Self-portrait of an Intensely Political Writer' *Age* (Melbourne) 11 October 1980, p.28; 'Truth and Fiction' *Sydney Morning Herald* 11 October 1980, p.20. Speech given at the National Book Council Awards Dinner, 10 October 1980. Reprinted in *Australian Literary Studies* v.10, 1981, p.99-101 and *Patrick White Speaks* (1989), p.81-85.

Misc 1981/1. 'An Interview with Patrick White' *Island Magazine* no.7, 1981, p.6-7.

Misc 1981/2. [Interview with Paul Murphy] *Nationwide* ABC TV, 12 March 1981. Published in the *Newcastle Herald* 19 March 1981, and reprinted in *Patrick White Speaks* (1989), p.87-92.

Misc 1981/3. 'Beware the Seductive Baubles, Says Patrick White' [Interview with ABC TV] *Sydney Morning Herald* 18 March 1981, p.2.

Misc 1981/4. 'Jack Mundey and the BLF' given in an open letter to the ACTU, September 1981. Reprinted in *Patrick White Speaks* (1989), p.95-97.

Misc 1981/5. 'Patrick White Speaks on Factual Writing and Fiction' *Australian Literary Studies* v.10, May 1981, p.99-101. Reprinted in *Patrick White: Selected Writings* ed. Alan Lawson (1994), p.277-281.

Misc 1981/6. 'Patrick White, Australian Puts his Country under the Microscope' *Beacon* May 1981, p.3-4.

Misc 1981/7. 'And if a Button is Pressed' given as a speech to People for Nuclear Disarmament in Melbourne, October 1981. Reprinted in *Patrick White Speaks* (1989), p.99-102.

Misc 1981/8. *Patrick White's Choice* (Art Gallery of New South Wales, [1981]). 21.1 x 29.8 cm. [6] p., gatefold. Contents: [1] title page; [2] 'Patrick White's Choice 22 December 1981 – 31 January 1982 For the Festival of Sydney 1982 [Introduction by] Edmund Capon | Director'; [3-4] [text by] 'Patrick White December 1981'; [5] [col. illust. of painting]; [6] 'Catalogue'. Reviewed in *National Times* 20-26 December 1981. Notes: the copy in White's own collection contains a letter from Brian Adams of the ABC (dated 21 December 1981) inviting White to participate in a video of the exhibition. The catalogue's essay is reprinted in *Patrick White: Selected Writings* ed. Alan Lawson (1994), p.291-293. There is also a typescript of White's essay for the catalogue.

See also *Sydney Morning Herald* 22 December 1981, p.8.

Misc 1981/9. Richard Coleman, 'P. White, Mother and Hat' [Interview] *Sydney Morning Herald* 22 December 1981, p.1.

Misc 1982/1. [Extract from *Flaws in the Glass*] *Waiguo Wenxue* [*Foreign Literatures*] v.4, 1982, p.17-28.

Misc 1982/2. 'Patrick White: The Inner Struggle' [Interview with Alan Roberts] *Advertiser* (Adelaide) 13 February 1982, p.21 and 26. Reprinted in *Sun-Herald* 28 February 1982, p.9.

Misc 1982/3. 'That Man White' [Interview with Leonard Radic] *Age* (Melbourne) 13 March 1982, Saturday Extra p.1.

Misc 1982/4. 'A Letter to Humanity' was an open letter read to the first of the Palm Sunday peace marches. Reprinted in *Patrick White Speaks* (1989), p.105-110.

Misc 1982/5. Geoffrey Dutton, 'A Prism's Light Shining in Flawed Glass: Patrick White at 70' [Article based on interviews, correspondence and personal knowledge] *Bulletin* (Sydney) 1 June 1982, p.62-66.

Misc 1982/6. 'A Warning from White' [Article quotes extensively from an unpublished letter to Neville

Wran] *Sydney Morning Herald* 6 July 1982, p.1.

Misc 1982/7. [Letter] *Guardian* (Manchester) 14 August 1982, p.8.

Misc 1983/1. 'Angus Wilson'. In: 'Talking about Angus Wilson', *Twentieth Century Literature* v.29, Summer 1983, p.115-141.

Misc 1983/2. 'The Role of the Australian Citizen in a Nuclear War' given as a speech to a symposium at the Australian National University, May 1983. First published in *Australia and Nuclear War* (Melbourne, 1983), p.252-264. Reprinted in *Best of the Science Show* (Sydney: ABC, 1983) and *Patrick White Speaks* (1989), p.113-126. Also published as an audiocassette entitled *Nuclear War* (Sydney: ABC, 1983).

Misc 1983/3. 'Finding the Faith to Save the World' *Age* (Melbourne) 1 June 1983, p.11.

Misc 1983/4. 'Novels? Patrick White Wants the Machine Gun Burst of Plays' [Interview with Michael Le Moignan] *Sydney Morning Herald* 23 July 1983, p.33.

Misc 1983/5. 'Patrick White Finds it Hard to Forgive' [Interview with Margaret Simons] *Age* (Melbourne) 24 September 1983, Saturday Extra p.3.

Misc 1983/6. 'No-one Realises How Frivolous Patrick White Can Be' [Interview with Geraldine O'Brien] *Sydney Morning Herald* 10 December 1983, p.31.

Misc 1983/7. 'A New Constitution' given as a speech to Citizens for Democracy in Sydney, 11 November 1983. First published in *Patrick White Speaks* (1989), p.129-131.

Misc 1983/8. 'Greece – My Other Country' was intended to be given as a speech in Athens, November 1983, but was never given. First published in *Patrick White Speaks* (1989), p.133-136.

Misc 1984/1. 'It Seems as though Life Itself Now Depends on Sport …' *Sydney Morning Herald* 26 January 1984, Supplement p.2. Reprinted in *Patrick White Speaks* (1989), p.139-143, and *Patrick White: Selected Writings* ed. Alan Lawson (1994), p.294-297.

Misc 1984/2. 'The Challenge and Hope of Patrick White' *Action for World Development Newsletter* February 1984, p.8-11.

Misc 1984/3. 'From Wigan to Wagga' given as a speech at the launch of *Australia and Nuclear War*, March 1984. First published in *Patrick White Speaks* (1989), p.145-148.

Misc 1984/4. 'Patrick White'
[Interview with Margaret Simons]
Tension no.3, April 1984, p.22-25.

Misc 1984/5. 'Search for an
Alternative to Futility' [Speech], La
Trobe University, 2 August 1984.
First published in *Arena* no.68, 1984,
p.7-13. Reprinted in *Patrick White
Speaks* (1989), p.151-158. See also
Sydney Morning Herald 3 August
1984, p.1 for 'Patrick White v
'Cockatoo Hairdo'.

Misc 1984/6. 'Hiroshima Day' given
as a speech at the Sydney Town Hall,
August 1984. First published in
Patrick White Speaks (1989), p.161-
165.

Misc 1984/7. 'Peace and Other
Matters' given as a speech in
Auckland, 2 November 1984. First
published in *Patrick White Speaks*
(1989), p.167-173.

Misc 1984/8. [Interview with
Gordon McLauchlan], TV-1 (New
Zealand), November 1984.

Misc 1985/1. 'Mrs Goodman Did
Die' [Extract from *The Aunt's Story*].
In: *Dear Mum: Australian Mothers
Then and Now* ed. Nancy Keesing
(North Ryde, NSW, 1985), p.130-
131.

Misc 1985/2. [Interview] *New
Zealand Listener* 19 January 1985.

Misc 1985/3. [Letter] *National Times*
17 May 1985, p.18.

Misc 1985/4. 'There's Still a Lot of
Black in White' [Interview with
Richard Glover] *Sydney Morning
Herald* 18 May 1985, Good
Weekend p.26-27 and 30.

Misc 1985/5. 'The 'Real' ABC
Audience Calls for Inquiry'
[Collective letter] *Sydney Morning
Herald* 12 August 1985, p.12.

Misc 1985/7. 'Monsterail' given as a
speech to one of the many rallies
against Sydney's monorail. First
published in *Patrick White Speaks*
(1989), p.175.

Misc 1986/1. [Interview with Janet
Hawley] *Age* (Melbourne) Extra, 8
February 1986, p.9.

Misc 1986/2. 'The Day the Nobel
Prize-winning Author Took on the
Premier of NSW' [Brief interview]
Sydney Morning Herald 24 March
1986, p.1,7.

Misc 1986/3. [Speech] given to a
symposium at the Australian Defence
Force Academy in Canberra, 11
November 1986. Published in
*Imagining the Real: Australian Writing
in the Nuclear Age* ed. Dorothy Green
and David Headon (Sydney: ABC,
1987) and reprinted in *Patrick White
Speaks* (1989), p.177-181. Also
published as an audiocassette
(Sydney: ABC, 1986).

Misc 1986/4. 'My Dog' [Pictorial]. In: *Australian Studies Project: Bulletin of the Committee to Review Australian Studies in Tertiary Education* no.4, October 1986.

Misc 1987/1. Michael Le Moignan and Larry Lucas, *Patrick White, His Life and Work* (Sydney: ABC, 1987). 5 audiocassettes (284 minutes). Includes extracts read by White from *Flaws in the Glass.*

Misc 1987/2. 'Patrick White' [Interview with Peter Ward] *Weekend Australian* 18-19 April 1987, Weekend Magazine p.1.

Misc 1988/1. 'Patrick White's Views on the Bicentenary' *Blast* no.5, Autumn 1988, p.5-6. Reprinted in *Patrick White Speaks* (1989), p.183-186.

Misc 1988/2. 'A Sense of Integrity' speech given at La Trobe University, July 1988. Extracts published in *Sydney Morning Herald* 22 July 1988, p.13. First published in *Arena* no.84, 1988, p.97-103. Reprinted in *Patrick White Speaks* (1989), p.189-195, and *Habitat Australia* v.17 no.4, August 1989, p.10-12.

Misc 1988/3. 'Credo' *Overland* no.111, June 1988, p.16. Reprinted in *Patrick White Speaks* (1989), p.197.

Misc 1988/4. 'Patrick White at seventy-five' [Interview with Ray Willbanks], *Antipodes* v.2, Spring 1988, and reprinted *Antipodes* v.14 no.1, June 2000, p.63-64.

Misc 1989/1. Anne Susskind, 'Educators Acting as "Virtual Censors"' [Includes quotes from White] *Sydney Morning Herald* 14 January 1989, p.5.

Misc 1989/2. [Interview: 'Books and Writing'] Radio National, 1 October 1989 (see *24 Hours* October 1989).

Misc 1989/3. 'White: Light and Shadow' [Interview with Angela Bennie] *Sydney Morning Herald* 11 November 1989, p.89.

Misc 1989/4. 'Writer replies', [Letter] *Sydney Morning Herald* 23 November 1989, p.14.

Misc 1990/1. [Extract from *Voss*]. In: *The Macmillan Anthology of Australian Literature* ed. Ken Goodwin and Alan Lawson (South Melbourne, 1990), p.41-44.

Misc 1992/1. [Two letters]. In: Barry Humphries, *More Please* (New York, 1992), p.327-328.

Appendix 6: Summary of Translations

Arabic
The Burnt Ones (part) In: [*Foreign literature*] v.6 no.1, July 1979 I.t6

Bulgarian
The Eye of the Storm Sofija: Narodna Kultura, 1984 M.t13
The Cockatoos Varna: Georgi Bakalov, 1986 N.t4
A Fringe of Leaves Plovdiv: Hr. G. Danov, 1981 O.t7

Chinese
The Tree of Man (extract) Beijing: Foreign Languages Institute, 1980 F.t12
The Tree of Man Shang-hai: Shang-hai i wen ch'u pan she, 1990 F.t18
Voss Beijing: Wai kuo wen hsüen ch'u pan she, 1991 G.t23
The Burnt Ones (part) In: [*Shijie Wenxue*] no.3, 1982 I.t7
The Eye of the Storm Kwein-lin Shih: Li-jiang ch'u pan she, 1986 M.t14
A Fringe of Leaves Beijing: Zhongguo Wenxue, 1993 O.t11a
A Fringe of Leaves Beijing: Zhongguo Wenxue, 1994 O.t11b
Flaws in the Glass Beijing: n.p., 1990 S.t3

Czech
The Tree of Man Prague: Státne Nakladetelstvi Krásné Literatury a Uměni, 1960 F.t3
The Tree of Man Prague: Nakladetelstvi Svoboda, 1984 F.t15
Voss Bratislava: Vavrin, 1977 G.t14
Voss Prague: Svobana, 1980 G.t17
The Eye of the Storm Prague: Odeon, 1978 M.t10
A Fringe of Leaves Prague: Odeon, 1983 O.t10a
A Fringe of Leaves Prague: Odeon / Klub Čtenářů, 1986 O.t10b

Danish
The Burnt Ones n.p.: Brøndums Forlag, 1974 I.t3

Dutch
Voss Amsterdam: Uitgeverij de Arbeiderspers, 1982 G.t18
The Vivisector Amsterdam: Uitgeverij de Arbeiderspers, 1980 L.t6

Estonian
The Tree of Man Tallin: Eesti raamat, 1983 F.t14
The Cockatoos (part) Tallin: LR, 1979 N.t3

Finnish
Voss Helsinki: Kustannusosakeyhtiö Otava, 1977 G.t13
Riders in the Chariot Helsinki: Kustannusosakeyhtiö Otava, 1967 H.t6
The Eye of the Storm Helsinki: Kustannusosakeyhtiö Otava, 1974 M.t3

French
Happy Valley Paris: Gallimard, 1951 C.t1a
The Living and the Dead Paris: Gallimard, 1990 D.t4
Voss Paris: Gallimard, 1967 G.t7
Riders in the Chariot Paris: Gallimard, 1965 H.t2a
Riders in the Chariot Paris: Gallimard, 1973 H.t2b
The Burnt Ones Paris: Gallimard, 1969 I.t1
The Solid Mandala Paris: Gallimard, 1970 K.t4
The Vivisector Paris: Gallimard, 1979 L.t5
The Eye of the Storm Paris: Gallimard, 1978 M.t11
A Fringe of Leaves Paris: Gallimard, 1981 O.t5a
A Fringe of Leaves Paris: Gallimard L'Imaginaire, 1985 O.t5b
The Twyborn Affair Paris: Gallimard, 1983 R.t2
Flaws in the Glass Paris: Gallimard, 1985 S.t2
Memoirs of Many in One Paris: Gallimard, 1988 V.t1
Three Uneasy Pieces Paris: Arléa, 1984 W.t1

German
The Tree of Man Köln and Berlin: Kiepenheuer & Witsch, 1957 F.t1a
The Tree of Man Frankfurt am Main, Vienna and Zurich: Büchergilde
Gutenberg, 1963 F.t1b
The Tree of Man Köln: Kiepenheuer & Witsch, 1973 F.t1c
The Tree of Man Münich: Deutscher Taschenbuch Verlag, 1973 F.t1d
The Tree of Man Münich: Deutscher Taschenbuch Verlag, 1974 F.t1e
The Tree of Man Münich: Deutscher Taschenbuch Verlag, n.d. F.t1f
The Tree of Man Münich: Deutscher Taschenbuch Verlag, 1988 F.t1g
The Tree of Man Stuttgart, Zürich and Salzburg: Europäischer Buchklub,
1960 F.t2a

The Tree of Man Zürich: Buchklub ex Libris, 1960 F.t2b

The Tree of Man Vienna, Darmstadt, Berlin: Deutsche Buchmeinschaft, 1963 F.t2c

Voss Köln and Berlin: Kiepenheuer & Witsch, 1958 G.t1a

Voss Köln and Berlin: Kiepenheuer & Witsch, 1958 G.t1b

Voss Reinbek bei Hamburg: Rowohlt, 1973 G.t1c

Voss Reinbek bei Hamburg: Rowohlt, 1974 G.t1d

Voss Berlin, Darmstadt, Vienna: Deutsche Büch-Gemeinschaft, 1961 G.t2a

Voss Stüttgart, Hamburg, Münich: Deutscher Bücherband, [1974] G.t2b

Voss Leipzig: Reclam, 1987 G.t3

Riders in the Chariot Köln and Berlin: Kiepenheuer & Witsch, 1969 H.t7a

Riders in the Chariot Köln and Berlin: Kiepenheuer & Witsch, n.d. H.t7b

Riders in the Chariot Köln and Berlin: Kiepenheuer & Witsch, n.d. H.t7c

Riders in the Chariot Zürich: Buchclub Ex Libris, 1973 H.t7d

Riders in the Chariot Reinbek bei Hamburg: Rowohlt, 1974 H.t7e

The Burnt Ones (part) Stuttgart: Philipp Reclam, Jun., 1975 I.t4

The Burnt Ones (part) Frankfurt am Main: Fischer Taschenbuch Verlag, 1991 I.t9

The Burnt Ones Frankfurt am Main: S. Fischer Verlag, 1992 I.t10

The Burnt Ones (part) Frankfurt am Main: S. Fischer Taschenbuch Verlag, 1995 I.t11

The Solid Mandala Düsseldorf: Claassen Verlag, 1978 K.t8

The Vivisector Hamburg und Düsseldorf: Claassen Verlag, 1972 L.t3a

The Vivisector Stüttgart, Hamburg, Münich: Deutscher Bucherband, 1974 L.t3b

The Vivisector Frankfurt am Main: Fischer Taschenbuch, 1974 L.t3c

The Vivisector Zurich: Buchclub Ex Libris, 1974 L.t3d

The Vivisector Munich, Zurich: Piper, 1989 L.t3e

The Eye of the Storm Düsseldorf: Claassen-Verlags; Zürich: Coron-Verlag; Paris: Les Editions Rombaldi, 1973 M.t1

The Eye of the Storm Düsseldorf: Claassen Verlag, 1974 M.t2a

The Eye of the Storm Zurich: Buchclub Ex Libris M.t2b

The Eye of the Storm Munich, Zurich: Piper, 1992 M.t2c

A Fringe of Leaves Düsseldorf: Claassen Verlag, 1982 O.t8a

A Fringe of Leaves Münich: Piper, 1990 O.t8b

A Fringe of Leaves Frankfurt am Main: Büchergilde Gutenberg, 1988 O.t9

The Twyborn Affair Düsseldorf: Claassen Verlag, 1986 R.t4a

The Twyborn Affair Munich: Zurich: Piper, 1991 R.t4b

Flaws in the Glass Frankfurt am Main: S. Fischer, 1994 S.t4

Memoirs of Many in One Düsseldorf: Claassen Verlag, 1988 V.t2

Greek

The Aunt's Story Athens: Hestia, 1988 E.t8

The Tree of Man Athens: Zarbanos, 1976 F.t7

Voss Athens: Ekdoseis Kanake, 1990 G.t24a

Voss Athens: Ekdoseis Kanake, 1995 G.t24b

Hebrew

The Aunt's Story Tel Aviv: Am Oved, 1992 E.t10

Voss Tel Aviv: Zmora-Bitan, 1990 G.t22

Riders in the Chariot Tel Aviv: Zmora, Bitan, Modan, 1980 H.t12

The Solid Mandala Tel Aviv: Zmora-Bitan, 1987 K.t9

The Eye of the Storm Lod: Zmora-Bitan, n.d. M.t15

A Fringe of Leaves Tel Aviv: Am Oved, 1978 O.t1

Hungarian

The Tree of Man Budapest: Magvető Kiadó, 1972 F.t5

The Burnt Ones (part) Budapest: Európa Könyvkiadó, 1988 I.t8

Big Toys Budapest: n.p., 1980 Q.t1

Italian

The Aunt's Story Rome: Casini, 1951 E.t1

The Aunt's Story Rome: Club degli Editori, 1974 E.t2

Voss Turin: Einaudi, 1965 G.t5a

Voss [not seen] G.t5b

Voss Turin: Einaudi, 1974 G.t5c

Voss [Rome]: UTET, 1974 G.t6

Riders in the Chariot Turin: Einaudi, 1976   H.t10

The Solid Mandala Milan: Valentino Bompiani, 1973 K.t5

The Eye of the Storm Milan: Bompiani, 1974 M.t4

Japanese

The Aunt's Story Tokyo: Suufu no Tomosha, 1976 E.t6

Voss Tokyo: The Simul Press, 1975 G.t12

The Burnt Ones (part) Tokyo: Kenkyusha, 1973 I.t2a

The Burnt Ones (part) Tokyo: Kenkyusha, 1982 I.t2b
The Eye of the Storm Tokyo: Mikasa Shobo, 1974 M.t5

Korean
The Tree of Man Seoul: Eulyoo Publishing Company, 1992 F.t19

Lithuanian
The Tree of Man Vilnius: Vaga, 1980 F.t11

Macedonian
Voss Skopje: Misla, 1986 G.t21

Malay
Voss Kuala Lumpur: Dewan Bahasa dan Pustaka, Kementerian Pendidikan Malaysia, 1995 G.t25

Norwegian
The Solid Mandala Oslo: Gyldendal, 1970 K.t3
The Vivisector Oslo: Gyldendal, 1971 L.t2

Polish
The Living and the Dead Warsaw: Państwowy Instytut Wydawniczy, 1985 D.t1
The Tree of Man Warsaw: Państwowy Instytut Wydawniczy, 1985 F.t16
Voss Warsaw: Państwowy Instytut Wydawniczy, 1979 G.t15
Voss Warsaw: Muza, 1993 G.t16
Riders in the Chariot Warsaw: Państwowy Instytut Wydawniczy, 1965 H.t3
The Solid Mandala Warsaw: Państwowy Instytut Wydawniczy, 1968 K.t1
The Vivisector Warsaw: Państwowy Instytut Wydawniczy, 1973 L.t4
The Vivisector Warsaw: Muza, 1993 L.t7
The Eye of the Storm Warsaw: Państwowy Instytut Wydawniczy, 1976 M.t9
A Fringe of Leaves Warsaw: Państwowy Instytut Wydawniczy, 1980 O.t3
A Fringe of Leaves Warsaw: Muza, 1995 O.t4

Portuguese
The Tree of Man Lisbon: Publições Dom Quixote, 1973 F.t6a
The Tree of Man Lisbon: Circulo de Lectores, 1974 F.t6b
The Tree of Man São Paolo; Circulo do Livro, 1981 F.t6c

Appendix Six – Summary of Translations

Voss Rio de Janeiro: Nova Fronteira, 1985 G.t20

Romanian
The Tree of Man Bucharest: Editura Univers, 1981 F.t13
The Solid Mandala Bucharest: Editura Univers, 1974 K.t6
The Solid Mandala Bucharest: Editura Orpheus, 1993 K.t10

Russian
The Tree of Man n.p.: n.p., 1976 F.t10a
The Tree of Man Moscow: Progress, 1979 F.t10b
Voss [not seen] G.t26
The Cockatoos (part) Moscow: Isvestija, 1986 N.t5
Flaws in the Glass [not seen] S.t5

Serbo-Croatian
The Aunt's Story Belgrade: Slovo Ljubve, 1979 E.t7
Voss Zagreb: Znanje, 1974 G.t11
The Eye of the Storm Zagreb: August Cesarec, 1979 M.t12
The Twyborn Affair Zagreb: August Cesarec, 1984 R.t3

Slovak
A Fringe of Leaves Bratislava: Edícia Eva Smena, 1981 O.t6

Slovene
Riders in the Chariot Ljubljani: Cankorjeva Založba, 1974 H.t11

Spanish
The Living and the Dead Barcelona: Barral Editores, 1974 D.t3
The Aunt's Story Barcelona: Luis de Caralt, 1974 E.t5
The Tree of Man Barcelona: Plaza & Janes, 1976 F.t8
The Tree of Man Barcelona: Plaza & Janes S.A., Editores, 1979 F.t9
Voss Barcelona: Luis de Caralt, 1962 G.t4a
Voss Madrid: Club Internacional del Libro, 1992 G.t4b
Riders in the Chariot Barcelona: Luis de Caralt, 1966 H.t4
Riders in the Chariot Barcelona: Orbis, 1985 H.t5
The Burnt Ones Barcelona: Biblioteca Universal Caralt, 1976 I.t5
The Solid Mandala Barcelona: Barral Editores, 1973 K.t7

The Eye of the Storm Barcelona: Luis de Caralt, 1974 M.t7
The Cockatoos Barcelona: Plaza & Janes S.A. Editores, 1976 N.t1
The Cockatoos Barcelona: Plaza & Janes S.A. Editores, 1979 N.t2

Swedish
The Aunt's Story Borås: Forum, 1991 E.t9
The Tree of Man Stockholm: Albert Bonniers, 1970 F.t4a
The Tree of Man Stockholm: Bokförlaget Aldus / Bonniers, 1973 F.t4b
Voss Stockholm, Forum, 1983 G.t19
Riders in the Chariot Stockholm: Albert Bonniers Förlag, 1964 H.t1a
Riders in the Chariot Stockholm: Bokförlaget Aldus / Bonniers, 1973 H.t1b
The Solid Mandala Stockholm: Albert Bonniers Förlag, 1969 K.t2
The Vivisector Stockholm: Bonniers, 1970 L.t1
The Eye of the Storm Stockholm: Forum, 1975 M.t8
A Fringe of Leaves Helsinborg: Forum, 1979 O.t2a
A Fringe of Leaves Stockholm: Månpocket, 1983 O.t2b
The Twyborn Affair Stockholm: Forum, 1981 R.t1
Flaws in the Glass [Stockholm]: Forum, 1984 S.t1
Memoirs of Many in One Oslo: Forum, [1989] V.t3

Turkish
The Living and the Dead Istanbul: Sander Yayinlari, 1973 D.t2
The Aunt's Story Istanbul: Milliyet Yayinlari, 1973 E.t3
The Aunt's Story Istanbul: Yayinlari Milliyet Yayin Ltd., 1974 E.t43
Voss Istanbul: Altin Yayinevi, 1973-1974 G.t8a-e
Voss Istanbul: Altin Kitaplar Yayinevi, 1974 G.t8f
Voss Istanbul: Altin Kitaplar Yayinevi, 1983 G.t9
Voss Istanbul: Cem Yayinevi, 1990 G.t10
Riders in the Chariot Istanbul: Milliyet Yayinlari, 1973 H.t8
Riders in the Chariot Istanbul: Cem Yayinevi, 1973 H.t9
The Eye of the Storm Istanbul: Hürriyet Yayinlari, 1974 M.t6

Vietnamese
The Tree of Man Hanoi: Nha Xuat Ban Van Hoc, 1987 F.t17

Appendix 7: Literary Manuscripts

As with his correspondence, Patrick White often burnt his literary manuscripts. The conflagrations at the time of his move from Castle Hill to Martin Road in 1964 and following his death in 1990 are the stuff of legend. Consequently, there are very few survivals. Two literary manuscripts (MS/3 and MS/18) were donated to good causes for the raising of funds, and a considerable number of playscripts have survived, mainly because of the collaborative nature of the medium. Barbara Mobbs, White's literary agent, has also been the source of a number of playscripts and also, more importantly, the two screenplays 'The Monkey Puzzle' and 'Last Words' previously thought to have been lost. Finally, some poems are held by the National Library of Australia in the papers of his cousin Betty Withycombe (MS/1), his confidant Pepé Mamblas (MS/2), and the composer Peter Sculthorpe (MS/4). It is expected that in the future more Patrick White manuscripts and letters will be discovered in private collections.

MS/1
Notebook
c1934
No.2 Canvas series
20.3 x 12.7
200 pages
Inscribed: 'Poems by P.V.M. White
Given to EGW [i.e. Elizabeth "Betty"
Withycombe]
National Library of Australia, Manuscript Collection MS 8649
Notes: Of 30 poems in the Notebook, 28 were published in *The Ploughman*. 'Soiree' and 'Interpretation' have never been published.

MS/2
BAENA, José Ruix de Arana y Bauer Duque de (Pepé Mamblas)
Papers relating to Patrick White
1936-1973
National Library of Australia, Manuscript Collection MS 7712

Notes: Includes typescripts of 2 unpublished poems, probably by Patrick White.

MS/3
ABORIGINAL TREATY COMMITTEE (A.C.T.)
Literary papers
1969-1981
National Library of Australia, Manuscript Collection MS 6326
Notes: Includes a single manuscript leaf in White's hand of the libretti for the projected opera based on the story of Eliza Fraser. For more information see the introduction to *A Fringe of Leaves* (1976).

MS/4
SCULTHORPE, Peter
Papers
1941-2002

National Library of Australia, Manuscript Collection MS 9676
Notes: Includes 2 folders of correspondence with Patrick White as well as a number of pages of poetic sketches relating to the story of Eliza Fraser. Sculthorpe published some of the sketches in his book *Sun Music* (1996). For more on the collaboration between White and Sculthorpe over a projected opera based on the story of Eliza Fraser, see the introduction to *A Fringe of Leaves* (1976).

MS/5
WHITE, Patrick
Sketch for the revue *The Swinging Gate*
British Library, Lord Chamberlain's Papers

MS/6
WHITE, Patrick
The Ham Funeral (Adelaide, 1961)
Typescript, 86 leaves
Copies: University of Queensland, Fryer Memorial Library (H1843); University of New England, Campbell Howard Collection; State Library of South Australia, Mortlock Library, Call no. D6317/1; State Library of New South Wales, Mitchell Library, Hedley Cullen Collection, MSS 6641 (also includes a copy of the printed program and numerous photographs of the production); State Library of New South Wales, Mitchell Library, MSS 7290, with corrections and notes in the hands of the author and director.

MS/7
WHITE, Patrick
The Ham Funeral (Sydney, 1962)
Typescript, 55 leaves
Copies: National Institute of Dramatic Art (NIDA) Library, Sydney, two copies (one of which was the director John Tasker's copy); University of New South Wales, Call no. VQ A822.9/WHI/3; National Library of Australia, Manuscript Collection, Norman Kessell Collection MS 6326; University of Melbourne, Baillieu Library, Special Collections, Call. no. A822.3/WHITE (Zoe Caldwell, Colin Roderick); Private collection, signed by John Tasker, sold by Nicholas Pounder in the mid-1990s.

MS/8
WHITE, Patrick
The Season at Sarsaparilla (Adelaide, 1961?)
Typescript
Copies: Flinders University of South Australia; State Library of New South Wales, Mitchell Library MSS 7290, with corrections and notes in the author's hand as well as a set diagram and inserted typescript page of 'Additional Corrections'.

MS/9
WHITE, Patrick
The Season at Sarsaparilla (Melbourne, 1962)
Typescript
Copies: State Library of New South Wales, Mitchell Library MSS 6160 (Colin Roderick's copy); National Library of Australia, Manuscript Col-

lection, Norman Kessell Collection
MS 6326; University of Queensland,
Fryer Memorial Library.

MS/10
WHITE, Patrick
A Cheery Soul (Melbourne, 1963)
Typescript, 107 leaves
Copies: National Institute of Dramatic Art (NIDA) Library, Sydney
(John Tasker's copy with some scene
sketches in the script); University of
New South Wales, Accession no.
661899G; State Library of South Australia, Mortlock Library, Call no.
D6317/2; State Library of New South
Wales, Mitchell Library MSS 6995,
presented by Barbara Mobbs in 2000,
with annotations and corrections by
the author and set diagrams by Desmond Digby.

MS/11
WHITE, Patrick
A Cheery Soul (Sydney, 1979)
Typescript, 73 leaves
Copies: University of Queensland,
Fryer Memorial Library.

MS/12
WHITE, Patrick
Night on Bald Mountain (Adelaide,
1964)
Typescript
Copies: State Library of New South
Wales, Mitchell Library, MSS 7290,
acquired from Nicholas Pounder in
2003, with typed corrections and notes
and corrections in the author's hand as
well as set diagrams by Desmond
Digby.

MS/13
WHITE, Patrick
Big Toys (Sydney, 1977)
Typescript, 92 leaves
Copies: University of Queensland,
Fryer Memorial Library.

MS/14
WHITE, Patrick
The Night the Prowler (Sydney,
1978)
Typescript, 127 leaves
Copies: University of Queensland,
Fryer Memorial Library; State Library
of New South Wales, Mitchell Li-
brary MSS 6995, presented by Barbara
Mobbs in 2000, with corrections in
the author's hand.

MS/15
WHITE, Patrick
The Monkey Puzzle
c1977
Typescript
Copies: State Library of New South
Wales, Mitchell Library, MSS
7008/1/1.
Notes: A typescript of the screenplay,
corrected by the author. The film was
never produced or published.

MS/16
WHITE, Patrick
Last Words
1979
Photocopied typescript
Copies: State Library of New South
Wales, Mitchell Library, MSS
7008/1/2.

Notes: A circulating typescript of the screenplay, with *dramatis personae* and editorial directions. The screenplay was never produced or published.

MS/17
WHITE, Patrick
Births, deaths and lotteries
Typescript, 11 pages
Copies: Private collection
Notes: Draft notes and sketches towards an opera libretto. See Appendix 4 for Carl Vine's *Aria* (1984).

MS/18
WHITE, Patrick
Athens 1983 – Patrick White at celebrations of the Student Uprising and the Fall of the Junta
Typescript, 3 leaves
Copies: Private collection, sold at Australian Book Auctions, 27-28 March 2000
Notes: First published as 'Οί λαοί απειλούνται από τηνΚισχύ των αρχηγών τους', in *Τα Νεα* 30 November 1983, and reprinted in *Patrick White Speaks* (1989).

MS/19
WHITE, Patrick
Memoirs of Many in One (London, 1986)
c1984-1985
Manuscript, 220 leaves
Copies: State Library of New South Wales, Mitchell Library MSS 5497 and the National Library of Australia, Manuscript Collection MS 8293. Acquired Sotheby's 1991.

Notes: Donated by White to the Canon Collins Educational Trust for South Africa in 1988, and acquired jointly by the State Library of New South Wales and the National Library of Australia from Sotheby's in 1991. For further discussion of this manuscript see the notes to V1a above.

INDEX